Shooter's Bible

ABOUT OUR COVER

The magnificent Perazzi shotguns displayed on our front cover are from the private collection of Mr. Dan Bonillas. Known as the ''Grand American 88,'' these models were custom designed by Mr. Daniele Perazzi and presented to Mr. Bonillas as a gift in 1988.

The exquisite engraving on the gun at left was crafted by Campana, while the equally impressive engraving on the right was the work of Angelo Galeazzi. Both shotguns are trap combos, each fitted with a 32-inch over/under barrel and a 34-inch single barrel.

ASK YOUR BOOKSELLER OR SPORTING GOODS DEALER FOR THESE OTHER FINE PUBLICATIONS FROM STOEGER

ADVANCED BOWHUNTING by Roger Maynard
ADVANCED MUZZLELOADER'S GUIDE by Toby Bridges
AMERICA'S GREAT GUNMAKERS by Wayne Von Zwoll
ANGLER'S GUIDE TO JIGS AND JIGGING by Ken Oberrecht
ANTIQUE GUNS: THE COLLECTOR'S GUIDE by John Traister
BLACK POWDER GUIDE, 2nd Edition, by George C. Nonte Jr.
BOOK OF THE 22: THE ALL-AMERICAN CALIBER by Sam Fadala
CLASSIC SALMON FLIES by Mikael Frodin
THE COMPLETE BOOK OF DEER HUNTING by Byron W. Dalrymple
THE COMPLETE FISH COOKBOOK by Dan & Inez Morris
COMPLETE GUIDE TO PHYSICAL FITNESS by Kiell & Frelinghuysen
DECEIVING TROUT by John Parsons
DRESS 'EM OUT by Captain James A. Smith
FIBERGLASS ROD MAKING by Dale P. Clemens
THE FLYTIER'S COMPANION by Mike Dawes
THE FLYTIER'S MANUAL by Mike Dawes
GAME COOKBOOK, New Revised Edition, by Geraldine Steindler
GREAT SHOOTERS OF THE WORLD by Sam Fadala
GUNSMITHING AT HOME by John E. Traister
GUN TRADER'S GUIDE, 15th Edition
THE HANDBOOK OF FLYTYING by Peter Gathercole
HANDLOADER'S GUIDE by Stanley W. Trzoniec
HANDLOADER'S MANUAL OF CARTRIDGE CONVERSION
   by John J. Donnelly
THE HANDY SPORTSMAN by Loring D. Wilson
HOW TO BUY AND SELL USED GUNS by John Traister
HUNTING PREDATORS FOR HIDES & PROFIT by Wilf E. Pyle
INTERNATIONAL GUIDE TO TROUT FLIES by Bob Church
LEGENDARY SPORTING RIFLES by Sam Fadala
MATCHING THE HATCH by Ernest G. Schwiebert, Jr.
MODERN WATERFOWL GUNS & GUNNING by Don Zutz
PISTOL GUIDE by George C. Nonte Jr.
THE PRACTICAL BOOK OF KNIVES by Ken Warner
PRECISION HANDLOADING by John Withers
RELOADER'S GUIDE, 3rd Edition, by R. A. Steindler
REVOLVER GUIDE by George C. Nonte Jr.
RIFLE GUIDE by R. A. Steindler
SHOOTER'S BIBLE 1940 REPRODUCTION
SMALL GAME AND VARMINT HUNTING by Wilf E. Pyle
TAXIDERMY GUIDE, New Revised 3rd Edition, by Russell Tinsley
TO RISE A TROUT by John Roberts
THE ULTIMATE IN RIFLE ACCURACY by Glenn Newick

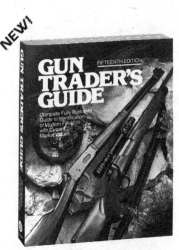

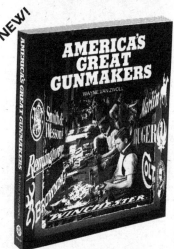

Shooter's Bible

NO. 84
1993 EDITION

EDITOR:
William S. Jarrett

PRODUCTION & DESIGN:
Charlene Cruson Step

FIREARMS CONSULTANTS:
Bill Meade, Vincent A. Pestilli,
Paul Rochelle, and
Robert A. Scanlon

COVER PHOTOGRAPHER:
Ray Wells

PUBLISHER:
Robert E. Weise

PRESIDENT
Brian T. Herrick

STOEGER PUBLISHING COMPANY

Published by Stoeger Publishing Company
55 Ruta Court
South Hackensack, New Jersey 07606

Library of Congress Catalog Card No.: 63-6200

International Standard Book No.: 0-88317-162-7

Manufactured in the United States of America

Distributed to the book trade and to the sporting goods trade by Stoeger Publishing Co., 55 Ruta Court, South Hackensack, New Jersey 07606

In Canada, distributed to the book trade and to the sporting goods trade by Stoeger Canada Ltd., Unit 16/1801 Wentworth St. P.O. Box 445, Whitby, Ontario, L1N 5S4, Canada

Contents

FOREWORD

As we unveil the 84th edition of SHOOTER'S BIBLE, it strikes us that the old adage—"The more things change, the more they remain the same"—certainly holds true in the shooter's world. That's one reason why we've decided to do a reprise of the popular series, "50 Years Ago in Shooter's Bible," to start off the article section. It comes complete with a month-by-month review of the major news and sports events of 1943, when America was still in the grip of World War ll.

Other articles prepared for your enjoyment and instruction—all heavily illustrated—include the fifth in a series on sporting art by Stephen Irwin, the Montana physician-hunter whose unmatched collection of powder flasks begins on p. 81. In further searching the past, we've added Jim Casada's colorful story about "Africa's Victorian Hunters and Their Guns," along with two articles taken from recently published books by Sam Fadala (on the Mauser) and Wayne van Zwoll (on Charles Parker and his marvelous shotgun).

For those who seek inspiration from today's world as well as the past, take a look at Wilf Pyle's piece on the current semiauto rifle, Don Lewis' appraisal of the wildcat cartridge, and Steve Sieberts' how-to article on pistol marksmanship. And last but not least, try veteran writer Ralph Quinn's analysis of "Big Game Hunting at Long-Range." Another new feature, called "Manufacturers' Showcase," makes its debut this year, highlighting new and popular products.

The catalog and specifications section starts on p. 97 ("Handguns") and covers updated facts and figures, including current suggested retail prices, on the products of more than 120 major manufacturers and distributors of firearms and related equipment. We regret the passing of Kimber rifles from these pages, but we welcome several newcomers, headed by the return of Harrington and Richardson, plus Wichita Arms, Ruko, Carl Gustaf, Feather Industries, Eagle Arms, Jarrett Rifles and Clifton Arms. All that is followed by a comprehensive section on scopes and sights. Next come more than 70 pages of information on cartridges, shotshells, bullets, powder and ballistics. A well-represented roundup of reloading equipment completes the catalog section.

The concluding portion of this year's edition—the Reference section—starts off with a review of recently published books on firearms and related subjects, then continues on with a listing of discontinued models. The ever popular and useful Gunfinder and Caliberfinder indexes will help readers find the information they seek for all gun products included in this edition.

In compiling this information, we've tried as always to be as accurate and complete as the restraints of time and space will allow. We invite your comments and suggestions and wish you a good new year of shooting, hunting, collecting, reloading and all the other pleasures of the shooting sports.

William S. Jarrett
Editor

Articles

50 YEARS AGO IN SHOOTER'S BIBLE

The following 12 pages from the 1943 SHOOTER'S BIBLE represent what was happening in the firearms industry half a century ago. In continuing our series, which began in 1988, we've selected a sampling of pages from the 1943 edition to give our readers a touch of nostalgia and perhaps a new perspective as well. For example, Winchester's Model 70 sold for $120 in 1943; today, it sells for $500 or more, depending on which of several "new" variations you select. And as before, we've added a month-by-month review of the major news and sports events in 1943. The U.S. was suffering through the second year of World War II, but already plans were underway to invade Europe and bring peace to the world. Meanwhile, SHOOTER'S BIBLE kept up its uninterrupted string of annual publications, providing its readers with all the gun news available in those war-time years.

WINCHESTER Model 70 Match Rifles
TRADE MARK

The new Winchester Model 70 target rifles, three in number, have been developed to meet the requirements of all long-range high power target shooting, and also to give service in long-range shooting at small game. All three have the same target start, differing only in the barrels.

All are characterized by a specially designed one-piece target stock of solid, close-grain selected black walnut—ample in size and weight, with large butt-stock, well rounded comb, large full pistol

grip, curving close to the guard, target butt plate and long, wide beaver-tail forestock. A new improvement is an adjustable forestock base for the forward sling swivel, which provides for adjustment to suit the shooter's reach. A sling accessory located here, bakelite hand-rest, raises the sling and avoids pinching the hand.

For .22 Win. Hornet, .250-3000 Savage, .270 Win., .30 Govt. M/06, 7 M/M, .257 Win. Roberts,—with 24" barrel. For .220 Win. Swift, .300 H. & H. Magnum with 26" barrel.

MODEL 70 NATIONAL MATCH RIFLE

SOLID FRAME

24" round Winchester Proof Steel barrel, floating type. Marksman design stock with full pistol grip and full fluted comb. Length of pull, 13¼"; drop at comb, 1⁹⁄₁₆"; drop at heel, 1⅞"; pitch down, 3".

Lyman No. 77 front sight on forged ramp sight base. Lyman No. 48WH receiver sight. Telescope mount bases. 1¼" Army type leather sling strap.

Order by symbol shown below

G7091C—National Match .30 Govt. M/06.... .... **$120.80**

MODEL 70 TARGET MODEL RIFLE WITH MEDIUM WEIGHT BARREL

SOLID FRAME

Medium weight Winchester Proof Steel barrel. Marksman design stock with full pistol grip and full fluted comb. Length of pull, 13¼"; drop at comb, 1⁹⁄₁₆"; drop at heel, 1⅞"; pitch down, 3".

Lyman No. 77 front sight, Lyman No. 48WH receiver sight. Telescope mount bases. 1¼" Army type leather sling strap.

Order by symbol shown below

G7041C—.22 Hornet
G7042C—.250-3000 Savage
G7043C—.270 Win.
G7044C—.30 Govt. M/06   } 24" barrel
G7045C—7 M/M
G7046C—.257 Roberts
G7047C—.35 Remington
.... **$131.90**

G7048C—.220 Swift   } 26" barrel
G7049C—.300 H. and H. Magnum

G7040C—.30 Govt. '06 (without sights)   24" barrel **$111.15**

MODEL 70 BULL GUN

SOLID FRAME

28" heavy Winchester Proof Steel barrel, floating type. Marksman design stock with full pistol grip and full fluted comb. Length of pull, 13¼"; drop at comb, 1⁹⁄₁₆"; drop at heel, 1⅞"; pitch down, 3".

Lyman No. 77 front sight, no ramp. Lyman No. 48WH receiver sight. Telescope mount bases. 1¼" Army type leather sling strap.

Order by symbol shown below

G7092C—.30 Govt. M/06   } 28" Rd. Barrel. **$142.70**
G7093C—.300 H. and H. Magnum

SAVAGE BOLT ACTION RIFLES

MODEL 40 SUPER SPORTER

CALIBERS:
.250-3000 Savage with 22 inch barrel.
.300 Savage with 24 inch barrel.

FOR BIG GAME

A rifle that American sportsmen have craved for years—embodying many features heretofore found only in expensive, imported rifles. Chambered for such outstanding cartridges as the famous .250-3000 and .300 Savage, the Sporter Rifle is a quality arm at a remarkably low price.

SPECIFICATIONS

Model 40—Standard Grade. Adjustable semi-buckhorn rear sight; white metal bead front sight.

SPECIFICATIONS—Bolt action, solid frame repeating rifle. Tapered round barrel with raised ramp front sight base. One-piece walnut stock with pistol grip and British type forestock, rubbed oil finish; corrugated steel butt plate. Four-shot, detachable magazine, 3-shot capacity. Weight about 7½ pounds.

For quality of materials, excellence of workmanship and mod-

The bolt is completely housed in against dirt, snow, etc. The ignition is exceptionally rapid, the firing pin having only ⅜-inch stroke. Another feature is the hunter's ability to insert a fresh magazine while the bolt is closed and a loaded cartridge is in the chamber.

erate price, the Super-Sporter equals the best commercial arms. The technical staff has put the fruit of its many years of experience into the design and manufacture of this fine rifle—and the hunter who owns one will find years of satisfactory service.

Model 40, Super Sporter.....................................$60.25
Extra for Lyman No. 40 Receiver Peepsight...................... 4.60
Extra Magazines, each....................................... 2.30

MODEL 23-D

FOR SMALL GAME

CALIBER: .22 Hornet

Model 23-D—.22 Hornet Bolt Action Repeating Rifle. High-speed lock. Five-shot detachable magazine. Hi-Power smokeless steel 25-inch barrel. New design, large size, one-piece pistol grip stock and forearm of selected walnut, oil finish. Flat top, adjustable sporting rear sight and gold bead front sight. Weight about 6½ pounds.

New High-Speed Lock—The speed of the new lock is less than 2-1000 of a second. This speed eliminates shift in aim between release of trigger and ignition.

The trajectory is extremely flat and a trained rifleman can make sure hits on small game and vermin up to 200 yards.

The .22 Hornet will be found the most satisfactory small game, woodchuck and target rifle. With it the skill of any rifleman should be increased and more satisfactory results secured.

Model 23-D—.22 Hornet Sporter Rifle $42.50
Extra Magazine for 23-B, C, or D............................ 1.45
Extras for the above rifle can be had as follows:
⅞-inch leather sling strap 2.30
1¼-inch leather sling strap 2.65

MODELS 23-B & 23-C

FOR SMALL GAME

CALIBERS: .25-20 and .32-20

Model 23-B—.25-20 Caliber Repeating, Bolt Action Rifle. 25-inch round barrel, one-piece walnut stock, full pistol grip. Four shot detachable box type magazine. Weight 6½ pounds.

Model 23-C—.32-20 (.32 Winchester) Repeating, Bolt Action Rifle. Same specifications as above.

In the introduction of the Models 23-B and 23-C Sporter Rifles, sportsmen were offered at a moderate price a bolt action rifle for small and medium game designed to handle the efficient .25-20 and .32-20 cartridges.

The barrels are made of Hi-Pressure steel and are carefully

made to insure extreme accuracy. The pistol grip stock was carefully designed to give perfect balance and to maintain the attractive appearance which characterizes Savage Rifles. The loading is quick and positive—detachable box magazines are interchangeable, allowing loaded magazines to be carried and quickly changed. Safety in rear of receiver can be operated by the hand in firing position.

Model 23-B—.25-20 caliber Sporter Rifle.....................$42.50
Model 23-C—.32-20 caliber Sporter Rifle..................... 42.50

MODEL 29

.22 Caliber, Hammerless, Takedown Repeating, Slide Action Rifle

Selected walnut stock, full pistol grip, checkered. Hard rubber butt plate. Extra long checkered walnut fore-end. Tubular magazine, capacity 20 short, 17 long or 15 long rifle cartridges.

Takedown receiver, one-piece bolt easily removed for cleaning. short fore-end stroke ejects and loads; positive operation. Push button type safety in rear of trigger guard. Adjustable flat top sporting rear sight, gold bead front sight. Stock tang drilled and tapped for all standard aperture sights, and especially for Savage No. 30 Rear Peep sight. Weight about 5¾ pounds.

Model 29—(As described above)...............................$30.75
Model 29-S—Same specifications as Model 29 except equipped with Savage No. 30 rear peep sight and Savage No. 31 folding middle sight..... 33.90

Chambered for .22 long rifle rim fire cartridges. Will also function and shoot without adjustment, .22 long or .22 short rim fire cartridges. Suitable for use with either "high speed" or "regular" cartridges. 24 inch octagon barrel of selected barrel steel, rifled with same four groove system used in Model 19 Target Rifle.

BIG VALUES IN MARLIN
.22 Cal. REPEATING RIFLES

← **MODEL 39-A—$35.95**

25-SHOT REPEATING RIFLE—World's Best All-Around .22

Marlin's Model 39A is the only lever action .22 cal. repeating rifle made, the only take down rifle exposing all working parts for cleaning and oiling by the turning of a single hand screw. Looks and handles like a custom job! 24″ semi-heavy, round-tapered blued steel barrel with Ballard type rifling. Crowned muzzle. Full magazine, holds 25 short, 20 long or 18 long rifle .22 cal. cartridges. Shoots regular and high-speed loads without adjustment. Side ejection. New unbreakable coiled main and trigger springs. Newly designed visible hammer. Solid top, case-hardened receiver. Silver bead front sight, flat top Rocky Mountain rear sight, drilled and tapped for tang peep sight. Low sighting plane for telescope mounting. Full pistol grip buttstock of genuine American black walnut, semi-beaver tail forearm designed to prevent canting. Overall length 41″, weight about 6½ lbs.

MODEL 81-C—$15.80 and MODEL 81-DL—$17.25
(Illustrated)

25-SHOT .22 CAL.
TUBULAR MAGAZINE REPEATER

Marlin's strong, reliable, bolt action repeater features important improvements. New military type one-piece buttstock with fluted comb and semi-beaver tail forearm, newly designed bolt handle, new OFF and ON safety. 24″ round tapered blue steel barrel, crowned muzzle, Ballard type rifling. New unique feeding mechanism, of simple positive action. Chrome-plated bolt assembly and trigger. Rocky Mountain type rear sight, silver bead front sight. Removable bolt assembly, flush take down screw, automatic side ejection, self-cocking action, quick-release trigger. Shoots .22 cal. short, long and long rifle; regular or high speed without adjustment. Magazine holds 25 short, 20 long, or 18 long rifle cartridges. Overall length 42½″; weight, about 6½ pounds. Designed for low mount telescopes.

MODEL 81-DL—Same specifications as Model 81-C but with peep sight, ramp front sight and hood and swivels.

MODEL A1-C—$16.80 and MODEL A1-DL—$18.20
(Illustrated)

6-SHOT .22 CAL.
AUTOMATIC REPEATER

Re-designed and improved; shoots as fast as the trigger can be pulled New military type, one-piece buttstock with fluted comb and semi-beaver tail forearm; equipped with Rocky Mountain type rear sight, silver bead front sight. 24″ round tapered blued steel barrel, crowned muzzle. Ballard type rifling. For regular and high speed .22 cal. long rifle greased cartridges only. Automatic side ejector, new OFF and ON safety. flush take down screw. Overall length 42½″; weight about 6 lbs. Packed 10 in case. Weight about 75 lbs.

MODEL A1-DL—Same specification as Model A1-C but with peep sight, ramp front sight and hood and swivels.

POPULAR AND MODERATELY PRICED

GENUINE BROWNING AUTOMATIC SHOTGUNS

SKEET MODEL
12, 16 and 20 GAUGES.

With Cutts Compensator.
All gauges chambered for 2¾" shells.

The Browning Automatic "Skeet Model" has proved itself to be an ideal skeet gun. The popularity of the Browning Automatic at skeet shooting, together with the outstanding records of thousands of Browning shooters is evidence of its performance and satisfaction.

A careful study by our technicians has developed the present Browning Skeet Model, which has proven to be the ideal skeet gun. Its dependability, perfect balance, "quick handling" and performance has earned for it a following among experienced skeet shooters unequalled by any other gun.

STOCK SPECIFICATIONS—Half pistol grip—drop at comb 1⅝ inches—drop at heel 2½ inches—length 14¼ inches.

Special Skeet Model, Either Gauge, 5- or 3-Shot, equipped with ventilated rib (as illustrated), and Cutts Compensator in 26" length only.....	$112.35
(Blued Steel Compensator with skeet and full choke tubes regularly supplied or blued aluminum furnished when specified).	
Extra for Beavertail Forearm...................	8.85
Cutts Compensator fitted to any other Browning Automatic Shotgun, blued steel or blued aluminum with skeet and full choke tubes (add to price of gun)	24.50
Additional Pattern Control Tubes—each........	3.60
Extra for barrel length other than 26", including Compensator with skeet tube (add to price of gun)	4.85

UTILITY FIELD GUN
12, 16 and 20 GAUGES.

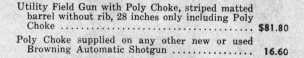

With Aero-Dyne Super Poly Choke.
All gauges chambered for 2¾" shells.

The Browning Utility Field Gun has been produced to meet the demand of field shooters. The utility feature of the Poly Choke which provides varying degrees of chokes is desirable to many.

The Browning Utility Field Gun now combines this flexible feature with all the advantages of the Browning Automatic described on pages 2 and 3.

STOCK SPECIFICATIONS—Half pistol grip—drop at comb 1⅝ inches—drop at heel 2½ inches, length 14¼ inches.

5 OR 3 SHOT

5-Shot is Adjustable to 3-Shot with Browning Magazine Adaptor (3-shot magazine plug) Furnished at no extra cost with all new 5-shot guns.

Utility Field Gun with Poly Choke, striped matted barrel without rib, 28 inches only including Poly Choke	$81.80
Poly Choke supplied on any other new or used Browning Automatic Shotgun	16.60

EXTRAS
(On New Guns Only)

Oil Finishing Stock........................	$3.00
Oil Finishing Forearm	2.00
Recoil Pad, any standard type, fitted (no extra charge for shortening stock)	6.75
Beavertail Forearm	8.85
Stock shortened up to 1 inch...............	3.75
Stocks made to special dimensions other than regular specifications of standard American Walnut.......................	19.80
Sights, Ivory or Red, fitted, each	1.50
Sights, Ivory or Red, fitted, per set front and middle.........	2.65
Sling Straps, leather, including swivels, fitted on new Automatic Shotguns	2.20

WINCHESTER
TRADE MARK

Model 40 Automatic (Self-Loading) Shotguns
Streamlined for Natural Pointing

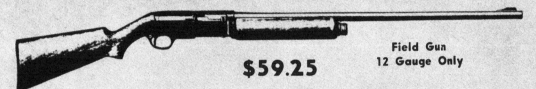

$59.25

**Field Gun
12 Gauge Only**

MODEL 40 FIELD GUN

This handsomely streamlined completely new design represents the latest development of the Winchester Automatic (self-loading) gun principle. It includes a number of new features that combine to make it an outstanding gun, with smoothness of operation, balance and handling feel, and mechanical precision.

Chambered for 2¾" shells. Pistol grip stock of standard grade American walnut. Stock and forearm not checkered. Dimensions: Length of pull, 14". Drop at comb, 1½". Drop at heel, 2½". Pitch down 2". Stock to special dimensions can be furnished at extra charge on special order only. Plain barrel of Winchester proof-steel in lengths and chokes as listed below. Magazine capacity of four shells. Furnished with wooden magazine plug to reduce capacity to three shots where required, and desired. Hard rubber, checkered butt plate. Weight approximately eight pounds. Solid raised matted rib and ventilated rib barrels cannot be furnished.

	Barrel Length	Choke	Price
G4006S	30 inches	full	$68.15
G4008S	30 inches	modified	68.15
G4003S	28 inches	full	68.15
G4005S	28 inches	Modified	68.15

MODEL 40 SKEET GUN
(With Cutts Compensator Attached)

You will find the Winchester Model 40 skeet gun a handsome, well balanced standard skeet gun. Replacing no other skeet model, this gun is introduced to give skeet shooters a gun of the automatic or self-loading type with the same superior type provided in Winchester double barrel and slide-operated repeater types of special skeet guns.

The Model 40 has a plain barrel with forged muzzle shoulder and Cutts compensator attached. Besides the compensators spreader tube for skeet there is a .705 full-choke tube which interchanges with the spreader, and a special wrench for seating the tubes. Overall length of barrel with choke tube attached is 25⅜ inches. Regular stock dimensions are: Length of pull 14"; drop at comb 1⅜"; drop at heel 2⅜"; pitch down, 2". The forearm is full, round, semi-beavertail, about 2" wide and 10⅜" long. Weight, approximately 8 pounds.

		Price
G4011S	Steel Compensator	$99.40
G4012S	Aluminum Compensator (bright)	99.40
G4013S	Aluminum Comp. (blacked)	99.40

Better balance, from improved distribution of receiver's weight. Note too, both hands in the same horizontal plane, which helps shooting speed and accuracy.

You can load the magazine of Model 40 with one hand. To unload just press down the shell carrier with your thumb, catch each shell with thumb and take them into your hand.

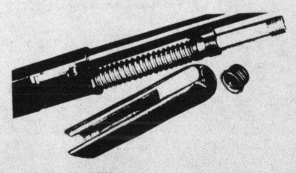

MODEL 40 IS AN OUTSTANDING GUN

PARKER SHOTGUNS

PARKER A. H. E.

Specially selected high grade figured walnut stock and fore-end, beautifully checkered. Solid gold name plate inlaid in pistol grip cap or in stock, engraved with name or monogram. Any stock measurements, including any style of grip, cheek piece, Monte Carlo or cast off. Rubber recoil pad or engraved skeleton steel butt plate. Tastefully applied engraving, English scroll or game scenes and scroll, as desired. Nickel plated triggers. Hinged front trigger. Ivory sights if desired. Automatic ejectors. Made in 10, 12, 16, 20, 28, and .410 gauges. Any boring of barrels.

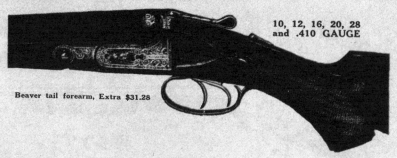

10, 12, 16, 20, 28 and .410 GAUGE

Beaver tail forearm, Extra $31.28

"A. H. E." Grade with double triggers $534.77
"A. H. E." Grade with selective single trigger 567.06
Raised ventilated rib, extra 35.32
Extra set of interchangeable barrels 227.03

PARKER A. A. H. E.

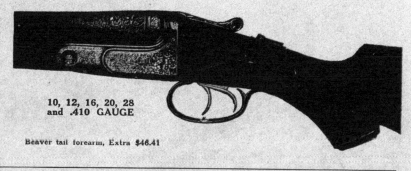

10, 12, 16, 20, 28 and .410 GAUGE

Beaver tail forearm, Extra $38.34

Beautifully figured selected curly walnut stock and fore-end, expertly fitted and shaped by hand to customer's individual needs. Artistically hand checkered. Solid gold name plate inlaid in pistol grip cap or in stock with engraved name or monogram. Any stock dimensions including cheek piece, Monte Carlo or cast off, and any style of grip. Choice of recoil pad or engraved skeleton steel butt plate. Highest quality engraving on barrels and frame—either scroll or a combination of game scenes and scroll. Silver plated triggers. Hinged front trigger. Ivory sights if desired. Automatic ejectors. Made in 10, 12, 16, 20, 28, and .410 gauges. Any boring of barrels.

"A. A. H. E." Grade with double triggers $756.75
"A. A. H. E." Grade with selective single trigger. 798.62
Raised ventilated rib, extra 46.41
Extra set of interchangeable barrels 325.91

PARKER A-1 SPECIAL

Made to order individually. Finest obtainable specially selected curly walnut stock and fore-end. Elaborate hand checkering. Any stock dimensions, including Monte Carlo, cheek piece or cast off, and any style of grip desired. Choice of recoil pad or engraved skeleton steel butt plate. Barrels and frame extensively engraved. Gold inlay if desired. Triggers gold plated. Hinged front trigger. Solid gold name plate inlaid in pistol grip cap or in stock with owner's name or monogram. Ivory sights if desired. Automatic ejectors. Made in 10, 12, 16, 20, 28, and .410 gauges. Any boring of barrels.

"A. 1. SPECIAL" Grade with double
  triggers $898.01
"A. 1. SPECIAL" Grade with selective
  single trigger 950.48
Raised ventilated rib, extra 46.41
Extra set of interchangeable barrels..... 393.51

10, 12, 16, 20, 28 and .410 GAUGE

Beaver tail forearm, Extra $46.41

PARKER SKEET GUNS

All double barrel PARKER guns from the "V. H. E." Grade up are furnished in Skeet models. These guns are built to the customer's individual specifications. They are thoroughly tested to insure the finest shooting qualities at Skeet ranges.

Made in 12, 16, 20, 28, and .410 gauges, 26-inch barrels. Bored for Skeet shooting. Right barrel marked "SKEET-OUT" for first shot at outgoing target. Left barrel marked "SKEET-IN" for incoming target. Option of any other barrel length and boring. Automatic ejectors. Non-automatic safety. Option of automatic safety. Selective single trigger. Ivory bead front and rear sights. Red bead front sight if desired. Beavertail fore-end. Stock dimensions, unless otherwise specified, 14 inches long, 2¼ inches drop at heel, 1½ inches drop at comb. Checkered butt on "V. H. E." and "G. H. E." grades. Skeleton steel butt on "D. H. E." to "A. 1. SPECIAL" grades. Straight grip. Option of full pistol grip with cap or half pistol grip. Stock measurements and other specifications will be varied in accordance with descriptions and prices given under separate grades. Quality of walnut, type of engraving, and other features correspond with respective

This Illustration Shows The

"V. H. E." Grade Skeet Gun

grades. Also supplied with raised ventilated rib at the extra charge.

"V. H. E." Grade Skeet Gun.................................$184.09
"G. H. E." Grade Skeet Gun................................. 204.27
"D. H. E." Grade Skeet Gun................................. 248.21
"C. H. E." Grade Skeet Gun................................. 350.12
"B. H. E." Grade Skeet Gun................................. 455.06
"A. H. E." Grade Skeet Gun................................. 598.34
"A. A. H. E." Grade Skeet Gun.............................. 836.97
"A. 1. SPECIAL" Grade Skeet Gun........................... 996.89

L. C. SMITH SHOTGUNS

"CROWN GRADE"

The L. C. Smith Royal Family of custom-built shotguns is perfectly represented by the Crown Grade. A small gold crown on the top-lever is symbolic of the beauty and quality of the complete gun. Selected walnut stock rich in finish, figure, color; fine, neat, hand-checkering; strong Nitro Steel Barrels carefully selected. Unsurpassed for artistic appointments. Delicately engraved hunting dogs on the lock-plates. Mechanical perfection. For the man of unusual discrimination.

With two triggers and Automatic Ejectors......................$315.50
With Automatic Ejectors and Selective Hunter One-trigger (EO)..... 347.85
With Automatic Ejectors, Selective Hunter One-trigger, Beavertail
Forend, (EOB) 383.80

Gauge	Barrels
12, 16 or 20 .410-caliber	26, 28, 30 or 32-inch Nitro Steel, proof tested, bored to order from full choke to cylinder, .410-caliber, 26 and 28-inch only.

Weights	Grip
12-gauge.........6 lbs. 6 oz. to 8¼ lbs.	Full-pistol is standard.
16-gauge....................6¼ to 7 lbs.	Half or straight
20-gauge...................5¾ to 6½ lbs.	to order.
.410-caliber................5½ to 5⅞ lbs.	

"MONOGRAM GRADE"

Custom-built to incorporate your personal requirements . . . engraved to attest our engravers' skill . . . monogrammed in gold to certify your ownership. Carefully shaped Circassian Walnut Stock of satin smoothness and beautiful curly grain. Exquisite engraving and a remarkable combination of English Scroll Work and Teutonic Relief. Barrels are of Sir Joseph Whitworth Fluid Steel . . . superior in hardness, tensile strength, and fine finish. A connoisseur's choice.

With Automatic Ejectors, Selective Hunter One-trigger (EO).......$639.65
With Automatic Ejectors, Selective Hunter One-trigger, Beavertail
Forend, (EOB) 702.60

L. C. SMITH DE LUXE GRADE

A quiet elegance surrounds the serene splendor of the L. C. Smith Premier. Its hand-worked Circassian Walnut Stock and skillfully hand-checkered matching forend are perfectly accentuated by the delicate engraving and hunting dogs depicted in gold on both lock-plates. Sir Joseph Whitworth Fluid Steel Barrels. A gold monogrammed seal inlet in the stock consummates a crowning achievement . . . a genteel work of the gun maker's art. Custom-made to any gauge, barrel length, grip, and stock specifications.

De Luxe Grade $1,458.45
With Automatic Ejectors, Selective Hunter One-trigger, Beavertail
Forend, (EOB) 1,530.35

DETAILS FOR THE MONOGRAM, PREMIER, AND DE LUXE	
Gauge	Barrels
12, 16 or 20 .410-caliber	26, 28, 30 or 32-inch Whitworth Fluid Steel, proof tested, bored to order from full choke to cylinder, .410-caliber, 26 and 28-inch only.

Weights	Grip
12-gauge.........6 lbs. 6 oz. to 8¼ lbs.	Full-pistol is standard.
16-gauge....................6¼ to 7 lbs.	Half or straight
20-gauge...................5¾ to 6½ lbs.	to order.
.410-caliber................5½ to 5⅞ lbs.	

OLYMPIC GRADE

SINGLE BARREL TRAP GUN

PRICES

Olympic	$100.00
Specialty	154.55
Crown	287.85
Monogram	476.20
De Luxe	1,190.25

Stock and fore-end from especially selected walnut. Grip: Full pistol, half pistol or straight. Barrels: 12 gauge, 30, 32 and 34 inches, Nitro steel, bored by the Smith system for perfection in trap shooting. Trigger Position: Rear, unless otherwise specified. The Olympic single-barrel is manufactured and sold only in the one standard stock dimension, 14½—1½—1⅞, full pistol grip, while the Specialty and better grades can be had in any reasonable stock dimensions and in the different style pistol grips. Recoil pad and Lyman sights included as regular equipment on all Smith single barrel trap guns.

EXTRA EQUIPMENT

If the combination you want is not listed on these pages, it may be made up from the prices shown below of the two trigger gun without ejector, the extra price of the features desired. Price combinations must be on the same grade. To obtain the price of any type combination on any L. C. Smith gun, add to the base price.

AUTOMATIC EJECTOR

Field, Skeet and Ideal—E $17.10
Trap, Specialty and Crown—E 21.60
Monogram, Premier and De Luxe—E 25.15

SELECTIVE HUNTER ONE-TRIGGER

Field Skeet and Ideal—O $24.55
Specialty and Crown—O 32.35
Monogram and De Luxe—O....................................... 39.50

NON-SELECTIVE HUNTER ONE-TRIGGER

Field and Ideal—N $16.05

BEAVER TAIL FORE-END

Ideal—B $18.95
Specialty—B 25.15
Crown—B 35.95
Monogram—B 62.95
De Luxe—B 79.90

VENTILATED RIB
Including Recoil Pad and Two Ivory Sights

Ideal, Specialty and Crown—V..................................$32.35
Monogram and De Luxe—V 39.50

ACCESSORIES

Recoil Pad (and grade) $5.75
Leather Covered Recoil Pad 6.90
Checkered Trigger (and grade) 2.30
Checkered Butt (except on Skeet) 4.05
Ivory Sights (per pair) 1.45
Oil Finished Stock (Field, Skeet Special, Ideal) 4.85

ZEPHYR SHOTGUNS

ZEPHYR CROWN GRADE

The Zephyr "Crown Grade" is a weapon of superior quality and particularly pleasing appearance. A gun available in all calibers and weights to meet any requirements. It is built on the well-known Anson & Deeley system and will find approval among those accustomed to seeking this quality of gun only in weapons of a much higher price.

Zephyr, Crown Grade, 12, 16 and 20 Ga.............$175.00
Zephyr, Crown Grade, 28 or .410 Ga.................. 190.00
Extra for Selective Single Trigger.................... 35.00

Zephyr
Crown Grade
Model 404E

ZEPHYR PREMIER GRADE

The Zephyr "Premier Grade" is of the same quality as the "Crown Grade" although built on slightly different lines including side plate thus allowing a large field for engraving for those who desire a gun embodying not only quality but extremely smart appearance as well. This gun, too, is available in a variety of calibers, barrel lengths, etc.

Zephyr, Premier Grade, 12, 16 or 20 Ga.............$195.00

Zephyr, Premier Grade, 28 or .410 Ga.............. 210.00

Extra for Selective Single Trigger.................... 35.00

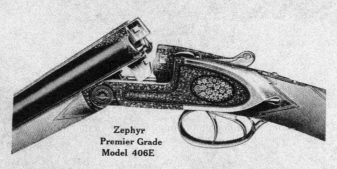

Zephyr
Premier Grade
Model 406E

Zephyr
Royal Grade
Model 410E

ZEPHYR ROYAL GRADE

The Zephyr "Royal Grade" has been built to satisfy the demands of the most discriminating shooters and those who have been accustomed to only the very finest in shotguns. The "Royal Grade" is a truly first quality gun built along the lines of the finest English first quality guns with which the "Royal Grade" compares most favorably although at but a fraction of the cost. The gun has genuine side locks, is of extremely smooth operation and perfect balance, made throughout of the best materials, and the engraving is of the finest English scroll type. This gun will bear comparison with guns selling at $1,000.00 and more.

Zephyr, Royal Grade, 12, 16 and 20 Ga..............$395.00
Zephyr, Royal Grade, 28 or .410 Ga.................. 415.00
Extra for Selective Single Trigger.................... 50.00

ZEPHYR DOUBLE RIFLES

ZEPHYR DOUBLE BARREL

To meet the demand for a really first quality double rifle at a fairly reasonable price, we offer the Zephyr "Double" which is patterned after the finest English double rifles and is more carefully built and executed in the very best of material, assuring easy and certainty of operation as well as ruggedness and high accuracy. This gun will be found dependable even under the most adverse and vigorous conditions. It is built only to order and may be had for any big game cartridge.

Zephyr Double Rifle.............................$475.00

Zephyr
Double Rifle
Model 420E

POWELL SHOTGUNS AND DOUBLE RIFLES

Chambered for the new 2-inch 12 gauge shells.

Anson & Deeley locks, Southgate ejector. Weight 5¼ pounds.

Ideal for ladies and elderly sportsmen. Lighter and more effective than a 20 bore.

Fine quality and well finished.

POWELL "TWO INCH" 12 GA.
Price in England........£47/5/0
Price in U. S. A.........$350.00

POWELL'S PIGEON AND WILDFOWL GUN

Price in England......£42/0/0
Price in U. S. A......$315.00

A handsome fine quality gun, 30-inch steel barrels, both full choke, chambered for 2¾-inch or 3-inch cartridges and specially bored to give dense patterns, dead level flat file cut rib, Anson & Deeley locks, treble grip with strong square concealed cross bolt and side clips. Half pistol grip stock. Handsomely engraved and finished. Weight 7½ pounds to 8 pounds.

A plain well made Hammerless Ejector of the Anson & Deeley type constructed under our personal supervision. English steel barrels, carefully bored, and shooting powers equal to the best productions. Well adapted for hard wear and Colonial use.

THE POWELL No. 9
Price in England........£36/15/0
Price in U. S. A.........$275.00

POWELL'S "MATCH" GUN
Designed Especially for Use in the U. S. A.

A sound well-made gun, 30-inch or 32-inch steel barrels, both full choke, chambered for 2¾-inch or 3-inch cartridges, flat file cut rib, Anson & Deeley locks, treble grip, concealed cross bolt, side clips. Half pistol grip stock. Engraved and well finished. Weight in 12 gauge, 7½ pounds to 8 pounds.

Price $275.00

POWELL DOUBLE RIFLES

AVAILABLE ON ORDER IN ALL CALIBERS FOR THE HEAVIEST GAME

Double barrel Hammerless Ejector, High Velocity. Best quality. Plain finish as illustrated. Made in all calibers to the individual requirements and specifications of the user.

Price in England..........£84
Price in U. S. A......$620.00

COLT AUTOMATIC PISTOLS

ACE .22 AUTOMATIC PISTOL CAL. .22 LONG RIFLE

The ACE is designed especially for shooters of the Government Model and Super .38 Automatic Pistols—and has also been in demand by shooters for all around service. Built on the same frame as the Government Model and has the same safety features. Special super-precisioned barrel and hand finished target action. Exceptionally smooth operation and unusually accurate. Rear sight is of target design with adjustments for both elevation and windage. Allows economical target practice for military men, using 22 caliber ammunition in an arm of the same design as the regular military model. For Regular and High Speed Greased Cartridges.

Price $53.75
Extra Magazine. 3.00

SPECIFICATIONS

Ammunition: .22 Long Rifle Greased cartridges. Regular or High Speed.
Magazine Capacity: 10 cartridges.
Length of Barrel: 4¾ inches.
Length Over All: 8¼ inches.

Action: Hand finished.
Weight: 38 ounces.
Sights: Front sight fixed. Rear sight adjustable for both elevation and windage.

Trigger and Hammer Spur: Checked.
Arched Housing: Checked.
Stocks: Checked Walnut.
Finish: Blued.

Price $44.75
Extra Magazine. 1.60

SUPER .38 AUTOMATIC PISTOL CALIBER .38

For the big game hunter, and the lover of the outdoors, the Super .38 offers an arm of unsurpassed power and efficiency. It is built on the same frame as the Government Model and has all of the safety features found in this famous gun. It is especially popular because of the powerful Super .38 cartridges which it handles—having a muzzle velocity of approximately 1300 foot seconds. Will stop any animal on the American continent and is a favorite for use as an auxiliary arm for big game hunting trips. Magazine holds 9 cartridges.

SPECIFICATIONS

Sights: Fixed Patridge type.
Trigger and Hammer Spur: Checked.
Arched Housing: Checked.
Stocks: Checked Walnut.
Finish: Blued. Nickel Finish at extra cost of $5.00.

Ammunition: .38 Automatic cartridges.
Magazine Capacity: 9 cartridges.
Length of Barrel: 5 inches.
Length Over All: 8½ inches.
Weight: 39 ounces.

GOVERNMENT MODEL AUTOMATIC PISTOL CAL. .45

The Colt Arched Housing is illustrated above—used on all heavy frame Colt models. It provides a more secure and more comfortable grip.

The Colt Government Model is the most famous Automatic Pistol in the world. It has for years been the Official side arm of the United States Army, Navy and Marine Corps, as well as the military organizations of many foreign countries. Extremely powerful and absolutely dependable. Magazine holds seven cartridges and magazines can be replaced with great speed. Rugged and simple, it has withstood the most rigorous tests by the United States Government and proved itself unsurpassed in reliability and efficiency.

Price $44.75
Extra Magazine. 1.80

SPECIFICATIONS

Ammunition: .45 Automatic cartridges.
Magazine Capacity: 7 cartridges.
Length of Barrel: 5 inches.
Length Over All: 8½ inches.
Sights: Fixed Patridge type.
Weight: 39 ounces.

Trigger and Hammer Spur: Checked.
Arched Housing: Checked.
Stocks: Checked Walnut.
Finish: Blued. Nickel Finish $5.00 extra.

Price $52.75

COLT NATIONAL MATCH CALIBER .45

The regulation Government Model side arm perfected for match competition. Identical in size and operation, but with velvet-smooth hand-honed target action and a super-precisioned match barrel. Full grip, fine balance, three safety features. Now with adjustable rear sight and ramp type front sight, Colt's National Match brings you accuracy, power and smoothness never before equalled in a caliber .45 automatic pistol.

COLT SUPER MATCH CALIBER .38

With the exception that it is chambered for the high-powered .38 automatic cartridge, the Super Match Automatic Pistol is identical in every way with the National Match Model. It has the same velvet-smooth action, precision match barrel, same dependable safety features, same checked arched housing, same firm non-slipping grip. Accuracy, of course, is further increased by the new sights now available; ramp type front and adjustable rear. The Colt Super Match answers every demand in a caliber .38 automatic for competitive shooting—and possesses tremendous power for the big game hunter.
Prices: National Match and Super Match with adjustable sight $52.75
National Match and Super Match with fixed sights 47.25

SPECIFICATIONS

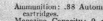

DOUBLE ADJUSTABLE REAR SIGHT AND A RAMP TYPE FIXED FRONT SIGHT WITH SERRATED FACE

Here is a beautiful and efficient new rear sight for the Colt National Match and Super Match Automatic Pistols. It is designed especially for these two arms, constructed with **precision**, and adjustable for both windage and elevation. Take a close look at the illustration. Note the simplicity of this new sight, how extremely easy it is to adjust and to set accurately. It's just the finest hand gun sight ever made. And we mean just that. A host of shooters are going to like the new ramp type rugged sight out front, too. All of which means cleaner definition, higher and more consistent scoring.

Ammunition: .38 Automatic cartridges.
Magazine Capacity: 9 cartridges.
Length of Barrel: 5 inches.
Length Over All: 8½ inches.
Weight: 39 ounces.

Action: Hand honed, velvet-smooth.
Stocks: Checked Walnut.
Sights: Adjustable rear, with Adjustments for elevation and windage. Ramp front sight.

Trigger and Hammer Spur: Checked.
Arched Housing: Checked.
Finish: Blued. Can be furnished in nickel finish at extra cost of $5.00.

ADJUSTABLE SIGHTS ON OLDER PISTOLS

You don't have to buy a new gun to enjoy the truly remarkable advantages of this new rear sight. For seven dollars and seventy-five cents, we will equip your Government Model and Super .38, as well as your National Match Model, or your Super Match, with this new sight combination. This includes the cost of the sight, recutting the sight slide cut, labor and targeting. It's a lot of value for $9.30.

TOPS IN HEAVY SERVICE REVOLVERS

SMITH & WESSON

.38/44 HEAVY DUTY

$37.50

An ideal gun for combatting automobile crime — particularly popular in recent years with leading State Police Departments and Highway Patrols from coast to coast.

The .38/44 Heavy Duty is manufactured specifically to meet the exacting requirements of severe usage and represents the highest point of accuracy, efficiency and ability to withstand hard wear.

Chambered for the entire line of .38 Special Cartridges right up to and including the ultra-modern High-Velocity, Metal-Piercing .38 Specials. This gun delivers tremendous power. Yet it has a marvelous "feel" and wonderful ease in shooting due to the weight and superb balance given by its .44 caliber frame and heavy, reinforced barrel.

SPECIFICATIONS

CALIBER: .38 S & W Special
NUMBER OF SHOTS: 6
BARREL: 4 or 5 inch
LENGTH: With 5-inch barrel, 10⅜ inches
WEIGHT: With 5-inch barrel, 40 ounces
SIGHTS: Fixed, 1/10-inch service type front; square notch rear
STOCKS: Checkered Circassian walnut with S & W Monograms.
Choice of square or Magna type
FINISH: S & W Blue or Nickel

AMMUNITION
.38 S & W Special High-Speed
.38 S & W Special Super Police
.38 S & W Special
.38 S & W Special Mid-Range
.38 Short Colt
.38 Long Colt
.38 Colt Special

$37.50

1926 MODEL .44 MILITARY

SPECIFICATIONS

CALIBER: .44 S & W Special
NUMBER OF SHOTS: 6
BARREL: 4, 5 or 6½ inches
LENGTH: With 6½-inch barrel, 11¾ inches
WEIGHT: With 6½-inch barrel, 39½ ounces
SIGHTS: Fixed, 1/10-inch service type front; square notch rear
STOCKS: Checkered Circassian walnut with S & W Monograms. Choice of square or Magna type
FINISH: S & W Blue or Nickel

AMMUNITION
.44 S & W Special
.44 S & W Russian

Immensely popular in the Southwest where Police, Sheriffs and Border Patrol traditionally prefer a heavy caliber, long range sidearm.

The large frame gives the 1926 Military all the weight it needs to handle the powerful .44 S & W Special cartridge with ease and comfort, while the reinforcing lug on the barrel contributes exceptional strength and perfect balance.

The .44 Military is justly considered by many as the finest large caliber revolver ever made. Its .44 S & W Special cartridge gives it all the muzzle energy and shock power of the .45, but with far greater accuracy and ranging power.

.45 CAL. 1917 ARMY

$37.50

The 1917 Army designed for use with the .45 Auto Rim cartridge or the regular .45 Auto cartridge in semi-circular clips, was chosen by the United States Army for use by American troops in the last war.

In actual Government test it gave greater penetration, velocity and accuracy than any other gun tested. In fact, the greater accuracy possible with this arm raised the former qualifying score in the National Pistol Course of the N. R. A. several points over that required when the Automatic Pistol was used.

A very powerful, fast handling gun for practical shooting up to 100 yards. Without doubt the quickest loading, safest and accurate arm made for the Service Cartridge.

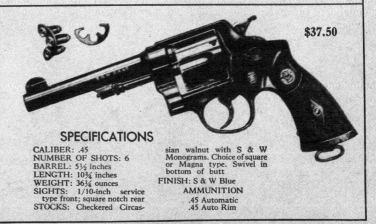

SPECIFICATIONS

CALIBER: .45
NUMBER OF SHOTS: 6
BARREL: 5½ inches
LENGTH: 10¾ inches
WEIGHT: 36¼ ounces
SIGHTS: 1/10-inch service type front; square notch rear
STOCKS: Checkered Circassian walnut with S & W Monograms. Choice of square or Magna type. Swivel in bottom of butt
FINISH: S & W Blue

AMMUNITION
.45 Automatic
.45 Auto Rim

PISTOL SHOOTING THE PROFESSIONAL WAY

by Steve Sieberts

One of the questions NRA Certified Instructors are most frequently asked is: "What is the secret to good shooting?" And their standard answer is: "There's no secret. To shoot well, you only have to do what any successful athlete must do—you must put out 100 percent and concentrate on using the basic fundamentals."

Pistol marksmanship in particular has seven such basic fundamentals, and all of them are followed by every successful shooter, whether he's the local club shooter or an Olympic competitor. The main difference between the two is that the Olympic shooter has refined his physical technique of shooting to a very high degree and has mastered the critical mental aspects of world class competition as well.

To explore all seven fundamentals of pistol shooting in depth would require several books. The purpose here is to provide shooters, old and new, with enough good, solid information to get them started in the right direction before they acquire bad habits. In addition, these pointers may also give shooters a new and different perspective on pistol marksmanship. Here, then, is a highly condensed overview of the seven fundamentals of pistol marksmanship:

1. STANCE

This is the foundation upon which all other fundamentals are built. Without a proper stance the entire shooting platform will be weakened. We will cover here the techniques for NRA bull's-eye and IPSC-style action shooting. In IPSC, the most common stance is called the "Isosceles," in which the body faces the target squarely, with the arms extended straight out. The feet should be set slightly wider than the shoulder width, especially for those who stand over six feet tall, to ensure proper balance. To counter the effect of recoil, about 60 percent of your weight should fall on the balls of your feet. The knees should be bent slightly to improve balance, and be sure to lean forward at the waist. This will also help control recoil and reduce strain in the back and shoulder muscles, as well as speed recovery after the shot. Always keep the head level, especially if you shoot with corrective lens, because the prescription is always ground better in the very center of the lens.

The arms should extend straight out, with enough muscle tension in the forearms and shoulders to keep the pistol as steady as possible without creating excessive strain. A lack of muscle tension in the arms, however, could also induce a malfunction (a point we'll cover in greater detail later on).

The bottom line in developing an effective stance is to maximize equilibrium and stability in the body to provide a solid shooting platform, and to do so without creating excessive strain in the muscles, or sacrificing mobility and flexibility.

Here the shooter takes the classic bull's-eye stance with the head kept level and the arm straight, with locked wrist and elbow.

Each shooter has a different body configuration, obviously, and so what works for one shooter may not be as effective for another. It follows that each person must develop the right combination of techniques that best matches that shooter's style. Watch other successful shooters in action and see what works for them. Don't be afraid to try a new technique—but don't change everything at once, either, because then it becomes difficult to isolate a specific technique.

In NRA-type shooting, all the above holds true, except you should face the target at a 45-degree angle, and use a little more tension in the hand and arm holding the pistol. During the timed and rapid fire stages, you need more tension in the arm to help aid recovery and keep your rhythm while you shoot.

Each shooter has a different body configuration, as these two men illustrate. It's important to find the combination that's best for you.

The shooting style shown above was popularized by Jeff Cooper. Note the bent left arm, with the body turned at a 45-degree angle to the target.

2. POSITION

This subtle aspect of shooting is one that many new shooters fail to understand fully. In order to acquire and maintain your hold in the center of the aiming area, it's necessary to establish a *natural point of aim*. You can do this by positioning your body relative to the target, so that the pistol recovers to the same spot it held prior to the shot—in the center of the aiming area.

It's really quite simple. Let's say you're firing two shots rapid fire at a target 15 yards away. At the first shot, the pistol goes into recoil and comes down slightly to the left of the target center. That means the natural point of aim was to the left of the target. You must then move the pistol to the right until it's once again in the center of the target. In rapid fire, whether it's bull's-eye or IPSC, this error in your natural point of aim could cause you to hesitate on firing the next shot until your

Finding his natural point of aim keeps this shooter centered in the target.

sights were centered, thereby ruining your shooting cadence by forcing you to speed up the next shot. That's the kiss of death for accurate shooting.

So, having learned what natural point of aim is, how do you go about achieving it? Simply by placing the body in a natural position relative to the target. It sounds easy, and it is. Assume your normal stance and hold the pistol out at a 45-degree angle to the target. Now close your eyes and raise the pistol to about the level of the target and open your eyes. You should be in the center of the target. If you're a little to the right or left, simply make an adjustment by moving your feet. I do this by pivoting on my left foot and moving my right foot forward or backward slightly. For NRA-style shooting, I'd pivot on my forward foot and move my trailing foot in the opposite direction of the error. You have to do this with your eyes closed, though, to find your true natural point of aim. Try this during your practice sessions and before firing each string.

3. GRIP

One of the most important aspects of the grip is the degree of muscle tension in the hand and forearm. If the grip is too loose, the pistol will shift in the hand during recoil, making it very difficult to re-acquire the sights. A grip that's too tight will cause the pistol to shake, forcing the shooter to apply erratic pressure to the trigger as the sights bounce around on the target. Try to maintain a grip that's firm, yet comfortable. When I first started shooting competitively, I found the proper grip by holding the pistol as if I were going to fire it. Then I'd squeeze my hand as hard as possible until the pistol began to shake. At that point, I'd back off slowly on the tension until the pistol stopped shaking. That's the point where most shooters will discover the grip tension that's right for them.

Every shooter needs a grip that allows recoil to travel straight up the arm. If the pistol twists away violently, that means the recoil is being transmitted to the base of the thumb. Make sure also that you keep a high grip on the pistol. This will help prevent the firearm from rotating around the axis of the wrist during recoil. I check for a natural grip the same way I check for natural position—by closing my eyes and raising the pistol up to the target, then opening my eyes. If the front sight is not centered in the rear sight notch, I know I must shift my hold on the pistol until I've achieved a natural sight alignment. This routine

A good shooter's grip should be firm, yet comfortable, as the shooter above demonstrates. The correct grip (below) allows the recoil to travel straight up the arm.

keeps me from having to make corrections in sight alignment during firing. Try not to exert excessive pressure in the hand, because this makes it difficult for the muscles in the trigger finger to move independently. It also makes the trigger pull seem heavier than it really is.

As noted earlier, a shooter whose grip, wrist or forearm lack sufficient muscle tension can actually induce a malfunction in a semiauto pistol. This is known as "limpwristing" a pistol, and the reason it occurs is because the recoil spring must have a firm surface to compress against. Without a firm grip and a locked wrist and elbow, the shooter can't provide that immovable surface, which in effect takes energy away from the spring, causing failures in feeding and ejecting. Another common problem with new shooters is known as "milking" the grip, or shifting the pistol in the hand while shooting.

Once you've achieved the proper grip and have

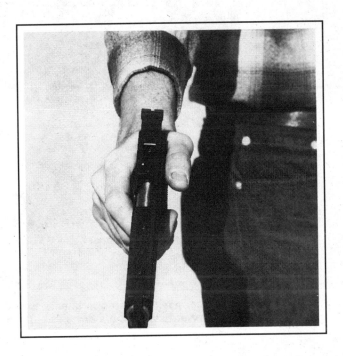

The proper stance, position and grip enable this shooter to control the pistol during rapid fire. Note how he leans forward slightly, his arms straight out to counter the effects of recoil.

This shooter's "high thumb" position can cause malfunctions, because the thumb will drag on the slide and slow it down.

begun to shoot, don't try making adjustments in the middle of a string of fire. Make sure you have the proper grip BEFORE you start shooting. Other common problems include wrapping the thumb of the non-firing hand over the top of the shooting hand (causing the recoiling slide to hit the thumb), and using the "cup and saucer" hold, in which the pistol is placed in the palm of the non-firing hand.

4. SIGHT ALIGNMENT

To shoot with any accuracy requires proper sight alignment, which means the front sight is centered in the rear sight notch, with equal daylight on both sides of the front sight, and with the top of the front sight level with the top of the rear sight.

It's important to focus your attention on the front sight only, unless the target is extremely close (five yards or less). Many new shooters are overwhelmed by how much the sights move on the target. They become convinced that in order to

achieve good scores they must look directly at the target. You must learn to disregard this movement and concentrate on maintaining good sight alignment. This point cannot be stressed enough. When I was a beginning shooter, my scores increased dramatically after I began to accept my arc of movement and focused instead on sight alignment.

All these things—a good stable stance, a proper grip, keeping a natural point of aim—will keep you in the center of the target. You must then concentrate on maintaining pinpoint focus on the front sight, accept your arc of movement (or "wobble area"), and mash the trigger. Everyone has a certain amount of movement when holding a pistol that cannot be totally eliminated; but by accepting this movement and not reacting to it, you can learn to fire a shot during the four to six seconds of peak concentration with the least amount of movement.

In speed shooting, where the targets are relatively large and the time limits short, small errors in sight alignment can still produce acceptable shots. But for bull's-eye shooting, sight alignment must be near perfect.

The truth is, pistol shooting goes against everything we were taught as children. For example, when you throw a baseball, do you look at the ball? Of course not. And when you drive a car, do you concentrate on the steering wheel, or do you look where you're driving? That explains why, when firing a pistol, we all have a tendency to look downrange at the target, not at the sights. This bad habit (for shooters) is difficult to break, but it must be if one is to become an effective shooter. By concentrating on sight alignment, you can develop the ability to call the location of the shot on the target. That's known as "follow-through," and it is essential to good marksmanship.

5. TRIGGER CONTROL

The smooth release of the trigger is another important factor in delivering a good shot. It doesn't matter if the trigger is mashed slowly or quickly, the keys to remember are *smoothness* and *consistency*. Notice we don't say "squeeze" the trigger. That's because the term implies squeezing the whole hand, which is something you want to avoid.

The technique of trigger control depends on whether you're firing a single shot or a string of shots. In firing a single shot, try to think of mashing the trigger as if you were falling off a cliff—once you start, you cannot stop, slow down, speed up, or go back. Trigger control is like that. Once you start to mash the trigger, you must apply steady pressure until the pistol fires. The only time

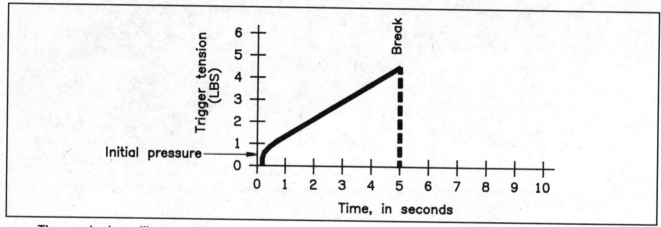

The graph above illustrates the positive, uninterrupted application of pressure to the trigger required for accurate pistol shots. The graph below shows what happens when the shooter hesitates while pulling the trigger, causing a poor shot.

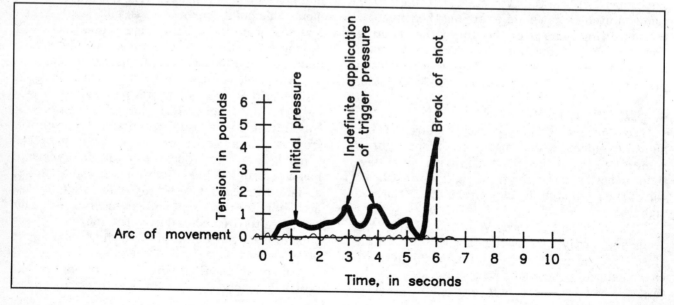

you can stop is when something breaks your concentration. When that happens, lower the pistol and start all over with the shot sequence. Many new shooters have what is known as "chicken finger," which means they hesitate to apply positive trigger pressure. Why? Because they are reacting to the movement of the sights on the target, and they are waiting until they achieve perfect sight alignment, causing them to yank on the trigger. They are also trying to catch the sights as they fly by the center of the target, again causing them to yank the trigger, hoping to force the shot in the center. This is also called "setting up the shot," or waiting until everything looks perfect before applying trigger pressure—and then applying it all at once. Normally, this causes the shot to go high right or low left on a right-handed shooter. As long as you are in the center of your aiming area, have good sight alignment, and apply smooth pressure to the trigger, you will get off a good shot.

In firing a series of shots, you need to establish a rhythm, or cadence. Try to think of your finger as being attached to a wheel. Each time it makes a revolution, the pistol fires. This technique works well when you have a set time limit, because it allows you to space your shots, thereby giving you an equal amount of time after each shot to realign the sights and re-apply trigger pressure. For IPSC shooting, there is no set time limit, but you still have to space your shots. Otherwise, you won't

have enough time to realign the sights and get the kind of quality shot you need. Every shooter has a comfort zone where speed is concerned. When you go too fast and exceed that comfort zone, the quality of the shot goes down—and so does your score. Shoot only as fast as you need to get the shot you want. And remember, a slow hit is better than a fast miss.

A word about placement of the finger on the trigger. When you're dry-firing and the front sight is jumping to the right or left, you either have too much of your finger on the trigger or too little. The trigger must be pressed straight to the rear without hesitation. No matter what your skill level may be, practice is the answer to this problem—as it is for all the others we've discussed.

6. BREATHING

Good breathing technique can do several things for you: it can oxygenate the blood to maximize visual acuity; it can relax the muscles so you can hold steadier; it can help to overcome "match nerves"; and it allows the shooter to minimize his movements while holding the pistol at arm's length. Prove this to yourself by taking three or four deep breaths, then holding one breath in about halfway. Now raise the pistol and align the sights. You'll notice the amount of movement gradually decreases. Then, after four to six seconds, the movement will slowly increase as the body runs

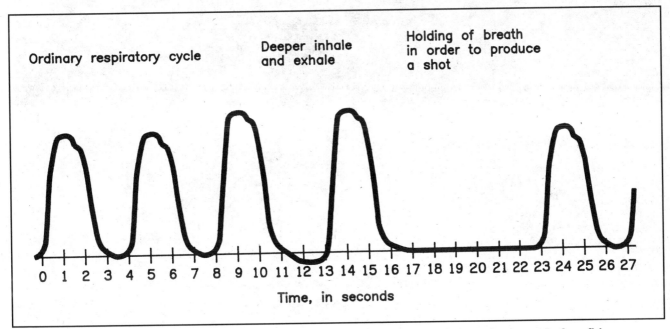

This graph illustrates the correct breathing technique needed to settle into the target before firing.

out of oxygen. It's during those few seconds of minimal movement that you should break off the shot. This "minimum arc of movement" is also the period when we have the highest amount of concentration and sharpest vision. So be sure to coordinate this short period with the smooth application of trigger pressure.

7. MENTAL DISCIPLINE (or SHOT MANAGEMENT)

Shooting is probably 95 percent mental, and it's the part with which shooters have the most trouble. Mental discipline includes thinking positively about your shooting ability, overcoming match pressure, establishing a systematic approach to shooting, using good visualization techniques, and having confidence in your ability to excel.

Many competitive shooters "psyche" themselves out before they even step up to the firing line. Some simply lack the confidence to duplicate their practice scores in a match environment.

We've all seen good shooters get so nervous before a big match that they are beaten before they step up to the line. Shooting is supposed to be fun, so relax and enjoy it. Your goal is to fire a score one point better than your best previous score. Keep telling yourself that if you can fire good scores in practice, you can certainly duplicate them in a match environment.

Sports psychologists teach us that visualization techniques are all-important. That means *seeing yourself in the act of shooting at your peak level.* That's an effective technique no matter what level your shooting ability happens to be. Establish a system that will help to organize your thinking before and during a match—and don't forget to organize your equipment as well before stepping up to the line.

Whether you're firing a single shot, a string of shots, or an entire match, your routine should go something like this:

1. Prepare. This includes all the details you need to attend to prior to the match: ammo, ear-

The concentration this shooter displays is critical to good shooting.

Bull's-eye shooting requires as much muscle tension in the arm as it does when shooting with two hands. The shooter must stay relaxed to reduce muscle tremors in the "wobble area."

plugs, glasses, magazines, scorebook, and so on. It's also the time to make the necessary mental preparations before stepping up to the line—telling yourself to relax, focusing your attention on the course of fire, and blocking out all outside interference.

2. Plan. Decide in advance how you will shoot the course of fire, where is the best place to reload, what's the best sequence to engage the targets.

3. Relax and Focus. Relax the body with the breathing techniques discussed earlier. Try to block out any negative thoughts, then focus your concentration on the shot.

4. Analysis. Check your performance constantly to make sure the plan you've formulated is working. If it isn't, analyze what went wrong and make the corrections.

5. Corrections. After you've analyzed the good and bad points of your plan, make the necessary corrections—even if the plan worked. There's always room for improvement. And that's what makes the shooting sports so challenging. There will always be new goals to strive after.

Whether you're a competitive shooter, hunter, or someone who simply enjoys plinking on the weekends, try to utilize and refine these proven techniques. You'll be well on your way to achieving a new level of shooting skill.

STEVE SIEBERTS has been involved with firearms professionally for 15 years, starting with a small arms maintenance shop in the U.S. Army's 82nd Airborne Division. He then spent four seasons with the Army Pistol team as a shooter and instructor. Sieberts holds the Distinguished Pistol Shot badge, the President's Hundred tab, and is a member of the prestigious 2600 Club. He is also an active IPSC competitor, an NRA Certified Law Enforcement Firearms instructor, and a graduate of four gunsmithing schools. Presently a senior gunsmith at a U.S. Department of Defense facility, he is involved in small arms research and development.

SOMEDAY ALL HANDGUNS WILL BE THIS GOOD.

While other companies were improving upon the technology of the past, GLOCK was busy perfecting the technology needed for the 21st Century.

Polymer technology.

You can see it in the complete line of GLOCK semi-automatic pistols. Hailed by police and sport shooters alike, these remarkable handguns fire even the most advanced ammunition with unfailing accuracy.

Find out for yourself what makes the GLOCK pistols so good. And why they have been setting new standards for simplicity, reliability, cost effectiveness and safety.

Contact your nearest dealer for a free GLOCK brochure. Or write or call GLOCK, INC. today.

ATTENTION: *All responsible firearms owners practice basic firearms safety.*

Thoroughly read and understand the users manual that is supplied with your firearm. Never use any firearm unless you completely understand its operation and safety features.

GLOCK®, INC.
P.O. Box 369 • Smyrna, Georgia 30081 • (404) 432-1202
Fax: (404) 433-8719 • Telex: 543353 Glock Atl UD

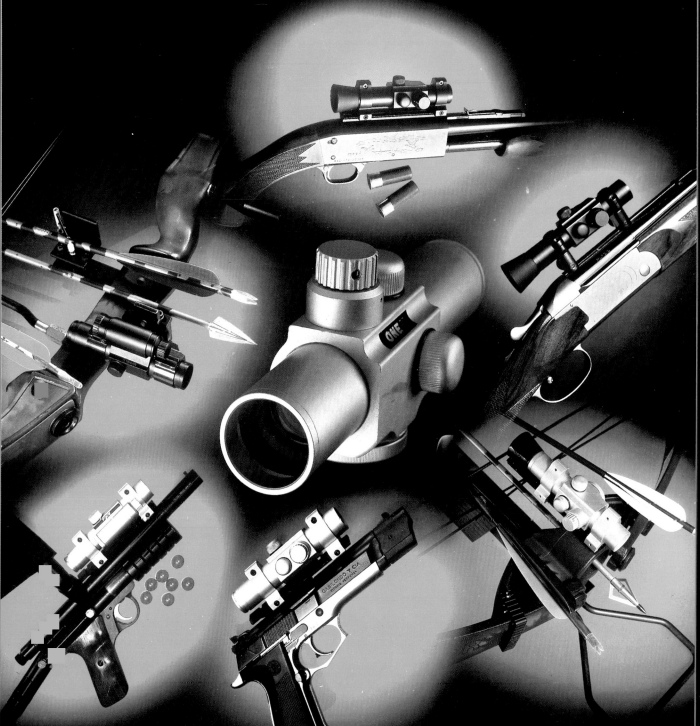

THE WILDCAT CARTRIDGE: MAKING A GOOD THING BETTER

by Don Lewis

The history of firearms began the moment someone discovered that Friar Roger Bacon's mixture of charcoal, saltpeter and sulfur could be used as a propulsive force. At that point, sometime in the 13th century, the armored knight was still greatly feared by the common foot soldier. Equipped with the best weapons and armor available, a knight on horseback was more than a match for the mud soldier who carried only a pitchfork or spear. But Friar Bacon's black dust, later called gunpowder, changed all that. Now, those gallant knights could be knocked off their steeds long before they could get close enough to swing an axe or throw a spear.

No one knows for certain when the first handheld gun was invented, but we do know that the first gun with an ignition system, the matchlock, was in use by 1475. For the next several hundred years, the search for a better form of ignition evolved from the matchlock to the wheel lock, flintlock and percussion cap. The quest ended in the mid-1800s with the metallic cartridge, which incorporated a self-contained primer. Because the spent primer was easily removed, the metallic case could then be reloaded simply by inserting a new primer along with a proper powder charge and bullet. Not only could this new cartridge be reloaded, its designers and amateur gun fanciers foresaw the possibility of modifying the metallic case to new physical dimensions. Hence, a new

cartridge name, "wildcat," was added to the lexicon of firearms terms.

The word *wildcat* is at once ambiguous, intriguing and somewhat formidable. Having nothing to do with the bobcat or the men who drilled for oil on unproved fields, wildcat here refers to a factory cartridge case that has been reformed (or fireformed) into a different version of itself. It is not, by definition, produced commercially. The primary reason for its invention and continued existence was to obtain high velocity and more striking power far beyond that of a conventional cartridge. Many wildcat versions came into being simply because their inventors wanted to modify a conventional factory case in order to fill a gap left open in the existing company lineup. Other wildcatters took a different approach by improving a factory case to a higher degree of performance. As a result, a mild controversy arose within the wildcatting ranks between those who favored the true wildcat cartridge and those who sought to improve existing cartridges.

This confrontation may have started when gunsmith Lyle D. Kilbourn first improved the case on the .22 Hornet, which was the first high-velocity, flat-trajectory .22 caliber wildcat to become factory-made. In its original version, muzzle velocity of this cartridge with a 45-grain bullet was about 2450 feet per second (fps). Kilbourn decided to blow out, or fire-form, the case so it could hold more powder. He achieved this by changing the shoulder angle of the Hornet from the original 5 degrees 38 minutes to a sharper 40-degree angle. Upon firing a factory round in his new chamber, Kilbourn found that the brass case expanded to the dimensions of the improved chamber. The result was more powder capacity, a sharper shoulder angle and better combustion. Back then, though, the main advantage of this modification was a significant gain of 400 fps in muzzle velocity using a 45-grain slug.

Some wildcat enthusiasts consider the .25 Niedner (sometimes known as the .25 Whelen) and the .25 High Power among the oldest "true" wildcats. The Niedner was made by running a .30-06 case into a .25 Niedner resizing die. The 17-degree 30-minute shoulder angle of the standard .30-06 case remained, but neck diameter was swaged down to accept a .25 caliber bullet. This change prevented the firing of the parent case in the .25 Niedner, thus creating a true wildcat cartridge in the purist's eye.

The .25 Niedner proved a super long-range

In 1966, H & R introduced its Model 317 Ultra Wildcat in a .17-223 cartridge. The case was made by necking down a military .223 to .17 caliber. In the photo above, the author's wife, Helen, (who took the photos for this article) zeros in on a chuck with a 317 Ultra Wildcat .17-223.

Custom rifle builder Jim Peightal feeds a chambering reamer into the spinning barrel. With his right hand on the feed wheel, he holds the lathe dog with his left hand to control reamer cut.

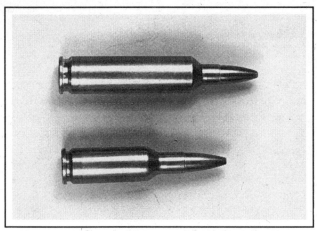

Wildcatting is alive and well. Two relatively new entries are the Mark I .22 CHeetah (top) and the 6mm PPC (below).

varmint cartridge and was subsequently offered by custom gunsmiths with shoulder angles as sharp as 40 degrees. The original 17-degree 30-minute angle of the .30-06, however, retained the strongest following. In 1969, almost half a century after Adolph Niedner introduced his original wildcat, Remington made it commercially available as the .25-06. The overall length of the factory round may be a trifle shorter than Niedner's version, but it carries the same shoulder angle.

FAMOUS WILDCAT CREATIONS

The indisputable heart of wildcatting lies in the modification of a given case so as to accept a smaller or larger bullet. In the beginning, most wildcatters simply pushed a conventional factory case into a die that necked the case up or down. While the majority of wildcatters reduced the neck diameter of a case to accept a smaller diameter bullet, it was not impossible to neck *up* a case as well. The .35 Whelen, for example, is a .30-06 case necked up to accept a .357 diameter bullet.

And not all wildcat creations are made only by reducing or increasing neck diameter. The .219 Donaldson Wasp was originally made from factory .219 Zipper brass by shortening, renecking and fire-forming the case. Swaging cases and shortening neck lengths with the old vise-type dies proved to be a time-consuming task. In that method, a factory case was shoved into a No. 1 Form Die; once started, it was then shoved completely in the die with a vise. A special casehardened pin was furnished with each die for knocking the case out of the die, resulting in high case losses.

Once the Winchester .219 Zipper came on the scene and Zipper cases were no longer available, .219 Wasp fans switched to Winchester .25-35 and .30-30 brass. This move saved that fine wildcat for a few years, but Remington's .222 soon sounded the death knell for it as well, as hundreds of Wasp adherents switched over to the new cartridge. The hassle over making the cases was reason enough to make the change, but it took the inherent accuracy of Remington's .222 to replace the wildcat. The Wasp remains one of the most accurate cartridges ever to hit the shooting range.

The heyday of wildcatting occurred between 1920 and 1940. Several gaps existed then between factory cartridges, and only wildcats could fill them. Literally hundreds of wildcat cartridges were cranked out, backed by unbridled claims about increased velocity. The truth is, most of the velocity figures were estimates that were never substantiated. Considering what top wildcatters—including the likes of Hervey Lovell, Ned Roberts, Jerry Gebby, Harvey Donaldson and P.O. Ackley—gave to the shooting world, their over-optimism can be excused.

Improvements were made on wildcat cartridges as well. The .22-3000 wildcat, developed in the mid-1930s by Lovell, is a case in point. Built on the .25-20 Single Shot case hot around the turn of the century, the .22-3000, armed with a 50-grain bullet and a heavy load of 4227 powder, could hit 3000 fps muzzle velocity. In 1937, New York gunsmith Harvey Donaldson improved the .22-3000 and called it a 2R Lovell, which became one of the most popular wildcat cartridges ever designed, almost matching the ballistics of Remington's .222. Eventually, the supply of .25-20 Single Shot cases

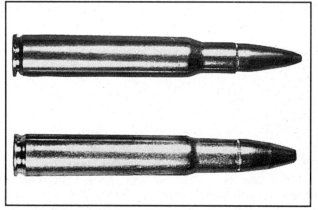

While many wildcat cases are necked down, the .35 Whelen (bottom) is a .30-06 case (top) necked up to accept the .35 caliber bullet.

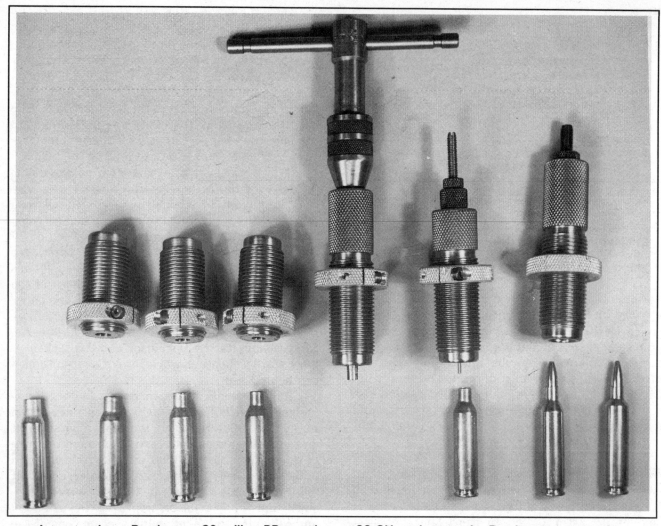

In converting a Remington .30 caliber BR case into a .22 CHeetah case, the Remington case neck is gradually swaged down to accept a .224 diameter bullet (first three dies on the left). The fourth die from the left reams the inside of the case neck to the proper diameter. The two dies on the right are conventional reloading dies. The case is loaded and fire-formed to obtain a sharp 40-degree shoulder angle on a .22 CHeetah Mark I.

was exhausted and the 2R Lovell fell by the wayside. Over the last few decades, owners of 2Rs have shot their brass sparingly, but now some light at the end of the tunnel can be seen. Huntington (Oroville, CA) is offering Bertram Brass made in Australia for many of the obsolete cases, including the .25-20 Single Shot.

Other varmint-type wildcats that have gained some degree of fame are the .218 Mashburn Bee, .219 Improved Zipper, .228 Ackley Magnum, .230 Ackley Magnum, .243 Rockchucker, .240 Page Pooper and the .25 Krag. Interestingly, the .230 Ackley was designed primarily to circumvent restrictions against the .224 caliber bullet then used for big game. In the mid-1950s, a few western

states decided that calibers below .23 were inadequate for big game. Since no .23 caliber cartridge existed, P.O. Ackley shortened and necked down the .30-06 case to accept custom-made .23 caliber bullets. According to Ackley, the .230 cartridge offered over 3450 fps muzzle velocity with a 75-grain bullet. Several other .23 caliber cartridges appeared later on, based on necked-down 6mm cases or necked-up Remington .222 Magnum brass.

Dozens of other wildcats died almost as soon as they were born. Some have been recorded merely for posterity's sake—the .17 Hornet, .17 Javelina, .20-222, .22 ICL Gopher, .22 Sabre, .22-30-30 Improved Ackley and .22 Newton. The list could go on, but only a few rifles chambered for these cartridges remain. Several others have survived and were finally standardized in factory rifles. The .22-250 Varminter, created by Captain Wotkyns and further improved by J.E. Gebby, began life in 1937. Since the .22-250 is nothing more than a Savage .250-3000 case necked down to .224 caliber, the Varminter nomenclature was soon changed to .22-250.

From its inception, the .22-250 was a winner. During the early days, it won more benchrest matches than Donaldson's .219 wasp. For some strange reason, the .22-250 remained a wildcat until 1967, when Remington standardized the cartridge for its Model 700 series of bolt-action rifles. At long last, the varmint hunter had an accurate long-range cartridge. Why the .22-250 was overlooked by ammo companies for nearly four decades remains a mystery.

The late Warren Page, former shooting editor at *Field & Stream*, worked with 6mm caliber bullets and designed the .240 Page Super Pooper, which eventually became (with minor alterations)

the Winchester .243. With a 1-in-10 twist, Page's .240 Super Pooper performed best with slow-burning powders, such as 4350 and 4831, behind a 105-grain bullet. Another old-timer that made it to the commercial ranks was the .25 Niedner, now known as the Remington .25-06. It earned the distinction of being the best of all .25 caliber creations, a reputation that rankled the fans of Ned Roberts' .257, which Remington standardized in 1934. It is fair to say the Remington .25-06 kept the .25 caliber on the market after it was almost taken over by the 6mm. Today, the .25-06 excels as a super varmint cartridge and is unquestionably a superb deer stopper as well. Varmint hunters should stick with bullets in the 75- to 87-grain range, while deer hunters will prefer slugs with 117 to 120 grain.

A LOOK AHEAD

Is wildcatting dead? No, not really. Wildcatters still dream of building the perfect cartridge. In the early 1980s, Jim Carmichel, shooting editor for *Outdoor Life*, and Fred Huntington, founder of

The author is shown firing a Mark I .22 CHeetah from an indoor benchrest. The CHeetah is built on a Mauser action using a Douglas Supreme 1-in-16 twist.

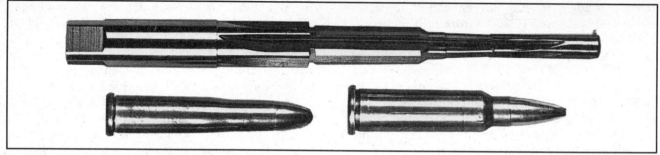

The Clymer .218 Mashburn Bee finishing reamer (top) is used to cut a .22 Hornet (left) to a .218 Mashburn Bee shown at right.

RCBS, introduced the .22 CHeetah. This latest wildcat, built on Remington's .22 BR case, contains standard .308 Winchester dimensions, except the BR case has the small primer pocket favored by many benchrest competitors. Because of its smaller volume of priming compound, this primer ignites less powder; moreover, the smaller flash hole helps control the primer's force. Carmichel felt that by making ignition more uniform, there'd be more consistent action and barrel vibration, both important elements in rifle accuracy.

Carmichel's published velocity figures show that the CHeetah, with a 55-grain bullet, has an instrumental velocity of 4042 fps 15 feet from the muzzle. It is truly a speedster; in fact, it is nearly 500 fps faster than a .22-250 with the same bullet weight. At 300 yards, the CHeetah can still travel faster than many .224 caliber cartridges.

True wildcatting may be beyond the scope of most hunters, shooters and gunsmiths; but improving a cartridge is not. Jim Peightal, a well-known custom rifle builder, rechambered my Ruger No. 3 Hornet to a .218 Mashburn Improved Bee simply by running a Clymer .218 Mashburn Bee finishing reamer into the chamber of the .22 Hornet. By firing a conventional .218 Bee round in the improved chamber, the brass expands to the new physical dimensions of the chamber. Since the .218 Bee is headspaced on its shell head rim, case loss is rare. The end result gives the varmint hunter a higher velocity and a greater degree of accuracy than that produced by the .218 Bee factory round.

With all the nostalgia that lingers around the .22 Hornet, it is still not an accurate cartridge, with an effective range of less than 200 yards. When Winchester's .218 Bee arrived in 1938, it was heralded as being vastly superior to the Hornet. That wasn't the truth. The Bee's larger case capacity produces slightly higher velocities with a wider range of powders, and it will handle heavier bullets

more efficiently than the Hornet. Common knowledge tells us that the Bee has precious little ballistic advantage over the .22 hornet.

Shortly after the inception of the .218 Bee, A.E. Mashburn (Oklahoma City, OK) realized that the factory .218 Bee contained flaws in its design. Designed originally for lever-action rifles, the Bee was introduced by Winchester in its Model 65. Since the factory cartridge produced relatively high pressures, the steep taper of the Bee's short body, coupled with its gentle 15-degree shoulder angle, caused the cases to stretch. After a few reloadings, case separation became a problem. Mashburn's Improved Bee solved this by minimizing body taper and creating a sharp 28-degree shoulder. More powder can be burned efficiently in this improved version, thus increasing velocity by several hundred feet per second. That gives the Mashburn Bee a higher muzzle velocity with a 55-grain bullet than the Hornet gets with a 45-grain bullet. In fact, the .218 Mashburn Bee's velocity (3100

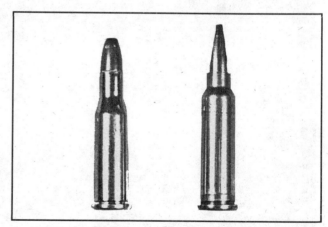

A Winchester factory .218 Bee (left) can also be transformed into the .218 Mashburn Bee (right) by modern wildcatting techniques. The result is improved accuracy for shooting enthusiasts.

fps) puts it in the same category as Remington's .222 (with both using 50-grain bullets). It is also more accurate than either the Hornet or the factory Bee. Cases are easily obtainable by firing factory shells in the improved chamber. Accuracy will be about the same when fire-forming, but with a slight loss in velocity. Reloading dies for the Mashburn Bee, by the way, are available from RCBS. Clymer Manufacturing (Rochester Hills, MN) carries .218 Mashburn Bee reamers in stock.

Wildcatting the Hornet to the Mashburn Bee makes a person step back in time to the days of Roberts, Gebby, Ackley and dozens of other wildcat specialists. Having little to work with but ingenuity and their innate skills, these men battled the quest for velocity without the aid of modern computer-type chronographs. The old-timer fired several cartridges of known velocity into a steel plate at a safe distance. He then fired his latest creation with identical weight and type of bullet into the same plate. By careful measuring of depth, he could tell if he'd reached a higher velocity. Crude and unscientific as this method may seem, the in-

ventions of these early wildcatters paved the way for the outstanding lineup of varmint cartridges we can enjoy and use in the 1990s.

That doesn't mean there's no room for improvement in the future. The true wildcatter always believes he can come up with a better cartridge. It's like the old prospector who fervently believed that "Thar's gold in them thar hills." Some are still looking for the mother lode. The same can be said for the modern wildcatter. May he never stop looking.

DON LEWIS is a retired corporate executive, who now spends most of his time testing and evaluating guns in his well-equipped shop in Kittanning, PA. A regular contributor to SHOOTER'S BIBLE, Lewis also writes about gun-related topics for *Pennsylvania Woods & Waters, Handloader's Digest* and other publications in the field. He is also the author of a book, *The Shooter's Corner,* (Pennsylvania Game News, Harrisburg, PA, 1989).

Jim Peightal chronographs a .218 Mashburn Bee after rechambering a No. 3 Ruger .22 Hornet to the .218 wildcat.

AFRICA'S VICTORIAN HUNTERS AND THEIR GUNS

by Jim Casada

During the 19th century, Africa was a sportsman's paradise. From the vast reaches of the savanna grassland south of the Sahara to the low veldt of the South African interior, from dense tropical jungles bordering the Congo to the slopes of Kilimanjaro, big game animals roamed in incredible profusion and variety. Their abundance first became known to Europeans in general, and the British in particular, through the pioneering of African explorers—men like Sir Samuel Baker, William Cornwallis Harris, James A. Grant and Joseph Thomson. Their best-selling books, in which they described their adventurous forays in the Dark Continent, were filled with tales of the incredible shooting Africa afforded. These early accounts enthralled a reading public that eagerly devoured any and all news coming out of Africa—whether it touched the uncertain fate of Dr. David Livingstone or the latest revelation in the unfolding mystery of the Nile's sources. Their tales also stimulated successive generations of hunters in a way that made the Victorian era synonymous with sport.

The result was a sort of sportsman's gold rush to Africa, with the combined lures of adventure, white gold in the form of ivory, and a chance to enjoy the kind of shooting that heretofore had been the stuff of dreams, drawing men like so many moths to a candle flame. As coincidence would have it, this great migration to Africa took place during the dramatic change from muzzleloading to breechloading weapons. Add to the equation the exciting and immensely readable accounts these hunters left behind of their travels, and the sum was incomparable armchair adventure. Indeed, Africa arguably offered the finest, most diverse sport that the world had ever known.

Without exception, the great African hunters were eccentrics, their exploits attracting the fancy not only of fellow sportsmen but the general public as well. Even their nicknames—"Baker of the Nile," "Lion Hunter Cumming" and "The Elephant Smasher" (Henry Bailey)—conveyed images of adventure and mystery. It was Sir Richard Burton, though, who best captured the allure of the Dark Continent's big game: "The theme [African hunting] has remoteness and obscurity of place, difference of custom, events passing strange yet credible, sometimes barbaric splendour, general luxuriance of nature, savage life, personal danger and suffering always borne with patience, dignity, and even enthusiasm."

WILLIAM CORNWALLIS HARRIS: AN INSPIRATIONAL PIONEER

The pioneer who brought Africa's wonderland of big game to public attention was William Cornwallis Harris, author of the first books devoted exclusively to African hunting. He found ample outlet for what he called the "delightful mania" in southern Africa in two major books describing his hunting experiences: *Wild Sports of Southern Africa* and *Portraits of the Game and Wild Animals of South Africa*. These works have left us a splendid literary and pictorial account of hunting's golden age.

Harris was the first man to kill a sable and bring its hide and horns back to Europe; and he was also accused, with some justification, of "lavish slaughter." He began his African adventure with 18,000 molded bullets, not to mention an abundance of uncast lead, and his descriptions of hunting read almost like a military campaign. Game animals were his "foes," excursions afield constituted a "campaign," and resting periods in camp were called "a cessation from hostilities." After repeatedly firing his double barrel rifle into a herd of elephants, he described the scene as "leaving the ground strewed with the slain." Still, it must be remembered that game was so plentiful then that neither Harris nor those who followed

in his footsteps could conceive of any amount of shooting seriously affecting animal populations.

From an overall perspective on sport in Africa, Harris was perhaps most important for his influence on others. All the great names in South Africa's sporting community—Roualeyn Gordon-Cumming, Cotton Oswell, Fred Selous, among others—paid tribute to Harris as their inspiration. The scenes he described in his books, along with his first-rate illustrations, compelled these men to venture into the vast, little known veldt.

ROUALEYN GORDON-CUMMING: THE LION HUNTER

The first hunter to follow Harris' lead was Gordon-Cumming, a Scot "remarkable for his great height and massive symmetry of build." Often called a "king of men," Gordon-Cumming focused his hunting fittingly on the king of beasts. He became so famous in this regard that he was widely referred to as "The Lion Hunter." For almost five

William Cornwallis Harris was a first-rate artist, as this drawing of a stately kudu from one of his books suggests.

William Cornwallis Harris, the pioneer who brought Africa's wonderland of big game to public attention, poses in dress clothes—with gun in hand.

courage bordering on foolhardiness, it is a miracle that Gordon-Cumming ever lived to write of his exploits. Of the 105 elephants he killed, only one died as a result of a single shot. More typical was an old bull that took 35 rounds from a 10 bore (all hits) and five more from a Dutch weapon (firing six balls to the pound) before it succumbed. Another time he faced an elephant "from half past eleven till the sun was under, when his tough old spirit fled, and the venerable monarch of the forest fell, pierced with 57 balls."

Gordon-Cumming regularly hunted elephant from horseback, an approach one modern authority has described as "probably the most foolhardy proceeding ever recorded." There was also the time

Roualeyn Gordon-Cumming shows off his full Scottish regalia, which he wore on lecture tour. Dubbed "The Lion Hunter," he was also known as a "king of men" because of his massive size.

years in the mid-1840s, he criss-crossed the remote interior, living in an ox-drawn wagon and using hunting techniques that today could only be described as foolhardy.

Gordon-Cumming's own description of his armory gives a good idea of the kind of weapons gentlemen adventurers took to Africa in those days: "My ordnance was as follows: 3 double barrelled rifles by Purdey, . . . one heavy single barrelled German rifle carrying 12 to the lb., . . . and 3 stout double barrelled guns for rough work when hard riding and quick loading is required." He also carried 300 pounds of lead, 50 pounds of pewter (to harden the lead), 10,000 prepared leaden bullets, some 20 bags of shot, 50,000 percussion caps, 100 pounds of fine gunpowder (and 300 pounds of coarse) and 2,000 gun flints.

Despite this armory, and blessed with a raw

when he dove into a crocodile-infested river, seized a wounded (but very much alive) hippopotamus by the tail, and while holding on with one hand, cut himself a better grip in its rump with a knife in his other hand.

Back home in England following his lengthy African sojourn, Gordon-Cumming must have cut quite a figure strolling down London's Regent Street "in a sailor's blue shirt, Highland kilt, and a belt garnished with knives and pistols, while his hair, which rivalled Absalom's, was confined in a bag of silk netting." He spent his later years there like so many of the great African hunters reliving treasured memories in a best-selling book, *A Hunter's Life in South Africa*, and a permanent museum housing his trophies. Ever an untamed figure, Gordon-Cumming died at the age of 46, leaving behind a hunting legacy few have matched and none surpassed.

WILLIAM COTTON OSWELL: DAREDEVIL AMONG DAREDEVILS

Unlike Gordon-Cumming and most of the other famous Victorian hunters in Africa, William Cotton Oswell was not a writer. Sir Samuel Baker once referred to him as "the Nimrod of South Africa par excellence, . . . the greatest hunter ever known in modern times, the truest friend, and the most thorough example of an English gentlemen," a man "with utter recklessness of danger in the moment of emergency."

Oswell first came to South Africa in 1844, and over the ensuing seven years made no less than five major sporting journeys into the unexplored interior, spending by his own account from 10 to 12 hours a day in the saddle. He carried fewer weapons than many of the noted hunters, relying primarily on a Purdey 10 bore and a 12 bore Westley Richards, which he once described as "a beast of a tool that once nearly cost me my life by stinging without seriously wounding a bull elephant. The infuriated brute charged me nine or ten times wickedly and the number would have been doubled had I not at last got hold of the Purdey, when he fell to the first shot."

The Purdey, which had been especially made for him, weighed 10 pounds and took balls wrapped "in waxed kid or linen patch, rolled between the hands and the folds cut off." The ball followed a paper cartridge—"the end bitten off and thrust into the barrel together with the paper covering"—in the loading process. Oswell loaned this trusted Purdey later on to Sam Baker, who

made good use of it during his treks along the headwaters of the upper Nile.

Unlike Gordon-Cumming, Oswell was a great believer in getting as close to his prey as possible before firing, usually killing even the largest game with a single shot. As a result, he was twice tossed by rhinos, being gored on one occasion, and chased by a lion that actually leaped on his horse's hindquarters. His closest brush with death, however,

Portrait of William Cotton Oswell as he appeared late in life. Samuel Baker once referred to Oswell as the Nimrod of South Africa par excellence.

came while following a wounded elephant. "I saw the burly brute from chest to tail as he passed directly over me lengthways, one foot between my knees and one fourteen inches beyond my head and not a graze! Five tons at least! . . . Of all my narrow escapes this was the only one that remained with me in recollection for any length of time. One hears of night-mares—well, for a month or more, I daresay, I had night-elephants!"

FREDERICK COURTENEY SELOUS: THE GREATEST OF THEM ALL

Oswell was one of many sporting predecessors who inspired the African adventures of Frederick Courteney Selous, a man whom Teddy Roosevelt once described as having "a heart of iron and frame of steel, the greatest of the world's big-game hunters." Used by H. Rider Haggard as a model for his famed fictional character, Allan Quatermain, Selous first set out alone for Africa when he was only 19 years of age. Once he had made his way into the unhunted interior, the great chieftain Lobengula described what must have been a typical reaction to the young hunter's features: "He asked what I had come to do. I said I had come to hunt elephants, upon which he burst out laughing and said, 'Was it not steinbucks that you came to hunt? Why, you're only a boy.'"

This collection of mounts in Selous' trophy room at his home in England attests to his hunting prowess.

During his early African years, the great hunter Frederick Selous had to rely on the heavy, battered muzzleloader shown above after his custom-made guns were stolen. Note his unusual costume, which he fashioned for himself for hunting in the veldt.

Boy or not, Selous proved during a quarter-century of near constant hunting a mettle second to none. Unfortunately, his expensive and favorite double-barreled, breechloading rifle was stolen from him at the outset of his first safari. For several years after that he had to rely on ponderous, smoothbore muzzleloaders called "Roers," which were the only weapons he could obtain. Even so, in 1873 alone he managed to kill 42 elephants, claiming that if he'd been armed with a modern .450 bore cordite rifle, "I would have laid low at least four of these animals for every one I actually brought to bag." In 1880 Selous obtained (from Gibbs of Bristol, England) a single-barreled .461 bore modified Express rifle, which he considered superior even to the .450, .500 and .577 bore Express blackpowder rifles. It was not until 1893, late in his African career, that Selous traded in his Gibbs rifle for a modern single-shot .303.

Prior to Teddy Roosevelt's great African safari in 1909, Selous recommended to the former president a double cordite rifle of .450 caliber or larger for big, dangerous game such as elephants, lions,

Frederick Selous relaxes in one of his African camps, surrounded by some of the day's catch.

rhinos, and buffaloes (he considered the latter the most dangerous of all African animals). He also suggested a selection of lighter rifles—chiefly .256, .275, and .303 calibers—for kudu, antelope and smaller game. Selous would himself have welcomed any of these highly functional and predictable weapons during some of his own adventures. On one occasion a wounded elephant forced him to run through thick thorns, tearing his clothing to shreds; and later that same day, his gunbearer gave him a double-loaded, four-bore elephant gun which, when fired at a charging bull elephant, had unexpected results. "The gun went off and I went off too! I was lifted clean from the ground . . . whilst the gun was carried yards away over my shoulder. Stunned, I found I could not lift my right arm. I was covered with blood, which

spurted from a deep wound under the right cheek-bone. The stock was shattered to pieces, and the only wonder was that the barrel did not burst."

Selous survived these incidents and many others, all of which make for good reading in his books, especially *A Hunter's Wanderings in Africa* and *Travels and Adventures in South-East Africa.* Some measure of the man's spirit and courage is offered by the circumstances of his death, which, fittingly enough, occurred in Africa. When World War I broke out, Selous, now well into his 60s, badgered officials until they finally gave him a commission in the East African theater. Having already earned the Distinguished Service Order for his work as an intelligence officer, Selous was shot by a German sniper while on reconnaissance early in 1917. Clad as was his custom in khaki shorts,

When World War I broke out, Selous was well into his 60s. Armed with a ''modern'' rifle with an adjustable sight, he did his part during the East African campaign in 1917, when he was shot by a German sniper. He was found under a tamarind tree which now, appropriately, lies in the vast Selous Game Preserve.

slouch bush hat, and with a bandana tied about his neck, he found his rest beneath a lone tamarind tree which now, appropriately, lies in the vast Selous Game Preserve.

SAMUEL BAKER: ELEPHANT HUNTING WITH KNIVES

When it came to a combination of sporting and literary skills, Selous' only real rival was Samuel Baker, who did most of his hunting in the central African regions at the headwaters of the Nile. Long before he first came to Africa, Baker was something of a legend in English sporting circles. Two books on his hunting experiences in Ceylon (now Sri Lanka)—*Eight Years in Ceylon* and *The Rifle and Hound in Ceylon*—had contributed to his fame, as had his feats in Scotland where he once killed a massive stag while armed only with a large knife.

A man of remarkable physical strength—he once shamed a circus strong man by wrapping chains around his biceps and snapping them by flexing his muscles—Baker brought exceptional verve to his sport in Africa. He first went to the Dark Continent supposedly to search for the sources of the Nile River, which he called "the greatest geographical secret after the discovery of America." But there is little doubt that Africa's incomparable sport is what really drew him there.

Certainly Baker's experiences in Africa did nothing to detract from his renown. Armed only with a double-edged sword, he hunted elephants from horseback, chasing them in the company of others until he could make a daring sword strike. Less dangerous was a special elephant gun made for him by George Gibbs, the noted Bristol gunsmith. Revolutionary in concept, it was a massive muzzleloader with a 36-inch barrel, featuring two rifling grooves capable of carrying a belted ball weighing a full three ounces (or a four-ounce conical ball). Its massive charge of 16 drams of powder gave it such force that it was considered "preposterous in the professional opinions of the trade." While only a powerful, broad-shouldered man such as Baker could have withstood its recoil, it had a telling effect on elephants and buffalo. "This weapon was in advance of the age," Baker wrote, "as it foreshadowed the modern Express, and the principle was thoroughly established to my own satisfaction, that a sporting rifle to be effective at long range must burn a heavy charge of powder, but the weight of the weapon must be in due proportion to the strain of the explosion."

Samuel Baker poses for a studio photo, circa 1865, in the hunting costume he designed for himself. Note the Holland & Holland double-barreled muzzleloader at his side.

In addition to this incredible rifle, Baker carried an impressive array of other guns. These included the 10 bore he had borrowed from Cotton Oswell, four double rifles, three single rifles, two double-barrel shotguns, a revolver, and a brace of pistols. The products of many of the finest gunmakers of the time—names like Tathem, Reilly, Beattie, Manton, and Purdey—they served Baker well. A man of inspiration and ingenuity while afield, he once ran out of lead balls during a particularly intense day's hunting. Undaunted, he reached into his pocket, grabbed several English coins, and rammed them home along with a hefty charge of powder. Amazingly, this highly unorthodox load of six pence did the desired trick.

Baker later described his adventures along the Nile in three books: *The Albert N'yanza, The Nile Tributaries of Abyssinia and the Sword Hunters of the Hamran Arabs,* and *Ismailia.* Even after his

African days were over, he and Selous remained at the center of the British sporting world. Indeed, Baker was planning a lion hunt in Somaliland when a sudden heart attacked felled him in 1893. Baker's life as a hunter was important in marking the transition from muzzleloading to breechloading weapons, prompting one authority to describe him as a "kind of fulcrum" in the evolution of big game hunting. Certainly he epitomized the active, strenuous sporting life which the Victorian era found so popular.

Countless other great and near-great hunters sampled Africa's incomparable sporting opportunities during this period, among them such great elephant hunters as "Old Bill" Finaughty, Bula N'Zau, James Sutherland and Arthur Neumann. Nor should we forget J.H. Patterson, who conquered the man-eating lions of Tsavo and gave Ernest Hemingway the real-life basis for his book, *The Short, Happy Life of Francis Macomber*. In addition, several explorers, including James Grant and Joseph Thomson, both of whom had gazelles named for them, were also devoted sportsmen.

To a man though, they were, as Baker once wrote of himself, "made up of queer materials (and) averse to beaten paths." The paths they chose were those suitable for wandering spirits, leading over the distant hill and on to the next valley rich with game. For the great hunters of Africa, it was roving—not civilization—that held their souls captive. Armchair adventurers everywhere benefit from their wanderlust and untiring devotion to sport. Thankfully, many of these great sportsmen saw fit to share in their timeless writings the wonders of their hunting, not to mention the glories of the skillfully crafted guns with which they went afield. To join them, even vicariously, is to sense some of the wonder of Africa.

JIM CASADA teaches history at Winthrop University (Rock Hill, SC) and contributes to outdoor publications on a variety of subjects. He is currently Senior Editor for *Sporting Classics*, Field Editor for *Sporting Clays*, and Contributing Editor for *Deer & Deer Hunting, The Flyfisher,* and *Flyfishing News & Reviews*. He also writes three weekly newspaper columns and is at work on a book about great African hunters, entitled *Africa Was Their World*, from which he drew much of the material for this article. In addition, Jim is the editor of *Hunting & Home in the Southern Heartland: The Best of Archibald Rutledge*.

FOR FURTHER READING

One of the finest ways to share the campfires and lonely trails of Africa's great hunters is through the books they wrote. Many of them, especially Baker, Selous and Gordon-Cumming, wrote prose that still cuts with razor-edged sharpness after more than a century. While original editions of books on early big game hunting are exceedingly rare, most of the truly classic works have been reprinted and can be purchased at reasonable prices. A number of modern anthologies, biographies, and related treatments also focus on the great Victorian hunters. Among the finest and most readable are:

Peter Beard, *The End of the Game* (1965)

Michael Brander, *The Big Game Hunters* (1988) and *The Perfect Victorian Hero: The Life and Times of Sir Samuel Baker* (1982)

Richard Hall, *Lovers on the Nile* [Sam and Florence Baker] (1980)

Geoffrey Haresnape (ed.), *The Great Hunters* (1974)

Kenneth Kemp, *Tales of the Big Game Hunters* (1986)

H.C. Maydon (ed.), *Big Game Shooting in Africa* (1932 and later editions)

Stephen Taylor, *The Mighty Nimrod: The Life of Frederick Courteney Selous* (1989)

Townsend Whelen (ed.), *Hunting Big Game*, 2 vols. (1946). Volume 2 deals with Asia and Africa.

CHARLES PARKER AND HIS SHOWCASE SHOTGUN

by Wayne van Zwoll

To name the finest automobile ever produced or the most exquisite piece of art, you might be hard pressed. But choosing the best American shotgun would be comparatively easy. All you'd have to say is "Parker," or be prepared to defend your alternative against an army of Parker shotgun enthusiasts who insist there *is* no alternative.

Parker shotguns aren't the sturdiest ever built, or the lightest. Their stocks have too much drop for shooters used to straight modern combs. Still, they've become celebrated guns—a legendary line that comprises not just steel and walnut, but the elusive ingredients of great art. To many connoisseurs, Parkers are simply what shotguns ought to be.

Their story begins with the birth of Charles Parker on January 2, 1809, in Cheshire, Connecticut. As a youngster, Charles was apprenticed to a nearby Southington shop, where he cast buttons. He moved to Meriden in 1828 to make coffee mills. Four years later, with a starting capital of $70, Parker launched his own coffee mill business. His first "power plant" was a blind horse attached to a pole sweep. The horse was replaced in 1844 by a steam engine, one of the first in Meriden.

That same year, ever in search of new opportunities, Parker became a partner in Snow, Hotchkiss and Company, which sold machinery of all kinds. By the end of the Civil War, the company's name had been changed to Meriden Manufacturing Company, with Charles Parker as its president.

THE FIRST PARKERS: PRODUCTS OF WAR

Before 1860, Parker had apparently never made a gun. He was an industrialist and an entrepreneur whose main interest seemed to lie in the manufacture of profitable items and the expansion of corporate holdings. The Civil War offered an excellent chance for him to acquire tooling and experience with little risk. His first gun contract came from the Kentucky Home Guard in 1860. It called for 5,000 caliber 50 Triplett and Scott cartridge rifles. This gun featured a tube magazine in its stock and a lever that released the barrel, which could be turned to free a fired case. After a fresh round was inserted and the action locked, the rifle was again ready to fire.

Because it could be reloaded so rapidly, the Confederacy appealed to President Lincoln to withdraw the gun from service on humanitarian grounds. Apparently Lincoln thought the complaint had merit, because he referred it to the Hague International Tribunal (the war ended before the Tribunal delivered its verdict).

The second Parker rifle was produced for the U.S. Government in 1864. Similar in appearance to the Colt and Whitney rifles of the day, Parker's was, by contrast, a breechloader. Very few of these 55-caliber guns saw service before Appomattox, although records show the contract was initiated on September 28, 1963, and the order for 15,000 rifles (at $19 each) was filled. Conflicting reports indicate that Parker and his companies built about 1,000 rifles for Union troops during the war, shipping as many as 100 per day.

PERFECTING THE DOUBLE SHOTGUN

Why did Charles Parker decide to build double-barrel shotguns? After all, America's pioneers were heading west then. They needed *rifles*—plain, sturdy guns with enough range and power to kill big game or fend off Indians. Conversely, Parker's expensive smoothbores smacked of southern plantations, still smoldering in the wake of Union troops.

Whatever his reasons, Charles Parker set about his new project right after the war. The final product—a 14-gauge with 29-inch barrels—came out in 1868 with the same crude-looking lock common among breechloading shotguns in those days.

Apparently shooters liked it anyway, because it stayed in use another 30 years, becoming the first sporting arm to be built in quantity for cartridges. It arrived just as blackpowder components were giving way to the self-contained shotshell. Its ammunition, like that of its contemporaries, comprised a brass hull containing powder, shot and wads. Priming was still external, consisting of a percussion cap on a hollow nipple that absorbed the blow of a hammer and channeled sparks to an opening at the base of the shell.

Parker's new double stayed on the market for six years before it was overhauled. A shrewd businessman, Charles Parker must have been aware of the huge changes convulsing gun design during the 1870s, surely the most productive decade ever for American armsmakers. In that period, Colt introduced its Single Action Army revolvers; Smith & Wesson produced its Schofield; John Marlin patented his first repeating mechanism; John Browning started to build his single-shot cartridge rifles; Winchester began pedaling

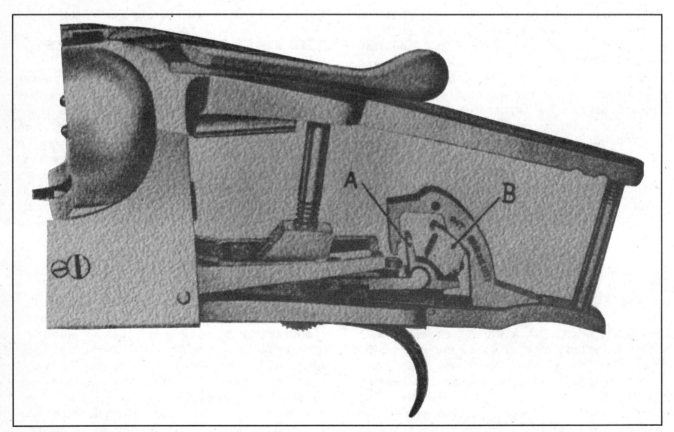

Parker's single trigger had a detent lever (A) that moved up into the hook of its housing when the first barrel fired. The housing stopped its movement until the trigger was released. A rebound block (B) prevented doubling under heavy recoil by backing into the housing.

its model 1873; and Remington had its Rolling Block.

To give his gun new life, Charles Parker sought a top-drawer engineer. He found one in Charles A. King, who quickly developed a hammerless shotgun and designed the first Parker gun with automatic ejectors. But his best known and most important contributions were to the gun's locking mechanism. Working closely with Parker, he reviewed the double-gun locking arrangements then in common use. Some were successful and would remain so, but King and Parker wanted something different. Eventually they came up with their own bolting, incorporating a combination bolt plate that prevented a gun from blowing open. It was so effective, in fact, that a Parker fired without the bolt engaged would not open. A Dealy & Edge-style forend lock replaced the earlier key design in 1880, and two years later the sliding lifter bar in front of the trigger guard was abandoned. In its place was a top-lever mechanism that locked the action by means of a pivoting lever and auxiliary round-bolt.

Within six years of its introduction—shortly after King's new bolting and lifter had been adopted—Parker claimed to have the "best and hardest shooting gun in the world." Sales supported the claim. By then, Parker was listing 11 models, priced from $45 to $250.

NEW STEEL, NO HAMMERS: "OLD RELIABLE"

"Grading" of Parker guns started as early as 1872, but while later grades were based primarily on embellishments, the first Parkers were priced according to the steel in their barrels. The first grades listed were, in ascending order, "PH," "GH," "DH" and "CH." The PH grade included "plain twist" barrels, while the better grades featured more complex patterns. The CH grade had a fancy "Bernard twist" and was considered Parker's best gun until Damascus barrels were replaced by those made of fluid steel right after World War I.

Parker's first hammerless guns appeared in 1889. The hammers were not actually abandoned; they were simply reshaped and moved inside. Unlike some hammerless guns, Parker's did not feature separate firing pins; rather, the hammer had an integral pin. A rebounding device on the base of each hammer brought the pin back away from the breech face as soon as it dented the primer. While Parker was not the first American firm to manufacture hammerless double shotguns, it mar-

keted a successful design that lasted, essentially unaltered, for 25 years.

Except for a change in barrel steels, the hammerless Parkers of 1889 differed little in appearance from those built after World War I. But in 1910, Parker technician James P. Hayes, who had engineered and patented the top-lever bolting system, came up with a simpler design. The old mechanism had 18 parts, the new one only four! The nickname "Old Reliable" stuck to Parker shotguns for many years—principally, said Parker owners, because Hayes' bolting mechanism was so strong and foolproof. Parkers closed crisply, and even prolonged hard use didn't cause discernible looseness.

Parker guns were made largely by hand. The barrels were filed to reduce weight or change their shape; stocks were selected by weight to ensure proper balance on individual guns; all locks and ribs were hand-fitted. Barrels had to be "soft-fitted" to the standing breech so closely that two pieces of tissue paper placed between them would be held tight, but without any metal contact.

All Parker shotguns were targeted at the plant. Each was clamped in a rest and fired at a white, 30-inch steel plate mounted on a trolley parked 40 yards away. A black bolt head in the middle of the plate served as an aiming point. After each shot, the pellet marks were counted and a fresh coat of paint applied. A gun that failed to shoot well had its barrels straightened or rebored.

While the company worked hard to build fine shotguns, it did relatively little to promote them. Parker literature is scarce, and few Parker magazine ads have surfaced. The gun's reputation and a comparatively small output kept orders coming in fast enough without extensive advertising. The company had only two sales rooms: one in Meriden, the other in New York City. Its salesmen, like those of other gun firms in pre-Depression days, often doubled as trick shooters. They not only talked a good line, but could shoot well enough to impress anyone in search of a better shotgun.

FRAMES, GRADES AND PRICES

For nearly 50 years, Parker maintained the most comprehensive line of double-barrel shotguns ever produced in America. The firm stuck to a narrow path, experimenting with repeating mechanisms and over/under shotguns but never building them for sale. A single-barrel trap gun, introduced late in the company's life, was its only deviation from the manufacture of side-by-side doubles.

From the turn of the century to the Depression, all Parker guns were built on six frame sizes:

#3 (8- and heavy 10-gauge)
#2 (10- and heavy 12-gauge)
#1½ (12- and heavy 16-gauge)
#1 (16-gauge)
#0 (20-gauge)
#00 (28-gauge)

This extensive selection of frames compelled Parker to keep a large inventory of parts on hand, but it also ensured buyers that any reasonable order could be filled with a perfectly balanced shot-

Parker's VHE (Vulcan) and A1 Special grades did not appear in company literature until after the turn of the century—sometime between 1899 and 1912. During this period the old lifter mechanism was finally discontinued, having been kept alive as an option for roughly 20 years after the introduction of King's superior bolting system.

The Parker Trojan first appeared in 1915, when a flyer inside the Parker catalog noted a price increase brought on by World War I. The war prompted changes in the design and manufacture of all sporting guns. Parker's products changed less than some, because they were still built mostly for

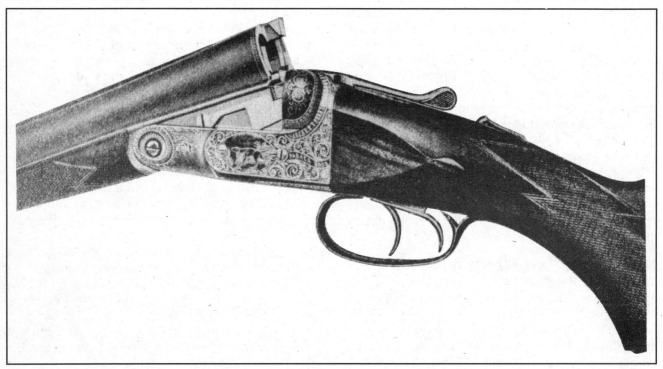

The DH, Parker's most popular mid-priced gun, accounted for about 41,000 sales. Its steel barrel was marked "Titanic," the company's own trade name.

gun. The firm listed its grades by number as well as by name, as follows (with average annual production percentages):

Trojan (Trojan)—40%
#0 (Vulcan)—25%
#1 (PHE)—3%
#2 (GHE)—10%
#3 (DHE)—15%
#4 (CHE)—1%
#5 (BHE)—5%
#7 (AHE)—½%
#8 (A1 Special)—½%

people who cared about tradition, balance, hand-fitting and those intangible qualities that make a gun feel alive.

In 1922 Parker announced its first single trigger model, and in 1923 the beavertail forend made its appearance. A ventilated rib arrived in 1926, followed by the first .410 Parker in 1927. By 1929 Parker was building about 5,000 guns a year.

The 200,000th Parker shotgun was numbered in the first months of the Great Depression. That shotgun, a 12-gauge with a straight grip, was given even more lavish treatment than the A1 Special. Parker called it "The Invincible," a top-of-the-line gun that was to be produced regularly but in small quantities and for a cost of $1,500. While such a price for the most ornate of double shotguns seems reasonable indeed by modern standards, it was comparatively high in 1930. An L.C. Smith Monogram Grade sold for $400 that year, a Purdey cost $650, and Parker's own A1 listed for $750.

Sadly, the Depression smashed hopes for The Invincible. The only Parker rivaling The Invincible in appearance was an A1 Special built for Tsar Nicholas of Russia, an avid shooter. A gold-inlaid stock of imported walnut and a gold Romanov eagle set in the trigger guard distinguished this unusual

The others were ordered destroyed when Parker decided not to produce any more 24-gauge guns. At its introduction in 1915, the Trojan was the least expensive Parker, listing at only $27.50. It quickly became the firm's best seller, differing from other Parkers in that it did not have automatic ejectors and wore double triggers for most of its life. Single triggers became an option for Trojan buyers in 1934; but the Parker Skeet gun introduced that year, and the double-barrel Trap model released in 1937, were not available as Trojans.

A Parker Trojan came standard with a hard

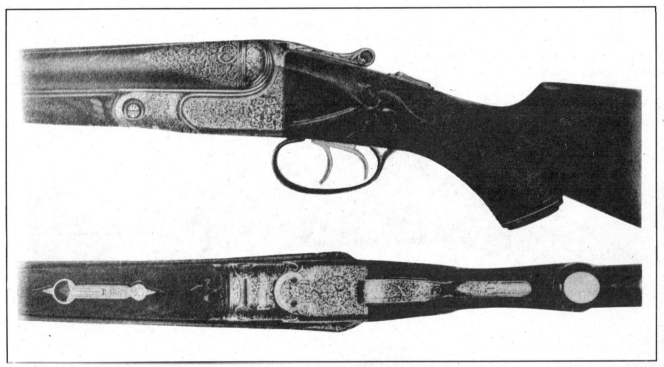

Parker's A1 Special (above) was the most valuable shotgun ever cataloged in the U.S. Only about 300 were made in 10, 12, 16, 20 and 28 gauge.

gun. Just before it was finished, though, the Bolsheviks overran the Russian palace and the shotgun was never delivered.

A SPARTAN ECONOMY AND ITS CONSEQUENCES

Another A1 with similar appeal to modern collectors is the 20-gauge presented by Buffalo Bill Cody, the famous sharpshooter, to Annie Oakley. A much plainer, though equally valuable Parker is a 24-gauge Trojan that was made for the United States Cartridge Company. Of the dozen Trojans so chambered, only one is known to have survived.

rubber buttpad, pistol-grip stock, and spartan finish. It was sold only in 12, 16 and 20 gauges, but any choke was available. The Trojan's forend was attached in such a way that only an extremely heavy force could snap it loose. Its casehardened frame lacked the gracefully curved forward shoulders of other Parkers. In 1939, its last year of production, the Trojan listed for $80—three times its introductory price and much higher than the prices of its competitors.

In 1917, Parker introduced its first competition model—the Single-Barrel Trap Gun. Available only with a 12-gauge, 2³/₄-inch chamber in barrel lengths of 30, 32 and 34 inches, this Parker came in several grades, with a beavertail forend and single trigger. It quickly proved itself on clay targets and remained unchanged and unchallenged until Parker announced its Double-Barrel Trap Gun in 1937. This double, which was manufactured for no more than seven years, became the last shotgun developed by Parker. It followed the Parker Skeet Gun, introduced in 1934. Cataloged with 26-inch barrels in 12, 16, 20, 28 and .410 chamberings, the Skeet Gun could be ordered with a ventilated rib at no extra charge. Both the Trap and Skeet models came with automatic ejectors.

The Great Depression summarily smashed many corporations, but gun firms weathered the blow surprisingly well. Parker was perhaps rocked the hardest. Its line comprised essentially one product (albeit in a heady number of configurations) that nobody needed. Many sportsmen wanted a Parker; but when money became tight, such fine double shotguns simply did not sell. Thus when the Remington Arms Company offered to buy manufacturing and marketing rights to Parker shotguns in 1932, the board of directors agreed and the deal was done.

During the next 3½ years, Remington continued to build shotguns at the Meriden plant, turning out 5,562 Parkers before transferring the operation to its Ilion (NY) factory in 1937. During this transition, Parker shotguns were manufactured exactly as before, by the same people with the same tools and machines. Nearly 80 percent of the original Parker work force made the move to Ilion, and for the next six years no substantial changes were made in the guns. Parkers were built regularly until 1944, with the final shipment completed in 1947.

The last Parker shotgun assembled bore the

Parker Models VHE (with ejectors) and VH (without ejectors) accounted for more sales—58,000— than any other Parker. The bottom-grade Trojan (shown here below the VH) ran a close second at 50,000.

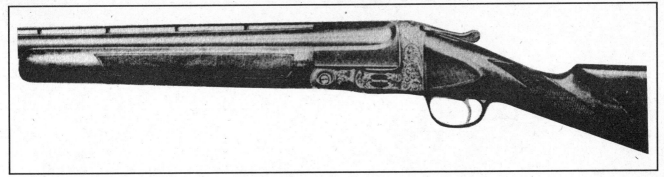

This Single Barrel Trap Gun was offered by Parker in five grades, but only one gauge —12.

serial number 242,385—a low number, considering that the firm was in business for nearly 80 years. Recently, Remington and Winchester have built limited quantities of replica Parkers. Materials and workmanship are surprisingly good, and prices— roughly, from $2,300 to $3,000—are about what you'd expect to pay for a well-built American double.

Collectors will insist these are not really Parkers, and that there's nothing like the original. They are right, of course. It is this same deep allegiance that made Charles Parker so successful with a gun built to higher standards of quality than anyone else dared risk in pioneer times. Thus it can still be said that in any Parker gun glows the glory days of shotgunning.

WAYNE VAN ZWOLL is a writer of books and magazine articles as well as a competitive rifleman, handloader and ballistician. The article that appears above is excepted from his new book, *Great American Gunmakers,* published by Stoeger Publishing Company (1992). It is the third in a series of articles in SHOOTER'S BIBLE tracing the history of the most successful and innovative gunmakers in the United States. Van Zwoll's first book, *Mastering Mule Deer,* was published in 1988.

THE CONTEMPORARY AUTO

by Wilf E. Pyle

Autoloaders historically have not been known for their fine accuracy or top-drawer reliability. Early autos did deliver sufficient accuracy to bring home deer and black bear taken at intermediate ranges, but tack-driving, target-quality accuracy was left to the single-shots. Today's models, however, provide hunters with all the accuracy needed to take a full list of big and small game anywhere in the world. For hunters, autoloader accuracy is no longer an issue, and any game within the capability of modern cartridges is well within range.

Somewhere, somehow, someone long ago decided it would be more dramatic and help sell more rifles if the autoloader feature was called "automatic." The word itself seems almost archaic now, but then it wasn't too long ago that something as mundane as an automatic transmission was considered high-end technology. "Automatic" spelled convenience, technology and speed. While well chosen to describe many consumer products, "automatic," when used in connection with a rifle, leaves the unfortunate impression of hunters armed with machine guns decimating the nation's game populations with rapid-fire shooting more befitting a war zone than the sporting field.

Other terms, such as "semi-auto," "self-loading" and "autoloading," were developed to define more clearly how the action on these firearms operated; but it was too late to help the image problem. Not that informed readers need to be told, but

it should be noted that the rifles under discussion are merely self-loading; i.e., the cartridge is extracted and ejected and a new one placed into the chamber at each pull of the trigger. The rifle does not fire "automatically." Thus, the term "automatic" is a misnomer, while the word "semi-automatic" improves the definition only marginally. The term "autoloader" is the best compromise available to the contemporary shooter and is now used in most advertising associated with this type of action.

Autoloaders are the fastest method for making available a loaded round. Levers are quick and pumps are even quicker, but in terms of getting off a second, well-aimed shot, the autoloader is king. Typically, about three seconds are needed to recover from the recoil of the first shot and then place the sights back on the moving target. That's half the time needed for a lever or a pump. Third and fourth shots can follow, and within 10 to 12 seconds all shots can be aimed and delivered at a cooperative target.

REMINGTON'S 7400 AND BROWNING'S BAR AUTOLOADING BESTSELLERS

Remington's Model 7400 and other similar contemporary rifles routinely deliver hunter-quality accuracy with factory cartridges and without special gunsmithing or fine tuning. Remington produced the first modern autoloading rifle in 1955 with its gas-operated Model 740 Woodmaster, later called Model 742. The rifle was improved and marketed in 1981 as the Model 7400. There was, for a short time, a Remington Model 4 as well. Introduced in 1981, it shared the same stock as the Model 742 and an economy model called the Sportsman 74.

These reasonably priced rifles have become famous in the cedar swamps of the eastern states and now hold a solid market share among serious hunters. The Remington has been around in various configurations for a long time now and has gained broad acceptability among hunters. In 17 years of continuous production, Model 7400 has sold over one million copies and dominated the market. Part of this success is due to the grand array of hunting-quality cartridges available for the rifle, namely: .243 Winchester, 6mm Remington, .308, .30-06 and .280 Remington. Another reason for the 7400's popularity is its gas-operated action, which helps dissipate recoil over an extended time period, thus softening felt recoil.

Another modern standard is the Browning Automatic Rifle, the BAR, which dates back to 1968. Its action is based loosely on Browning's military BAR, but the similarity ends there. The non-military BAR is a gas-operated autoloading rifle with a seven-lug locking bolt and rotary head. It has a five-shot, trap-door-style magazine, 22-inch barrel, folding leaf rear sight, and weighs only 7³⁄₈ pounds.

The BAR's popularity is based on three criteria: (1) the rifle simply looks good. It's well appointed with a French walnut pistol-grip stock and forend with hand-checkering that is sharp and runs 18 lines to the inch. Fit and finish are near perfect, with all metal surfaces highly polished and richly blued. (2) A trap-door floorplate holds the magazine, so that the magazine can be removed or reloaded in place. This feature actually combines the benefit of a fixed magazine—a solid and reliable cartridge-holding system—with the advantage of a clip (easily removed and replaced). And (3) the BAR is available in five good hunting-quality cartridges: .270, .280, .243, .308 and .30-06.

The BAR also ranks as the most powerful autoloading rifle in the world. It's chambered in 7mm Magnum and .300 Winchester Magnum, both of which have earned their magnum status. The 7mm Magnum pushes a 150-grain bullet at 3110 fps at the muzzle and leaves behind just under 1800 foot-pounds of energy at 300 yards. This is surpassed by the .300 Winchester Magnum, which drives a 220-grain bullet at 2680 fps and offers nearly a ton of stopping power at 300 yards.

The BAR, moreover, is now catalogued in the powerful .338 Winchester, which disappeared from the Browning list in 1977. The rifle's gas-powered mechanism helps reduce apparent recoil, giving the rifle a reputation as the answer to controlling magnum-level kick. This combination of less recoil and more power is a tantalizing one for shooters.

THE VENERABLE .284 WINCHESTER CARBINE

No rifle article is complete without the writer's nostalgic lament for an older rifle, or one long since

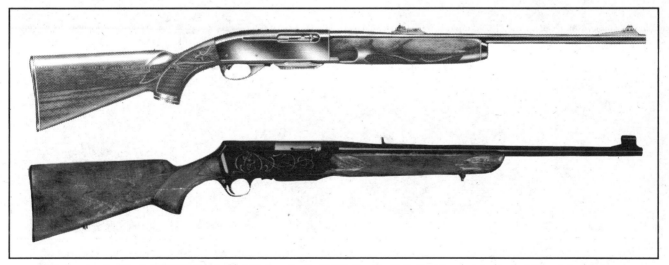

Remington's Model 7400 (top) and Browning's BAR Grade II (below) are two popular autoloaders that deliver hunter-quality accuracy with factory cartridges.

The author's .284 Model 100 Winchester carbine consistently produces two-inch five-shot groups at 100 yards. This is acceptable shooting even in today's accuracy-conscious world.

made unavailable or consigned to the junk pile. One such rifle is the Winchester Model 100 carbine in .284 Winchester. By now, many shooters have forgotten this cartridge, with its .270-like ballistics contained in a short, tight package. The case is greatly shortened and features a rebated rim and a short neck that allows high powder capacity. Developing 2860 fps at the muzzle, the .284 Winchester yields about a ton of striking energy at 200 yards. For those who go after deer, the .284 remains all the cartridge a hunter will ever need to do the job.

As a representative of the modern autoloading rifle, the Model 100 broke new ground in many ways. It achieved its light weight (7 lbs.) decades before the word "lightweight" became synonymous with sporting rifles. And with its handy size—the barrel is only 18 inches—Winchester's fine old carbine comes close to being the Holy Grail of deer-hunting tools. The rifle is gas-operated with a cam action rotating bolt featuring three massive locking lugs. Ejection is off the right-hand side through a large, cut-open receiver. A crossbolt safety housed in an all-aluminum trigger guard tops off the package. A forward barrel band supports the sling swivel, but unlike other models, this does not interfere with the barrel.

Winchester's Model 100 autoloading rifle first appeared on the market in 1960, followed in 1968

by the carbine. At first, it was available only in .308 with a 12-inch twist and in .243 with a 10-inch twist. The .284 appeared some years later. The magazine in the .308 and .243 holds four cartridges, while the .284 contains three. The carbine in .284 is the rarest—hence the least written about—autoloader of all times. It was slow to catch on with hunters, who remained skeptical of the squat, European-looking cartridge. The author's own .284 Model 100 carbine produces two-inch five-shot group at 100 yards with consistency. This is acceptable shooting even in today's accuracy-conscious world. From time to time, the odd un-accountable flyer will spoil a target group, but in the field it produces results equal to any auto-loader on the market today. The load—51 grains of IMR 4320—is no secret. Thrown from an aging Lyman powder measure into Winchester brass behind a 139-grain flat base Hornady spire-point bullet, it has proven itself time and again on deer, antelope, blacktailed prairie dogs and big jackrabbits sitting at the 225-yard mark.

THE .30 M1 AUTOLOADER, FRONT AND CENTER

Following World War II, the U.S. Military M1 autoloader contributed to a mild rebirth of interest in autoloading firearms. It really picked up steam in 1963, when the NRA sold 175,000 copies of the

The autoloader has appeared in a number of useful cartridges. They include (left to right): .300 Winchester Magnum, 7mm Remington Magnum, .270 Winchester, .30-06 Springfield, .243 Winchester, .284 Winchester, .308 Winchester, .223 Remington, .222 Remington, .44 Magnum and 9mm Parabellum.

Following World War II, the U.S. Military M1 autoloader, which this hunter is demonstrating, contributed to a mild rebirth of interest in shooting autoloading firearms.

M1 carbine to its membership. The rifle sports a dramatic-looking, compact autoloading design and still generates excitement among small game shooters and plinkers. Barrel length is 18 inches and rifling is one turn in 20 inches with a right-hand twist. While never promoted as a hunting round, the .30 M1 cartridge moves a 110-grain bullet at 1990 fps and develops a chamber pressure of about 40,000 psi, providing an effective range of just under 300 yards. The cartridge is often compared to the .32-20 Winchester developed for the 1873 and 1892 repeating rifles. The .30 M1 cartridge offers plenty for Sunday afternoon plinking or small game hunting, but it lacks the power to be an effective big game cartridge.

Many companies have offered M1 look-alikes based on the military version. Iver Johnson now markets a Model PM 30HB, and plenty of Plainfield Model MLs are in the hands of plinkers and casual target shooters. Universal was a once-prominent player, offering five separate styles, including two models that handled the .256 cartridge. Johnson Arms formerly carried four different versions. At one point during 1967, in fact, 24 versions of this rifle were in production. Second-hand M1s are available as well, and gun dealers claim it is the most commonly traded rifle in America today.

Some postwar models were assembled from a combination of newly manufactured and old surplus parts. The configurations made at different times over the years dwarf the availabilities of other companies who offer autoloaders. Styles range from deluxe versions sporting Monte Carlo stocks to commando types with telescoping stocks. The 15-shot clip is standard in these retreads, but 5-, 10- and 30-shots are available.

Military or Civilian? The M1 merits comment as a contemporary firearm for two reasons. First, nearly every shooter has one. Not only does it exist in such great numbers, but a myriad of styles abound. Second, and more important, is the M1's place in modern autoloader shooting history. The U.S. carbine .30 M1 is the first autoloader to cross the line from a full military type to a civilian sporting arm, thereby ushering in two debates among shooters and hunters: (1) the ethical use of the autoloader as a legitimate hunting gun; and (2) the proper place for the paramilitary rifle in today's society.

Ever since Bonnie and Clyde were gunned down with a .401 Winchester Model 1910 auto-

The M-16, shown here in the hands of an infantryman, personifies the two debates currently raging among shooters and hunters. One involves the ethics of using an autoloader as a hunting gun; the other promotes the value of the paramilitary rifle in today's society.

loading rifle, gun owners have associated auto arms with bad guys and blue coats. The debate has reached the hunting fields, where some claim that autoloading firearms take away the sporting chance inherent in the sport. Fully disclaiming the fact that some people must still hunt to survive, quick follow-up shots and rapid fire mask the notion of sport in their eyes, suggesting a blood lust for helpless game without hope of escape.

The paramilitary role of the autoloader is even more fractious. The number of autoloaders in the military or paramilitary configuration grows each year. Old favorites, such as the author's prized Model 100 Winchester, have long since given way to more than three dozen paramilitary models on today's market. The current success of the paramilitary rifle is an embarrassment to the rifle manufacturing establishment and the gun lobby in general. Indeed, demographers can produce statistics showing that the gun-owning constituency is shifting away from hunters and outdoorsmen to those with an interest solely in paramilitary arms.

Gun companies, sensitive to the public mood and ever mindful of the potential for law suits, have kept the number of autoloaders they produce deliberately low. Indeed, many companies offer autoloading arms as law enforcement equipment only. The unfortunate outcome of all this is that the hunter loses. Such benefits as quick follow-up shots, which reduce the opportunity for wounded game to escape and die a lingering death, are denied. Legislation is also more strict where the use of autoloading rifles is concerned. Such is the creeping reality of the current environment in which autoloading firearms must carve their market share.

To be sure, the autoloading rifle has not benefited from the experimentation and development experienced by the bolt gun. This is apparent in the available cartridge choices. For example, where is the Browning BAR or the Remington Model 7400 in .223 or .222 Remington? Where are the carbine versions in the current line of big game hunting autoloaders? Can shooters look forward to a return of the Remington 742 carbine in .30-06 and .308 that was so popular in the mid-1960s? What about the Ruger 44 autoloading carbine in .44 Magnum, with an 18½-inch barrel, or the Ruger International with its Mannlicher-style stock? And whatever happened to the Ruger autoloader XGI? Are gun manufacturers overreacting, and have they become too cautious about introducing new models?

RUGER'S MIGHTY LITTLE MINI-14

The Ruger line of autoloaders began with the .44 Magnum Standard Carbine. The .44 Magnum cartridge is a brute in a handgun and only a little less so in a rifle, producing 1760 fps at the muzzle and 661 foot-pounds of energy at 200 yards with a 240-grain factory bullet. It was designed to offer shooters a rifle that allows cartridge interchange with handguns, a need that dates back to the days of the old .44-40. A look-alike Ruger Model 10/22 became available in 1964, nearly matching the design and style of the .44, which disappeared from the Ruger line in 1986.

The great success story in the autoloading world is the Ruger-designed Mini-14 in .223. Actually a re-design of the U.S. military Garand-type rifles (M1 and M14), this little rifle illustrates what fun autoloading rifles really are. Weighing in at only 6 pounds 6 ounces, with an 18½-inch barrel and 37¼-inch overall length, these rifles are easy to carry and handle in the field, store readily in a vehicle, and can get on target in a hurry. Introduced in 1972 following five years of design, the Mini-14 was available at first only to police and quasi-military institutions. Following an expansion of production facilities, it finally became available to the public.

The gas system of the Mini-14 includes a fixed piston and a moving cylinder designed to expel unburned powder from within the system. This improves reliability under extended use. Other features include a one-piece stock reinforced with steel liners at points of stress and high heat; also, the hand guard and forearm are separated from the barrel to enhance cooling. A stainless steel version of the Mini-14, incorporating these features while adding the corrosion-resistant quality of stainless steel, appeared in 1978. The Mini-14 was improved in 1984 to accept a scope more readily. Designated the Ranch Rifle, it featured integral bases in the receiver to accept the proven solid steel Ruger mountain rings.

The most successful sporting grade autoloader ever produced is the Ruger Mini-14, which this shooter is about to fire. Popular, lightweight and fast, it remains the best of its kind.

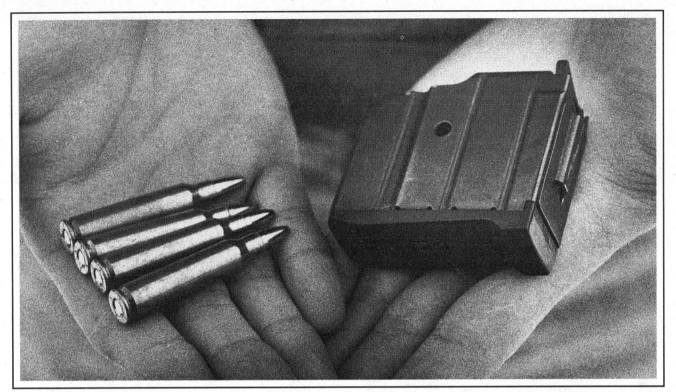

Clips are an important feature in all autoloading rifles. They are quick and easy to use—and easy to misplace as well.

The autoloader owner can choose from a reasonable selection of hunting cartridges for big and small game, as exemplified by the .223 Remington. But it still falls far short of the choices available to bolt action owners.

How much fun is the Mini-14? The answer is: "A lot!" Its accuracy in taking predators is excellent, and where follow-up shots are called for the little rifle does well. Light in weight, maneuverable, with less report and mild recoil, all these factors help put hides on the stretcher.

Ruger modified its Ranch Rifle in 1988 to create the Mini-30 chambered for the 7.62×39mm Russian. Originally developed in 1943 by the Russians as an infantry small arms cartridge, it came into general use in the 1960s. The Russian bullet weighs 123 grains and travels at 2300 fps, producing 860 foot-pounds of striking energy at 200 yards.

All centerfire autoloaders produced today load with a separate clip. This is a great invention that makes reloading much easier and quicker. Other than some Sako models and a few Parker-Hales, bolt rifles lack this feature. Because clips are easily lost and expensive to replace, a hunter going afield with an autoloader should carry a replacement clip or two so that the misplaced part won't mean failure in the field. All hunters should carry their clips in handy belt pouches or web gear to ensure cleanliness and availability.

One final point often forgotten in technical

Levers are fast and pumps are faster, but nothing beats the autoloader for ease in delivering that quick follow-up shot—a sentiment this successful hunter surely echoes.

discussions involving autoloaders should be made: when all is said and done, *autoloaders are fun to shoot*. Successive shots delivered quickly and accurately add a great dimension to all hunting and make plinking a challenging diversion. For many shooters, fun is reason enough to pick an autoloader and keep it in the rifle rack for those grand occasions when a good time is the order of the day.

WILF PYLE is an avid sportsman who has hunted nearly all species of game, most successfully with his favorite Model 100 Winchester, which inspired this article. A well-known authority on sporting firearms in the U.S. and Canada, he is also an enthusiastic reloader and ballistician. Pyle's recent books include *Small Game and Varmint Hunting* and *Hunting Predators for Hides and Profits*, both Stoeger publications, as well as the *Hunter's Book of the Pronghorn Antelope* (New Century).

In Your Mind You Always Knew A Shotgun Should Feel This Good.

Remember how, as a kid, you used to make a "gun?" By pointing and swinging your arms, you developed the natural hand/eye coordination and aiming instincts you depend on to this day. In

OUR NEW LIGHT CONTOUR SHOTGUNS:
THE MODEL 11-87™ PREMIER®
AND MODEL 870™ WINGMASTER®

your mind you've always known just how an ideally balanced shotgun should feel. That's what you'll feel when you mount the new Remington® Model 11-87™ Premier® and

Model 870™ Wingmaster® shotguns. Thanks to their new light contour barrels, these 12-gauge field guns are a half-pound lighter overall. Yet they still have the benefits of all-steel receivers. These new Premier and Wingmaster light contour shotguns are superbly balanced, with the weight ideally centered where you want it—between your hands. They come up quicker, letting you point and swing them so smoothly and effortlessly you'll swear they're "20s." And, because these American-made shotguns are so much lighter, you won't be tired out as your hunting day winds down. Both these light contour shotguns are avail-able with a choice of 26," 28"* or 30" barrels, each with three Rem™ Choke tubes. What's more, when you buy any Remington shotgun with light contour

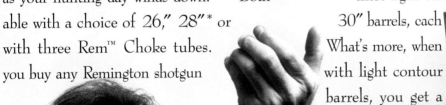

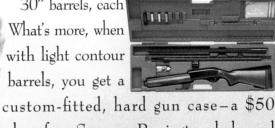

barrels, you get a custom-fitted, hard gun case—a $50 value—free. See your Remington dealer and shoulder our new Model 11-87 Premier and Model 870 Wingmaster shotguns.** You won't believe how great they feel.

Remington. DUPONT
IT'S WHAT YOU'RE SHOOTING FOR.

There's something new about these custom features...
NOW THEY'RE STANDARD.

New angled rear slide serrations, once found only on Gold Cup models, are now standard on all enhanced Colt pistols.

New scalloped ejection port for more efficient ejection.

New flat top slide is now standard on all enhanced Colt pistols. Some models available with new high-profile 3-dot sighting system for rapid target acquistion.

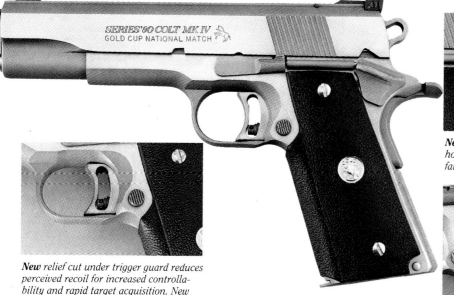

New combat-style hammer with elongated hole through spur provides faster hammer fall for increased accuracy.

New beavertail grip safety creates a more comfortable and natural grip, and eliminates "hammer bite."

New relief cut under trigger guard reduces perceived recoil for increased controllability and rapid target acquisition. New long trigger comes in stainless steel or black composite.

Introducing the New Enhanced Colt Semiautomatic Pistols.

Serious shooters have always chosen Colt's Government Model pistols as the starting point for a host of costly enhancements from America's custom pistolsmiths. Now, these custom extras are available as standard features from Colt, designed-in, rather than tacked on. Look for these enhancements on all our new Model "O" pistols — Gold Cup, Delta Elite, Combat Elite, Government Model, Combat Commander, Lightweight Commander, Officer's ACP and Officer's ACP Lightweight. For positive reloading,

every enhanced Colt pistol now comes with a new beveled magazine well. In addition, the Combat Elite now has adjustable sights and is available in both 45 ACP and 38 Super. Custom-molded carry case with two magazines is furnished with each pistol.

See the wide range of enhanced Model "O" pistols at your Colt dealer's. Whatever your preference, there's only one choice...Colt.

COLT *The Legend Lives*

Colt's Manufacturing Company, Inc.
P.O. Box 1868, Hartford, CT 06144-1868

Warning: Be a safe shooter — never chamber a round until you are ready to shoot. Be aware of state and local firearms regulations. Always read and follow the instruction manuals which accompany each firearm. Free instruction manuals and catalogs are available from the factory upon request.

Above All...
Tasco World Class Plus™
Performance Level Uniquely Superior

Tasco World Class Plus™ 3X-9X Riflescope with 44mm Objective, Black Gloss Finish

Tasco World Class Plus™
15X-45X 60mm Spotting Scope with Tripod

Tasco World Class Plus™
7X42mm Binocular

Tasco World Class Plus,™ a line of optics sold through serious firearm dealerships only, takes the quality of World Class to a new level of excellence. Riflescopes with fully and multi-coated lenses and large, light-gathering 44mm and extra-large 50mm objectives provide the clearest, brightest view possible for dusk to dawn hunting. A *15X-45X60mm spotting scope* offers a sharp, clear, distortion-free image throughout the zoom range while a *60mm spotter* with optional eyepieces accommodates individual needs. Completing the line, full size wide angle *binoculars* and a convenient *compact*, all with BAK-4 prisms, fully coated PLUS multi-coated optics, extra long eye relief and a sleek, rubber armored exterior, are designed for the look of quality inside and out.

Covered by an extraordinary No Fault Limited Lifetime Warranty, Tasco World Class Plus™ has taken its well-deserved place in the industry...clearly, above all.

FINLAND
TIKKA

A DELICATE BLEND OF INNOVATION AND "OLD WORLD CRAFTSMANSHIP"

BY

FINLAND
sako

BIG GAME HUNTING
AT
LONG RANGE

by Ralph F. Quinn

Big game hunters who have spent better than half their lives pursuing trophies worldwide are bound to have definite opinions on the subject of taking big game at long range. Any among the thousands of hunters who take whitetail deer regularly from 50 to 150 yards will claim there's no need to discuss the subject. If the hunter scouts properly, they argue, and positions himself correctly, the animal will come to him, making the long-range debate a moot one.

Yet every season, long-shot chances present themselves all across the U.S. and Canada. In northern New York, it might be at the far edge of a timber slash. In Mississippi, vast bean plots act as buck magnets, but seldom are the animals attracted to the hunter's side. The dune country of Michigan's lower peninsula is a patchwork of timber and sand, so hunters must be equally talented there. And in the Plains states and far West, huge, open places exist between brush and timber, harboring plenty of deer and antelope. If any devotee of the hunting art wants to cash in on the bounty, however, he'll have to do his homework.

DEFINING LONG RANGE

How far is far, exactly, and what is long-range shooting? Any game animal that lurks beyond the 400-yard mark is on the outer edge of reasonable rifle distances. As a matter of fact, anything beyond 300 yards is a tough shot, even for experi-enced shooters. True, a number of high-intensity cartridges are capable of delivering the necessary foot-pounds of energy for one-shot kills at 500 yards, but few riflers can handle the punishing recoil generated by a load like that. The goal of the long-range shooter, after all, is not to shoot from county to county, but to place that first shot on target with precision.

Reduced to its essence, the hunter's problem is simply to hit the game at long range. That may sound easy enough, and usually it is for the shooter who uses good judgment, estimates range distances accurately, and has a reasonable grasp of ballistics (trajectory). Add to those attributes the accuracy of both rifle and shooter as integral facets of successful long-range shooting, and you get the idea that hitting the target is not all that easy. And let's not forget such ungovernable human factors as nerves, flinches and wobbles! The truth is, not even the most accurate centerfire rifle in the world can make up for poor shooting skills.

GETTING THE RANGE

Typically, the biggest problem in long-distance shooting is range estimation. Most hunters can judge distances to 200–250 yards with some accuracy, but beyond that it becomes a matter of speculation. At 300 yards and beyond, it's not unusual to make errors of 100 yards, plus or minus. And at 400–450 yards, faulty estimates can balloon to 150–175 yards. Granted, that may not be important if the hunter uses a flat-shooting, high-stepping cartridge. Unfortunately, it's at the outside edge of long range, where precise ranging becomes most critical. A quick look at one of the trajectory (ballistic) tables in the back of this book or in your favorite ammo catalog will demonstrate that fact.

Let's say you've selected for your western mule deer hunt the inveterate 30-06 loaded with a 150-grain boat-tail bullet. With the scope mounted 1½ inches above line of sight and zeroed at 200 yards, the bullet will strike −7.4 inches low at 300 yards. At 400 yards, that figure zooms to −23.1 inches, and at 500 yards it's −43.7! At 300 yards, moreover, the bullet has slowed down by some 700 feet-per-second and has begun a rapid downward trajectory.

At 400 yards, the energy/foot-pounds factor is fast approaching the magical 1200 foot-pounds required for one-shot kills. And at 500 yards, the same bullet plods along at only 1880 fps. Suppose a mature mulie buck with a maximum allowable kill area of 14 inches is spotted at 400 yards, and the hunter makes an error in estimating range of 100 yards, plus or minus. His bullet will hit over or under the animal by a significant amount. At 500 yards, remember, vertical drop is almost four feet. Toss in the added variables of wind drift, mirage and marksmanship, and it's a pretty safe bet the bullet will pass harmlessly by the target.

To be sure, some shooters can anchor big game with consistency at 250 and 300 yards, but most of them use yardage markers to take all guesswork out of their range estimation. By ranging expected crossings and feeding points before the hunt begins, you'll have solved one of the biggest problems in long-range shooting.

Because he knows the allowable kill area on full-size big game targets, this hunter is on his way to long-range success.

By sighting in at the longest possible zero, and by tailoring load to rifle properly, this hunter can assure solid hits at long-range. Note the bullet drop compensator scope.

Winston Elrod, one of North America's most consistent long-range riflemen, uses the combination of a flatshooting .25-06 and a quality, high-resolution optic to take the guesswork out of estimating how far off the target lies. And when sighting in, he uses the longest possible zero point for a 120-grain Speer bullet.

Under ideal conditions, 10X rangefinders can take a lot of the guesswork out of estimating distances to targets. Of course, it's necessary to learn how to use the device under hunt conditions—and to practice. Another good idea is to use scopes that incorporate bullet-drop compensators or range-finding reticules. These work to a degree, but at best they yield only approximations. The most reliable tactic is to develop an accurate load for your particular rifle, to know the trajectory of that particular bullet and powder combination, and to shoot as often as you can.

For those who are not avowed handloaders,

it's a good idea to buy factory brands, such as Federal's Premium or Winchester's Supreme loads. These rounds are loaded to provide maximum velocities and uniform pressures. They're more expensive, but consider them wise investments in accuracy for the coming seasons and beyond.

Bullet selection is, in fact, a vital component in successful long-range hunting. Since expansion is the name of the game in this area, point design and jacket construction become all-important. Well-constructed bullets—Silvertips, Bronze Points and Partitions, for example—are poor choices because at low velocities their points fail to expand the thin copper jackets. The pointed Soft Point bullet has proven to be among the most reliable for long-range expansion uniformity. In most cases, where the lungs or shoulder area have been hit, this bullet expands well, creating a wide wound channel. If a bullet doesn't do that, then it simply isn't traveling fast enough.

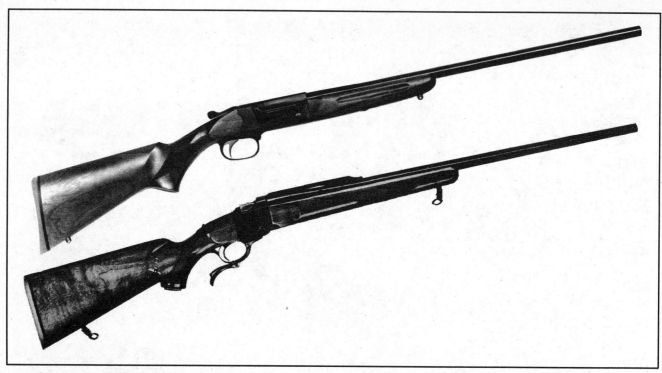

Since velocity/energy foot-pounds is important for long-range kills, many hunters prefer single-shot rifles like the Thompson/Center TCR '87 Hunter (top) and the Ruger No. 1B Standard. Both have barrels of about 26 inches in length.

MAKING THE SHOT

Taking a chapter from the ranks of world-class shooters like Schuetzen, Wimbledon and the silhouette champions, long-range accuracy is only a matter of repeating each phase of shooting exactly the same way, round after round. Basically, these specialists load, take a solid rest, and fire. The only difference is, they're shooting at stationary targets, and they have a specific time limit in which to get the shot off. Most important, they know the exact distance to the target. There are no such luxuries in big game riflery.

Ideally, the hunter should get into the steadiest position possible. Sometimes the terrain will allow the shooter to use the prone position with a tight sling; but with the exception of big game in rough terrain, these are rare instances. When the opportunity arises, the shooter should rest the forend or barrel on a surface that is reasonably soft, such as a rolled-up down sweater or day pack. If nothing like that is available, use your hand as a pad atop a log, tree limb or ridge comb as a cushion against recoil. Never rest the forend or barrel on a hard surface, because that will cause the rifle to jump and the shot to strike high.

Also, when angling shots up or downhill, hold low on the chest region. Bullets traveling through the normal trajectory curve have a tendency to rise above line of sight; a normal hold will therefore put the shot high, particularly at high altitude.

Some experienced long-range shooters get on target by adopting a sitting position, with elbows on both knees, and using a military-style sling. A setup like that assures a definite edge over the off-hand position. But first it's important to practice getting your arm into the sling and dropping into the sitting position until it becomes second nature. The name of this game is to get into position fast.

At this point, the brain should be running through a series of check-offs: rifle, load, position, aim, squeeze and follow-through. Here, again, we come back to the question: How far is the game? An animal will appear closer or farther away depending on the time of day, light levels, terrain and vegetation. There's precious little time to assess the situation. Obviously, it's necessary when aiming at 300 yards to allow for the bullet to drop below point of aim. But how can you do this quickly and subconsciously under field conditions?

That's where cartridge selection becomes all-important. At 300 yards, the trusty .30-06 loaded with the 150-grain boat-tail has begun its downward flight, a path that steepens rapidly beyond 350 yards. Most spitzer (pointed) bullets with good ballistic coefficients (i.e., a bullet's ability to overcome the resistance of air in flight) experience a 300-yard drop of 7 to 10 inches when zeroed at 200. That is the critical number to remember when selecting a long-range cartridge and bullet.

If the mulie is anything less than 200 yards away, hold dead on and you'll be on target. At 300 yards, lay the horizontal crosshair level with the mulie's back and squeeze the trigger. Since most mature deer have a 14- to 15-inch vital zone, and assuming you've made a reasonably good estimate of distance, you should be in the money. This system works well with sheep, goats and caribou as well. On moose and elk with larger kill areas, you can drop down a bit. For pronghorns, be sure the yardage isn't much beyond 300. If it is, try to get closer, or take a solid rest.

SELECTING THE RIGHT CARTRIDGE

In selecting the ideal long-range cartridge, consider three things: the shooter, the rifle-cartridge combination, and the amount of energy foot-pounds delivered. Experienced riflemen are better prepared to cope with the heavy recoil normally associated with high-velocity cartridges, and for the most part they do extremely well with them. Some of the best all-round long-range specialists in the business use the potent .257 Weatherby

Magnum with 120-grain loads to collect western whitetail every season at distances of 350 yards or more. With some 25 foot-pounds of free recoil, that's tough to hold consistently. But if you can handle increased recoil in a hunting-weight rifle, magnums may be the right choice.

For most hunters, though, the moderate cartridges—.25-06 and 7mm-08 in both factory and custom chamberings—are preferable. For part-time shooters, this may be the best route to go. A lot of mulies and Canadian whitetails have been taken at distances over 300 yards with a Sako Standard in .270 Winchester. Another fine choice is the .280 Remington, which was introduced in 1957. Fred Huntington shot the works with it in Africa that year using 150 grain loads.

In the magnums, it's hard to beat the 7mm Remington and .338 for long-range work on elk-size animals. Bill and Tracy Hardy, one of the best father-son hunting teams in Arizona's Rincon Mountains, use a glass-stocked 7mm Magnum they affectionately call the "Green Monster" with which they collect trophy Coues and Burro mule deer at ranges to 450 yards. Zeroed at 300 yards, bullet drop for the 150-grain spitzer is a scant six inches!

Since long-range shooting is a calculated sport, its devotees take extreme care to put their first shot on the mark. Even if they fail to connect, there's always time to make corrections for a second shot. A growing number of long-range specialists are discovering that single-shot rifles like

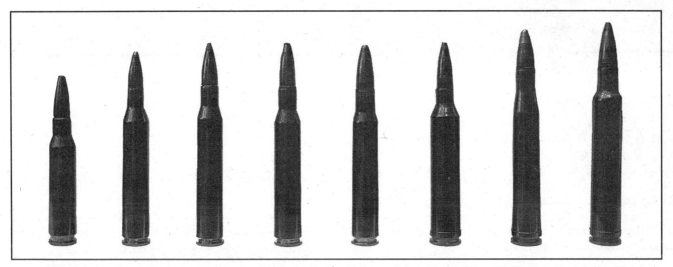

This lineup of potent long-range cartridges includes (left to right): 7mm-08, .25-06 Remington, .280 Remington, .270 Winchester, .30-06, 7mm Remington Magnum, .300 Winchester Magnum and .300 Weatherby Magnum.

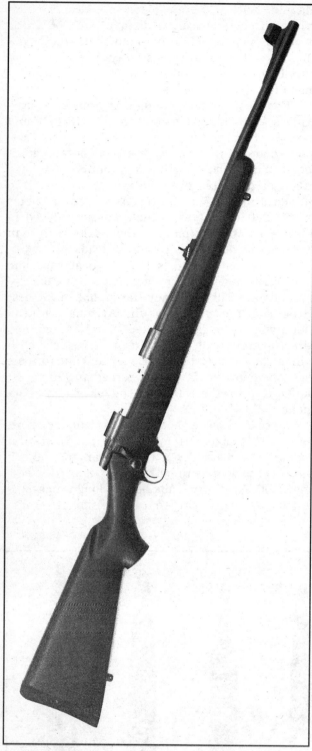

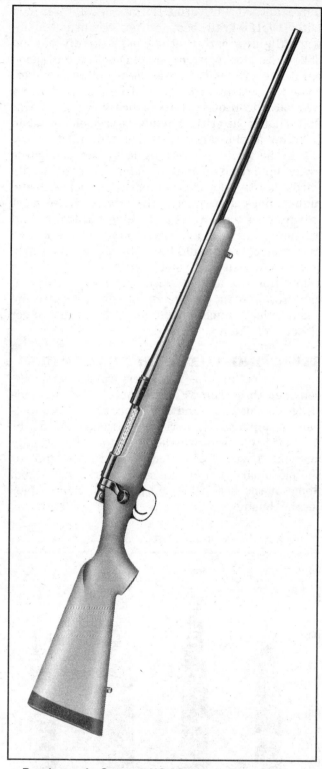

Sako's Fiberclass rifle in its long action version offers top accuracy under all hunt conditions. This model is chambered for .25-06 Remington, .270 Winchester, .280 Remington, .30-06, 7mm Remington Magnum, .300 Winchester Magnum and .338 Winchester Magnum.

Remington's Custom KS Mountain Rifle is a good out-of-the-box choice for long-range work. This rifle is offered in .270 Winchester, .280 Remington, 7mm Remington Magnum, .30-06, .300 Winchester Magnum, .338 H&H and .375 H&H Magnum.

Ruger's No. 1 or Browning's Model 1885 are ideal tools simply because their barrels average four inches longer than bolt guns of the same overall length. Energy foot-pounds and velocity are critical elements in long-range shooting, making these rifles logical choices.

Another fine selection is a medium-barreled (24 inches) glass-stocked bolt-action rifle, either magazine-fed or single-shot. Depending on one's budget, the choices include Sako's Fiberclass, Remington's 700 KS, Ruger's M-77 Mark II All-Weather, Browning's A-Bolt Stalker, and Weatherby's Fibermark series. All offer long-range chamberings to fit the needs of most big game hunters. In each case, solid lockup of bolt to receiver is a time-honored design, and off-the-shelf accuracy is good.

As for customized long-range pieces, one that is guaranteed to yield maximum velocity, this big game hunter recommends the following: screw on a 24- or 26-inch, medium-weight barrel chambered for the .280 Remington or 7mm Magnum. Also, have the metal work accurized, square the barrel to the receiver, turn the bolt face, and replace the factory trigger with a target model. Finally, glass-bed the works in a top-of-the line fiberglass stock and free-float the barrel. With such an outfit, any hunter can be relatively assured of hitting the mark—provided, of course, he does his job!

Choosing optics for such a formidable long-range piece is a matter of personal preference, but most will opt for nothing less than a quality 3–9X variable with a 40mm or 44mm objective lens. Some long-range shooters prefer fixed powers in 6-X, particularly when shots under 150 yards are the exception. A 4-X is a fine compromise for this kind of hunting—if the hunter uses it wisely.

USE ENOUGH GUN ... KNOW YOUR GAME

Over 25 years ago, Parker Ackley, the noted wildcatter and gunsmith, published his classic work, *The Handbook for Shooters and Reloaders.* In his chapter on "Killing Power," Ackley discussed the energy needed to kill various animals at game ranges. Sheep, goats, deer and antelope, he wrote, require 1200 foot-pounds, while larger beasts—elk, moose and bear—take 2000. Regardless of a bullet's weight, it should have the specified energy when it hits game in the vital chest area. Ackley's numbers are only rough estimates, of course, but few experienced hunters will disagree with them.

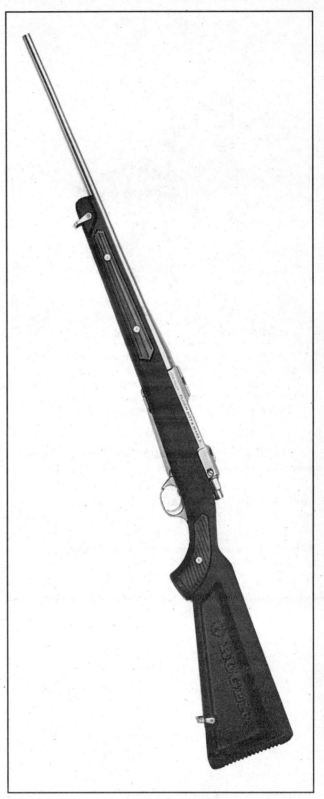

Ruger's new Mark II M-77 All-Weather rifle is an excellent choice for long-range big game hunting when chambered in .270 Winchester, .30-06, 7mm Remington or .300 Magnum.

Pronghorn antelope typically inhabit flat, barren terrain, making long-range estimating difficult. To assure success, the hunter should sight in his rifle for maximum point-blank range, and he should know the bullet trajectory by heart.

With Ackley's two numbers as a guide, it's a relatively easy matter to sift through ballistic tables for cartridges capable of delivering the energy foot-pounds required at 200 to 500 yards. For example, you'll find that the popular .270 Winchester in 150-grain delivers 1290 fps at 500 yards. Does this mean the .270 is a good 500-yard deer car-

tridge? In a purely hypothetical sense, yes, provided the hunter delivers the bullet on target under field-shooting conditions. Even with the .270 sighted for 275 yards, anything beyond 325 yards becomes a tough shot. The same applies to the 30-06 in 150-grain.

Summing up, legitimate long-range game shooting requires a liberal dose of good judgment before pulling the trigger. Any hunter should avoid attempting a shot from an unsteady position, or when the animal is able to move out of sight quickly. It's always better, when possible, to stalk to within sure hitting range than to attempt an uncertain shot, particularly when dealing with dangerous game.

By controlling the variables inherent in rifle, load and rest, and by using a flat-shooting, high-velocity cartridge, the big game hunter is well on the way to tagging a trophy using the long-range methods described here. Even the most proficient shooter will have a rough time hitting, though, if he doesn't know how far the target is. To avoid failure, be sure to limit your shots to the existing conditions, use a solid rest and some common sense, and you'll stay on top of the game.

RALPH QUINN is an award-winning, full-time freelance writer who regularly contributes to national hunting and shooting publications. A video and film producer as well, he travels throughout the world and the U.S. in search of fresh, new subjects. He is a dedicated big game hunter and the advice he offers in this article comes from more than 25 years of hunting experience worldwide.

SPORTING MAUSERS: POTENT AND ACCURATE

by Sam Fadala

The .30-06 cartridge had a great deal to do with the fame of the Model 1903 Springfield as a sporting rifle. The original military Springfield could be "cleaned up" through sporterizing using the original barrel, sometimes turned down, polished and blued. Modern handloads for the .30-06 provide maximum velocities of almost 3100 feet per second (fps) for a 150-grain bullet and a shade over 2800 fps for a 180-grain bullet. The .30-06 remains the No. 1 big game cartridge west of the Mississippi River and more than a little popular east of it.

However, at the close of World War II, a great many German Mauser rifles found their way into the U.S. A large number of them were chambered for the 8mm Mauser (7.9mm), a round not all that much shorter than the .30-06 and about .32 caliber instead of .30. The 8mm Mauser was a fine hunting cartridge capable of good work on all big game when a crack shot was in charge of directing the bullet. But it was impossible for the 8mm Mauser to compete with the .30-06, especially since American factory loads were not up to par; i.e., a popular load being a 170-grain bullet at modest velocity.

When the Mauser Model 98 came out in the latter days of the 19th century, the rifle was a military number, chambered for the 8mm Mauser cartridge. Very soon the rifle became a sporting arm. Both versions were made by Mauser-Werke in Oberndorf, Germany, which also sold Model 98 actions to different arms companies around the world, so the actions were plentiful.

The 8mm Mauser cartridge came to be considered a sporting round and was chambered in various hunting rifles. The round is also known as the 7.9×57mm, meaning a bullet of 7.9mm diameter and a case 57mm long. The 7×57mm is actually an 8×57mm necked down to 7mm. Originally, the bullet diameter was .318 inch and weighed 236 grains in round-nosed configuration for a muzzle velocity of 2100 fps. Improved since then, the bullet diameter of the 8mm is now .323 inch with bullet weight at 154 grains for 2900 fps.

The American loading of the 8mm Mauser never credited the round for its potential. Today, the round is loaded with a 170-grain bullet at 2360 fps. A good .30-30 load projects a 170-grain bullet at 2100 to 2200 fps. To be fair about it, some problems have been reported with imported 8mm Mauser rifles. These problems stem mainly from variations in bore size, according to data, and it could be that American ammo companies wanted to load mildly to accommodate potential bore size discrepancy. Furthermore, a good many 8mm Mauser rounds found their way into rifles chambered for the .30-06 cartridge. Squeezing a .32-caliber bullet through a .30-caliber bore is never a

The handsome Kimber Model 89 embodies features from the Mauser military action.

good idea. No doubt some rifles were seriously damaged when the ammo mixup occurred. Meanwhile, European companies continued to load the 8mm Mauser more in line with its potential.

Today, the German firm of RWS offers the 8mm Mauser sporting cartridge in various loadings. There is a 187-grain bullet at 2625 fps and another bullet of the same weight, different design, at 2690 fps. RWS ammo generally comes out "on the button" when independently chronographed. A heavier 196-grain bullet is shown at 2620 fps and a 198-grain bullet leaves the muzzle at the same velocity. These are, in order, muzzle energies of 2862, 3005, 2988 and 3019 foot-pounds. Energy levels in the 3000 foot-pound range suffice for North American big game with proper bullet placement. Compare these 8mm Mauser figures with the American loading, which develops 2103 foot-pounds; it's easy to see that the U.S. shooter/hunter either had to handload to boost 8mm Mauser cartridge performance or look for foreign ammo.

Mild factory 8mm ammo was a major reason for full-blown sporterizing of the Mauser Model 98 rifle. While the Springfield was fine "as is," the Mauser was not. To be sure, some Mausers were rechambered to a wildcat known as the 8mm-06 so that the original barrel could be retained. The 8mm-06 was simply the .30-06 case necked up to accept 8mm bullets. Properly handloaded, the 8mm-06 was a powerful cartridge. Nonetheless, many American sportsmen who wanted to use the German rifle found it advisable to remove the action and use it as the starting point for a whole new sporting arm. The success of the Mauser was so complete that a number of companies built rifles using commercial Mauser actions with no, or limited, changes.

MAUSER: FATHER OF THE BOLT ACTION RIFLE

A list of commercial Mausers past and present is a long one. One of the latest Mauser copies is the beautiful Kimber Model 89. This rifle boasts an action designed after the Mauser plus the pre-64 Model 70 Winchester, with traits of both. Herter's (then of Waseca, Minnesota) offered a rifle based on the Mauser 98 action, although not an exact copy of it. Smith & Wesson made a Mauser. The Centurion rifle of Golden State Arms was a Mauser, too, as was the Parker-Hale bolt-action rifle. The Santa Barbara action carried the Mauser pattern all the way in a Spanish-made version. P.O.

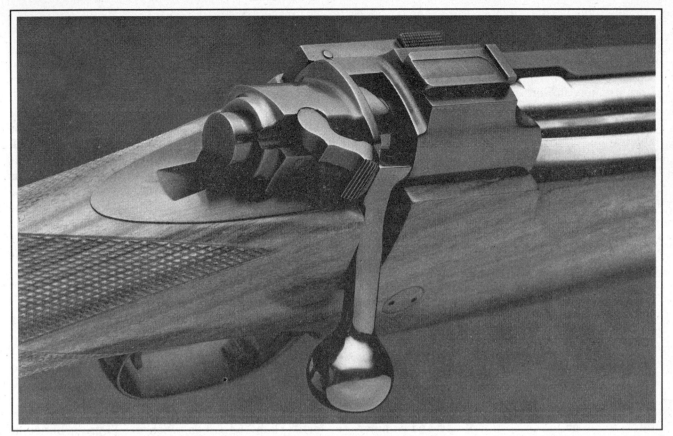

A close-up view of the Kimber Model 89 shows the Mauser-like action with the inclusion of a three-position safety and integral square-bridge scope mount bases.

Ackley's riflemaking operation included a Mauser action as well. The French-made Brevex Magnum Mauser was well-liked by gunsmiths who wanted to chamber a rifle for the big ones, such as the .416 Rigby, which has become relatively popular in America. The Mark X Mauser remains widely available and is considered a bargain, especially in the barreled-action version. The early Husqvarna rifle of Sweden, once a popular rifle in U.S. catalogues, is another Mauser. The Brno Czech sporting rifle is not exactly a Mauser, but neither does it depart radically from the Mauser design.

In a very real sense, the Mauser 98 is the father of most of our popular bolt-action rifles, and that certainly includes the Springfield, which relied heavily on Model 98 design. The Mauser is so important to arms history in general, as well as sporting rifle history specifically, that there is no end of literature on the subject. A book of special interest is *Mauser Bolt Rifles* by Ludwig Olson, a 1976 title that is well-read to this today. Olson is known as one of the most intelligent and resourceful of our firearms researchers. Paul Mauser (June 27, 1838–May 29, 1914) certainly deserves recognition as the father of the Mauser Model 98 as we know it, but he was not entirely responsible for every facet of Mauser rifle development. As always, many inventions preceded the Mauser 98, with a host of models that were superseded one at a time by better rifles. There were blackpowder Mausers, a Model 71/84 with a turnbolt action, a Model 87 and an 88, as well as a 91 and 93, a 95 still found as a used military arm, a 94 and so on until we reach the advent of the Model 98 Mauser, the apex of development.

The workings of the Model 98 are today considered pedestrian, because we are so used to this type of action. However, the 98 is in fact an extremely sound design that has not been vastly improved by its followers. Two big locking lugs turn to secure the bolt. A third lug appears forward of the bolt handle, which is considered a backup lug should the bolt set back for any reason. The action is cocked primarily on the opening of the bolt. Some cocking effort was applied when the locking lugs were rotated into the locked position. Some riflemen have blasted the 98 because the bolt does tend to wobble around at its most withdrawn position; however, that is not a problem. The design, if anything, promotes reliability, for the 98 tends to function when less than perfectly clean. Furthermore, any notion that this particular idiosyncrasy means weakness must be dispelled immediately. It's fairly well agreed that the actions which followed the 98, including the Model 70 and the Springfield, were not quite as strong as the 98.

After the Spanish-American War of 1898, American soldiers were forced to admit that the Mauser Model 98 rifle was better than the Krag. A new rifle was put on the drawing board immediately, and when the sketches turned from paper to metal, the Model 1903 Springfield emerged. There is no denying that the Springfield was bred and born of the Mauser. Both enjoyed many similar traits, including the staggered magazine box, claw-type extractor, two forward locking lugs as well as other features. Anyone who questions the family resemblance should be reminded that the U.S. Government paid Mauser a royalty for infringement.

The Mauser action lives on today only slightly modified in many sporting rifles built everywhere, and that the action in both military and commercial form is used by some of the world's greatest gunmakers in building fine, expensive firearms. On the threshold of the 21st century, in other words, a 19th-century idea clings because it is sound. We have mentioned a number of rifles of commercial manufacture; let's look at what can be done by the custom gunmaker.

GIL VAN HORN'S CUSTOM SPORTING MAUSERS

Gil Van Horn, custom gunmaker noted for building some of the most powerful and elegant rifles of all time, prefers Mauser actions. In one instance, he was challenged to produce a rifle capable of stopping the world's most dangerous game. This meant the Cape buffalo of Africa, as well as lions and elephants. The rifle had to be handy and fast-working despite its projected large size and of course with an action smoother than an oiled ball bearing.

Van Horn tamped a bowlful of data into his pipe of invention and puffed up the .500 Express cartridge for starters, a round that could be called the .510 Express, for it is .51 caliber not .50, with a bullet diameter of .510 inch. The thrust of the .500 Van Horn Express is this: the power of the fabled .505 Gibbs in a standard-length action. If it delivered power equal with its size, the .505 would drop an elephant the way a .22 varmint rifle handles a woodchuck.

The Van Horn creation came out more powerful than the Gibbs, with a 500-grain bullet at 2500 fps muzzle velocity and a 600-grain bullet departing the muzzle at close to 2300 fps. Muzzle energy was a whopping 6941 foot-pounds for the 500-grain bullet and 7050 for the 600-grain one. (The Gibbs is generally loaded with a 525-grain

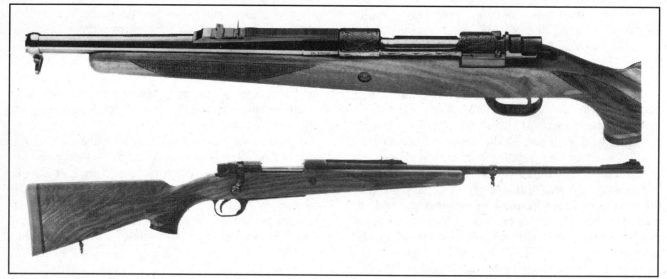

The Parker-Hale M81 African rifle, now made in America by the Gibbs Rifle Company, is a fine commercial example of a modern sporting rifle built around the original Mauser 98 action.

The configuration of the .500 Van Horn case conforms to the ideals of accuracy—short and squat, rather than tall and thin—with 100% loading density capability. Because cartridge design adheres to efficiency standards, the entire powder charge is applied to propel the projectile. A zone of diminishing returns is not suffered with IMR-3031 or IMR-4064 powders.

The appearance of the Van Horn rifle is nothing short of stunning. The French walnut (also known as California English walnut) stock is big, but not bulky, and commensurate with the power of the cartridge. The choice of this type of walnut is designed to reduce the effects of "felt" recoil. The rifle was fitted to the customer who ordered it in true custom-made rifle fashion with a rubber recoil pad fitted to the buttstock. The stock finish appears to be in the wood, not on it. The stock is embellished with a forend tip and pistol-grip cap

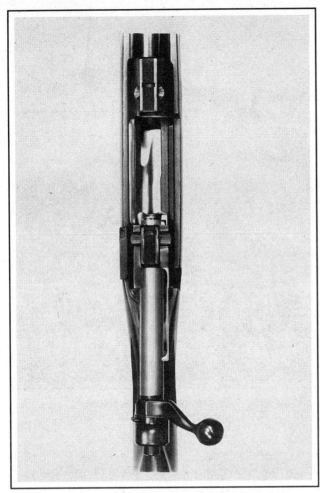

The successful Ruger Model 77 is a separate action from the Model 98, but it carries several 98 distinctions, including a claw-type extractor.

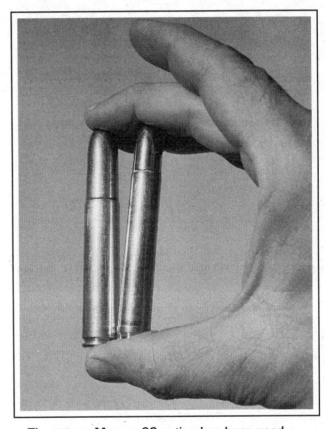

The strong Mauser 98 action has been used for chambering hundreds of different cartridges. One of the largest is the Van Horn .500 Express (left) compared here with a .458 Winchester cartridge. The VH .500 Express shoots a .510-inch, 600-grain bullet at over 2200 fps.

bullet at a muzzle velocity of around 2300 fps or a 525-grain bullet doing 2390 fps with 105 grains of HiVel #2. Van Horn wanted similar potency without the long action required for a .505 bolt-gun.) The Gibbs case length is 3.15 inches; the Van Horn, 2.75 inches. The head size of the Gibbs is .635 inch, while the 500 VH Express is .585 inch with a 40-degree shoulder and neck length of .375 inch. The shoulder may be slight, but it is entirely adequate for headspacing. The cartridge is prepared from B.E.L.L. .416 brass, or by turning the belts from .460 Weatherby Magnum cases, trimming to length, working through a full-length resize die, then fireforming the brass to produce final dimensions. Van Horn prefers a beltless case headspacing on the shoulder, rather than a belted case headspacing on the belt.

The Gil Van Horn .500 Express custom rifle is a highly potent arm built around a hand-selected Mauser action. Completely reworked, with exquisite features, the rifle weighs 11½ pounds and sells in the hefty 5-digit range.

made of dry ebony, which is very difficult to locate nowadays. A nice touch of metalwork was the engraved sterling silver inlay on the cap. The rear swivel stud is from the pre-64 Model 70 Super Grade rifle—very strong.

Van Horn uses three or four methods of ensuring stock/action integrity, including a second recoil lug installed near the first lug on some of his rifles. (The Weatherby .460 uses this system, a second recoil lug close to the main lug—at least this is so on a .460 Weatherby of my investigation.) Surprisingly, this rifle does not include the second recoil lug, for the gunmaker does not believe in the small additional lug that is usually placed down-barrel. Van Horn has found that by adhering to microscopic tolerances in the action mortise and barrel channel of the stock, along with ample reinforcers, the metalwork has never broken away from the wood, even on a .500 Express rifle. Because certain reinforcers are vital, key points are glassed in and reinforcing stock bolts are used. Furthermore, wood inserts are installed behind the magazine, and wooden reinforcers are epoxied in place with the grain of the stock. On some rifles,

he also uses a secondary stock bolt built into the web area. He may also employ a wooden reinforcer behind the tang, the latter job accomplished in a mill with a slot cutter.

The wrist of the rifle is on the thick side. Many old-time English-made big-bore double rifles ended up with split stocks because of thin wrists, which are graceful and pleasing to the eye, but not necessarily correct on high-recoil rifles.

The action? It is a Venezuelan "FN" made in the 1930s—a Mauser all the way and reputed to carry excellent steel. Van Horn chooses only the best actions to begin with, which is part of the reason for the fluidity of his finished products. Here his goal is a marble-smooth action for safari work. For perfection of fit, the lugs are lapped into their recesses. The cocking cam is also lapped, and sometimes the opening cam in the bolt handle root as well. No compound is used on the bolt proper (Mauser bolts are inherently loose-fitted). The metal finish—Gun Koat—is also conducive to smoothness of operation. The rifle handles well—even fast, considering its weight. The comparative shortness of bolt-throw also lends speed of operation in the field. The action is non-binding. No matter that the bolt handle is torqued, slick operation prevails.

Further metalwork appointments include a handcrafted trigger guard, floorplate and magazine box after the pre-64 Model 70 style, but with an Oberndorf-type guard bow floorplate release. The follower is made from du Pont Delron, which is light, tough and dent-resistant. Moreover, the follower does not slam forward against the front of the magazine box. Metal followers can batter the magazine box in a high-recoil rifle. This magazine box is extra thick and made of spring steel. It is hardened in the frontal area to resist damage from heavy bullets during recoil. The stainless steel barrel has a 1:20 rate of twist. The integral muzzle break is one of the highlights of the rifle. The front eye is located on the barrel. The trigger is a modified Timney, with an extended bow welded in place. The safety is a Grisel.

The sights of this custom Mauser 98 are unique, in part because they are bulky. Having witnessed sight failures on several safaris, Van Horn was determined to build his own sight style with massive construction. He calls his special sight, which he builds by hand, the "Disappearing Head." The front sight collapses into the ramp and is returned to full battery position by depressing a button on the side of the ramp. The sight base is made of stainless steel and the rear sight V-notch is built from hardened tool steel. Considerable time and effort go into the construction of these special sights, adding a full $1000 to the cost of the finished product.

In the bushveldt, accuracy in a hunting rifle is vital. In a well-bedded rifle, the stiff Mauser 98 action is known for its accuracy capability. To test the .500 Van Horn Express, it was shot from the bench and, as expected, it passed admirably. The test range was 50 yards in deference to the iron sights (the rifle wore no scope). Three-shot cloverleafs were the rule, and no sandbag was used between the buttpad and the shooter's shoulder.

So here is a powerhouse rifle built on a slick-working action whose design dates back almost a century. With a four-round magazine and a round chambered in the barrel, the hunter has a cargo of five powerful blows to use against any big game. Both rifle and round have been proven where it counts, in the field.

This account of a well-crafted Mauser sporter could be relived hundreds of times with different riflemakers' works. For the Mauser 98 remains high on the list of great actions in the building of great rifles. Not only has it withstood the test of time, it is guaranteed safe passage into the 21st century as one of the most widely used and copied action designs ever.

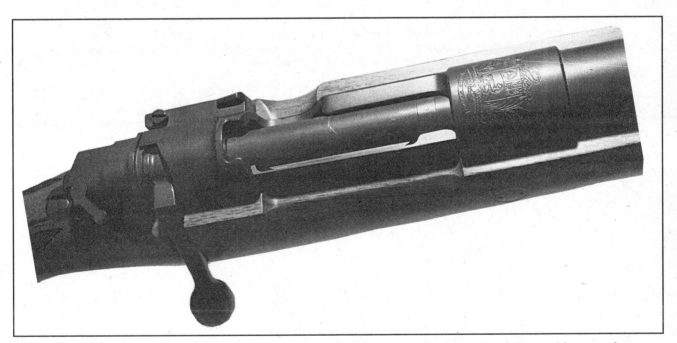

The Venezuelan "FN" Mauser action made in the 1930s serves as the basis of the marble-smooth action of Gil Van Horn's outstanding custom rifle.

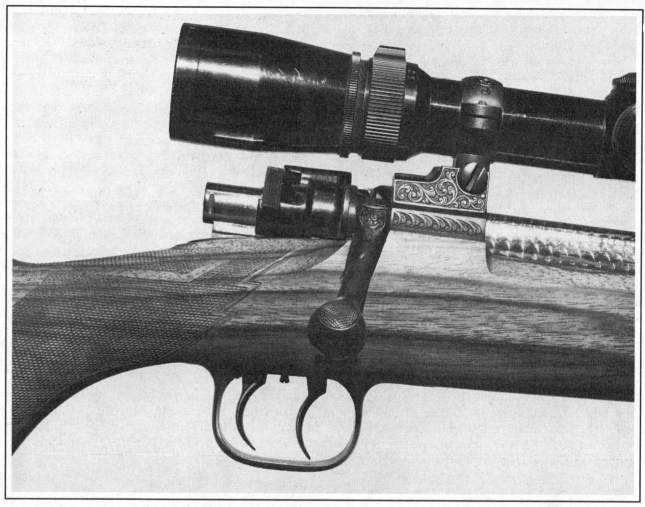

This close-up view of the Dean Zollinger 7mm Rem. Mag., another customized Mauser, illustrates the attention to detail that distinguishes a custom rifle from the ordinary. Note the double-set triggers, engraved receiver and bolt handle and the fine checkering.

SAM FADALA is a well-known author of firearms articles and books. This excerpt is taken from his latest book, *Legendary Sporting Rifles* (1992, Stoeger Publishing Co.). He is presently Technical Editor for *Handloader/Rifle* magazines, Feature Editor for *Muzzleloader Magazine,* and Special Projects Editor for *Guns Magazine.* A frequent contributor to SHOOTER'S BIBLE, he also writes for such national publications as *Gun World, Outdoor Life, Sports Afield* and *Bow and Arrow Hunter.*

POWDER FLASKS: INTRIGUING RELICS OF THE PAST

by R. Stephen Irwin, M.D.

Never has the discovery of any chemical had a greater impact on the course of world history and the lives of human beings everywhere than the discovery of gunpowder. No potion from any apothecary, no substance from any laboratory has changed the boundaries of nations or altered the lives of people more than this simple compound. And yet, for all its importance, the origins of gunpowder remain shrouded in mystery. No one knows for certain who invented it, nor even the general area of the world in which it was discovered. Claims and counterclaims have been made by China, India, Arabia and Europe.

One fact is certain: Friar Roger Bacon of England at least knew of the compound and wrote about it in 1248. Indeed, he may have been the original discoverer. Bacon hid his formula in an anagram because he thought the substance was too dangerous for general publication, but scholars have since broken his code.

The earliest gunpowder, known as meal or serpentine powder, was a simple mixture of charcoal, sulfur and saltpeter. The original formulation was a weak powder requiring huge quantities to fire a gun with any force. Around the mid-1300s, soon after the discovery of gunpowder, the first true hand-held firearms were developed. Guns became portable, so naturally ammunition had to be as well. Thus began the search for the safest, most efficient way to carry gunpowder. Since early guns

of the 14th and 15th centuries took large charges of the weak powder—sometimes one-third to one-half of the bore was filled with it—soft leather pouches were used to carry the powder. Because moisture ruins gunpowder, these were replaced by solid containers. Hollowed-out gourds and animal horns were fitted with stoppers to become the first true powder flasks. Tusks, teeth, large nuts, rare woods, shells, ostrich eggs, rhinoceros horns, and stag antlers were all converted into powder flasks,

Three examples of flasks with panel motifs include a Hawksley (left), a Dixon (center) and the rare George Washington flask.

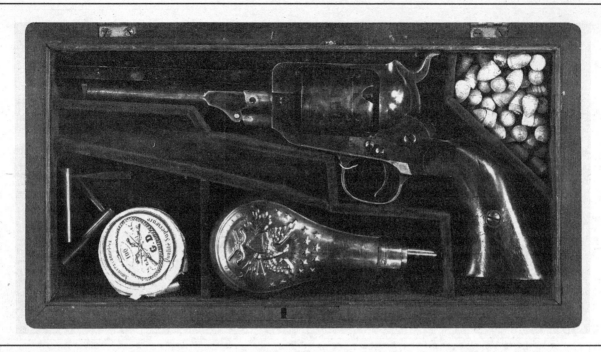

Many cased sets, like this Whitney Pocket Model Percussion Revolver (Second Type, c. 1850–1860) included a vintage powder flask. (Courtesy of Buffalo Bill Historical Society, Cody, WY)

most of which were closed by simple stoppers. Metal, mostly brass, became the flask material of choice for routine use, and by 1550 the basic flask shapes and stoppering mechanisms had evolved and proved effective enough to last for the next two centuries or more.

When paper cartridges appeared in Europe after 1550, loose gunpowder underwent a transition to semi-fixed ammunition. These early cartridges were simply individual charges of powder rolled into paper tubes, with the balls carried separately. Around 1600, a new method of attaching ball to paper charge was devised, thus becoming the first true form of fixed ammunition.

Despite these early advances, the conventional means of charging a firearm—by pouring loose powder down the end of a gun barrel—did not change for the next two and a half centuries, making the flask an essential and permanent accouterment for the firearm.

MAKING POWDER SAFE AND EFFECTIVE

Meal or serpentine powder presented a number of problems. For one thing, kegs of this powder gave off a highly explosive dust when they were moved about. For another, the three ingredients had different specific gravities; after the powder

had been stored for a length of time, these elements tended to separate according to their specific weights, rendering the powder useless. And because meal powder attracted moisture, it often failed to ignite at all.

These problems were largely solved when corned powder was developed in the early 1400s. This improved mixture, which was essentially the same as the black powder of today, presented less of a danger from explosive dust. Corned powder also resisted dampness better and generated more power by burning faster. For these reasons, the new corned powder became the preferred choice for a propellant. Following this development, it became common practice to carry two flasks—a large one containing corned powder for the propelling charge, and a small priming flask containing serpentine powder for the priming charge. Carrying two flasks was by no means universal, however. The majority of armsmen probably continued to carry one flask, using corned powder for both propellant and priming.

The priming flask may have been developed during the 15th century for use in association with the bandoleer. Consisting of a leather strap worn over the shoulder, the bandoleer contained a dozen or so cylinders, each holding enough powder for one charge. The priming flask was a necessary adjunct to the propellant charges and was itself attached to the bandoleer at the bottom of a loop located under the arm. The bandoleer was probably first used in Germany and then gained acceptance throughout northern and western Europe. Because of the incessant noise it made as the charge cylinders clattered against each other, it became the bane of hunters and militiamen alike.

THE MAKEUP OF A FLASK

The metal used in the production of flasks was most commonly brass, which is basically an alloy of copper and zinc. The proportions of the two metals present in this alloy govern the color of the flask, ranging from brown to pink to golden yellow. Rarely was pewter used to make flasks.

The first production flasks of the 19th century were severely plain. Later, flask-makers employed artists and designers to create more appealing patterns and eye-catching motifs. The pear-shaped flask became the standard configuration, but an infinite variety of size, color, material, face design

These versatile flasks contain separate compartments in which to carry caps, balls, patches or extra flints. The oak leaf design at left has two compartments on the bottom with covers that swing open; the plain flask on the right has a single receptacle on top.

and shape have evolved. Many flasks were lavishly decorated; only among production military flasks was there a degree of uniformity and style.

In his authoritative work, *The Powder Flask Book*, published in 1953, Ray Riling states that not one single forming die for manufacturing flasks has ever been unearthed for study. Nor has an illustration of forming machinery or any records pertaining to the process of flask fabrication ever been located. Hence, many of the details of manufacture of the production flask during the 19th century remain buried with the secrets of the past.

Basically, the body of the powder flask is formed by the union of two halves. Each half is formed and imprinted by stamping sheet metal between two formed and polished steel dies. After being removed from the die, the fin, or flash (i.e., that portion of metal extending beyond the die impression) is trimmed away. The two halves of the flask are then joined by sweating, followed by a finish of prepared stains or lacquers applied by brush or by dipping.

As noted, the earliest flasks had simple friction-fit stoppers, a style that never completely disappeared from some of the lower quality examples. Today, most have spring closures in the spout or nozzle, a handy device that facilitates quick use. Being an integral part of the flask,

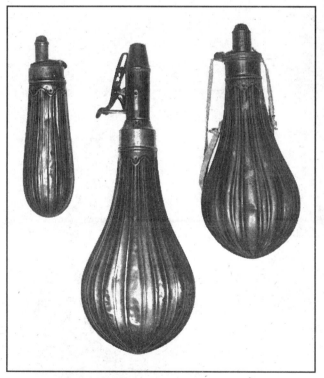

Fluting was a common decoration, which afforded a sturdy surface to resist denting. The two examples on the right were designed by the Capewell family. The third was used for loading powder into shotshells and helped continue the use of flasks into the breechloading era.

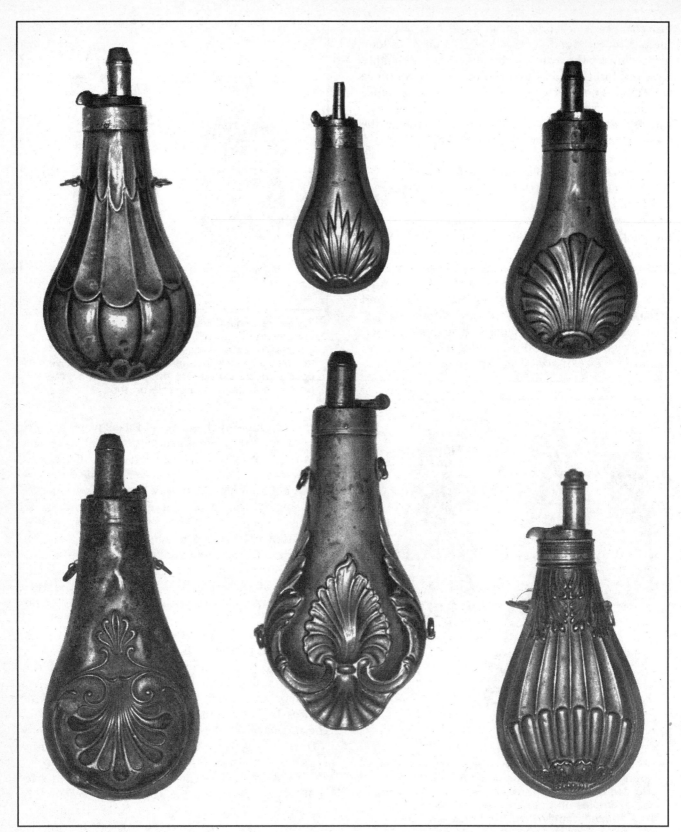

The shell and bush decorations shown above were common embellishments on 19th century powder flasks.

moreover, the nozzle end cannot be readily detached and lost.

Another refinement that became standard issue was the spring top that, with each use, dispensed a proper measure of powder charge into the barrel. These spring top charges brought with them some inherent dangers, however. Should the spring weaken with use, or if the seal between the intended charge and the reservoir of powder inside the flask was not sufficiently tight, a terrible explosion could result. An overheated gun could, for example, ignite the powder, as could a particle of ignited wad that remained in the gun barrel.

In 1814, Thomas Sykes of Sheffield, England, was awarded British patent #3828 for what he termed a "fire-proof powder flask." Sykes' spring top charger was indeed a giant leap forward in safety, and from then on most flask chargers conformed to the basic style of Sykes' device. These new flask chargers were made with spring stop plates, or cutters; as a result, once the charger chamber had been filled with powder, it could not mix with the main powder reservoir in the body of the flask. An added refinement was to conceal the spring inside the collar of the flask, lending it a cleaner profile.

NOTABLE FLASK MAKERS

Plunger-type powder flasks dispense their charges whenever pressure is exerted (on the open end of the nozzle) against the gun muzzle. These self-measuring chargers saw their greatest use in America with various forms of pepperbox pistols. Charger design was carried to its zenith by Samuel Colt, whose ingenious powder-and-ball flask was used to charge his famous Paterson revolver. Five nozzles were located on the flask so as to fit all chambers of the firearm cylinder simultaneously. By turning a knurled hand, properly measured charges dropped into each chamber. The opposite end of the flask, which held the balls, was designed to drop a single ball into each chamber through a double gate.

Flask-making has always been predominantly a British industry. In his book, Ray Riling lists 127 British makers to a scant 19 in America. Most production in England took place in and around the cities of Birmingham, London and Sheffield. The major flask manufacturers, including Thomas Sykes, James Dixon and Sons, and J.W. Hawksley, supplied not only British sportsmen, but hunters, shooters, arms manufacturers and militia from many foreign markets as well.

The American flask manufacturing scene, on the other hand, was made up largely of a series of desultory, short-lived production efforts by individuals and small companies which, for the most part, failed to meet foreign price competition.

These flasks were all produced by Geo. and J. W. Hawksley of Sheffield, England. This firm, founded in 1840, made flasks until at least 1889. Hawksley flasks are of high quality and typically sport concealed top springs. Their narrow throat contour, another Hawksley characteristic, is designed to fit the hand comfortably.

Flasks with motifs depicting game birds, scenes from the hunt, and hanging game were obviously created to appeal to the sportsman. Today, they've become specimens for the collector. The flask at the lower right is a rare example of a flask made with pewter.

family in Hereford, England. Upon emigrating to America in 1840, the original Capewells brought with them "machinery to manufacture sporting goods, including shot tops, powder flasks, etc." Their innovative charger for loading powder into fixed shotshells helped carry the use of the powder flask over into the era of breech-loading weapons.

Finally, the American Flask and Cap Company of Waterbury, Connecticut, organized in 1857, produced flasks until the late 1860s, when it merged with the American Brass Company. The remainder of the American flask manufacturing industry occurred mainly in the small shops of gunsmiths and craftsmen who, in addition to flasks, produced shot bags, game bags, duck calls, and other miscellany as adjuncts to their primary lines of guns.

Traditionally, flasks have been used to charge pistols, rifles and shotguns of every conceivable make and caliber. Certainly the size of the flask and the capacity of the charger gave some indication of the type gun for which it was intended. One major frustration of arms historians and collectors alike is that an absolute connection between a given flask and a particular firearm is difficult at best, and usually impossible. The very nature of flask manufacture and distribution precluded such precise relationships. Colt and other manufacturers usually made it optional as to which flask

While primarily an armsmaker, John H. Hall is credited with producing the first American-made flask. It was produced (with Hall's rifles) under a contract dated March 19, 1819, specifying that the U.S. had the right to manufacture 1000 rifles and flasks at a public armory. Harpers Ferry Armory was selected as the place of manufacture and Hall was hired under the contract as assistant armorer at a salary of $60 per month, plus a royalty of $1 for each rifle and flask produced.

Other American flask-makers included John T. and Joseph H. Batty of Springfield, Massachusetts, who made the famous (to collectors) "Peace" and "Fouled Anchor" martial flasks from 1847 to 1858. John Matthewman of New Haven, Connecticut, a distinguished American flask-maker of the mid-19th century, supplied the plunger-type flasks for Walker Arms. And the Capewells of Woodbury, Connecticut, were flask-making descendants of a

These flasks displaying the national emblem were made by American manufacturers, including the American Flask and Cap Company and J. Matthewman of New Haven, Connecticut.

was to be supplied with a given firearm. Adaptation and innovation were hallmarks of the day, and not infrequently has a flask been discovered with its nozzle or charge capacity altered to fit a gun differently from what was originally intended.

Early in the 19th century, as the U.S. Government began mass-producing paper cartridges for use with its smoothbore arms, the powder flask continued to serve its rifled arms. It became increasingly apparent, however, that a practical paper cartridge was inevitable. Its advantages were many, among them quickness in loading, safety, bullets of uniform size, standardization of powder charges, and ease in transportation and carrying. By mid-century, after the self-contained cartridge had been perfected, the powder flask continued to enjoy acceptance among the sporting fraternity. But clearly, its death knell had sounded.

Martial flasks made by and for the U.S. Government were severely plain (left photo) or well appointed (right photo). The public property flask (center) was made in France and sold to the military through a contract with James Baker of Philadelphia in 1827.

Today, powder flasks offer collectors and gun enthusiasts an intriguing insight into several important centuries of firearm development. The myriad of style, shapes, materials, sizes and decors of flasks, along with the clever innovations and adaptations designed to serve shooters better, provide a fascinating study, as witnessed by several illustrated examples reproduced on these pages.

STEPHEN IRWIN This is the fourth in a series of articles by Dr. Stephen Irwin on the sporting arts to appear in SHOOTER'S BIBLE. An avid big game hunter and sport fisherman, Dr. Irwin has been writing for many years on the history of hunting and fishing, including such specialized areas as antique fishing lures, duck decoys and firearms. His articles have appeared in most of the major outdoor publications. He has also authored *The Providers: Hunting and Fishing Methods of the Indians and Eskimos.*

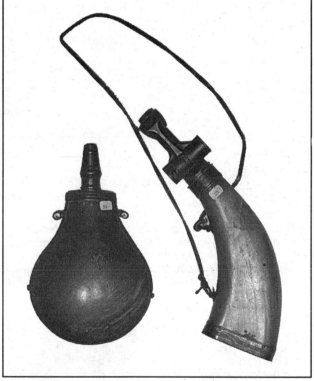

These production horn flasks, known as "lanthorns," featured horns that were thinned to transparency, shaped, and fitted with metal edging and nozzles.

MANUFACTURERS' SHOWCASE

With this edition, SHOOTER'S BIBLE proudly unveils a new feature—the "Manufacturers' Showcase." In it, a wide variety of new and popular products will be brought to our readers' attention each year that we hope will be of special interest to shooters of all kinds.

SWIFT INSTRUMENTS, INC.

SCOPE MODEL 656
3-9X, 40mm

Universally useful, the SWIFT Model 656 has proven to be a most popular scope. It has a maximum field of 40 feet at 100 yards at 3X, and a field of 14 feet at the highest power—9X. Maximum R.L.E. 266 to 30 is provided by a 40mm objective lens. The optical system has 11 lens elements and Quadraplex reticle. Model 656 is waterproof, sports a wide angle field of view and is multi-coated.

SWIFT INSTRUMENTS, INC.
952 Dorchester Ave., Boston, MA 02025 or
P.O. Box 562, San Jose, CA 95106

SNAIL WET TRAP SYSTEMS

The Passive Bullet Trap—SNAIL®—is a free-standing, self-contained unit that passively captures a projectile and then progressively breaks down its stored energy in a deceleration chamber. By providing controlled deflection, the bullet is not impacted to a sudden stop and remains extensively intact. The projectile enters into a gyroscopic pattern, using centrifugal force to create friction and deceleration. This patented design, along with use of a lubricating liquid, eliminates lead dust that is normally a by-product of dry "smash" plate-type traps. Particles of bullets or jackets returning into the room are no longer a concern for the shooter, nor are they an environmental issue.

PASSIVE BULLET TRAPS INC.
Springdale Road, Westfield, MA 01085
(413) 568-7001

BIOMETRIC SCANNING SAFE

Introducing the Guardian Security Closure, the world's only instant access safe. Handguns are locked away in a case of heavy steel construction that can be opened in less than one second, even in the dark. Activated by touch, not sight, this newly developed access system scans for your individual finger pattern. Instantly it decides if you are the proper user and, if so, pulls the cam. It also keeps track of—and stops—unauthorized users. The Guardian can be programmed for one- or two-handed use as well as multiple users. Write or call:

BEDFORD TECHNOLOGIES, INC.
P.O. Box 328, Miami, OK 74355 1-800-467-FREE (7233)

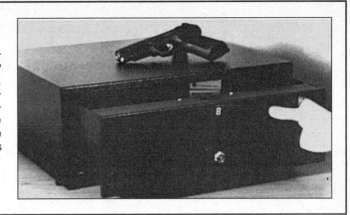

MARBLE ARMS

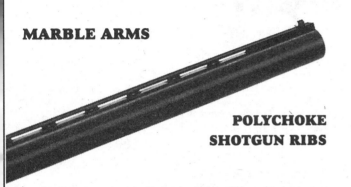

POLYCHOKE
SHOTGUN RIBS

MARBLE ARMS offers a truly fine raised ventilated rib for your shotgun. Created for all over-and-under and single barrel shotguns—pump, auto or single shot—it is made of anodized aluminum in gauges 12, 16, 20, 28 and .410. The rib is lightweight—less than two ounces—and can be custom mounted without drilling and tapping the barrel. Custom installation includes front and mid-rib sights. And if you already have a factory-ribbed barrel, an International Top Rib can be installed directly on the existing rib to raise the sight plane.

MARBLE ARMS CORPORATION
P.O. Box 111, 420 Industrial Park
Gladstone, MI 49837 (906) 428-3711

MANUFACTURERS' SHOWCASE

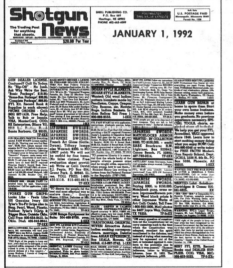

THE SHOTGUN NEWS

Established in 1946, THE SHOTGUN NEWS offers some of the finest gun buys in the United States. Published three times each month, with over 150,000 readers, this national publication has helped thousands of gun enthusiasts locate, buy, trade and sell antique, modern, military and sporting firearms and accessories. As the cover says, SHOTGUN NEWS is "The Trading Post for Anything That Shoots." Call TOLL FREE 1-800-345-6923 and receive a one-year subscription (36 issues) for just $20.00 (use your Master or Visa card). For more information, call 1-402-463-4589 or write:

THE SHOTGUN NEWS
P. O. Box 669, Hastings, NE 68902

MARK II AUTOMATIC CASTER

BALLISTI-CAST's fully automatic 265-pound casting machine boasts five essential elements: **1. Drive**, featuring an easy access, gear-driven, rack and pinion drive system. **2. Electrical**, with timed lead control, electronic counter, indicator working lights, solid thermostat, dust-sealed control panel and two heavy-duty air blowers. **3. Furnace**, containing a 2600-watt heating element and thermostatic control. **4. Moulds**, all made by Hensley & Gibbs. Each mould and sprue cutter is highly polished, hardened and treated with a special substance that eliminates sticking. **5. Carrier System**, featuring positive indexing, easy access, quiet operation, and quick mould replacement and adjustment.

BALLISTI-CAST, INC.
Box 383, Parshall, ND 58770 (701) 862-3324

GLASER SAFETY SLUG AMMO

GLASER SAFETY SLUG's state-of-the-art, professional-grade personal defense ammunition is now offered in two bullet styles: BLUE uses a #12 compressed shot core for maximum richochet protection, and SILVER uses a #6 compressed shot core for maximum penetration. The manufacturing process results in outstanding accuracy, with documented groups of less than an inch at 100 yards! That's why Glaser has been the top choice of professional and private law enforcement agencies worldwide for over 15 years. Currently available in every caliber from 25 ACP through 30-06, including 40 S&W, 10mm, 223 and 7.62×39. For a free brochure contact:

GLASER SAFETY SLUG, INC.,
P.O. Box 8223, Foster City, CA 94404

☒ WIDEVIEW™
NEW BLACK POWDER MOUNT

The new WIDEVIEW Black Powder Mount pictured above fits the Thompson/Center Renegade and Hawken rifles with no drilling or tapping. The barrel still comes off for easy cleaning, and the original iron sight is used. With Wideview's Ultra Precision See-Thru mounts included, you may use a scope or iron sights. No hammer modification is needed.

WIDEVIEW SCOPE MOUNT CORP.
26110 Michigan Ave., Inkster, MI 38141 (313) 274-1238

MANUFACTURERS' SHOWCASE

DIXIE GUN WORKS CATALOG

The greatest blackpowder catalog of them all! Over 600 pages of guns, equipment and supplies for the hunter, shooter and historical enthusiast. The DIXIE GUN WORKS catalog also features a section dealing with facts and figures designed to improve anyone's knowledge of this fascinating field. We also stock parts for antique and replica guns, re-enactor items—patterns, uniforms, boots—and other equipment.

DIXIE GUN WORKS, INC.
Gunpowder Lane, Union City, TN 38261 (901) 885-0700

BELL & CARLSON
CARBELITE GUN STOCKS

Tough, accurate and beautiful—these performance advantages of the B&C CARBELITE gun stocks for bolt-action rifles, two-piece rifles and shotguns are well known to demanding hunters everywhere. These fiberglass, graphite Kevlar stocks, which are designed to reduce recoil, have proven accurate in every type of climate. All stocks are available in two beautiful and realistic woodgrain finishes or in durable baked-on finishes in gray, black or camo. All have a lifetime warranty. B&C also maintains a fully staffed service department for custom fitting CARBELITE stocks to customers' actions. For a free color brochure and list of available models, contact:

BELL & CARLSON, INC.
Dept. SB, 509 N. 5th, Atwood, KS 67730

HODGDON CLAYS POWDER

This new powder developed for 12 gauge clay target shooters is perfect for 1⅛ and 1 oz. loads. Trap, skeet and sporting clays shooters will love it. Clays also performs well in many handgun applications. These include .38 Special, .40 S&W and .45 ACP. This exclusive HODGDON introduction will surprise even veteran shooters with its performance characteristics. Velocity for .45 ACP is 974 fps with 185 grain bullet and 4.9 gr. charge. In 12 gauge (1⅛ oz. shot), velocity is 1200 fps with WWAA12 Wad (18.9 gr. charge) or Fig. 8 Wad (19.2 gr. charge).

HODGDON POWDER COMPANY
6231 Robinson, P. O. Box 2932
Shawnee Mission, KS 66201 (913) 362-9455

Rooster LABORATORIES

ROOSTER LABORATORIES offers a wide lineup of "Pacesetter" Products for reloaders: • **Zambini** Pistol Bullet Lubricant • **HVR** Rifle Bullet Lubricant • **Rooster Jacket** Liquid Bullet Lube • **CFL-56** Case Forming Lubricant • **CSL-71** Case Sizing Lubricant • **CL-WR-14** Water-Removable Case Lube • **Rooster Bright** Brass Case Polish • **Black Powder** Bullet Lubricants • **Heater** for Manual Lubrisizers

ROOSTER LABORATORIES
P.O. Box 412514, Kansas City, Missouri 64141 (816) 474-1622

MANUFACTURERS' SHOWCASE

CATALOG

ED BROWN PRODUCTS, the premium quality handgun accessory parts manufacturer, offers their 1992 catalog packed full of goodies for custom, competition, and serious carry use. Designed primarily for the 1911 Government pistol, this catalog also features Smith & Wesson auto and revolver parts. Send $2.00 (refundable on your first order) to:

ED BROWN PRODUCTS
Route 2, Box 2922, Dept. SB, Perry, MO 63462

M/ASH SHOULDER HOLSTER

The all-new "M/ASH" Modular/Ambidextrous Shoulder Holster™ from SHOOTING SYSTEMS offers the highest level of performance ever made available in a fabric horizontal shoulder holster. The M/ASH System™ is loaded with patent pending features like Power Band™ adjustable drawing tension, Nichols Sight Strip™ internal sight protector, and the Deltab™ fully articulated shoulder harness. And M/ASH holsters are made from quilted layers of the toughest ballistic nylon. See your local SHOOTING SYSTEMS dealer for more information, or send $3.00 for a color catalog describing the complete line of ballistic nylon holsters, rifle cases, luggage and gear bags.

SHOOTING SYSTEMS, INC.
Dept. M-H, 1075 Headquarters Park, Fenton, MO 63026-2478

Aimpoint® 2X RED DOT SIGHT

AIMPOINT introduces its new 30mm AIMPOINT 500 2 Power, a fixed, low-power electronic sight with a floating red dot. It's the only unit of its kind with built-in magnification. The shooter now has the speed and accuracy of a red dot sight combined with the advantages of a low-power scope. Because the magnification is in the objective lens instead of the ocular lens (as with previous screw-in attachments), the dot covers only 1.5" at 200 yards. The 5000 2 Power can be used on all types of firearms and comes complete with 30mm rings and all accessories. Suggested retail price is $399.95. For more information write:

AIMPOINT
580 Herndon Parkway, Suite 500, Herndon, VA 22070
(703) 471-6828

ADULT PELLET GUN CATALOG

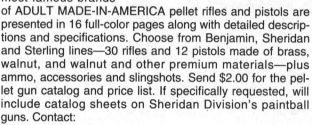

Benjamin, Sheridan and Sterling Airguns & Accessories

The latest models of the nation's three most famous brands of ADULT MADE-IN-AMERICA pellet rifles and pistols are presented in 16 full-color pages along with detailed descriptions and specifications. Choose from Benjamin, Sheridan and Sterling lines—30 rifles and 12 pistols made of brass, walnut, and walnut and other premium materials—plus ammo, accessories and slingshots. Send $2.00 for the pellet gun catalog and price list. If specifically requested, will include catalog sheets on Sheridan Division's paintball guns. Contact:

BENJAMIN AIR RIFLE CO.
2684 Chicory Road, Racine WI 53403

MANUFACTURERS' SHOWCASE

GLASER/CHEROKEE FEATHERWEIGHT BIPOD

At less than six ounces—half the usual weight—the GLASER/CHEROKEE bipod offers the discriminating shooter the ultimate in strength and sleek beauty. A frontal area 4½ times smaller than other bipods greatly reduces snag hazards. Uneven terrain is automatically compensated for up to 33 degrees. Deployment and retraction require only single and silent one-hand movements that take less than a second. The bipod fits all sporter, varmint and most paramilitary firearms. The basic mount permits front or rear mounting to the forearm, rather than the barrel, for target accuracy. Hidden or quick-detachable, customized mounting accessories are available. For a free brochure contact:

GLASER SAFETY SLUG, INC.
P. O. Box 8223, Foster City, CA 94404

SWIFT INSTRUMENTS, INC. SCOPE MODEL 666 SHOTGUN 1X, 20mm

At last, a high-quality shotgun scope with SWIFT's special features of multi-coating, waterproof integrity, and the popular Quadraplex reticle. The Model 666 is lightweight (9.6 oz.), has an eye relief of 3.2, a field of 113 feet at 100 yards, is 7.5 inches long, and is equally good for use on shotguns and bows. Black anodized one-inch tube and shockproof. Gift boxed.

Swift Instruments, Inc.
952 Dorchester Ave., Boston, MA 02025 or
P.O. Box 562, San Jose, CA 95106

Mitchell ARMS

1992 MITCHELL ARMS CATALOG

Receive a maroon and silver shoulder patch with the new '92 Mitchell Arms catalog. It features fine guns—from Bat Masterson's revolver to the latest combat rifles—along with the new P-08 Parabellum pistol. The best from the old days to the modern guns of today are included in this fully illustrated catalog, available (with shoulder patch) at $5.00. Call or write:

MITCHELL ARMS INC.
3400 W. MacArthur Blvd., Suite 1, Santa Ana, CA 92704
(714) 957-5711

GunVault

HANDGUN SAFE

The GunVault is a rapid-access handgun safe. It is designed to keep your gun out of the reach of others, yet remain right at your fingertips. The hand-shaped control panel is touch-operated with Braille-like dots. A computer stores your personal access code. Enter your code, the door pops open and you withdraw your gun. Tamper-proof programming frustrates youngsters. The GunVault mounts anywhere, even upside down, and comes with its own mounting hardware and backup keylock. The case is high-impact plastic with a steel liner. Fits most handguns. Battery life is 1 year.

GUNVAULT, INC.
200 Larkin Drive, Wheeling, IL 60090 (800) 622-4903

MANUFACTURERS' SHOWCASE

 **MODULAR-CONCEPT SIGNATURE GRIP**

The latest addition to PACHMAYR's storied line of Signature grips for semiauto pistols is the Model SW-5904/6—an all-new modular design that allows different backstraps and/or a finger groove front to be fitted. It puts the gripping power of genuine Neoprene plus the patented wrap-around clam shell pattern to work for 3rd Generation S&W owners. The combination of CAD/CAM design and material improvements results in better recoil absorption and a gun that naturally "points right." Fits S&W 3rd Generation models 5906, 5904 and 4006. Call toll free: 1-800-423-9704 or write:

PACHMAYR, LTD.
1875 S. Mountain Ave., Monrovia, CA 91016 (818) 357-7771

NATIONAL HOME GUARD SHOTGUN

H&R made the gun and CHOATE MACHINE & TOOL makes the stocks. This shotgun, which retails for $149.95, features quick thumb screw breakdown and is available in 12 and 20 gauge. The storage in the forearm and buttstock will accommodate a dozen 3″ shells. The gun has a 22″ barrel and comes with detachable sling swivel studs, plus a lifetime warranty on the stocks. For a limited time only, a FREE pistol grip worth $19.00 that interchanges with the buttstock is included. In addition to the stocks, CHOATE MACHINE & TOOL makes a conventional forearm and buttstock with recoil pad and a pistol grip forearm. For more details and free information contact:

CHOATE MACHINE & TOOL, INC.
P.O. Box 218, Bald Knob, AR 72010-0218 (501) 724-6193

WOLFE PUBLISHING

WOLFE PUBLISHING is America's foremost firearms publisher of quality magazines and books for sportsmen. *Hunting Horizons* is the only journal dedicated to the finest pursuits of the hunt. *Handloader* is the only journal emphasizing the fine art of ammunition reloading. And *Rifle* is the technical magazine for sporting firearms. Over 150 books and wildlife art prints are described in detail in their free catalog. Why not write or call today for your copy and get acquainted with the publications that are respected by those who know firearms.

WOLFE PUBLISHING
6471 Airpark Drive, Prescott, AZ 86301 (800) 899-7810

LYMAN CARTRIDGE GAUGES

Rifle cartridge gauges measure both head-space and overall case length. For safety and better accuracy, LYMAN recommends that all cartridge cases be inspected after resizing to ensure that the proper headspace and case length is maintained. Rifle gauges are available initially in .223, .243, .308 and .30-06, or set of 4. LYMAN's new pistol gauges check most critical cartridge dimensions to ensure proper functioning in semiautomatic pistols. Pistol gauges are available in 9mm, 10mm, 40 S&W and 45 ACP, or set of 4. Special Trial Offer: Mention you saw them in SHOOTER'S BIBLE and get any rifle or pistol gauge at $12.95. To order call: 1-800-22-LYMAN

LYMAN PRODUCTS CORPORATION
Route 147, Dept. 168, Middlefield, CT 06455

MANUFACTURERS' SHOWCASE

SWIFT INSTRUMENTS

MODEL 664
4-12X, 40mm

Spot that mountain goat with 4X, then bring him 12 times closer for the kill. Because of its parallax adjustment from 5mm to infinity, this SWIFT scope is highly adaptable. It is also excellent for use in gas-powered air rifles. Externally adjustable caps amplify corrections in elevation and drift. Self-centering Quadraplex reticle and multi-coated optics bring you on the target with clarity. Hard anodized 1″ tube. Fogproof. Gift boxed.

SWIFT INSTRUMENTS, INC. 952 Dorchester Ave., Boston, MA 02025 or P.O. Box 562, San Jose, CA 95106

BEEMAN CROW MAGNUM

AIR RIFLE

The BEEMAN Crow Magnum air rifle boasts incredible power, coupled with superb accuracy and truly outstanding craftsmanship. The power plant of this unusual gun represents the full flowering of a really great idea—the gas spring—which was used orginally in the now-famous BEEMAN RX. The Crow Magnum resulted from a leap forward in design and sophistication, namely the H-E ("High Efficiency") system, which allows more power with less cocking effort. The pellet seems to leave the muzzle instantly. For more information and a FREE catalog write:

BEEMAN PRECISION ARMS 3440-C16 Airway Drive, Santa Rosa, CA 95403-2024 (707) 578-7900

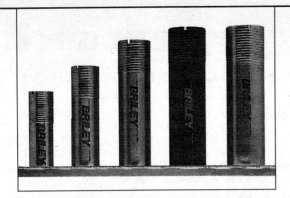

BRILEY SCREW-IN CHOKES

The famous BRILEY screw-in chokes are known throughout the country by competition target shooters and hunters for their consistent, reliable patterns and quality of manufacture. The BRILEY system gives the shooter the choke control needed to utilize the full spectrum of ammunition, from steel shot to lead, in all sizes. The sporting clays boom has made it almost mandatory that competitors have a quality screw-in choke system for total versatility at all stations and target situations. Shooters in this exciting game have embraced the BRILEY system. As for steel shot compatibility, BRILEY offers the finest screw-in chokes for steel shot available anywhere.

BRILEY MANUFACTURING COMPANY
1085-B Gessner, Houston, Texas 77055

E.M.F. SINGLE ACTION REVOLVER CATALOG

Specializing in a complete line of genuine Western "Cowboy Guns," E.M.F.'s new gun catalog offers a huge selection of Colt, Remington and Winchester-type firearms, plus an outstanding array of all single action revolvers from E.M.F.'s Custom Shop. E.M.F. is a major supplier of parts for Colt 1st, 2nd and 3rd Generation single action revolvers. Also many hard-to-find and specialty gun accessories and parts, as well as all the original Colt and Remington percussion revolver reproductions. For those interested in the finest quality and authenticity, this catalog is a must.

E.M.F. COMPANY, Inc.
1900 East Warner Ave., Suite 1-D, Santa Ana, CA 92705
(714) 261-6611

MANUFACTURERS' SHOWCASE

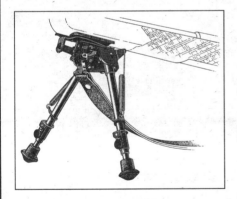

 **BIPODS**

HARRIS bipods clamp securely to most stud-equipped bolt action rifles and are quick-detachable. With adapters, they can fit other guns as well. HARRIS bipods are the result of time-proven design and quality, and are made with heat-treated steel and hard alloys. Folding legs on the bipods have completely adjustable spring-return extensions (except Model LM). The sling swivel attaches to the clamp. Series S Bipods rotate 45 degrees for instant leveling on uneven ground. The hinged base has tension adjustment and buffer springs to eliminate tremor or looseness in the crotch area of the bipod. Otherwise, all Series S models are similar to the non-rotating Series 1A2.

HARRIS ENGINEERING, INC.
Barlow, Kentucky 42024 (502) 334-3633

A few years ago, in response to Colonel Jeff Cooper's concept of the general all-purpose rifle — which he calls the Scout Rifle — CLIFTON ARMS developed the integral, retractable bipod and its accompanying state-of-the-art composite stock. Further development resulted in an integral butt magazine well for storage of cartridges inside the buttstock. These and other components make up the CLIFTON Scout Rifle. Built to the customer's choice of action, the rifle incorporates all the features specified by Colonel Cooper. A comprehensive catalog is available for $4.00 from:

CLIFTON ARMS, Inc.
P.O. Box 531258, Grand Prairie, TX 75053

CLIFTON ARMS SCOUT RIFLE

MODERN MUZZLELOADING MK-85 HUNTER

The original blackpowder rifle that changed the sport of muzzleloading hunting forever, this 50-caliber MK-85 Hunter is truly the safest, most accurate and highly versatile rifle ever forged. It features an American-made, patented double safety system, Magnum sure-fire ignition system, tapered 24" blued, non-glare barrel with open breech system, 1:28" twist, Timney featherweight deluxe trigger, and walnut stock with Pachmayr vented recoil pad. Plus the MK-85's hammer, nipple and breech plug are all stainless steel. A Williams fully adjustable rear sight and front gold bead sight with removable hood are standard, as are sling swivel studs (installed), with receiver drilled and tapped for easy scope mounting. Also in 54 caliber. Each rifle comes with a limited lifetime warranty.

MODERN MUZZLELOADING, INC. P.O. Box 130, Centerville, Iowa 52554

K.B.I./FEG
SINGLE ACTION PISTOL MODEL PJK-9HP

All FEG pistols are manufactured in Hungary by skilled craftsmen using the finest material available. The 9mm single action pistol PJK-9HP is patterned after the military pistol of most NATO nations. In addition to its high luster, blued steel frame and slide, hand-checkered walnut grips and manual slide release, the PJK-9HP has a rounded combat-serrated external hammer, ramp front sight and rear dovetail sight adjustable for windage. This model comes with two 13-round magazines and a cleaning rod. Barrel length is 4 ³/₄" and weight is 32 oz.

K.B.I.
P.O. Box 6346, Harrisburg, PA 17112

MANUFACTURERS' SHOWCASE

TRIUS TRAPS

Since 1955, TRIUS traps have set the standard for the industry. From "behind-the-barn" casual shooters to upstart Sporting Clay ranges, the easy cocking, lay-on loading and wide cocking surface of the TRIUS traps make them simple and fun to operate. Singles and doubles, as well as piggy-back doubles (birds stacked on top of each other), offer variety not found in other portable traps. TRIUS has four models: **Birdshooter**—quality at a budget price; **Model 92**—a bestseller with high-angle clip and can thrower; **Trapmaster**—sit-down comfort plus pivoting action; and **RabbitMaster**—designed to throw "rabbit disc" clay targets along the ground. Contact Hart Luebkeman at (513) 941-5682 or write:

TRIUS PRODUCTS, INC.
P.O. Box 25, Cleves, Ohio 45002

DAKOTA ARMS INC
76 AFRICAN SERIES

The DAKOTA 76 African Series rifles are specifically designed to satisfy the requirements of professional guides and clients who hunt dangerous game. Each rifle is individually crafted to the customer's specifications, and each is thoroughly tested to provide absolute reliability. Special features include a four-round magazine plus one in the chamber for a five-round capacity; select wood fitted with recoil pad, forearm tip, crossbolts, cheekpiece and longer grip; and front and rear island blade sights.

DAKOTA ARMS, INC.
HC 55, Box 326, Sturgis, SD 57785 (605) 347-4686

Foolproof Safety and Double Action Readiness...

HIGH CONTRAST SIGHTS for rapid target acquisition even in low light conditions. Unique dovetail sights are easily interchangeable. Betalight night sights available on some models.

STEEL-TO-STEEL LOCKUP and hard coat, anodized frame for outstanding durability.

PATENTED AUTOMATIC FIRING PIN SAFETY BLOCK permits carrying of loaded, decocked pistol. Pistol will not fire until trigger is pulled.

DECOCKING LEVER puts hammer in perfect register with safety intercept notch in one smooth motion. Tactical advantage over two-step slide mounted decocking levers.

THUMB-LEVEL MAGAZINE RELEASE for rapid magazine changes can be easily switched to accommodate both left- and right-handed shooters.

ERGONOMICALLY-DESIGNED GRIP DIMENSIONS and grip angle for easy, thumb-level manipulation of all controls including decocking lever. Ideal weight distribution for maximum shooting comfort.

SIG SAUER: The Tactical Edge

All SIG SAUER Small Arms are distinguished by their dependable performance in the field, and double action readiness for enhanced first shot potential.

For over 125 years, the SIG name has been synonymous with highly accurate, safe handling firearms. We build the finest guns in the world because we build safety, reliability and accuracy into every firearm we manufacture.

Contact SIGARMS today for the name of your local SIG SAUER Dealer. He's anxious to show you how SIG SAUER Handguns give you the tactical edge.

SIG SAUER HANDGUNS...THE TACTICAL EDGE!

SIGARMS

SIGARMS INC.
Industrial Drive
Exeter, NH 03833

SIG SAUER P 220: 7 + 1 ROUND, .45 ACP
SIG SAUER P 225: 8 + 1 ROUND 9mm PARA
SIG SAUER P 226: 15 + 1 ROUND (20 + 1 OPTIONAL) 9mm PARA
SIG SAUER P 230: 7 + 1 ROUND .380 ACP STAINLESS or BLUED

SIG encourages safe shooting. Consult your local District Attorney's office or police authorities for rules and regulations governing firearms ownership in your area. When handling firearms, follow safety guidelines in owner's manual. If a manual is not accompanied with your weapon, please contact SIGARMS for a replacement manual.

LLAMA M-87

THE ULTIMATE COMP PISTOL

FINLAND SAKO
CLASSIC GRADE

THE SAKO CLASSIC GRADE MODEL...
THE UNDERSTATED ELEGANCE OF
A TRADITIONALLY STYLED RIFLE.
THE TRUE RIFLEMAN'S RIFLE.

CLASSIC ELEGANCE CAN
BEST DESCRIBE SAKO'S LATEST
MODEL—THE CLASSIC GRADE.
CONSTRUCTED WITH OLD WORLD
CRAFTSMANSHIP THAT THROUGHOUT THE
YEARS HAS BECOME A SAKO TRADITION.
A TRUE SAKO MASTERPIECE.

STOEGER IGA
SHOTGUNS

Handguns

For addresses and phone numbers of manufacturers and distributors included in this section, turn to *DIRECTORY OF MANUFACTURERS AND SUPPLIERS* at the back of the book.

AMERICAN ARMS PISTOLS

MODEL PK-22 DA SEMIAUTO
$199.00

SPECIFICATIONS
Caliber: 22 LR
Capacity: 8-shot clip
Barrel length: 3¹/₃″
Overall length: 6¹/₃″
Weight: 22 oz. (empty)
Sights: Fixed; blade front, "V"-notch rear
Grip: Black polymer

MODEL P-98 CLASSIC SEMIAUTO
$219.00

SPECIFICATIONS
Caliber: 22 LR
Capacity: 8-shot clip
Barrel length: 5″
Overall length: 8¹/₈″
Weight: 26 oz. (empty)
Sights: Fixed blade front; adjustable square-notch rear
Grip: Black polymer

MODEL CX-22 DA SEMIAUTO
$189.00

SPECIFICATIONS
Caliber: 22 LR
Capacity: 8-shot clip
Barrel length: 3¹/₃″
Overall length: 6¹/₃″
Weight: 22 oz. (empty)
Sights: Fixed; blade front, "V"-notch rear
Grip: Black polymer
Also available:
MODEL PX-25—$199.00

REGULATOR SINGLE ACTION REVOLVER
$299.00
REGULATOR DELUXE $369.00
TWO-CYLINDER SET $349 ($399 DELUXE MODEL)

SPECIFICATIONS
Calibers: 45 Long Colt, 44-40, 357 Mag.
Barrel lengths: 4³/₄″ and 7¹/₂″
Action: Single Action
Sights: Fixed
Safety: Half cock
Features: Brass trigger guard and back strap (**Deluxe** model has casehardened steel trigger guard); two-cylinder combinations available (45 L.C./45 ACP and 44-40/44 Special)

AMERICAN DERRINGER PISTOLS

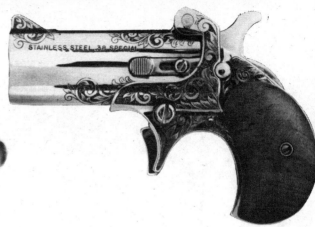

MODEL 1

SPECIFICATIONS
Overall length: 4.82″
Barrel length: 3″
Weight: 15 oz. (in 45 Auto)
Action: Single action w/automatic barrel selection
Number of shots: 2

Calibers	Prices
380 Auto, 9mm Luger	$208.00
38 Special	215.00
38 Super	235.00
38 Special +P+ (Police)	225.00
38 Special Shot Shells	235.00
32-20	215.00
22 LR, 22 Magnum Rimfire	237.50
357 Magnum	247.00
357 Maximum	265.00
10mm Auto, 40 S&W, 45 Auto, 30 M-1 Carbine	250.00
45-70 (single shot)	312.00
45 Colt, 2½″ Snake (45 cal.rifled barrel), 44-40 Win., 44 Special	320.00
45 Win. Mag., 44 Magnum, 41 Magnum, 30-30 Winchester, 223 Rem. Comm. Ammo dual calibers	375.00

MODEL 1 ENGRAVED
$325.00 (add'l)

Also available:
MODEL 7 Ultra Lightweight (7½ oz.) Single Actions

22 LR	$212.50
22 Magnum Rimfire	215.00
32 Magnum, 32 S&W Long	202.50
38 Special	202.50
380 Auto	199.95
44 Special	500.00

MODEL 10 (10 oz.)

45 Colt	$320.00
45 Auto	250.00

MODEL 11 Light Weight (11 oz.) Double Derringer

38 Special	$205.00

LADY DERRINGER (Stainless Steel Double)

38 Special, 32 Magnum, 32 S&W	$250.00
Engraved	695.00

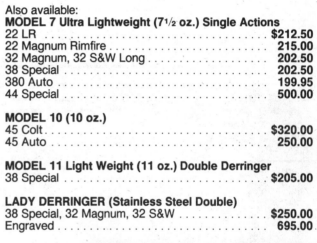

MODEL 3
Stainless Steel Single Shot Derringer
(not shown)

SPECIFICATIONS
Calibers: 32 Magnum, 38 Special
Barrel length: 2.5″
Overall length: 4.9″
Weight: 8.5 oz.
Safety: Manual "Hammer-Block"
Grips: Rosewood
Price: ... $120.00

38 DOUBLE ACTION DERRINGER (14.5 oz.)

38 Special	$245.00
38 Special Lady Derringer w/syn. ivory grips	265.00
9mm Luger	257.00
357 Magnum	300.00

AMERICAN DERRINGER PISTOLS

MODEL 4
Stainless Steel Double Derringer

SPECIFICATIONS
Calibers: 45 Colt or 3″ .410
Barrel length: 4.1″
Overall length: 6″
Weight: 16.5 oz.
Number of shots: 2
Finish: Satin or high polish stainless steel
Price: **$350.00**
Also available:
In 45 Auto, 45 Colt, 44 Special, 357 Magnum, 357 Maximum,
   50-70 (single shot only) **$382.00–495.00**
Alaskan Survival Model in 45-70 .... 387.50

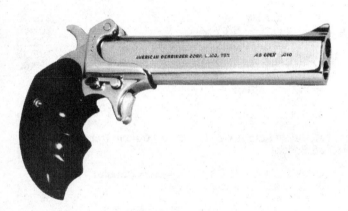

MODEL 6
Stainless Steel Double Derringer

SPECIFICATIONS
Calibers: 357 Magnum, 3″ .410, 45 Auto, 45 Colt
Number of shots: 2
Barrel length: 6″
Overall length: 8.2″
Weight: 21 oz.
Price: Grey matte finish $350.00
        Satin finish 362.50
        High polish finish 387.50
        W/oversize grips **add** 35.00

SEMMERLING LM-4 DOUBLE ACTION

SPECIFICATIONS
Caliber: 45 ACP or 9mm
Action: Double action
Capacity: 5 rounds
Overall length: 5″
Price: Blued finish (manual repeating) $1750.00
        Stainless steel 1875.00

COP AND MINI-COP 4-SHOT DA DERRINGERS
(not shown)

22 Magnum Rimfire (Mini-Cop) $312.50
357 Mag., 9mm Luger or 38 Special (Cop) 375.00

125th ANNIVERSARY DOUBLE DERRINGER
COMMEMORATIVE (1866–1991)

38 Special $215.00
44-40 or 45 Colt 320.00
Engraved models 695.00

AMT PISTOLS

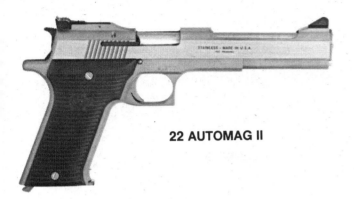

22 AUTOMAG II

AMT 380 BACKUP

22 AUTOMAG II RIMFIRE MAGNUM
$375.95

The only production semiautomatic handgun in this caliber, the Automag II is ideal for the small-game hunter or shooting enthusiast who wants more power and accuracy in a light, trim handgun. The pistol features a bold open-slide design and employs a unique gas-channeling system for smooth, trouble-free action.

SPECIFICATIONS
Caliber: 22 Rimfire Magnum
Barrel lengths: 3³/₈″, 4¹/₂″ or 6″
Magazine capacity: 9 shots (4¹/₂″ & 6″), 7 shots (3³/₈″)
Weight: 32 oz.
Sights: Millett adjustable (white outline rear; red ramp)
Features: Squared trigger guard; grooved carbon fiber grips

AMT 380 BACKUP
$265.95 ($285.95 DA ONLY)

SPECIFICATIONS
Caliber: 380
Capacity: 5 shots
Barrel length: 2¹/₂″
Overall length: 5″
Weight: 18 oz.
Width: ¹¹/₁₆″
Sights: Open
Grips: Carbon fiber

ON DUTY DOUBLE ACTION PISTOL
(not shown)
$529.99 ($569.99 in 45 ACP)

SPECIFICATIONS
Caliber: 40 S&W, 45 ACP and 9mm Luger
Capacity: 13 rounds
Barrel length: 4¹/₂″
Overall length: 7³/₄″
Weight: 32 oz.
Features: Stainless steel slide and barrel; carbon fiber grips; inertia firing pin; steel recoil shoulder; white 3 dot sighting system; trigger disconnector safety; light let-off double action.
Also available: Decocker model (same price).

45 ACP LONGSLIDE (not shown)
$649.99

SPECIFICATIONS
Caliber: 45 ACP
Capacity: 7 shots
Barrel length: 7″
Overall length: 10¹/₂″
Weight: 46 oz.
Sights: Millett adjustable
Features: Wide adjustable trigger; Neoprene wraparound grips
Also available:
45 ACP Government $575.95
45 ACP Hardballer 625.95

AMT PISTOLS

JAVELINA
$675.95

SPECIFICATIONS
Caliber: 10mm
Capacity: 8 shots
Barrel lengths: 7″
Overall length: 10½″
Weight: 48 oz.
Sights: Millett adjustable
Features: Long grip safety; wraparound Neoprene grips; beveled magazine; wide adjustable trigger

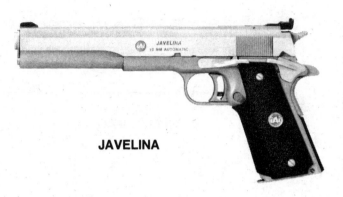

JAVELINA

AUTOMAG III
$629.99

SPECIFICATIONS
Caliber: 30 M1 Carbine, 9mm Win. Mag.
Capacity: 8 shots
Barrel length: 6⅜″
Overall length: 10½″
Weight: 43 oz.
Sights: Millett adjustable
Grips: Carbon fiber
Finish: Stainless steel

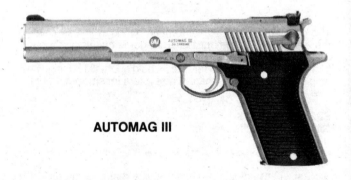

AUTOMAG III

AUTOMAG IV
$675.95

SPECIFICATIONS
Caliber: 45 Win. Mag., 10mm
Capacity: 7 shots
Barrel length: 6½″
Overall length: 10½″
Weight: 46 oz.
Sights: Millett adjustable
Grips: Carbon fiber
Finish: Stainless steel

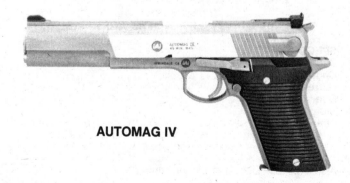

AUTOMAG IV

ANSCHUTZ PISTOLS

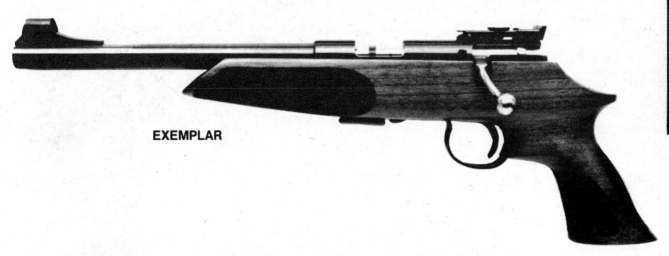

EXEMPLAR

EXEMPLAR
$480.00

SPECIFICATIONS
Calibers: 22 LR
Capacity: 5-shot clip
Barrel length: 10″
Overall length: 19″
Weight: 3 1/3 lbs.
Action: Match 64
Trigger pull: 9.85 oz., two-stage adjustable

Safety: Slide
Sights: Hooded ramp post front; open notched rear; adjustable for windage and elevation
Stock: European walnut

Also available:
EXEMPLAR LEFT featuring right-hand operating bolt.
Price: $492.50

EXEMPLAR XIV
$509.50

SPECIFICATIONS
Calibers: 22 LR
Barrel length: 14″
Overall length: 23″
Weight: 4.15 lbs.
Action: Match 64
Trigger pull: 9.85 oz., two-stage
Safety: Slide

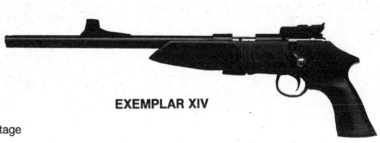

EXEMPLAR XIV

EXEMPLAR HORNET

EXEMPLAR HORNET
$822.00

A centerfire version with Match 54 action.

SPECIFICATIONS
Caliber: 22 Hornet
Trigger pull: 19.6 oz.
Barrel: 10″
Overall length: 20″
Weight: 4.35 lbs.
Features: Tapped and grooved for scope mounting; wing safety

AUTO-ORDNANCE PISTOLS

MODEL 1911A-1 THOMPSON

SPECIFICATIONS
Calibers: 45 ACP, 9mm and 38 Super; also 10mm, 40 S&W
Capacity: 9 rounds (9mm & 38 Super); 7 rounds (45 ACP)
Barrel length: 5″
Overall length: 8 1/2″
Weight: 39 oz.
Sights: Blade front; rear adjustable for windage
Stock: Checkered plastic with medallion
Prices:
MODEL 1911A-1
In 45 ACP $368.95
In 9mm, 10mm & 38 Super 404.25
In 40 S&W 415.95
Satin nickel finish (45 cal. only) 390.80
PIT BULL MODEL (45 ACP w/3 1/2″ barrel) 404.25

**MODEL 1911A-1 THOMPSON
(9mm)**

MODEL 1911 "THE GENERAL"
(not shown)

SPECIFICATIONS
Caliber: 45 ACP
Capacity: 7 rounds
Barrel length: 4 1/2″
Overall length: 7 3/4″
Weight: 37 oz.
Stock: Black textured, rubber wraparound with medallion
Feature: Full-length recoil guide system
Price: $410.50

**MODEL 1911A-1 THOMPSON
PIT BULL**

MODEL 1927A-5

SPECIFICATIONS
Caliber: 45 ACP
Capacity: 30 rounds
Barrel length: 13 1/2″ (finned)
Overall length: 26″
Weight: 7 lbs.
Sights: Blade front; adjustable open rear
Stock: Walnut rear grip, vertical forend
Price: $704.00

**MODEL 1927A-5
(Shown w/50-round L-Type Drum)**

BEEMAN PISTOLS

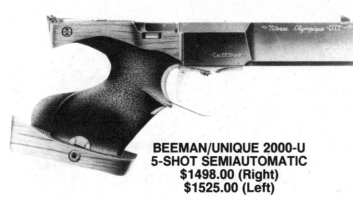

BEEMAN/UNIQUE 2000-U 5-SHOT SEMIAUTOMATIC
$1498.00 (Right)
$1525.00 (Left)

SPECIFICATIONS
Caliber: 22 Short. **Weight:** 2.7 lbs. **Features:** This improved version of the 823-U includes a reshaped grip, a redesigned dry-firing mechanism that is easier to use and a faster falling hammer. Trigger weight is only 3.5 oz.; special light alloy frame and solid steel slide and shock absorber; five vents reduce recoil; three removable vent screws adjust for jump control and velocity; counterweights available.
Also available: **Beeman/Unique DES/32** (32 LG) . **$1235.00**

BEEMAN P-08 SEMIAUTOMATIC (not shown)
$389.00

SPECIFICATIONS
Caliber: 22 LR. **Capacity:** 8 rounds. **Action:** Toggle joint. **Barrel length:** 3.8″. **Overall length:** 7.8″. **Weight:** 1.9 lbs. **Sights:** Military style. **Grip:** Checkered hardwood.

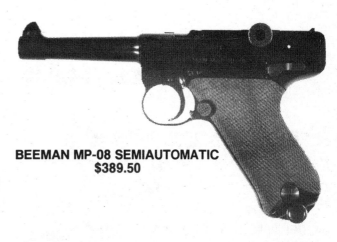

BEEMAN MP-08 SEMIAUTOMATIC
$389.50

SPECIFICATIONS
Caliber: 380 ACP. **Capacity:** 6 rounds. **Action:** Toggle joint. **Barrel length:** 3.5″. **Overall length:** 7.4″. **Weight:** 1.4 lbs. **Sights:** Military style. **Grip:** Checkered hardwood.

BEEMAN/UNIQUE 69U TARGET PISTOL
$1459.00 (Right)
$1498.00 (Left)

SPECIFICATIONS
Caliber: 22 LR. **Capacity:** 5-shot magazine. **Sight radius:** 8.7″. **Weight:** 2.2 lbs. **Grips:** Adjustable, anatomically shaped. **Features:** Trigger adjusts for position and pull weight; several barrel counterweights available; dry-firing device; meets all U.I.T. requirements.

BEEMAN/KORTH SEMIAUTOMATIC
$399.00

SPECIFICATIONS
Calibers: 30 Luger, 9×21 MI (all calibers plus changeable barrel available. **Barrel lengths:** 4″ and 5″. **Features:** All-steel construction; locked breech; recoil-operated semiautomatic (barrel is locked together with slide until bullet has left barrel); 6 grooves, right-hand twist; rebounding hammer moves automatically into safety notch when pistol is decocked; rear sight adjustable in height and sideways via slotted head screws.

BEEMAN REVOLVERS

SPECIFICATIONS
Calibers: 357 Mag. or 22 LR w/interchangeable combo cylinders of 357 Mag./9mm Para or 22 LR/22 WMR. **Barrel lengths:** 3″, 4″, 6″ (Combat or Target). **Features:** The metal parts of these revolvers are hammer-forged steel super-hardened to high tensile strength; cylinder gap of .002″ eliminates stretching of the frame while firing, reduces flash and increases velocity.

**BEEMAN/KORTH REVOLVER
$4342.00 (6″ barrel)**

BEEMAN/HÄMMERLI PISTOLS

MODEL 208S TARGET PISTOL
$1955.00

SPECIFICATIONS:
Caliber: 22 LR
Barrel length: 6″
Overall length: 10.2″
Weight: 37.3 oz. (w/accessories)
Capacity: 9 rounds
Sight radius: 8.3″
Sights: Micrometer rear sight w/notch width; standard front blade

MODEL 212 TARGET PISTOL
$1662.00

SPECIFICATIONS
Caliber: 22 LR
Barrel length: 5″
Overall length: 8.6″
Weight: 31 oz.
Capacity: 8 rounds
Sights: Blade front; notched rear

MODEL 232 RAPID FIRE PISTOL
$1545.00

SPECIFICATIONS:
Caliber: 22 Short
Barrel length: 5.1″
Overall length: 10.5″
Weight: 44 oz.
Sight radius: 9.6″
Capacity: 6 rounds
Grips: Adjustable, wraparound grips and left-hand version also available

**MODEL 232—$1800.00
(W/Wraparound Grips)**

BEEMAN/HÄMMERLI PISTOLS

MODEL 280 SPORT PISTOL
$1650.00 ($1655.00 in 32 S&W)

SPECIFICATIONS
Calibers: 22 LR and 32 S&W
Capacity: 6 rounds (22 LR); 5 rounds (32 S&W)
Barrel length: 4.58″
Weight: (excluding counterweights) 34.92 oz. (22 LR); 38.8 oz. (32 S&W)
Sight radius: 8.66″

MODEL 150 FREE PISTOL
$2139.00 ($2217.00 Left Hand)

SPECIFICATIONS
Caliber: 22 LR
Overall length: 17.2″
Weight: 45.6 oz.
Trigger action: Infinitely variable set trigger weight; cocking lever located on left of receiver; trigger length variable along weapon axis
Sights: Sight radius 14.8″; micrometer rear sight adj. for windage and elevation
Locking action: Martini-type locking action w/side-mounted locking lever

Barrel: Free floating, cold swaged precision barrel w/low axis relative to the hand
Ignition: Horizontal firing pin (hammerless) in line w/barrel axis; firing pin travel 0.15″
Grips: Selected walnut w/adj. hand rest for direct arm to barrel extension

MODEL 152 ELECTRONIC PISTOL
$2333.00 ($2389.00 Left Hand)

SPECIFICATIONS:
Same as **Model 150** except trigger action is electronic. Features short lock time (1.7 milliseconds between trigger actuation and firing pin impact), light trigger pull, and extended battery life.

BERETTA PISTOLS
SMALL FRAME

MODEL 21

MODEL 21 DA SEMIAUTOMATIC
$235.00 ($260.00 Nickel)

A safe, dependable, accurate small-bore pistol in 22 LR or 25 Auto. Easy to load with its unique barrel tip-up system.

SPECIFICATIONS
Caliber: 22 LR or 25 Auto. **Magazine capacity:** 7 rounds (22 LR); 8 rounds (25 Auto). **Overall length:** 4.9″. **Barrel length:** 2.4″. **Weight:** 11.5 oz. (25 ACP); 11.8 oz. (22 LR) **Sights:** Blade front; V-notch rear. **Safety:** Thumb operated. **Grips:** Walnut. **Frame:** Special alloy.
Also available:
Model 21 Engraved $285.00
W/Plastic Matte Finish 185.00

MODEL 950 BS
(22 Short)

MODEL 950 BS
SINGLE ACTION SEMIAUTOMATIC

SPECIFICATIONS
Calibers: 25 ACP and 22 Short. **Barrel length:** 2¹/₂″. **Overall length:** 4¹/₂″. **Overall height:** 3.4″. **Safety:** External, thumb-operated. **Magazine:** 8 rounds (25 cal.); 6 rounds (22 Short). **Sights:** Blade front; V-notch rear. **Weight:** 10.2 oz. in 22 cal.; 9.9 oz. in 25 cal. **Frame:** Special alloy.

Model 950 BS $180.00
Model 950 BS Nickel 210.00
Model 950 EL Engraved 260.00
Model 950 BS Plastic Matte Finish (25 ACP only) . .   150.00

MEDIUM FRAME

MODEL 84F

This pistol is pocket size with a large magazine capacity. The lockwork is of double-action type. The first shot (with hammer down, chamber loaded) can be fired by a double-action pull on the trigger without cocking the hammer manually.

The pistol also features a favorable grip angle for natural pointing, positive thumb safety (uniquely designed for both right- and left-handed operation), quick takedown (by means of special takedown button) and a conveniently located magazine release. Black plastic grips. Wood grips available at extra cost.

MODEL 84F

SPECIFICATIONS
Caliber: 380 Auto (9mm Short). **Weight:** 1 lb. 7 oz. (approx.). **Barrel length:** 3³/₄₄″. (approx.) **Overall length:** 6¹/₂″. (approx.) **Sights:** Fixed front and rear. **Magazine capacity:** 13 rounds. **Height overall:** 4¹/₄″ (approx.).

Model 84F w/Plastic $525.00
Model 84F w/Wood 555.00
Model 84F w/Wood Nickel 600.00

BERETTA PISTOLS
MEDIUM FRAME PISTOLS
Calibers 22 LR and 380

MODEL 85F

This double-action semiautomatic pistol features walnut or plastic grips, matte black finish on steel slide, barrel and anodized alloy frame, ambidextrous safety, and a single line 8-round magazine.

SPECIFICATIONS
Caliber: 380 Auto. **Barrel length:** 3.82″. **Weight:** 21.8 oz. (empty). **Overall length:** 6.8″. **Overall height:** 4.8″. **Capacity:** 8 rounds. **Sights:** Blade integral with slide (front); square notched bar, dovetailed to slide (rear).
Price: **$455.00**
Also available:
Model 85 w/Plastic (8 rounds) **$485.00**
Model 85 w/Wood **510.00**
Model 85 w/Wood Nickel **550.00**

Also available:
Model 87 w/Wood (22 LR) **$490.00**
Model 87 (Long barrel, SA) **510.00**

MODEL 85F

MODEL 86

MODEL 86

SPECIFICATIONS
Caliber: 380 Auto. **Barrel length:** 4.33″. **Overall length:** 7.33″. **Capacity:** 8 rounds. **Weight:** 23 oz. **Sight radius:** 5.0″. **Overall height:** 4.8″. **Overall width:** 1.4″. **Grip:** Walnut or plastic. **Features:** Same as other Medium Frame, straight blow-back models, plus safety and convenience of a tip-up barrel (rounds can be loaded directly into chamber without operating the slide).
Price: **$555.00**

MODEL 89 STANDARD TARGET

This sophisticated single-action, target pistol features an 8-round magazine, adjustable target sights, and target-style contoured walnut grips with thumb rest.

SPECIFICATIONS
Caliber: 22 LR. **Barrel length:** 6″. **Overall length:** 9½″. **Height:** 5.3″. **Weight:** 41 oz.
Price: **$735.00**

MODEL 89 TARGET

BERETTA PISTOLS
LARGE FRAME

MODEL 92FS (9mm)

This 9mm Parabellum semiautomatic pistol is specifically designed for use by law enforcement agencies. It has also been adopted as the official sidearm of the U.S. Armed Forces. Its 15-round firepower combines with flawless reliability and safety to make it the ideal police and military sidearm. Its firing mechanism will handle thousands of rounds without malfunction. And the ambidextrous triple-safety mechanism features a passive firing pin catch, a slide safety that acts as a decocking lever, plus a unique firing pin to ensure that a falling hammer can never break safety and discharge accidentally. Available in two compact versions; 3-dot and tritium night sights available.

SPECIFICATIONS
Caliber: 9mm Parabellum. **Overall length:** 8.54″. **Height:** 5.4″. **Barrel length:** 4.9″. **Weight** (empty): 34 oz. **Magazine:** 15 rounds, removable floorplate. **Sights:** Front, blade integral with slide; rear, square-notched bar, dovetailed to slide. **Slide stop:** Holds slide open after last round, manually operable.

Model 92FS	$625.00
(Wood grips **$20.00** additional)	
Model 92F Stainless	755.00
Also available:	
Model 92FS Compact (8 round)	625.00
With wood grips	645.00
Model 92FS Plastic Centurion w/3-Dot Sight	625.00
Model 92D (DA only) w/bobbed hammer and 3-Dot	
Sight	585.00
w/Trijicon Sight	650.00

Optional: 3-Dot Sights (same price) and Trijicon Sights (**$75.00** additional)

MODEL 92F (9mm)

MODEL 92D

MODEL 92F-EL

MODEL 92F-EL

This deluxe version of the 92FS features exquisite gold trim on the safety levers, trigger, magazine release and grip screws. Top of barrel has Beretta logo with gold inlay. Richly grained walnut grips are ergonomically designed and also have engraved Beretta logo. High polish, blued finish on barrel, slide and frame. All other specifications same as the standard 92F.

Model 92F-EL Stainless	$1240.00
Model 92F-EL Gold	790.00

MODEL 96

MODEL 96

Same specifications as the Model 92FS, except in 40 caliber with a 10-shot magazine capacity (9 shot in Compact version).

Model 96	$640.00
With Trijicon Sight	710.00

BERSA AUTOMATIC PISTOLS

MODEL 23 DOUBLE ACTION
$274.95 ($306.95 in Nickel)

SPECIFICATIONS
Caliber: 22 LR
Barrel length: 4″
Action: Blowback
Sights: Front blade on barrel; rear, square-notched adjustable for windage
Capacity: 10 shots
Grips: Custom wood
Finish: Blue

MODEL 23 DOUBLE ACTION

MODEL 83 DOUBLE ACTION
$274.95 ($306.95 in Nickel)

SPECIFICATIONS
Caliber: 380 Auto
Capacity: 7 shots
Barrel length: 3¹/₂″
Weight: 25³/₄ oz.
Width: 1¹/₃″
Action: Blowback
Sights: Front blade sight integral on slide; rear sight square notched adjustable for windage
Grips: Custom wood

MODEL 83 DOUBLE ACTION

MODEL 85 DOUBLE ACTION
$324.95 ($383.95 in Nickel)

SPECIFICATIONS
Caliber: 380 Auto
Capacity: 13 shots
Barrel length: 3¹/₂″
Overall length: 6⁵/₈″
Weight: 22 oz.
Width: 1⁷/₁₆″

Also available:

MODEL 86 CUSTOM UNDERCOVER DA (not shown)
$366.95 ($399.95 in Nickel)

SPECIFICATIONS
Same as Model 85, except Model 86 has military non-glare matte finish and 3 dot sight system.

MODEL 85 DOUBLE ACTION

BROWNING AUTOMATIC PISTOLS

**9mm HI-POWER
SINGLE ACTION**

9mm HI-POWER
SINGLE ACTION

The Browning 9mm Parabellum, also known as the 9mm Browning Hi-Power, has a 14-cartridge capacity and weighs 2 pounds. The push-button magazine release permits swift, convenient withdrawal of the magazine.

The 9mm is available with either a fixed-blade front sight and a windage-adjustable rear sight or a non-glare rear sight, screw adjustable for both windage and elevation. The front sight is an 1/8-inch-wide blade mounted on a ramp. The rear surface of the blade is serrated to prevent glare. All models have an ambidextrous safety.

Prices:

Standard Mark III w/matte finish, molded grip	**$469.95**
Polished blue with adjustable sights	**554.95**
Polished blue with fixed sights	**509.95**
Practical w/fixed sights, Pachmayr rubber grip	**549.95**
w/adjustable sights	**594.95**
Silver chrome w/adjustable sights, Pachmayr rubber grip	**564.95**

9MM SEMIAUTOMATIC PISTOL

	SINGLE ACTION FIXED SIGHTS	SINGLE ACTION ADJUSTABLE SIGHTS
Finish	Polished Blue, Matte, or Nickel	Polished Blue
Capacity of Magazine	13	13
Overall Length	7 3/4″	7 3/4″
Barrel Length	4 21/32″	4 21/32″
Height	5″	5″
Weight (Empty)	32 oz.	32 oz.
Sight Radius	6 5/16″	6 3/8″
Ammunition	9mm Luger, (Parabellum)	9mm Luger, (Parabellum)
Grips	Checkered Walnut or Contoured Molded	Checkered Walnut or Contoured Molded
Front Sights	1/8″	1/8″ wide on ramp
Rear Sights	Drift adjustable for windage and elevation.	Drift adjustable for windage and elevation. Square Notch.

MODEL BDM 9mm DOUBLE ACTION

Browning's Model BDM (for Browning Double Mode) pistol brings shooters into a new realm of convenience and safety by combining the best advantages of double-action pistols with those of the revolver. In just seconds, the shooter can set the BDM to conventional double-action "pistol" mode or to the all-new double-action "revolver" mode.

SPECIFICATIONS
Caliber: 9mm Luger
Capacity: 15 rounds
Barrel length: 4.73″
Overall length: 7.85″
Weight: 31 oz. (empty)
Sight radius: 6.26″
Sights: Low-profile front (removable); rear screw adjustable for windage; includes 3-dot sight system
Finish: Matte blue
Features: Dual-purpose ambidextrous decocking lever/safety designed with a short stroke for easy operation (also functions as slide release); contoured grip is checkered on all four sides
Price: **$514.95**

**MODEL BDM
9mm DOUBLE ACTION**

BROWNING AUTOMATIC PISTOLS

MODEL BDA-380

MODEL BDA-380

A high-powered, double-action semiautomatic pistol with fixed sights in 380 caliber. See specifications on preceding page.

Nickel Finish **$594.95**
Standard Finish **564.95**

BUCK MARK 5.5 TARGET

MICRO BUCK MARK

MICRO BUCK MARK

Features light weight, Pro Target Sight, bull barrel and black molded composite grips.

BUCK MARK PISTOLS SPECIFICATIONS

	MICRO BUCK MARK	BUCK MARK BUCK MARK PLUS	BUCK MARK* 5.5 TARGET/FIELD	BUCK MARK* SILHOUETTE	BUCK MARK* VARMINT	BUCK MARK* UNLTD. SILHOUETTE
Capacity	10	10	10	10	10	10
Overall length	8″	9 1/2″	9 5/8″	14″	14″	18 11/16″
Barrel length	4″	5 1/2″	5 1/2″	9 7/8″	9 7/8″	14″
Height	5 3/8″	5 3/8″	5 5/16″	5 15/16″	5 5/16″	5 15/16″
Weight (empty)	32 oz.	32 oz.	35 oz.	53 oz.	48 oz.	64 oz.
Sight radius	6 1/2″	8″	8 1/4″	13″	—	15″
Ammunition	22 LR	22 LR	22 LR	22 LR	22 LR	22 LR
Grips	Laminated Wood	Black, Molded; Impregnated Hardwood	Contoured Walnut	Contoured Walnut	Contoured Walnut	Contoured Walnut
Front Sights	Ramp front	1/8″ wide	Interchangeable Post*	Interchangeable Post*	None*	Interchangeable Post*
Rear Sights	Pro Target Sight	Pro Target Sight	Pro Target Sight	Pro Target Sight	None*	Pro Target Sight
Prices	$224.95 (Std.) $259.95 (Nickel) $269.95 (Plus)	$224.95 $269.95 (Buck Mark PLUS) $259.95 (Nickel)	$359.95 ($379.95 Gold Target)	$379.95	$334.95	$449.95

* Bark Mark Target, Silhouette and Varmint models supplied with full length top rib designed to accept most standard clamp style scope rings. Additional accessories for the Silhouette and Target models are available. New finger groove grip option on all target models.

CHARTER ARMS REVOLVERS

**357 MAGNUM REVOLVER
BULLDOG "TRACKER"**

357 MAGNUM REVOLVER
BULLDOG "TRACKER"

SPECIFICATIONS
Caliber: 357 Magnum. **Type of action:** 5-shot. **Barrel length:** 2½". **Overall length:** 7½" (2½ bbl.). **Height:** 5⅛". **Weight:** 21 oz. **Grips:** Hand-checkered walnut, square butt design. **Sights:** Ramp front; adjustable square-notched rear; elevation reference lines; definite click indicator. **Finish:** Service blue.

Price:
Blue finish and Neoprene or Bulldog grips **$240.00**

**BULLDOG PUG
44 SPECIAL**

BULLDOG 44 SPECIAL

SPECIFICATIONS
Caliber: 44 Special. **Type of action:** 5-shot, single- and double-action. **Barrel length:** 3". **Overall length:** 7¾". **Height:** 5". **Weight:** 19 oz. **Grips:** Neoprene or American walnut hand-checkered bulldog grips. **Sights:** Patridge-type, 9/64" wide front; square-notched rear. **Finish:** High-luster Service Blue or stainless steel.

Prices:
Blue finish Pug **$267.00**
Stainless steel Pug **320.00**

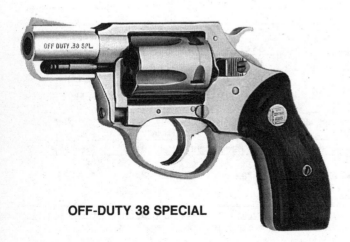

OFF-DUTY 38 SPECIAL

OFF-DUTY 38 SPECIAL

SPECIFICATIONS
Calibers: 22 LR and 38 Special. **Type of action:** 5-shot, single and double action. **Barrel length:** 2". **Overall length:** 6¼". **Height:** 4¼". **Weight:** 16 oz. (matte black); 17 oz. (stainless). **Grips:** Select-a-grip (9 colors) or Neoprene. **Sights:** Patridge-type ramp front (with "red dot" feature); square-notch rear on stainless.

Prices:
Matte black finish **$210.00**
Stainless steel **257.00**

CHARTER ARMS REVOLVERS

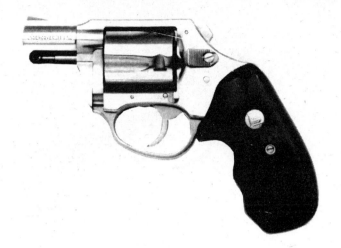

POLICE UNDERCOVER

SPECIFICATIONS
Caliber: 32 H&R Magnum and 38 Special. **Type of action:** 6-shot, single and double action. **Barrel length:** 2″. **Height:** 4 1/2″. **Weight:** 17 1/2 oz. (2″ barrel) and 19 oz. (4″ barrel.) **Grips:** Checkered walnut panel. **Sights:** Patridge-type ramp front; square-notch rear. **Finish:** Blue.

Price $240.00
Stainless steel and checkered walnut panel 270.00

UNDERCOVER 38 SPECIAL

SPECIFICATIONS
Caliber: 38 Special (Mid-Range & Standard). **Type of Action:** 5-shot, single and double action. **Barrel length** (with shroud): 2″. **Overall length:** 6 1/4″. **Height:** 4 1/4″. **Weight:** 16 oz. **Grips:** American walnut hand-checkered. **Sights:** Patridge-type or standard ramp front, square-notched rear. **Finish:** Stainless steel.

Price: $275.00

PATHFINDER
22 L.R.

SPECIFICATIONS
Caliber: 22 LR. **Type of action:** 6-shot, single and double action. **Barrel length:** 3″ or 6″. **Overall length:** 7 3/4″ (3″ bbl.); 10 5/8″ (6″ bbl.). **Height:** 4 3/4″ (3″ bbl.); 5″ (6″ bbl.). **Weight:** 20 oz. (3″ bbl.); 22 1/2 oz. (6″ bbl.). **Grips:** Hand-checkered square butt or checkered walnut panel. **Sights:** Patridge-type ramp front sight; fully adjustable notch rear sight. **Finish:** High-luster Service Blue.

Prices:
With 3″ barrel $220.00
With 6″ barrel 223.00
With 3″ barrel in stainless steel 280.00

CHARTER ARMS REVOLVERS

BONNIE

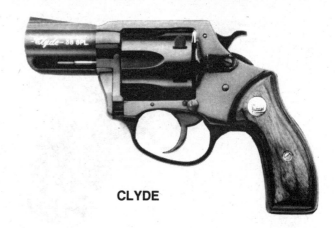

CLYDE

BONNIE AND CLYDE

This matching pair of handguns in 32 Magnum and 38 Special are designed for couples who like to go to the shooting range together. Both guns come with their own "gun rug" identified by name. Each model also offers a scrolled name on the barrel and features Select-A-Grip color-coordinated grips. The fully shrouded barrels are 2½" long with an attractive blue finish.

Price: (per set) . . . .**$256.00.**

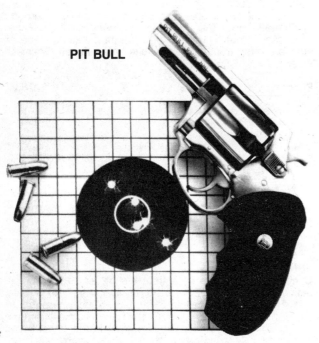

PIT BULL

Actual target group at 40 feet.

PIT BULL

SPECIFICATIONS
Calibers: 9mm, 357 Mag., 38 Special. **Capacity:** 5 rounds.
Barrel lengths: 2½", 3½" and 4". **Overall length:** 7", 7¼",
8¼", 8½" and 8¾". **Height:** 5". **Weight:** 21½ oz. (357 Mag.
w/2½" barrel); 24 oz. (38 Special w/4" barrel); 25 oz. (9mm
w/2½" barrel); 26 oz. (9mm w/3½" barrel); 26½ oz. (38 Special
w/4" barrel); 28 oz. (357 Mag. w/4" barrel). **Finish:** Stainless
steel; 2½" 357 Mag. and 4" 38 Special in Service Blue only.

Prices:
Service Blue finish **$276.00**
Stainless finish **360.00**

CHINASPORTS

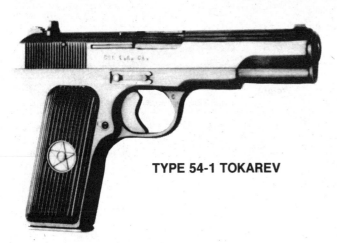

TYPE 54-1 TOKAREV

TYPE 59 MAKAROV

TYPE 54-1 TOKAREV
$199.00

SPECIFICATIONS
Calibers: 38 Super or 7.62×25mm (9mm in Compact Model only)
Action: Single semiauto
Capacity: 8 rounds
Barrel length: 4½" (3.8" Compact Model)
Overall length: 7.7" (7" Compact Model)
Weight: 29 oz. (27 oz. Compact Model)
Sights: Fixed

TYPE 59 MAKAROV
$299.00

SPECIFICATIONS
Caliber: 9×18mm or 380 ACP
Action: Single and double
Capacity: 8 rounds
Barrel length: 3½"
Overall length: 6.3"
Weight: 24 oz.
Sights: Fixed and adjustable

TYPE 77B
$329.00

NORINCO TYPE M1911-A1 PISTOL

SPECIFICATIONS
Caliber: 9mm×19mm
Action: Single
Capacity: 8 rounds
Barrel length: 5"
Overall length: 7½"
Weight: 34 oz.
Sights: Adjustable rear
Features: Trigger guard cocking

NORINCO TYPE M1911-A1 PISTOL
$399.00

SPECIFICATIONS
Caliber: 45 ACP
Capacity: 8 rounds (7+1)
Barrel length: 5"
Overall length: 8½"
Weight: 39 oz.
Sights: Blade front; square-notched rear
Finish: Blued

COLT AUTOMATIC PISTOLS

DOUBLE EAGLE MK SERIES 90

SPECIFICATIONS

Model	Caliber	Barrel Length (inches)	Finish	Sights	Approx. Weight (ozs.)	Overall Length (inches)	Sight Radius (inches)	Rounds	Price
Double Eagle	45ACP	5	STS	WDS	39	8½	6½	8	$695.95
Double Eagle	45ACP	5	STS	AS	39	8½	6¾	8	725.95
Double Eagle	10mm Auto	5	STS	WDS	39	8½	6½	8	715.95
Double Eagle	10mm Auto	5	STS	AS	39	8½	6¾	8	745.95
D.E. Combat Com.	40 S&W	4¼	STS	WDS	36	7¾	5¾	8	695.95
D.E. Combat Com.	45ACP	4¼	STS	WDS	36	7¾	5¾	8	695.95
D.E. Officer's ACP	45ACP	3½	STS	WDS	35	7¼	5¼	8	695.95
D.E. Officer's L.W.	45ACP	3½	B	WDS	25	7¼	5¼	8	N/A

DOUBLE EAGLE

COMBAT COMMANDER
4¼″ barrel only

COMBAT COMMANDER MKIV SERIES 80

The semiautomatic Combat Commander, available in 45 ACP and 38 Super, boasts an all-steel frame that supplies the pistol with an extra measure of heft and stability. This outstanding Colt also offers 3-Dot high-profile sights, lanyard-style hammer and thumb and beavertail grip safety.

SPECIFICATIONS

Caliber	Weight	Overall Length	Magazine Rounds	Finish	Price
45 ACP	36 oz.	7¾″	8	Blue	$639.95
45 ACP	36 oz.	7¾″	8	Stainless	689.95
38 Super	37 oz.	7¾″	9	Stainless	689.95

LIGHTWEIGHT COMMANDER MKIV SERIES 80
(not shown)

This lightweight, shorter version of the Government Model offers increased ease of carrying with the firepower of the 45 ACP. The Lightweight Commander features alloy frame, 3-Dot high-profile sights, long trigger, lanyard-style hammer and rubber stocks; also thumb and beavertail grip safety, and firing pin safety.

SPECIFICATIONS
Magazine capacity: 8 rounds
Barrel length: 4¼″
Overall length: 7¾″
Weight: 27½ oz.
Finish: Blue
Price: $639.95

COLT AUTOMATIC PISTOLS

MKIV SERIES 80

GOLD CUP NATIONAL MATCH

SPECIFICATIONS
Caliber: 45 ACP
Capacity: 8 rounds
Barrel length: 5″
Weight: 39 oz.
Overall length: 8½″
Sights: Colt Elliason sights; adjustable rear for windage and elevation
Hammer: Serrated rounded hammer
Stock: Rubber combat
Finish: Colt blue, stainless or "Ultimate" bright stainless steel
Prices: $819.95 Blue
     874.95 Stainless steel
     940.95 Bright stainless
Also available:
COMBAT ELITE 45 ACP and 38 Super; features Accro Adjustable sights, beavertail grip safety. **Price: $774.95** (45 ACP)

GOLD CUP NATIONAL MATCH

GOVERNMENT MODEL

GOVERNMENT MODEL

These full-size automatic pistols, available exclusively with 5-inch barrels, may be had in 45 ACP, 40 S&W and 38 Super. The Government Model's special features include high-profile 3 dot sights, grip and thumb safeties, and rubber combat stocks.

SPECIFICATIONS
Calibers: 40 S&W, 38 Super and 45 ACP
Barrel length: 5″
Overall length: 8½″
Capacity: 9 rds.; 7 rds. (45 ACP)
Weight: 38 oz.
Prices: $639.95 45 ACP blue
     679.95 45 ACP and 40 S&W stainless
     749.95 45 ACP bright stainless
     649.95 38 Super blue
     684.95 38 Super stainless
     754.95 38 Super bright stainless

GOVERNMENT MODEL 380 AUTOMATIC

This scaled-down version of the 1911 A1 Colt Government Model does not include a grip safety. It incorporates the use of a firing pin safety to provide for a safe method to carry a round in the chamber in a "cocked and locked" mode. Available in matte stainless steel finish with black composition stocks.

SPECIFICATIONS
Caliber: 380 ACP
Magazine capacity: 7 rounds
Barrel length: 3.25″
Overall length: 6″
Height: 4.4″
Weight (empty): 21.75 oz., 14¾ oz. (Lightweight)
Sights: Fixed ramp blade front; fixed square notch rear
Grip: Composition stocks
Prices: $419.95 Blue
     469.95 Satin Nickel
     449.95 Stainless steel
Now available: **Pocklite Model (14¾ oz.), blue finish only.**
Price: $419.95

380 GOVERNMENT POCKLETLITE

COLT AUTOMATIC PISTOLS

MKIV SERIES 80

DELTA ELITE AND DELTA GOLD CUP

The proven design and reliability of Colt's Government Model has been combined with the powerful 10mm auto cartridge to produce a highly effective shooting system for hunting, law enforcement and personal protection. The velocity and energy of the 10mm cartridge make this pistol ideal for the serious handgun hunter and the law enforcement professional who insist on down-range stopping power.

SPECIFICATIONS
Type: 0 Frame, semiautomatic pistol
Caliber: 10mm
Magazine capacity: 8 rounds
Barrel length: 5″
Overall length: 8½″
Weight (empty): 38 oz.
Sights: 3-dot, high-profile front and rear combat sights; Accro rear sight adj. for windage and elevation (on Delta Gold Cup only)
Sight radius: 6½″ (3 dot sight system), 6¾″ (adjustable sights)
Grips: Rubber combat stocks with Delta medallion
Safety: Trigger safety lock (thumb safety) is located on left-hand side of receiver; grip safety is located on backstrap; internal firing pin safety

DELTA ELITE

Rifling: 6 groove, left-hand twist, one turn in 16″
Prices: $704.95 Blue
714.95 Stainless steel
784.95 "Ultimate" Bright Stainless
Also available:
DELTA GOLD CUP. Same specifications as Delta Elite, except 39 oz. weight and 6¾″ sight radius. Stainless. **$899.95**

COLT MUSTANG .380

This backup automatic has four times the knockdown power of most 25 ACP automatics. It is a smaller version of the 380 Government Model.

SPECIFICATIONS
Caliber: 380 ACP
Capacity: 6 rounds
Weight: 18.5 oz.
Overall length: 5.5″
Height: 3.9″
Prices: $419.95 Standard blue
469.95 Nickel
449.95 Stainless steel
Also available:
MUSTANG POCKETLITE 380 with aluminum alloy receiver; ½″ shorter than standard Govt. 380; weighs only 12.5 oz. **Price: $419.95.**
MUSTANG PLUS II features full grip length (Govt. 380 model only) with shorter compact barrel and slide (Mustang .380 model only). **Price: $419.95** Blue; **$449.95** Stainless steel.

COLT MUSTANG .380

COLT OFFICER'S 45 ACP

SPECIFICATIONS
Caliber: 45 ACP
Barrel length: 3½″
Overall length: 7¼″
Weight: 34 oz.
Prices: $624.95 Matte finish
679.95 Stainless steel
639.95 Standard blue
749.95 Ultimate stainless
Also available:
Officer's LW w/aluminum alloy frame (24 oz.). **Price: $639.95** Matte finish.

COLT OFFICER'S 45 ACP

COLT AUTOMATIC PISTOLS

**ALL AMERICAN MODEL 2000
(Right view)**

COLT ALL AMERICAN MODEL 2000

Colt's new 9mm semiautomatic pistol combines a 15-round magazine capacity with the smooth double action and simple operation of a revolver. The All American shares important technology with the famous Colt M16 military rifle: locked breech; recoil-operated action with locking lugs integral to the barrel; barrel and slide lock together and work as a unit. This precise rotary action reduces felt recoil by slowing down the unlocking cycle.

SPECIFICATIONS
Caliber: 9mm
Capacity: 15 + 1 standard
Barrel length: 4$\frac{1}{2}$"
Overall length: 7$\frac{1}{2}$"
Weight (empty): 29 oz. (approx.)
Sights: Fixed, ramped blade (glare proof) front; square notch (glare proof) rear, 3-Dot system
Sight radius: 6$\frac{3}{8}$"
Rifling: 6 grooves, left-hand twist, 1 turn in 14"
Safety system: Internal striker block
Magazine: Can be fired without magazine; magazine release located behind trigger guard and readily reversible
Finish: Non-glare carbon steel blue slide; electroless nickel-plated carbon steel barrel, polymer receiver
Price: $575.00

Rotary barrel action reduces recoil and straightline design promotes shot-to-shot accuracy.

Three-dot sight system allows rapid target acquisition even under low light conditions.

Safe, simple operation with internal striker block safety and no external safety or decocking lever—simplifies and reduces training time.

Roller-bearing mounted trigger features smooth, straight double action pull with no overtravel.

Checkered trigger guard and grip improve handling and pointability during firing.

Magazine release is reversible for left- or right-handed shooters, and is operated without shifting your grip.

Slide release operates easily without shifting grip.

Easy assembly and disassembly for field maintenance. Field strips to 7 parts (8 including magazine).

The All American can be fired without a magazine.

**ALL AMERICAN MODEL 2000
(Left view)**

COLT PISTOLS/REVOLVERS

MODEL M1991 A1

MODEL M1991 A1 PISTOL

SPECIFICATIONS
Caliber: 45 ACP
Capacity: 7 rounds
Barrel length: 5″
Overall length: 8½″
Sight radius: 6½″
Grips: Black composition
Finish: Parkerized
Features: Custom-molded carry case
Price: $499.95

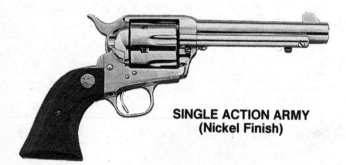

SINGLE ACTION ARMY
(Nickel Finish)

SINGLE ACTION ARMY REVOLVER

Colt's maintains the tradition of quality and innovation that Samuel Colt began more than a century and a half ago. Single Action Army revolvers continue to be highly prized collectible arms and are offered in full nickel finish or in Royal Blue with color casehardened frame, without engraving unless otherwise specified by the purchaser. Grips are American walnut.
Price: **$1119.95**

SINGLE ACTION ARMY SPECIFICATIONS

SINGLE ACTION ARMY
(Royal Blue Finish)

Caliber	Bbl. Length (inches)	Finish	Approx. Weight (ozs.)	O/A Length (inches)	Grips	Medallions
45LC	4¾	CC/B	40	10¼	Walnut	Gold
45LC	4¾	N	40	10¼	Walnut	Nickel
45LC	5½	CC/B	42	11	Walnut	Gold
45LC	5½	N	42	11	Walnut	Nickel
45LC	7½	CC/B	43	13	Walnut	Gold
44-40	4¾	CC/B	40	10¼	Walnut	Gold
44-40	4¾	N	40	10¼	Walnut	Nickel
44-40	5½	CC/B	42	11	Walnut	Gold
44-40	5½	N	42	11	Walnut	Nickel

—Overall   N—Nickel   CC/B—Colorcase frame, Royal Blue cylinder & barrel

COLT REVOLVERS

KING COBRA DOUBLE ACTION

This "snake" revolver features a solid barrel rib, full-length ejector rod housing, red ramp front sight, white outline adjustable rear sight, and "gripper" rubber combat grips.

SPECIFICATIONS
Calibers: 357 Magnum and 38 Special
Capacity: 6 rounds
Barrel lengths: 2 1/2", 4", 6", 8" (stainless and "Ultimate" bright stainless)
Overall length: 8" (2 1/2" bbl.); 9" (4" bbl.); 11" (6" bbl.); 13" (8" bbl.)
Weight: 36 oz. (2 1/2"), 42 oz. (4"), 46 oz. (6"), 48 oz. (8")
Prices:
Blue **$409.95**
Stainless **434.95**
"Ultimate" Bright Stainless **469.95**

KING COBRA (8" barrel) in "Ultimate" Bright Stainless Steel

ANACONDA (6" barrel)

ANACONDA DOUBLE ACTION

SPECIFICATIONS
Caliber: 44 Magnum
Capacity: 6 rounds
Barrel lengths: 4", 6", 8"
Overall length: 9 5/8", 11 5/8", 13 5/8"
Weight: 47 oz. (4"), 53 oz. (6"), 59 oz. (8")
Sights: Red insert front; adjustable white outline rear
Sight radius: 5 3/4" (4"), 7 3/4" (6"), 9 3/4" (8")
Grips: Black neoprene combat-style with finger grooves
Finish: Matte stainless steel
Price: All barrel lengths **$539.95**

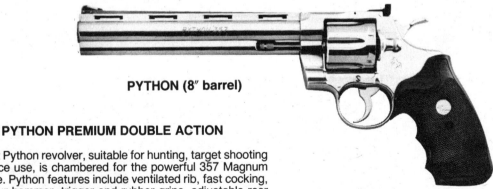

PYTHON (8" barrel)

PYTHON PREMIUM DOUBLE ACTION

The Colt Python revolver, suitable for hunting, target shooting and police use, is chambered for the powerful 357 Magnum cartridge. Python features include ventilated rib, fast cocking, wide-spur hammer, trigger and rubber grips, adjustable rear and ramp-type front sights, grooved.

SPECIFICATIONS
Calibers: 357 Mag. and 38 Special
Barrel lengths: 2 1/2", 4", 6", 8"
Overall length: 8" to 13 1/2"
Weight: 33 oz. (2 1/2"), 38 oz. (4"), 43 1/2 oz. (6"), 48 oz. (8")
Stock: Rubber combat (2 1/2", 4") or rubber target (6", 8")

Finish: Colt high-polish royal blue, stainless steel and "Ultimate" bright stainless steel
Prices:
Royal Blue **$775.95**
Stainless steel **864.95**
"Ultimate" Bright Stainless Steel **894.95**

DAEWOO

MODEL DP51 9mm PISTOL
$499.00

SPECIFICATIONS
Caliber: 9mm Parabellum
Capacity: 13 rounds
Barrel length: 4¹/₈″
Overall length: 7¹/₂″
Weight: 28.2 oz.
Sights: Blade front (¹/₈″) with self-luminous dot (optional); square notch rear, drift adjustable with 2 self-luminous dots
Finish: Sand-blasted black or polished
Muzzle velocity: 1150 fps
Safety: Ambidextrous manual safety, half-cocking and automatic firing pin block

DAVIS PISTOLS

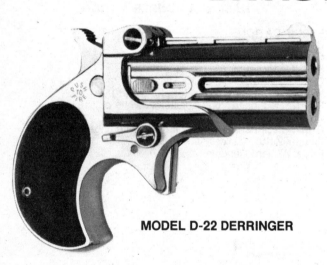

MODEL D-22 DERRINGER

D-SERIES DERRINGERS
$64.90

SPECIFICATIONS
Calibers: 22 LR, 22 Mag., 25 Auto, 32 Auto
Barrel length: 2.4″
Overall length: 4″
Height: 2.8″
Weight: 9.5 oz.
Capacity: 2 shot
Grips: Laminated wood
Finish: Black teflon or chrome
Also available:
BIG BORE 38 SPECIAL D-SERIES. Barrel length: 2.75″.
  Overall length: 4.65″. **Weight:** 11.5 oz. **Price:** . . **$87.90**

MODEL P-380 (not shown)
$98.00

SPECIFICATIONS
Caliber: 380 Auto
Magazine capacity: 5 rounds
Barrel length: 2.8″
Overall length: 5.4″
Height: 4″
Weight: 22 oz. (empty)

MODEL P-32
$87.50

SPECIFICATIONS
Caliber: 32 Auto
Magazine capacity: 6 rounds
Barrel length: 2.8″
Overall length: 5.4″
Height: 4″
Weight (empty): 22 oz.
Grips: Laminated wood
Finish: Black teflon or chrome

MODEL P-32

EMF/DAKOTA

SINGLE ACTION REVOLVERS

1873 DAKOTA REVOLVER

1873 DAKOTA SINGLE ACTION REVOLVER
$490.00   ($636.00 in Nickel)

SPECIFICATIONS
Calibers: 357 Mag., 44-40, 45 Long Colt. **Barrel lengths:** 4³/₄″, 5¹/₂″ and 7¹/₂″. **Finish:** Blued, casehardened frame. **Grips:** One-piece walnut. **Features:** Set screw for cylinder pin release; parts are interchangeable with early Colts.

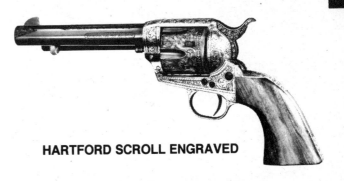

HARTFORD SCROLL ENGRAVED

HARTFORD SCROLL ENGRAVED
SINGLE ACTION REVOLVER
$840.00   ($1000.00 in Nickel)

SPECIFICATIONS
Calibers: 22, 45 Long Colt, 357 Magnum, 44-40. **Barrel lengths:** 4⁵/₈″, 5¹/₂″ and 7¹/₂″. **Features:** Classic original-type scroll engraving.

HARTFORD MODEL

HARTFORD MODELS
$600.00   ($760.00 in Nickel)

EMF's Hartford Single Action revolvers are available in the following calibers: 32-20, 38-40, 44-40, 44 Special and 45 Long Colt. **Barrel lengths:** 4³/₄″, 5¹/₂″ and 7¹/₂″. All models feature steel back straps, trigger guards and forged frame. Identical to the original Colts.

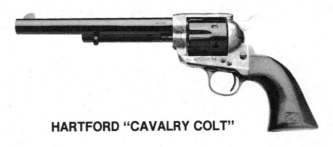

HARTFORD "CAVALRY COLT"

HARTFORD MODELS
"CAVALRY COLT" AND "ARTILLERY"
$655.00

The Model 1873 Government Model Cavalry revolver is an exact reproduction of the original Colt made for the U.S. Cavalry in caliber 45 Long Colt with barrel length of 7¹/₂″. The Artillery Model has 5¹/₂″ barrel.

EMF/DAKOTA

MODEL 1873 (With Extra Cylinder)
$665.00

SPECIFICATIONS
Calibers: 32-20, 38-40, 44-40, 357 Mag., 45 Long Colt, 30 M1 Carbine. **Barrel lengths:** 4¾", 5½", 7½". **Finish:** Engraved models, blue or nickel. **Special feature:** Each gun is fitted with second caliber.

DAKOTA TARGET
$500.00

SPECIFICATIONS
Calibers: 45 Long Colt, 357 Magnum, 22 LR. **Barrel lengths:** 5½" and 7½". **Finish:** Polished blue. **Special features:** Casehardened frame, one-piece walnut grips, brass back strap, ramp front blade target sight and adjustable rear sight.

MODEL 1875 "OUTLAW"
$465.00 ($550.00 in Nickel)

SPECIFICATIONS
Calibers: 44-40, 45 Long Colt, 357 Magnum. **Barrel length:** 7½". **Finish:** Blue or nickel. **Special features:** Casehardened frame, walnut grips; an exact replica of the Remington No. 3 revolver produced from 1875 to 1889.
Factory Engraved Model $600.00
In nickel 710.00

MODEL 1890 REMINGTON POLICE
$470.00   ($560.00 in Nickel)

SPECIFICATIONS
Calibers: 44-40, 45 Long Colt and 357 Magnum. **Barrel length:** 5¾". **Finish:** Blue or nickel. **Features:** Original design (1891–1894) with lanyard ring in buttstock; casehardened frame; walnut grips.
Engraved Model $620.00
In nickel 725.00

ERMA TARGET ARMS

MODEL 777 SPORTING REVOLVER

SPECIFICATIONS
Caliber: 357 Magnum
Capacity: 6 cartridges
Barrel length: 4″ and 5½″
Overall length: 9.7″ and 11.3″
Weight: 43.7 oz. w/5½″ barrel
Sight radius: 6.4″ and 8″
Grip: Checkered walnut
Price: $1200.00

Also available:
MODEL 773 MATCH (32 S&W Wadcutter). Same specifications as Model 777 (5½″ barrel), but with adjustable match grip and 6″ barrel. **Weight:** 47.3 oz. $1345.00
MODEL 772 MATCH (22 LR). Same specifications as Model 773, except weight is 47¼ oz. $1345.00
Both Match revolvers feature micrometer rear sights (adjustable for windage and elevation), interchangeable front and rear sight blades, adjustable triggers, polished blue finish and 6-shot capacity.

MODEL 777

MODEL 777
(With Match Grip)

MODEL ESP 85

MODEL ESP 85 SPORTING PISTOL

SPECIFICATIONS
Caliber: 22 LR or 32 S&W Wadcutter (interchangeable)
Action: Semiautomatic
Capacity: 5 cartridges (8 in 22 LR optional)
Barrel length: 6″
Overall length: 10″
Weight: 40 oz.
Sight radius: 7.8″
Sights: Micrometer rear sight; fully adjustable interchangeable front and rear sight blade (3.5mm/4.0mm)
Grip: Checkered walnut grip with thumbrest

Prices:
ESP 85A SPORTING 22 LR	**$1228.00**
Chrome slide (22 LR only), **add**	165.00
In 32 S&W	1284.00
Target adjustable grip, **add**	169.50
Left hand, **add**	199.00
ESP 85A MATCH 22 LR	1345.00
Left hand	1375.00
ESP 85A CHROME MATCH 22 LR	1568.00
In 32 S&W	1400.00
Conversion Units 22 LR	689.00
In 32 S&W	746.00

FREEDOM ARMS

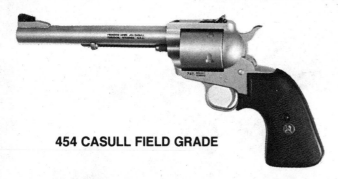

454 CASULL FIELD GRADE

**MODEL 353 REVOLVER
FIELD GRADE 7½" BARREL**

MODEL 353

454 CASULL PREMIER & FIELD GRADES

SPECIFICATIONS
Calibers: 454 Casull, 44 Rem. Mag.
Action: Single action
Capacity: 5 rounds
Barrel lengths: 4¾", 6", 7½", 10"
Overall length: 14" (w/7½" barrel)
Weight: 3 lbs. 2 oz. (w/7½" barrel)
Safety: Patented sliding bar
Sights: Notched rear; blade front (optional adjustable rear and replaceable front blade)
Grips: Impregnated hardwood
Finish: Brushed stainless
Features: Patented interchangeable forcing cone bushing (optional); Bo-Mar silhouette, Millett competition and express sights are optional; SSK T'SOB 3-ring scope mount optional

Prices:
MODEL FA-454AS (Premier Grade)
W/adjustable sights **$1340.00**
W/fixed sights (7½" barrel only) **1263.00**
No sight model (7½" barrel only), drilled
   and tapped for scope base **1245.00**
44 Remington w/adjustable sights
   (7½" or 10" barrel only) **1340.00**
MODEL FA-454FGAS (Field Grade)
With stainless steel matte finish, adj. sight,
   Pachmayr presentation grips **1063.00**
W/fixed sights (4¾" barrel only) **1000.00**
44 Remington w/adjustable sights
   (7½" or 10" barrel only) **1063.00**
MODEL FA-454ASM U.S. Deputy Marshall
With adj. sights (3" barrel only) **1509.00**
With fixed sights **1432.00**
HUNTER PAKS available: **$1342.15 to $1558.45**

SPECIFICATIONS
Caliber: 357 Magnum
Action: Single action
Capacity: 5 shots
Barrel lengths: 7½", 9"
Sights: Removable front blade; adjustable rear
Grips: Pachmayr Presentation grips (Premier Grade has impregnated hardwood grips
Finish: Non-glare Field Grade (standard model); Premier Grade finish (all stainless steel)
Prices:
Field Grade **$1063.00**
Premier Grade **1340.00**

**MODEL 252 REVOLVER
SILHOUETTE CLASS 10" BARREL**

MODEL 252

SPECIFICATIONS
Caliber: 22 LR (optional 22 Magnum cylinder)
Barrel lengths: 7½" (Varmint Class) and 10" (Silhouette Class)
Sights: Silhouette competition sights (Silhouette Class); adjustable rear express sight; removable front express blade
Grips: Black micarta (Silhouette Class); black and green laminated hardwood (Varmint Class)
Finish: Stainless steel
Features: Dual firing pin; lightened hammer; pre-set trigger stop; accepts all sights and/or scope mounts
Prices:
Silhouette Class **$1295.00**
Varmint Class **1248.00**

SILHOUETTE AND COMPETITION MODELS
(not shown)

SPECIFICATIONS
Calibers: 22 LR (Model 252), 357 Magnum, 44 Rem. Mag., 454 Casull
Barrel lengths: 9" (357 Mag.), 10" (22 LR, 44 Rem. Mag., 454 Casull)
Sights: Adjustable ISGW rear sight; removable Patridge front blade

Grips: Pachmayr Presentation (black micarta in 22 LR)
Trigger: Pre-set stop; trigger overtravel screw
Finish: Matte
Prices:
357 Mag., 44 Rem. Mag., 454 Casull **$1131.95**
22 LR **1295.00**

Get SHOOTING TIMES and get everything you need to know about handguns, rifles, shotguns and more!

- The most in-depth gun reviews anywhere, from the world's top gun experts
- Tips on reloading that will help you save money and improve performance
- Article after article on hunting, metallic silhouette, IPSC, target shooting, plinking
- News on accessories, scopes, reloading equipment, hunting gear and more
- Answers to your questions, law updates, gunsmithing how-to's, and "gun buff" news

Send for your FREE trial issue today!

1/2 PRICE DEAL!

Get your biggest savings ever on the best gun magazine around. It all starts with your FREE trial issue!

etach this card and mail today!

Get it all only in

Exclusive gun reviews Take an exclusive first look at the newest guns on the market. Plus get specs on new models and the lowdown on how old favorites perform.

Ammunition Learn which powder works best with which caliber…if casting your own bullets is the way to go…which reloading press is best for you…and lots more.

Hunting & shooting how-to's Discover a wealth of tips and expert advice sure to make your sport more fun, more exciting, or just more enjoyable.

The best gun writers in the business Get your shooting sports know-how from the best — from American Handgunner Award Winner Bill Jordan to noted rifleman Rick Jamison.

SHOOTING TIMES brings you 12 big issues a year including…

- Special February Reloading Issue
- Special March Handgun Issue
- Special September Rifle/Handgun Hunting Issue

Compare SHOOTING TIMES to any gun magazine. You'll quickly discover that it is the most info-loaded resource for anyone who enjoys the shooting sports.

Send for your free trial issue today!

GLOCK PISTOLS

MODEL 17

MODEL 17L COMPETITION

MODEL 17
$579.95

SPECIFICATIONS
Caliber: 9mm Parabellum
Magazine capacity: 17 rounds (19 rounds optional)
Barrel length: 4½″ hexagonal profile with right-hand twist
Overall length: 7.21″
Weight: 22 oz. (without magazine)
Sights: Fixed or adjustable rear sights
Also available: **MODEL 22** (Sport and Service models) in 40 S&W. **Overall length:** 7.4″. **Capacity:** 15 rounds. **Price:** $579.95.

MODEL 17L COMPETITION
$963.15

SPECIFICATIONS
Caliber: 9mm Parabellum
Magazine capacity: 17 rounds
Barrel length: 6.02″
Overall length: 8.77″
Weight: 23.35 oz. (without magazine)
Sights: Fixed or adjustable rear sights

MODEL 19 COMPACT

MODEL 20

MODEL 19 COMPACT
$579.95

SPECIFICATIONS
Caliber: 9mm Parabellum
Magazine capacity: 15 rounds
Barrel length: 4″
Overrall length: 6.74″
Weight: 21 oz. (without magazine)
Sights: Fixed or adjustable rear sights

Also available: **MODEL 23** (Compact Sport and Service models) in 40 S&W. **Overall length:** 6.97″. **Capacity:** 13 rounds. **Price:** $579.95.

MODEL 20
$638.49

SPECIFICATIONS
Caliber: 10mm
Magazine capacity: 15 rounds
Action: Double action
Barrel length: 4.6″
Overall length: 8.27″
Height: 5.2″ (w/sights)
Weight: 27.55 oz. (empty)
Sights: Fixed or adjustable
Features: 3 safeties, "safe action" system, polymer frame
Also available: **MODEL 21** in 45 ACP (13 round capacity). **Price:** $638.49.

GRENDEL PISTOLS

MODEL P-30
$225.00   ($250.00 in Nickel)

SPECIFICATIONS
Caliber: 22 WRF Magnum
Capacity: 30 rounds
Barrel length: 5″
Overall length: 8½″
Weight: 21 oz. (empty)
Sight radius: 7.2″
Features: Fixed barrel, flat trajectory, low recoil, ambidextrous safety levers, front sight adjustable for windage.
Also available: **Model P-30M** (w/removable muzzle brake); **barrel length: 5.6″; overall length: 10″. Price: $235.00 ($260.00** in Nickel)

MODEL P-30

MODEL P-12
$175.00   ($195.00 in Nickel)

SPECIFICATIONS
Caliber: 380 ACP
Capacity: 12 rounds
Barrel length: 3″
Overall length: 5.3″
Weight: 13 oz. (empty)
Sight radius: 4½″
Features: Low inertia safety hammer system; glass reinforced Zytel magazine; solid steel slide w/firing pin and extractor; polymer DuPont ST-800 grip

MODEL P-12

HARRINGTON & RICHARDSON

SPORTSMAN 999 REVOLVER

SPORTSMAN 999 REVOLVER
$229.95

SPECIFICATIONS
Calibers: 22 Short, Long, Long Rifle
Action: Single and double action
Capacity: 9 rounds
Barrel lengths: 4″ and 6″ (both fluted)
Weight: 30 oz. (w/4″ barrel); 34 oz. (w/6″ barrel)
Sights: Windage adjustable rear; elevation adjustable front
Grips: Walnut-finished hardwood
Finish: Blue
Features: Top-break loading with auto shell ejection

HECKLER & KOCH PISTOLS

MODEL P7M8
$999.00 (w/2 mag.)
$1039.00 (Nickel)

MODEL P7M10
$1799.00 (Nickel)
$1659.00 (Blue)

MODEL P7M8 SELF-LOADING PISTOL

SPECIFICATIONS
Caliber: 9mm × 19 (Luger)
Capacity: 8 rounds
Barrel length: 4.13″
Overall length: 6.73″
Weight: 1.75 lbs. (empty)
Sight radius: 5.83″
Sights: Adjustable rear
Also available: **MODEL P7M13** with same barrel length, but slightly longer overall, heavier and 13-round capacity **$1219.00** (**$1259.00** Nickel).

MODEL P7M10

SPECIFICATIONS
Caliber: 40 S&W
Capacity: 10 rounds
Barrel length: 4.13″
Overall length: 6.9″
Weight: 2.69 lbs. (empty)
Sights: Adjustable rear
Operating system: Recoil operated; retarded inertia bolt

MODEL P7K3
$999.00 (w/2 mag.)

MODEL SP89
$1299.00

MODEL P7K3

SPECIFICATIONS
Calibers: 22 LR, 380
Capacity: 8 rounds
Barrel length: 3.8″
Overall length: 6.3″
Weight: 1.65 lbs. (empty)
Sight radius: 5.5″
Sights: Adjustable rear
Also available:
22 LR or 380 Conversion Kit **$524.00**

MODEL SP89

This multi-purpose sporting/security pistol features a rotary-aperture rear sight adjustable for windage and elevation; a hooded front sight; and a shape designed to accept H&K claw-lock mounts for adding a telescopic sight.
SPECIFICATIONS
Caliber: 9mm
Action: Semiautomatic, recoil-operated, delayed roller-locked bolt system
Capacity: 15 rounds
Barrel length: 4 1/2″
Overall length: 13″
Weight: 4.4 lbs.

KBI PISTOLS

MODEL PSP-25

MODEL 941 JERICHO
$649.00 (Full Frame)
$629.00 ("Baby")

MODEL PSP-25
$249.00   ($299.00 Hard Chrome)

SPECIFICATIONS
Caliber: 25 ACP
Barrel length: 2$\frac{1}{8}$"
Overall length: 4$\frac{1}{8}$"
Weight: 9.5 oz. (empty)
Height: 2$\frac{7}{8}$"
Features: Dual safety system; all-steel construction; honed, polished and blued.

SPECIFICATIONS
Calibers: 9mm and 40 S&W
Magazine capacity: 11 shots (40 S&W); 16 shots (9mm)
Barrel length: 4.4"
Rifling: 1 turn in 10" (9mm); 1 turn in 18.5" (40 S&W)
Overall length: 8.8"
Height: 5.5"
Weight: 33 oz.

Also available:
41 AE Conversion Kit (Full Frame only) **$299.00**

FEG MODEL MBK-9HP
$349.00

FEG MODEL PMK-380
$199.00

See the table below for specifications on all FEG pistols imported from Hungary by KBI, including the **MBK-9HPC ($349.00)** and **PJK-9HP ($329.00)**, which are not shown.

Model	Article Number	Caliber	Barrel Length in.	Overall Length in.	Weight Empty oz.	Magazine Capacity
MBK-9HP	GR1031	9mm	4$\frac{2}{3}$"	8"	36	14
MBK-9HPC	GR1082	9mm	4"	7$\frac{1}{3}$"	34	14
PJK-9HP	GR1066	9mm	4$\frac{3}{4}$"	8"	32	13
PMK-380	GR1007	.380 ACP	4"	7"	21	7

L.A.R. GRIZZLY

MARK I
GRIZZLY 45 WIN MAG
$893.00

This semiautomatic pistol is a direct descendant of the tried and trusted 1911-type .45 automatic, but with the added advantage of increased caliber capacity.

SPECIFICATIONS
Calibers: 45 Win. Mag., 45 ACP, 357 Mag., 10mm
Barrel length: 6 1/2"
Overall length: 10 1/2"
Weight (empty): 48 oz.
Height: 5 3/4"
Sights: Fixed, ramped blade (front); fully adjustable for elevation and windage (rear)

Magazine capacity: 6 rounds
Grips: Checkered rubber, nonslip, combat-type
Safeties: Grip depressor, manual thumb, slide-out-of-battery disconnect
Materials: Mil spec 4140 steel slide and receiver with noncorrosive, heat-treated, special alloy steels for other parts
Same model in 357 Magnum **$920.00**
Also available:
Grizzly 44 Magnum Mark 4 w/adj. sights 920.00
Grizzly Win Mag Conversion Units 207.00
Win Mag Compensator 107.00

**GRIZZLY WIN MAG
6 1/2" BARREL**

MARK 4 GRIZZLY 44 MAG.

**GRIZZLY WIN MAG
8" BARREL**

**MARK 4 GRIZZLY 44 MAG
5 1/2" Barrel, Parkerized Finish**

Also available:
Grizzly Win Mag with 8" and 10" barrels in 45 Win. Mag., 357 Magnum, 45 ACP and 357/45 Grizzly Win. Mag.
Model G-WM8 (8" barrel in 45 Win. Mag., 45 ACP or 357/45 Grizzly Win. Mag. **$1313.00**

Model G357M8 (8" barrel in 357 Magnum) **$1337.50**
Model G-WM10 (10" barrel in 45 Win Mag, 45 ACP or 357/45 Grizzly Win. Mag. 1375.00
Model G357M10 (10" barrel in 357 Magnum) 1400.00

LLAMA REVOLVERS

COMANCHE III
357 Mag.
Satin Chrome
4″ and 6″ barrels

LLAMA COMANCHE

IN REVOLVERS TODAY, THERE'S A NEW NAME IN EXCELLENCE: THE LLAMA COMANCHE® SERIES. Designed for you and incorporating every feature worth having to make these Llamas the finest revolvers made today . . . at any price.

The sledgehammer 357 Magnum caliber utilizes massively forged solid-steel frames for tremendous strength and enduring reliability.

Up front, Llama added a precision-bored heavyweight barrel of target quality, complete with a solid shroud to protect the ejector rod, and a raised ventilated-rib that dissipates heat from the barrel to give you a clear, sharp sight image even when the action gets hot.

On the inside, everything is finely fitted and polished, for a double action that's slick and smooth, and a single-action trigger pull that's light, crisp and clean. Llama gave all Comanches a floating firing pin for greater safety and dependability. The hammer is mounted on an eccentric cam, whose position is controlled by the trigger. Only when the trigger is fully depressed can the firing pin contact the primer.

357 Mag. Standard Blue 4″, 6″ **$339.00**
357 Mag. Satin Chrome 4″, 6″ **395.00**

SPECIFICATIONS COMANCHE III

CALIBERS:	357 Magnum
BARRELL LENGTH:	4 and 6-inch
NUMBER OF SHOTS:	6 shots
FRAME:	Forged high tensile strength steel. Serrated front and back strap.
ACTION:	Double-action.
TRIGGER:	Wide grooved target trigger
HAMMER:	Wide spur target hammer with serrated gripping surface.
SIGHTS:	Square notch rear sight with windage and elevation adjustments; serrated quick-draw front sight on ramp.
SIGHT RADIUS:	With 4-inch barrel—5³/₄″; and 6-inch barrel—7³/₄″.
GRIPS:	Oversized target, walnut. Checkered.
WEIGHT:	w/4″ bbl.—2 lbs., 4 ozs. w/6″ bbl.—2 lbs. 7 ozs.
OVER-ALL LENGTH:	With 4-inch barrel—9¹/₄″; with 6-inch barrel—11″.
FINISH:	High-polished, deep blue. Deluxe models, satin chrome (.357 w/4″ & 6″ bbl.)
SAFETY FEATURE:	The hammer is mounted on an eccentric cam, the position of which is controlled by the trigger. Only when the latter is fully depressed can the firing pin contact the primer.

LLAMA REVOLVERS

SUPER COMANCHE IV
44 Magnum $440.00
Available in 6″ and 8½″ barrels

LLAMA SUPER COMANCHE 44 MAGNUM

If ever a handgun was conceived, designed and built to fit the requirements of big bore handgunners, this one is it. The frame, for example, is massive. The weight and balance are such that the heavy recoil generated by the powerful .44 Magnum cartridge is easily and comfortably controlled.

Instead of a single cylinder latch, the Llama has two. In addition to the conventional center pin at the rear of the ratchet, there's a second latch up front that locks the crane to the frame, resulting in a safer, more secure lockup. The hammer is mounted on an eccentric cam, the position of which is controlled by the trigger. Only when the trigger is fully depressed can the firing pin contact the primer.

To minimize leading and to enhance accuracy, Llama has perfected a new honing process that imparts a mirror-smooth finish to the bore.

Additional features include a precision-lapped, heavyweight bull barrel with target accuracy. A matte finish, ventilated rib for more efficient heat dissipation, less glare and less target mirage. Oversized grips that soak up recoil for better control and a faster recovery for a second shot. A super-wide trigger for a more comfortable, controlled pull.

A three-point crane/cylinder provides support for a stronger, more rigid lockup.

The finish is highly polished and deeply blued with genuine walnut grips.

SPECIFICATIONS

	Super Comanche .44 Mag.	
Type:	Double action	
Calibers:	.44 Magnum	
Barrel Length:	6″	8½″
Number of Shots:	6	
Frame:	Forged high tensile strength steel.	
Trigger:	Smooth extra wide	
Hammer:	Wide spur, deep positive serrations.	
Sights:	Rear-click adjustable for windage and elevation, leaf serrated to cut down on glare. Front-ramped blade.	
Sight Radius:	8″	10³/₈″
Grips:	Oversized target, walnut. Checkered.	
Weight:	3 lbs., 2 ozs.	3 lbs., 8 ozs.
Overall Length:	11³/₄″	14½″
Finish:	High polished, deep blue	

LLAMA AUTOMATIC PISTOLS

Llama's newest 9mm single action is a compact version of its 9mm semi-auto, a gun which over the years has earned the kind of trust that has made it the issue side arm of countless military and law enforcement agencies throughout the world. It is also available in 45 and 38 Super calibers.

The small-frame Llama models, available in 22 LR, 32 and 380 Auto, are impressively compact handguns. All frames are precision machined of high strength steel, yet weigh a featherlight 23 ounces. In addition, two safeties, a thumb side lever and grip are incorporated into this Llama.

Every small-frame Llama offers a wide-spur serrated target-type hammer and adjustable rear sight.

The large-frame Llama models, available in potent 45 ACP, are completely crafted of high strength steel.

**9mm PARABELLUM
STANDARD BLUE
$385.00**

**LLAMA COMPACT 45 & 38 SUPER
$385.00**

**LLAMA SMALL-FRAME
AUTOMATIC WITH
DEEP BLUE FINISH
22, 32 and 380 Caliber
$325.00**

LLAMA AUTOMATIC PISTOLS

**LLAMA SMALL-FRAME
AUTOMATIC PISTOL IN
SATIN CHROME FINISH
22 and 380 Caliber
$399.00**

LLAMA AUTOMATIC PISTOL SPECIFICATIONS

TYPE:	SMALL FRAME AUTO PISTOLS			COMPACT FRAME AUTO PISTOLS			LARGE FRAME AUTO PISTOLS
CALIBERS:	22 LR	32	380 Auto	9mm Parabellum	38 Super	45 Auto	45 Auto
FRAME:	Precision machined from high-strength steel. Serrated front strap, checkered (curved) backstrap.			Precision machined from high-strength steel. Serrated front strap, checkered (curved) backstrap.			Precision machined from high-strength steel. Plain front strap, checkered (curved) backstrap.
TRIGGER:	Serrated			Serrated			Serrated
HAMMER:	External. Wide spur, serrated.			External. Wide spur, serrated.			External. Wide spur, serrated.
OPERATION:	Straight blow-back.			Locked breech.			Locked breech.
LOADED CHAMBER INDICATOR:	No	Yes	Yes	No	No	No	Yes
SAFETIES:	Side lever thumb safety, grip safety.			Side lever thumb safety, grip safety.			Side lever thumb safety, grip safety.
GRIPS:	Modified thumbrest black plastic grips.			Matte black polymer.			Matte black polymer.
SIGHTS:	Square notch rear, and Patridge-type front, adjustable rear sight for windage			Square notch rear, and Patridge-type front, adjustable rear sight for windage.			Square notch rear, and Patridge-type front, adjustable rear sight for windage
SIGHT RADIUS:	4 1/4"			6 1/4"			6 1/4"
MAGAZINE CAPACITY:	8-shot	7-shot	7-shot	9-shot	8-shot	7-shot	7-shot
WEIGHT:	23 ounces			34 ounces			36 ounces
BARREL LENGTH:	3 11/16"			5"			5"
OVERALL LENGTH:	6 1/2"			7 7/8"			8 1/2"
HEIGHT:	4 3/8"			5 7/16"			5 1/3"
FINISH:	Std. models: High-polished, deep blue. Deluxe models: Satin chrome (22 & 380 Auto) Duo-Tone (380 Auto)			Std. models: High-polished, deep blue. Deluxe models: Satin chrome (9mm & 45 Auto) Duo-Tone (9mm & 45 Auto)			Std. models: High-polished, deep blue. Deluxe models: Satin chrome (45) Duo-Tone (45 Auto)

LLAMA AUTOMATIC PISTOLS

Machined and polished to perfection. These truly magnificent firearms offer a wide-spur checkered target-type hammer, windage adjustable rear sight and black polymer grips.

In addition to High Polished Deep Blue, the following superb handguns are available in handsome Satin Chrome 22 LR, 380 Auto, 9mm and 45 ACP.

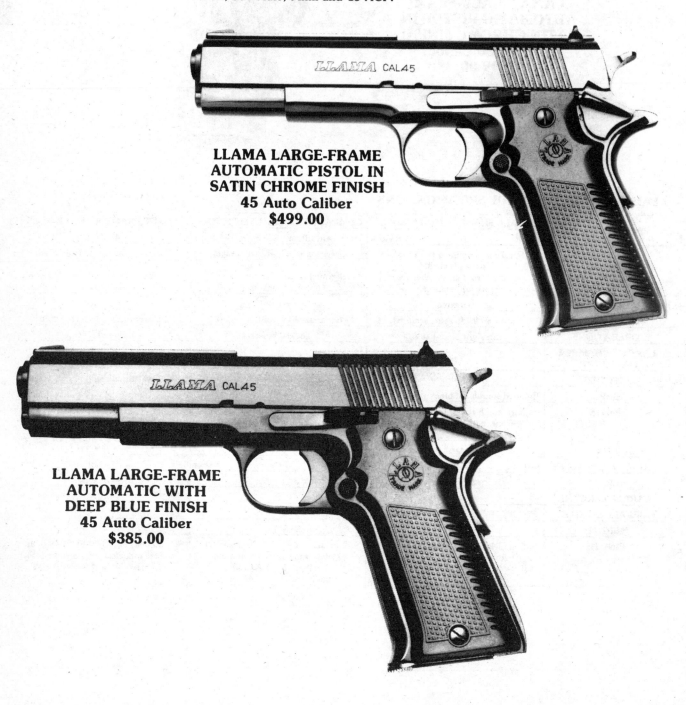

**LLAMA LARGE-FRAME
AUTOMATIC PISTOL IN
SATIN CHROME FINISH**
45 Auto Caliber
$499.00

**LLAMA LARGE-FRAME
AUTOMATIC WITH
DEEP BLUE FINISH**
45 Auto Caliber
$385.00

LLAMA PISTOLS

MODEL M-82
9mm DOUBLE ACTION
$975.00

SPECIFICATIONS
Caliber: 9mm Parabellum
Magazine: 15 cartridges (15 + 1 shot)
Barrel length: 4¼″
No. of barreling grooves: 6
Overall length: 8″
Height: 5⁵⁄₁₆″
Maximum width: 1³⁄₈″
Weight: 39 oz. (empty)
Sights: High visibility, 3-dot sights; rear sight drift adj.
Sight radius: 6″
Grips: Matte black polymer
Stocks: Plastic
Finish: Blued satin

After nearly a decade of research, development and testing, the new Llama M-82 is being offered to the gun buying public. Representing the state-of-the-art in double action, semiauto pistol design, this handgun offers a unique blend of highly innovative technical features, combined with the kind of ergonomic design and practical performance that are so important in day-to-day use. It's the kind demanded by military and law enforcement personnel, as well as by competitive combat shooters and otherwise knowledgeable handgunners.

Whatever criteria are used in judging a DA semiauto—whether accuracy, reliability, simplicity of design, looks, compactness, quality of fit, or finish—all are effectively combined in the M-82. The following features indicate why pistol experts are already hailing this new Llama as the world's finest production combat handgun.

1. MINIMAL BARREL/SLIDE DISPLACEMENT: As the slide moves rearward during the firing cycle, the lineal displacement required to unlock the action is but a fraction of that in other double action designs. This translates into less wear and tear on the mechanism, as well as allowing tighter tolerances. That, in turn, means greater accuracy, greater durability.

2. POSITIVE SAFETY MECHANISM: Even when at rest and with the safety disengaged, the hammer does not contact the firing pin, making this gun one of the safest handguns available today.

3. TWIN LUG LOCK-UP: Unlike other DA's, which rely on a single locking lug engagement in the ceiling of the slide, the M-82 has two lugs in the "three and nine o'clock" position. This unique system provides greater strength, greater rigidity. . . . and greater accuracy.

4. FULL-LENGTH GUIDE RAILS: For more positive, accurate alignment of barrel, slide and frame, the Llama's slide is engaged by guide rails the entire length of its movement (some autos allow as much as two inches of unsupported slide movement).

5. MAXIMUM FIREPOWER: The M-82's staggered magazine holds 15 rounds, plus one in the chamber. This potent firepower is made possible by an overall grip dimension small enough to fit comfortably in the average hand.

6. RECESSED BREECH FACE: Unlike other guns featuring flat breech faces, the Llama's is recessed, much like most modern high-powered rifles. This additional support in the critical case head area means greater safety.

7. AMBIDEXTROUS SAFETY: Allows the M-82 to be used with equal speed and convenience by both right- and left-handed shooters.

8. CHANGEABLE MAGAZINE RELEASE: Normally positioned on the left side of the grip for right-handed shooters, the clip release button on the M-82 can be changed easily to the other side for southpaw use.

9. ARTICULATED FIRING PIN: Another excellent Llama feature is its virtually unbreakable firing pin. In fact, it's guaranteed not to break—for life.

10. COMPACT SIZE: Despite its 16-shot capability, the M-82 is neither heavy nor bulky. Its overall dimensions are short—8¼″ in length, 5 ⁵⁄₆″ in height, and 1 ³⁄₈″ in extreme width. Empty weight is 39 ounces.

11. ENLARGED EJECTION PORT: To preclude any sort of ejection problems brought about by variation in loads or in slide velocity, the ejection port is slightly oversize.

12. MODULAR GRIP DESIGN: The hammer strut and main spring are housed in a separate sub-assembly which easily detaches from the frame for routine cleaning and maintenance.

13. INSTANT DISASSEMBLY: The M-82 can be field stripped in less than five seconds—without tools.

LLAMA PISTOLS

LLAMA M-87 COMP PISTOL (9mm)
$1450.00

Llama, located in the heart of the Basque region of Spain, has been manufacturing high-grade quality handguns since 1903 and has recently made a substantial investment in high tech computer-controlled machining centers. This 21st-century hi-tech machinery has enabled the factory to produce the "match ready" LLAMA M-87 Comp pistol designed specifically for the professional shooter. All of the features demanded by the serious competitive shooter are already built into the M-87 so that it is virtually "out-of-the-box" ready for the range.

COMPENSATOR: Full profile • reduces muzzle lift • increased speed to get back "on target" • dual port internal expansion chamber • reduces recoil.
TRIGGER: Clean • crisp • smooth • positive • creep-free • concave, checkered and extended trigger guard.
SAFETIES: Manual thumb safety allows for quick release • oversized and extended lever for speed • conventional hammer block safety with ambidextrous (dual) levers.
MAGAZINE: 15 rounds • ambidextrous magazine release button is oversized and extended • tapered top allows for quick insertion • bumper pad ensures positive seating • pad also minimizes damage from dropping while rapid firing.

FRAME: Investment casting from Llama's state-of-the-art investment casting factory • beavertail extension for greater hand control and comfort • magazine well flared and beveled, providing for rapid magazine insertion.
SIGHTS: Low-profile combat sights • rapid target acquisition.
TILTING-BLOCK LOCK-UP MECHANISM: Operates "in line" with the barrel • eliminates downward drop to unlock • no separate barrel bushing, which in turn provides a more solid and stable enclosure at the muzzle for greater accuracy.

SPECIFICATIONS
Caliber: 9mm double action
Capacity: 15 round magazine plus 1 in the chamber
Finish: Satin-nickel finish frame: matte black grip panels, operating levers, slide and compensator
Front sights: Low-profile combat; micrometer click; adjustable for windage
Grips: 2-piece polymer
Barrel length: 5 1/4″
Overall length: 9 1/2″
Weight: 40 oz.

LLAMA PISTOLS
DUO-TONE FINISH

LLAMA DUO-TONE LARGE FRAME 45 CALIBER AUTOMATIC
$475.00

New and potent. That describes Llama's latest offering for its large-frame 45 caliber automatic. The high-luster deep blued finish combined with a rich satin chrome finish offers a very distinctive appearance. In addition, this fine firearm offers a matte rib for maximum heat dissipation, a wide-spur serrated target-type hammer, adjustable rear sight and polymer black high-impact grips.

LLAMA DUO-TONE COMPACT FRAME 9mm AUTOMATIC
$475.00

The combination of high-luster blue with soft satin chrome provides an extraordinary finish and appearance to this fine handgun. Features include a matte rib, wide-spur serrated target-type hammer and dense black high-impact grips.

LLAMA DUO-TONE SMALL FRAME 380 CALIBER AUTOMATIC
$385.00

New from Llama is this impressive handgun that attractively combines deep luster blue and satin chrome finishes. The frame is precision machined of high-strength steel, yet weighs a feather-light 23 ounces. Incorporated into the firearm is a thumb side lever and grip safety. Additional features: matte rib, wide-spur serrated target-type hammer and adjustable rear sight for windage.

MAGNUM RESEARCH

DESERT EAGLE PISTOLS

SPECIFICATIONS	357 MAGNUM	41/44 MAGNUM
Length, with 6-inch barrel	10.6 inches	10.6 inches
Height	5.6 inches	5.7 inches
Width	1.25 inches	1.25 inches
Trigger reach	2.75 inches	2.75 inches
Sight radius (wh 6-inch barrel)	8.5 inches	8.5 inches
Additional available barrels	14 inch	14 inch & 10 inch
Weight	See below	See below
Bore rifling — Six rib	Polygonal: 1 turn in 14 inches	Polygonal: 1 turn in 18 inches
Method of operation	Gas operated	Gas operated
Method of locking	Rotating bolt	Rotating bolt
Magazine capacity	9 rounds (plus one in chamber)	8 rounds (plus one in chamber)

**DESERT EAGLE MARK I
(10″ Barrel)**

DESERT EAGLE PISTOLS

357 MAGNUM
$789.00 Standard Parkerized
    Finish (6″ Barrel)
  839.00 Stainless Steel (6″)
  939.00 Standard (10″ barrel)
  989.00 Stainless (10″ barrel)
  949.00 Standard (14″ barrel)
  999.00 Stainless (14″ barrel)

41 MAGNUM (6″ & 14″ Barrels)
$799.00 Std. Parkerized Finish
  849.00 Stainless Steel

44 MAGNUM (6″, 10″, 14″ Barrels)
$ 839.00 Standard Parkerized Finish
  889.00 Stainless Steel (6″ Barrel)
  979.00 Standard (10″ Barrel)
1019.00 Stainless (10″ Barrel)
  989.00 Standard (14″ Barrel)
1029.00 Stainless (14″ Barrel)
  839.00 Alloy Frame

Also available:
50 MAGNUM ACTION EXPRESS
$1189.00

DESERT EAGLE — WEIGHT TABLES
357 Magnum

Frame	Without Magazine		With Empty Magazine	
	6″ Barrel	14″ Barrel	6″ Barrel	14″ Barrel
	ounces	ounces	ounces	ounces
Aluminum	47.8	55.0	51.9	59.1
Steel	58.3	65.5	62.4	96.6
Stainless	58.3	65.5	62.4	69.6

41/44 Magnum

Frame	Without Magazine		With Empty Magazine	
	6″ Barrel	14″ Barrel	6″ Barrel	14″ Barrel
	ounces	ounces	ounces	ounces
Aluminum	52.3	61.0	56.4	65.1
Steel	62.8	71.5	66.9	75.6
Stainless	62.8	71.5	66.9	75.6

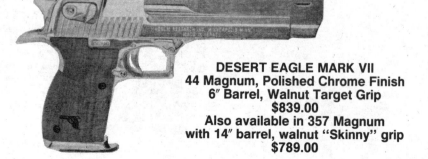

DESERT EAGLE MARK VII
44 Magnum, Polished Chrome Finish
6″ Barrel, Walnut Target Grip
$839.00
Also available in 357 Magnum
with 14″ barrel, walnut "Skinny" grip
$789.00

MAGNUM RESEARCH

MOUNTAIN EAGLE
$199.00

This affordable, lightweight triangular barreled pistol with minimum recoil is ideal for plinkers, target shooters and varmint hunters. The barrel is made of hybrid injection-molded polymer and steel, and the standard 15-round magazine is made of high-grade, semi-transparent polycarbonate resin. It uses a constant force spring to load all 15 rounds easily. The receiver is made of machined T-6 alloy.

SPECIFICATIONS
Caliber: 22 LR
Barrel length: 6½"
Overall length: 10.6"
Weight: 21 oz.
Sights: Standard orange in front, black in rear (adjustable for windage and elevation
Grip: One-piece injection-molded, checkered conventional contour side panels, horizontally textured front and back panels

BABY EAGLE
$569.00

SPECIFICATIONS
Calibers: 9mm, 40 S&W, 41 AE
Capacity: 10 rounds (40 S&W), 11 rounds (41 AE), 16 rounds (9mm)
Barrel length: 4.72"
Overall length: 8.14"
Weight: 35.37 oz. (empty)
Sights: Combat
Features: Extra-long slide rail; combat-style trigger guard; decocking safety; polygonal rifling; ambidextrous thumb safety; all-steel construction; double action
Also available: Conversion Kit (9mm to 41 AE). **Price: $239.00**

SSP-91 SINGLE SHOT PISTOL

SSP-91 SINGLE SHOT PISTOL
$299.00

This new SSP-91 specialty pistol is designed for hunters, silhouette enthusiasts, long-range target shooters and other marksmen. The pistol can fire 17 different calibers of ammunition, more than any other single-shot pistol. Available with interchangeable 14-inch barreled actions, the gun is accurate and engineered to handle the high internal pressures of centerfire rifle ammunition. The design of the grip and its placement toward the center of the barrel provide the SSP-91 with balance, reduced actual and felt recoil, and a high level of comfort for the shooter. **Calibers:** 22-250, 223 Remington, 22 Hornet, 22 LR, 22 Win. Mag., 243 Rem., 30-30, 30-06 Springfield, 308 Win., 357 Mag., 358 Win., 35 Rem., 44 Mag., 444 Marlin, 6mm Bench Rest 7mm-08, 7mm Bench Rest.

MAUSER PISTOLS

MODEL 80-SA
$416.00

NEW HIGH POWER 9MM PISTOLS

These three new models from Mauser are basic Hi-power designs. Available in caliber 9mm Parabellum only, with blued finish, wooden grips and fixed sights, they are each packaged with an extra magazine and cleaning rod. See specifications in the chart below.

MODEL 90-DA
$467.00

MODEL 90-DAC COMPACT
$502.00

SPECIFICATIONS

	Action	Capacity	Barrel Length	Overall Length	Weight
Model 80-SA	Single	13 rounds	4.67″	8″	31.5 oz.
Model 90-DA	Double	14 rounds	4.67″	8″	35 oz.
Model 90-DAC Compact	Double	14 rounds	4.13″	7.4″	33.25 oz.

MITCHELL ARMS

SINGLE ACTION ARMY REVOLVERS

The Mitchell Arms Single Action Army Model Revolver is a modern version of the original "gun that won the West," adopted by the U.S. Army in 1873. Faithful to the original design, these revolvers—Bat Masterson, Cowboy, U.S. Army and U.S. Cavalry—are made of modern materials and use up-to-date technology.

SPECIFICATIONS
Calibers: 357 Mag., 44 Mag., 45 Colt
Barrel lengths: 4³/₄″, 5¹/₂″, 6¹/₂″ and 7¹/₂″
Frame: Forged steel, fully machined with traditional color casehardening; two-piece style backstrap made of solid brass
Action: Traditional single action with safety position and half-cock position for loading and unloading
Sights: Rear sight is fully adjustable for windage and elevation. Front sight is two-step ramp style with non-glare serrations. Fixed sight models feature deep notch with fixed blade front sight.
Grip: One-piece solid walnut grip built in the style of the old blackpowder revolvers
Accuracy: High-grade steel barrel honed for accuracy with smooth lands and grooves; precise alignment between cylinder and barrel. Fully qualified for big game hunting or silhouette shooting.
Prices:
Fixed and Adjustable Sight Models **$389.00–495.00**

SINGLE ACTION ARMY MODEL
(44 Magnum)
$450.00 (w/Adjustable Sights)

1875 REMINGTON REVOLVER

SINGLE SHOT SHARPSHOOTER (not shown)

SPECIFICATIONS
Calibers: 22 LR, 22 Magnum, 223, 45 Colt and 357 Magnum
Barrel: Half-round, half-octagonal
Grips: Walnut
Sights: Adjustable rear sight, ramp front
Features: Rolling-block action
Price: **$395.00**

PISTOL PARABELLUM '08
THE GERMAN LUGER

SPECIFICATIONS
Caliber: 9mm Parabellum
Barrel length: 4″
Features: Stainless steel frame; American walnut grips; loaded chamber indicator; American Eagle engraving
Price: **$695.00**

1875 AND 1890 REMINGTON REVOLVERS

SPECIFICATIONS
Calibers: 45 Colt, 45 Colt/45 ACP (Interchangeable) and 357 Magnum
Barrel lengths: 5¹/₂″ and 7¹/₂″
Grips: Walnut
Finish: Blue with color case or nickel
Features: Hardened frame; solid brass trigger guard
Prices:
357 Magnum and 45 Colt (7¹/₂″ barrel) **$399.00**
45 Colt (5¹/₂″ barrel). 399.00
45 Colt/45 ACP 450.00
45 Colt Nickel 475.00
45 Colt/45 ACP Nickel 499.00

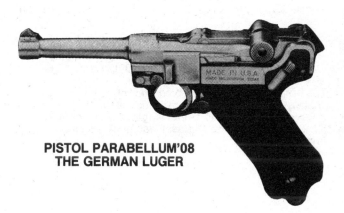

PISTOL PARABELLUM'08
THE GERMAN LUGER

MOA MAXIMUM PISTOL

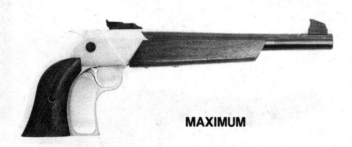

MAXIMUM

MAXIMUM

This single-shot pistol with its unique falling-block action performs like a finely tuned rifle. The single piece receiver of chromoly steel is mated to a Douglas barrel for optimum accuracy and strength.

SPECIFICATIONS
Calibers: 22 Hornet to 358 Win.
Barrel lengths: 8³/₄″, 10¹/₂″ and 14″
Weight: 3 lbs. 8 oz. (8³/₄″ bbl.); 3 lbs. 13 oz. (10¹/₂″ bbl.); 4 lbs. 3 oz. (14″ bbl.)
Prices:
Armoloy receiver, blued barrel **$534.00**
Armoloy receiver, stainless barrel 584.00
Stainless receiver, blued barrel 566.00
Stainless receiver and barrel 616.00

NAVY ARMS REPLICAS

1873 SINGLE ACTION

1873 COLT-STYLE SINGLE ACTION REVOLVERS

The classic 1873 Single Action is the most famous of all the "six shooters." From its adoption by the U.S. Army in 1873 to the present, it still retains its place as America's most popular revolver. **Calibers:** 44-40 or 45 Long Colt. **Barrel lengths:** 3″, 4³/₄″, 5¹/₂″ or 7¹/₂″. **Overall length:** 10³/₄″ (5¹/₂″ barrel). **Weight:** 2¹/₄ lbs. **Sights:** Blade front; notch rear. **Grips:** Walnut.
Prices: . . . . **$325.00 to $410.00**

1873 U.S. CAVALRY MODEL (not shown)

An exact replica of the original U.S. Government issue Colt Single Action Army, complete with Arsenal stampings and inspector's cartouche. **Caliber:** 45 Long Colt. **Barrel length:** 7¹/₂″. **Overall length:** 13¼″. **Weight:** 2 lbs. 7 oz. **Sights:** Blade front; notch rear. **Grips:** Walnut.
Price: $495.00

1895 U.S. ARTILLERY MODEL (not shown)

Same specifications as the U.S. Cavalry Model, but with a 5¹/₂″ barrel as issued to Artillery units. **Caliber:** 45 Long Colt.
Price: $495.00

TT-OLYMPIA PISTOL

TT-OLYMPIA PISTOL

The TT-Olympia is a faithful reproduction of the famous Walther .22 target pistol that won the gold medal at the 1936 Olympics in Berlin. **Caliber:** 22 LR. **Barrel length:** 4⁵/₈″. **Overall length:** 8″. **Weight:** 1 lb. 11 oz. **Sights:** Blade front; adjustable rear.
Price: $300.00

NEW ENGLAND FIREARMS

STANDARD REVOLVER
$119.95 ($129.95 in Nickel)

SPECIFICATIONS
Calibers: 22 S, L or LR
Capacity: 9 shots
Barrel lengths: 2¹/₂" and 4"
Overall length: 7" (2¹/₂" barrel) and 8¹/₂" (4" barrel)
Weight: 25 oz. (2¹/₂" bbl.) and 2. (4" bbl.)
Sights: Blade front; fixed rear
Grips: American hardwood, walnut finish
Finish: Blue or nickel
Also available in 5-shot 32 H&R Mag. $114.95 (Blue)

STANDARD MODEL
(22 LR, 2¹/₂" Barrel)

ULTRA MAG.

ULTRA MODEL (6" Barrel)

ULTRA AND ULTRA MAG. REVOLVERS
$149.95

SPECIFICATIONS
Calibers: 22 LR, 22 Win. Mag. and 32 H&R Mag.
Capacity: 9 shots (22 LR); 6 shots (22 Win. Mag.,); 5 shots
   (32 H&R Mag.)
Barrel lengths: 3" and 6"
Overall length: 7⁵/₈" (3" barrel) and 10⁵/₈" (6" barrel)
Weight: 31 oz. (3" bbl.); 36 oz. (6" bbl.)
Sights: Blade on rib front; fully adjustable rear
Grips: American hardwood, walnut finish
Also available:
LADY ULTRA in 5-shot 32 H&R Magnum. **Barrel length:** 3".
   Overall length: 7¹/₂". **Price:** $149.95

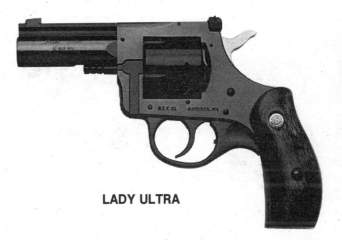

LADY ULTRA

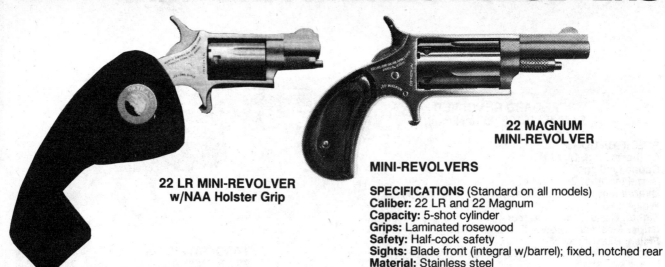

**22 LR MINI-REVOLVER
w/NAA Holster Grip**

**22 MAGNUM
MINI-REVOLVER**

MINI-REVOLVERS

SPECIFICATIONS (Standard on all models)
Caliber: 22 LR and 22 Magnum
Capacity: 5-shot cylinder
Grips: Laminated rosewood
Safety: Half-cock safety
Sights: Blade front (integral w/barrel); fixed, notched rear
Material: Stainless steel
Finish: Matte with brushed sides

SPECIFICATIONS: MINI-REVOLVERS & MINI-MASTER SERIES

Model	Weight	Barrel Length	Overall Length	Overall Height	Overall Width	Prices
NAA-MMT-M	10.7 oz.	4″	7³/₄″	3⁷/₈″	⁷/₈″	$265.50
NAA-MMT-L	10.7 oz.	4″	7³/₄″	3⁷/₈″	⁷/₈″	265.50
*NAA-BW-M	8.8 oz.	2″	5⁷/₈″	3⁷/₈″	⁷/₈″	223.50
*NAA-BW-L	8.8 oz.	2″	5⁷/₈″	3⁷/₈″	⁷/₈″	223.50
NAA-22LR	4.5 oz.	1¹/₈″	4¹/₄″	2³/₈″	¹³/₁₆″	162.50
NAA-22LLR	4.6 oz.	1⁵/₈″	4³/₄″	2³/₈	¹³/₁₆″	162.50
*NAA-22MS	5.9 oz.	1¹/₈″	5″	2⁷/₈″	⁷/₈″	182.50
*NAA-22M	6.2 oz.	1⁵/₈″	5³/₈″	2⁷/₈″	⁷/₈″	182.50

* Available with Conversion Cylinder chambered for 22 Long Rifle (**$217.50**).

**MINI-MASTER NAA-MMT-M
(22 Mag. 4″ Barrel)**

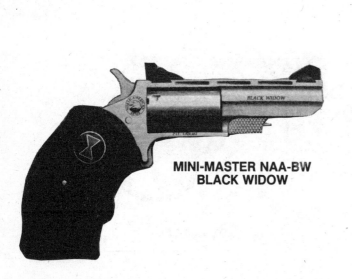

**MINI-MASTER NAA-BW
BLACK WIDOW**

MINI-MASTER SERIES

SPECIFICATIONS (Standard on all models)
Calibers: 22 LR (NAA-MMT-L, NAA-BW-L) and 22 Magnum
   (NAA-MMT-M, NAA-BW-M)
Barrel: Heavy vent
Rifling: 8 land and grooves, 1/12 R.H. button broach twist
Grips: Oversized black rubber
Cylinder: Bull
Sights: Front integral with barrel; rear Millett adjustable white
   outlined (elevation only) or low-profile fixed

QFI-QUALITY FIREARMS REVOLVERS

WESTERN RANGER SINGLE ACTION

SPECIFICATIONS
Caliber: 22 LR or 22 LR/22 Magnum
Capacity: 6 rounds
Barrel lengths: 3¼", 4¾", 6½", 9"
Weight: 31 to 37 oz.
Sights: Blade front
Finish: Blue with gold accents
Features: Smooth walnut grips; rotating hammer block safety
Prices:
22 LR (3¼", 4¾", 6½" barrel). **$104.95**
   With 9" barrel **111.95**
22 Magnum (3¼" barrel only) **134.95**
   With 9" barrel only **139.95**
   With 4¾" or 6½" barrel **119.95**

PLAINS RIDER SINGLE ACTION

SPECIFICATIONS
Calibers: 22 Short, Long, Long Rifle or 22 Magnum
Capacity: 6 rounds
Barrel length: 3¼", 4¾", 6½", 9"
Weight: 28 oz. (3¼" bbl.); 32 oz. (6½" bbl.)
Finish: Blue with ebony nylon grips
Sights: Blade front, fixed rear
Features: Floating firing pin, manual shell extraction
Prices:
22 LR . . . . **$ 99.95**
22 LR (9" barrel) **110.95**
22 Magnum **125.95**
22 Magnum (9" barrel) **136.95**
Also available: Convertible models supplied with 22 LR and
   22 Magnum cylinders. **Price: $119.95**

"RP" REVOLVER SERIES
$104.95 – $129.95

SPECIFICATIONS
Calibers: 38 Special, 32 S&W, 32 H&R Magnum, 32 S&W
   Long, 22 LR, 22 LR/22 Magnum
Capacity: 6 rounds
Barrel length: 2" or 4"
Finish: Blue or chrome
Features: Checkered composition grips; internal hammer block
   safety; additional safety plug in cylinder

QFI-QUALITY FIREARMS PISTOLS

VICTORY MC5
$465.00

SPECIFICATIONS
Calibers: 9×19 Parabellum (Luger), 38 Super, 40 S&W, 10mm, 45 ACP
Capacity: 10 + 1 (45 ACP); 12 + 1 (40 S&W & 10mm); 15 + 1 (9mm Para, 38 Super)
Barrel lengths: 4½″, 5⅞″, 7½″
Overall length: 8½″ (4½″ barrel)
Weight: 45 oz. (empty, 9mm Para.)
Sights: Patridge high-visibility ramp sight, adjustable for elevation (interchangeable blades)
Finish: Service matte black; custom high-luster blue
Features: Push-button ambidextrous magazine catch; ambidextrous CM5 multi-function safety catch; loaded chamber indicator; high-impact plastic grip panels; manual decocking; automatic safeties
Also available: **Conversion Kits: $180.00**

MODEL SA25 SEMIAUTOMATIC
$54.95

SPECIFICATIONS
Caliber: 25 ACP
Barrel length: 2½″
Weight: 12 oz.
Sights: Ramp front, fixed rear
Hammer: Serrated external
Grips: European walnut
Trigger lock: Thumb operated
Also available: $ 64.95 Dyna-Chrome
154.95 Titan Tigress (Ladies' Pistol)

MODEL 722TP SILHOUETTE PISTOL
$269.95

SPECIFICATIONS
Caliber: 22 LR
Capacity: 10 rounds
Action: Bolt action with adjustable trigger and bolt retainer
Barrel length: 10⅜″ (free floating)
Weight: 3.4 lbs.
Finish: Walnut
Sights: Globe front (insert-type with match post); square-notch rear, fully adjustable

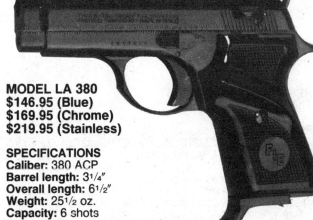

MODEL LA 380
$146.95 (Blue)
$169.95 (Chrome)
$219.95 (Stainless)

SPECIFICATIONS
Caliber: 380 ACP
Barrel length: 3¼″
Overall length: 6½″
Weight: 25½ oz.
Capacity: 6 shots
Finish: Blue
Grip: European walnut
Sights: Integral tapered post front sight; windage adjustable rear sight

REMINGTON LONG-RANGE PISTOLS

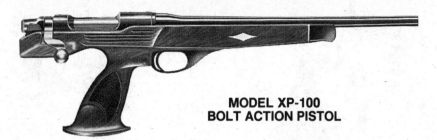

MODEL XP-100
BOLT ACTION PISTOL

MODEL XP-100 SILHOUETTE TARGET AND "VARMINT SPECIAL" PISTOLS

These unique single-shot centerfire, bolt-action pistols have become legends for their strength, precision, balance and accuracy. Chambered for the 35 Rem. and 223 Rem. with a 14½″ barrel, they are also available in 7mm BR, which many feel is the ideal factory-made metallic silhouette handgun for "unlimited" events. All XP-100 handguns have one-piece Du Pont "Zytel" nylon stocks with universal grips, two-position thumb safety switches, receivers drilled and tapped for scope mounts or receiver sights, and match-type grooved triggers.

SPECIFICATIONS
Calibers: 35 Rem., 7mm BR Rem., 223 Rem.
Barrel length: 14½″
Overall length: 21¼″
Weight: 4⅛ lbs.
Prices:
7mm BR Rem. **$427.00**
223 Rem. **419.00**
35 Rem. **441.00**

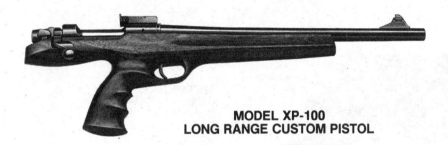

MODEL XP-100
LONG RANGE CUSTOM PISTOL

"XP-100" LONG RANGE CUSTOM PISTOLS

Remington's Model XP-100 Custom pistol is chambered for the 22-250 Rem., 6mm BR Rem., 223 Rem., 250 Savage, 7mm BR, 7mm-08 Rem., 308 Win. and 35 Rem. All XP-100 Custom pistols are hand crafted from select English walnut in right- and left-hand versions. All chamberings except the 35 Rem. (standard barrel only) are offered in a choice of standard

14½″ barrels with adjustable rear leaf and front bead sights or 15½″ barrels without sights. Receivers are drilled and tapped for scope mounts. **Weight** averages 4½ lbs. for standard models and 5½ lbs. for heavy barrel models.

Price: **$945.00**

MODEL XP-100R KS CUSTOM REPEATER
BOLT ACTION CENTERFIRE
**Calibers: 22-250, 223 Rem., 250 Savage,
7mm-08 Rem., 308 Win., 35 Rem., 350 Rem. Mag.
$800.00**

Same specifications as the XP-100, but with Kevlar-reinforced stock and sling swivel studs.

ROSSI REVOLVERS

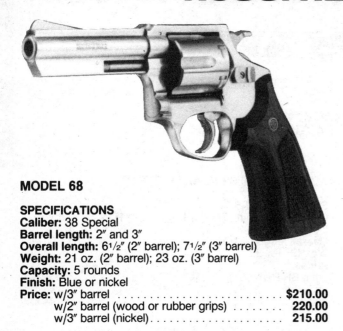

MODEL 68

SPECIFICATIONS
Caliber: 38 Special
Barrel length: 2″ and 3″
Overall length: 6½″ (2″ barrel); 7½″ (3″ barrel)
Weight: 21 oz. (2″ barrel); 23 oz. (3″ barrel)
Capacity: 5 rounds
Finish: Blue or nickel
Price: w/3″ barrel **$210.00**
w/2″ barrel (wood or rubber grips) **220.00**
w/3″ barrel (nickel) **215.00**

MODEL M88
$240.00 (3″ Barrel)
$255.00 (2″ Barrel)

SPECIFICATIONS
Caliber: 38 Special
Barrel length: 2″, 3″
Capacity: 5 rounds, swing-out cylinder
Weight: 21 oz.
Sights: Ramp front, square notch rear adjustable for windage
Finish: Stainless steel

MODEL 720 (not shown)
$310.00

SPECIFICATIONS
Caliber: 44 S&W Special
Capacity: 5 shots
Barrel length: 3″
Overall length: 8″
Weight: 27½ oz.
Sights: Adjustable rear; red insert front
Finish: Stainless steel
Features: Rubber combat grips; full ejector rod shroud

MODEL 971
$263.33 Blue
$298.33 Stainless

SPECIFICATIONS
Caliber: 357 Magnum
Capacity: 6 rounds
Barrel length: 4″ (blue only) and 6″
Overall length: 9″ (blue only), 9³⁄₁₆″, 11³⁄₁₆″
Weight: 35.4 oz., 36 oz. (blue only), 40.5 oz.
Finish: Blue or stainless steel

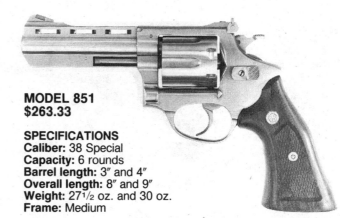

MODEL 515 (not shown)
$248.33

SPECIFICATIONS
Calibers: 22 LR and 22 Magnum
Capacity: 6-shot cylinder
Barrel length: 4″
Overall length: 9″
Weight: 30 oz.
Sights: Fully adjustable square notch rear; red insert front
Finish: Stainless steel
Features: Shrouded ejector rod; checkered custom wood grips; classic kit gun design

MODEL 851
$263.33

SPECIFICATIONS
Caliber: 38 Special
Capacity: 6 rounds
Barrel length: 3″ and 4″
Overall length: 8″ and 9″
Weight: 27½ oz. and 30 oz.
Frame: Medium

RUGER REVOLVERS

ALLOY STEEL REDHAWK

The popular Ruger Redhawk® double-action revolver is available in an alloy steel model with blued finish in 44 Magnum caliber. The newest Redhawk is constructed of hardened chrome-moly and other alloy steels. The revolver is satin polished to a high lustre and finished in a rich blue.

Catalog Number	Caliber	Barrel Length	Overall Length	Approx. Weight (Ounces)	Price
RUGER BLUED REDHAWK REVOLVER					
RH-445	44 Mag.	5½″	11″	52	$458.50
RH-44	44 Mag.	7½″	13″	52	458.50
RH-44R*	44 Mag.	7½″	13″	52	496.50

*Scope model, with Integral Scope Mounts, 1″ Ruger Scope rings.

REDHAWK DOUBLE-ACTION REVOLVER

There is no other revolver like the Ruger Redhawk. Knowledgeable sportsmen reaching for perfection in a big bore revolver will find that the Redhawk demonstrates its superiority at the target, whether silhouette shooting or hunting. The scope sight model incorporates the patented Ruger integral Scope Mounting System with 1″ stainless steel Ruger scope rings.

Catalog Number	Caliber	Barrel Length	Overall Length	Approx. Weight (Ounces)	Price
RUGER STAINLESS REDHAWK REVOLVER					
KRH-445	44 Mag.	5½″	11″	52	$516.75
KRH-44	44 Mag.	7½″	13″	52	516.75
KRH-44R*	44 Mag.	7½″	13″	52	557.25

*Scope model, with Integral Scope Mounts, 1″ Stainless Steel Ruger Scope rings.

SUPER REDHAWK STAINLESS DOUBLE-ACTION REVOLVER

The **Super Redhawk** double-action revolver in stainless steel features a heavy extended frame with 7½″ and 9½″ barrels. Cushioned grip panels contain Goncalo Alves wood grip panel inserts to provide comfortable, nonslip hold. Comes with integral scope mounts and 1″ stainless steel Ruger scope rings.

SPECIFICATIONS
Caliber: 44 Magnum
Barrel length: 7½″ and 9½″
Overall length: 13″ w/7½″ bbl.; 15″ w/9½″ bbl.
Weight (empty): 3 lbs. 5 oz. (7½″ bbl.); 3 lbs. 10 oz. (9½″ bbl.)
Sight radius: 9½″ (7½″ bbl.); 11¼″ (9½″ bbl.)
Finish: Stainless steel; satin polished

KSRH-7 (7½″ barrel) $589.00
KSRH-9 (9½″ barrel) 589.00

RUGER REVOLVERS

BLACKHAWK SINGLE ACTION REVOLVER

SPECIFICATIONS
Caliber: 357 Magnum (interchangeable with 38 Special); 41 Magnum, 45 Long Colt
Barrel lengths: $4^5/8''$ and $6^1/2''$
Frame: Chrome molybdenum steel with bridge reinforcement and rear-sight guard
Springs: Music wire springs throughout
Weight: 40 oz. w/$4^5/8''$ barrel and 42 oz. w/$6^1/2''$ barrel (in 357 Mag.); 38 oz. w/$4^5/8''$ barrel and 40 oz. w/$6^1/2''$ barrel (41 Mag.); 40 oz. w/$4^5/8''$ barrel and 39 oz. w/$7^1/2''$ barrel (45 Long Colt)
Sights: Patridge style, ramp front matted blade $1/8''$ wide; rear sight click adjustable for windage and elevation
Grips: Genuine walnut
Finish: Polished and blued or brushed satin stainless steel (357 Mag. only)

Catalog No./Specifications	Prices
BN-34 357 Mag.; 38 Special interchangeably; $4^5/8''$ barrel	$328.00
KBN-34 Same as BN-34 in stainless steel	404.00
BN-36 357 Mag.; 38 Special interchangeably; $6^1/2''$ barrel	328.00
KBN-36 Same as BN-36 in stainless steel	404.00
BN-34X/36X Same as BN-34/BN-36 fitted with 9mm Parabellum extra cylinder (not available in stainless steel)	343.50
BN-41 41 Magnum; $4^5/8''$ barrel	328.00
BN-42 41 Magnum; $6^1/2''$ barrel	328.00
BN-44 45 Long Colt; $4^5/8''$ barrel, blue	328.00
BN-45 45 Long Colt; $7^1/2''$ barrel, blue	328.00
KBN44 45 Long Colt; $4^5/8''$, $7^1/2''$ bbl., stainless	424.20

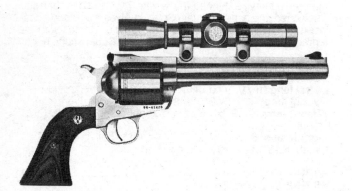

BLACKHAWK SINGLE ACTION REVOLVER
(In 30 Carbine Caliber)
$315.00

SPECIFICATIONS
Caliber: 30 Carbine
Barrel length: $7^1/2''$; 6-groove rifling; 20-inch twist
Overall length: $13^1/8''$
Weight: 44 oz.
Springs: Unbreakable music wire springs used throughout; no leaf springs
Screws: For security, Nylok® screws are used at all five locations that might be affected by recoil
Sights: Patridge-style, ramp front sight with $1/8''$ wide blade, matted to eliminate glare; rear sight adjustable for windage and elevation
Ignition system: Independent alloy steel firing pin, mounted in frame, transfer bar
Frame: Same cylinder frame as 44 Mag. Super Blackhawk
Grips: Genuine walnut
Finish: Polished, blued and anodized

SUPER BLACKHAWK HUNTER REVOLVER
$479.50

Ruger's new Super Blackhawk Hunter revolver combines modern mechanical reliability with the frontier values of strength and simplicity. Mounting a telescopic sight on such guns has always been difficult, because most were not designed to accept scopes. Rib and barrel of the Hunter are machined to accept Ruger one-inch stainless steel scope rings with integral bases supplied with each gun. This model also has metal sights with a front sight blade using interchangeable colored nylon inserts or a steel gold bead and a blued steel rear sight adjustable for windage and elevation.

SPECIFICATIONS
Caliber: 44 Magnum
Capacity: 6 rounds
Barrel length: $7^1/2''$ (with solid full-length rib)
Overall length: $13^1/2''$
Weight: 54 oz. (empty)
Sight radius: $9^1/4''$
Grips: Smooth laminated wood
Finish: Buffed satin

RUGER REVOLVERS

**SUPER BLACKHAWK
SINGLE ACTION REVOLVER**

SUPER BLACKHAWK
SINGLE ACTION REVOLVER

SPECIFICATIONS
Caliber: 44 Magnum; interchangeable with 44 Special
Barrel lengths: 7¹/₂″, 10¹/₂″
Overall length: 13³/₈″
Weight: 48 oz. (7¹/₂″ bbl.) and 51 oz. (10¹/₂″ bbl.)
Frame: Chrome molybdenum steel or stainless steel
Springs: Music wire springs throughout
Sights: Patridge style, ramp front matted blade ¹/₈″ wide; rear sight click and adjustable for windage and elevation
Grip frame: Chrome molybdenum or stainless steel, enlarged and contoured to minimize recoil effect

Trigger: Wide spur, low contour, sharply serrated for convenient cocking with minimum disturbance of grip
Finish: Polished and blued or brushed satin stainless steel

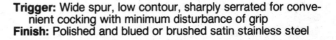

KS45N	5¹/₂″ barrel, stainless steel	$413.75
KS47N	7¹/₂″ barrel, stainless steel	413.75
KS411N	10¹/₂″ barrel, stainless steel	413.75
KSH7NH	7¹/₂″ barrel, scope rings, stainless	479.50
S45N	5¹/₂″ barrel, blued	378.50
S47N	7¹/₂″ barrel, blued	378.50
S411N	10¹/₂″ barrel, blued	378.50

SUPER SINGLE-SIX

SUPER SINGLE-SIX REVOLVER

SPECIFICATIONS
Caliber: 22 LR (fitted with WMR cylinder)
Barrel lengths: 4⁵/₈″, 5¹/₂″, 6¹/₂″, 9¹/₂″; stainless steel model in 5¹/₂″ and 6¹/₂″ lengths only
Weight (approx.): 33 oz. (with 5¹/₂″ barrel)
Sights: Patridge-type ramp front sight; rear sight click adjustable for elevation and windage; protected by integral frame ribs
Finish: Blue or stainless steel
Prices:
In blue $281.00
In stainless steel (convertible 5¹/₂″ and 6¹/₂″ barrels only) 354.00

SINGLE-SIX SSM™ REVOLVER

SINGLE-SIX SSM™ REVOLVER

SPECIFICATIONS
Caliber: 32 H&R Magnum; also handles 32 S&W and 32 S&W Long
Barrel lengths: 4⁵/₈″, 5¹/₂″, 6¹/₂″, 9¹/₂″
Weight (approx.): 34 oz. (with 6¹/₂″ barrel)
Price: $270.00

RUGER REVOLVERS

RUGER SP101
38 Special

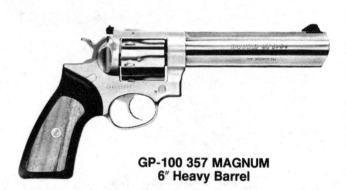

GP-100 357 MAGNUM
6″ Heavy Barrel

MODEL SP101
$408.00

This critically acclaimed small frame SP101 model has added 6-shot capacity in 32 Magnum and 5-shot capacity in 9mm and 357 Magnum.

SPECIFICATIONS

Catalog Number	Caliber	Capacity	Sights	Barrel Length	Approx. Wt. (oz.)
KSP-221	22 LR	6	Adj.	2¼″	32
KSP-240	22 LR	6	Adj.	4″	33
KSP-241	22 LR	6	Adj.	4″	34
KSP-3231	32 Mag.	6	Adj.	3¹/₁₆″	30
KSP-921	9×19mm	5	Fixed	2¼″	25
KSP-931	9×19mm	5	Fixed	3¹/₁₆″	27
KSP-821	38 + P	5	Fixed	2¼″	25
KSP-831	38 + P	5	Fixed	3¹/₁₆″	27
KSP-321	357 Mag.*	5	Fixed	2¼″	25
KSP-331	357 Mag.*	5	Fixed	3¹/₁₆″	27

* Revolvers chambered for the .357 Magnum cartridge also accept the 38 Special cartridge.
Model KSP-240 has short shroud; all others have full.

BISLEY REVOLVER (not shown)

SPECIFICATIONS
Calibers: 357 Mag., 41 Mag., 44 Mag., 45 Long Colt
Barrel length: 7½″
Weight (approx.): 48 oz.
Sights: Adjustable rear sight, ramp-style front sight
Special features: Unfluted cylinder rollmarked with classic foliate engraving pattern (or fluted cylinder without engraving); hammer is low with smoothly curved, deeply checkered wide spur positioned for easy cocking.
Price: **$391.00**

Also available in 22 LR and 32 H&R Mag. Weight: 41 oz.
   Barrel length: 6½″. **Sights:** Adjustable or fixed.
Price: **$328.75**

GP-100 357 MAGNUM

The GP-100 is designed for the unlimited use of 357 Magnum ammunition in all factory loadings; it combines strength and reliability with accuracy and shooting comfort. (Revolvers chambered for the 357 Magnum cartridge also accept the 38 Special cartridge.)

SPECIFICATIONS

Catalog Number	Finish*	Sights†	Shroud††	Barrel Length	Wt. (oz.)	Prices
GP-141	B	A	F	4″	41	$413.50
GP-160	B	A	S	6″	43	413.50
GP-161	B	A	F	6″	46	413.50
GPF-330	B	F	S	3″	35	397.00
GPF-331	B	F	F	3″	36	397.00
GPF-340	B	F	S	4″	37	397.00
GPF-341	B	F	F	4″	38	397.00
KGP-141	S	A	F	4″	41	446.50
KGP-160	S	A	S	6″	43	446.50
KGP-161	S	A	F	6″	46	446.50
KGPF-330	S	F	S	3″	35	430.00
KGPF-331	S	F	F	3″	36	430.00
KGPF-340	S	F	S	4″	37	430.00
KGPF-341	S	F	F	4″	38	430.00
KGPF-830*	S	F	S	3″	35	430.00
KGPF-831*	S	F	F	3″	36	430.00
KGPF-840*	S	F	S	4″	37	430.00
KGPF-841*	S	F	F	4″	38	430.00

* B = blued; S = stainless. † A = adjustable; F = fixed. †† F = full; S = short. * 38 Special only.

RUGER PISTOLS

MODEL P90DAC

MODEL P90 AUTO PISTOL

SPECIFICATIONS
Caliber: 45 Auto
Action: Double action
Capacity: 7 rounds
Barrel length: 4 1/2″
Overall length: 7.84″
Weight: 2.38 lbs. (loaded)
Sight radius: 6.12″
Mechanism type: Recoil-operated, semiautomatic
Breech locking mode: Tilting barrel, link actuated
Sights: Rear drift adjustable for windage
Feature: Ambidextrous decocking levers (KP90DAC)
Prices:
KP90C Stainless steel, safety **$488.65**
KP90DAC Stainless steel, decocker 488.65

MODEL P91 AUTO PISTOL

SPECIFICATIONS
Caliber: 40 Auto
Action: Double action
Capacity: Double column magazine holds 12 rounds
Barrel length: 4 1/2″
Overall length: 7.84″
Weight: 2.38 lbs. (loaded)
Sight radius: 6.12″
Mechanism type: Recoil-operated, semiautomatic
Breech locking mode: Tilting barrel, link actuated
Sights: Rear drift adjustable for windage
Feature: Decocking lever enables the shooter to decock without pulling the trigger
Prices:
KP91DC Stainless steel, decocker **$488.65**
KP91DAO Stainless steel, double action only 488.65

MODEL P91DC

MODEL P85 MARK II AUTO PISTOL

**MODEL P85 MARK II
9mm AUTO PISTOL**

SPECIFICATIONS
Caliber: 9mm
Action: Double action
Capacity: 15 rounds
Barrel length: 4 1/2″
Overall length: 7.84″
Weight: 2.38 lbs. (loaded)
Sight radius: 6.12″
Mechanism type: Recoil-operated, semiautomatic
Breech locking mode: Tilting barrel, link actuated
Sights: Rear adjustable for windage
Prices:
P85CMKII   Blued, safety **$410.00**
P85MKIIDCC   Blued, decocker 410.00
KP85CMKII   Stainless steel, safety 452.00
KP89DCC   Stainless steel, decocker 452.00
KP89DAO   Stainless steel, double action only 452.00

RUGER 22 AUTOMATIC PISTOLS

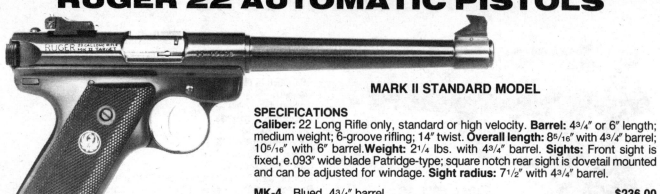

MARK II STANDARD MODEL

SPECIFICATIONS
Caliber: 22 Long Rifle only, standard or high velocity. **Barrel:** 4³/₄" or 6" length; medium weight; 6-groove rifling; 14" twist. **Overall length:** 8⁵/₁₆" with 4³/₄" barrel; 10⁵/₁₆" with 6" barrel. **Weight:** 2¹/₄ lbs. with 4³/₄" barrel. **Sights:** Front sight is fixed, e.093" wide blade Patridge-type; square notch rear sight is dovetail mounted and can be adjusted for windage. **Sight radius:** 7¹/₂" with 4³/₄" barrel.

MK-4	Blued, 4³/₄" barrel	$236.00
MK-6	Blued, 6" barrel	236.00
KMK-4	Stainless steel, 4³/₄" barrel	314.25
KMK-6	Stainless steel, 6" barrel	314.25

MARK II TARGET MODEL

SPECIFICATIONS
Same as for Mark II Model with the following exceptions. **Barrel:** 5¹/₄" and 6⁷/₈" tapered, button rifled. **Overall length:** 11¹/₈". **Weight:** Approx. 2⁵/₈ lbs. **Sights:** Patridge-type front blade, .125" wide, undercut to prevent glare; rear sight with click adjustments for windage and elevation. **Sight radius:** 9¹/₄" for 6⁷/₈" barrel.

MK-514	Blued, 5¹/₄" barrel	$294.50
MK-678	Blued, 6⁷/₈" barrel	294.50
KMK-514	Stainless steel, 5¹/₄" barrel	373.00
KMK-678	Stainless steel, 6⁷/₈" barrel	373.00
MK678G	Blued, 5¹/₂" bull barrel, Govt. Model	340.50
KMK678G	Stainless steel, 5¹/₂" bull barrel	411.29
KMK678GC	Stainless steel, 6⁷/₈" Govt. Competition barrel, scope rings	425.00

MARK II BULL BARREL MODEL

The Mark II Bull barrel pistol is identical to the Mark II Target Model except that it is equipped with a heavier Bull barrel offered in two lengths, 5¹/₂ inches/10 inches. The Bull barrel configuration was developed to meet the needs of those shooters who prefer a greater concentration of weight at the muzzle. The longer barrel model meets all IHMSA regulations.

SPECIFICATIONS
Same as for Mark II model with the following exceptions. **Barrel:** 5¹/₂" or 10"; button rifled; shorter barrel untapered, longer barrel has slight taper. **Weight:** Approx. 2⁵/₇ lbs. with 5¹/₂" barrel; 3¹/₄ lbs. with 10" barrel. **Sights:** Patridge-type front sight. Rear sight with click adjustments for windage and elevation. **Sight radius:** 7⁷/₈" for 5¹/₂" barrel, 12³/₈" for 10" barrel.

MK-512	Blued, 5¹/₂" barrel	$294.50
MK-10	Blued, 10" barrel	294.50
KMK-512	Stainless steel, 5¹/₂" barrel	373.00
KMK-10	Stainless steel, 10" barrel	373.00

SIG SAUER PISTOLS

MODEL P220 "AMERICAN"

MODEL P220 "AMERICAN"

SPECIFICATIONS
Calibers: 38 Super, 9mm Parabellum, 45 ACP
Capacity: 9 rounds; 7 rounds in 45 ACP
Barrel length: 4.4″
Overall length: 7.79″
Weight (empty): 26½ oz.; 25.7 oz. in 45 ACP
Finish: Blue
Prices:
45 ACP Blued $780.00
  W/"Siglite" night sights 880.00
  W/Nickel slide 805.00
  W/Nickel slide & "Siglite" night sights 905.00
  W/K-Kote 850.00
  W/K-Kote and "Siglite" night sights 950.00

MODEL P225

SPECIFICATIONS
Caliber: 9mm Parabellum
Capacity: 8 rounds
Barrel length: 3.85″
Overall length: 7″
Weight (empty): 26.1 oz.
Finish: Blue
Prices:
Blued finish $775.00
Blued w/"Siglite" night sights 875.00
W/K-Kote 845.00
W/K-Kote and "Siglite" night sights 945.00
W/Nickel slide 800.00
W/Nickel slide and "Siglite" night sights 900.00

MODEL P225

MODEL P226

MODEL P226

SPECIFICATIONS
Caliber: 9mm Parabellum
Capacity: 15 rounds
Barrel length: 4.4″
Overall length: 7¾″
Weight (empty): 26.5 oz.
Finish: Blue
Prices:
Blued finish $805.00
Blued w/"Siglite" night sights 905.00
W/K-Kote 875.00
K-Kote w/"Siglite" night sights 975.00
W/Nickel slide 830.00
W/Nickel slide & "Siglite" night sights 930.00
Double action only 805.00
  W/"Siglite" night sight 905.00
  W/Nickel slide 830.00

SIG SAUER PISTOLS

MODEL P228

MODEL P228

SPECIFICATIONS
Caliber: 9mm
Capacity: 13 rounds
Barrel length: 3.86″
Overall length: 7.08″
Weight (empty): 26.01 oz.
Finish: Blue, K-Kote or nickel
Prices:
Blued finish **$805.00**
Blued w/"Siglite" night sights **905.00**
W/Nickel slide **830.00**
W/Nickel slide & "Siglite" night sights **930.00**
W/K-Kote. **875.00**
W/K-Kote and "Siglite" night sights **975.00**

MODEL P229

SPECIFICATIONS
Caliber: 40 S&W
Capacity: 12 rounds
Barrel length: 3.86″
Overall length: 7.08″
Weight (empty): 27.54 oz.
Finish: Blue
Features: Blue stainless steel slide; DA/SA or DA only; automatic firing pin lock
Prices:
Model P229 . . . . **$875.00**
  W/"Siglite night sight **975.00**

MODEL P229

MODEL P230 SL

SPECIFICATIONS
Caliber: 380 ACP
Capacity: 7 rounds
Barrel length: 3.6″
Overall length: 6.6″
Weight (empty): 16¼ oz.; 20.8 oz. in stainless steel
Finish: Blue or stainless steel
Prices:
Blued finish **$510.00**
Stainless steel **595.00**

MODEL P230 SL

SMITH & WESSON AUTO PISTOLS

MODEL 422
22 SINGLE ACTION
$214.00 (Fixed Sight)
$267.00 (Adjustable Sight)

Caliber: 22 LR
Capacity: 10 rounds (magazine furnished)
Barrel lengths: 4½" and 6"
Overall length: 7½" (4½" barrel) and 9" (6" barrel)
Weight: 22 oz. (4½" barrel) and 23½ oz. (6" barrel)
Stock: Plastic (field version) and checkered walnut w/S&W monogram (target version)
Front sight: Serrated ramp w/.125" blade (field version); Patridge w/.125" blade (target version)
Rear sight: Fixed sight w/.125" blade (field version): adjustable sight w/.125" blade (target version)
Hammer: .250" internal
Trigger: .312" serrated
Also available:
MODEL 622. Same specifications as Model 422 in stainless steel. **Price: $259.00.** (Add **$52.00** for adj. sights).

MODEL 422

MODEL 2206 (not shown)
$259.00 (6" Bbl., Fixed Sights)
$299.00 (Fixed Sights)
$311.00 (Adj. Sights)

Caliber: 22 LR. **Capacity:** 12 rounds. **Barrel length:** 4½" and 6". **Overall length:** 7½" and 9". **Weight:** 35 oz. (4½" bbl.); 39 oz. (6" bbl.). **Finish:** Stainless steel.

MODEL NO. 41
$738.00 (Blue Only)

Caliber: 22 Long Rifle
Magazine capacity: 12 rounds
Barrel lengths: 5½" and 7"
Weight: 44 oz. (5½" barrel)
Sights: Front, ⅛" Patridge undercut; rear, S&W micrometer click sight adjustable for windage and elevation
Stocks: Checkered walnut with modified thumb rest, equally adaptable to right- or left-handed shooters
Finish: S&W Bright Blue
Trigger: .365" width; with S&W grooving and an adjustable trigger stop

MODEL NO. 41

MODEL 2214 RIMFIRE
"SPORTSMAN" (not shown)
$245.00 (Fixed Sights)

Caliber: 22 LR. **Capacity:** 8 rounds. **Barrel length:** 3". **Overall length:** 6⅛". **Weight:** 18 oz. **Finish:** Blue carbon steel slide and alloy frame (**Model 2213** has stainless steel slide w/alloy frame)

38 MASTER MODEL NO. 52
SINGLE ACTION CENTERFIRE PISTOL
$890.00 (Bright Blue Only)

Calibers: 38 S&W Special and 32 S&W Long (for Mid-Range Wad Cutter only)
Magazine capacity: 5 rounds (2 five-round magazines furnished)
Barrel length: 5"
Overall length: 8⅞"
Sight radius: 6¹⁵/₁₆"
Weight: 40 oz. with empty magazine
Sights: Front, ⅛" Patridge on ramp base; rear, new S&W micrometer click sight with wide ⅞" sight slide
Stocks: Checkered walnut with S&W monograms
Finish: S&W Bright Blue with sandblast stippling around sighting area to break up light reflection
Trigger: .365" width; with S&W grooving and an adjustable trigger stop

MODEL NO. 52

SMITH & WESSON PISTOLS

THIRD GENERATION DOUBLE ACTION PISTOLS

Smith & Wesson's double-action semiautomatic Third Generation line includes 8 series of compact and full-size custom-built pistols combining the following features: fixed barrel bushing for greater accuracy • smoother trigger pull plus a slimmer, contoured grip and lateral relief cut where trigger guard meets frame • three-dot sights • wraparound grips • beveled magazine well for easier reloading • ambidextrous safety lever secured by spring-loaded plunger • low-glare bead-blasted finish.

MODEL 1000 SERIES

Caliber: 10mm
Capacity: 9 rounds
Barrel length: 4¼″ and 5″
Overall length: 7⅞″ and 8⅝″
Weight: (w/fixed sights) 38 oz. (4¼″); 38½ oz. (5″)
Sights: Post with white dot front; fixed with white dot rear
Finish: Stainless steel
Prices:
MODEL 1006 (5″ barrel, fixed sights) $747.00
  With adjustable sights 773.00
MODEL 1066 (4¼″ barrel, fixed sights) 730.00
MODEL 1076 (4¼″ barrel w/straight backstrap
  grip, frame-mounted decocking lever) 755.00
MODEL 1086 Same as Model 1076 in DA only 730.00

MODEL 1026

**MODEL 3913 DA
Fixed Sight**

MODEL 3900 COMPACT SERIES

Caliber: 9mm Parabellum DA Autoloading Luger
Capacity: 8 rounds
Barrel length: 3½″
Overall length: 6⅞″
Weight (empty): 25 oz.
Sights: Post w/white dot front; fixed rear adj. for windage only w/2 white dots. Adjustable sight models include micrometer click, adj. for windage and elevation w/2 white dots. Deduct **$25** for fixed sights.
Finish: Blue (Model 3913); satin stainless (Model 3914)
Prices:
MODEL 3913 . . . . $585.00
MODEL 3914 . . . . 528.00

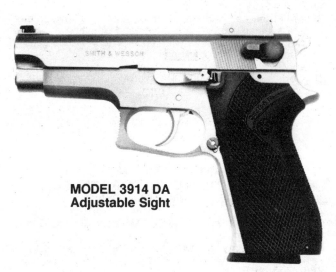

**MODEL 3914 DA
Adjustable Sight**

Also available:
MODEL 3913 LADYSMITH $603.00
MODEL 3953 (Double action only, stainless) 585.00
MODEL 3954 (Double action only, blue) 528.00

SMITH & WESSON PISTOLS

THIRD GENERATION DOUBLE ACTION PISTOLS

MODEL 4000 SERIES

Caliber: 40 S&W
Capacity: 11 rounds
Barrel length: 4″
Overall length: 7⅞″
Weight: 38½ oz. (with fixed sights)
Sights: Post w/white dot front; fixed or adjustable w/2 white dots rear
Stocks: Straight backstrap, Xenoy wraparound
Finish: Stainless steel
Prices:

MODEL 4003 Blue finish	**$643.00**
Stainless steel	691.00
MODEL 4006 w/fixed sights	708.00
Same as above w/adj. sights	736.00
MODEL 4026 w/decocking lever	724.00
W/fixed Tritium night sight	812.00
MODEL 4043 Double action only, blue finish	643.00
Stainless steel	691.00
MODEL 4046 w/fixed sights	708.00
Double action, fixed Tritium night sight	812.00

MODEL 4046

**MODEL 4506 DA
Fixed Sight**

MODEL 4500 SERIES

Caliber: 45 ACP Autoloading DA
Capacity: 8 rounds (Model 4506); 7 rounds (Model 4516)
Barrel length: 5″ (Model 4506); 3¾″ (Model 4516)
Overall length: 8⅝″ (Model 4506); 7⅛″ (Model 4516)
Weight (empty): 38½ oz. (Model 4506); 34½ oz. (Model 4516)
Sights: Post w/white dot front; fixed rear, adj. for windage only. Adj. sight incl. micrometer click, adj. for windage and elevation w/2 white dots. Add **$29.00** for adj. sights.
Stocks: Delrin one-piece wraparound, arched backstrap, textured surface
Finish: Satin stainless
Prices:

MODEL 4506 w/adj. sights, 5″ bbl.	**$765.00**
With fixed sights	735.00
MODEL 4566 w/4¼″ bbl., fixed sights	735.00
MODEL 4576 w/decocking lever, 4¼″ bbl.	762.00
MODEL 4586 Double action only, 4¼″ bbl.	735.00

SMITH & WESSON PISTOLS

THIRD GENERATION DOUBLE ACTION PISTOLS

MODEL 5900 SERIES

Caliber: 9mm Parabellum DA Autoloading Luger
Capacity: 15 rounds
Barrel length: 4″
Overall length: 7¹/₂″
Weight (empty): 28¹/₂ oz. (Model 5903); 26¹/₂ oz. (Model 5904); 37¹/₂ oz. (Model 5906)
Sights: Post w/white dot front; fixed rear, adj. for windage only w/2 white dots. Adjustable sight models include micrometer click, adj. for windage and elevation w/2 white dots. Add **$30** for adj. sights.
Finish: Blue (Model 5904); satin stainless (Models 5903 and 5906)
Prices:

MODEL 5903	**$686.00**
With fixed sights	655.00
MODEL 5904	639.00
With fixed sights	610.00
MODEL 5906	704.00
With fixed sights	672.00
With Tritium night sight	776.00

Also available:

MODEL 5926 w/frame-mounted decocking lever	**$697.00**
MODEL 5946 in double action only	672.00

MODEL 5904 DA
Fixed Sight

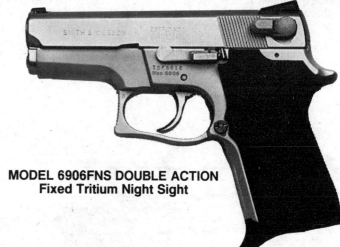

MODEL 6906FNS DOUBLE ACTION
Fixed Tritium Night Sight

MODEL 6904 DA
Fixed Sight

MODEL 6900 COMPACT SERIES

Caliber: 9mm Parabellum DA Autoloading Luger
Capacity: 8 rounds
Barrel length: 3¹/₂″
Overall length: 6⁷/₈″
Weight (empty): 26¹/₂ oz.
Sights: Post w/white dot front; fixed rear, adj. for windage only w/2 white dots
Stocks: Delrin one-piece wraparound, arched backstrap, textured surface
Finish: Blue (Model 6904); clear anodized/satin stainless (Model 6906)
Prices:

MODEL 6904	**$578.00**
MODEL 6906	637.00
MODEL 6906FNS Fixed Tritium night sight	741.00

SMITH & WESSON REVOLVERS

SMALL FRAME

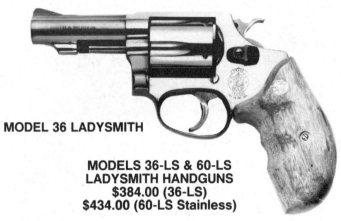

MODEL 36 LADYSMITH

MODELS 36-LS & 60-LS
LADYSMITH HANDGUNS
$384.00 (36-LS)
$434.00 (60-LS Stainless)

Caliber: 38
Capacity: 5 shots
Barrel length: 2″
Weight: 20 oz.
Sights: Serrated ramp front; fixed notch rear

MODEL 60 LADYSMITH

Grips: Contoured laminated rosewood
Finish: Glossy deep blue or stainless
Features: Both models come with Soft Side LadySmith case

MODEL 36
38 CHIEFS SPECIAL
$351.00 Blue $363.00 Nickel

Caliber: 38 S&W Special
Number of shots: 5
Barrel length: 2″ or 3″
Overall length: 6¹/₂″ with 2″ barrel
Weight: 19¹/₂ oz. (2″ barrel); 21¹/₂ oz. (3″ barrel)
Sights: Serrated ramp front; fixed square notch rear
Grips: Checkered walnut Service
Finish: S&W blue carbon steel or nickel
Features: .312″ smooth combat-style trigger; .240″ service hammer
MODEL 37 AIRWEIGHT: Same as Model 36, except finish is blue or nickel aluminum alloy; wt. 13¹/₂ oz.
Blue **$372.00**
With nickel finish . . . . **307.00.**

MODEL 36
38 CHIEFS SPECIAL

MODEL 60
38 CHIEFS SPECIAL STAINLESS
$401.00 ($426.00 w/Full Lug Barrel)

Caliber: 38 S&W Special
Number of shots: 5
Barrel lengths: 2″ and 3″ (3″ full lug barrel optional)
Weight: 19¹/₂ oz. (2″ barrel); 21¹/₂ oz. (3″ barrel); 24¹/₂ oz. (3″ full lug barrel)
Sights: Micrometer click rear, adj. for windage and elevation; pinned black front (3″ full lug model only); standard sights as on Model 36
Grips: Checked walnut Service with S&W monograms; Santoprene combat-style on 3″ full lug model
Finish: Stainless steel
Features: .312″ smooth combat-style trigger (.347″ serrated trigger on 3″ full lug model); .240″ service hammer (.375″ semi-target hammer on 3″ full lug model)

MODEL 60
38 CHIEFS SPECIAL

SMITH & WESSON REVOLVERS

SMALL FRAME

38 BODYGUARD "AIRWEIGHT"
MODEL 38
$394.00 Blue
$408.00 Nickel

Caliber: 38 S&W Special
Number of shots: 5
Barrel length: 2″
Overall length: 6³/₈″
Weight: 14 oz.
Sights: Front, fixed ¹/₁₀″ serrated ramp; rear square notch
Stocks: Checked walnut Service with S&W monograms
Finish: S&W blue or nickel aluminum alloy

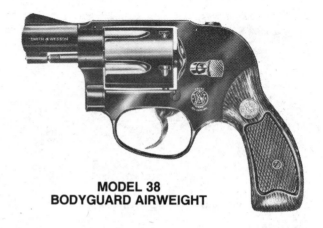

**MODEL 38
BODYGUARD AIRWEIGHT**

38 BODYGUARD MODEL 49
$373.00

Caliber: 38 S&W Special
Number of shots: 5
Barrel length: 2″
Overall length: 6¹/₄″
Weight (empty): 20 oz.
Sights: Serrated ramp (front); fixed square notch (rear)
Finish: S&W blue

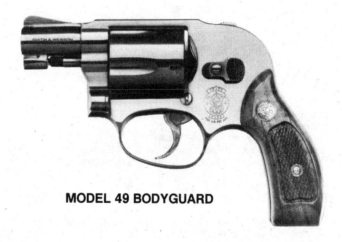

MODEL 49 BODYGUARD

MODEL 649 BODYGUARD
$424.00

Caliber: 38 Special
Capacity: 5 shots
Barrel length: 2″
Overall length: 6¹/₄″
Weight: 20 oz.
Sights: Serrated ramp front, fixed square notch rear
Grips: Round butt; checkered walnut service
Finish: Stainless steel

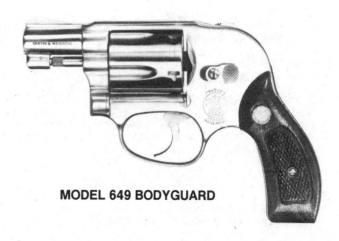

MODEL 649 BODYGUARD

SMITH & WESSON REVOLVERS

SMALL FRAME

MODEL 63
22/32 KIT GUN
$418.00

Caliber: 22 Long Rifle
Number of shots: 6
Barrel lengths: 2″ and 4″
Weight: 22 oz. (2″ barrel); 24½ oz. (4″ barrel)
Sights: ⅛″ red ramp front sight; rear sight is black stainless steel S&W micrometer click square-notch, adjustable for windage and elevation
Stocks: Square butt
Finish: Satin stainless

MODEL 63 22/32 KIT GUN

MODEL 642 CENTENNIAL AIRWEIGHT
$426.00

Caliber: 9mm Parabellum (+ P)
Barrel length: 2″
Weight: 15.8 oz.
Sights: Serrated ramp front; fixed square notch rear
Grips: Santoprene combat grips
Finish: Stainless steel and aluminum alloy
Features: .312″ smooth combat trigger; fully concealed hammer
Also available:
MODEL 640. Same specifications as Model 642, except available in 3″ barrel also; features smooth hardwood Service stock and stainless steel finish

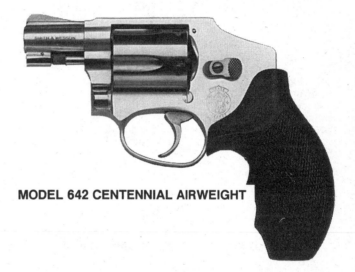

MODEL 642 CENTENNIAL AIRWEIGHT

MODEL 940 CENTENNIAL
$429.00

Caliber: 9mm Parabellum
Barrel lengths: 2″ and 3″
Weight: 23 oz. (2″ barrel); 25 oz. (3″ barrel)
Sights: Serrated ramp front; fixed square notch rear
Grips: Santoprene combat grips
Feature: Fully concealed hammer

22 MAGNUM KIT GUN
MODEL 651 (not shown)
$412.00

Caliber: 22 Magnum
Number of shots: 6
Barrel length: 4″
Weight: 24½ oz.
Sights: Red ramp front; micrometer click rear, adjustable for windage and elevation
Grips: Checkered premium hardwood Service
Finish: Stainless steel
Features: .375″ hammer; .312″ smooth combat trigger

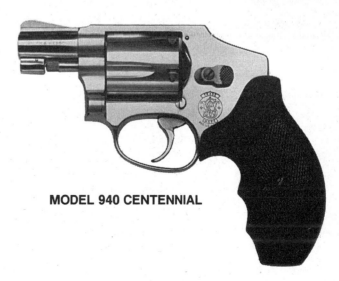

MODEL 940 CENTENNIAL

SMITH & WESSON REVOLVERS

MEDIUM FRAME

38 MILITARY & POLICE
MODEL 10
$346.00 Blue
$358.00 Nickel (4″ barrel only)

Caliber: 38 S&W Special
Capacity: 6 shots
Barrel length: 2″, 4″ (also 4″ heavy barrel)
Weight: 33½ oz. with 4″ barrel
Sights: Front, fixed ⅛″ serrated ramp; rear square notch
Stocks: Checkered walnut service with S&W monograms, round or square butt
Finish: S&W blue or nickel

MODEL 10

357 MILITARY & POLICE (HEAVY BARREL)
MODEL 13
$353.00

Caliber: 357 Magnum and 38 S&W Special
Capacity: 6 shots
Barrel length: 3″ and 4″
Overall length: 9¼″ (w/4″ barrel)
Weight: 34 oz. (w/4″ barrel)
Sights: Front, ⅛″ serrated ramp; rear square notch
Stocks: Checkered walnut service with S&W monograms, square butt (3″ barrel has round butt)
Finish: S&W blue

MODEL 13

357 MILITARY & POLICE (HEAVY BARREL)
MODEL 65
$383.00

Same specifications as Model 13, except Model 65 is stainless steel.

MODEL 65

38 MILITARY & POLICE STAINLESS
MODEL 64
$383.00

Calibers: 38 S&W Special, 38 S&W Special Mid Range
Capacity: 6 shots
Barrel length: 4″ heavy barrel, square butt; 3″ heavy barrel, round butt; 2″ regular barrel, round butt
Overall length: 9¼″ w/4″ barrel; 7⅞″ w/3″ barrel; 6⅞″ w/2″ barrel
Weight: With 4″ barrel, 33½ oz.; with 3″ barrel, 30½ oz.; with 2″ barrel, 28 oz.
Sights: Fixed, ⅛″ serrated ramp front; square notch rear
Stocks: Checkered walnut service with S&W monograms
Finish: Satin stainless

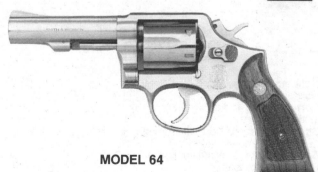

MODEL 64

SMITH & WESSON REVOLVERS

MEDIUM FRAME

MODEL 14

K-38 MASTERPIECE
MODEL 14
$425.00

Caliber: 38 S&W Special
Barrel length: 6″ full lug barrel
Weight: 47 oz.
Sights: Micrometer click rear, adjustable for windage and elevation; pinned black Patridge-style front
Grips: Combat-style premium hardwood
Finish: Blue carbon steel
Features: .500 target hammer; .312″ smooth combat trigger

MODEL 15

38 COMBAT MASTERPIECE
MODEL 15
$375.00

Caliber: 38 S&W Special
Number of shots: 6
Barrel length: 4″
Overall length: 9⁵/₁₆″
Weight (loaded): 32 oz.
Sights: Serrated ramp front; S&W micrometer click sight adjustable for windage and elevation
Stocks: Checkered walnut service with S&W monograms
Finish: S&W blue

32 H&R MAGNUM MASTERPIECE
MODEL 16 (not shown)
$419.00

Caliber: 32 H&R Magnum
Barrel length: 6″ full lug barrel
Weight: 47¹/₂ oz.
Sights: Micrometer click rear, adjustable for windage and elevation; pinned black Patridge-style front
Finish: Blue carbon steel
Features: .500 target hammer; .400″ serrated trigger

MODEL 17

K-22 MASTERPIECE
MODEL 17
$394.00 (4″ barrel)
$444.00 (8³/₈″ barrel)
$433.00 (6″ barrel w/target trigger, hammer)

Caliber: 22 Long Rifle
Number of shots: 6
Barrel length: 4″, 6″, 8³/₈″
Overall length: 9⁵/₁₆″ (4″ barrel); 11¹/₈″ (6″ barrel); 13¹/₂″ (8³/₈″ barrel)
Weight (loaded): 38¹/₂ oz. with 6″ barrel; 42¹/₂ oz. with 8³/₈″ barrel
Sights: Front, ¹/₈″ plain Patridge; rear, S&W micrometer click sight adjustable for windage and elevation
Stocks: Checkered walnut Service with S&W monograms
Finish: S&W blue

SMITH & WESSON REVOLVERS

MEDIUM FRAME

357 COMBAT MAGNUM
MODEL 19
$369.00—$400.00

Caliber: 357 Magnum (actual bullet dia. 38 S&W Spec.)
Number of shots: 6
Barrel length: 2½″, 4″ and 6″
Overall length: 9½″ with 4″ barrel; 7½″ with 2½″ barrel; 11½″ with 6″ barrel
Weight: 30½ oz. (2½″ barrel); 36 oz. (4″ barrel); 39 oz. (6″ barrel)
Sights: Front, ⅛″ Baughman Quick Draw on 2½″ or 4″ barrel, ⅛″ Patridge on 6″ barrel; rear, S&W micrometer click sight adjustable for windage and elevation
Stocks: Checkered Goncalo Alves Target with S&W monograms
Finish: S&W bright blue

MODEL 19

357 COMBAT MAGNUM
MODEL 66
$420.00–$468.00 Stainless Steel

Caliber: 357 Magnum (actual bullet dia. 38 S&W Spec.)
Number of shots: 6
Barrel length: 6″ or 4″ with square butt; 2½″ with round butt
Length overall: 9½″ with 4″ barrel; 7½″ with 2½″ barrel; 11⅜″ with 6″ barrel
Weight: 36 oz. with 4″ barrel; 30½ oz. with 2½″ barrel; 39 oz. with 6″ barrel
Sights: Front: ⅛″. Rear: S&W Red Ramp on ramp base, S&W Micrometer Click Sight, adjustable for windage and elevation
Stocks: Checked Goncalo Alves target with square butt with S&W monograms
Finish: Satin stainless
Trigger: S&W grooving with an adjustable trigger stop
Ammunition: 357 S&W Magnum, 38 S&W Special Hi-Speed, 38 S&W Special, 38 S&W Special Mid Range

MODEL 66

Also available:
MODEL 617 (22 LR)
With 4″ or 6″ barrel, stainless or blue finish **$416.00**
W/targer hammer & trigger, 6″ only **447.00**
8⅜″ only w/target hammer & trigger **458.00**

DISTINGUISHED COMBAT MAGNUM
MODEL 586
$417.00–$421.00

Caliber: 357 Magnum
Capacity: 6 shots
Barrel lengths: 4″, 6″
Overall length: 9¾″ with 4″ barrel; 11½″ with 6″ barrel; 13¹³⁄₁₆″ with 8⅜″ barrel
Weight: 42 oz. with 4″ barrel; 46 oz. with 6″ barrel; 53 oz. with 8⅜″ barrel
Sights: Front is S&W Red Ramp; rear is S&W Micrometer Click adjustable for windage and elevation; White outline notch. Option with 6″ barrel only—plain Patridge front with black outline notch
Stocks: Checkered Goncalo Alves with speedloader cutaway
Finish: S&W Blue
MODEL 686: Same as Model 586 except also available with 2½″ barrel and finish is stainless steel **$439.00** (2½″) to **$479.00** (6″ w/adj. front sight)

MODEL 586

SMITH & WESSON REVOLVERS

LARGE FRAME

357 MAGNUM MODEL 27
$440.00

Caliber: 357 Magnum (actual bullet dia. 38 S&W Spec.)
Number of shots: 6
Barrel length: 6″
Weight: 45½ oz.
Sights: Front, Patridge on ramp base; rear, S&W micrometer click sight adjustable for windage and elevation
Stocks: Checkered hardwood target
Frame: Finely checked top strap and barrel rib
Finish: Blue carbon steel

MODEL 27

44 MAGNUM MODEL 29
$501.00 (4″ and 6″) $512.00 (8³/₈″)

Caliber: 44 Magnum
Number of shots: 6
Barrel lengths: 4″, 6″ and 8³/₈″
Overall length: 11⁷/₈″ with 6½″ barrel
Weight: 44 oz. with 4″ barrel; 47 oz. with 6″ barrel; 51½ oz. with 8³/₈″ barrel
Sights: Front, Red ramp on ramp base; rear, S&W micrometer click sight adjustable for windage and elevation; white outline notch
Stocks: Checkered, highly grained hardwood target type
Hammer: Checkered target type
Trigger: Grooved target type
Finish: Blue carbon steel
Also available:
MODEL 29 CLASSIC in blue carbon steel w/full lug barrel, interchangeable front sights, Hogue combat grips.
  With 5″ and 6½″ barrels **$540.00**
  With 8³/₈″ barrels 551.00
MODEL 29 CLASSIC DX. Same as above with two sets of grips and five interchangeable front sights and proof target.
  With 5″ and 6½″ **$713.00**
  With 8³/₈″ barrels 728.00

MODEL 29

MODEL 625 (not shown)
$535.00

Caliber: 45 ACP
Capacity: 6 shots
Barrel length: 5″
Overall length: 10³/₈″
Weight (empty): 46 oz.
Sights: Front, Patridge on ramp base; S&W micrometer click rear, adjustable for windage and elevation
Stock: Pachmayr SK/GR gripper, round butt
Finish: Stainless steel

SMITH & WESSON REVOLVERS

LARGE FRAME

41 MAGNUM MODEL 57
$444.00

Caliber: 41 Magnum
Number of shots: 6
Barrel length: 6″ and 8³/₈″
Overall length: 11³/₈″ (6″ barrel)
Weight: 48 oz. (6″ barrel); 52¹/₂ oz. (8³/₈″ barrel)
Sights: Front, serrated ramp on ramp base; rear, S&W micrometer click sight adjustable for windage and elevation; white outline notch
Stocks: Checkered hardwood target
Trigger: Serrated target type
Finish: Blue carbon steel

MODEL 57

MODEL 657 STAINLESS
$490.00 (8³/₈″)
$473.00 (6″)

Caliber: 41 Magnum
Capacity: 6 shots
Barrel lengths: 6″, 8³/₈″
Overall length: 11³/₈″ (6″ barrel); 13¹⁵/₁₆″ (8³/₈″ barrel)
Weight (empty): 48 oz. (6″ barrel); 52¹/₂ oz. (8³/₈″ barrel)
Sights: Serrated ramp on ramp base (front); Blue S&W micrometer click sight adj. for windage and elevation (rear)
Finish: Satin stainless steel

MODEL 657

MODEL 629 (not shown)
$530.00 (4″ and 6″ Barrels)
$548.00 (8³/₈″ Barrel)

Calibers: 44 Magnum, 44 S&W Special
Capacity: 6 shots
Barrel lengths: 4″, 6″, 8³/₈″
Overall length: 9⁵/₈″, 11³/₈″, 13⁷/₈″
Weight (empty): 44 oz. (4″); 47 oz. (6″ barrel); 51¹/₂ oz. (8³/₈″)
Sights: S&W red ramp front; plain blade rear w/S&W micrometer click; adj. for windage and elevation; scope mount
Stock: Checkered hardwood target
Finish: Stainless steel
Also available:
MODEL 629 CLASSIC w/interchangeable front sight, square butt, synthetic grips, white outline rear sight, 5″ and 6¹/₂″ barrels **$569.00**
With 8³/₈″ barrel **588.00**
MODEL 629 CLASSIC DX. Same features as above plus two sets of grips and five interchangeable front sights and proof target. With 5″ and 6¹/₂″ barrels **$755.00**
With 8³/₈″ barrel **780.00**

SPRINGFIELD ARMORY

**MODEL 1911-A1
STANDARD**

MODEL 1911-A1 STANDARD

An exact duplicate of the M1911-A1 pistol that served the U.S. Armed Forces for more than 70 years, this model has been precision manufactured from forged parts, including a forged frame, then hand-assembled.

SPECIFICATIONS
Calibers: 9mm Parabellum, 38 Super, 40 S&W and 45 ACP
Capacity: 9 in mag. 1 in chamber (9mm); 8 in mag. 1 in chamber (45 ACP)
Barrel length: 5.04″
Overall length: 8.59″
Weight: 35.62 oz.
Trigger pull: 5 to 6.5 lbs.
Sight radius: 6.481″
Rifling: 1 turn in 16; right-hand, 4-groove (9mm); left-hand, 6-groove (45 ACP)

**MODEL 1911-A1
CHAMPION**

MODEL 1911-A1	
45 ACP/9mm, blued	**$539.00**
45 ACP/9mm, Parkerized finish	**499.00**
45 ACP/9mm, Duotone finish	**599.00**
40 S&W, blued	**689.00**
40 S&W, Parkerized	**649.00**
1911-A1 DEFENDER w/fixed combat sights, bobbed hammer, walnut grips, beveled magazine well, extended thumb safety, 40 S&W and 45 ACP, Duotone	**999.00**
1911-A1 CHAMPION with 1/2″ shortened slide and barrel, 45 ACP, stainless finish	**749.00**
With blued finish	**609.00**
1911-A1 38 SUPER w/Parkerized finish	**599.00**
With blued finish	**629.00**
1911-A1 COMPACT w/blued finish	**609.00**
With stainless finish	**749.00**
1911-A1 FACTORY COMP 38 Super, blued	**869.00**
In 45 ACP	**839.00**
GULF VICTORY in 45 ACP w/blued finish	**869.00**

MODEL 1911-A2 S.A.S.S.
(Springfield Armory Single Shot)

SPECIFICATIONS
Calibers: 22 LR, 243, 44 Mag., 357 Mag., 7mm BR (10.7″ barrel); 223, 243, 7mm-08, 7mm BR, 308 and 358 Win. (14.9″ barrel)
Barrel length: 10.7″ or 14.9″ (interchangeable)
Prices:

1911-A2 S.A.S.S. 14.9″ barrel	**$749.00**
10.7″ barrel	**749.00**
Conversion Units 14.9″ barrel	**399.00**
10.7″ barrel	**399.00**

**1911-A2 S.A.S.S.
SPRINGFIELD ARMORY SINGLE SHOT**

SPRINGFIELD ARMORY

MODEL P9 DOUBLE ACTION

SPECIFICATIONS
Calibers: 9mm Parabellum, 40 S&W, 45 ACP
Capacity: 15 rounds (9mm), 11 rounds (40 S&W), 10 rounds (45 ACP)
Barrel length: 4.72″
Overall length: 8.1″
Weight: 35.3 oz.
Rifling: Right-hand; 1 turn in 10″, 4-groove
Grips: Checkered walnut
Features: Serrated front and rear frame straps; frame-mounted thumb safety, Commander-style hammer

Prices P9 PISTOLS

Standard Parkerized in 45 ACP and 40 S&W	**$549.00**
In 9mm, 40 S&W Compact & Sub-Compact	**519.00**
In 9mm Compact & Sub-Compact..............	**499.00**
In 45 Ultra LSP	**709.00**
In 40 S&W Ultra LSP	**639.00**
In 9mm Ultra LSP	**609.00**
Standard Blued in 45 ACP	**579.00**
In 40 S&W	**569.00**
In 9mm, 40 S&W Compact & Sub-Compact	**549.00**
In 9mm Compact & Sub-Compact..............	**519.00**
In 45 Ultra LSP	**739.00**
In 40 S&W Ultra LSP	**669.00**
Standard Stainless Steel in 45 ACP & 40 S&W ..	**629.00**
In 9mm	**599.00**
In 45 Ultra LSP	**859.00**
In 40 S&W Ultra LSP	**799.00**
In 9mm Ultra LSP	**769.00**

MODEL P9 DOUBLE ACTION

"R" SERIES PISTOLS

Springfield Armory's new "R" Series stands for "Recreational Shooting" and comprises four pistols that share common characteristics, including ergonomically designed grips, superior sights and sensible safety systems.

PANTHER
$609.00

SPECIFICATIONS
Calibers: 9mm, 40 S&W, 45 ACP
Capacity: 15 rounds (9mm); 9 rounds (45 ACP); 11 rounds (40 S&W)
Barrel length: 3.79″
Overall length: 7.04″
Weight: 28.96 oz.
Trigger pull: 4.0 lbs
Sight radius: 5.34″
Finish: Non-glare blue
Features: Narrow profile walnut grips; serrated front and rear strap; hammer drop and firing pin safeties; frame-mounted slide stop

"R" SERIES PANTHER

SPRINGFIELD ARMORY

"R" SERIES PISTOLS

FIRECAT
$569.00

SPECIFICATIONS
Calibers: 9mm, 40 S&W
Capacity: 8 rounds (9mm); 7 rounds (40 S&W)
Barrel length: 3.51″
Overall length: 6.52″
Weight: 25.76 oz.
Trigger pull: 4.0 lbs
Sight radius: 4.84″
Action: Single-action semiautomatic

"R" SERIES FIRECAT

BOBCAT
$449.00

SPECIFICATIONS
Calibers: 380 ACP
Capacity: 13 rounds
Barrel length: 3.52″
Overall length: 6.6″
Weight: 21.92 oz.
Trigger pull: 4.0 lbs
Sight radius: 4.63″
Action: Single- or double-action semiautomatic

"R" SERIES BOBCAT

LYNX
$269.00

SPECIFICATIONS
Caliber: 25 ACP
Capacity: 7 rounds
Barrel length: 2.23″
Overall length: 4.43″
Weight: 10.56 oz.
Trigger pull: 5.0 lbs
Sight radius: 3.1″
Action: Single-action semiautomatic

"R" SERIES LYNX

STAR AUTOMATIC PISTOLS

STAR MODELS 31P & 31PK
9mm Parabellum or 40 S&W

The Model 31 features a staggered 15-round button release magazine, square notch rear sight (click-adjustable for windage) and square front sight (notched to diffuse light). Removable backstrap houses complete firing mechanism. All-steel frame (Model 31PK has alloy frame).
Barrel length: 3.86″. **Overall length:** 7″. **Weight:** 39.4 oz. (Model 31P); 30 oz. (Model 31PK)
Model 31P Blue finish, 40 S&W $610.00
  Blue finish, 9mm Para. 550.00
  Starvel finish, 40 S&W 640.00
  Starvel finish, steel frame 580.00
Model 31PK Alloy frame, 9mm Para. 550.00

MODEL 31PK

MODEL M40 AND M43 FIRESTAR
9mm Parabellum or 40 S&W

This pocket-sized Firestar pistol features all-steel construction, a triple-dot sight system (fully adjustable rear), and ambidextrous safety. The Acculine barrel design reseats and locks the barrel after each shot. Checkered rubber grips.
Barrel length: 3.39″. **Overall length:** 6½″. **Weight:** 30.35 oz.
Capacity: 7 rounds (6 rounds in 40 S&W).
Firestar M40 Blue finish $456.67
  Starvel finish 486.67
Firestar M43 Blue finish 431.67
  Starvel finish 461.67
Megastar Blue finish, 10mm and 45 ACP 658.35
Megastar Starvel finish, 10mm and 45 ACP 688.35

MODEL M43 FIRESTAR

TAURUS PISTOLS

MODEL PT 22

SPECIFICATIONS
Caliber: 22 LR
Action: Semiautomatic
Capacity: 9 shots
Barrel length: 2³⁄₄″
Overall length: 5¹⁄₄″
Weight: 12.3 oz.
Sights: Fixed
Grips: Brazilian hardwood
Finish: Blue
Also available:
MODEL PT 25. Same price and specifications as Model PT 22, except magazine holds 8 rounds in 25 ACP.

MODEL PT 22
$182.00

TAURUS PISTOLS

MODEL PT 58

SPECIFICATIONS
Caliber: 380 ACP
Action: Semiautomatic double action
Capacity: Staggered 13 shot
Barrel length: 4″
Overall length: 7.2″
Weight: 30 oz.
Hammer: Exposed
Sights: Front, drift adjustable; rear, notched bar dovetailed to slide, 3-dot combat
Grips: Smooth Brazilian walnut
Finish: Blue, satin nickel or stainless steel

MODEL PT 58
$423.00 (Blue)
$454.00 (Nickel)
$481.00 (Stainless)

MODEL PT 92

Caliber: 9mm Parabellum
Action: Semiautomatic double action
Capacity: Staggered 15-shot magazine
Hammer: Exposed
Barrel length: 5″
Overall length: 8½″
Height: 5.39″
Width: 1.45″
Weight: 34 oz. (empty)
Rifling: R.H., 6 grooves
Sights: Front, fixed; rear, drift adjustable, 3-dot combat
Safeties: (a) Ambidextrous manual safety locking trigger mechanism and slide in locked position; (b) half-cock position; (c) inertia operated firing pin; (d) chamber loaded indicator
Slide: Hold open upon firing last cartridge
Grips: Smooth Brazilian walnut
Finish: Blue, satin nickel or stainless steel
Also available:
MODEL PT 99. Same specifications as Model PT 92, but has micrometer click-adjustable rear sight. **$512.00** (Blue); **$554.00** (Nickel); **$582.00** (Stainless).

MODEL PT 92
$473.00 (Blue)
$511.00 (Nickel)
$538.00 (Stainless)

MODEL PT 92C

SPECIFICATIONS
Caliber: 9mm Parabellum
Capacity: 13 rounds
Barrel length: 4.25″
Overall length: 7.5″
Weight: 31 oz.
Sights: Fixed front; drift-adjustable rear, 3-dot combat
Stocks: Brazilian hardwood
Slide: Last shot held open
Safety: Manual, ambidextrous hammer drop; inertia firing pin; chamber load indicator
Finish: Blue, satin nickel or stainless steel

MODEL PT 92C
$473.00 (Blue)
$511.00 (Nickel)

TAURUS PISTOLS/REVOLVERS

MODEL PT 99
$483.00 (Blue)
$523.00 (Nickel)

MODEL PT 99

Caliber: 9mm Parabellum
Action: Semiautomatic double action
Capacity: Staggered, 15-shot magazine
Hammer: Exposed
Barrel length: 5″
Overall length: 8½″
Height: 5.39″
Width: 1.45″
Weight: 34 oz. (empty)
Rifling: R.H., 6 grooves
Sights: Fixed front; rear, micrometer click adjustable for elevation and windage, 3-dot combat
Safeties: (a) Ambidextrous manual safety locking trigger mechanism and slide in locked position; (b) half-cock position; (c) inertia-operated firing pin; (d) chamber loaded indicator
Slide: Hold open upon firing last cartridge
Grips: Smooth Brazilian walnut
Finish: Blue, satin nickel or stainless steel

MODEL PT 101

MODEL PT 100
$482.00 (Blue)
$521.00 (Nickel)
$547.00 (Stainless)

MODEL PT 100

Caliber: 40 S&W
Capacity: 15 shots
Barrel length: 5″
Weight: 34 oz. (empty)
Sights: Fixed front; adjustable rear, 3-dot Combat
Grips: Brazilian hardwood
Finish: Blue, satin nickel or stainless steel
Also available:
MODEL PT 101. Same specifications as Model PT 100, but features micrometer click-adjustable rear sight. **$522.00** (Blue); **$564.00** (Nickel); **$592.00** (Stainless).

MODEL 65
$249.00 (Blue)
$264.00 (Nickel)

MODEL 65

SPECIFICATIONS
Caliber: 357 Magnum
Capacity: 6 shot
Barrel length: 3″, 4″
Weight: 34 oz.
Sights: Rear square notch; serrated front ramp
Action: Double
Stock: Brazilian hardwood
Finish: Royal blue or satin nickel

MODEL 66
$274.00 (Blue) $289.00 (Nickel)
$348.00 (Stainless Steel)

MODEL 66

SPECIFICATIONS
Caliber: 357 Magnum
Action: Double
Capacity: 6 shot
Barrel length: 3″, 4″, 6″
Weight: 35 oz. (4″ barrel)
Sights: Serrated ramp front; rear micrometer click adjustable for windage and elevation
Stock: Brazilian hardwood
Finish: Royal blue, satin nickel or stainless steel

TAURUS REVOLVERS

MODEL 73
$223.00 (Blue)
$243.00 (Nickel)

SPECIFICATIONS
Caliber: 32 H&R Magnum
Capacity: 6 shot
Barrel length: 3″ heavy barrel
Weight: 20 oz.
Sights: Rear, square notch
Action: Double
Stock: Brazilian hardwood
Finish: Blue or satin nickel
Also available:
MODEL 76 w/6″ barrel, target hammer, adj. target trigger, weight of 34 oz. **$308.00**

MODEL 83
$228.00 (Blue)
$241.00 (Nickel)

SPECIFICATIONS
Caliber: 38 Special
Action: Double
Number of shots: 6
Barrel length: 4″
Weight: 34 oz.
Sights: Patridge-type front; rear micrometer click adjustable for windage and elevation
Stock: Brazilian hardwood
Finish: Blue or satin nickel

MODEL 85
$237.00 (Blue) $257.00 (Nickel)
$297.00 (Stainless Steel)

SPECIFICATIONS
Caliber: 38 Special
Capacity: 5 shot
Action: Double
Barrel length: 2″ and 3″
Weight: 21 oz. (2″ barrel)
Sights: Notch rear sight, fixed sight
Stock: Brazilian hardwood
Finish: Blue, satin nickel (3″ only) or stainless steel

MODEL 85CH
$237.00 (Blue)
$297.00 (Stainless Steel)

Same specifications as Model 85, except has concealed hammer and 2″ barrel only. Not available in nickel.

TAURUS REVOLVERS

MODEL 80
$216.00 (Blue)
$231.00 (Nickel)

SPECIFICATIONS
Caliber: 38 Special
Capacity: 6 shot
Action: Double
Barrel lengths: 3″, 4″
Weight: 30 oz. (4″ barrel)
Sights: Notched rear; serrated ramp front
Stock: Brazilian hardwood
Finish: Blue or satin nickel

MODEL 80

MODEL 82
$216.00 (Blue)
$231.00 (Nickel)

SPECIFICATIONS
Caliber: 38 Special
Capacity: 6 shot
Action: Double
Barrel lengths: 3″, 4″
Weight: 34 oz. (4″ barrel)
Sights: Notched rear; serrated ramp front
Stock: Brazilian hardwood
Finish: Blue or satin nickel

MODEL 82

MODEL 94
$249.00 (Blue)
$296.00 (Stainless Steel)

SPECIFICATIONS
Caliber: 22 LR
Number of shots: 9
Action: Double
Barrel lengths: 3″ and 4″
Weight: 25 oz.
Sights: Serrated ramp front; rear micrometer click adjustable
     for windage and elevation
Stock: Brazilian hardwood
Finish: Blue or stainless steel

Also available:
MODEL 941 in 22 Magnum, 8-shot capacity; ejector
     shroud . . . .**$274.00 (Blue)**
In stainless steel **326.00**

MODEL 941

TAURUS REVOLVERS

MODEL 86 TARGET MASTER
$308.00

SPECIFICATIONS
Caliber: 38 Special
Capacity: 6 shot
Action: Double
Barrel length: 6″
Weight: 34 oz.
Sights: Patridge-type front; micrometer click adjustable rear for windage and elevation
Stock: Brazilian hardwood
Finish: Bright royal blue

MODEL 86 TARGET MASTER

MODEL 96
$308.00

SPECIFICATIONS
Caliber: 22 LR
Number of shots: 6
Action: Double
Barrel length: 6″
Weight: 34 oz.
Sights: Patridge-type front; rear micrometer click adjustable for windage and elevation
Stock: Brazilian hardwood
Finish: Blue only

MODEL 96

MODEL 669
$284.00 (Blue)
$356.00 (Stainless Steel)

SPECIFICATIONS
Caliber: 357 Magnum
Capacity: 6 shots
Action: Double
Barrel lengths: 4″ and 6″
Weight: 37 oz. (4″ barrel)
Sights: Serrated ramp front; rear micrometer click adjustable for windage and elevation
Stock: Brazilian hardwood
Finish: Royal blue or stainless

MODEL 669

MODEL 689
$295.00 (Blue)
$370.00 (Stainless Steel)

The Model 689 has the same specifications as the Model 669, except vent rib is featured.

A **Limited Edition** is also available, featuring Laser Aim Sight, accessories and custom case. **Prices:**
Blue $668.00
Stainless steel 739.00

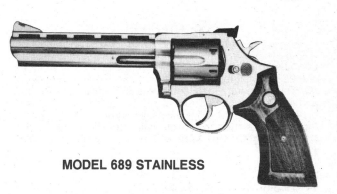

MODEL 689 STAINLESS

THOMPSON/CENTER

BULL BARREL

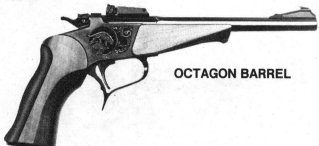

OCTAGON BARREL

CONTENDER
OCTAGON BARREL MODELS

This standard barrel is interchangeable with any model listed here. Available in 10-inch length, it is supplied with iron sights. Octagon barrel is available in 22 LR. No external choke in this model. **Price:** **$405.00**

Also available:
25th Anniversary Model **$700.00**

CONTENDER SUPER "14"

CONTENDER
SUPER "14" MODELS

Chambered in 12 calibers (17 Rem., 22 LR, 222 Remington and 223 Remington, 7-30 Waters, 7mm T.C.U., 10mm Auto, 30/30 Winchester, 357 Rem. Max., 35 Remington, 375 Win. and 44 Mag. and 445 Super Mag.), this gun is equipped with a 14-inch bull barrel, fully adjustable target rear sight and Patridge-style ramped front sight with 13½-inch sight radius. **Overall length:** 18¼″. **Weight:** 3½ lbs. **Price:** . . . **$415.00** Add **$30.00** for 17 Rem.

Also available
14″ Vent Rib Model in 45 Colt/.410 . . . . **$445.00**

CONTENDER
BULL BARREL MODELS

This pistol with 10-inch barrel features fully adjustable Patridge-style iron sights.

Standard and Custom calibers available:
22 Long Rifle, 22 Hornet, 22 Win. Mag., 7-30 Waters, 223 Rem., 270 Rem., 10mm Auto, 32-20 Win., 7mm T.C.U., 30-30 Win., 357 Mag., 44 Mag., 44 Super, 357 Rem. Max. and 30 M1 Carbine.
Bull Barrel (less internal choke) **$405.00**
Standard calibers available w/internal choke:
45 Colt/.410 . . . . 410.00
Vent Rib Model 425.00
With **Match Grade Barrel** (22 LR only) 415.00

CONTENDER HUNTER

Chambered in 7-30 Waters, 223 Rem., 30-30 Win., 35 Rem., 45-70 Government, 357 Rem. Max., 375 Win. and 44 Rem. Mag., the most popular commercially loaded cartridges available to handgunners. **Barrel length:** 12″ or 14″. **Overall length:** 16″. **Weight:** 4 lbs. (approx.). **Features:** T/C Muzzle Tamer (to reduce recoil); a mounted T/C Recoil Proof 2.5X scope with lighted reticle, QD sling swivels and nylon sling, plus suede leather carrying case.
12″ Barrel **$685.00**
14″ Barrel 695.00

CONTENDER SUPER "16"
VENTILATED RIB/INTERNAL CHOKE MODELS
(not shown)

Featuring a raised ventilated (7/16-inch wide) rib, this Contender model is available in 45 Colt/.410 caliber. A patented detachable choke (1 7/8 inches long) screws into the muzzle internally. **Barrel length:** 16¼″ inches. **Price** . . . . **$450.00** Add **$20.00** for 45-70 Govt.

Also available:
10″ Vent Rib Model w/internal choke **$425.00**

A. UBERTI REPLICAS

1871 ROLLING BLOCK TARGET PISTOL
$380.00

SPECIFICATIONS
Calibers: 22 LR, 222 Rem., 223 Rem., 22 Magnum, 357 Magnum, 45 L.C.
Capacity: Single shot
Barrel length: 9¹/₂″ (half-octagon/half-round or full round Navy Style)
Overall length: 14″
Weight: 2.75 lbs.
Sights: Fully adjustable rear; ramp front or open sight on Navy Style barrel
Grip and forend: Walnut
Trigger guard: Brass
Frame: Color casehardened steel

1871 ROLLING BLOCK TARGET PISTOL

1873 CATTLEMAN QUICK DRAW
$365.00 (Brass)
$415.00 (Steel)

SPECIFICATIONS
Calibers: 38-40, 357 Magnum, 44 Special, 44-40, 45 L.C., 45 ACP
Capacity: 6 shots
Barrel lengths: 4³/₄″, 5¹/₂″, 7¹/₂″; round tapered
Overall length: 10³/₄″ w/5¹/₂″ barrel
Weight: 2.42 lbs.
Grip: One-piece walnut
Frame: Color casehardened steel; also available in charcoal blue (**$25.00** extra) or nickel (**$45.00** extra)
Also available:
45 L.C./45 ACP Convertible **$455.00**
   In brass **415.00**

1873 CATTLEMAN QUICK DRAW

1875 REMINGTON ARMY S.A. "OUTLAW"

1875 REMINGTON ARMY S.A. "OUTLAW"
$405.00

SPECIFICATIONS
Calibers: 357 Magnum, 45 Long Colt, 44-40, 45 ACP
Capacity: 6 shots
Barrel length: 7¹/₂″ round tapered
Overall length: 13³/₄″
Weight: 2.75 lbs.
Grips: Two-piece walnut
Frame: Color casehardened steel
Also available:
In nickel plate **$450.00**
45 L.C./45 ACP Convertible **450.00**

BUCKHORN SINGLE ACTION LARGE FRAME
$420.00

SPECIFICATIONS
Calibers: 357 Magnum, 45 Long Colt, 44-40, 44 Magnum
Capacity: 6 shots
Barrel length: 4³/₄″ or 7¹/₂″
Overall length: 11³/₄″
Weight: 2.5 lbs.
Sights: Open or target
Finish: Black
Also available:
In nickel plate **$455.00**
44-40 Mag. Convertible **460.00**

BUCKHORN SINGLE ACTION LARGE FRAME

WALTHER PISTOLS

DOUBLE-ACTION AUTOMATIC PISTOLS

The Walther double-action system combines the principles of the double-action revolver with the advantages of the modern pistol without the disadvantages inherent in either design.

Models PPK and PPK/S differ only in the overall length of the barrel and slide. Both models offer the same features, including compact form, light weight, easy handling and absolute safety. Both models can be carried with a loaded chamber and closed hammer, but ready to fire either single- or double-action. Both models are provided with a live round indicator pin to signal a loaded chamber. An automatic internal safety blocks the hammer to prevent accidental striking of the firing pin, except with a deliberate pull of the trigger. Sights are provided with white markings for high visibility in poor light. Rich Walther blue/black finish is standard and each pistol is complete with an extra magazine with finger rest extension.

**MODEL PPK & PPK/S
6-SHOT AUTOMATICS**

MODEL PPK & PPK/S 6-SHOT AUTOMATICS

Caliber: 380 ACP
Barrel length: 3.2″
Overall length: 6.1″
Height: 4.28″
Weight: 23 oz.
Finish: Walther blue or stainless steel
Price: $585.00

MODEL TPH DOUBLE ACTION

Walther's Model TPH is considered by government agents and professional lawmen to be one of the top undercover/back-up guns available. A scaled-down version of Walther's PP-PPK series.

SPECIFICATIONS
Caliber: 22 LR
Barrel length: 2¹/₄″
Overall length: 5³/₈″
Weight: 14 oz.
Finish: Stainless steel
Price: $445.00

MODEL TPH

WALTHER PISTOLS

MODEL P-38 DOUBLE ACTION

The Walther P-38 is a double-action, locked breech, semiautomatic pistol with an external hammer. Its compact form, light weight and easy handling are combined with the superb performance of the 9mm Luger Parabellum cartridge. The P-38 is equipped with both a manual and automatic safety, which allows it to be carried safely while the chamber is loaded.

SPECIFICATIONS
Caliber: 9mm Parabellum
Barrel length: 5″
Overall length: 8 1/2″
Weight: 28 oz. (alloy); 34 oz. (steel)
Finish: Blue or non-reflective black
Price: **$950.00**
Also available: **100 YEAR P-38 COMMEMORATIVE**
w/Presentation case **950.00**

MODEL P-38

MODEL P-5 DA

SPECIFICATIONS
Caliber: 9mm Parabellum
Capacity: 8 rounds
Barrel length: 3 1/2″
Overall length: 7″
Weight: 28 oz.
Finish: Blue
Features: Four automatic built-in safety functions; lightweight alloy frame; supplied with two magazines
Price: **$1233.00**
MODEL P-5 COMPACT **1660.00**

MODEL P-5 DA

MODEL PP DOUBLE ACTION (not shown)

SPECIFICATIONS
Caliber: 22 LR, 32 ACP or 380 ACP
Barrel length: 3.8″
Overall length: 6.7″
Weight: 23.5 oz.
Prices:
In 22 LR . . . . **$ 900.00**
In 32 ACP **1250.00**
In 380 ACP **1075.00**

MODEL P-88 DA

SPECIFICATIONS
Caliber: 9mm Parabellum
Capacity: 15 rounds
Barrel length: 4″
Overall length: 7 3/8″
Weight: 31 1/2 oz.
Finish: Blue
Sights: Rear adjustable for windage and elevation
Features: Internal safeties; ambidextrous de-cocking lever and magazine release button; lightweight alloy frame; loaded chamber indicator
Price: **$1550.00**

MODEL P-88 DA

WALTHER TARGET PISTOLS

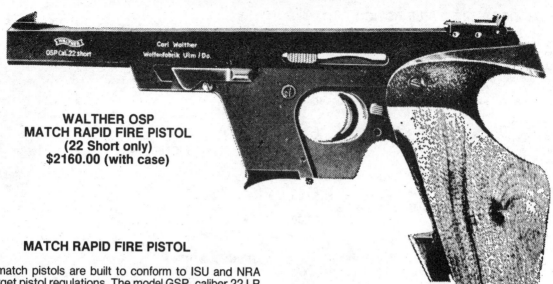

WALTHER OSP
MATCH RAPID FIRE PISTOL
(22 Short only)
$2160.00 (with case)

MATCH RAPID FIRE PISTOL

Walther match pistols are built to conform to ISU and NRA match target pistol regulations. The model GSP, caliber 22 LR is available with either 2.2 lb. (1000 gm) or 3.0 lbs. (1360 gm) trigger, and comes with 4½-inch barrel and special hand-fitting designed walnut stock. Sights consist of fixed front and adjustable rear sight. The GSP-C 32 S&W wadcutter centerfire pistol is factory tested with a 3.0 lb. trigger. The 22 LR conversion unit for the model GSP-C consists of an interchangeable barrel, a slide assembly and two magazines.

MATCH PISTOL SPECIFICATIONS
Calibers: 22 Short, 22 LR and 32 S&W Wadcutter
Magazine capacity: 5 shots
Weight: 44.8 oz. (22 LR); 49.4 oz. (32 S&W)
Overall length: 11.8″

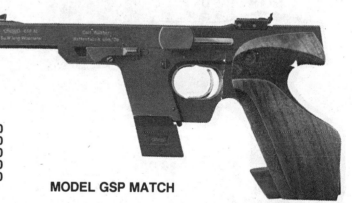

WALTHER GSP MATCH PISTOL
22 LR & 32 S&W Wadcutter

Prices:
GSP—22 Long Rifle w/carrying case $1750.00
GSP-C—32 S&W wadcutter w/carrying case 2250.00
22 LR conversion unit for GSP-C 1000.00
22 Short conversion unit for GSP-C 1420.00
32 S&W wadcutter conversion unit for GSP-C ... 1250.00

MODEL GSP MATCH

GSP JR. SEMIAUTOMATIC (not shown)
$1810.00 (w/Carrying Case)

Caliber: 22 LR
Capacity: 5 rounds
Barrel length: 4½″
Overall length: 11.8″
Weight: 40.1 oz.

DAN WESSON REVOLVERS

357 MAGNUM REVOLVERS

Introduced in 1935, the 357 Magnum iis still the top selling handgun caliber. It makes an excellent hunting sidearm, and many law enforcement agencies have adopted it as a duty caliber. Take your pick of Dan Wesson 357s; then, add to its versatility with an additional barrel assembly option to alter it to your other needs.

SPECIFICATIONS

Action: Six-shot double and single action. **Ammunition:** 357 Magnum, 38 Special Hi-speed, 38 Special Mid-range. **Typical dimension:** 4″ barrel revolver, 9¼″×5¾″. **Trigger:** Smooth, wide tang (³/₈″) with overtravel adjustment. **Hammer:** Wide spur (³/₈″) with short double-action travel. **Sights: Models 14 and 714,** ¹/₈″ fixed serrated front; fixed rear integral with frame. **Models 15 and 715,** ¹/₈″ serrated interchangeable front blade; red insert standard, yellow and white available; rear notch (.125, .080, or white outline) adjustable for windage and elevation; graduated click. 10″ barrel assemblies have special front sights and instructions. **Rifling:** Six lands and grooves, right-hand twist, 1 turn in 18.75 inches (2½″ thru 8″ lengths); six lands & grooves, right-hand twist, 1 turn in 14 inches (10″ bbl.). **Note:** All 2½″ guns shipped with undercover grips. 4″ guns are shipped with service grips and the balance have oversized target grips.

357 MAGNUM

Price:
Pistol Pac Models 14-2 thru 715-VH10 . . . . **$456.00 to $888.00**

MODEL	CALIBER	TYPE	BARREL LENGTHS & WEIGHT IN OUNCES					FINISH
			2½″	4″	6″	8″	10″	
14-2	.357 Magnum	Service	30	34	38	NA	NA	Satin Blue
14-2B	.357 Magnum	Service	30	34	38	NA	NA	Brite Blue
15-2	.357 Magnum	Target	32	36	40	44	50	Brite Blue
15-2V	.357 Magnum	Target	32	35	39	43	49	Brite Blue
15-2VH	.357 Magnum	Target	32	37	42	47	55	Brite Blue
714	.357 Magnum	Service	30	34	40	NA	NA	Satin Stainless Steel
715	.357 Magnum	Target	32	36	40	45	50	Satin Stainless Steel
715-V	.357 Magnum	Target	32	35	40	43	49	Satin Stainless Steel
715-VH	.357 Magnum	Target	32	37	42	49	55	Satin Stainless Steel

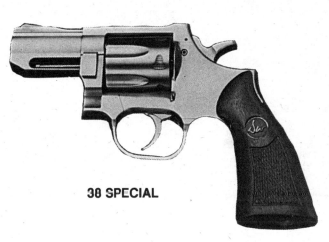

38 SPECIAL

38 SPECIAL REVOLVER

For decades a favorite of security and law enforcement agencies, the 38 special still maintains it's reputation as a fine caliber for sportsmen and target shooters. Dan Wesson offers a choice of many barrel lengths in either the service or target configuration.

SPECIFICATIONS

Action: Six-shot double and single action. **Ammunition:** 38 Special Hi-speed, 38 Special Mid-range. **Typical dimension:** 4″ barrel revolver, 9¼″ × 5¾″. **Trigger:** Smooth, wide tang (³/₈″) with overtravel adjustment. **Hammer:** Wide spur (³/₈″) with short double travel. **Sights:** Models 8 and 708, ¹/₈″ fixed serrated front; fixed rear integral with frame. Models 9 and 709, ¹/₈″ serrated interchangeable front blade; red insert standard, yellow and white available; rear, standard notch (.125, .080, or white outline) adjustable for windage and elevation; graduated click. **Rifling:** Six lands and grooves, right-hand twist, 1 turn in 18.75 inches. **Note:** All 2½″ guns shipped with undercover grips. 4″ guns are shipped with service grips and the balance have oversized target grips.

Price:
38 Special Pistol Pacs (Blue) . . . . **$615.00—805.00**
Stainless Steel . . . . **689.00—888.88**

MODEL	CALIBER	TYPE	BARREL LENGTHS & WEIGHT IN OUNCES				FINISH
			2½″	4″	6″	8″	
8-2	.38 Special	Service	30	34	38	NA	Satin Blue
8-2B	.38 Special	Service	30	34	38	NA	Brite Blue
9-2	.38 Special	Target	32	36	40	44	Brite Blue
9-2V	.39 Special	Target	32	35	39	43	Brite Blue
9-2VH	.38 Special	Target	32	37	42	47	Brite Blue
70B	.38 Special	Service	30	34	38	NA	Satin Stainless Steel
709	.38 Special	Target	32	36	40	44	Satin Stainless Steel
709-V	.38 Special	Target	32	35	39	43	Satin Stainless Steel
709-VH	.38 Special	Target	32	37	42	47	Satin Stainless Steel

DAN WESSON REVOLVERS

22 SILHOUETTE REVOLVER

SPECIFICATIONS
This six-shot, single-action-only revolver is available with 10″ vented or vent heavy barrel assembly; incorporates a new cylinder manufacturing process that enhances the inherent accuracy of the Wesson revolver. Shipped with a combat-style grip, .080 narrow notch rear sight blade, a Patridge-style front sight blade to match. **Caliber:** 22 rimfire. **Type:** Target. **Weight:** 55 to 62 oz. **Finish:** Bright blue or stainless steel.
Price: . . . . **$430.00 to $485.00**

22 SILHOUETTE REVOLVER

GOLD SERIES (not shown)

SPECIFICATIONS
Barrel length: 6″ or 8″; slotted shroud with bright blued barrel, stamped ''Gold Series.'' **Hammer and trigger:** Polished smooth with high bright finish. **Sights:** White triangle imprinted on rear blade; orange dot Patridge front blade. Additional specifications available from manufacturer on request.
Price: **$554.00**

MODEL 738P "L'IL DAN"

SPECIFICATIONS
Caliber: 38 + P. **Capacity:** 5 shots. **Barrel length:** 6½″. **Weight:** 24.6 oz. **Sights:** Fixed. **Finish:** Stainless steel or blue. **Grip:** Pauferro wood or rubber.
Price: Stainless **$270.00**
(Blue model price not set)

MODEL 738P "L'IL DAN"

ACTION CUP/P.P.C. REVOLVER (not shown)

SPECIFICATIONS
Caliber: 38 Special or 357 Magnum. **Barrel length:** 6″, bull shroud with removeable underweight. **Action:** Double action (single action on request). **Finish:** Bright blue or stainless steel (Action Cup in stainless only). **Grip:** Hogue gripper. **Sights:** Tasco PRO Point II (Action Cup) or Aristocrat (P.P.C. model).
Prices:
Action Cup **$913.00**
P.P.C. 38 Special **780.00**
P.P.C. 357 Magnum **857.00**

DAN WESSON REVOLVERS

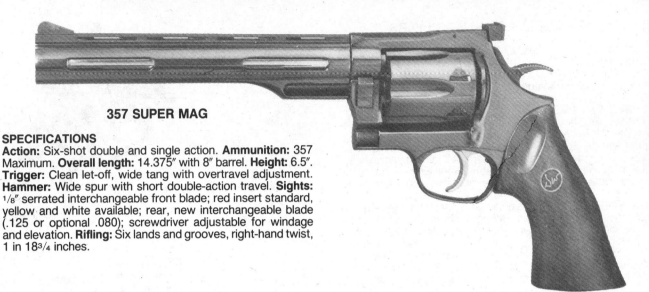

357 SUPER MAG

SPECIFICATIONS

Action: Six-shot double and single action. **Ammunition:** 357 Maximum. **Overall length:** 14.375″ with 8″ barrel. **Height:** 6.5″. **Trigger:** Clean let-off, wide tang with overtravel adjustment. **Hammer:** Wide spur with short double-action travel. **Sights:** 1/8″ serrated interchangeable front blade; red insert standard, yellow and white available; rear, new interchangeable blade (.125 or optional .080); screwdriver adjustable for windage and elevation. **Rifling:** Six lands and grooves, right-hand twist, 1 in 18¾ inches.

SPECIFICATIONS

Model	Caliber	Type	Barrel lengths & Weight (oz.)				Finish	Prices*
			4″	6″	8″	10″		
740-V	357 Max	Target	56	59.5	65	69	Stainless	
740-VH	357 Max	Target	58	62	72	76	Stainless	$550.00—$642.00
740-V8S	357 Max	Target			64		Stainless	

*Model 40 (Blue): $488.00–575.00

32/.32-20 MAGNUM SIX SHOT

This target and small-game gun offers a high muzzle velocity and a flat trajectory for better accuracy. **Action:** Six-shot double and single. **Calibers:** 32 H&R Magnum, 32 S&W Long, 32 Colt new police cartridges interchangeable. **Barrel length:** 4″. **Overall length:** 9¼″. **Trigger:** Smooth, wide tang (3/8″) w/overtravel adjustment. **Hammer:** Wide spur (3/8″) w/short double-action travel. **Sights:** Front—1/8″ serrated, interchangeable blade, red insert standard (yellow and white available); rear—interchangeable blade for wide or narrow notch sight picture (wide notch standard, narrow notch available), adj. for windage and elevation, graduated click. **Rifling:** Six lands and grooves, right-hand twist 1:18¾″. **Finish:** Blue or stainless steel.

SPECIFICATIONS

Model	Caliber	Type	Barrel lengths & Weight in ounces				Finish	Pistol Pac Prices*
			2½″	4″	6″	8″		
32	.32 Magnum	Target	35	39	43	48	Brite Blue	
32V	.32 Magnum	Target	35	39	43	48	Brite Blue	$615.00–$805.00
32VH	.32 Magnum	Target	35	40	46	53	Brite Blue	
732	.32 Magnum	Target	35	39	43	48	Satin Stainless Steel	
732V	.32 Magnum	Target	35	39	43	48	Satin Stainless Steel	$689.00–$888.00
732VH	.32 Magnum	Target	35	40	46	53	Satin Stainless Steel	

DAN WESSON REVOLVERS

41 AND 44 MAGNUM REVOLVERS

The Dan Wesson 41 and 44 Magnum revolvers are available with a patented "Power Control" to reduce muzzle flip. Both the 41 and the 44 have a one-piece frame and patented gain bolt for maximum strength.

SPECIFICATIONS
Action: Six-shot double- and single-action. **Ammunition:** Models 41 and 741, 41 Magnum; Models 44 and 744, 44 Magnum and 44 Special. **Typical dimension:** 6″ barrel revolver, 12″×6.″ **Trigger:** Smooth, wide tang (³/₈″) with overtravel adjustment. **Hammer:** Wide checkered spur with short double-action travel. **Sights:** Front, ¹/₈″ serrated interchangeable blade; red insert standard, yellow and white available; rear, standard notch (.125, .080, or white outline) adjustable for windage and elevation; click graduated. **Rifling:** Eight lands and grooves, right-hand twist, 1 turn in 18.75 inches. **Note:** 4″, 6″, and 8″ 44 Magnum guns will be shipped with unported and Power Control barrels. 10″ 44 Magnum guns available only without Power Control. Only jacketed bullets should be used with the 44 Mag. Power Control or excessive leading will result.

Prices:
Pistol Pac Model 41 (Blue) . . . . **$624.00—672.00**
   Stainless Steel . . . . **690.00—739.00**
Pistol Pac Model 44 (Blue) . . . . **708.00—758.00**
   Stainless Steel . . . . **814.00—867.00**

41/44 MAGNUM REVOLVER

Model	Caliber	Type	Barrel Lengths & Wt. in Ounces				Finish
			4″	6″	8″	10″**	
41-V	.41 Magnum	Target	48	53	58	64	Brite Blue
41-VH	.41 Magnum	Target	49	56	64	69	Brite Blue
44-V	.44 Magnum	Target	48	53	58	64	Brite Blue
44-VH	.44 Magnum	Target	49	56	64	69	Brite Blue
741-V	.41 Magnum	Target	48	53	58	64	Satin Stainless Steel
741-VH	.41 Magnum	Target	49	56	64	69	Satin Stainless Steel
744-V	.44 Magnum	Target	48	53	58	64	Satin Stainless Steel
744-VH	.44 Magnum	Target	49	56	64	69	Satin Stainless Steel

445 SUPERMAG REVOLVERS

With muzzle velocities in the 1650 fps range, and chamber pressures and recoil comparable to the 44 Magnum, the 445 Supermag has already won considerable renown in silhouette competition. As a hunting cartridge, it is more than adequate for any species of game on the American continent. **Action:** Six-shot double and single. **Type:** Target. **Caliber:** 445 Supermag. **Overall length:** 14.375″ w/8″ barrel. **Trigger:** Clean let-off, widg tane with overtravel adjustment. **Hammer:** Wide spur with short double-action travel. **Sights:** ¹/₈″ serrated, interchangeable front blade, red insert standard (yellow and white available); rear—interchangeable blade for wide or narrow notch sight picture, wide notch standard (narrow notch available), adj. for windage and elevation. **Rifling:** Six lands and grooves, right-hand twist 1:18³/₄″.

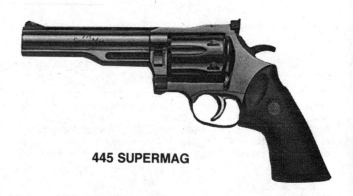

445 SUPERMAG

Model	Barrel Length & Weight in Ounces			Finish	Prices
	6″	8″	10″		
445-V	59.5	62	65	Bright Blue	
445-VH	62	72	76	Bright Blue	$516.00–$615.00
445-VHS	—	64	—	Bright Blue	
445-VS	—	60	64	Bright Blue	
7445-V	59.5	62	65	Stainless Steel	
7445-VH	62	72	76	Stainless Steel	$592.00–$683.00
7445-VHS	—	64	—	Stainless Steel	
7445-VS	—	60	64	Stainless Steel	

DAN WESSON REVOLVERS

22 RIMFIRE and 22 WIN. MAGNUM REVOLVERS

Built on the same frames as the Dan Wesson 357 Magnum, these 22 rimfires offer the heft and balance of fine target revolvers. Affordable fun for the beginner or the expert.

SPECIFICATIONS

Action: Six-shot double and single action. **Ammunition:** Models 22 & 722, 22 Long Rifle; Models 22M & 722M, 22 Win. Mag. **Typical dimension:** 4″ barrel revolver, $9\frac{1}{4}″ \times 5\frac{3}{4}″$. **Trigger:** Smooth, wide tang ($\frac{3}{8}″$) with overtravel adjustment. **Hammer:** Wide spur ($\frac{3}{8}″$) with short double-action travel. **Sights:** Front, $\frac{1}{8}″$ serrated, interchangeable blade; red insert standard, yellow and white available; rear, standard wide notch (.125, .080, or white outline) adjustable for windage and elevation; graduated click. **Rifling:** Models 22 and 722, six lands and grooves, right-hand twist, 1 turn in 12 inches; Models 22M and 722M, six lands and grooves, right-hand twist, 1 turn in 16 inches. **Note:** All $2\frac{1}{2}″$ guns are shipped with undercover grips. 4″ guns are shipped with service grips and the balance have oversized target grips.

Prices:
Pistol Pac Models 22 thru 722M . . . . . . $637.00 (Blue)—
$923.00 (Stainless)

22 RIMFIRE/22 WIN. MAG. (Blue)

22 RIMFIRE/22 WIN. MAG. (Stainless)

Model	Caliber	Type	Barrel Lengths & Wt. in Ounces				Finish
			2¼″	4″	6″	8″	
22	.22 L.R.	Target	36	40	44	49	Brite Blue
22-V	.22 L.R.	Target	36	40	44	49	Brite Blue
22-VH	.22 L.R.	Target	36	41	47	54	Brite Blue
22-M	.22 Win Mag	Target	36	40	44	49	Brite Blue
22M-V	.22 Win Mag	Target	36	40	44	49	Brite Blue
22M-VH	.22 Win Mag	Target	36	41	47	54	Brite Blue
722	.22 L.R.	Target	36	40	44	49	Satin Stainless Steel
722-V	.22 L.R.	Target	36	40	44	49	Satin Stainless Steel
722-VH	.22 L.R.	Target	36	41	47	54	Satin Stainless Steel
722M	.22 Win Mag	Target	36	40	44	49	Satin Stainless Steel
722M-V	.22 Win Mag	Target	36	40	44	49	Satin Stainless Steel
722M-VH	.22 Win Mag	Target	36	41	47	54	Satin Stainless Steel

HUNTER PACS

Offered in all magnum calibers and include the following:
1. Gun with vent heavy 8″ shroud.
2. A vent 8″ shroud only, equipped with Burris scope mounts and Burris scope in either 1½x4X variable or fixed 2X.
3. Barrel changing tool and Wesson emblem packed in a custom-fitted carrying case. Available in either bright blue or stainless steel.

Prices: $691.00 (32 Mag. w/blue finish, mounts only) to **$1145.00** (445 Supermag, stainless steel w/1½X-4X scope)

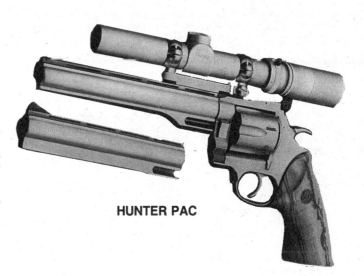

HUNTER PAC

WICHITA ARMS PISTOLS

SILHOUETTE PISTOL
$1100.00

SPECIFICATIONS
Calibers: 308 Win. F.L., 7mm IHMSA and 7mm×308
Barrel length: 14¹⁵/₁₆″
Weight: 4¹/₂ lbs.
Action: Single-shot bolt action
Sights: Wichita Multi-Range Sight System
Grips: Right-hand center walnut grip or right-hand rear walnut grip
Features: Glass bedded; bolt ground to precision fit; adjustable Wichita trigger

SILHOUETTE PISTOL
(Right Hand Rear Grip)

Also available:
WICHITA CLASSIC PISTOL **$2950.00**
Engraved Model 4850.00

INTERNATIONAL PISTOL
$510.00 (10″ Barrel)
$544.00 (14″ Barrel)

SPECIFICATIONS
Calibers: 7-30 Waters, 7mm Super Mag., 7R (30-30 Win. necked to 7mm), 30-30 Win., 357 Mag., 357 Super Mag., 32 H&H Mag., 22 RFM, 22 LR
Barrel lengths: 10″ and 14″ (10¹/₂″ for centerfire calibers)
Weight: 3 lbs. 2 oz. (10″ barrel); 4 lbs. 7 oz. (14″ barrel)
Action: Top-break, single-shot, single action only
Sights: Patridge front sight; rear sight adjustable for windage and elevation
Grips and Forend: Walnut
Safety: Cross bolt

INTERNATIONAL PISTOL

WILDEY PISTOLS

These gas-operated pistols are designed to meet the needs of hunters who want to use handguns for big game. The Wildey pistol includes such features as: • Ventilated rib • Reduced recoil • Double-action trigger mechanism • Patented hammer and trigger blocks and rebounding fire pin • Sights adjustable for windage and elevation • Stainless construction • Fixed barred for increased accuracy • Increased action strength (with 3-lug and exposed face rotary bolt) • Selective single or autoloading capability • Ability to handle high-pressure loads

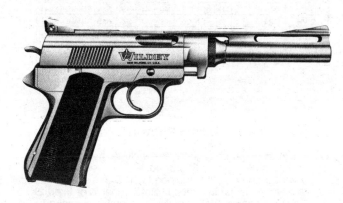

SPECIFICATIONS
Calibers: 45 Win. Mag., 475 Wildey Mag.
Capacity: 7 shots
Barrel lengths: 5″, 6″, 7″, 8″, 10″, 12″
Overall length: 11″ with 7″ barrel
Weight: 64 oz. with 5″ barrel
Height: 6″
Prices:
SURVIVOR MODEL in 45 Win. Mag.,
5″, 6″ and 7″ models **$1175.00**
   With square trigger guard, **add** 35.00
   Same model w/8″ or 10″ barrels 1195.00
   With square trigger guard, **add** 35.00
   With new vent rib, **add** 30.00
SURVIVOR MODEL in 475 Wildey Mag., 8″ or 10″
barrels 1195.00
   With square trigger guard, **add** 35.00
   With new vent rib, **add** 30.00

HUNTER MODEL in 45 Win. Mag., 8″, 10″, 12″
barrels 1315.95
   With square trigger guard, **add** 35.00
HUNTER MODEL in 475 Wildey Mag., 8″, 10″,
barrels 1315.95
   With 12″ barrel 1345.95
   W/square trigger guard (8″, 10″, 12″ barrels)
   add 35.00

Also available:
Interchangeable barrel extension assemblies **$474.95** (5″ barrel) to **$589.95** (12″ barrel).

Discover

HAND GUNNING

Loaded with excitement!

6 BIG ISSUES A YEAR FEATURING...

- In-depth reviews of auto pistols, revolvers, and single-shot handguns

- Handloading how-to's that help you get maximum performance out of every shot

- Special reports on handgun hunting, personal defense, law enforcement, and more

- Accurate info on how factory loads perform on the range and in the field

- Modifications you can make at home to turn your factory handgun into a custom shooting piece

- The nation's *best* handgun writers, including Wiley Clapp, Dick Metcalf, Charles E. Petty, and law enforcement specialist Bob Hoelscher

HALF-PRICE DEAL

Get your BIGGEST savings on the best handgun magazine around. And your first issue's FREE!

You'll get more out of HandGunning. GUARANTEED.

If **HandGunning** doesn't help you get more out of your sport, just say so. We'll refund **100%** of the subscription price, no questions asked.

Only 1 magazine covers it all — with lively news, authoritative information, and issues of special interest to <u>you</u>.

Send for your FREE trial issue today!

HandGunning FREE TRIAL ISSUE OFFER

☐ **YES!** Please send me a free trial issue of **HandGunning**. If I like it and want more, I'll pay the $9.99 invoice for a full year of handgun action (5 additional issues, 6 in all). **I save HALF OFF** the regular subscription value!

If I don't choose to subscribe, I'll return the invoice, marked "cancel." The trial issue is mine to keep — FREE!

K8SB5

Please Print

Name _____

Address _____ Apt _____

City _____

State _____ Zip _____

Offer expires July 1, 1993.

Your first issue will arrive in two to ten weeks. Outside U.S., add $8 postage, payable in U.S. funds drawn on a U.S. bank. Canada (includes postage & GST): $19.25 U.S.

Get *MORE* out of *HandGunning*

TOP GUNS

See what's new in handguns today! **HandGunning** expert bring you the most thorough evaluations in the business.

HOT SHOTS

Whether you're a big game hunter or backyard plinker, you'll get more out of your sport with **HandGunning**. It's packed with valuable tips and techniques for handgun hunting…target shooting…handloading… home defense…and more.

BIG ADVENTURES

Join us on high-adventure hunting expeditions. See the latest in high-tech equipment. And share in the unique perspective of men and women for whom handgunning is more than a hobby — from the military to officers on the beat.

6 big issues a year including the exclusive Handgun Buyer's Guide

Essential reading for anyone who's thinking of buying a handgun. **HandGunning's** annual report on more than 200 SA, DA and single-shot handguns, featuring complete specs and suggested prices.

It all starts with your FREE trial issue.
Mail this card today!

Rifles

For addresses and phone numbers of manufacturers and distributors included in this section, turn to *DIRECTORY OF MANUFACTURERS AND SUPPLIERS* at the back of the book.

ACTION ARMS

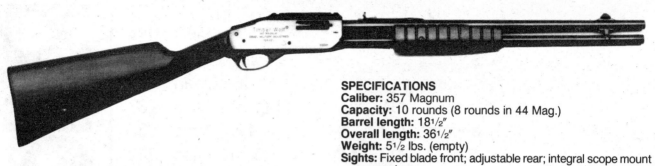

TIMBER WOLF
$319.00 ($379.00 Chrome)

SPECIFICATIONS
Caliber: 357 Magnum
Capacity: 10 rounds (8 rounds in 44 Mag.)
Barrel length: 18½"
Overall length: 36½"
Weight: 5½ lbs. (empty)
Sights: Fixed blade front; adjustable rear; integral scope mount on receiver
Stock: Walnut
Operation: Locked breech
Safety system: Push button on trigger guard

AMT RIFLES

LIGHTNING (Stock Folded)

LIGHTNING
$279.99

This stainless steel rifle features a tapered or bull barrel, diamond finished and Pope crowned, grooved for scope mount. Fixed sights and recoil pad are standard.

SPECIFICATIONS:
Caliber: 22 LR Semiautomatic
Capacity: 30 rounds
Barrel length (stock folded): 17½"
Overall length: 26½" (37" w/stock extended)
Weight: 6¼ lbs. (tapered barrel); 6½ lbs. (bull barrel)
Features: Checkered handle and forearm are black matte fiberglass filled nylon

SPECIFICATIONS
Caliber: 22 LR Semiautomatic
Capacity: 10 rounds
Barrel length: 22"
Overall length: 40½"
Weight: 6 lbs.
Features: Uncle Mike's swivel studs for strap attachment; removable recoil pad provides storage for ammo, cleaning rod and survival knife; grooves for scope mount; synthetic stock is black matte fiberglass filled nylon, checkered at forearm and grip
Also available:
22 MAGNUM RIMFIRE (MATCH GRADE) free-floating
barrel $359.99

SMALL GAME HUNTER II RIFLE
$299.99
(Scope not included)

ANSCHUTZ SPORTER RIFLES

SPORTER MODELS

MODEL 1700D CUSTOM
$1237.00 (22 LR)
$1389.00 (22 Hornet & 222 Rem.)
$1189.00 (Featherweight)
$1399.00 (Featherweight Deluxe)

BAVARIAN 1700
$1237.00 (22 LR)
$1360.00 (22 Hornet & 222 Rem.)

MODEL 1700D CLASSIC
$1199.00 (22 LR)
$1360.00 (22 Hornet & 222 Rem.)

MODEL 1700 GRAPHITE CUSTOM
$1229.00

SPECIFICATIONS

	Custom	Bavarian	Classic	Graphite Custom
	22 Long Rifle, 22 Magnum, 22 Hornet, 222 Remington			22 LR
Length—Overall	43″	43″	43″	41″
Barrel	24″	24″	24″	22″
Pull	14″	14″	14″	14″
Drop at—Comb	1¼″	1¼″	1¼″	1¼″
Monte Carlo	1″	—	—	1″
Heel	1½″	1½″	1½″	1½″
Average Weight	7½ lbs.	7½ lbs.	6¾ lbs.	7¼ lbs.
Trigger—Single Stage 5096 (.222 Rem., 5095)	•	•	•	•
Rate of Twist	Right Hand—one turn in 16.5″ for .22 LR; 1-16″ for .22 Hornet; 1-14″ for .222 Rem.			

ANSCHUTZ SPORTER RIFLES

MATCH 64 SPORTER MODELS

MODEL 1416DCL (22 LR) AND 1516DCL (22 Magnum) CLASSIC
$665.00 (1416DCL) $689.00 (1516DCL)
$698.00 (22 LR Left Hand)

1418D (22 LR) AND 1518D (22 Magnum) MANNLICHER
$1029.00 (22 LR) $1049.00 (22 Magnum)

MODEL 525 SPORTER
$519.00

MODEL 1416D (22 LR) AND 1516D (22 Magnum) CUSTOM
$679.00 (22 LR) $699.00 (22 Magnum)
(not shown)

SPECIFICATIONS

	Classic 1416D** 1516D	Custom 1416D 1516D	Mannlicher 1418D 1518D	Model 525 Sporter
Length—Overall	41″	41″	38″	43″
Barrel	22½″	22½″	19¾″	24″
Pull	14″	14″	14″	14″
Drop at—Comb	1¼″	1¼″	1¼″	1⅛″
Monte Carlo	1½″	1½″	1½″	1¾″
Heel	1½″	2½″	2½″	2⅝″
Average Weight	5½ lbs.	6 lbs.*	5½ lbs.	6½ lbs.
Rate of Twist Right Hand—one turn in 16.5″ for .22 LR; 1–16″ for .22 Mag				
Take Down Bolt Action With Removable Firing Pin	•	•	•	
¾″ Swivel			•	
Swivel Studs	•	•		•

* 5¼ lbs. in 1416D Fiberglass

ANSCHUTZ MATCH RIFLES

MODEL 1827 BIATHLON RIFLE

BIATHLON RIFLES SPECIFICATIONS

Model	1827B	1827BT	1403B
Barrel	21$\frac{1}{2}$″ ($\frac{3}{4}$″ dia.)	21$\frac{1}{2}$″ ($\frac{3}{4}$″ dia.)	21$\frac{1}{2}$″ ($\frac{3}{4}$″ dia.)
Action	Super Match 54	T. Bolt	Match 64
Trigger	1 lb. 3.5 oz. 2 stage #5020 adjustable* from 3$\frac{1}{2}$ oz. to 2 lbs.	1 lb. 3.5 oz., 2 stage #5020 adjustable* from 3$\frac{1}{2}$ oz. to 2 lbs.	1 lb. 5 oz. 2 stage #5092
Safety	Slide safety	Slide safety	Slide safety
Stock	European Walnut, cheek piece, stippled pistol grip and front stock	European Walnut, cheek piece, stippled pistol grip and front stock.	Blond finished European hardwood, stippled pistol grip.
Sights	6827 Sight Set with snow caps furnished with rifle and 10 click adjustment.	6827 Sight Set with snow caps furnished with rifle and 10 click adjustment.	6560 front sight with snow cap furnished. Rear sight is extra.
Overall length	42$\frac{1}{2}$″	42$\frac{1}{2}$″	42$\frac{1}{2}$″
Weight	8$\frac{1}{2}$ lbs. with sights	8$\frac{1}{2}$ lbs. with sights	8$\frac{1}{2}$ lbs. with sights
Price	$2284.00	$3550.00 ($3880.00 L.H.)	$997.50

MODEL 64MS

MODEL 54.18MS-REP DELUXE

SPECIFICATIONS AND FEATURES (22 LR)

METALLIC SILHOUETTE RIFLES

Prices:

64MS	$ 889.00
Left Hand	948.00
54.18MS	1465.00
Left Hand	1539.00
54.18MS-REP	1789.00
54.18MS-REP DELUXE	1999.00
1700 FWT	1189.00
1700 FWT DELUXE	1399.00

	64MS	54.18MS	54.18MS-REP*	1700 FWT*
Grooved for scope	•	•	•	•
Tapped for scope mount	•	•	•	•
Overall length	39.5″	41″	41–49″	41″
Barrel length	21$\frac{1}{2}$″	22″	22–30″	22″
Length of pull	13$\frac{1}{2}$″	13$\frac{3}{4}$″	13$\frac{3}{4}$″	14″
High cheekpiece with Monte Carlo effect	•	•	•	
Drop at Comb	1$\frac{1}{2}$″	1$\frac{1}{2}$″	1$\frac{1}{2}$″	1$\frac{1}{4}$″
Average weight	8 lbs.	8 lbs. 6 oz.	7 lbs. 12 oz.	6$\frac{1}{4}$ lbs.
Trigger:	#5091	#5018	#5018	#5096
Stage	Two	Two	Two	Single
Factory adjusted weight	5.3 oz.	3.9 oz.	3.9 oz.	2.6 lbs.
Adjustable weight	4.9–7 oz.	2.1–8.6 oz.	2.1–8.6 oz.	2.6–4.4 lbs.
Safety	Slide	Slide	Slide	Wing
True Left-hand Model	•	•	•	

* **Deluxe** model features Fibergrain Finish

ANSCHUTZ INTERNATIONAL TARGET RIFLES

**MODEL 1913
SUPER MATCH**
$2899.00 ($3094.00 Left Hand)

MODEL 1910 SUPER MATCH II
(not shown)
$2589.00 ($2767.00 Left Hand)

MODEL 1803D (not shown)
$1012.00

**MODEL 1911
PRONE MATCH**
$2049.00 ($2188.00 Left Hand)

**MODEL 1808DRT (not shown)
SUPER RUNNING $1729.00**

MODEL 1903D (not shown)
$1049.00 ($1115.00 Left Hand)

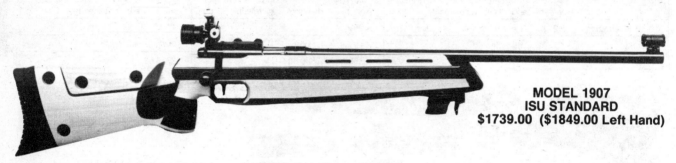

**MODEL 1907
ISU STANDARD**
$1739.00 ($1849.00 Left Hand)

INTERNATIONAL MATCH RIFLES: SPECIFICATIONS AND FEATURES

	1913	1911	1910	1907	1808DRT-Super
Barrel Length O/D	27¹/₄" ⁷/₈" (23.4 mm)	27¹/₄" ⁷/₈" (23.4 mm)	27¹/₄" ⁷/₈" (23.4 mm)	26" ⁷/₈" (22 mm)	32¹/₂" ⁷/₈" (22 mm)
Stock	Int'l.- Thumb Hole Adj. Palm Rest Adj. Hand Rest	Prone	Int'l.- Thumb Hole	Standard	Thumb Hole
Cheek Piece Butt Plate	Adj. Adj. Hook 10 Way Hook	Adj. Adj. 4 Way	Adj. Adj. Hook 10 Way Hook	Removable Adj. 4 Way	Adj. Adj. 4 Way
Recommended Sights	6820, 6823 *6820 Left	6820, 6823 *6820 Left	6820, 6823 *6820 Left	6820, 6823 *6820 Left	Grooved for Scope Mounts
Overall Length	45"-46"	45"-46"	45"-46"	43³/₄"-44¹/₂"	50¹/₂"
Overall Length to Hook	49.6"-51.2"		49.6"-51.2"		
Weight (approx) without sights	15.2 lbs.	11.7 lbs.	13.7 lbs.	11.2 lbs.	9.4 lbs.
True Left-Hand Version	1913 Left	1911 Left	1910 Left	1907 Left	1808 Left
Trigger Stage Factory Set Wt. Adjust. Wt.	#5018 Two 3.9 oz. 2.1-8.6 oz.	#5018 Two 3.9 oz. 2.1-8.6 oz.	#5018 Two 3.9 oz. 2.1-8.6 oz.	#5018 Two 3.9 oz. 2.1-8.6 oz.	5020D Single 1.2 lbs. 14 oz.-2.4 lbs.

ANSCHUTZ TARGET RIFLES

THE ACHIEVER
$395.00

This rifle has been designed especially for young shooters and is equally at home on range or field. It meets all NRA recommendations as an ideal training rifle.

SPECIFICATIONS
Caliber: 22 LR
Capacity: 5- or 10-shot clips available

Action: Mark 2000-type repeating
Barrel length: 19$\frac{1}{2}$″
Overall length: 35$\frac{1}{2}$″–36$\frac{2}{3}$″
Weight: 5 lbs.
Trigger: #5066-two stage (2.6 lbs.)
Safety: Slide
Sights: Hooded ramp front; marble folding-leaf rear, adjustable for windage and elevation
Stock pull: 12″
Stock: European hardwood

MODEL 2013
$3577.00

SPECIFICATIONS
Caliber: 22 LR
Barrel length: 19$\frac{3}{4}$″
Overall length: 43″ to 45$\frac{1}{2}$″
Weight: 12.5 lbs. (without sights)
Trigger: #5018, two-stage, 3.9 oz. (factory set wt.)
Sights: #6820
Stock: International with adjustable palm rest and hand rest
Feature: Adjustable cheekpiece

MODEL 2007 ISU STANDARD (not shown)
$2526.00

SPECIFICATIONS
Caliber: 22 LR
Barrel length: 19$\frac{3}{4}$″
Overall length: 43$\frac{1}{2}$″ to 44$\frac{1}{2}$″
Weight: 10.8 lbs. (without sights)
Trigger: #5018, two-stage, 3.9 oz. (factory set wt.)
Sights: #6820
Stock: Standard ISU
Feature: Adjustable cheekpiece

A-SQUARE RIFLES

CAESAR MODEL (Left Hand)
$2250.00

SPECIFICATIONS
Calibers: Groups I, II and III only (see Hannibal Model)
Features: Selected Claro walnut stock with oil finish; three-position safety; three-way adjustable target trigger

CAESAR MODEL (416 Hoffman)
w/2x7 Variable Scope and
3-Leaf Express Sights

HANNIBAL MODEL (416 Rigby)
w/2xLER Scope and 3-Leaf
Express Sights

HANNIBAL MODEL
$2195.00

SPECIFICATIONS
Calibers:
Group I: 30-06
Group II: 7mm Rem. Mag., 300 Win. Mag., 416 Taylor, 425 Express, 458 Win. Mag.
Group III: 300 H&H, 300 Weatherby, 8mm Rem. Mag., 340 Weatherby, 375 H&H, 375 Weatherby, 404 Jeffrey, 416 Hoffman, 416 Rem. Mag., 450 Ackley, 458 Lott
Group IV: 338 A-Square Mag., 375 A-Square Mag., 378 Weatherby, 416 Rigby, 416 Weatherby, 460 Short A-Square Mag., 460 Weatherby, 495 A-Square Mag., 500 A-Square Mag.

Barrel lengths: 20″ to 26″
Length of pull: 12″ to 15¼″
Finish: Deluxe walnut stock; oil finish; matte blue
Features: Flush detachable swivels, leather sling, ammo carrier, dual recoil lugs, coil spring ejector, ventilated recoil pad, premium honed barrels, contoured ejection port, adjustable target-style trigger, Mauser-style claw extractor and controlled feed, positive safety

AUTO-ORDNANCE

THOMPSON MODEL M1 CARBINE
$712.50

SPECIFICATIONS
Caliber: 45 ACP
Barrel length: 16½″
Overall length: 38″
Weight: 11½ lbs.
Sights: Blade front; fixed rear
Stock: Walnut stock and forend
Finish: Military black
Features: Side cocking lever; frame and receiver milled from solid steel

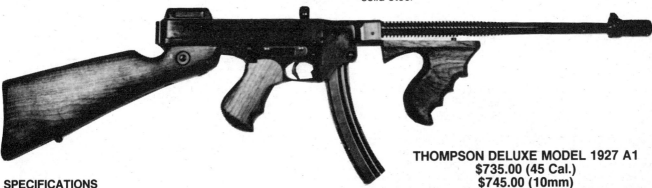

THOMPSON DELUXE MODEL 1927 A1
$735.00 (45 Cal.)
$745.00 (10mm)

Also available:
THOMPSON 1927A-1C LIGHTWEIGHT. Same as the 1927A1 model, but 20% lighter. **Price: $707.00**
THOMPSON MODEL 1927A3. Same as above, but in caliber 22 LR. **Weight:** 7 lbs. **Price: $487.50**

VIOLIN CARRYING CASE (for gun, drum & extra magazines)
$105.00

SPECIFICATIONS
Caliber: 45 ACP and 10mm
Barrel length: 16″
Overall length: 42″
Weight: 11½ lbs.
Sights: Blade front; open rear adjustable
Stock: Walnut stock; vertical forend

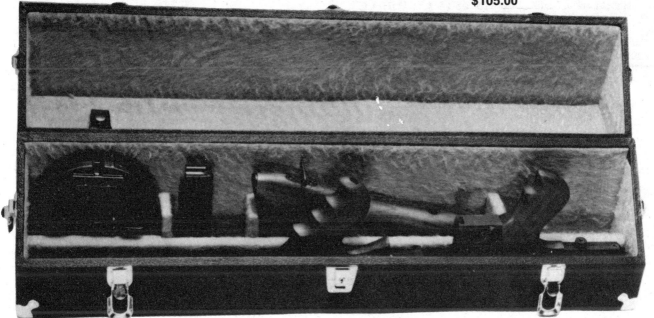

BEEMAN RIFLES

BEEMAN/WEIHRAUCH HW 60M SMALLBORE RIFLE
$798.00 (Right) $878.95 (Left)

Caliber: 22 LR, single shot. Improved bolt action. Adjustable match trigger with push button safety. Precision rifled barrel. Stippled forearm and pistol grip. Precision aperture sights, hooded front sight ramp. **Barrel length:** 26.8″. **Overall length:** 45.7″. **Weight:** 10.8 lbs.

BEEMAN/WEIHRAUCH HW 60J-ST BOLT-ACTION RIFLE
$889.50 (60J) $584.95 (60J-ST)

Calibers: 222 Rem. (60J); 22 LR (60J-ST). Features include: walnut stock with cheekpiece; cut-checkered pistol grip and forend; polished blue finish; oil-finished wood. **Sights:** Hooded blade on ramp front; open rear adjustable. **Barrel length:** 22.8″. **Overall length:** 41.7″. **Weight:** 6½ lbs. Imported from West Germany by Beeman.

BEEMAN/WEIHRAUCH HW 660 MATCH RIFLE
$889.50 (Right Hand)

Caliber: 22 LR. Match-type walnut stock with adjustable cheekpiece and buttplate. Adjustable match trigger; stippled pistol grip and forend; forend accessory rail. **Sights:** Globe front; match aperture rear. **Barrel length:** 26″. **Overall length:** 45.3″. **Weight:** 10.7 lbs. Imported from West Germany by Beeman.

BEEMAN/FWB 2600
$1398.00 (Right) $1575.00 (Left)

Caliber: 22 LR. Designed as an identical small-bore companion to the Beeman/FWB 600 Match air rifle. Super rigid stock made of laminated hardwood. Bull barrel free floats. Stock is cut low to permit complete ventilation around barrel. Match trigger has fingertip weight adjustment dial. Adjustable comb; match sights; single shot.

BLASER RIFLES

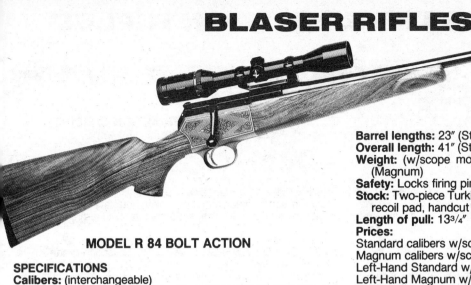

MODEL R 84 BOLT ACTION

SPECIFICATIONS
Calibers: (interchangeable)
    Standard: 22-250, 243 Win., 6mm Rem., 25-06, 270 Win., 280 Rem., 30-06
    Magnum: 257 Weatherby Mag., 264 Win. Mag., 7mm Rem. Mag., 300 Win. Mag., 300 Weatherby Mag., 338 Win. Mag., 375 H&H

Barrel lengths: 23″ (Standard) and 24″ (Magnum)
Overall length: 41″ (Standard) and 42″ (Magnum)
Weight: (w/scope mounts) 7 lbs. (Standard) and 7¼ lbs. (Magnum)
Safety: Locks firing pin and bolt handle
Stock: Two-piece Turkish walnut stock and forend; solid black recoil pad, handcut checkering (18 lines/inch, borderless)
Length of pull: 13¾″
Prices:

Standard calibers w/scope mounts	**$2250.00**
Magnum calibers w/scope mounts	2250.00
Left-Hand Standard w/scope mounts	2300.00
Left-Hand Magnum w/scope mounts	2300.00
Interchangeable barrels	545.00
Deluxe Model (Right Hand)	2500.00
(Left Hand)	2550.00
Super Deluxe Model (Right Hand)	2850.00
(Left Hand)	2900.00

BRNO RIFLES

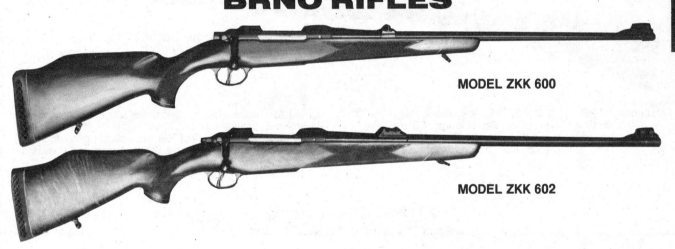

MODEL ZKK 600

MODEL ZKK 602

MODEL ZKK SPECIFICATIONS

Model	Action Type	Caliber	Barrel Specifications			Overall Length	Weight	Magazine Capacity	Sighted In
			Length	Rifling Twist	#Lands				
ZKK 600	bolt	270 Win. 30.06 Spring	23.5 in	1 in 10″ 1 in 9″	4 4	44.0 in.	7 lbs. 2 oz.	5	110 yd.
ZKK 601	bolt	243 Win. 308 Win.	23.5 in.	1 in 12″ 1 in 10″	4 4	43.0 in.	6 lbs. 3 oz.	5	110 yd.
ZKK 602	bolt	300 Win. Mag. 375 H&H 458 Win. Mag.	25.0 in.	1 in 10″ 1 in 12″	4 4	45.5 in.	9 lbs. 4 oz.	5	110 yd.

Model ZKK 600 Standard	**$519.00**	Model ZKK 602 Standard	**$779.00**
Model ZKK 601 Monte Carlo Stock	519.00	In 458 Win. Mag.	795.00

BROWNING LEVER ACTION RIFLES

MODEL 1886 LEVER ACTION CARBINE
$749.95

The Model 1886 rifle was John Browning's first lever-action repeater design to be manufactured. Winchester realized the opportunity to carry this unique, stronger action design and paid Browning ''more money than there is in Ogden'' (Utah, where Browning lived and worked) for the rights to produce the 1886 rifle. Virtually identical to the original, the new Model 1886 has the following specifications.

Caliber: 45-70 Government. **Capacity:** 8 rounds. **Action:** Lever action. **Barrel length:** 22″, round. **Overall length:** 40³/₄″. **Weight:** 8 lbs. 3 oz. **Sights:** Adjustable folding-leaf rear. **Fea-**

tures: Full-length magazine, classic-style forearm with barrel bands; saddle ring; metal crescent buttplate; select walnut with satin finish (all metal surfaces deeply blued).

Also available:
LIMITED EDITION HIGH GRADE. Features high-grade select walnut stock and forearm with finely cut checkering in a gloss finish. Receiver and lever are grayed steel embellished with scroll engraving depicting scenes of mule deer and grizzly bear. **Price: $1175.00**

MODEL 1885 SINGLE SHOT
$771.95

Calibers: 22-250; 223, 30-06, 270, 7mm Rem. Mag., 45-70 Govt. **Bolt system:** Falling block. **Barrel length:** 28″ (recessed muzzle). **Overall length:** 43¹/₂″. **Weight:** 8 lbs. 12 oz. **Action:** High wall type, single shot, lever action. **Sights:** Drilled and

tapped for scope mounts; two-piece scope base available. **Hammer:** Exposed, serrated, three-position with inertia sear. **Stock and Forearm:** Select Walnut, straight grip stock and Schnabel forearm with cut checkering. Recoil pad standard.

MODEL 81 BLR LEVER ACTION
$499.95 (with Sights)

Calibers: 223 Rem., 22-250 Rem., 243 Win., 257 Roberts, 7mm-08 Rem., 284 Win., 308 Win. and 358 Win. **Action:** Lever action with rotating head, multiple lug breech bolt with recessed bolt face. Side ejection. **Barrel length:** 20″. Individually machined from forged, heat treated chrome-moly steel; crowned muzzle. **Rifling:** 243 Win., one turn in 10″; 308 and 358 Win., one turn in 12″. **Magazine:** Detachable, 4-round capacity. **Overall length:** 39³/₄″. **Approximate Weight:** 6 lbs. 15 oz. **Trigger:** Wide, grooved finger piece. Short crisp pull of 4¹/₂ pounds. Travels with lever. **Receiver:** Non-glare top. Drilled and tapped to accept most top scope mounts. Forged and milled steel. All parts are machine-finished and hand-fitted. Surface deeply polished. **Sights:** Low profile, square notch,

screw adjustable rear sight. Gold bead on a hooded raised ramp front sight. Sight radius: 17³/₄″. **Safety:** Exposed, 3-position hammer. Trigger disconnect system. Inertia firing pin. **Stock and forearm:** Select walnut with tough oil finish and sure-grip checkering, contoured for use with either open sights or scope. Straight grip stock. Deluxe recoil pad installed.

Also available:
MODEL 81 BLR LONG ACTION. Calibers: 30-06, 270, 7mm Magnum. **Barrel length:** 22″ (30-06, 270) and 24″ (7mm Mag.). **Overall length:** 42¹/₂″ (30-06, 270) and 44¹/₂″ (7mm Mag.). **Weight:** 8 lbs. 8 oz. (30-06, 270) and 8 lbs. 13 oz. (7mm Mag.). **Price: $529.95**

BROWNING RIFLES

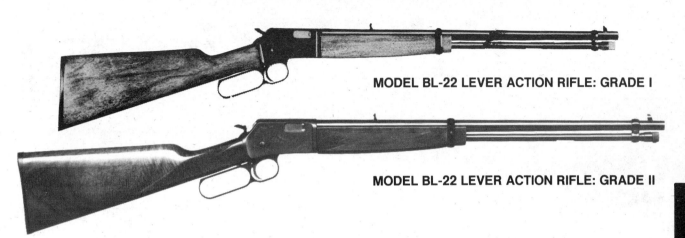

MODEL BL-22 LEVER ACTION RIFLE: GRADE I

MODEL BL-22 LEVER ACTION RIFLE: GRADE II

MODEL BL-22 SPECIFICATIONS

Action: Short throw lever action. Lever travels through an arc of only 33 degrees and carries the trigger with it, preventing finger pinch between lever and trigger on the upward swing. The lever cycle ejects the fired shell, cocks the hammer and feeds a fresh round into the chamber. **Magazine:** Rifle is designed to handle 22 caliber ammunition *in any combination* from tubular magazine. Magazine capacity is 15 Long Rifles, 17 Longs and 22 Shorts. The positive magazine latch opens and closes easily from any position. **Safety:** A unique disconnect system prevents firing until the lever and breech are fully closed and pressure is released from and reapplied to the trigger. An inertia firing pin and an exposed hammer with a half-cock position are other safety features. **Receiver:** Forged and milled steel. Grooved. All parts are machine-finished and hand-fitted. **Trigger:** Clean and crisp without creep. Average pull 5 pounds. Trigger gold-plated on Grade II model. **Stock and forearm:** Forearm and straight grip butt stock are shaped

from select, polished walnut. Hand checkered on Grade II model. Stock dimensions:

Length of Pull	13 1/2″
Drop at Comb	1 5/8″
Drop at Heel	2 1/4″

Sights: Precision, adjustable folding leaf rear sight. Raised bead front sight. **Scopes:** Grooved receiver will accept the Browning 22 riflescope (Model 1217) and two-piece ring mount (Model 9417) as well as most other groove or tip-off type mounts or receiver sights. **Engraving:** Grade II receiver and trigger guard are engraved with tasteful scroll designs. **Barrel length:** 20″; recessed muzzle. **Overall length:** 36 3/4″. **Weight:** 5 pounds.

Price:		
	Grade I	$301.50
	Grade II	343.50

MODEL A-BOLT 22 BOLT ACTION
$374.95   ($384.95 w/Sights)

Caliber: 22 LR. **Barrel length:** 22″. **Overall length:** 40 1/4″. **Average weight:** 5 lbs. 9 oz. **Action:** Short throw bolt. Bolt cycles a round with 60° of bolt rotation. Firing pin acts as secondary extractor and ejector, snapping out fired rounds at prescribed speed. **Magazine:** Five and 15-shot magazine standard. Magazine/clip ejects with a push on magazine latch button. **Trigger:** Gold colored, screw adjustable. Pre-set at approx. 4 lbs. **Stock:** Laminated walnut, classic style with pistol grip. **Length of pull:** 13 3/4″. **Drop at comb:** 3/4″. **Drop at heel:** 1 1/2″. **Sights:** Available with or without sights (add **$10** for sights). Ramp front and adjustable folding leaf rear on open sight model. **Scopes:** Grooved receiver for 22 mount. Drilled and tapped for full-size scope mounts.

Available in 22 Magnum (with open sights)	**$431.95**
Without sights	429.95
Gold Medallion Model	496.95

SPECIFICATIONS RIMFIRE RIFLES

Model	Caliber	Barrel Length	Sight Radius	Overall Length	Average Weight
A-Bolt 22	22 Long Rifle	22″	17 5/8″	40 1/4″	5 lbs. 9 oz.
22 Semi-Auto	22 Long Rifle	19 1/4″	16 1/4″	37″	4 lbs. 4 oz.
BL-22	22 Long Rifle, Longs, Shorts	20″	15 3/8″		5 lbs.

BROWNING RIFLES

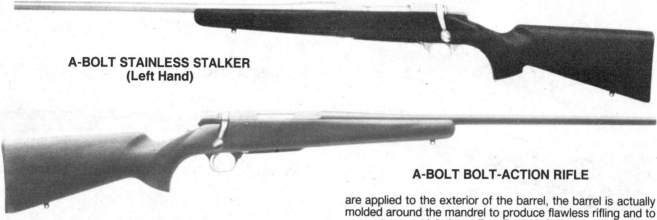

A-BOLT STAINLESS STALKER
(Left Hand)

A-BOLT BOLT-ACTION RIFLES

Calibers: 25-06 Rem., 270 Win., 280 Rem., 30-06 Sprg., 375 H&H, 7mm Rem. Mag., 300 Win. Mag., 338 Win. Mag. **Action:** Short throw bolt of 60 degrees. Plunger-type ejector. **Magazine:** Detachable. Depress the magazine latch and the hinged floorplate swings down. The magazine can be removed from the floorplate for reloading or safety reasons. **Trigger:** Adjustable within the average range of 3 to 6 pounds. Also grooved to provide sure finger control. **Stock and forearm:** Stock is select grade American walnut cut to the lines of a classic sporter with a full pistol grip.

Scopes: Closed. Clean tapered barrel. Receiver is drilled and tapped for a scope mount; or select **Hunter** model w/open sights. **Barrel length:** 24". Hammer forged rifling where a precision machined mandrel is inserted into the bore. The mandrel is a reproduction of the rifling in reverse. As hammer forces

A-BOLT BOLT-ACTION RIFLE

are applied to the exterior of the barrel, the barrel is actually molded around the mandrel to produce flawless rifling and to guarantee a straight bore. Free floated. **Overall length:** 44¼". **Weight:** 7 lbs. 8 oz. in Magnum; 6 lbs. 8 oz. in Short Action; 7 lbs. in Standard (Long Action).

Short Action A-Bolt available in 22 Hornet (Micro Medallion), 223 Rem., 22-250 Rem., 243 Win., 257 Roberts, 7mm-08 Rem., and 308 Win.

Prices:

Hunter	**$499.95**
Hunter w/open sights	563.95
Medallion (no sights)	584.95
Medallion Left-Hand Model	609.95
Medallion 375 H&H (open sights)	682.95
Micro Medallion (no sights)	584.95
Gold Medallion	794.95
Stainless Stalker (no sights)	651.95
Stainless Stalker Left Hand Model	671.95
Stainless Stalker 375 H&H (open sights)	749.95
Same as above in Left Hand	771.95

A-BOLT COMPOSITE STALKER
$514.95

Browning's new graphite-fiberglass composite stock resists the nicks and scrapes of hard hunting and is resistant to weather and humidity. Its recoil-absorbing properties also make shooting a more pleasant experience. This series is available in three models: Stainless Stalker, Composite Stalker and Camo Stalker. The newest of these—the A-Bolt Composite Stalker—has the same features as Browning's A-Bolt Hunter plus the graphite-fiberglass composite stock, which helps ensure accuracy as well as durability. The stock is checkered for a good grip and has a nonglare textured finish. All exposed metal surfaces have a nonglare matte blued finish.

BROWNING RIFLES

MODEL 52 LIMITED EDITION
$499.95

During its 72 years of production by Winchester, the Model 52 gained a worldwide reputation for accuracy. The new Browning Model 52 is nearly identical to the original Model 52C Sporter. Its Micro-Motion trigger system remains as good as the original; indeed, the trigger travel on Model 52 is almost imperceptible. The trigger adjusts for pull and over-travel with two screws found just forward of the trigger guard. Other original features include a five-shot, curved magazine that is removed by pressing the release button next to the magazine on the right side of the stock. The new Browning 52 is smooth-barreled, with the receiver drilled and tapped to accommodate different commercially available rear peep sights or scope mounts. The stock is high-grade walnut with an oil-like finish. Cut checkering is standard with a rosewood forend and metal grip cap accenting the stock. All exposed metal surfaces are polished and deeply blued. **Caliber:** 22LR. **Barrel length:** 24″. **Weight:** 7 lbs.

22 SEMIAUTOMATIC RIMFIRE RIFLES
GRADES I AND VI

SPECIFICATIONS

Caliber: 22 LR. **Overall length:** 37″. **Barrel length:** 19 1/4″. **Weight:** 4 lbs. 4 oz. **Safety:** Cross-bolt type. **Capacity:** 11 cartridges in magazine, 1 in chamber. **Trigger:** Grade I is blued; Grade VI is gold colored. **Sights:** Gold bead front, adjustable folding leaf rear; drilled and tapped for Browning scope mounts. **Length of pull:** 13 3/4″. **Drop at comb:** 1 3/16″. **Drop at heel:** 2 5/8″. **Stock & Forearm:** Grade I, select walnut with checkering (18 lines/inch); Grade VI, high-grade walnut with checkering (22 lines/inch).

Grade I $344.95
Grade VI 708.95

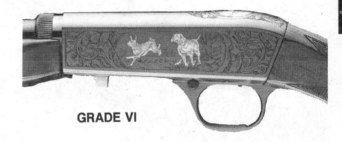

GRADE VI

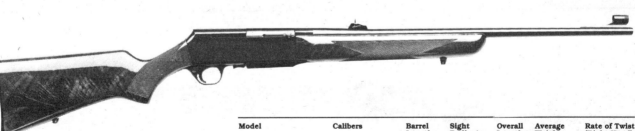

BAR SEMIAUTOMATIC RIFLES
(Grade I with Sights)

Standard Calibers $632.95
Magnum Calibers 679.95
(Deduct $16 without scopes)

Model	Calibers	Barrel Length	Sight Radius*	Overall Length	Average Weight	Rate of Twist (Right Hand)
Magnum	338 Win. Mag.	24″	19 1/2″	45″	8 lbs. 6 oz.	1 in 12″
Magnum	300 Win Mag.	24″	19 1/2″	45″	8 lbs. 6 oz.	1 in 10″
Magnum	7mm Rem Mag.	24″	19 1/2″	45″	8 lbs. 6 oz.	1 in 9 1/2″
Standard	30-06 Sprg.	22″	17 1/2″	43″	7 lbs. 6 oz.	1 in 10″
Standard	280 Rem.	22″	17 1/2″	43″	7 lbs. 9 oz.	1 in 10″
Standard	270 Win.	22″	17 1/2″	43″	7 lbs. 9 oz.	1 in 10″
Standard	308 Win.	22″	17 1/2″	43″	7 lbs. 9 oz.	1 in 12″
Standard	243 Win.	22″	17 1/2″	43″	7 lbs. 10 oz.	1 in 10″

*All models are available with or without open sights. All models drilled and tapped for scope mounts.

CHAPUIS RIFLES

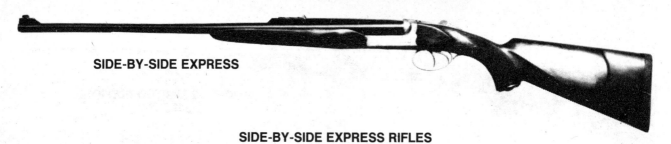

SIDE-BY-SIDE EXPRESS

SIDE-BY-SIDE EXPRESS RIFLES

Manufactured in France by Chapuis Armes, these side-by-side double rifles are imported and distributed exclusively in the U.S. by Armes de Chasse (see Directory of Manufacturers and Distributors for details). The rifles have specially reinforced boxlock actions with various styles of hand-engraved ornamentation. They have Blitz actions with coil springs (very important on safari, where repairs may be difficult), double underbites, automatic ejectors and 25.5″ or 23.6″ barrels (depending upon caliber).

SPECIFICATIONS
Calibers: 375 H&H, 470 N.E., 9.3×74R, 7×65R, 8×57JRS, 30-06
Barrel lengths: 23.6″ and 25.5″
Weight: 8 to 10 lbs.
Stock: French walnut with Monte Carlo comb
Prices:
Express Progress Agex Jungle 470 N.E. **$12,000.00**
   In 375 H&H **10,000.00**
Express Progress Agex Savanna **10,000.00**
REX Express in 9.3×74R, 7×65R, 8×57JRS,
   30-06 . . . . **7,000.00**

CHINASPORTS

MODEL EM-321
$169.00

SPECIFICATIONS
Caliber: 22 LR
Capacity: 9 rounds
Action: Pump
Barrel length: 19 1/2″
Overall length: 37″
Weight: 6 lbs.
Sights: Iron sights

NORINCO TYPE EM-332
BOLT ACTION REPEATER
$239.00

SPECIFICATIONS
Caliber: 22 LR
Capacity: 5 rounds
Barrel length: 18 1/2″
Overall length: 41 1/2″
Weight: 4 1/2 lbs.
Feature: Double magazine holder (underside of stock)

CLIFTON ARMS

SCOUT RIFLE
$2500.00

Five years ago, in response to Colonel Jeff Cooper's concept of an all-purpose rifle, which he calls the "Scout Rifle," Clifton Arms developed the integral, retractable bipod and its accompanying state-of-the-art composite stock. Further development resulted in an integral butt magazine well for storage of cartridges inside the buttstock. These and other components make up the Clifton Scout Rifle. Built to the customer's choice of action, the rifle incorporates all the features specified by Col. Cooper.

SPECIFICATION
Calibers: 308, 7mm-08, 243, 30-06, 350 Rem. Mag.
Barrel length: 19″ to 19½″ (longer or shorter lengths available; made with Shilen stainless premium match-grade steel)
Weight: 7–8 lbs.
Sights: Forward-mounted Burris 2¾X Scout Scope attached to integral scope base pedestals machined in the barrel; Warner rings; reserve iron sight is square post dovetailed into a ramp integral to the barrel, plus a large aperture "ghost ring" mounted on the receiver bridge.
Features: Standard action is Ruger 77 MKII stainless; metal finish options include Polymax, NP3 and chrome sulphide; left-hand rifles available.

COLT RIFLES

COLT SPORTER LIGHTWEIGHTS

The Colt Sporter semiautomatic rifle fires from a closed bolt, is easy to load and unload, and has a buttstock and pistol grip made of tough nylon. A round, ribbed handguard is fiberglass-reinforced to ensure better grip control. **Calibers:** 223 Rem. and 9mm. **Barrel length:** 16″. **Weight:** 6.7 lbs. to 7.1 lbs. **Capacity:** 5 rounds. **Price: $859.95.**

SPORTER COMPETITION HBAR

sories. **Caliber:** 223 Rem. **Barrel length:** 20″. **Weight:** 8 lbs. to 10½ lbs. **Capacity:** 5 rounds. **Price: $969.95.**

This new Colt sporter is range-selected for top accuracy. It has a 3-9X rubber armored variable power scope mount, carry handle with iron sight, Cordura nylon case and other acces-

Also available:
MATCH H-BAR $919.95
TARGET GOV'T MODEL 879.95

DAKOTA ARMS

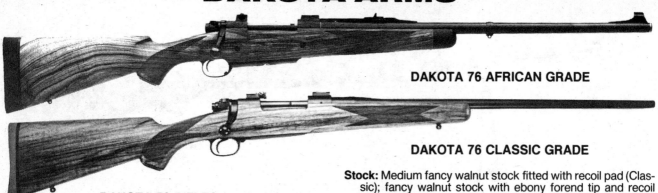

DAKOTA 76 AFRICAN GRADE

DAKOTA 76 CLASSIC GRADE

DAKOTA 76 RIFLES

Stock: Medium fancy walnut stock fitted with recoil pad (Classic); fancy walnut stock with ebony forend tip and recoil pad (Safari)

SPECIFICATIONS
Calibers:
  Safari Grade: 338 Win. Mag., 300 Win. Mag., 375 H&H Mag., 458 Win. Mag.
  Classic Grade: 257 Roberts, 270 Win., 280 Rem., 30-06, 7mm Rem. Mag., 338 Win. Mag., 300 Win. Mag., 375 H&H Mag., 458 Win. Mag.
Barrel lengths: 21″ or 23″ (Alpine and Classic); 23″ only (Safari); 24″ (African)
Weight: 7½ lbs. (Alpine & Classic); 8 lbs. (African); 8½ lbs. (Safari)
Safety: Three-position striker-blocking safety allows bolt operation with safety on
Sights: Ramp front sight; standing leaf rear sight

Prices:
Safari Grade	**$2950.00**
Classic Grade	2150.00
Alpine Grade (Blind magazine)	1995.00
African Grade	3500.00
Barreled actions:	
Safari Grade	1850.00
Classic Grade	1550.00
Alpine Grade	1450.00
African Grade	2500.00
Actions:	
Safari Grade	1500.00
Classic Grade	1300.00
Alpine Grade	1200.00

DAKOTA 10 SINGLE SHOT

SPECIFICATIONS
Calibers: Most rimmed and rimless commercially loaded calibers
Barrel length: 23″
Overall length: 39½″
Weight: 5½ lbs.
Features: Receiver and rear of breech block are solid steel without cuts or holes for maximum lug area (approx. 8 times

DAKOTA 10 SINGLE SHOT

more bearing area than most bolt rifles); crisp, clean trigger pull (trigger plate is removable, allowing action to adapt to single set triggers); straight-line coil spring action and short hammer fall combine for extremely fast lock time; unique top tang safety is smooth and quiet (it blocks the striker forward of the main spring); strong and positive extractor and manual ejector equally adapted to rimmed or rimless cases.

Price:	**$2150.00**
Barreled actions	1550.00
Action	1300.00

DAKOTA 22 LR SPORTER

DAKOTA 22 LR SPORTER

SPECIFICATIONS
Calibers: 22 LR and 22 Hornet
Capacity: 5-round clip

Barrel length: 22″ (chrome-moly, 1 turn in 16″)
Weight: 6½ lbs.
Stock: X Clara or English walnut with hand-cut checkering
Features: Plain bolt handle; swivels and single screw studs; ½-inch black pad; 13⅝″ length of pull

Price:	**$995.00**

EAGLE ARMS RIFLES

MODEL EA-15 RIFLES

All EA-15 rifles include these standard features: upper and lower receivers precision machined from 7075 T6 aluminum forgings • receivers equipped with push-type pivot pin for easy disassembly • EZ-style forward assist mechanism that clears jammed shells from the chamber • trapdoor-style buttstock • full-size 30-round magazine

MODEL EA-15 MATCH RIFLE
(With Action Master Accessories)
$1075.00

SPECIFICATIONS
Caliber: .223
Barrel length: 20″ Douglas Premium fluted barrel
Weight: 8 lbs. 5 oz.
Stock: Fixed

Features: One-piece international-style upper receiver; solid aluminum handguard tube (allows for a free-floating barrel); compensator for reducing muzzle climb; NM Match Trigger Group & Bolt Carrier Group

MODEL EA-15 GOLDEN EAGLE MATCH RIFLE
$1075.00

SPECIFICATIONS
Caliber: .223
Barrel length: 20″ Douglas Premium extra heavy w/1:9″ twist
Weight: 12 lbs. 12 oz.
Sights: Elevation adjustable NM front sight w/set screw; E-2 style NM rear sight assembly w/1/2 MOA adjustments for windage and elevation
Stock: Fixed

Also available:
EA-15 STANDARD (Wt. 7 lbs.) **$800.00**
EA-15 w/E-2 Accessories (Wt. 8 lbs. 14 oz.) **895.00**
   Same as above with NM sights 890.00
EA-15 CARBINE w/E-1 Accessories 16″ barrel,
   Sliding buttstock (Wt. 5 lbs. 14 oz.) 845.00
   Same as above w/E-1 accessories
   (Wt. 6 lbs. 12 oz.) 895.00

EMF RIFLES

1875 "OUTLAW" REMINGTON-STYLE REVOLVING CARBINE
$880.00

Includes walnut stock, brass trim, blued finish and casehardened frame.
Calibers: 357, 44-40, 45 Colt
Barrel length: 20″
Overall length: 38″
Weight: 5 lbs.

FEATHER RIFLES

MODEL AT-22

MODEL F2 AT-22

SPECIFICATIONS
Caliber: 22 LR
Capacity: 20 rounds
Type: Autoloader
Operation: Blowback
Barrel length: 17″
Overall length: 35″ (26″ w/stock folded)
Weight: 3.25 lbs.
Price: **$249.95**

MODEL AT-22

This 22 LR rifle breaks down to a compact, easy-to-stow and transportable 17″ package. It will accommodate any kind of 22 LR ammo and has set a new standard for autoloading rimfire rifles.

Also available:
MODEL F2 AT-22. Same as Model AT-22, but with fixed buttstock made of high-impact polymer for a more traditional look. **Price:** **$279.95**

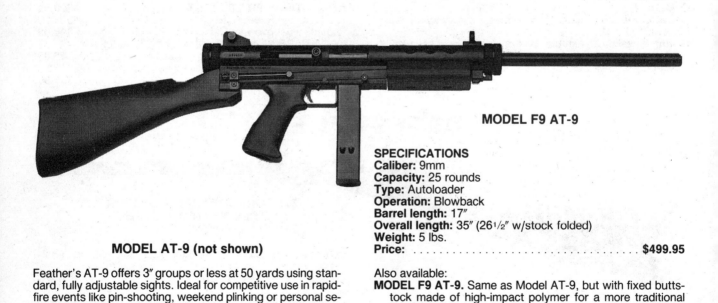

MODEL F9 AT-9

SPECIFICATIONS
Caliber: 9mm
Capacity: 25 rounds
Type: Autoloader
Operation: Blowback
Barrel length: 17″
Overall length: 35″ (26 1/2″ w/stock folded)
Weight: 5 lbs.
Price: **$499.95**

MODEL AT-9 (not shown)

Feather's AT-9 offers 3″ groups or less at 50 yards using standard, fully adjustable sights. Ideal for competitive use in rapid-fire events like pin-shooting, weekend plinking or personal security.

Also available:
MODEL F9 AT-9. Same as Model AT-9, but with fixed buttstock made of high-impact polymer for a more traditional look. **Price:** **$534.95**

FRANCOTTE RIFLES

BOLT ACTION RIFLE

August Francotte rifles are available in all calibers for which barrels and chambers are made. All guns are custom made to the customer's specifications; there are no standard models. Most bolt-action rifles use commercial Mauser actions; however, the magnum action is produced by Francotte exclusively for its own production. Side-by-side and mountain rifles use either boxlock or sidelock action. Francotte system sidelocks are back-action type. Options include gold and silver inlay, special engraving and exhibition and museum grade wood. Francotte rifles are distributed in the U.S. by Armes de Chasse (see Directory of Manufacturers and Distributors for details).

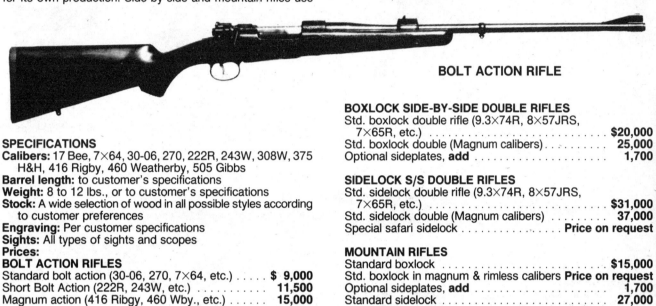

BOLT ACTION RIFLE

SPECIFICATIONS
Calibers: 17 Bee, 7×64, 30-06, 270, 222R, 243W, 308W, 375 H&H, 416 Rigby, 460 Weatherby, 505 Gibbs
Barrel length: to customer's specifications
Weight: 8 to 12 lbs., or to customer's specifications
Stock: A wide selection of wood in all possible styles according to customer preferences
Engraving: Per customer specifications
Sights: All types of sights and scopes
Prices:
BOLT ACTION RIFLES
Standard bolt action (30-06, 270, 7×64, etc.) . . . . . **$ 9,000**
Short Bolt Action (222R, 243W, etc.) **11,500**
Magnum action (416 Ribgy, 460 Wby., etc.) **15,000**

BOXLOCK SIDE-BY-SIDE DOUBLE RIFLES
Std. boxlock double rifle (9.3×74R, 8×57JRS, 7×65R, etc.) **$20,000**
Std. boxlock double (Magnum calibers) **25,000**
Optional sideplates, **add** **1,700**

SIDELOCK S/S DOUBLE RIFLES
Std. sidelock double rifle (9.3×74R, 8×57JRS, 7×65R, etc.) **$31,000**
Std. sidelock double (Magnum calibers) **37,000**
Special safari sidelock . . . . **Price on request**

MOUNTAIN RIFLES
Standard boxlock **$15,000**
Std. boxlock in magnum & rimless calibers **Price on request**
Optional sideplates, **add** **1,700**
Standard sidelock **27,000**

CARL GUSTAF RIFLES

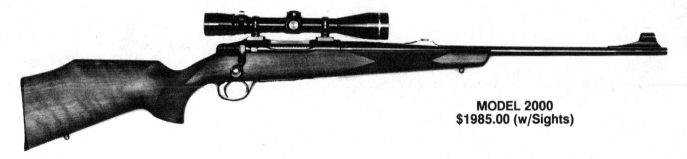

MODEL 2000
$1985.00 (w/Sights)

The Carl Gustaf 2000 rifle, created by one of the oldest rifle-makers in the world, uses the latest Swedish hi-tech engineering, design and manufacturing methods to produce this fine hunting piece, while retaining the balance and sleek lines of its famous predecessor, the *Husqvarna*. Each rifle bears the "Crowned C" stamp, the exclusive Royal Swedish symbol of quality and durability.

SPECIFICATIONS
Calibers: 30-06, 308 Win., 6.5×55, 7×64, 9.3×63, 243, 270, 7mm Rem. Mag., 300 Win. Mag.
Capacity: 3-round clip (4-round clip optional)
Action: Bolt
Barrel length: 24″
Overall length: 44″
Weight: 7½ lbs.
Sights: Hooded ramp front; open rear (drilled and tapped for scope mounting)
Stock: Cheekpiece with Monte Carlo; Wundhammer palm swell on pistol grip (see also above)
Length of pull: 13¾″

HECKLER & KOCH RIFLES

**MODEL HK PSG-1 HIGH PRECISION
MARKSMAN'S RIFLE
$8859.00**

SPECIFICATIONS
Caliber: 308 (7.62mm). **Capacity:** 5 rounds and 20 rounds.
Barrel length: 25.6″. **Rifling:** 4 groove, polygonal. **Twist:** 12″,
right hand. **Overall length:** 47.5″. **Weight:** 17.8 lbs. **Sights:**
Hensoldt 6×42 telescopic. **Stock:** Matte black, high-impact
plastic. **Finish;** Matte black, phosphated.

SPECIFICATIONS
Caliber: 308 Win. **Capacity:** 5 rounds. **Barrel length:** 19 1/2″.
Overall length: 42 3/8″. **Weight:** 10 1/2 lbs. **Sights:** Post front;
aperture rear, adjustable for windage and elevation. **Stock:**
Kevlar-reinforced fiberglass (wood grain) with thumbhole
buttstock. **Features:** Bull barrel; PSG1 Marksman trigger
group; clawlock scope mounts.

**MODEL SR-9
$1369.00**

**MODEL SR-9(T) TARGET RIFLE
$1799.00**

SPECIFICATIONS
Same specifications as Model SR-9, but has adjustable MSG90
buttstock and PSG1 trigger group plus adjustable contoured
grip.

HEYM RIFLES

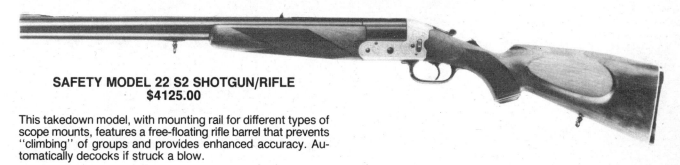

SAFETY MODEL 22 S2 SHOTGUN/RIFLE
$4125.00

This takedown model, with mounting rail for different types of scope mounts, features a free-floating rifle barrel that prevents "climbing" of groups and provides enhanced accuracy. Automatically decocks if struck a blow.

SPECIFICATIONS
Shotgun gauges: 20 ga. (2³/₄″), 20 ga. (3″), 16 ga. (2³/₄″), 12 ga. (2³/₄″)

Rifle calibers: 22 Hornet, 222 Rem. Mag., 223 Rem., 22-250, 243 Win., 308 Win. and 30-06 (metric calibers available on request).

MODEL SR20 CLASSIC SPORTER SERIES

SPECIFICATIONS
Standard (N) calibers: 22-250, 243 Win., 270 Win., 308 Win. and 30-06 (metric calibers available on request)
Barrel length: 22″ (N)
Overall length: 43″
Weight: 7 lbs. (with iron sights)
Price: $2120.00 ($2050.00 without iron sights)

Magnum (G) calibers: 7mm Rem. Mag., 300 Win. Mag., 338 Win. Mag., 375 H&H Mag. (metric calibers available on request)
Barrel length: 24″
Overall length: 45″
Weight: 7¹/₂ lbs.
Price: $2235.00 ($2165.00 without iron sights)

MODEL SR20 TROPHY SERIES
$2815.00 ($2935.00 Magnum)

SPECIFICATIONS
Calibers: 243 Win., 270 Win., 308 Win., 30-06, 7mm Rem. Mag., 300 Win. Mag., 338 Win. Mag., 375 H&H and 6.5×55 (additional metric calibers available on request)

Other specifications are the same as the Classic Sporter Series, but include Krupp-Special steel shaped in tapered octagon form with classic quarter rib, rear open sight and raised front sight rib.

HEYM RIFLES

MODEL SR20 ALPINE SERIES
BOLT ACTION CARBINE
$2335.00

SPECIFICATIONS
Calibers: 243 Win., 270 Win., 308 Win., 30-06 (metric calibers available on request)
Capacity: 5 rounds
Barrel length: 20″
Overall length: 41″
Weight: 7¹/₂″ lbs.
Safety: 3-position style
Trigger: Single adjustable
Sights: Adjustable front and rear
Features: European walnut stock w/sculptured cheekpiece; ''Old English'' recoil pad; quick detachable swivel studs

MODEL EXPRESS
$6245.00

SPECIFICATIONS
Calibers: 338 Lapua Magnum, 375 H&H, 416 Rigby, 378 Weatherby Magnum, 460 Weatherby Magnum, 450 Ackley, 500 A-Square, 500 Nitro Express

Also available:
MODEL EXPRESS 600 in 600 Nitro Express. **Price: $10,900.00** (add **$555.00** for left-hand model)

MODEL SR20 CLASSIC SAFARI SERIES
BIG GAME RIFLE (not shown)
$2725.00

SPECIFICATIONS
Calibers: 375 H&H, 425 Express, 458 Win. Mag.
Capacity: 3 rounds
Barrel length: 24″
Overall length: 43¹/₂″
Weight: 8¹/₄ lbs.
Sights: 3-leaf express (regulated for 50, 100 & 200 meters)
Features: Barrel-mounted, ring-type front Q.D. swivel and stock-mounted rear Q.D. swivel; European walnut stock w/sculptured cheekpiece; double recoil lug bolts

MODEL SR20 ALPINE CLASSIC (not shown)
$2165.00

SPECIFICATIONS
Calibers: 243 Win., 270 Win., 308 Win., 30-06 and 6.5×55
Barrel length: 20″
Weight: 7¹/₂″ lbs.
Feature: Mannlicher-style forend

HEYM RIFLES

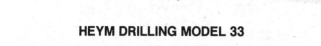

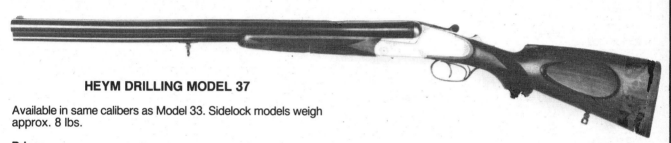

HEYM DRILLING MODEL 33

The Heym Drilling Model 33 is offered (limited availability) in Standard or Deluxe boxlock versions in **calibers:** 222 Rem., 243 Win., 270 Win., 308 Win., and 30-06. **Weight:** approx. 6.8 lbs.

Prices:
Standard with arabesque engraving **$8685.00**
Deluxe with hunting scene engraving **9240.00**

HEYM DRILLING MODEL 37

Available in same calibers as Model 33. Sidelock models weigh approx. 8 lbs.

Prices:
Standard with border engraving **$11,975.00**
Deluxe with hunting scene engraving **13,910.00**

Also available:
MODEL 37B Double Rifle Drilling **$15,220.00**
MODEL 37B DELUXE **17,780.00**

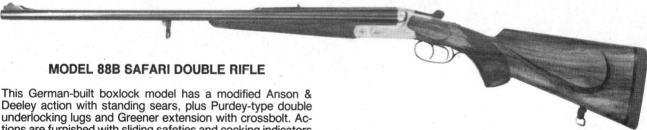

MODEL 88B SAFARI DOUBLE RIFLE

This German-built boxlock model has a modified Anson & Deeley action with standing sears, plus Purdey-type double underlocking lugs and Greener extension with crossbolt. Actions are furnished with sliding safeties and cocking indicators on the top tang, nonbreakable coil springs, front single set triggers and steel trigger guards.

SPECIFICATIONS
Calibers: 8×57 JRS, 9.3×74R and 30-06
Weight: 8 lbs.
Features: Ejectors, small action
Price: **$12,435.00**
In 375 H&H Mag. **13,860.00**

Also available:
MODEL 88B/SS. Sidelock version of above **$15,820.00**
MODEL 88B "SAFARI." **Calibers:** 375 H&H, 458 Win. Mag., 470 Nitro Express, 500 Nitro Express. **Weight:** 10 lbs., large frame **15,640.00**

HOWA RIFLES

TROPHY SPORTING RIFLES
$528.33
($548.33 in 7mm Rem. Mag., 300 Win. Mag., and 338 Win. Mag.)

SPECIFICATIONS

	Varmint	Trophy		Barreled Actions	
	Heavy Barrel	Standard	Magnum	Standard	Magnum
Capacity	5 rounds	5 rounds	3 rounds	5 rounds	3 rounds
Sights	No	Yes	Yes	No	No
Barrel Length	24″	22″	24″	22″	24″
Overall Length	44″	42″	44″	29¼″	31¼″
Weight	9 lbs. 12 ozs.	7 lbs. 8 ozs.	7 lbs. 12 ozs.	5 lbs. 5 ozs.	5 lbs. 9 ozs.
Caliber 223	X	X		X	
22-250	X	X		X	
243		X		X	
270		X		X	
308	X	X		X	
30-06		X		X	
7mm Mag.			X		X
300 WM			X		X
338 WM			X		X

IVER JOHNSON RIFLES

M-1 CARBINE

SPECIFICATIONS
Calibers: 30 Carbine and 9mm
Capacity: 15 and 30 rounds
Barrel length: 18″
Overall length: 35½″
Weight: 5½ lbs.

Sights: Military front; peep rear, adjustable for windage and elevation
Finish: Blue
Stock: Hardwood or walnut
Prices:
M-1 Carbine (30 caliber, hardwood stock) $349.95
    With walnut stock 384.95
M-1 Paratrooper w/telescoping stock 433.00
M-1 Carbine Full Auto 560.00
M-1 Carbine (9mm, hardwood stock) 365.75
    With walnut stock 399.00
M-1 Paratrooper (9mm telescoping stock) 448.95

LONG-RANGE RIFLE MODEL 5100A1
SINGLE SHOT BOLT ACTION
(not shown)

SPECIFICATIONS
Caliber: 50
Barrel length: 29″
Overall length: 51½″
Weight: 36 lbs.
Features: Folding legs
Price: . . . . $3750.00 to $5000.00

JARRETT CUSTOM RIFLES

ACCURACY LEGEND SERIES

All Jarrett "Accuracy Legend" rifles include the following features: Metal finish • Top-mounted bolt release • Break-in and load development with 20 rounds • Setup for switch barrel • Serial number

MODELS 2 AND 3
$3495.00

MODEL 2 features: McMillan Mountain Rifle stock • Remington 700 Magnum receiver • Hart #4 tapered barrel (.308 bore w/1 in 12" twist) • Remington conversion trigger • Olive drab Teflon metal finish • Forest camo stock • 3.5x10x50 Leupold scope with A.O. matte finish • Pachmayr decelerator brake and Jarrett brake kit

MODEL 3 offers: Caliber 7mm STW • Schneider .284 bore barrel w/1 in 10" twist (25½" at crown) • Black textured stock • Hard chrome receiver, rings and bases • Leupold base w/30mm Redfield rings. Other specifications same as Model 1. Also available in 300 Win. Mag. with black Teflon metal and Old English Pachmayr 1" pad.

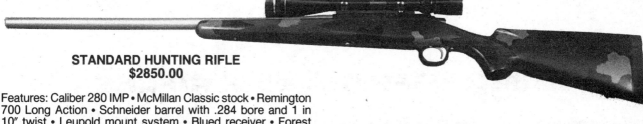

STANDARD HUNTING RIFLE
$2850.00

Features: Caliber 280 IMP • McMillan Classic stock • Remington 700 Long Action • Schneider barrel with .284 bore and 1 in 10" twist • Leupold mount system • Blued receiver • Forest camo stock finish • 1" decelerator pad

LIGHTWEIGHT VARMINT RIFLE
$2850.00

Features: Caliber 223 • Remington XP-100 action • Schneider barrel w/.224 bore and 1 in 14" twist (#4 tapered to 23" at crown) • Leupold mount system • Black Teflon metal finish • Gray textured-finish stock • 6.5x20 scope (optional) • Remington conversion trigger

SNIPER RIFLE
$3425.00 (w/o Scope)

Features McMillan stock • Remington 700 short action receiver • #6 taper Hart 308 barrel (1 in 12" twist) • Jewel trigger set at 15 oz. • Leupold mount system • Kahles 10X sniper scope • Black teflon finish • Black texture paint on stock • Pachmayr decelerator (1" pad) • Jarrett muzzle brake • Group average: 5-5 shot groups-.297

KDF RIFLES

MODEL K15
$1950.00 ($2000.00 in Magnum)

SPECIFICATIONS
Calibers: Standard—22-250, 243, 6mm Rem., 25-06, 270 Win., 280 Rem., 308 Win., 30-06; **Magnum**—270 Wby., 7mm Rem., 300 Win., 300 Wby., 338 Win., 340 Wby., 375 H&H, 411 KDF, 416 Rem., 458 Win.
Capacity: 4 rounds (3 rounds in Magnum)
Barrel lengths: 24″ (26″ in Magnum)
Overall length: 44¹/₂″ (46¹/₂″ in Magnum)
Weight: 8 lbs. (approx.)
Receiver: Drilled and tapped for scope mounts (KDF bases available to take 1″ or 30mm rings)

Trigger: Competition-quality single stage; adjustable for travel, pull and sear engagement
Safety: Located on right-hand side
Stocks: Kevlar composite or laminate stock; Pachmayr decelerator pad; quick detachable swivels; AAA grade walnut stocks with 22-line hand-checkering; ebony forend; pistol grip cap and crossbolts (walnut stocks may be ordered in classic, schnabel or thumbhole style)
Features and options: Iron sights; recoil arrestor; choice of metal finishes; 3 locking lugs w/large contact area; 60-degree lift for fast loading; box-style magazine system; easily accessible bolt release catch; fully machined, hinged bottom metal

KRIEGHOFF DOUBLE RIFLES

MODEL TECK OVER/UNDER

SPECIFICATIONS
Calibers: 308, 30-06, 300 Win. Mag., 9.3×74R, 8×57JRS, 7×65R, 458 Win. Mag.
Barrel length: 25″
Action: Boxlock; double greener-type crossbolt and double barrel lug locking, steel receiver
Weight: 7¹/₂ lbs.
Triggers: Double triggers; single trigger optional
Safety: Located on top tang
Sights: Open sight with right angle front sight
Stock: German-styled with pistol grip and cheekpiece; oil-finished
Length of stock: 14³/₈″
Finish: Nickel-plated steel receiver with satin grey finish
Prices:
Model Teck (Boxlock) . . . .$ 8,300.00
   In 9.3×74R and 458 Win. Mag. **9,445.00**
Teck-Handspanner (16 ga. receiver only;
   7×65R, 30-06, 308 Win.) **9,975.00**
Also available:
TRUMPF SBS (Side-by-side boxlock) **13,900.00**

MODEL ULM OVER/UNDER

SPECIFICATIONS
Calibers: 308 Win., 30-06, 300 Win. Mag., 375 H&H, 458 Win. Mag.
Barrel length: 25″
Weight: 7.8 lbs.
Triggers: Double triggers (front trigger=bottom; rear trigger=upper
Safety: Located on top tang
Sights: Open sight w/right angle front sight
Stock: German-styled with pistol grip and cheekpiece; oil-finished
Length of stock: 14³/₈″
Forearm: Semi-beavertail
Prices:
Model ULM (Sidelock) $13,900.00
Primus (Deluxe Sidelock) **17,750.00**
Also available:
NEPTUN DRILLING **14,500.00**

LAKEFIELD SPORTING RIFLES

MODEL 92S
$415.95

SPECIFICATIONS

Model:	90B	92S
Caliber:	.22 Long Rifle Only	.22 Long Rifle
Capacity:	5-shot metal magazine	5-shot metal magazine
Action:	Self-cocking bolt action, thumb-operated rotary safety	Self-cocking bolt action, thumb-operated rotary safety
Stock:	One-piece target-type stock with natural finish hardwood; comes with clip holder, carrying & shooting rails, butt hook and hand stop	One-piece high comb, target-type with walnut finish hardwood
Barrel Length:	21″ w/snow cover	21″
Sights:	Receiver peep sights with 1/4 min. click micrometer adjustments; target front sight with inserts	None (receiver drilled and tapped for scope base)
Overall Length:	39⁵/₈″	39⁵/₈″
Approx. Weight:	8¼ lbs.	8 lbs.

MARK I
$116.95

MODEL 64B
$129.95

Also available:
MARK I "SMOOTH BORE" (20½″ barrel) $116.95
MARK II YOUTH (19″ barrel) 137.95
MARK II LEFT HAND (20½″ barrel) 137.95

SPECIFICATIONS

Model:	MARK I	MARK II ($124.95)	64B
Caliber:	.22 Short, Long or Long Rifle	.22 Long Rifle Only	.22 Long Rifle Only
Capacity:	Single Shot	10 Shot Clip Magazine	10 Shot Clip Magazine
Action:	Self Cocking Bolt Action. Thumb Operated Rotary Safety.	Self-Cocking Bolt Action. Thumb Operated Rotary Safety.	Semi-Automatic Side Ejection. Bolt Hold Open Device. Thumb Operated Rotary Safety.
Stock:	One Piece, Walnut Finish Hardwood, Monte Carlo Type with Full Pistol Grip. Checkering on Pistol Grip and Forend.		
Barrel Length:	20½″	20½″	20″
Sights:	Open Bead Front Sight, Adjustable Rear Sight, Receiver Grooved for Scope Mounting.		
Overall Length:	39½″	39½″	40″
Approx. Weight:	5½ lbs.	5½ lbs.	5½ lbs.

LAKEFIELD SPORTING RIFLES

MODEL 91T
$415.95

MODEL 91TR
$442.95

Model	91TR	91T
Caliber:	.22 Long Rifle	.22 Short, Long or Long Rifle
Capacity	5-shot clip magazine	Single shot
Action:	Self-cocking bolt action, thumb-operated rotary safety	Self-cocking bolt action thumb-operated rotary safety
Stock:	One-piece, target-type with walnut finish hardwood (also available in natural finish); comes with shooting rail and hand stop	One-piece, target-type walnut finish hardwood (also available in natural finish); comes with shootng rail and hand stop
Sights:	Receiver peep sights with 1/4 min. click micrometer adjustments, target front sight with inserts	Receiver peep sights with 1/4 min. click micrometer adjustments, target front sight with inserts
Overall Length:	43⁵/₈″	43⁵/₈″
Approx. Weight:	8 lbs.	8 lbs.

MARK X RIFLES
ACTIONS & BARRELED ACTIONS

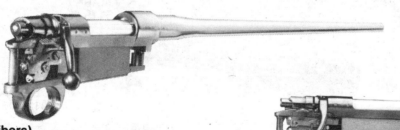

BARRELED ACTIONS
$333.00 (Standard Calibers)
$353.00 (7mm Rem. Mag., 300 Win. Mag.)
$413.00 (375 H&H, 458 Win. Mag.)
$333.00 (223, 7.62×39)

Hand-fitted with premium hammer-forged barrels created from corrosion resistant chrome vanadium steel. Each barreled action is carefully proofed and marked under close government control, ready to drop into the stock of your choice.

Calibers: 223, 22-250, 243, 25-06, 270, 7×57, 7mm Rem. Mag., 300 Win. Mag., 308, 30-06. **Barrel length:** 24″. **Weight:** 5½ lbs. (5¾ lbs. in 22-250, 243, and 25-06). **Rifling twist:** 10 (14 in 22-250 and 9.5 in 7×57).

    Also available in 375 H&H Mag. and 458 Win. Mag. Same barrel length but different weights: 6 lbs. (375 H&H Mag.) and 5.75 lbs. (458 Win. Mag.). **Rifling twist:** 12 (375 H&H Mag.) and 14 (458 Win. Mag.).

MAUSER SYSTEM ACTIONS
$230.00 (Single Shot)

Type A: 7×57mm to 30-06. Standard magazine (3³/₈″) and bolt face (.470″) **$270.00**
Type B: 22-250 to 308. Short magazine (2⁷/₈″); standard bolt face **270.00**
Type C: 7mm Rem. Mag. to 458 Win. Mag. Standard magazine and Magnum bolt face (.532″) **275.00**
Type D: 300 Win. Mag. to 375 H&H. Magnum magazine (3¹¹/₁₆″) and Magnum bolt face **300.00**
Mini-Mark X (.17 to .223) **270.00**

MARK X RIFLES

MINI-MARK X
$500.00 (Without sights)

SPECIFICATIONS
Caliber: 223, 7.62×39
Capacity: 5 rounds
Barrel length: 20″
Twist: I turn in 10″
Overall length: 39³/₄″
Weight: 6.35 lbs.
Trigger: Adjustable

MARK X VISCOUNT SPORTER
$539.00 ($559.00 Magnum calibers)

SPECIFICATIONS
Calibers: 22-250, 243 Win., 25-06, 270 Win., 7×57, 308 Win., 30-06; 7mm Rem. Mag., 300 Win. Mag.
Capacity: 5 rounds; 3 in 7mm Rem. Mag., 300 Win. Mag.
Barrel length: 24″
Overall length: 45″
Twist: 1 turn in 10″
Weight: 7½ lbs.
Stock: Carbolite

MARK X WHITWORTH
$665.00 ($685.00 Magnum calibers)

Features forged and machined Mauser System actions . . . Hammer-forged, chrome, vanadium steel barrels . . . Drilled and tapped for scope mounts and receiver sights . . . Hooded ramp front and fully adjustable rear sight . . . All-steel button release magazine floor plate . . . Detachable sling swivels . . . Silent sliding thumb safety . . . Prime European walnut stocks . . . Sculpted, low-profile cheekpiece . . . Rubber recoil butt plate . . . Steel grip cap.

Calibers: 22-250, 243 Win., 25-06, 270 Win., 7 × 57, 308 Win., 30-06, 7mm Rem. Mag., 300 Win. Mag. **Barrel length:** 24″. **Overall length:** 44″. **Weight:** 7 lbs. **Capacity:** 5 rounds.

Also available: **VISCOUNT MAUSER SYSTEM SPORTING RIFLES.** Same as American Field, but without European walnut stock: **$499.00.** In 7mm Rem. Mag. or 300 Win. Mag.: **$519.00**

MARLIN 22 RIFLES

MODEL 60
$144.50

SPECIFICATIONS
Caliber: 22 Long Rifle
Capacity: 14-shot tubular magazine with patented closure system
Barrel length: 22"
Weight: 5½ lbs.
Overall length: 40½"

Sights: Ramp front sight; adjustable open rear, receiver grooved for scope mount
Action: Self-loading; side ejection; manual and automatic "last-shot" hold-open devices; receiver top has ser-rated, non-glare finish; cross-bolt safety
Stock: One-piece walnut-finished hardwood Monte Carlo stock with full pistol grip; Mar-Shield® finish

MODEL 70HC
$164.15

SPECIFICATIONS
Caliber: 22 LR
Capacity: 7- and 15-shot clip magazine
Barrel length: 18"
Overall length: 36¾"
Weight: 5½ lbs.

Action: Self-loading; side ejection; manual bolt hold-open; receiver top has serrated, non-glare finish; cross-bolt safety

Sights: Adjustable open rear, ramp front; receiver grooved for scope mount
Stock: Monte Carlo walnut-finished hardwood with full pistol grip and Mar-Shield® finish

MODEL 70P "PAPOOSE"
$181.95

SPECIFICATIONS
Caliber: 22 LR
Capacity: 7-shot clip
Barrel length: 16¼"
Overall length: 35¼"
Weight: 3¼ lbs.

Action: Self-loading; side ejection; manual and "last-shot" bolt hold-open; receiver top has serrated non-glare finish; cross bolt safety
Sights: Adjustable open rear; ramp front; receiver grooved for scope mount

Stock: Walnut-finished hardwood with full pistol grip and Mar-Shield® finish
Features: Zippered carrying case included

MARLIN 22 RIFLES

MODEL 882L
$247.35

SPECIFICATIONS
Caliber: 22 Win. Mag. Rimfire (not interchangeable with other 22 cartridges)
Capacity: 7-shot clip magazine
Barrel length: 22" Micro-Groove®

Overall length: 41"
Weight: 6 1/4 lbs.
Sights: Ramp front w/brass bead and removable Wide-Scan hood; adj. folding semi-buckhorn rear

Stock: Laminated hardwood Monte Carlo w/Mar-Shield® finish
Features: Swivel studs; rubber rifle butt pad; receiver grooved for scope mount; positive thumb safety; red cocking indicator

MODEL 990L
$209.45

SPECIFICATIONS
Caliber: 22 LR (self-loading)
Capacity: 14 rounds
Barrel length: 22" Micro-Groove®
Overall length: 40 1/2"
Weight: 5.75 lbs.

Sight: Folding semi-buckhorn rear
Stock: Laminated hardwood Monte Carlo
Features: Cross-bolt safety; manual and automatic last-shot bolt hold-open;

solid locking, spring-loaded magazine with patented closure system; swivel studs; rubber rifle butt pad; rustproof receiver grooved for scope mount; gold-plated steel trigger

MODEL 995
$193.20

SPECIFICATIONS
Caliber: 22 Long Rifle
Action: Self-loading
Capacity: 7-shot clip magazine
Barrel: 18" with Micro-Groove® rifling (16 grooves)
Overall length: 36 3/4"

Stock: Monte Carlo genuine American black walnut with full pistol grip; checkering on pistol grip and forend
Sights: Adjustable folding semi-buckhorn rear; ramp front sight with brass bead, Wide-Scan™ hood

Weight: 5 lbs.
Features: Receiver grooved for tip-off scope mount; bolt hold-open device; cross-bolt safety

MARLIN BOLT ACTION RIFLES

MARLIN 15YN "LITTLE BUCKAROO™"
Single Shot 22 Beginner's Rifle
$147.85

SPECIFICATIONS
Caliber: 22 Short, Long or Long Rifle
Capacity: Single shot
Action: Bolt action; easy-load feed throat; thumb safety; red cocking indicator

Barrel length: 16¼" (16 grooves)
Overall length: 33¼"
Weight: 4¼ lbs.
Sights: Adjustable open rear; ramp front sight

Stock: One-piece walnut finish hardwood Monte Carlo with full pistol grip; tough Mar-Shield® finish

MODEL 25MN
$175.40

SPECIFICATIONS
Caliber: 22 Win. Mag Rimfire (not interchangeable with any other 22 cartridge)

Capacity: 7-shot clip magazine
Barrel length: 22" with Micro-Groove® rifling
Overall length: 41"
Weight: 6 lbs.

Sights: Adjustable open rear, ramp front sight; receiver grooved for scope mount
Stock: One-piece walnut-finished hardwood Monte Carlo with full pistol grip; Mar-Shield® finish

MODEL 25N
$153.55

Same specifications as Model 25MN, except **caliber** 22 LR and **weight** 5½ pounds.

MARLIN 880
$211.65

SPECIFICATIONS
Caliber: 22 Long Rifle
Capacity: 7-shot clip magazine
Action: Bolt action; positive thumb safety; red cocking indicator
Barrel: 22" with Micro-Groove® rifling (16 grooves)

Sights: Adjustable folding semi-buckhorn rear; ramp front with Wide-Scan™ with hood; receiver grooved for scope mount
Overall length: 41"
Weight: 5½ lbs.

Stock: Monte Carlo genuine American black walnut with full pistol grip; checkering on pistol grip and forend; tough Mar-Shield® finish; rubber butt pad; swivel studs

MARLIN BOLT ACTION RIFLES

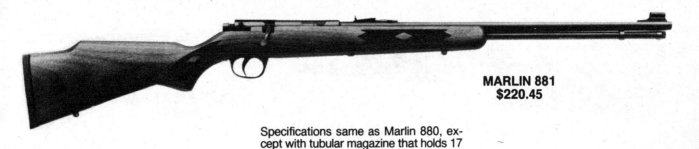

MARLIN 881
$220.45

Specifications same as Marlin 880, except with tubular magazine that holds 17 Long Rifle cartridges. **Weight:** 6 lbs

MARLIN 882 MAGNUM
$233.30

Specifications same as Model 883 Magnum, except with 7-shot clip magazine.

MARLIN 883 MAGNUM
$241.85

SPECIFICATIONS

Caliber: 22 Win. Mag. Rimfire (not interchangeable with any other 22 cartridge)
Capacity: 12-shot tubular magazine with patented closure system
Action: Bolt action; positive thumb safety; red cocking indicator

Barrel: 22″ with Micro-Groove® rifling (20 grooves)
Sights: Adjustable folding semi-buckhorn rear; ramp front with Wide-Scan™ hood; receiver grooved for scope mount
Overall length: 41″

Weight: 6 lbs.
Stock: Monte Carlo genuine American black walnut with full pistol grip; checkering on pistol grip and underside of forend; rubber butt pad; swivel studs; tough Mar-Shield® finish

MODEL 883N
(Electroless Nickel-plated)
$266.95

MARLIN RIFLES

MODEL 2000 TARGET
$543.75

SPECIFICATIONS
Caliber: 22 Long Rifle
Capacity: Single-shot; 5-shot adapter kit available
Action: Bolt action, 2-stage target trigger, red cocking indicator

Barrel length: 22″ Micro-Groove with match chamber, recessed muzzle
Overall length: 41″
Weight: 8 lbs.

Sights: Hooded Lyman front sight with 7 aperture inserts; fully adjustable Lyman target rear peep sight
Stock: Fiberglass + Kevlar, textured blue paint

MODEL 9 CAMP CARBINE
$363.50

SPECIFICATIONS
Caliber: 9mm
Capacity: 4-shot clip (12-shot magazine available)
Action: Self-loading. Manual bolt hold-open. Garand-type safety, magazine safety, loaded chamber indicator. Solid-top, machined steel receiver is sandblasted to prevent glare, and is drilled and tapped for scope mounting.
Barrel length: 16½″ with Micro-Groove® rifling
Overall length: 35½″
Weight: 6¾ lbs.
Sights: Adjustable folding rear, ramp front sight with high visibility, orange front sight post; Wide-Scan™ hood. Receiver drilled and tapped for scope mount.
Stock: Walnut finished hardwood with pistol grip; tough Mar-Shield® finish; rubber rifle butt pad; swivel studs
Also available: **MODEL 9N** (electroless nickel-plated): **$410.01**

MODEL 45
$363.50

SPECIFICATIONS
Caliber: 45 Auto
Capacity: 7-shot clip
Barrel length: 16½″
Overall length: 35½″

Weight 6.75 lbs.
Sights: Adjustable folding rear; ramp front sight with high visibility, orange front sight post; Wide-Scan™ hood

Stock: Walnut finished hardwood with pistol grip; rubber rifle butt pad; swivel studs

MARLIN LEVER ACTION CARBINES

MODEL 30AS
$334.50

SPECIFICATIONS
Caliber : 30-30
Capacity: 6-shot tubular magazine
Action: Lever action w/hammer block safety; solid top receiver w/side ejection
Barrel: 20″ Micro-Groove® barrel
Overall length: 38¼″

Weight: 7 lbs.
Sights: Tapped for scope mount and receiver sight; also available in combination w/4x, 32mm, 1″ scope
Stock: Walnut-finish hardwood stock w/ pistol grip; Mar-Shield® finish

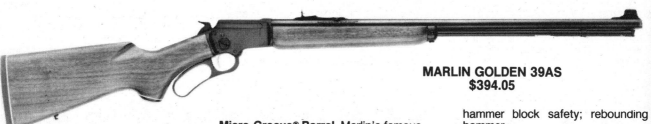

MARLIN GOLDEN 39AS
$394.05

The Marlin lever-action 22 is the oldest (since 1891) shoulder gun still being manufactured.
Solid Receiver Top. You can easily mount a scope on your Marlin 39 by screwing on the machined scope adapter base provided. The screw-on base is a neater, more versatile method of mounting a scope on a 22 sporting rifle. The solid top receiver and scope adapter base provide a maximum in eye relief adjustment. If you prefer iron sights, you'll find the 39 receiver clean, flat and sandblasted to prevent glare. Exclusive brass magazine tube.

Micro-Groove® Barrel. Marlin's famous rifling system of multi-grooving has consistently produced fine accuracy because the system grips the bullet more securely, minimizes distortion, and provides a better gas seal.

And the Model 39 maximizes accuracy with the heaviest barrels available on any lever-action 22.

SPECIFICATIONS
Caliber: 22 Short, Long and Long Rifle
Capacity: Tubular magazine holds 26 Short, 21 Long and 19 Long Rifle Cartridges
Action: Lever action; solid top receiver; side ejection; one-step takedown; deeply blued metal surfaces; receiver top sandblasted to prevent glare;

hammer block safety; rebounding hammer
Barrel: 24″ with Micro-Groove® rifling (16 grooves)
Overall length: 40″
Weight: 6½ lbs.
Sights: Adjustable folding semi-buckhorn rear, ramp front sight with new Wide-Scan™ hood; solid top receiver tapped for scope mount or receiver sight; scope adapter base; offset hammer spur for scope use—works right or left
Stock: Two-piece genuine American black walnut with fluted comb; full pistol grip and forend; blued-steel forend cap; swivel studs; grip cap; white butt and pistol-grip spacers; tough Mar-Shield® finish; rubber rifle butt pad

MODEL 39 TAKE-DOWN
$418.95 (Incl. Carrying Case)

SPECIFICATIONS
Caliber: 22 Short, Long or Long Rifle
Capacity: Tubular magazine holds 16 Short, 12 Long, or 11 Long Rifle cartridges

Action: Lever action; solid top receiver; side ejection; rebounding hammer; one-step take-down; deep blued metal surfaces; gold-plated trigger
Barrel length: 16½″ lightweight barrel (16 grooves)
Overall length: 32⅝″
Weight: 5¼ lbs.
Safety: Hammer block safety

Sights: Adjustable semi-buckhorn folding rear, ramp front with brass bead and Wide-Scan™ hood; top receiver tapped for scope mount and receiver sight; scope adapter base; offset hammer spur (right or left hand) for scope use
Stock: Two-piece straight-grip American black walnut with scaled-down forearm and blued steel forend cap; Mar-Shield® finish

MARLIN LEVER ACTION CARBINES

MODEL 1894 CLASSIC
$474.25

SPECIFICATIONS
Calibers: 218 Bee, 25-20 Win. and 32-20 Win.
Capacity: 6-shot tubular magazine
Barrel length: 22″ (6-groove rifling)
Overall length: 38³/₄″

Weight: 6¹/₄ lbs.
Action: Lever action with squared finger lever; side ejection; solid receiver top sandblasted to prevent glare; hammer block safety
Sights: Adjustable semi-buckhorn fold-

ing rear, brass bead front; solid top receiver tapped for scope mount and receiver sight; offset hammer spur
Stock: Straight-grip American black walnut with Mar-Shield® finish; blued steel forend cap

MARLIN 1894S
$441.95

SPECIFICATIONS
Calibers: 44 Rem. Mag./44 Special, 45 Colt
Capacity: 10-shot tubular magazine
Action: Lever action w/square finger lever; hammer block safety

Barrel: 20″ Micro-Groove® barrel
Sights: Ramp front sight w/brass bead; adjustable semi-buckhorn folding rear and Wide-Scan™ hood; solid top receiver tapped for scope mount or receiver sight

Overall length: 37¹/₂″
Weight: 6 lbs.
Stock: American black walnut stock w/ Mar-Shield® finish; blued steel forend cap; swivel studs

MARLIN 1894CS 357 MAGNUM
$441.95

SPECIFICATIONS
Calibers: 357 Magnum, 38 Special
Capacity: 9-shot tubular magazine
Action: Lever action w/square finger lever; hammer block safety; slde ejection; solid top receiver; deeply blued metal surfaces; receiver top sandblasted to prevent glare

Barrel: 18¹/₂″ long with Micro-Groove® rifling (12 grooves)
Sights: Adjustable semi-buckhorn folding rear, bead front; solid top receiver tapped for scope mount or receiver sight; offset hammer spur for scope use—adjustable for right- or left-hand use

Overall length: 36″
Weight: 6 lbs.
Stock: Straight-grip two-piece genuine American black walnut with white butt plate spacer; tough Mar-Shield® finish; swivel studs

MARLIN LEVER ACTION CARBINES

MARLIN 1895SS
$476.45

SPECIFICATIONS
Caliber: 45/70 Government
Capacity: 4-shot tubular magazine
Action: Lever action; hammer block safety; receiver top sandblasted to prevent glare

Barrel: 22″ Micro-Groove® barrel
Sights: Ramp front sight w/brass bead; adjustable semi-buckhorn folding rear and Wide-Scan™ hood; receiver tapped for scope mount or receiver sight

Overall length: 40½″
Weight: 7½ lbs.
Stock: American black walnut pistol grip stock w/rubber rifle butt pad and Mar-Shield® finish; white pistol grip and butt spacers

MARLIN 336CS
$392.90 (Without Scope)

SPECIFICATIONS
Calibers: 30-30 Win., and 35 Rem.
Capacity: 6-shot tubular magazine
Action: Lever action w/hammer block safety; deeply blued metal surfaces; receiver top sandblasted to prevent glare

Barrel: 20″ Micro-Groove® barrel
Sights: Adjustable folding semi-buckhorn rear; ramp front sight w/brass bead and Wide-Scan™ hood; tapped for receiver sight and scope mount; offset hammer spur for scope use (works right or left)

Overall length: 38½″
Weight: 7 lbs.
Stock: American black walnut pistol-grip stock w/fluted comb and Mar-Shield® finish; rubber rifle butt pad; swivel studs

MODEL 444SS
$476.45

Caliber: 444 Marlin
Capacity: 5-shot tubular magazine
Barrel: 22″ Micro-Groove®
Overall length: 40½″
Weight: 7½ lbs.

Stock: American black walnut pistol grip stock with rubber rifle butt pad; swivel studs

Sights: Ramp front sight with brass bead and Wide-Scan® hood; adjustable semi-buckhorn folding rear; receiver tipped for scope mount or receiver sight

MAUSER RIFLES

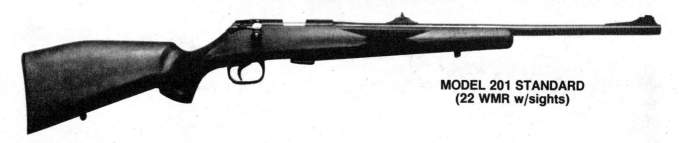

**MODEL 201 STANDARD
(22 WMR w/sights)**

MODEL 201 RIMFIRE

SPECIFICATIONS
Calibers: 22 LR or 22 WMR
Capacity: 5 shots (optional 8-shot available)
Barrel length: 21″
Overall length: 40″
Weight: 6½ lbs.
Sights: Metallic (optional)
Features: Receiver drilled and tapped for scope mounts; single-stage trigger (adj. from 1½ to 7 lbs.); positive silent tang safety locks bolt, sear and trigger; dual extractors for positive extraction of empty cases; hammer-forged steel barrels w/6 lands and grooves

Also available:
LUXUS MODELS with European walnut stocks, hand-checkered rosewood forends, rubber butt pad and 1″ quick disconnect sling swivels
Prices:
Standard 22 LR (without sights) $529.00
Standard 22 WMR (with sights) 599.00
Luxus 22 LR (without sights) 695.00
Luxus 22 WMR (with sights) 781.00

MODEL 107

MODEL 107

SPECIFICATIONS
Caliber: 22 LR
Capacity: 5 rounds (optional 8-shot available)
Barrel length: 21.6″
Overall Length: 40″
Weight: 5.1 lbs.
Length of pull: 13½″

Sights: Sliding rear sight adjustable to 200 meters
Features: 60° bolt throw locks into receiver groove; dual extractors for positive extraction of empty cases; all-steel floor plate and trigger guard; hammer-forged steel barrel with 6 lands and grooves; receiver accepts all rail scope mounts; two-stage trigger adjustable for weight and travel; positive silent tang safety locks bolt, sear and trigger
Price: $370.00

MODEL 86 SPECIALTY RIFLE
(not shown)

SPECIFICATIONS
Caliber: 308 Win. (7.62×51)
Capacity: 9 shots (+ 1 in chamber)
Barrel length: 28.8″ (with muzzle break)
Overall length: 47.7″ (maximum)
Weight: 10.8 lbs.

Features: Match trigger adjustable for two-stage or single stage; trigger slack, pull and position adjustable externally; scope mount; detachable receiver sight; receiver of chrome/moly steel
Prices:
Model 86 w/Fiberglass stock $4400.00
Model 86 w/Match Thumbhole wood stock 4650.00

MAUSER RIFLES

MODEL 66 STUTZEN

MODEL 66

These bolt-action centerfire repeating rifles feature a telescopic short-stroke action that allows the receiver to be two inches shorter than in most standard bolt-action rifles. Model 66 also provides interchangeability of barrels.

SPECIFICATIONS
Calibers: Standard—243 Win., 270 Win., 30-06, 308 Win. Magnum—7mm Rem., 300 Win., 300 Wby. Safari—375 H&H, 458 Win.
Capacity: 3-shot internal magazine
Barrel lengths: 21″ (Stutzen); 24″ (Standard); 26″ (Magnum & Safari)
Overall lengths: 39″ (Stutzen); 42″ (Standard); 44″ (Magnum & Safari)

Weight: 7 1/2 lbs. (Stutzen & Standard); 7.9 lbs. (Magnum); 9.3 lbs. (Safari)
Sights: Rectangular front blade and cover; open rear adjustable for windage and elevation
Features: Silent safety catch; barrel band front sling swivel; two large front bolt-locking lugs; mini-claw extractor for positive extraction of spent cases; single-stage adjustable trigger
Prices:
Standard calibers	**$1998.00**
Magnum calibers	2104.00
Safari calibers	2332.00
Stutzen full stock models	2104.00

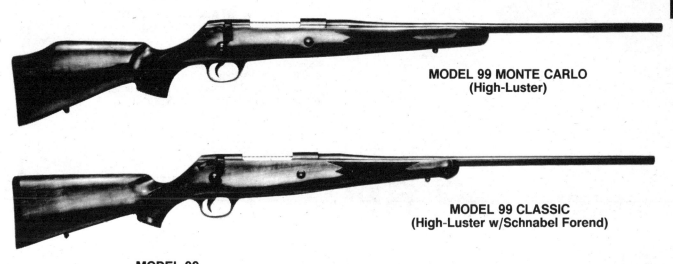

MODEL 99 MONTE CARLO
(High-Luster)

MODEL 99 CLASSIC
(High-Luster w/Schnabel Forend)

MODEL 99

SPECIFICATIONS
Calibers:
   Standard—243 Win., 25-06 Win., 270 Win., 30-06, 308 Win.
   Magnum—7mm Rem., 257 Wby., 270 Wby., 300 Wby., 300 Win., 338 Win., 375 H&H
Capacity: 4 shots (Standard); 3 shots (Magnum)
Barrel lengths: 24″ (Standard); 26″ (Magnum)
Overall lengths: 44″ (Standard); 46″ (Magnum)
Weight: 8 lbs.
Sights: None
Features: Chrome/Moly hammer-forged steel barrels; 60° bolt throw; 3 front bolt-locking lugs; stellite insert for strong lockup between receiver and barrel; jeweled bolt; dual cocking cam and patented two-stage floating firing pin for

fast lock time (1.6 milli-seconds); mini-claw extractor for positive extraction of spent cases; single-stage trigger (adj. from 1 1/2 to 7 lbs.); steel floor plate and trigger guard
Prices:
MODEL 99 CLASSIC
Standard calibers (w/oil finish)	**$1267.00**
With High-Luster finish	1426.00
Magnum calibers (w/oil finish)	1320.00
With High-Luster finish	1479.00

MODEL 99 MONTE CARLO STOCK
Standard calibers (w/oil finish)	1267.00
With High-Luster finish	1479.00
Magnum calibers (w/oil finish)	1320.00
With High-Luster finish	1479.00

McMILLAN SIGNATURE RIFLES

CLASSIC SPORTER
$2299.00

SPECIFICATIONS
Calibers:
    Model SA: 22-250, 243, 6mm Rem., 6mm BR, 7mm BR, 7mm-08, 284, 308, 350 Rem. Mag.
    Model LA: 25-06, 270, 280 Rem., 30-06
    Model MA: 7mm STW, 7mm Rem. Mag., 300 Win. Mag., 300 Weatherby, 300 H&H, 338 Win. Mag., 340 Weatherby, 375 H&H, 416 Rem.

Capacity: 4 rounds; 3 rounds in magnum calibers
Weight: 7 lbs; 7 lbs. 9 oz. in long action
Barrel lengths: 22″, 24″, 26″
Options: Fibergrain; wooden stock, optics, 30mm rings, muzzle brakes, steel floor plates, iron sights

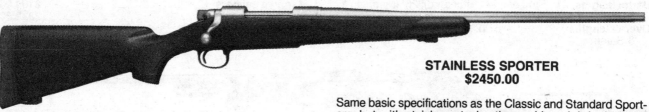

STAINLESS SPORTER
$2450.00

Same basic specifications as the Classic and Standard Sporters, but with stainless steel action and barrel. It is designed to withstand the most adverse weather conditions. Accuracy is guaranteed (3 shot in ½″ at 100 yards). Choice of wood, laminate or McMillan fiberglass stock.

ALASKAN
$3225.00

SPECIFICATIONS
Calibers:
    Model LA: 270, 280, 30-06
    Model MA: 7mm Rem. Mag., 300 Win. Mag., 300 H&H, 300 Weatherby, 358 Win., 340 Weatherby, 375 H&H, 416 Rem.

Other specifications same as the Classic Sporter, except McMillan action is fitted to a match-grade barrel, complete with single-leaf rear sight, barrel band front sight, 1″ detachable rings and mounts, steel floorplate, electroless nickel finish. Monte Carlo stock features cheekpiece, palm swell and special recoil pad.

McMILLAN SIGNATURE RIFLES

TALON SPORTER
$2541.00

The all-new action of this model is designed and engineered specifically for the hunting of dangerous (African-type) game animals. Patterned after the renowned pre-64 Model 70, the Talon features a cone breech, controlled feed, claw extractor, positive ejection and three-position safety. Action is available in chromolybdenum and stainless steel. Drilled and tapped for scope mounting in long, short or magnum, left or right hand.

Same basic specifications as McMillan's Signature series, but offered in the following **calibers:**
Standard Action: 22-250, 243, 6mm Rem., 6mm BR, 7mm BR, 7mm-08, 284, 308, 350 Rem. Mag.
Long Action: 25-06, 270, 280 Rem., 30-06
Magnum Action: 7mm STW, 7mm Rem. Mag., 300 Win. Mag., 300 Weatherby, 300 H&H, 338 Win. Mag., 340 Weatherby, 375 H&H, 416 Rem.

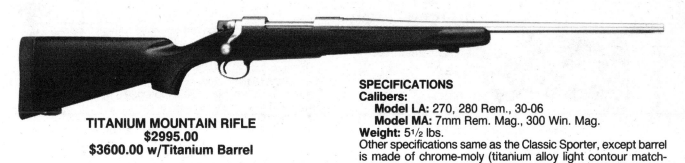

VARMINTER
$2370.00

SPECIFICATIONS
Calibers: 223, 22-250, 220 Swift, 243, 6mm Rem., 25-06, 7mm-08, 308, 350 Rem. Mag.
Other specifications same as the Classic Sporter, except the Super Varminter comes with heavy contoured barrel, adjustable trigger, field bipod and hand-bedded fiberglass stock.

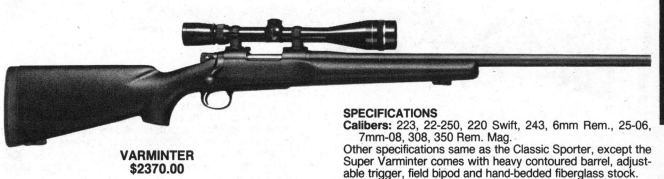

TITANIUM MOUNTAIN RIFLE
$2995.00
$3600.00 w/Titanium Barrel

SPECIFICATIONS
Calibers:
   Model LA: 270, 280 Rem., 30-06
   Model MA: 7mm Rem. Mag., 300 Win. Mag.
Weight: 5 1/2 lbs.
Other specifications same as the Classic Sporter, except barrel is made of chrome-moly (titanium alloy light contour match-grade barrel is available at additional cost of **$500.00**).

.300 PHOENIX
$2995.00

SPECIFICATIONS
Caliber: 300 Phoenix
Barrel length: 27 1/2"
Weight: 12 1/2 lbs.
Stock: Fiberglass with adjustable cheekpiece
Feature: Available in left-hand action

McMILLAN SIGNATURE RIFLES

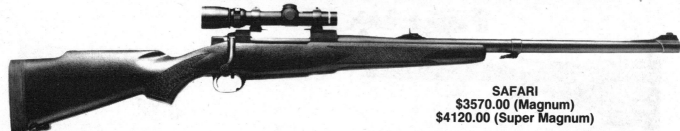

SAFARI
$3570.00 (Magnum)
$4120.00 (Super Magnum)

Super Magnum: 300 Phoenix, 338 Lapua, 378 Wby., 416 Rigby, 416 Wby., 460 Wby.
Other specifications same as the Classic Sporter, except for match-grade barrel, positive extraction McMillan Safari action, quick detachable 1″ scope mounts, positive locking steel floorplate, multi-leaf express sights, barrel band ramp front sight, barrel band swivels, and McMillan's Safari stock.

SPECIFICATIONS
Calibers:
  Magnum: 300 Win. Mag., 300 Weatherby, 300 H&H, 338 Win. Mag., 340 Weatherby, 375 H&H, 404 Jeffrey, 416 Rem., 458 Win.

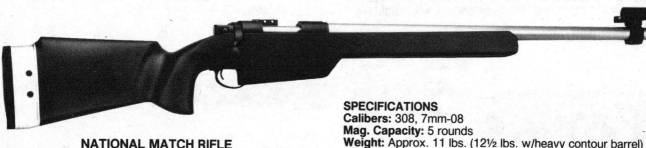

NATIONAL MATCH RIFLE
$2598.00

SPECIFICATIONS
Calibers: 308, 7mm-08
Mag. Capacity: 5 rounds
Weight: Approx. 11 lbs. (12½ lbs. w/heavy contour barrel)
Available for right-hand shooters only. Features modified ISU fiberglass stock with adjustable butt plate, stainless steel match barrel with barrel band and Tompkins front sight; McMillan repeating bolt action with clip shot and Canjar trigger. Barrel twist is 1:12″.

LONG RANGE RIFLE
$2598.00

SPECIFICATIONS
Calibers: 300 Win. Mag., 300 Phoenix, 7mm Mag., 338 Lapua
Weight: 14 lbs.
Barrel length: 26″
Available in right-hand only. Features a fiberglass stock with adjustable butt plate and cheekpiece. Stainless steel match barrel comes with barrel band and Tompkins front sight. McMillan solid bottom single-shot action and Canjar trigger. Barrel twist is 1:12″.

McMILLAN BENCHREST RIFLE
$2800.00 (not shown)

SPECIFICATIONS
Calibers: 6mm PPC, 243, 6mm BR, 6mm Rem., 308
Built to individual specifications to be competitive in hunter, light varmint and heavy varmint classes. Features solid bottom or repeating bolt action, Canjar trigger, fiberglass stock with recoil pad, stainless steel match-grade barrel and reloading dies. Right- or left-hand models.

MITCHELL ARMS

REPRODUCTIONS

1858 HENRY RIFLE
$975.00

This classic reproduction features an octagonal barrel, solid brass frame, shiny brass receiver, original loading system and solid European walnut stock. **Caliber:** 44-40.

1866 WINCHESTER RIFLE
$799.00

This lever-action Winchester with octagonal barrel has a solid brass frame, original loading system and solid European walnut stock. **Caliber:** 44-40.

1873 WINCHESTER RIFLE
$895.00

Features steel side plates, color casehardened frame and side plates, octagonal barrel, solid walnut buttstock and forend. Lever action. Uses centerfire ammo. **Calibers:** 44-40, 45 Colt, 357 Mag.

22 CAL. MILITARY-STYLE RIFLES

MODEL M-16A1/22
$349.00

MODEL CAR-15/22
$349.95

These full-size, full-weight 22 caliber versions of the U.S. Army M-16 and CAR-15 models feature the new round hand guards and basket flash hiders. A 15-round magazine is concealed within each full-size magazine well.

NAVY ARMS RIFLES

No. 2 CREEDMOOR TARGET RIFLE
$695.00

SPECIFICATIONS
Caliber: 45-70
Barrel length: 30″, tapered
Overall length: 46″
Weight: 9 lbs.
Sights: Globe front, adjustable Creedmoor rear
Stock: Checkered walnut stock and forend

This reproduction of the Remington No. 2 Creedmoor Rifle features a color casehardened receiver and steel trigger guard, tapered octagon barrel, and walnut forend and buttstock with checkered pistol grip.

REMINGTON-STYLE ROLLING BLOCK BUFFALO RIFLE
$500.00

SPECIFICATIONS
Caliber: 45-70
Barrel length: 26″ or 30″; full octagon or half-round
Sights: Blade front, open notch rear
Stock: Walnut stock and forend
Feature: Shown with optional 32¹/₂″ Model 1860 brass telescopic sight **$125.00**; Compact Model (18″) is **$130.00**

This replica of the rifle used by buffalo hunters and plainsmen of the 1800s features a casehardened receiver, solid brass trigger guard and walnut stock and forend. The tang is drilled and tapped to accept the optional Creedmoor sight.

MODEL TU-KKW
$200.00

SPECIFICATIONS
Caliber: 22 LR
Barrel length: 26″
Overall length: 44″
Weight: 8 lbs.
Sights: Open military style

Also available:
MODEL TU-33/40 w/20³/₄″ barrel **$200.00**
MODEL TU-KKW SNIPER TRAINER w/26″ barrel and
   2.75 power Type 89 scope **275.00**

The TU-KKW is a replica of the ''Kleine Kaliber Wehrsport Gewehr'' 22-caliber training rifle used by the Germans in World War II. A full-size, full-weight 98K, it is complete with Mauser-style military sights, bayonet lug and cleaning rod. Unlike the original, this replica model features a 5-round detachable magazine.

NAVY ARMS RIFLES

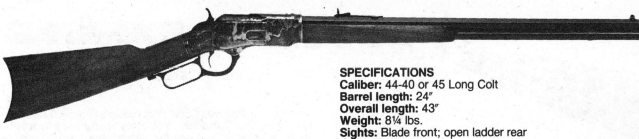

1873 WINCHESTER-STYLE RIFLE
$840.00

Known as "The Gun That Won the West," the "1873" was the most popular lever-action rifle of its time. This fine replica features a casehardened receiver.

SPECIFICATIONS
Caliber: 44-40 or 45 Long Colt
Barrel length: 24″
Overall length: 43″
Weight: 8¼ lbs.
Sights: Blade front; open ladder rear
Stock: Walnut

Also available:
1873 WINCHESTER-STYLE CARBINE
(19″ barrel) $815.00
1873 WINCHESTER-STYLE SPORTING RIFLE
(30″ full octagon bbl.) 895.00

SHARPS CAVALRY CARBINE
$650.00

This Cavalry version of the Sharps rifle features a side bar and saddle ring.

SPECIFICATIONS
Caliber: 45-70
Barrel length: 22″
Overall length: 39″
Weight: 7¾ lbs.
Sights: Blade front; military ladder rear
Stock: Walnut

COWBOYS COMPANION
$160.00

The Cowboys Companion is a hard-hitting, economical semi-automatic sporting carbine. The 7.62×39 cartridge is fast becoming a popular deer cartridge, similar to the 30-30. The gun is one of the shortest, lightest 30 sporting carbines available to the American hunter.

SPECIFICATIONS
Caliber: 7.62×39
Capacity: 10 rounds (5-round hunting magazine available)
Barrel length: 16″
Overall length: 36″
Weight: 7½ lbs.
Sights: Post front; U-notch rear
Also available:
SKS "PARA" CARBINE. A military version of the Cowboys Companion, equipped with a folding bayonet. **Price: $170.00**

NAVY ARMS REPLICA RIFLES

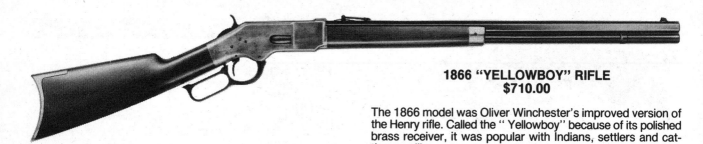

1866 "YELLOWBOY" RIFLE
$710.00

The 1866 model was Oliver Winchester's improved version of the Henry rifle. Called the "Yellowboy" because of its polished brass receiver, it was popular with Indians, settlers and cattlemen alike.

SPECIFICATIONS
Caliber: 44-40
Barrel length: 24″, full octagon
Overall length: 42½″
Weight: 8½ lbs.
Sights: Blade front; open ladder rear
Stock: Walnut

1866 "YELLOWBOY" CARBINE
$685.00

This is the "saddle gun" variant of the rifle described above.

SPECIFICATIONS
Caliber: 44-40
Barrel length: 19″, round
Overall length: 38¼″
Weight: 7¼ lbs.
Sights: Blade front; open ladder rear
Stock: Walnut

SHARPS PLAINS RIFLE
$650.00

A replica of the classic Sharps rifle, the Plains model was used by buffalo hunters and sportsmen in the late 19th century.

SPECIFICATIONS
Caliber: 45-70
Barrel length: 28½″
Overall length: 45¾″
Weight: 8 lbs. 10 oz.
Sights: Blade front; folding leaf rear
Stock: Walnut

NAVY ARMS REPLICA RIFLES

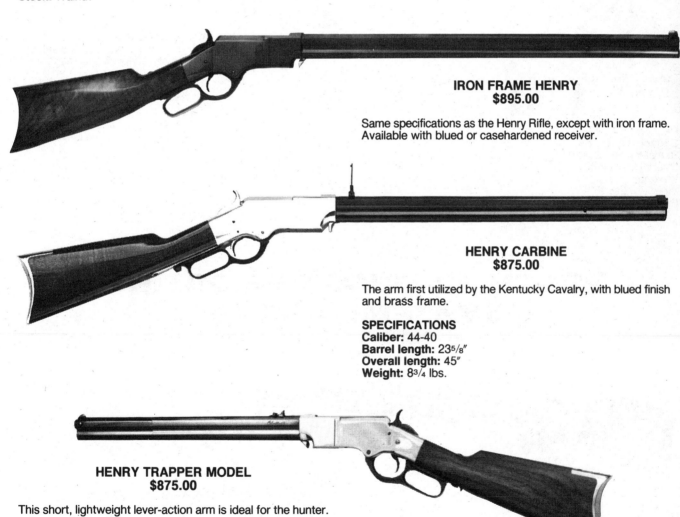

HENRY MILITARY RIFLE
$875.00

Features a highly polished brass frame and blued barrel; sling swivels to the original specifications are located on the left side.

SPECIFICATIONS
Calibers: 44-40 and 44 rimfire
Barrel length: 24″
Overall length: 43″
Weight: 9¼ lbs.
Stock: Walnut

IRON FRAME HENRY
$895.00

Same specifications as the Henry Rifle, except with iron frame. Available with blued or casehardened receiver.

HENRY CARBINE
$875.00

The arm first utilized by the Kentucky Cavalry, with blued finish and brass frame.

SPECIFICATIONS
Caliber: 44-40
Barrel length: 23⅝″
Overall length: 45″
Weight: 8¾ lbs.

HENRY TRAPPER MODEL
$875.00

This short, lightweight lever-action arm is ideal for the hunter.

SPECIFICATIONS
Caliber: 44-40
Barrel length: 16½″
Overall length: 34½″
Weight: 7¼ lbs.

NORINCO RIFLES

MODEL 22 ATD

MODEL 22 ATD
$158.33

SPECIFICATIONS
Caliber: 22 LR
Capacity: 11 rounds
Barrel length: 19.4″
Overall length: 36.6″
Weight: 4.6 lbs.
Sight radius: 16.3″
Finish: Blue
Features: Mauser-style flat-top steel receiver with integral rib (fits all popular rimfire scope mounts); Model 70-style safety (locks both firing pin and bolt); detachable 5-shot magazine

MODEL JW-15 "BUCKHORN" (not shown)
$110.00

SPECIFICATIONS
Caliber: 22 LR
Capacity: 5 rounds
Barrel length: 23.8″
Overall length: 41.5″
Weight: 5.5 lbs.
Sight radius: 18.8″
Finish: Blue

NORTH AMERICAN SHOOTING SYSTEMS RIFLES

CUSTOM HUNTER RIFLE
$1545.00

North American Shooting Systems (NASS) has an exclusive licensing arrangement to produce rifles chambered for the "Imperial Magnum" calibers. Among the many features are Sako AV action, match grade barrels and hand-bedded McMillan fiberglass stocks

SPECIFICATIONS
Calibers: 7mm Imp. Mag., 300 Imp. Mag., 311 Imp. Mag., 360 Imp. Mag.
Capacity: 3 rounds
Barrel length: 24″ or 26″
Overall length: 42″ or 44″
Weight: 8 lbs. (24″ barrel) or 8½ lbs. (26″ barrel)
Also available:
Custom Hunter with Fibergrain stock **$1675.00**

PARKER-HALE RIFLES

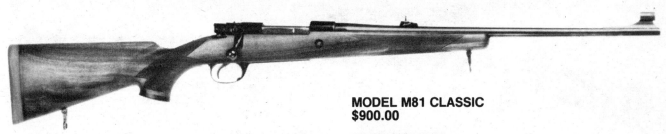

MODEL M81 CLASSIC
$900.00

SPECIFICATIONS
Calibers: 22-250, 243 Win., 6mm Rem., 270 Win., 6.5×55, 7×57, 7×64, 308 Win., 30-06
Barrel length: 24″
Overall length: 44¹/₂″
Capacity: 4 rounds
Weight: 7.75 lbs.
Length of pull: 13¹/₂″
Stock: Checkered walnut
Features: All-steel trigger guard; adjustable trigger

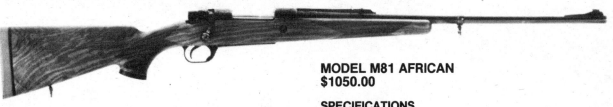

MODEL M81 AFRICAN
$1050.00

SPECIFICATIONS
Calibers: 375 H&H, 9.3 × 62mm
Capacity: 3 rounds
Barrel length: 24″
Overall length: 44¹/₂″
Weight: 7.75 lbs.
Stock: Checkered walnut
Features: All-steel trigger guard, adjustable trigger, barrel band front swivel, African express rear sight, hand-engraved receiver

MODEL 1100 LIGHTWEIGHT
$595.00

SPECIFICATIONS
Calibers: 22-250, 243 Win., 6mm Rem., 270 Win., 308 Win., 30-06
Barrel length: 22″
Overall length: 43″
Weight: 6¹/₂ lbs.
Capacity: 4 rounds
Length of pull: 13¹/₂″
Stock: Monte Carlo style, satin finished walnut with schnabel forend and wraparound checkering
Features: Slim profile barrel, alloy trigger guard and anodized bolt handle

PARKER HALE RIFLES ARE MANUFACTURED BY GIBBS RIFLE COMPANY, DISTRIBUTED BY NAVY ARMS

PARKER-HALE RIFLES

MODEL 2100 MIDLAND
$375.00

SPECIFICATIONS
Calibers: 22-250, 243 Win., 6mm Rem., 270 Win., 308 Win., 30-06
Capacity: 4 rounds
Barrel length: 22″ (24″ in cal. 22-250)
Overall length: 43″
Weight: 7 lbs.
Length of pull: 13½″

Stock: Checkered walnut
Sights: Hooded ramp front; adjustable flip-up rear

Also available:
MODEL 2600 MIDLAND SPECIAL in 22-250, 243 Win., 6mm Rem., 6.5×55, 7×57, 7×64, 30-06, 308 and 270. **Price: $360.00**
MODEL 2700 LIGHTWEIGHT in 22-250, 243 Win., 6mm Rem., 270 Win., 6.5×55, 7×57, 7×64, 308 Win. and 30-06 **Weight:** 6½ lbs. **Price: $415.00**

MODEL 1200 SUPER
$595.00

SPECIFICATIONS
Calibers: 22-250, 243 Win., 6mm Rem., 270 Win., 308 Win., 30-06
Capacity: 4 rounds
Barrel length: 24″
Overall length: 44½″

Weight: 7½ lbs.
Length of pull: 13½″

Also available:
MODEL 1200 SUPER CLIP in 22-250, 243 Win., 6mm Rem., 270 Win., 30-06 and 308 Win. Same specifications as Model 1200 Super, but weighs 7½ lbs. **Price: $640.00**

MODEL 1000 CLIP
$535.00

SPECIFICATIONS
Calibers: 22-250, 243 Win., 6mm Rem., 270 Win., 6.5×55, 7×57, 7×64, 308 Win. and 30-06

Capacity: 4 rounds
Barrel length: 22″
Overall length: 43″
Weight: 7¼ lbs.
Stock: Checkered walnut, Monte Carlo style
Features: Detachable magazine, Mauser-style 98 action

Also available:
MODEL 1000 STANDARD. Same specifications as the Model 1000 Clip, but with fixed 4-round magazine. **Price: $495.00**

PARKER HALE RIFLES ARE MANUFACTURED BY GIBBS RIFLE COMPANY, DISTRIBUTED BY NAVY ARMS

PARKER-HALE RIFLES

MODEL 1100M AFRICAN MAGNUM
$930.00

SPECIFICATIONS
Calibers: 357 H&H Magnum, 458 Win. Mag.
Capacity: 4 rounds
Barrel length: 24″
Overall length: 46″

Weight: 9½ lbs.
Stock: Checkered walnut, weighted, with two recoil lugs
Features: Vented recoil pad, shallow "V" rear sight, steel magazine with hinged floorplate

MODEL 1300C "SCOUT"
$595.00

SPECIFICATIONS
Calibers: 243 Win., 308 Win.
Capacity: 10 rounds
Barrel length: 20″

Overall length: 41″
Weight: 8½ lbs.
Stock: Checkered laminated birch wood
Features: Detachable magazine, muzzle brake

M-85 SNIPER RIFLE
$1950.00

SPECIFICATIONS
Caliber: 308 Win. (7.62 NATO)
Capacity: 10 or 20 rounds
Barrel length: 24¼″
Overall length: 45″
Weight: 12 lbs. 6 oz. (with scope)
Sights: Blade front (adjustable for windage); folding aperture rear (adjustable for elevation)

Stock: Fiberglass McMillan, adjustable for length of pull
Features: M-14 type detachable magazine; adjustable trigger; "quick-detach" bipod

**PARKER HALE RIFLES ARE MANUFACTURED BY GIBBS RIFLE COMPANY,
DISTRIBUTED BY NAVY ARMS**

REMINGTON BOLT ACTION RIFLES

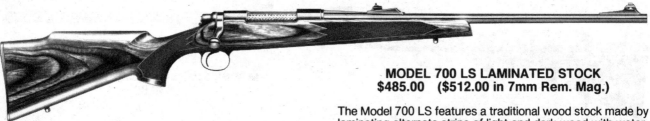

MODEL 700 LS LAMINATED STOCK
$485.00   ($512.00 in 7mm Rem. Mag.)

The Model 700 LS features a traditional wood stock made by laminating alternate strips of light and dark wood with water-proof adhesive and impregnating it with a phenolic resin for greater stability. Other features include low-gloss satin finish, cut checkering, sling swivel studs and open factory sights. **Calibers:** 243 Win., 270 Win., 30-06 and 7mm Rem. Mag. **Capacity:** 5 (4 in 7mm Rem. Mag.). **Barrel length:** 22″ (24″ in 7mm Rem. Mag.). **Weight:** 7¼ lbs. **Stock dimensions:** drop at heel 1⁵/₁₆″; drop at comb ¹¹/₁₆″; length of pull 13³/₈″.

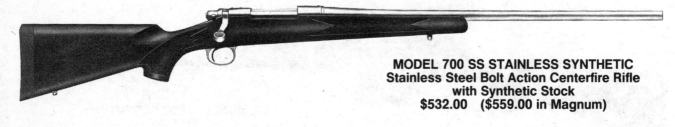

MODEL 700 SS STAINLESS SYNTHETIC
Stainless Steel Bolt Action Centerfire Rifle with Synthetic Stock
$532.00   ($559.00 in Magnum)

MODEL 700 MOUNTAIN RIFLE
$519.00

A special lightweight version of the Remington Model 700 bolt action centerfire rifle. **Calibers:** 243 Win., 257 Roberts, 25-06 Rem., 270 Win., 7mm-08 Rem., 7mm Mauser, 280 Rem., 30-06 and 308 Win. **Weight:** 6³/₄ lbs. **Barrel length:** 22″. **Overall length:** 41⁵/₈″. **Stock:** Straight-line comb with cheekpiece; satin stock finish.

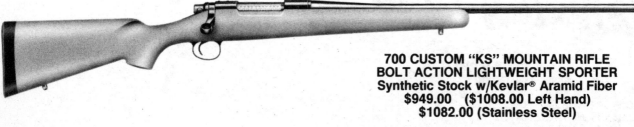

700 CUSTOM "KS" MOUNTAIN RIFLE
BOLT ACTION LIGHTWEIGHT SPORTER
Synthetic Stock w/Kevlar® Aramid Fiber
$949.00   ($1008.00 Left Hand)
$1082.00 (Stainless Steel)

Calibers: 270 Win., 280 Rem., 30-06, 7mm Rem. Mag., 300 Win. Mag., 300 Weatherby Mag., 35 Whelen, 338 Win. Mag., 8mm Rem. Mag., and 375 H&H Mag. All calibers except 35 Whelen and 8mm Rem. Mag. are for right-hand only.
Also available in wood-grained Kevlar® stock (same calibers). **Price: $1056.00 ($1114.00 Left Hand).**

REMINGTON BOLT ACTION RIFLES

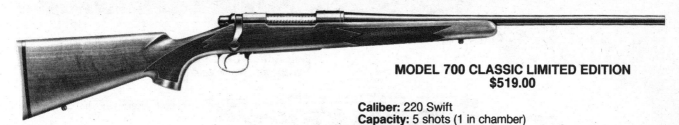

MODEL 700 CLASSIC LIMITED EDITION
$519.00

Caliber: 220 Swift
Capacity: 5 shots (1 in chamber)
Barrel length: 24″
Overall length: 44½″
Weight: 7½ lbs.
Bolt: Jeweled with shrouded firing pin
Receiver: Drilled and tapped for scope mounts; fixed magazine with or without hinged floor plate
Stock: Cut-checkered select American walnut with quick detachable sling swivels installed; recoil pad standard equipment on Magnum rifles; installed at extra charge on others

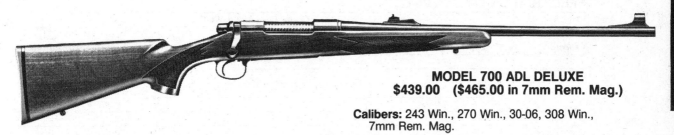

MODEL 700 ADL DELUXE
$439.00   ($465.00 in 7mm Rem. Mag.)

Calibers: 243 Win., 270 Win., 30-06, 308 Win., 7mm Rem. Mag.

MODEL 700 CS (Camo Synthetic)
$563.00   ($589.00 in 7mm Rem. Mag.)

The Model 700® is bedded to a synthetic stock fully camouflaged in Mossy Oak® Bottomland™. Stronger than wood and unaffected by weather, this stock will not warp or swell in rain, snow or heat. The Model 700 Camo Synthetic comes with a non-reflective matte finish on the bolt and is available in nine calibers (see table below and on the following page).

	Calibers	Mag. Capacity	Barrel Length	Overall Length	Twist R-H 1 turn in	Avg. Wt. (lbs.)
Model 700™ CS Camo-Synthetic Stock	22-250 Rem.	4	24″	43⅝″	14″	6½
	243 Win.	4	22″	41⅝″	9⅛″	6½
	270 Win.	4	22″	42½″	10″	6½
	280 Rem.	4	22″	42½″	9¼″	6½
	30-06	4	22″	42½″	10″	6½
	308 Win.	4	22″	41⅝″	10″	7
	7mm Rem. Mag.	3	24″	44½″	9¼″	6¾
	300 Weatherby Mag.	3	24″	44½″	12″	7
	7mm-08 Rem.	4	22″	42½″	9¼″	7¼″

REMINGTON BOLT ACTION RIFLES

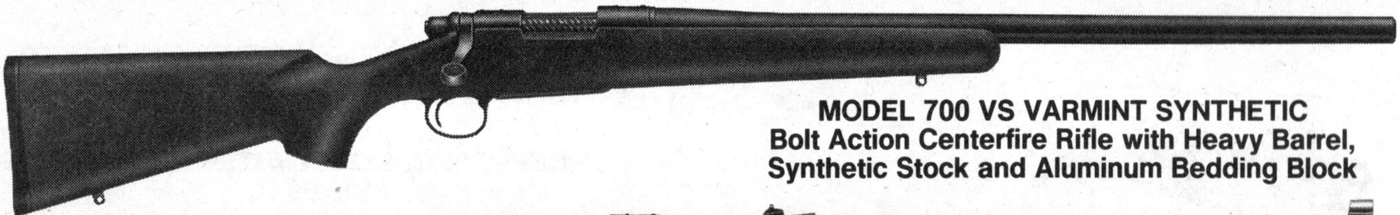

MODEL 700 VS VARMINT SYNTHETIC
Bolt Action Centerfire Rifle with Heavy Barrel, Synthetic Stock and Aluminum Bedding Block

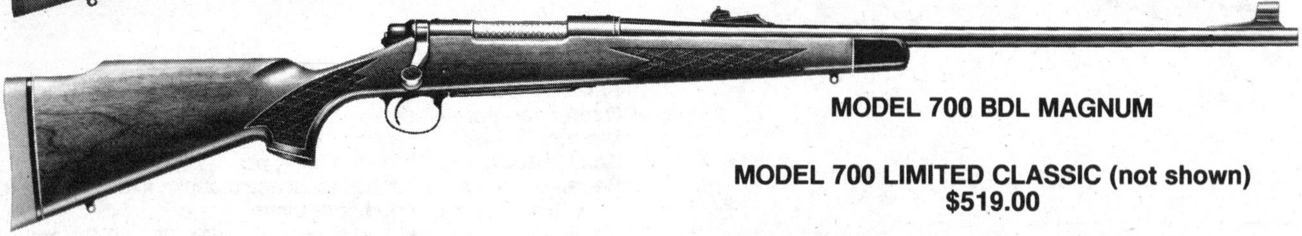

MODEL 700 BDL MAGNUM

MODEL 700 LIMITED CLASSIC (not shown)
$519.00

This new addition to the Model 700 line is chambered for caliber 220 Swift. It features a 5-shot magazine, barrel length of 24″ with right-hand twist of 1:14″, overall length of 44 1/2″ and weight of 7 1/2 pounds.

SPECIFICATIONS MODEL 700

			Overall Length/Avg. Wt. (lb.)						
				Varmint Special[1]					Twist
Calibers	Mag. Cap.	Barrel Lth.	"Mtn. Rifle"*	Wood	Synthetic	Camo Synthetic	Stainless Synthetic	ADL & BDL	R-H 1 turn in
17 Rem.	5	24″	—	—	—	—	—	43 5/8″/7 1/4	9″
222 Rem.	5	24″	—	43 1/2″/9	—	—	—	43 5/8″/7 1/4	14″
22-250 Rem.	4	24″	—	43 1/2″/9	43 1/2″/8 1/2	43 5/8″/7 1/4	—	43 5/8″/7 1/4	14″
	4	24″	—	—	—	—	—	14 5/8″/7 1/4	14″
223 Rem.	5	24″	—	43 1/2″/9	43 1/2″/8 1/2	—	—	43 5/8″/7 1/4	12″
6mm Rem.	4	22″	—	43 1/2″/9	—	—	—	41 5/8″/7 1/4	9 1/8″
243 Win.	4	22″	41 5/8″/6 3/4	43 1/2″/9	—	41 5/8″/7 1/4	—	41 5/8″/7 1/4	9 1/8″
	4	22″	—	—	—	—	—	41 5/8″/7 1/4	9 1/8″
25-06 Rem.	4	24″	—	—	—	—	42 1/2″/6 1/4	44 1/2″/7 1/2	10″
	4	22″	42 1/2″/6 3/4	—	—	—	—	—	10″
257 Roberts	4	22″	41 5/8″/6 3/4	—	—	—	—	—	10″
270 Win.	4	22″	42 1/2″/6 3/4	—	—	42 1/2″/7 1/4	—	42 1/2″/7 1/4	10″
	4	22″	—	—	—	—	—	42 1/2″/7 1/4	10″
	4	24″	—	—	—	—	42 1/2″/6 1/4	—	10″
280 Rem.	4	22″	42 1/2″/6 3/4	—	—	42 1/2″/7 1/4	42 1/2″/6 1/4	42 1/2″/7 1/4	9 1/4″
7mm-08 Rem.	4	22″	41 5/8″/6 3/4	43 1/2″/9	—	42 1/2″/7 1/4	—	41 5/8″/7 1/4	9 1/4″
7mm Mauser (7 × 57)	4	22″	41 5/8″/6 3/4	—	—	—	—	—	9 1/4″
7mm Rem. Mag.[2]	3	24″	—	—	—	44 1/2″/7 1/2	44 1/2″/7	44 1/2/7 1/2	9 1/4″
	3	24″	—	—	—	—	—	44 1/2″/7 1/4	9 1/4″
7mm Wby. Mag.	3	24″	—	—	—	—	44 1/2″/7	—	9″ 1/4
300 Savage	4	22″	—	—	—	—	—	42 1/2″/7 1/4	12″
30-06	4	22″	42 1/2″/6 3/4	—	—	42 1/2″/7 1/4	—	42 1/2″/7 1/4	10″
	4	22″	—	—	—	—	—	42 1/2″/7 1/4	10″
	4	24″	—	—	—	—	42 1/2″/6 1/4	—	10″
308 Win.	4	22″	41 5/8″/6 3/4	—	—	41 5/8″/7 1/4	—	41 5/8″/7 1/4	10″
	4	24″	—	43 1/2″/9	43 1/2″/8 1/2	—	—	—	12″
	4	22″	—	—	—	—	—	41 5/8″/7 1/2	10″
300 Win. Mag.[2]	3	24″	—	—	—	—	44 1/2″/7	44 1/2″/7	10″
300 Wby. Mag.[2]	3	24″	—	—	—	44 1/2″/7 1/2	—	—	12″
35 Whelen[2]	4	22″	—	—	—	—	—	42 1/2″/7 1/4	16″
338 Win. Mag.[2]	3	24″	—	—	—	—	44 1/2″/7	44 1/2″/7 1/2	10″
	3	24″	—	—	—	—	—	44 1/2″/7 1/2	10″

[1] Varmint Special equipped only with a 24″ barrel only. [2] Recoil pad included. LS = Laminated Stock.
Adjustable open sights are on Model 700® ADL, Camo, BDL, Safari, and Seven®. The Mountain Rifle, Limited Classic, Stainless Synthetic and Varmint Specials do not have sights.

REMINGTON RIFLES
SAFARI GRADE BOLT ACTION RIFLES

Model 700 Safari Grade bolt-action rifles provide big game hunters with a choice of two stock materials. Model 700 Safari Monte Carlo (with Monte Carlo comb and cheekpiece) and Model 700 Safari Classic (with straight-line classic comb and no cheekpiece) are the wood-stocked models. Both Monte Carlo and Classic models are supplied with a satin wood finish decorated with hand-cut checkering 18 lines to the inch and fitted with two reinforcing cross bolts covered with rosewood plugs. The Monte Carlo model also has a rosewood pistol grip cap and forend tip. All models are fitted with sling swivel studs and 24″ barrels. Synthetic stock is available with simulated wood-grain finish and is reinforced with Kevlar® (KS). **Calibers:** 8mm Rem. Mag., 375 H&H Magnum, 416 Rem. Mag. and 458 Win. Mag. **Capacity:** 3 rounds. **Average weight:** 9 lbs. **Overall length:** 44½″. **Rate of twist:** 10″ (8mm Rem. Mag.); 12″ (375 H&H Mag.); 14″ (416 Rem. Mag., 458 Win. Mag.).
Prices:
Classic Stock (Right Hand) . . . . $ 953.00
Left Hand 1012.00
Monte Carlo Stock (Right Hand) 953.00

Kevlar®-reinforced Stock (Right Hand) 1098.00
Left Hand 1157.00
Wood-grained Kevlar®-reinforced Stock (R.H.) . 1205.00
Left Hand 1264.00

			Prices		Varmint Special[1]	
Mtn. Rifle	Camo Synthetic	Stainless Synthetic	ADL	BDL	Wood	Synthetic
—	—	—	—	$545	—	—
—	—	—	—	519	$552	—
—	$563	—	—	519	552	$625
—	—	—	—	577 LH	—	—
—	—	—	—	519	552	625
—	—	—	—	519	552	—
$519	563	—	$439	519	552	—
—	—	—	485 LS	577 LH	—	—
—	—	$532	—	519	—	—
519	—	—	—	—	—	—
519	—	—	—	—	—	—
519	563	—	439	519	—	—
—	—	—	485 LS	577 LH	—	—
—	—	532	—	—	—	—
519	563	532	—	519	—	—
519	563	—	—	519	522	—
519	—	—	—	—	—	—
—	589	532	465	545	—	—
—	—	—	512 LS	604 LH	—	—
—	—	559	—	—	—	—
—	—	—	—	519	—	—
519	563	—	439	519	—	—
—	—	—	485 LS	577 LH	—	—
—	—	559	—	—	—	—
519	563	—	439	519	—	—
—	—	—	—	—	552	625
—	—	—	—	577 LH	—	—
—	—	559	—	545	—	—
—	589	—	—	—	—	—
—	—	—	—	545	—	—
—	—	559	—	545 LH	—	—
—	—	—	—	604 LH	—	—

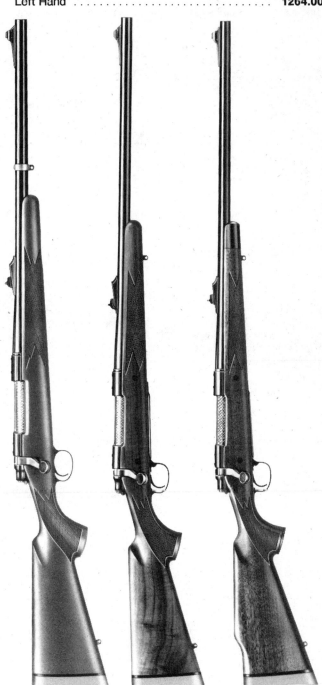

MODEL 700 SAFARI KS   **MODEL 700 SAFARI CLASSIC**   **MODEL 700 SAFARI MONTE CARLO**

REMINGTON BOLT ACTION RIFLES

Every **Model Seven** is built to the accuracy standards of our famous Model 700 and is individually test fired to prove it. Its 18½" Remington special steel barrel is free-floating out to a single pressure point at the forend tip. And there is ordnance-quality steel in everything from its fully enclosed bolt and extractor system to its steel trigger guard and floor plate. Ramp front and fully adjustable rear sights, sling swivel studs are standard.

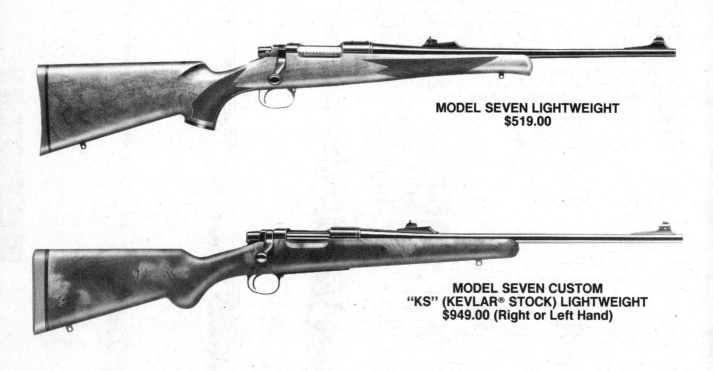

MODEL SEVEN LIGHTWEIGHT
$519.00

MODEL SEVEN CUSTOM
"KS" (KEVLAR® STOCK) LIGHTWEIGHT
$949.00 (Right or Left Hand)

Models	Calibers	Clip Mag. Capacity	Barrel Length	Overall Length	Twist R-H 1 turn in	Avg. Wt. (lbs.)
MODEL SEVEN™	223 Rem.	5	18½"	37¾"	12"	6¼
	243 Win.	4	18½"	37¾"	9⅛"	6¼
	6mm Rem.	4	18½"	37¾"	9⅛"	6¼
	7mm-08 Rem.	4	18½"	37¾"	9¼"	6¼
	308 Win.	4	18½"	37¾"	10"	6¼
MODEL 7400™ AND MODEL 7600™	243 Win.		22"	42⅝"	9⅛"	7½
	270 Win.		22"	42⅝"	10"	7½
	280 Rem.		22"	42⅝"	9¼"	7½
	30-06 Carbine		18½"	39⅛"	10"	7¼
	30-06		22"	42⅝"	10"	7½
	308 Win.		22"	42⅝"	10"	7½
	35 Whelen*		22"	42⅝"	16"	7¼

STOCK DIMENSIONS: 13³⁄₁₆" length of pull, ⁵⁄₁₆" drop at heel, ⁹⁄₁₆" drop at comb. Model 7600 also accepts 30-06 and 308 Accelerator® cartridges. Each has a positive cross-bolt safety switch.
* Model 7600 only.

REMINGTON RIFLES

MODEL 7400 (High Gloss Stock)
$503.00

Calibers: 243 Win., 270 Win., 280 Rem., 30-06, 308 Win., and 30-06 Carbine (see below)
Capacity: 5 centerfire cartridges (4 in the magazine, 1 in the chamber); extra 4-shot magazine available
Action: Gas-operated; receiver drilled and tapped for scope mounts
Barrel length: 22″
Weight: 7½ lbs.

Overall length: 42″
Sights: Standard blade ramp front; sliding ramp rear
Stock: Satin or high-gloss (270 Win. and 30-06 only) walnut stock and forend; curved pistol grip
Length of pull: 13⅜″
Drop at heel: 2¼″
Drop at comb: 1¹³/₁₆″

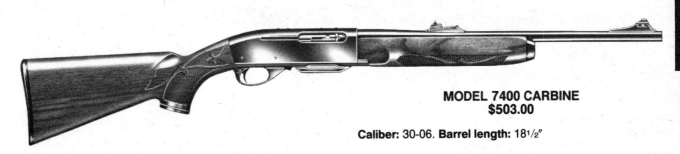

MODEL 7400 CARBINE
$503.00

Caliber: 30-06. **Barrel length:** 18½″

MODEL 7600 (High Gloss Stock)
$480.00

Calibers: 243 Win., 270 Win., 280 Rem., 30-06, 308 Win., 35 Whelen, and 30-06 Carbine (see below)
Capacity: 5-shot capacity in all six calibers (4 in the removable magazine, 1 in the chamber)
Action: Pump action
Barrel length: 22″ (18½″ in 30-06 Carbine)
Overall length: 42″
Weight: 8 lbs.

Sights: Standard blade ramp front sight; sliding ramp rear, both removable
Stock: Satin or high-gloss walnut
Length of pull: 13⅜″
Drop at heel: ¹⁵/₁₆″
Drop at comb: ⁹/₁₆″
Also available:
MODEL 7600 CARBINE with 18½″ barrel; chambered for 30-06 cartridge

REMINGTON RIMFIRE RIFLES

MODEL 541-T BOLT ACTION
$356.00

RIMFIRE RIFLE SPECIFICATIONS

Model	Action	Barrel Length	Overall Length	Average Wt. (lbs.)	Magazine Capacity
541-T	Bolt	24″	42½″	5⅞	5-Shot Clip
581-S	Bolt	24″	42½″	5⅞	5-Shot Clip
552 BDL Deluxe Speedmaster	Auto	21″	40″	5¾	15 Long Rifle
572 BDL Deluxe Fieldmaster	Pump	21″	40″	5½	15 Long Rifle

MODEL 552 BDL DELUXE SPEEDMASTER
$213.00

A deluxe model with dependable mechanical features on the inside, plus special design and appearance extras on the outside. The 552 BDL rimfire semiautomatic rifle sports Remington custom-impressed checkering on both stock and forend.

Tough DuPont RK-W lifetime finish brings out the lustrous beauty of the walnut while protecting it. Sights are ramp-style in front and rugged big-game type fully adjustable in rear.

MODEL 572 BDL DELUXE FIELDMASTER
$224.00

MODEL 572 DELUXE

Features of this rifle with big-game feel and appearance are: DuPont's tough RK-W finish; centerfire-rifle-type rear sight fully adjustable for both vertical and horizontal sight alignment; big-game style ramp front sight; Remington impressed checkering on both stock and forend.

Action: Pump repeater
Caliber: 22 Short, Long and Long Rifle rimfire
Capacity: Tubular magazine holds 20 Short, 17 Long, 15 Long Rifle cartridges
Barrel length: 21″
Overall length: 40″
Average weight: 5½ lbs.
Safety: Positive cross bolt
Receiver: Grooved for "tip-off" scope mounts
Sights: Fully adjustable rear; ramp front; screw removable
Stock and forend: American walnut with DuPont RK-W lustrous finish and fine-line custom checkering

REMINGTON TARGET RIFLES

**MODEL 40-XR KS
Rimfire Position Rifle
$1205.00 (w/Kevlar Stock)**

Stock designed with deep forend for more comfortable shooting in all positions. Butt plate vertically adjustable. Exclusive loading platform provides straight line feeding with no shaved bullets. Crisp, wide, adjustable match trigger. Meets all International Shooting Union standard rifle specifications.

Action: Bolt action, single shot
Caliber: 22 Long Rifle rimfire
Capacity: Single loading
Sights: Optional at extra cost. Williams Receiver No. FPTK and Redfield Globe front match sight
Safety: Positive serrated thumb safety

Receiver: Drilled and tapped for receiver sight
Barrel: 24″ medium weight target barrel countersunk at muzzle. Drilled and tapped for target scope blocks. Fitted with front sight base
Bolt: Artillery style with lock-up at rear. 6 locking lugs, double extractors
Trigger: Adjustable from 2 to 4 lbs.
Overall length: 43½″
Average weight: 10½ lbs.
Stock: Position style with Monte Carlo, cheekpiece and thumb groove; five-way adjustable butt plate and full-length guide rail

**MODEL 40-XC KS
National Match Course Rifle
$1281.00 (w/Kevlar Stock)**

Chambered solely for the 7.62mm NATO cartridge, this match rifle was designed to meet the needs of competitive shooters firing the national match courses. Position-style stock, five-shot repeater with top-loading magazine, anti-bind bolt and receiver and in the bright stainless steel barrel. Meets all International Shooting Union Army Rifle specifications.

Action: Bolt action, single shot
Caliber: 7.62mm NATO
Capacity: Single loading
Barrel: 24″ heavy barrel
Overall length: 43½″

Average weight: 11 lbs.
Bolt: Heavy, oversized locking lugs and double extractors
Trigger: Adjustable from 1½ to 3 lbs.
Safety: Positive thumb safety
Sights: Optional at extra cost. Williams Receiver No. FPTK and Redfield Globe front match sight
Receiver: Drilled and tapped for receiver sight or target scope blocks
Stock: Position style with front swivel block on forend guide rail
Length of pull: 13½″

REMINGTON TARGET RIFLES

MODEL 40-XB "RANGEMASTER"
Centerfire Rifle
$1056.00   ($1114.00 Left Hand)

Barrels, in either standard or heavy weight, are unblued steel. Comb-grooved for easy bolt removal. Mershon White Line non-slip rubber butt plate supplied.

Action: Bolt—single shot in either standard or heavy barrel versions; repeater in heavy barrel only; receiver bedded to stock; barrel is free floating
Calibers: Single-shot, 220 Swift, 222 Rem., 223 Rem., 22-250 Rem., 6mm Rem., 222 Rem. Mag., 243 Win., 7.62mm NATO (308 Win.), 30-06, 30-338, 300 Win. Mag., 25-06 Rem., 6mm BR Rem., 7mm Rem. Mag., 7mm BR Rem.
Sights: No sights supplied; target scope blocks installed

Safety: Positive thumb operated
Receiver: Drilled and tapped for scope block and receiver sights
Barrel: Drilled and tapped for scope block and front target iron sight; muzzle diameter S2—approx. 3/4", H2—approx. 7/8"; unblued stainless steel only, 27 1/4" long
Trigger: Adjustable from 1 1/2 to 3 lbs. pull; special 2-oz. trigger available at extra cost; single shot models only
Stock: American walnut; adjustable front swivel block on rail; rubber non-slip butt plate
Overall length: Approx. 47"
Average weight: H2—11 1/4 lbs.

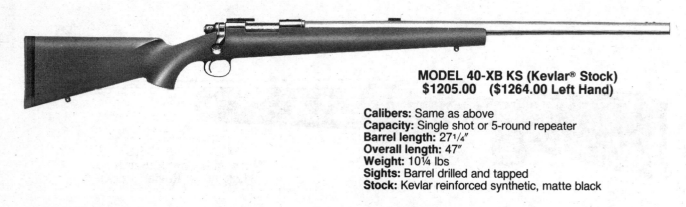

MODEL 40-XB KS (Kevlar® Stock)
$1205.00   ($1264.00 Left Hand)

Calibers: Same as above
Capacity: Single shot or 5-round repeater
Barrel length: 27 1/4"
Overall length: 47"
Weight: 10 1/4 lbs
Sights: Barrel drilled and tapped
Stock: Kevlar reinforced synthetic, matte black

MODEL 40-XBBR KS (Kevlar® stock)
BENCH REST CENTERFIRE RIFLE
$1281.00

Built with all the features of the extremely accurate Model 40-XB but modified to give the competitive bench rest shooter a standardized rifle that provides the inherent accuracy advantages of a short, heavy, extremely stiff barrel. Wider, squared off forend gives a more stable rest on sandbags or other supports and meets weight limitations for the sporter and light-varmint classes of National Bench Rest Shooters Association competition.

Action: Bolt, single shot only
Calibers: 222 Rem., 222 Rem. Mag., 22 Bench Rest Rem., 7.62 NATO (308 Win.), 6mm Bench Rest Rem., 223 Rem., 6×47

Barrel: 20" and 24"; unblued stainless steel only
Overall length: 38" to 42"
Average weight: 10 1/2 to 13 1/2 lbs.
Sights: Supplied with target scope blocks
Receiver: Drilled and tapped for target scope blocks
Safety: Positive thumb operated
Trigger: Adjustable from 1 1/2 to 3 1/2 lbs.; special 2-oz. trigger available at extra cost
Stock: Kevlar®; 12" or 13" length of pull

ROSSI RIFLES

PUMP-ACTION GALLERY GUNS

MODEL M62 SAC
$215.00   ($231.67 Nickel)

SPECIFICATIONS
Caliber: 22 LR
Capacity: 12 rounds
Barrel length: 16¹/₂″
Overall length: 32³/₄″
Weight: 4¹/₄″
Finish: Blue

MODEL M62 SA
$215.00   ($231.67 Nickel)

SPECIFICATIONS
Caliber: 22 LR
Capacity: 13 rounds
Barrel length: 23″
Overall length: 39¹/₄″
Weight: 5¹/₂″ lbs.
Finish: Blue
Model M62 SA w/Octagonal barrel **$240.00**
Model 59 22 Magnum **265.00**

PUMA LEVER-ACTION CARBINES

MODEL M92 SRS
$331.67 (not shown)

SPECIFICATIONS
Caliber: 38 Special or 357 Magnum
Capacity: 7 rounds
Barrel length: 16″
Overall length: 33″
Weight: 5 lbs.
Finish: Blue

MODEL M92 SRC
$331.67

SPECIFICATIONS
Caliber: 38 Special or 357 Magnum
Capacity: 10 rounds
Barrel length: 20″
Overall length: 37″
Weight: 5³/₄″
Also available:
Model M65SRC in 44 Magnum **$348.33**

RUGER CARBINES

RUGER MINI-14

Materials: Heat-treated chrome molybdenum and other alloy steels as well as music wire coil springs are used throughout the mechanism to ensure reliability under field-operating conditions. **Safety:** The safety blocks both the hammer and sear. The slide can be cycled when the safety is on. The safety is mounted in the front of the trigger guard so that it may be set to Fire position without removing finger from trigger guard. **Firing pin:** The firing pin is retracted mechanically during the first part of the unlocking of the bolt. The rifle can only be fired when the bolt is safely locked. **Stock:** One-piece American hardwood reinforced with steel liner at stressed areas. Handguard and forearm separated by air space from barrel to pro-

mote cooling under rapid-fire conditions. **Field stripping:** The Carbine can be field stripped to its eight (8) basic sub-assemblies in a matter of seconds and without use of special tools.

MINI-14 SPECIFICATIONS
Caliber: 223 (5.56mm). **Length:** 37¼″. **Weight:** 6 lbs. 8 oz. **Magazine:** 5-round, detachable box magazine. **Barrel length:** 18½″.

Mini-14/5 Blued **$491.50**
K-Mini-14/5 Stainless Steel **542.00**
(Scopes not included)

MINI-14 RANCH RIFLE

Caliber: 223 (5.56mm). **Length:** 37¼″. **Weight:** 6 lbs. 8 oz. **Magazine:** 5-round detachable box magazine. Barrel length: 18¼″.

Mini-14/5R Blued **$530.00**
K-Mini-14/5R Stainless Steel **580.00**

MINI THIRTY

This modified version of the Ruger Ranch rifle is chambered for the 7.62 × 39mm Russian service cartridge (used in the SKS carbine and AKM rifle). Designed for use with telescopic sights, it features a low, compact scope mounting for greater accuracy and carrying ease. **Barrel length:** 18½″. **Overall**

length: 37¼″. **Weight:** 6 lbs. 14 oz. (empty). **Magazine capacity:** 5 shots. **Rifling:** 6 grooves, right-hand twist, one turn in 10″. **Finish:** polished and blued overall.

Price **$530.00**
In Stainless steel **580.00**

RUGER CARBINES

STANDARD 10/22 CARBINE

DELUXE 10/22 SPORTER

MODEL K10/22 RB STAINLESS CARBINE

MODEL 10/22 CARBINE
22 LONG RIFLE CALIBER

Identical in size, balance and style to the Ruger 44 Magnum Carbine and nearly the same in weight, the 10/22 is a companion to its high-power counterpart. Construction of the 10/22 Carbine is rugged and follows the Ruger design practice of building a firearm from integrated sub-assemblies. For example, the trigger housing assembly contains the entire ignition system, which employs a high-speed, swinging hammer to ensure the shortest possible lock time. The barrel is assembled to the receiver by a unique dual-screw dovetail system that provides unusual rigidity and strength—and accounts, in part, for the exceptional accuracy of the 10/22.

SPECIFICATIONS
Caliber: 22 Long Rifle, high-speed or standard-velocity loads.
Barrel: 18½" long; barrel is assembled to the receiver by unique dual screw dovetail mounting for added strength and rigidity.

Weight: 5 lbs. **Overall length:** 37¼". **Sights:** 1/16" gold bead front sight; single folding leaf rear sight, adjustable for elevation; receiver drilled and tapped for scope blocks or tip-off mount adapter. **Magazine:** 10-shot capacity, exclusive Ruger rotary design; fits flush into stock. **Trigger:** Curved finger surface, 3/8" wide. **Safety:** Sliding cross-button type; safety locks both sear and hammer and cannot be put in safe position unless gun is cocked. **Stocks:** 10/22 R Standard Carbine is walnut; 10/22 RB is birch; 10/22 SP Deluxe Sporter is American walnut. **Finish:** Polished all over and blued or anodized or brushed satin bright metal.

Model 10/22 RB Standard (Birch stock) **$201.50**
Model 10/22 DSP Deluxe (Hand-checkered
   American walnut) **254.50**
Model K10/22 RB Stainless **206.00**

RUGER SINGLE-SHOT RIFLES

The following illustrations show the variations currently offered in the Ruger No. 1 Single-Shot Rifle Series. Ruger No. 1 rifles come fitted with selected American walnut stocks. Pistol grip and forearm are hand-checkered to a borderless design. Price for any listed model is **$634.00** (except the No. 1 RSI International Model: **$656.00**). Barreled Actions (blued only): **$429.50**.

NO. 1A LIGHT SPORTER

Calibers: 243 Win., 30-06, 270 Win., 7×57mm. **Barrel length:** 22″. **Sight:** Adjustable folding-leaf rear sight mounted on quarter rib with ramp front sight base and dovetail-type gold bead front sight; open. **Weight:** 7¼ lbs.

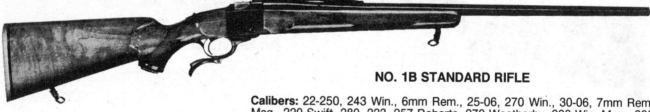

NO. 1S MEDIUM SPORTER

Calibers: 7mm Rem. Mag., 300 Win. Mag., 45-70, 338 Win. Mag. **Barrel length:** 26″ (22″ in 45-70). **Sights:** (same as above). **Weight:** 8 lbs. (7¼ lbs. in 45-70).

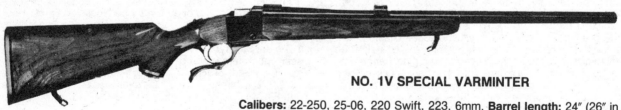

NO. 1B STANDARD RIFLE

Calibers: 22-250, 243 Win., 6mm Rem., 25-06, 270 Win., 30-06, 7mm Rem. Mag., 220 Swift, 280, 223, 257 Roberts, 270 Weatherby, 300 Win. Mag., 300 Weatherby, 338 Win. Mag. **Barrel:** 26″. **Sights:** Ruger 1″ steel tip-off scope rings. **Weight:** 8 lbs.

NO. 1V SPECIAL VARMINTER

Calibers: 22-250, 25-06, 220 Swift, 223, 6mm. **Barrel length:** 24″ (26″ in 220 Swift). **Sights:** Ruger target scope blocks, heavy barrel and 1″ tip-off scope rings. **Weight:** 9 lbs.

See following page for additional Single-Shot models

RUGER RIFLES

NO. 1H TROPICAL RIFLE

Calibers: 375 H&H Mag., 458 Win. Mag., 416 Rigby. **Barrel length:** 24″ (heavy). **Sights:** Adjustable folding-leaf rear sight mounted on quarter rib with ramp front sight base and dovetail-type gold bead front sight; open. **Weight:** 8¼ lbs. for 375; 9 lbs. for 458. **Price:** $634.00

NO. 1RSI INTERNATIONAL
With Mannlicher Style Forearm

Calibers: 243 Win., 270 Win., 30-06 and 7×57mm. **Barrel length:** 20″ (lightweight). **Overall length:** 36½″. **Weight:** 7¼ lbs. **Sights:** Adjustable folding leaf rear sight mounted on quarter rib with ramp front sight base and dovetail-type gold bead front sight. **Price:** $656.00

BOLT ACTION RIFLES

MODEL 77/22 RS

MODEL 77/22 BOLT-ACTION RIMFIRE RIFLE

The Ruger 22-caliber rimfire 77/22 bolt-action rifle represents a blend of characteristics long associated with the famous Ruger M-77 rifle and the internationally popular Ruger 10/22 semiautomatic rimfire rifle. It has been built especially to function with the patented Ruger 10-Shot Rotary Magazine concept. The magazine throat, retaining lips, and ramps that guide the cartridge into the chamber are solid alloy steel that resists bending or deforming.

The bolt assembly is built to military rifle standards of quality, but it has been modified to function with the 22 rimfire cartridge. Accordingly, the front part of the bolt is nonrotating and the locking lugs have been moved back to the middle of the action. The rear part of the bolt rotates and cams like that of the Ruger M-77 rifle.

The 77/22 weighs just under six pounds and provides the smallbore shooter with a compact, reliable featherweight arm. The heavy-duty receiver incorporates the integral scope bases of the patented Ruger Scope Mounting System, with 1-inch Ruger scope rings. With the 3-position safety in its "lock" position, a dead bolt is cammed forward, locking the bolt handle down. In this position the action is locked closed and the handle cannot be raised.

A simplified bolt stop fits flush with the left side of the receiver and permits the bolt to be withdrawn from receiver merely by pressing down tightly. The bolt locking system ensures positive lock-up by two large locking lugs on rotating part of bolt. A nonadjustable trigger mechanism is set for medium weight trigger pull. Lock time is 2.7 milliseconds.

All metal surfaces are finished in a non-glare deep blue. Stock is select straight-grain American walnut, hand checkered and finished with durable polyurethane.

An All-Weather, all-stainless steel **MODEL K77/22RS** features a stock made of 6/6 glass-fiber reinforced nylon. **Weight:** approx. 6 lbs.

SPECIFICATIONS
Calibers: 22 LR and 22 Magnum. **Barrel length:** 20″. **Overall length:** 39¼″. **Weight:** 5 lbs. 14 oz. (w/o scope, magazine empty). **Feed:** Detachable 10-Shot Ruger Rotary Magazine.
Prices:

77/22R plain barrel w/o sights, 1″ Ruger rings	$402.00
77/22RM walnut stock, plain barrel, no sights, 1″ Ruger rings, 22 Mag.	402.00
77/22RS sights included, 1″ Ruger rings	424.00
77/22-RP Synthetic stock, plain barrel with 1″ Ruger rings	330.75
77/22-RSP Synthetic stock, gold bead front sight, folding-leaf rear sight and Ruger 1″ rings	353.00
K77/22-RP Synthetic stock, stainless steel, plain barrel with 1″ Ruger rings	397.00
K77/22-RMP Synthetic stock, stainless steel, plain barrel, 1″ Ruger rings	419.00
K77/22-RSP Synthetic stock, stainless steel, gold bead front sight, folding-leaf rear, Ruger 1″ rings	419.00
77/22RSM American walnut, 22 Mag.	424.00
K77/22RMP Synthetic stock, stainless	419.00
K77/22RSMP Synthetic stock, stainless	445.20

RUGER BOLT ACTION RIFLES

MODEL M-77RS

Integral Base Receiver, Ruger steel 1″ rings, open sights. **Calibers:** 270, 30-06 (with 22″ barrels), 25-06, 7mm Rem. Mag., 300 Win. Mag., 35 Whelen, 338 Win. Mag. (with 24″ barrels). **Weight:** Approx. 7 lbs.

Price $616.35

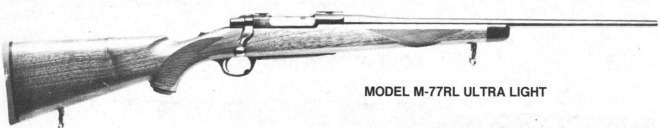

MODEL M-77RL ULTRA LIGHT

New 6-pound big game rifle in both long- and short-action versions, with Integral Base Receiver and 1″ Ruger scope rings. Luxury detailing throughout. **Calibers:** 22-250, 270, 30-06, 257. **Barrel length:** 20″. **Weight:** Approx. 6 lbs.

Price $592.46

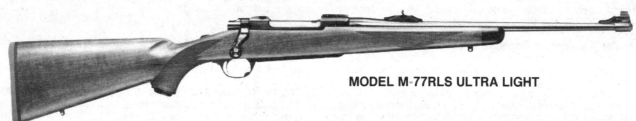

MODEL M-77RLS ULTRA LIGHT

This big game bolt-action rifle encompasses the traditional features that have made the Ruger M-77 one of the most popular centerfire rifles in the world. It includes a sliding top tang safety, a one-piece bolt with Mauser-type extractor and diagonal front mounting system. American walnut stock is hand-checkered in a sharp diamond pattern. A rubber recoil pad, pistol grip cap and studs for mounting quick detachable sling swivels are standard. **Calibers:** 270, 30-06. **Barrel length:** 18½″. **Overall length:** 38⅞″. **Weight:** 6 lbs. (empty). **Sights:** Open.

Price $592.46

RUGER BOLT ACTION RIFLES

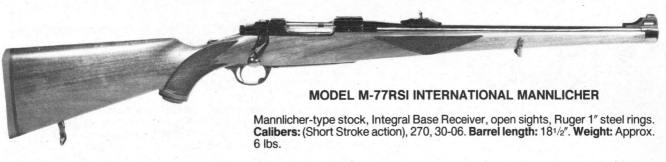

MODEL M-77RSI INTERNATIONAL MANNLICHER

Mannlicher-type stock, Integral Base Receiver, open sights, Ruger 1″ steel rings. **Calibers:** (Short Stroke action), 270, 30-06. **Barrel length:** 18½″. **Weight:** Approx. 6 lbs.

Price **$623.44**

MODEL M-77R

Integral Base Receiver, 1″ scope rings. No sights. **Calibers:** (Magnum action) 270, 7×57mm, 257 Roberts, 280 Rem., 30-06 (all with 22″ barrels); 25-06, 7mm Rem. Mag., 300 Win. Mag., 338 Win. Mag. (all with 24″ barrels); and (Short Stroke action) 22-250 (22″ barrels); 220 Swift (with 24″ barrel). **Weight:** Approx. 7 lbs.

Price **$557.81**

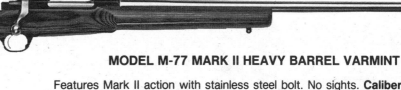

MODEL M-77 MARK II HEAVY BARREL VARMINT

Features Mark II action with stainless steel bolt. No sights. **Calibers:** 22-250, 220 Swift, 25-06, 223, 243 and 308. **Barrel length:** 26″, hammer-forged, free-floating stainless steel. **Weight:** 9¾ lbs. **Stock:** Laminated American hardwood with flat forend.

Price . . . . **Upon request**

M-77 MARK II ALL-WEATHER

M-77RMKII Receiver w/integral dovetails to accommodate Ruger 1″ rings, no sights. **Calibers:** 223, 6mm, 243, 270, 308, 30-06 (all 22″ barrels); 7mm Rem. Mag. (24″ only) **$557.81**
M-77RLMKII Ultra-Light, 6 lbs., black forend tip, receiver w/integral dovetails to accommodate Ruger 1″ rings, no sights. **Calibers:** 223, 243, 308 (all 20″ barrels) **558.00**
KM 77RPMKII ALL WEATHER Receiver w/integral dovetails to accommodate Ruger 1″ rings, no sights, stainless steel, synthetic stock. **Calibers:** 223 (20″ barrel only); 243, 270, 308, 30-06, (all 22″ barrels); 7mm, 300 Win. Mag., 338 Win. Mag. (24″ barrels) **558.00**
M-77LRMKII LEFT HAND. Calibers 270, 30-06 (22″ barrels), 7mm, 300 Mag. (24″ barrels) **573.56**

RUGER BOLT ACTION RIFLES

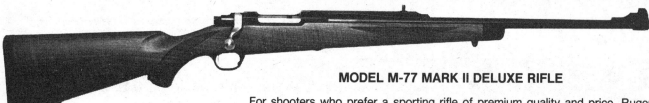

MODEL M-77 MARK II DELUXE RIFLE

For shooters who prefer a sporting rifle of premium quality and price, Ruger offers the M-77 Mark II Deluxe rifle. Its stock is precision machined from a single blank of medium quality walnut. Forend and pistol grip are hand-checkered in a diamond pattern with 18 lines per inch. Pistol grip cap, trigger guard and floorplate are blued steel. A black buttpad of live rubber, black forend cap and steel studs for quick detachable sling swivels are standard.

Action is standard short or long length in blued chrome-moly steel with stainless steel bolt. A fixed blade-type ejector working through a slot under the left locking lug replaces the plunger-type ejector used in the earlier M-77 models. A three-position wing safety allows the shooter to unload the rifle with safety on. The trigger guard houses the patented floorplate latch, which holds the floorplate closed securely to prevent accidental dumping of cartridges into the magazine.

An integral, solid sight rib extends from the front of the receiver ring. Machined from a solid chrome-moly steel barrel blank, the rib has cross serrations on the upper surface to reduce light reflections. Each rifle is equipped with open metal sights. A blade front sight of blued steel is mounted on a steel ramp with curved rear surface serrated to reduce glare. Rear sights (adjustable for windage and non-folding) are mounted on the sighting rib. The forward rear sight is folding and adjustable for windage. A set of Ruger 1″ scope rings with integral bases is standard.

Calibers: A wide variety of popular American and European calibers. **Barrel lengths:** 22″ and 24″ (depending on caliber). **Capacity:** 4 rounds. **Overall length:** 42 1/8″ (approx.). **Weight:** 7 3/4 lbs. (avg., loaded); 7 1/2 lbs. (unloaded). **Length of pull:** 13 1/2″.

Price **$1450.00**

RUGER MAGNUM RIFLE

This "Bond Street" quality African safari hunting rifle features a sighting rib machined from a single bar of steel; Circassian walnut stock with black forend tip; steel floorplate and latch; a new Ruger Magnum trigger guard with floorplate latch designed flush with the contours of the trigger guard (to eliminate accidental dumping of cartridges); a three-position safety mechanism (*see* illustrations); Express rear sight; and front sight ramp with gold bead sight.

Calibers: 375 H&H, 416 Rigby and 458 Win. Mag. **Capacity:** 4 rounds (375 H&H) and 3 rounds (416 Rigby, 458 Win. Mag.). **Barrel thread diameter:** 1 1/8″. **Weight:** 9 1/4 lbs. (375 H&H); 10 1/4 lbs. (416 Rigby and 458 Win. Mag.).

Price **$1550.00**

RUKO-ARMSCOR RIFLES

MODEL M14P
$109.00

SPECIFICATIONS
Type: Bolt action
Caliber: 22 LR
Capacity: 5 rounds
Barrel length: 23″
Overall length: 41¹⁄₂″

Weight: 7 lbs.
Trigger pull: 14″
Stock: Mahogany
Finish: Blued
Also available:
MODEL M14D Bolt Action Deluxe $119.00

MODEL M1500
$149.00

SPECIFICATIONS
Type: Bolt action deluxe
Caliber: 22 Win. Mag.
Capacity: 5 rounds
Barrel length: 21¹⁄₂″

Overall length: 41¹⁄₄″
Weight: 6.8 lbs.
Trigger pull: 14″
Stock: Mahogany
Finish: Blued

MODEL M20P
$99.00

SPECIFICATIONS
Type: Semiautomatic
Caliber: 22 LR
Capacity: 15 rounds
Barrel length: 21″
Overall length: 39³⁄₄″

Weight: 6¹⁄₂ lbs.
Trigger pull: 13″
Stock: Mahogany
Finish: Blued
Also available:
MODEL M2000 with deluxe stock $115.00
MODEL M20C (16¹⁄₂″ barrel; 5¹⁄₄″ lbs.) 129.00

SAKO RIFLES

HUNTER RIFLE

HUNTER LIGHTWEIGHT

Here's one case of less being more. Sako has taken its famed bolt-action, centerfire rifle, redesigned the stock and trimmed the barrel contour. In fact, in any of the short action (A1) calibers—17 Rem., 222 or 223 Rem.—the Hunter weighs in at less than 7 pounds, making it one of the lightest wood stock production rifles in the world.

The same cosmetic upgrading and weight reduction have been applied to the entire Hunter line in all calibers and action lengths, standard and magnum. All the precision, quality and accuracy for which this Finnish rifle has been so justly famous are still here. Now it just weighs less.

The Sako trigger is a rifleman's delight—smooth, crisp and fully adjustable. If these were the only Sako features, it would still be the best rifle available. But the real quality that sets Sako apart from all others is its truly outstanding accuracy.

While many factors can affect a rifle's accuracy, 90 percent of any rifle's accuracy potential lies in its barrel. And the creation of superbly accurate barrels is where Sako excels.

The care that Sako takes in the cold-hammering processing of each barrel is unparalleled in the industry. As an example, after each barrel blank is drilled, it is diamond-lapped and then optically checked for microscopic flaws. This extra care affords the Sako owner lasting accuracy and a finish that will stay "new" season after season.

You can't buy an unfired Sako. Every gun is test fired using special overloaded proof cartridges. This ensures the Sako owner total safety and uncompromising accuracy. Every barrel must group within Sako specifications or it's scrapped. Not

recycled. Not adjusted. Scrapped. Either a Sako barrel delivers Sako accuracy, or it never leaves the factory.

And hand-in-hand with Sako accuracy is Sako beauty. Genuine European walnut stocks, flawlessly finished and checkered by hand.

Available with either a matte lacquer or oil finish.

Prices:
Short Action (AI)
In 17 Rem., 222 Rem., 223 Rem. . . . . $ 975.00
Medium Action (AII)
In 22-250 Rem., 7mm-08, 243 Win. &
   308 Win. 975.00
Long Action (AV)
In 25-06 Rem., 270 Win., 280 Rem., 30-06 . . . . . 1000.00
In 7mm Rem. Mag., 300 Win. Mag.,
   338 Win. Mag. 1020.00
In 300 Wby. Mag., 375 H&H Mag.,
   416 Rem. Mag. 1035.00

LEFT-HANDED MODELS (Matte Lacquer Finish)
Medium Action (AII)
In 22-250 Rem., 7mm-08, 243 Win. &
   308 Win. $1055.00
Long Action (AV)
In 25-06 Rem., 270 Win., 280 Rem., 30-06 . . . . . 1085.00
In 7mm Rem. Mag., 300 Win. Mag.,
   338 Win. Mag. 1100.00
In 375 H&H Mag., 416 Rem. Mag. 1115.00

SAKO RIFLES

DELUXE

All the fine-touch features you expect of the deluxe grade Sako are here—beautifully grained French walnut, superbly done high-gloss finish, hand-cut checkering, deep rich bluing and rosewood forend tip and grip cap. And of course the accuracy, reliability and superior field performance for which Sako is so justly famous are still here too. It's all here—it just weighs less than it used to. Think of it as more for less.

In addition, the scope mounting system on these Sakos is among the strongest in the world. Instead of using separate bases, a tapered dovetail is milled right into the receiver, to which the scope rings are mounted. A beautiful system that's been proven by over 20 years of use. Sako scope rings are available in *low, medium,* and *high* in one-inch only.

Prices:
Short Action (AI)
In 17 Rem., 222 Rem. & 223 Rem. **$1325.00**
Medium Action (AII)
In 22-250 Rem., 243 Win., 7mm-08
    and 308 Win. **1325.00**
Long Action (AV)
In 25-06 Rem., 270 Win., 280 Rem., 30-06 . . . . . **1365.00**
In 7mm Rem. Mag., 300 Win. Mag. &
    338 Win. Mag. **1380.00**
In 300 Wby. Mag., 375 H&H Mag.,
    416 Rem. Mag. **1395.00**

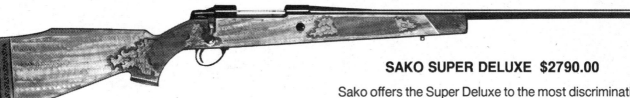

SAKO SUPER DELUXE $2790.00

Sako offers the Super Deluxe to the most discriminating gun buyer. This one-of-a-kind beauty is available on special order.

SAKO RIFLES

CLASSIC

Classic elegance best describes SAKO'S latest model—
the CLASSIC —designed for discriminating shooters
who demand quality and the traditional clean, graceful
lines of the classic style. Available in two action lengths
and the most popular calibers (see below). Also available
in a left-handed model.

Calibers: 243 Win., 270 Win., 30-06, 7mm Rem. Mag.
Barrel length: 22″ and 24″ (Magnum action only). **Ca-
pacity:** 5 rounds (Medium and Long action); 3 rounds
(Magnum action). **Overall length:** 42″ and 44″ (Magnum
action only). **Weight:** 6⅞ lbs. (243 Win.); 7 lbs. (270
Win. and 30-06); 7¼ lbs. (7mm Rem. Mag.). **Finish:**
Matte lacquer.

Prices:
Medium Action (All)
In 243 Win. . . . . $ 975.00
Long Action (AV)
In 270 Win., 30-06 . . . . 1000.00
In 7mm Rem. Mag. 1020.00

LEFT-HANDED MODELS (Long Action Only)
In 270 Win. $1085.00
In 7mm Rem. Mag. 1100.00

SAKO CARBINE

SAKO MANNLICHER-STYLE CARBINE

Sako's Mannlicher-style Carbine combines the handiness and carrying qualities of the traditional, lever-action "deer rifle" with the power of modern, high-performance cartridges. An abbreviated 18½-inch barrel trims the overall length of the Carbine to just over 40 inches in the long (or AV) action calibers, and 38 inches in the medium (or AII) action calibers. Weight is a highly portable 7 and 6½ pounds, respectively (except in the 338 and 375 H&H calibers, which measures 7½ pounds).

As is appropriate for a rifle of this type, the Carbine is furnished with an excellent set of open sights; the rear is fully adjustable for windage, while the front is a nonglare serrated ramp with protective hood.

The Mannlicher Carbine is available in the traditional wood stock of European walnut done in a contemporary Monte Carlo style with hand-rubbed oil finish. Hand-finished checkering is

standard. The Mannlicher-style full stock Carbine wears Sako's exclusive two-piece forearm, which joins beneath the barrel band and also features an oil finish. This independent forward section of the forearm eliminates the bedding problems normally associated with the full forestock. A blued steel muzzle cap puts the finishing touches on this European-styled Carbine.

Sako Mannlicher-Style Carbine Prices:
Medium Action
In 243 Win. and 308 Win. $1130.00
Long Action
In 270 Win. and 30-06 . . . . 1165.00
In 338 Win. Mag. 1180.00
In 375 H&H Mag. 1200.00

SAKO WHITETAIL/BATTUE

This unique rifle was originally designed to meet the needs of wild boar shooting in France. Because of its versatility and success there, it is now being introduced to North American hunters. The primary purpose of the rifle is for snap-shooting when quickness is required. The raised quarter-rib, coupled with the wide "V"-shaped rear sight, allow the shooter a wide field of view, enabling him to get on a moving target fast.

The 18½" barrel (overall length 38") is perfectly balanced and honed to ensure Sako's acclaimed accuracy. The stock

features a soft matte lacquered finish that enhances its beauty and durability. Weight is 7½ pounds.

Prices:
Medium Action
In 22-250 Rem., 243 Win., 308 Win., 7mm-08 . . $1000.00
Long Action
In 25-06 Rem., 270 Win., 280 Rem., 30-06 . . . . . 1030.00
In 7mm Mag., 300 Win. Mag., 338 Win. Mag. . . 1045.00
In 375 H&H Mag. 1060.00

SAKO RIFLES

Ever since Dr. Lou Palmisano and Farris Pindel introduced their custom-made PPC ammo in 1975, it has become widely recognized as the "world's most accurate cartridge," having broken well over 200 records since its debut. The impossible dream of making one-hole targets with five cartridges may never be realized, but PPC cartridges have come closer to that goal of perfection than anything in today's market.

Under an agreement with Dr. Palmisano, Sako has manufactured the PPC benchrest, heavy barrel, single-shot rifle in both 6 PPC and 22 PPC since late 1987; in 1988 they introduced factory-made ammo and brass. Because of its outstanding success with the benchrest model, Sako now makes both calibers available in a repeater version of its new Hunter and Deluxe models. Each model features a soft, luxurious matte lacquer finish and is built to the demanding specifications and workmanship that have become synonymous with Finnish gunmakers.

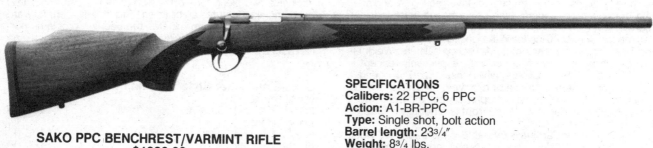

SAKO PPC BENCHREST/VARMINT RIFLE
$1330.00

SPECIFICATIONS
Calibers: 22 PPC, 6 PPC
Action: A1-BR-PPC
Type: Single shot, bolt action
Barrel length: 23³/₄″
Weight: 8³/₄ lbs.
Finish: Oil-finished stock

SAKO PPC HUNTER
$1245.00

SPECIFICATIONS
Calibers: 22 PPC, 6 PPC
Action: A1-PPC
Magazine capacity: 4
Barrel length: 21¹/₂″
Weight: 6¹/₄ lbs.
Finish: Matte-lacquer stock

SAKO PPC DELUXE
$1565.00

SPECIFICATIONS
Calibers: 22 PPC, 6 PPC
Action: A1-PPC
Capacity: 4
Barrel length: 21¹/₂″
Weight: 6¹/₄ lbs.
Finish: Matte-lacquer stock
Features: Deep-cut checkering; rosewood pistol-grip and forend caps; engraved floorplate; high-luster blue on barreled action

SAKO RIFLES

VARMINT
$1100.00

The Sako Varmint is specifically designed with a prone-type stock for shooting from the ground or bench. The forend is extra wide to provide added steadiness when rested on sandbags or makeshift field rests.

Calibers: 17 Rem., 222 Rem. & 223 Rem. (Short Action); 22-250, 243 Win. and 308 Win. (Medium Action). Also available in 6mm PPC and 22 PPC (single shot). **Price: $1330.00.**

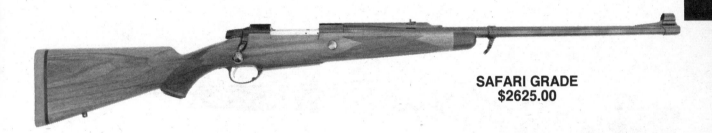

SAFARI GRADE
$2625.00

Crafted in the tradition of the classic British express rifles, Safari Grade is truly a professional's rifle. Every feature has been carefully thought out and executed with one goal in mind: performance. The magazine is extended, allowing four belted magnums to be stored inside (instead of the usual three). The steel floorplate straddles the front of the trigger guard bow for added strength and security.

An express-style quarter rib provides a rigid, non-glare base for the rear sight, which consists of a fixed blade. The front swivel is carried by a contoured barrel band to keep the stud away from the off-hand under the recoil of big calibers. The front sight assembly is also a barrel-band type for maximum strength. The blade sits on a non-glare ramp and is protected by a steel hood.

The Safari's barreled action carries a subtle semi-matte blue, which lends an understated elegance to this eminently practical rifle. The functional, classic-style stock is of European walnut selected especially for its strength with respect to grain orientation as well as for color and figure. A rosewood forend tip, rosewood pistol grip cap with metal insert suitable for engraving, an elegant, beaded cheekpiece and presentation—style recoil pad complete the stock embellishments.

Calibers: 338 Win. Mag., 375 H&H Mag. and 416 Rem. Mag. See also **Specifications Table.**

SAKO RIFLES

LAMINATED STOCK MODELS

In response to the growing number of hunters and shooters who seek the strength and stability that a fiberglass stock provides, coupled with the warmth and feel of real wood, Sako features its Laminated Stock models.

Machined from blanks comprised of 36 individual layers of 1/16-inch hardwood veneers that are resin-bonded under extreme pressure, these stocks are virtually inert. Each layer of hardwood has been vacuum-impregnated with a permanent brown dye. The bisecting of various layers of veneers in the shaping of the stock results in a contour-line appearance similar to a piece of slab-sawed walnut. Because all Sako Laminated Stocks are of real wood, each one is unique, with its own shading, color and grain.

These stocks satisfy those whose sensibilities demand a rifle of wood and steel, but who also want state-of-the-art performance and practicality. Sako's Laminated Stock provides both, further establishing it among the most progressive manufacturers of sporting rifles—and the *only* one to offer hunters and shooters their choice of walnut, fiberglass or laminated stocks in a wide range of calibers and left-handed models.

Laminated Stock Model Prices:
Medium Action
In 22-250, 243 Win., 308 Win. and 7mm-08 . . . . **$1110.00**
Long Action
In 25-06 Rem., 270 Win., 280 Rem. & 30-06 . . . **1155.00**
In 7mm Rem. Mag., 300 Win. Mag. and
    338 Win. Mag. **1175.00**
In 375 H&H Mag., 416 Rem. Mag. **1185.00**

FIBERGLASS MODEL

In answer to the increased demand for Sako quality and accuracy in a true "all-weather" rifle, this fiberglass-stock version of the renowned Sako barreled action has been created. Long since proven on the bench rest circuit to be the most stable material for cradling a rifle, fiberglass is extremely strong, light in weight, and unaffected by changes in weather. Because fiberglass is inert, it does not absorb or expel moisture, hence it cannot swell, shrink or warp. It is impervious to the high humidity of equatorial jungles, the searing heat of arid deserts, or the rain and snow of the high mountains.

Not only is this rifle lighter than its wood counterpart, it appeals to the performance-oriented hunter who seeks results over appearance.

Prices:
Long Action (AV)
In 25-06 Rem., 270 Win., 280 Rem., 30-06 . . . . . **$1310.00**
In 7mm Rem. Mag., 300 Win. Mag. and
    338 Win. Mag. **1325.00**
In 375 H&H Mag., 416 Rem. Mag. **1340.00**

SAKO RIFLES

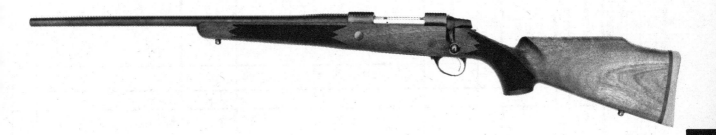

LEFT-HANDED MODELS

Sako's Left-Handed models are based on mirror images of the right-handed models enjoyed by Sako owners for many years, with handle, extractor and ejection port all located on the port side. Naturally, the stock is also reversed, with the cheekpiece on the opposite side and the palm swell on the port side of the grip.

Otherwise, these guns are identical to the right-hand models. That means hammer-forged barrels, one-piece bolts with integral locking lugs and handles, integral scope mount rails, three-way adjustable triggers and Mauser-type inertia ejectors.

Sako's Left-Handed rifles are available in all Long Action models. The Hunter Grade carries a durable matte lacquer finish with generous-size panels of hand-cut checkering, a presentation-style recoil pad and sling swivel studs installed. The Deluxe model is distinguished by its rosewood forend tip and grip cap, its skip-line checkering and gloss lacquer finish atop a select-grade of highly figured European walnut. The metal work carries a deep, mirro-like blue that looks more like black chrome.

Prices:
Hunter Lightweight (Medium Action)
In 22-250 Rem. 243 Win., 308 Win., 7mm-08 . . . **$1055.00**
Hunter Lightweight (Long Action)
In 25-06, 270 Win., 280 Rem. & 30-06 . . . . **$1085.00**
in 7mm Rem. Mag., 300 Win. Mag. and
  338 Win. Mag. 1100.00
In 375 H&H Mag., 416 Rem. Mag. 1115.00

Deluxe (Long Action)
In 25-06, 270 Win. Mag., 280 Rem. & 30-06 . . . . **$1430.00**
In 7mm Rem. Mag., 300 Win. Mag. and
  338 Win. Mag. 1445.00
In 375 H&H Mag., 416 Rem. Mag. 1460.00

Classic Left-Handed (Long Action, Matte Lacquer Finish)
In 270 Win. **$1085.00**
In 7mm Rem. Mag. 1100.00

SAKO RIFLES

BRASS AND AMMO ARE AVAILABLE FOR BOTH 6 PPC AND 22 PPC. BALLISTIC INFORMATION ON THESE TWO CALIBERS AVAILABLE UPON REQUEST FROM STOEGER INDUSTRIES.

For varmint shooting, benchrest competition, target or hunting

	PPC DELUXE	PPC HUNTER	BENCHREST VARMINT	CUSTOM VARMINT	CUSTOM SAFARI	CARBINE MANNLICHER STYLE	WHITETAIL / BATTUE	LAMINATED	FIBERCLASS	SUPERDELUXE	CLASSIC	DELUXE	HUNTER
Model — Action*	AI	AI	AI	AI / AII	AV	AI / AV	AII / AV	AI / AII / AV	AI / AII / AV	AI / AII / AV	AII / AV	AI / AII / AV	AI / AII / AV
Left-handed												• • •	• • •
Dimensions — Total length (inches)	41½	41½	43¾	43¼ / 42¾	43	40½	39 / 39	39½ / 39½	41½ / 42½ / 43½	41½ / 43½ / 45½	42½ / 44	41½ / 42½ / 44 / 46	41¼ / 42½ / 44 / 46
Barrel length (inches)	21½	21½	23¾	23¾ / 22¾	22	18¼	21½ / 21½	18¼ / 18¼	21¾ / 22 / 24	21¾ / 24	21¾ / 24	21½ / 21¾ / 22 / 24	21¼ / 21¾ / 22 / 24
Weight (lbs)	6½	6½	8¾	8¾ / 8½	8½	8	7¾ / 7	7 / 7	5¾ / 6½ / 7¾	7¾ / 7¾ / 8¼	6¾ / 7½	5¾ / 6½ / 7¾ / 8¼	5¾ / 6½ / 7¾ / 8¼
Caliber/Rate of Twist — 17 Rem / 10"				•						•			•
222 Rem / 14"				•						•			•
223 Rem / 12"				•						•			•
22 PPC / 14"	PPC	PPC	PPC	•									
6mm PPC / 14"	PPC	PPC	PPC										•
22-250 Rem / 14"				•			•	•		•		•	•
243 Win / 10"				•			•	•	•	•		•	•
7mm-08 / 9½"							•	•	•	•		•	•
308 Win / 12"				•			•	•	•	•		•	•
25-06 Rem / 10"							•	•	•	•		•	•
270 Win / 10"							•	•	•	•		•	•
280 Rem							•	•	•	•		•	•
30-06 / 10"				•			•	•	•	•	•	•	•
7mm / Rem Mag / 9½"								•	•	•	•	•	•
300 Win Mag / 10"								•	•	•		•	•
300 Wby Mag / 10"									•	•			•
338 Win Mag / 10"					•				•	•		•	•
375 H&H Mag / 12"					•				•	•		•	•
416 Rem Mag / 12"					•				•				•
Stock Finish — Lacquered										•		•	•
Matte Lacquered							•	•			•		•
Oiled				•	•							•	•
Sights — Without sights*				•	•			•	•	•	•	•	•
Open sights*							•						•
Base for telescopic sight mounts	•	•	•	•	•	•	•	•	•	•	•	•	•
Mag. — Magazine capacity	5	5	0	6 / 5	4	3	3	5 / 3	5 / 3	6 / 5 / 3	5 / 3	6 / 5 / 3	6 / 5 / 3
Buttplate — Rubber				•	•		•	•	•	•	•	•	•

SAKO ACTIONS

Only by building a rifle around a Sako action do shooters enjoy the choice of three different lengths, each scaled to a specific family of cartridges. The AI (Short) action is miniaturized in every respect to match the 222 family, which includes everything from 17 Remington to 223 Remington. The AII (Medium) action is scaled down to the medium-length cartridges of standard bolt face—22-250, 243, 308, 7mm-08 or similar length cartridges. The AV (Long) action is offered in either standard or Magnum bolt face and accommodates cartridges of up to 3.65 inches in overall length, including rounds like the 300 Weatherby and 375 H&H Magnum. **For left-handers, the Medium and Long actions are offered in either standard or Magnum bolt face.** All actions are furnished in-the-white only.

AI-1 (SHORT ACTION)
CALIBERS:
17 Rem., 222 Rem.
222 Rem. Mag.
223 Rem.
$495.00

AI PPC (Short Action)
Hunter 22 PPC and 6 PPC
$540.00

AI PPC (Short Action)
Single Shot 22 PPC and 6 PPC
$595.00

AII-1 (MEDIUM ACTION)
CALIBERS:
22-250 Rem. (AII-3)
243 Win.
308 Win.
7mm-08
$495.00

AV-4 (LONG ACTION)
CALIBERS:
25-06 Rem. (AV-1)
270 Win. (AV-1)
280 Rem. (AV-1)
30-06 (AV-1)
7mm Rem. Mag. (AV-4)
300 Win. Mag. (AV-4)
300 Wby. Mag. (AV-4)
338 Win. Mag. (AV-4)
375 H&H Mag. (AV-4)
$495.00

Also available:
LEFT-HANDED ACTIONS
Medium and Long: $525.00

SAUER RIFLES

MODEL 90 LUX

MODEL 90

SPECIFICATIONS
Calibers: 25-06, 270, 30-06, 7mm Rem. Mag., 300 Win. Mag., 300 Wby. Mag., 338 Win., 375 H&H
Barrel lengths: 24" (standard calibers); 26" (Magnum calibers)
Overall length: 44" (46.13" for Magnums)
Weight: 7¼ lbs. to 8 lbs.
Sights: None furnished; drilled and tapped for scope mount
Stock: "Lux" Model has satin-gloss oil-finished European walnut stock; "Supreme" Model has high-gloss lacquer-finished American walnut stock. Both models feature Monte Carlo cut with sculptured cheekpiece, hand-checkered pistol grip and forend, rosewood pistol grip cap and forend tip, black rubber recoil pad, and fully inletted sling swivel studs.

Features: Rear bolt cam-activated locking lug action; jeweled bolt with an operating angle of 65°; fully adjustable gold-plated trigger; chamber loaded signal pin; cocking indicator; tang-mounted slide safety with button release; bolt release button (to operate bolt while slide safety is engaged); detachable 3 or 4-round box magazine; sling side scope mounts; leather sling (extra)

Engravings: Four distinctive hand-cut patterns on gray nitride receiver, trigger housing plate, magazine plate and bolt handle (extra)

Prices:
LUX or SUPREME MODEL 90 . . . . $1495.00
  w/Engraving #1 . . . . 2495.00
  w/Engraving #2 . . . . 3095.00
  w/Engraving #3 . . . . 3395.00
  w/Engraving #4 . . . . 3995.00

MODEL 90 ENGRAVING #2

MODEL 90 ENGRAVING #4

SAUER .458 SAFARI

The Sauer .458 Safari features a rear bolt cam-activated locking-lug action with a low operating angle of 65°. It has a gold plated trigger, jeweled bolt, oil finished bubinga stock and deep luster bluing. Safety features include a press bottom slide safety that engages the trigger sear, toggle joint and bolt. The bolt release feature allows the sportsman to unload the rifle while the safety remains engaged to the trigger sear and toggle joint. The Sauer Safari is equipped with a chamber loaded signal pin for positive identification. Specifications include: **Barrel Length:** 24" (heavy barrel contour). **Overall length:** 44". **Weight:** 10 lb. 6 oz. **Sights:** Williams open sights (sling swivels included). **Price: $1995.95**

SAVAGE CENTERFIRE RIFLES

MODEL 110GC

MODEL 110 BOLT ACTION CENTERFIRE RIFLES
Standard and Magnum Calibers

The Savage 100 Series features solid lockup, positive gas protection, precise head space, precision-rifled barrels, and select walnut-finished Monte Carlo stocks. See specifications table below for full details.

Prices:

Model 110G	$370.00
Model 110GC	
In 270 and 30-06	370.00
In 7mm Rem. and 300 Win.	385.00
Model 110GNS	360.00
Model 110F	395.00
Model 110FNS	380.00
Model 110GV	400.00
Model 110FP	500.00
Model 110CY	370.00

RIFLES

SPECIFICATIONS

Model	Calibers	Capacity (1) in Chamber	Barrel Length	Length	Pull	Avg. Wt. Lbs.	Twist R.H.	Stock	Sights†
110G*	.22–250	5	22″	43¹/₂″	13¹/₂″	7¹/₂″	1 in 14″	Cut Checkered Walnut Finished Hardwood with Recoil Pad	110G Adj.
110GNS*	.223 .243	5 5	22″ 22″	43¹/₂″ 43¹/₂″	13¹/₂″ 13¹/₂″	7¹/₂″ 7¹/₂″	1 in 14″ 1 in 10″		110 GNS None
110F**	.308	5	22″	43¹/₂″	13¹/₂″	7¹/₂	1 in 10″	Black Rynite® Recoil Pad	110F Adj.
110FNS	30–06 .270	5 5	22″ 22″	43¹/₂″ 43¹/₂″	13¹/₂″ 13¹/₂″	7¹/₂ 7¹/₂	1 in 10″ 1 in 10″		
110GC	.270 30-06 7mm Rem. Mag. .300 Win. Mag.	5 5 4 4	22″ 22″ 24″ 24″	43¹/₂″ 43¹/₂″ 45¹/₂″ 45¹/₂″	13¹/₂″ 13¹/₂″ 13¹/₂″ 13¹/₂″	6³/₄ 6³/₄ 7 7	1 in 10″ 1 in 10″ 1 in 9¹/₂″ 1 in 10″	Cut Checkered Walnut Finished Hardwood with Recoil Pad	Adj.
110GV	.22–250 .223	5 5	24″ 24″	45¹/₂″ 45¹/₂″	13¹/₂″ 13¹/₂″	7³/₄ 7³/₄	1 in 14″ 1 in 14″	Cut Checkered Walnut Finished Hardwood with Recoil Pad	None
110FP	.223 .308	5 5	24″ 24″	45¹/₂″ 45¹/₂″	13¹/₂″ 13¹/₂″	9 9	1 in 14″ 1 in 10″	Black Rynite® Recoil Pad	None
110CY	.243 .300 Sav.	5	22″	42¹/₂″	12¹/₂″	6¹/₂″	1 in 10″ 1 in 10″	Cut Checkered Walnut Finished Hardwood with Recoil Pad	Adj.

* Left hand models available in 270, 30-06, 7mm Rem. Mag.   **Also available in 338 Mag.   † All receivers drilled and tapped for scope mount.

All Models 110's are packed with a gunlock, ear puffs, safety glasses and target.

SAVAGE CENTERFIRE RIFLES

MODEL 112FV
$380.00

To meet the demand for a 26″ heavy barrel varmint rifle, Savage is introducing the new Model 112FV. The 112FV includes the best features of the Savage Model 110, which is famous for its accuracy and dependability. Available with black DuPont Rynite® stock and recoil pad, the 112FV is drilled and tapped for scope mounting. Shipped from the factory with gunlock, ear puffs, target and shooting glasses.

SPECIFICATIONS
Calibers: 22-250 and 223
Capacity: 5 rounds
Barrel length: 26″
Overall length: 47½″
Weight: 9 lbs.
Stock: Black Rynite®
Also available:
MODEL 112FVS. Heavy barrel varmint rifle with rigid solid bottom receiver. Same specifications and features as Model 112FV. **Price: $370.00**

MODEL 114CU
$480.00

Savage's Model 114CU is a high-grade sporting firearm designed with a straight classic American black walnut stock. Cut-checkering, fitted grip cap and recoil pad are complemented by a high-gloss luster metal polish finish. The staggered box-type magazine is removed with a push of a button, making loading and reloading quick and easy.

SPECIFICATIONS
Calibers: 270, 30-06, 7mm Rem Mag., 300 Win. Mag.
Capacity: 4 rounds (Magnum); 5 rounds (270 and 30-06)
Barrel length: 22″ (270 and 30-06) and 24″ (Magnum)
Overall length: 43½″ (270 and 30-06) and 45½″ (Magnum)
Sights: Deluxe adjustable; receivers drilled and tapped for scope mounts
Length of pull: 13½″

MODEL 116FSS
$530.00

Savage Arms has combined the strength of a black DuPont Rynite® stock and the durability of a stainless steel barrel and receiver to create this new bolt-action rifle. The new Model 116FSS weds rugged materials with the features of the highly accurate Savage Model 110 to make a rifle that satisfies the needs of demanding sportsmen. Major components are made from stainless steel, honed to a low reflective satin finish. Drilled and tapped for scope mounts, the 116FSS is offered in popular long-action calibers. Packed with gunlock, ear puffs, shooting glasses and target.

SPECIFICATIONS
Calibers: 223, 243, 270, 30-06, 7mm Rem Mag., 300 Win. Mag., 338 Win. Mag.
Capacity: 4 (7mm Rem. Mag., 300 Win. Mag., 338 Win. Mag.); 5 (223, 243, 270, 30-06)
Barrel length: 22″ (223, 243, 270, 30-06); 24″ (7mm Rem. Mag., 300 Win. Mag., 338 Win. Mag.)
Overall length: 43½″–45½″
Weight: 7½–7¾ lbs.
Stock: Black Rynite® with recoil pad

SAVAGE CENTERFIRE RIFLES

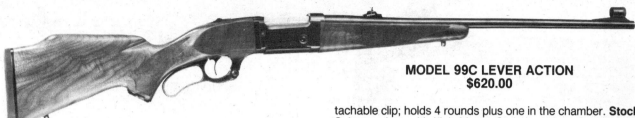

MODEL 99C LEVER ACTION
$620.00

Clip magazine allows for the chambering of pointed, high-velocity big-bore cartridges. **Calibers:** 243 Win., 308 Win. **Action:** Hammerless, lever action, top tang safety. **Magazine:** De-

tachable clip; holds 4 rounds plus one in the chamber. **Stock:** Select walnut with high Monte Carlo and deep fluted comb. Cut checkered stock and forend with swivel studs. Recoil pad and pistol grip cap. **Sights:** Detachable hooded ramp front sight, bead front sight on removable ramp adjustable rear sight. Tapped for top mount scopes. **Barrel length:** 22″. **Overall length:** 42³/₄″. **Weight:** 7³/₄ lbs.

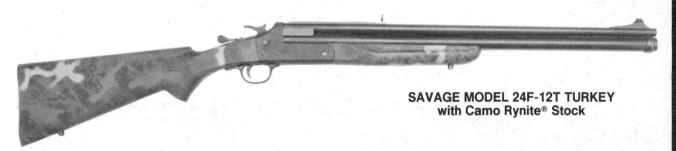

SAVAGE MODEL 24F-12T TURKEY
with Camo Rynite® Stock

RIFLES

SAVAGE MODEL 24F COMBINATION RIFLE/SHOTGUN

Match a 12- or 20-gauge shotgun with any of three popular centerfire calibers. Frame is color casehardened and barrel is a deep, lustrous blue and tapped, ready for scope mounting. Two-way top opening lever. All models are stocked with tough Du Pont Rynite™, plus hammerblock safeties that limit hammer

travel in the safe position. Other features include interchangeable chokes (extra full tube supplied), and factory swivel studs.
Prices:
Model 24F-20	$410.00
Model 24F-12	410.00
Model 24F-12T	420.00

SPECIFICATIONS MODEL 24F COMBINATION RIFLE/SHOTGUN

O/U Comb. Model	Gauge Caliber	Choke	Chamber	Barrel Length	O.A. Length	Twist R.H.	Stock
24F-20	20 ga./22 Hor.	Mod Barrel	3″	24″	40¹/₂″	1 in 14″	Black Rynite®
	20 ga./223					1 in 14″	
	20 ga./30/30					1 in 12″	
24F-12	12 ga./22 Hor.	Full Mod, IC Choke Tubes	3″	24″	40¹/₂″	1 in 14″	Black Rynite®
	12 ga./223					1 in 14″	
	12 ga./30/30					1 in 12″	
24F-12T Turkey	12 ga./22 Hor.	Full Mod, IC Choke Tubes	3″	24″	40¹/₂″	1 in 14″	Camo Rynite®
	12 ga./223					1 in 14″	

Features: Hammer block safety, Tough Dupont Rynite® stocks and positive extraction.

SPRINGFIELD ARMORY RIFLES

SPRINGFIELD M1A STANDARD

SPRINGFIELD M1A STANDARD

SPECIFICATIONS
Caliber: 308 Win./7.62mm NATO (243 or 7mm-08 optional)
Capacity: 5, 10 or 20-round box magazine
Barrel length: 18¼"
Overall length: 40½"
Weight: 8¾ lbs.

Sights: Military square post front; military aperture rear, adjustable for windage and elevation
Sight radius: 22¾"
Rifling: 6 groove, RH twist, 1 turn in 11"
Finish: Walnut, camo fiberglass, or GI wood stocks
Price: **$1129.00**

SPRINGFIELD M1A MATCH RIFLE

MIA MATCH

SPECIFICATIONS
Caliber: 308 Win. (243 or 7mm-08 optional)
Barrel length: 22"
Over length: 44.375"
Trigger pull: 4½ lbs.
Weight: 10.06 lbs.

Features: Comes with National Match barrel, flash suppressor, gas cylinder, special glass-bedded walnut stock and match-tuned trigger assembly.
Price: **$1499.00**

Also available:
M1A SUPER MATCH. Features heavy match barrel and permanently attached figure-8-style operating rod guide, plus special heavy walnut match stock, longer pistol grip and contoured area behind rear sight for better grip. **Price: $1799.00**

SPRINGFIELD M1A-A1 BUSH RIFLE

SPECIFICATIONS
Caliber: 308 Win./7.62mm (243 or 7mm-08 optional)
Barrel length: 22"
Overall length: 44.375"
Weight: 9 lbs.

Sight radius: 26.688"
Features: Other specifications same as MIA Standard
Prices:
W/Camo GI Fiberglass stock **$1229.00**
W/Walnut stock **1229.00**

STEYR-MANNLICHER RIFLES

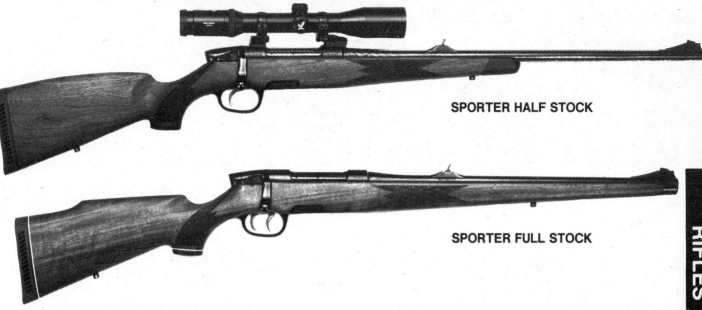

SPORTER HALF STOCK

SPORTER FULL STOCK

SPORTER SERIES

All Sporter models feature hand-checkered wood stocks, a five-round detachable rotary magazine, and a choice of single or double-set triggers. M actions are available in left-hand models. S (Magnum) action are available in half stock only. **Calibers:** See table on following page. **Barrel length:** 20″ (Full Stock); 23.6″ (Half Stock). **Overall length:** 39″ (Full). **Weight:** Model SL—6.16 lbs. (Full) and 6.27 lbs. (Half Stock); Model L—6.27 lbs. (Full) and 6.38 lbs. (Half); Model M—6.82 lbs. (Full) and 7 lbs. (Half). **Features:** SL and L Models have rifle-type rubber butt pad.

Prices:
Models SL, L, M Full Stock	**$1743.00**
Models SL, L, M Half Stock	1618.00
Model M Left Hand Full Stock	1868.00
Model M Left Hand Half Stock	1743.00
Model M Professional (w/black synthetic stock and iron sights)	1368.00
Varmint Rifle Half stock, 26″ heavy barrel	1743.00

MODEL M PROFESSIONAL

STEYR-MANNLICHER RIFLES

MANNLICHER LUXUS
(Half Stock)

MANNLICHER LUXUS

The Mannlicher Luxus is the premier rifle in the Steyr lineup. It features a hand-checkered walnut stock, smooth action, combination shotgun set trigger, steel in-line three-round magazine (detachable), rear tang slide safety, and European-designed receiver. **Calibers:** See table below. **Barrel length:** 20″ (Full Stock); 23.6″ (Half Stock).

Prices:
Luxus Models
Half Stock $2118.00
Full Stock 2243.00
Luxus S (Magnum) Models (26″ barrel,
Half Stock only) 2243.00

MODELS:	222 Rem.	222 Rem. Mag.	223 Rem.	5.6×50 Mag.	5.6×57	243 Win.	308 Win	6.5×57	270 Win.	7×64	30-06 Spr.	9.3×62	6.5×68	7mm Rem. Mag.	300 Win. Mag.	8×685	22-250 Rem.	6mm Rem.	6.5×55	7.5 Swiss	7×57	8×57 JS	375 H&H Mag.	458 Win. Mag.
Sporter (SL)	●	●	●	●																				
(L)					●	●	●										●	●						
(M)								●	●	●	●	●							●	●	●	●		
S and S/T													●	●	●	●							●	●
Professional (M)								●	●	●	●	●							●	●	●	●		
Luxus					●	●	●																	
(M)								●	●	●	●	●									●	●		
(S)											●	●	●	●										
Varmint	●		●		●	●	●								●									
Match UIT							●																	
SSG					●	●																		

STEYR SSG

STEYR SSG

The Steyr SSG features a black synthetic Cycolac stock (walnut optional), heavy Parkerized barrel, five-round standard (and optional 10-round) staggered magazine, heavy-duty milled receiver. **Calibers:** 243 Win. and 308 Win. **Barrel length:** 26″. **Overall length:** 44.5″. **Weight:** 8.5 lbs. **Sights:** Iron sights; hooded ramp front with blade adjustable for elevation; rear standard V-notch adjustable for windage. **Features:** Sliding safety; 1″ swivels.

Prices:
Model SSG Cycolac Half Stock $1634.00
 With Walnut Half Stock 2082.00
Model SSG Scope Mount 194.00
Model SSG P-II Sniper (308 Win.) 1783.00
 With Walnut Stock 2231.00
Model SSG P-III (26″ heavy barrel) 2529.00
Model SSG P-IV Urban (16½″ heavy barrel) 2082.00

STEYR-MANNLICHER RIFLES

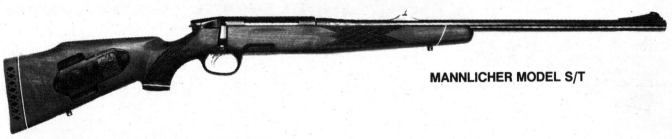

MANNLICHER MODEL S/T

MANNLICHER MODEL S-S/T MAGNUM

The Mannlicher S/T is a heavy-barreled version of the Sporter S Model designed specifically for big game hunting. It features a hand-checkered walnut stock, five-round rotary magazine, optional butt stock magazine, and double-set or single trigger. **Calibers:** 6.5×68, 7mm Rem. Mag., 300 Win. Mag., 8×685, 375 H&H Mag., 338 Win. **Barrel length:** 26″. **Weight:** 8.36 lbs. (Model S); 9 lbs. (Model S/T).

Prices:
Model S **$1743.00**
Model S/T (w/optional butt magazine) **1868.00**

RIFLES

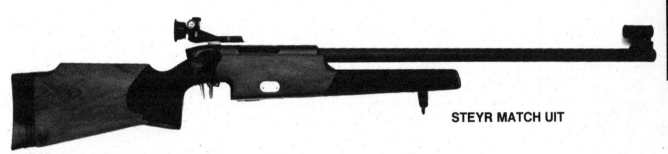

STEYR MATCH UIT

STEYR MATCH UIT

Designed especially for target competition, the Steyr Match UIT features a walnut competition stock, stipple-textured pistol grip, adjustable straight and wide trigger, adjustable first-stage trigger pull, enlarged bolt handle for rapid fire, cold hammer-forged barrel, and non-glare band for sighting. **Caliber:** 308 Win. **Overall length:** 44″. **Weight:** 10 lbs.

Price:
Steyr Match UIT **$4562.00**
10-shot magazine **143.00**

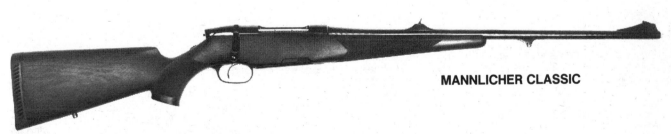

MANNLICHER CLASSIC

MANNLICHER CLASSIC

The new Classic Model features an all-new stock tailored to the American shooter's preference for a classic stock design. The walnut half stock has a straight comb buttstock (as opposed to the Monte Carlo stock on earlier Mannlichers). The schnabel has been eliminated from the forestock. The Classic stock is available in all Mannlicher and Luxus models except the Varmint, S and S/T Magnum series. For additional specifications and prices, contact Gun South Inc.

THOMPSON/CENTER RIFLES

TCR DELUXE RIFLE

TCR HUNTER SINGLE SHOT RIFLE
$595.00
Calibers: 22 Hornet, 222 Rem., 223 Rem., 22/250 Rem.,
243 Win., 270 Win., 7mm-08, 308 Win., 32-40 Win., 30-06,
7mm Rem. Mag., 300 Win. Mag., 338 Win. Mag., 220 Swift,
375 H&H and 416 Rem.

Barrels quickly interchange from one caliber to the next

Chambered for most of the popular hunting cartridges, this superbly accurate sports rifle offers the simplicity and strength of a break-open design coupled with the unique feature of interchangeable barrels. Triggers function double set or single stage. A positive lock cross-bolt safety offers maximum security. Wood is hand-selected American black walnut from the Thompson/Center mill. All barrels are equipped with iron sights, removable for scope mounting. **Muzzle Tamer** available in 375 H&H Mag. and 416 Rem. Mag. **Price: $615.00 ($695.00 Deluxe Model)**

SPECIFICATIONS
Barrel lengths: 23″ (Light Sporter) and 25⅞″ (Medium Sporter)
Overall length: 39½″ (Light Sporter) and 43⅜″ (Medium Sporter)
Weight: 6 lbs. 11 oz. (Light Sporter) and 7 lbs. 4 oz. (Medium Sporter)
Also available: **TCR DELUXE RIFLE** w/Light or Medium Sporter barrel $675.00

THE CONTENDER CARBINE
$430.00

Available in 14 **calibers:** 17 Rem., 22 LR, 22 LR Match, 22 Hornet, 22 WMR, 223 Rem., 7mm T.C.U., 7×30 Waters, 30-30 Win., 35 Rem., 375 Win., 44 Mag., 45-70 and 357 Rem. Max. **Barrels** are 21 inches long and are interchangeable, with adjustable iron sights and tapped and drilled for scope mounts. **Weight:** Only 5 lbs. 3 oz.
Also available:
Contender Vent Rib Carbine
With standard walnut stock $470.00
With 21″ 17 Rem. barrel 480.00

Contender Youth Model Carbine w/Walnut Youth
stock 415.00
With 16½″ 45 Colt/.410 barrel 445.00
Contender Carbine
w/Match Grade barrel & Rynite stock 425.00
w/Match Grade 22LR barrel 460.00
w/Rynite Stock & 21″ barrel (not available in
22 WMR or 45-70) 415.00
In 17 Rem. 445.00

TIKKA RIFLES

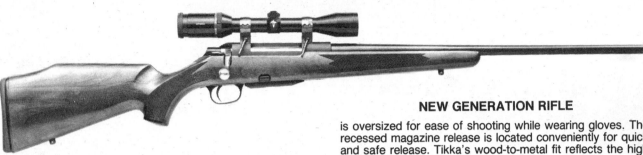

NEW GENERATION RIFLE

is oversized for ease of shooting while wearing gloves. The recessed magazine release is located conveniently for quick and safe release. Tikka's wood-to-metal fit reflects the high standards of Finnish craftsmanship throughout. **Calibers:** 223 Rem., 22-250 Rem., 243 Win., 308 Win., 270 Win., 30-06, 7mm Rem. Mag., 300 Win. Mag., and 338 Win. Mag. **Barrel length:** 22" (24" in Magnum). **Weight:** 7 1/8 lbs.

Prices NEW GENERATION:
Calibers 223 Rem., 22-250 Rem., 243 Win., 308 Win., 270 Win. and 30-06 . . . . **$835.00**
Calibers 7mm Rem. Mag., 300 Win. Mag., 338 Win. Mag. **860.00**
Magazines (5 rounds) **66.50**
           (3 rounds) **55.00**

With the consolidation of three renowned Finnish firearms manufacturers—Tikka, Sako and Valmet—a "new generation" of Tikka rifles becomes a reality. These new rifles feature a "smooth as silk" bolt action made possible by a sleeve constructed of a space-age synthetic Polyarylamide material reinforced with fiberglass. The overall look of the rifle is enhanced by a walnut stock with matte lacquer finish and diamond point checkering. A short bolt throw allows for rapid firing, and a free-floating barrel increases accuracy. Barrel quality itself is ensured through Tikka's cold-hammered forging process. The trigger guard, made of synthetic materials for added strength,

PREMIUM GRADE RIFLE

eliminate unnecessary weight and each trigger is designed and built to be crisp, clean and travel-free. For those who demand the very finest, the TIKKA Premium is a must. Available in a wide assortment of calibers.

Prices PREMIUM GRADE:
Calibers 223 Rem., 22-250 Rem., 243 Win., 308 Win., 270 Win., 30-06 . . . . **$1030.00**
Calibers 7mm Rem. Mag., 300 Win. Mag., 338 Win. Mag. **1070.00**
Magazines (5 rounds) **66.50**
           (3 rounds) **55.00**

The TIKKA Premium Grade rifle is designed and crafted by Sako of Finland for the discriminating shooter. This superb firearm features a detachable magazine, along with a "smooth as silk" bolt that is encased in a polymer sleeve. The luxurious matte lacquer stock incorporates a roll-over cheek-piece, rosewood pistol grip cap and forend tip and hand-checkered throughout. The cold-hammered barrel is deeply blued and free floated for maximum accuracy. The two action lengths

MODEL 412S DOUBLE RIFLE
$1470.00

Finland. Tikka's double rifle offers features and qualities no other action can match: rapid handling and pointing qualities and the silent, immediate availability of a second shot. As such, this model overcomes the two major drawbacks usually associated with this type of firearm: price and accuracy.
SPECIFICATIONS
Calibers: 9.3×74R
Barrel length: 24"
Overall length: 40"
Weight: 8 1/2 lbs.
Stock: European walnut
Other: Automatic ejectors

The renowned Valmet 412S line of fine firearms is now being produced under the Tikka brand name and is being manufactured to the same specifications as the former Valmet. As a result of a joint venture entered into by Sako Ltd., the production facilities for these firearms are now located in Italy. The manufacture of the 412S series is controlled under the rigid quality standards of Sako Ltd., with complete interchangeability of parts between firearms produced in Italy and

TIKKA RIFLES

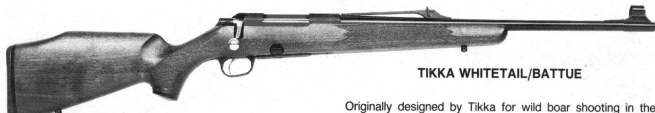

TIKKA WHITETAIL/BATTUE

Originally designed by Tikka for wild boar shooting in the French marketplace, this unique rifle is now being introduced to the North American audience because of its proven success. The primary purpose of the rifle is for snap-shooting when quickness is a requirement in the field. The raised quarter-rib, coupled with the wide "V"-shaped rear sight, allow the shooter a wide field of view. This enables him to zero in on a moving target swiftly. Also features a hooded front sight. A 3-round detachable magazine is available as an option.

The 20½" barrel (overall length: 40½") is perfectly balanced and honed to ensure the accuracy for which Tikka is famous. The stock is finished in soft matte lacquer, enhancing its beauty and durability. Weight is 7 pounds.

Prices:
In 308 Win., 270 Win., 30-06 . . . . **$860.00**
In 7mm Mag., 300 Win. Mag., 338 Win. Mag. **895.00**

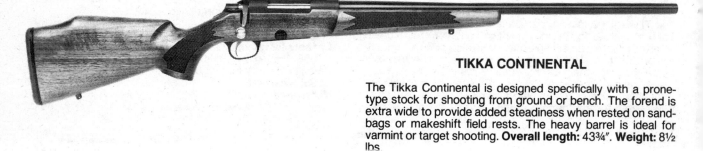

TIKKA CONTINENTAL

The Tikka Continental is designed specifically with a prone-type stock for shooting from ground or bench. The forend is extra wide to provide added steadiness when rested on sand-bags or makeshift field rests. The heavy barrel is ideal for varmint or target shooting. **Overall length:** 43¾". **Weight:** 8½ lbs

Price:
In 223 Rem., 22-250 Rem., 243 Win., 308 Win. . . **$1090.00**

A. UBERTI REPLICA RIFLES & CARBINES

ALL UBERTI FIREARMS AVAILABLE IN SUPER GRADE, PRESTIGE AND ENGRAVED FINISHES

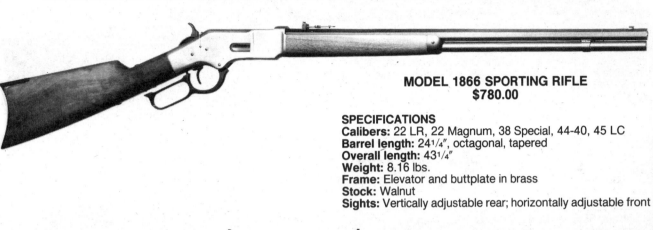

MODEL 1866 SPORTING RIFLE
$780.00

SPECIFICATIONS
Calibers: 22 LR, 22 Magnum, 38 Special, 44-40, 45 LC
Barrel length: 24¼", octagonal, tapered
Overall length: 43¼"
Weight: 8.16 lbs.
Frame: Elevator and buttplate in brass
Stock: Walnut
Sights: Vertically adjustable rear; horizontally adjustable front

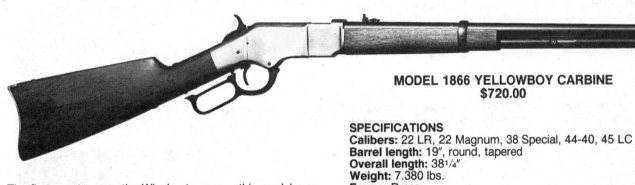

MODEL 1866 YELLOWBOY CARBINE
$720.00

SPECIFICATIONS
Calibers: 22 LR, 22 Magnum, 38 Special, 44-40, 45 LC
Barrel length: 19", round, tapered
Overall length: 38¼"
Weight: 7.380 lbs.
Frame: Brass
Stock and forend: Walnut
Sights: Vertically adjustable rear; horizontally adjustable front

The first gun to carry the Winchester name, this model was born as the 44-caliber rimfire cartridge Henry and is now chambered for 22 LR and 44-40.

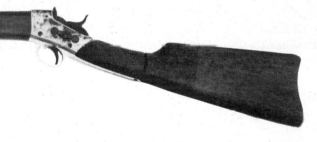

MODEL 1871 ROLLING BLOCK
BABY CARBINE
$460.00

SPECIFICATIONS
Calibers: 22 LR, 22 Magnum, 357 Magnum
Barrel length: 22"
Overall length: 35½"
Weight: 4.85 lbs.
Stock & forend: Walnut
Trigger guard: Brass

Sights: Fully adjustable rear; ramp front
Frame: Color casehardened steel

A. UBERTI REPLICA
RIFLES & CARBINES

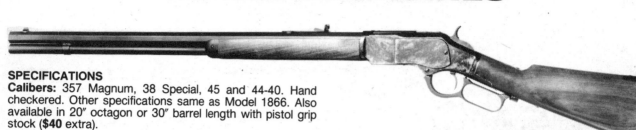

SPECIFICATIONS
Calibers: 357 Magnum, 38 Special, 45 and 44-40. Hand checkered. Other specifications same as Model 1866. Also available in 20″ octagon or 30″ barrel length with pistol grip stock (**$40** extra).

MODEL 1873 SPORTING RIFLE
$900.00

SPECIFICATIONS
Calibers: 38 Special, 44-40, 45 LC, 357 Mag.
Barrel length: 19″ round, tapered
Overall length: 38¼″
Weight: 7.38 lbs.
Sights: Fixed front; vertically adjustable rear

1873 CARBINE
$890.00

SPECIFICATIONS
Calibers: 44-40, 45 LC, 44 Special
Barrel length: 24¼″ (half-octagon, with tubular magazine)
Overall length: 43¾″
Weight: 9.26 lbs.
Frame: Brass
Stock: Varnished American walnut

HENRY RIFLE
$895.00 (44-40 Cal.)
$900.00 (45 LC & 44 Spec.)

HENRY CARBINE (not shown)
$900.00

SPECIFICATIONS
Caliber: 44-40
Capacity: 12 shots
Barrel length: 22¼″
Weight: 9.04 lbs.

Also available: **HENRY TRAPPER. Barrel length:** 16¼″ or 18″. **Overall length:** 35¾″ or 37¾″. **Weight:** 7.383 lbs. or 7.934 lbs. **Capacity:** 8 or 9 shots. **Price: $900.00**

ULTRA LIGHT ARMS

MODEL 28
(7mm Rem. Mag.)

MODEL 20 SERIES
$2400.00 ($2500.00 Left Hand)

SPECIFICATIONS
Calibers (Short Action): 6mm Rem., 17 Rem., 22 Hornet, 222
Rem., 222 Rem. Mag., 223 Rem., 22-250 Rem., 243 Win.,
250-3000 Savage, 257 Roberts, 257 Ackley, 7mm Mauser,
7mm Ack., 7mm-08 Rem., 284 Win., 300 Savage, 308 Win.,
358 Win.
Barrel length: 22″
Weight: 4.75 lbs.

Safety: Two-position safety allows bolt to open or lock with
sear blocked
Stock: Kevlar/Graphite composite; choice of 7 or more colors

Also available:
MODEL 24 SERIES (Long Action) in 270 Win.,
30-06, 25-06, 7mm Express **$2500.00**
Same as above in Left-Hand Model **2600.00**
MODEL 28 SERIES (Magnum Action) in 264 Win.,
7mm Rem., 300 Win., 338 . . . . **2900.00**
Same as above in Left-Hand Model **3000.00**

WALTHER TARGET RIFLES

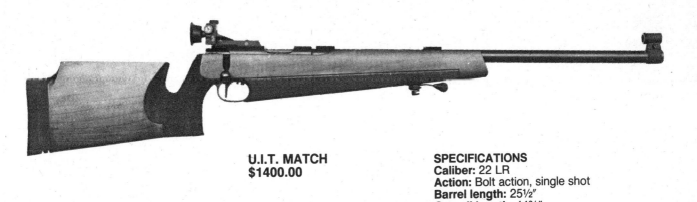

U.I.T. MATCH
$1400.00

SPECIFICATIONS
Caliber: 22 LR
Action: Bolt action, single shot
Barrel length: 25½″
Overall length: 44¾″
Weight: 13 lbs.

WEATHERBY RIFLES

MARK V FIBERMARK
$1376.00 ($1494.00 w/26" Barrel)

The Fibermark's hand-molded fiberglass stock is impervious to climatic changes. It shoots with constant accuracy no matter what the weather—from desert heat to mountain snow. The stock is finished with a non-glare black wrinkle finish for a positive grip, even in wet, humid weather. See table below.

MARK V DELUXE RIFLE

MARK V LAZERMARK

With its intricately carved stock pattern, this Mark V model captures the beauty of Old World craftsmanship using today's most modern laser technology. Available in right- or left-hand models, unless stated otherwise. See table below.

Prices:

With 24" barrel	$1355.00
With 26" barrel	1383.00
In 378 Weatherby Magnum	1565.00
In 416 Weatherby Magnum	1727.00
In 460 Weatherby Magnum	1811.00

MARK V RIFLE SPECIFICATIONS

Caliber	Barreled Action	**Weight w/o Sights	Overall Length	Magazine Capacity	Barrel	Rifling
224 Wby Mag.	Right hand 24" or 26" bbl.	6½ lbs.	43⅜" or 45⅜" dependent on barrel length	4, +1 in chamber	24" Standard or 26" Semi-target	1–14" twist
22-250	Left hand model not available	6½ lbs.		3, +1 in chamber	24" Standard or 26" Semi-target	1–14" twist
240 Wby Mag.		7¼ lbs.		4, +1 in chamber	24" #1 contour or 26" #2 contour	1–10" twist
257 Wby Mag.	Right or left hand 24" bbl.	7¼ lbs.		3, +1 in chamber	24" #1 contour or 26" #2 contour	1–10" twist
270 Wby Mag.	Right hand 26" bbl.	7¼ lbs.	44⅝" or 46⅝" dependent on barrel length	3, +1 in chamber	24" #1 contour or 26" #2 contour	1–10" twist
7mm Wby. Mag.	Left hand 26" bbl. **available in .300 cal. only**	7¼ lbs.		3, +1 in chamber	24" #1 contour or 26" #2 contour	1–10" twist
30-06		7¼ lbs.		4, +1 in chamber	24" #1 contour or 26" #2 contour	1–10" twist
300 Wby Mag.		7¼ lbs.		3, +1 in chamber	24" #1 contour or 26" #2 contour	1–10" twist
340 Wby. Mag.	Right or left hand 26" bbl. only	8½ lbs.	46⅝"	3, +1 in chamber	26" #2 contour	1–10" twist
378 Wby. Mag.	Right or left hand 26" bbl. only	8½ lbs.	46⅝"	2, +1 in chamber	26" #3 contour	1–12" twist
416 Wby. Mag.	Right or left hand 24" or 26" bbl.*	9½ lbs.	44¾" or 46¾"	2, +1 in chamber	24" or 26" #3.5 contour	1–14" twist
460 Wby. Mag.	Right or left hand 24" or 26" bbl.*	10½ lbs.	44¾" or 46¾"	2, +1 in chamber	24" or 26" #4 contour*	1–16" twist

*Available with muzzle brake only.   **Weight varies due to wood density and bore diameter.

WEATHERBY RIFLES

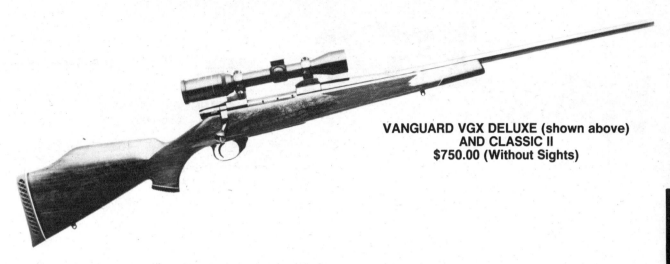

**VANGUARD VGX DELUXE (shown above)
AND CLASSIC II
$750.00 (Without Sights)**

VANGUARD SPECIFICATIONS (see also following page)

	VGX DELUXE AND CLASSIC II								
CALIBER	22/250 Rem.	.243 Rem.	.270 WBY. MAG.	.270 Win.	7mm Rem. Mag.	.30-06	.300 Win. Mag.	.300 WBY. MAG.	.338 Win. Mag.
Barrel Length	24″	24″	24″	24″	24″	24″	24″	24″	24″
Barrel Contour	No. 3	No. 2	No. 2	No. 2	No. 2	No. 2	No. 2	No. 2	No. 2
**Approx. Weight	8 lb. 8 oz.	7 lb. 4 oz.	7 lb.	7 lb.	7 lb.	7 lb.	7 lb.	7 lb.	7 lb.
Overall Length	*44″	*44″	44 1/2″	44 1/2″	44 1/2″	44 1/2″	44 1/2″	44 1/2″	44 1/2″
Magazine Capacity	5 rnds.	5 rnds.	3 rnds.	5 rnds.	3 rnds.	5 rnds.	3 rnds.	3 rnds.	3 rnds.
Rifling	1-14″	1-10″	1-10″	1-10″	1-10″	1-10″	1-10″	1-10″	1-10″

	CLASSIC I AND WEATHERGUARD						
Caliber	.223 Rem.	.243 Win.	.270 Win.	7 mm/08 Rem.	7 mm Rem. Mag.	.30-06	.308 Win.
Barrel Length	24″	24″	24″	24″	24″	24″	24″
Barrel Contour	No. 1	No. 1	No. 1	No. 1	No. 1	No. 1	No. 1
**Weight—Classic I	7 lb. 5 oz.	7 lb. 5 oz.	7 lb. 7 oz.	7 lb. 5 oz.	7 lb. 7 oz.	7 lb. 7 oz.	7 lb. 5 oz.
Weight—Weatherguard	7 lb 14 oz.	7 lb. 14 oz.	8 lbs.	7 lb. 14 oz.	8 lbs.	8 lbs.	7 lb. 14 oz.
Overall Length	44″	44″	44 1/2″	44″	44 1/2″	44 1/2″	44″
Magazine Capacity	5 rnds.	5 rnds.	5 rnds.	5 rnds.	3 rnds.	5 rnds.	5 rnds.
Rifling	1-12″	1-10″	1-10″	1-9.5″	1-10″	1-10″	1-10″

ALL MODELS	
Sights	Scope or iron sights available at extra cost.
Stocks: Classic II	American walnut, 13 5/8″ pull, custom hand checkered, satin finish, 90 degree black tip and pistol grip cap, solid black recoil pad.
VGX Deluxe	American walnut, 13 5/8″ pull, custom checkering, recoil pad, high lustre finish; 45 degree rosewood fore end tip and pistol grip cap.
Classic I	American walnut, 13 5/8″ pull, hand checkered, satin finish, black butt pad. (Recoil pad on 7mm Rem. Mag.)
Weatherguard	Synthetic checkered stock, wrinkle finish, 13 7/8″ pull, black butt pad. (Recoil pad on 7mm Rem. Mag.)
Action	Vanguard action of the improved Mauser type.
Safety	Side operated, forward moving release, accessible and positive.
Mounts	Vanguard action accepts same bases as Mark V action.

**Weight Approximate—varies due to stock density.

RIFLES

WEATHERBY RIFLES

VANGUARD CLASSIC I
$568.00

Available in 223 Rem., 243 Rem., 270 Win., 7mm-08, 7mm Rem. Mag., 30-06 and 308 Win. Features include black recoil pad (on magnum calibers) and solid black butt pad on regular calibers. See table on the previous page for additional information and specifications.

VANGUARD CLASSIC II
$750.00

Utilizing the classic styling of an American walnut stock with oil finish, the Classic II stock design features a 90-degree black forend tip (rather than Weatherby's original 45-degree models). The black pistol grip cap with a walnut diamond inlay and a solid black recoil pad make this a distinctive stock. All **barrels** are 24″ with matte finish bluing. Available in **calibers:** 22-250, 243 Win., 270 Win., 7mm Rem. Mag., 30-06, 270 Wby. Mag., 300 Win. Mag., 300 Wby. Mag., and 338 Win. Mag. For additional information and specifications, see table on the previous page.

VANGUARD WEATHERGUARD
$495.00

Weatherby's new Weatherguard features a 24″ barrel and a synthetic injection molded stock designed to resist weather and humidity. Normal scratches from wear and tear are not visible because the black finish penetrates the entire stock. Stock comes complete with basket-weave checkering, solid black recoil pad, and front and rear swivel studs. **Calibers:** 223 Rem., 243 Rem., 270 Win., 7mm-08, 7mm Rem. Mag., 30-06 and 308 Win. For additional information and specifications, see table on the previous page.

WEATHERBY RIFLES

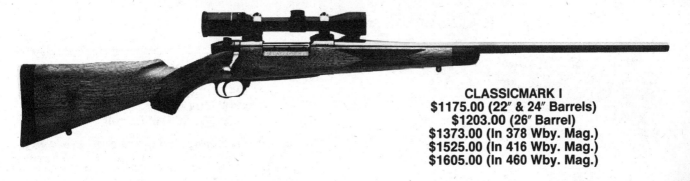

CLASSICMARK I
$1175.00 (22″ & 24″ Barrels)
$1203.00 (26″ Barrel)
$1373.00 (In 378 Wby. Mag.)
$1525.00 (In 416 Wby. Mag.)
$1605.00 (In 460 Wby. Mag.)

CLASSICMARK II
$1775.00 (22″ & 24″ Barrels)
$1803.00 (26″ Barrel)
$1976.00 (In 378 Wby. Mag.)
$2128.00 (In 416 Wby. Mag.)
$2207.00 (In 460 Wby. Mag.)

CLASSICMARK I, II WEATHERMARK AND ALASKAN RIFLE SPECIFICATIONS (see also following page)

Caliber	Barreled Action	**Weight w/o Sights	Overall Length	Magazine Capacity	Barrel	Rifling	Sights
.240 WBY MAG		8 lbs.		4, +1 in chamber	24″ #1 contour or 26″ #2 contour	1-10″ twist	
.257 WBY MAG	Right or left hand 24″ bbl. Right hand 25″ bbl.	8 lbs.	44⅝″ or 46⅝″ dependent on barrel length	3, +1 in chamber	24″ #1 contour or 26″ #2 contour	1-10″ twist	Drilled and tapped for scope. Iron sights extra.
.270 WBY MAG		8 lbs.		3, +1 in chamber	24″ #1 contour or 26″ #2 contour	1-10″ twist	
.270 WIN	Right or left hand 22″ bbl.	8 lbs.	42⅝″	4, +1 in chamber	22″ #1 contour	1-10″ twist	
7mm REM MAG	Right or left hand 24″ bbl.	8 lbs.	44⅝″	3, +1 in chamber	24″ #1 contour	1-10″ twist	
7mm WBY MAG	Right or left hand 24″ bbl. Right hand 26″ bbl.	8 lbs.	44⅝″ or 46⅝″ dependent on barrel length	3, +1 in chamber	24″ #1 contour or 26″ #2 contour	1-10″ twist	
.30-06	Right or left hand 22″ bbl.	8 lbs.	42⅝″	4, +1 in chamber	22″ #1 contour	1-10″ twist	
.300 WBY MAG	Right or left hand 24″ bbl. Right hand 26″ bbl. Left hand 26″ bbl.	8 lbs.	44⅝″ or 46⅝″ dependent on barrel length	3, +1 in chamber	24″ #1 contour or 26″ #2 contour	1-10″ twist	
.340 WBY MAG	Right or left hand 26″ bbl. only	8½ lbs.	46⅝″	3, +1 in chamber	26″ #2 contour	1-10″ twist	
.375 H&H MAG	Right hand 24″ bbl. only	8½ lbs.	44⅝″	2, +1 in chamber	24″ #3 contour	1-12″ twist	Drilled and tapped includes ½ rib and hooded front sight.
.378 WBY MAG	Right or left hand 26″ bbl. only	8½ lbs.	46⅝″	2, +1 in chamber	26″ #3 contour	1-12″ twist	
.416 WBY MAG*	Right or left hand 24″ or 26″ bbl.	9 lbs.	44¾″ or 46¾″	2, +1 in chamber	24″ or 26″ #3.5 contour	1-14″ twist	Drilled and tapped for scope. Iron sights extra.
.460 WBY MAG*	Right or left hand 24″ or 26″ bbl.*	10 lbs.	44¾ or 46¾″	2, +1 in chamber	24″ or 26″ #4 contour	1-16″ twist	

*Available with muzzle brake only.   **Weight varies due to wood density and bore diameter.   All rifles measure ¾″ drop at comb; drop at heel 1½″.

CLASSIMARK II: Right hand only.   WEATHERMARK: Right hand only.   FIBERMARK: Left hand only.   LAZERMARK: Available all models.   Accubrake: Available all models except .240 WBY MAG.   Mk V Specs Apply.

WEATHERBY RIFLES

WEATHERMARK ALASKAN
$1180.00 (22″ & 24″ Barrels)
$1207.00 (26″ Barrel)

The Alaskan model rifle with Mark V bolt action features Weatherby's Weathermark® composite stock with special non-glare finish. The electroless nickel finish is stainless and impervious to rust. The stock, which features raised point checkering, is color impregnated for a durable, scratch-resistant finish and is teamed with satin-finished metalwork to reduce game-spooking glare. See table on previous page for specifications.

WEATHERMARK
$1000.00 (22″ & 24″ Barrels)
$1027.00 (26″ Barrel)

Also available:
LIMITED EDITION SAFARI CLASSIC (not shown) in 375 H&H caliber. Features Weatherby's new Classicmark stock design with Mark V bolt action. The classic line stock is hand-selected American walnut, with straight comb, rounded forend, and shadow-line cheekpiece. Oil-finished, it carries a steel grip cap and Old English recoil pad and boasts wraparound point checkering. It also sports a quarter rib express sight, hooded front sight, and a barrel band sling swivel. Accuracy of 1½″ or less for a 3-shot group at 100 yards is guaranteed. Price on request.

The new Weathermark® rifle features the Mark V bolt action and features a special composite stock that is guaranteed not to warp, preserving accuracy. The stock is the same as the Alaskan model (see above). For complete specifications, see the table on the previous page.

WINCHESTER BOLT ACTION RIFLES

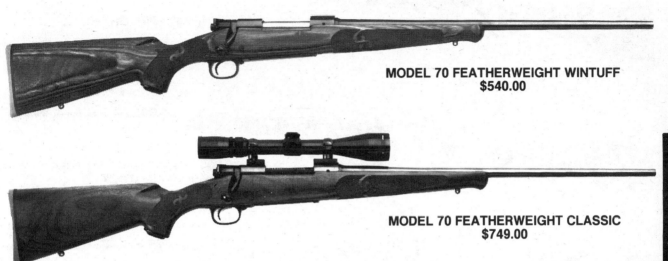

MODEL 70 FEATHERWEIGHT WINTUFF
$540.00

MODEL 70 FEATHERWEIGHT CLASSIC
$749.00

Model		Caliber	Magazine Capacity*	Barrel Length	Overall Length	Nominal Length Of Pull	Nominal Drop At Comb	Heel	Nominal Weight (Lbs.)	Rate of Twist 1 Turn In	Bases Rings or Sights
70 WALNUT FEATHERWEIGHT		22-250 Rem.	5	22"	42"	13 1/2"	9/16"	7/8"	7	14"	B + R
Standard Grade Walnut		223 Rem.	6	22	42	13 1/2	9/16	7/8	7	12	B + R
		243 Win.	5	22	42	13 1/2	9/16	7/8	7	10	B + R
		6.5×55mm Swedish	5	22	42 1/2	13 1/2	9/16	7/8	7	7.87	B + R
		270 Win.	5	22	42 1/2	13 1/2	9/16	7/8	7 1/4	10	B + R
		280 Rem.	5	22	42 1/2	13 1/2	9/16	7/8	7 1/4	10	B + R
	New	7mm-08 Rem.	3	22	42	13 1/2	9/16	7/8	7	9.5	B + R
		7mm Rem. Mag	5	24	44 1/2	13 1/2	9/16	7/8	7 1/2	9.5	B + R
		30-06 Spfld.	5	22	42 1/2	13 1/2	9/16	7/8	7 1/4	10	B + R
		308 Win.	3	22	42	13 1/2	9/16	7/8	7	12	B + R
		300 Win. Mag.	3	24	44 1/2	13 1/2	9/16	7/8	7 1/2	10	B + R
70 WINTUFF FEATHERWEIGHT	**New**	22-250 Rem.	5	22	42	13 1/2	9/16	7/8	6 3/4	14	B + R
Brown Laminate	**New**	223 Rem.	6	22	42	13 1/2	9/16	7/8	6 3/4	12	B + R
	New	243 Win.	5	22	42	13 1/2	9/16	7/8	6 3/4	10	B + R
	New	270 Win.	5	22	42 1/2	13 1/2	9/16	7/8	7	10	B + R
	New	308 Win.	5	22	42	13 1/2	9/16	7/8	6 3/4	12	B + R
	New	30-06 Spfld.	5	22	42 1/2	13 1/2	9/16	7/8	7	10	B + R
70 WALNUT CLASSIC	**New**	270 Win.	5	22	42 1/2	13 1/2	9/16	7/8	7 1/4	10	B + R
Standard Grade Walnut	**New**	280 Rem.	5	22	42 1/2	13 1/2	9/16	7/8	7 1/4	10	B + R
Controlled Round Feeding	**New**	30-06 Spfld.	5	22	42 1/2	13 1/2	9/16	7/8	7 1/4	10	B + R

* For additional capacity, add one round in chamber when ready to fire. Drops are measured from center line of bore. Rate of twist is right-hand.

WINCHESTER BOLT ACTION RIFLES

MODEL 70 LIGHTWEIGHT RIFLE

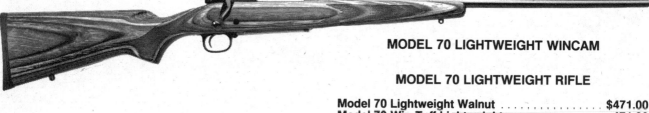

**MODEL 70 LIGHTWEIGHT WIN-TUFF
LAMINATED STOCK**

MODEL 70 LIGHTWEIGHT WINCAM

MODEL 70 LIGHTWEIGHT RIFLE

Model 70 Lightweight Walnut	$471.00
Model 70 Win-Tuff Lightweight	471.00
Model 70 Win-Cam Lightweight	471.00

SPECIFICATIONS: MODEL 70 LIGHTWEIGHT

Model	Caliber	Magazine Capacity (A)	Barrel Length	Overall Length	Nominal Length Of Pull	Nominal Drop At Comb	Nominal Drop At Heel	Nominal Drop At MC	Nominal Weight (Lbs.)	Rate of Twist 1 Turn In
70 WALNUT Checkered, No Sights	22-250 Rem.	5	22"	42"	13¾"	9/16"	7/8"	—	6¼	14"
	223 Rem.	6	22	42	13¾	9/16	7/8	—	6¼	12
	243 Win.	5	22	42	13¾	9/16	7/8	—	6¼	10
	270 Win.	5	22	42½	13¾	9/16	7/8	—	6½	10
	280 Rem.	5	22	42½	13¾	9/16	7/8	—	6½	10
	30-06 Spgfld.	5	22	42½	13¾	9/16	7/8	—	6½	10
	308 Win.	5	22	42	13¾	9/16	7/8	—	6¼	12
70 WIN-TUFF Warm Brown Laminate, Checkered, No Sights	223 Rem.	6	22	42	13¾	9/10	7/8	—	6¾	12
	243 Win.	5	22	42	13¾	9/16	7/8	—	6¾	10
	270 Win.	5	22	42½	13¾	9/16	7/8	—	7	10
	30-06 Spgfld.	5	22	42½	13¾	9/16	7/8	—	7	10
	308 Win.	5	22	42	13¾	9/16	7/8	—	6¾	12
70 WIN-CAM Camo Green Laminate	270 Win.	5	22	42½	13¾	9/16	7/8	—	7	10
	30-06 Spgfld.	5	22	42½	13¾	9/16	7/8	—	7	10

(A) For additional capacity, add one round in chamber when ready to fire. Drops are measured from center line of bore. Rate of twist is right-hand. No sights.

WINCHESTER BOLT ACTION RIFLES

MODEL 70 SUPER GRADE
$997.00 (not shown)

The Winchester Model 70 Super Grade features a bolt with true claw-controlled feeding of belted magnums. The stainless steel claw extractor on the bolt grasps the round from the magazine and delivers it to the chamber and later extracts the spent cartridge. A gas block doubles as bolt stop and the bolt guard rail assures smooth action. Winchester's 3-position safety and field-strippable firing pin are standard equipment. Other features include a satin finish select walnut stock with sculptured cheekpiece designed to direct recoil forces rearward and away from the shooter's cheek; an extra-thick honeycomb recoil; all-steel bottom metal; and chrome molybdenum barrel with cold hammer-forged rifling for optimum accuracy. Specifications are listed in the table below.

Also available:
MODEL 70 CUSTOM EXPRESS in calibers 375 H&H Mag., 375 JRS, 416 Rem. Mag., 458 Win. Mag. and 470 Capstick. **Price: $2125.00**

WINCHESTER MODEL 70 SUPER GRADE RIFLE

Model	New Symbol Number	Caliber	Magazine Capacity*	Barrel Length	Overall Length	Nominal Length of Pull	Nominal Drop at Comb	Nominal Drop at Heel	Nominal Drop at MC	Nominal Weight (Lbs.)	Rate of Twist 1 Turn in	Bases & Rings or Sights
70 SUPER GRADE	3821	270 Win.	5	24″	44¾″	14	9/16″	13/16″	—	7¾	10	B + R
	3870	30-06 Spfld.	5	24	44¾	14	9/16	13/16	—	7¾	10	B + R
	3862	7mm Rem. Mag.	3	24	44¾	14	9/16	13/16	—	7¾	9½	B + R
	3888	300 Win. Mag.	3	24	44¾	14	9/16	13/16	—	7¾	10	B + R
	3904	338 Win. Mag.	3	24	44¾	14	9/16	13/16	—	7¾	10	B + R

* For additional capacity, add one round in chamber when ready to fire. Drops are measured from center line of bore. Rate of twist is right-hand.

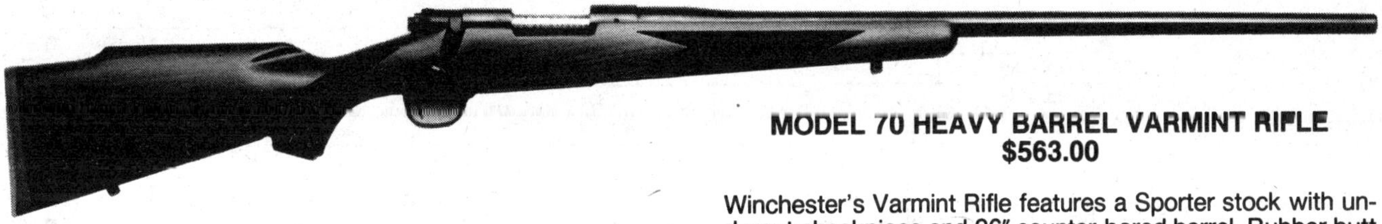

MODEL 70 HEAVY BARREL VARMINT RIFLE
$563.00

Winchester's Varmint Rifle features a Sporter stock with undercut cheekpiece and 26″ counter-bored barrel. Rubber butt pad, swivel studs and receiver drilled and tapped for scope are standard, as is Winchester's 3-position safety. Also available in composite stock and matte finished barrel and receiver.

MODEL 70 HEAVY BARREL VARMINT RIFLE SPECIFICATIONS

Model	Caliber	Magazine Capacity (A)	Barrel Length	Overall Length	Nominal Length Of Pull	Nominal Drop At Comb	Nominal Drop At Heel	Nominal Drop At MC	Nominal Weight (Lbs.)	Rate of Twist 1 Turn In	Sights
70 VARMINT	22-250 Rem.	5	26″	46″	13¾″	9/16″	1 5/16″	¾″	9	14″	—
	223 Rem.	6	26	46	13¾	9/16	1 5/16	¾	9	12	—
	243 Win.	5	26	46	13¾	9/16	1 5/16	¾	9	10	—
	308 Win.	5	26	46	13¾	9/16	1 5/16	¾	9	12	—
70 SHB	308 Win.	5	26″	46″	13¾	9/16	13/16	—	9	12	—

(A) For additional capacity, add one round in chamber when ready to fire. Drops are measured from center line of bore. Rate of twist is right-hand.

WINCHESTER BOLT ACTION RIFLES

MODEL 70 SPORTER & SUPER EXPRESS RIFLES
$540.00 ($816.00 SUPER EXPRESS)

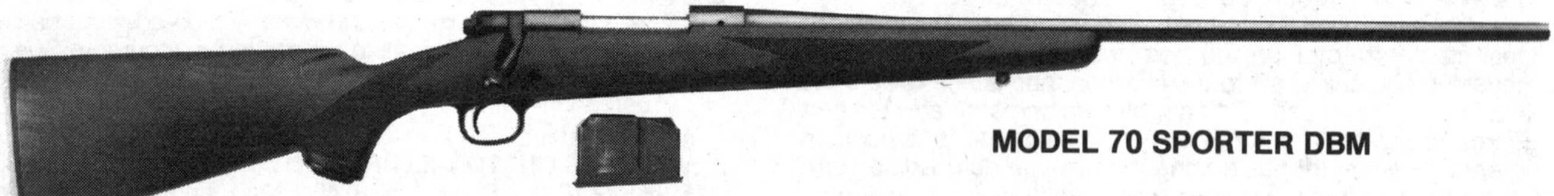

MODEL 70 SPORTER DBM

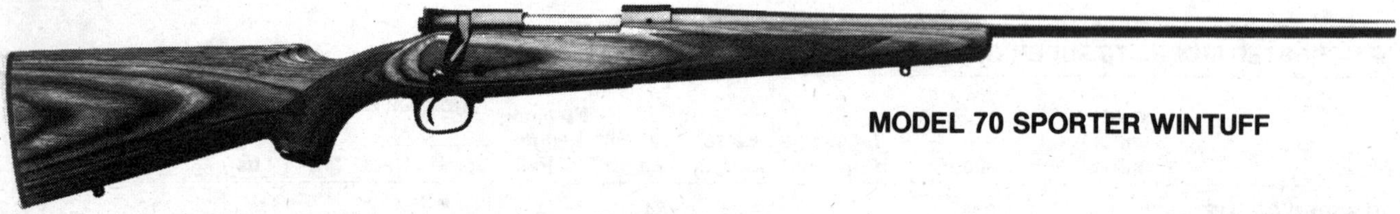

MODEL 70 SPORTER WINTUFF

SPECIFICATIONS: MODEL 70 SPORTER & SUPER EXPRESS

Model	Caliber	Magazine Capacity (A)	Barrel Length	Overall Length	Nominal Length Of Pull	Nominal Drop At Comb	Nominal Drop At Heel	Nominal Drop At MC	Nominal Weight (Lbs.)	Rate of Twist 1 Turn In	Bases & Rings or Sights
70 SPORTER WALNUT	22-250 Rem.	5	24″	44″	13½″	9/16″	13/16″	¾″	7⅞″	14″	Sights
	22-250 Rem.	5	24	44	13½	9/16	13/16	¾	7⅞	14	B + R
	223 Rem.	6	24	44	13½	9/16	13/16	¾	7⅝	12	Sights
	223 Rem.	6	24	44	13½	9/16	13/16	¾	7⅝	12	B + R
	243 Win.	5	24	44	13½	9/16	13/16	¾	7⅝	10	Sights
	243 Win.	5	24	44	13½	9/16	13/16	¾	7⅝	10	B + R
	25-06 Rem.	5	24	44	13½	9/16	13/16	¾	7⅞	16	Sights
	25-06 Rem.	5	24	44	13½	9/16	13/16	¾	7⅞	16	B + R
	264 Win. Mag.	3	24	44½	13½	9/16	13/16	¾	7⅞	9	Sight
	264 Win. Mag.	3	24	44½	13½	9/16	13/16	¾	7⅞	9	B + R
	270 Win.	5	24	44½	13½	9/16	13/16	¾	7⅞	10	Sights
	270 Win.	5	24	44½	13½	9/16	13/16	¾	7⅞	10	B + R
	270 Weath. Mag.	3	24	44½	13½	9/16	13/16	¾	7⅞	10	Sights
	270 Weath. Mag.	3	24	44½	13½	9/16	13/16	¾	7⅞	10	B + R
	7mm Rem. Mag.	3	24	44½	13½	9/16	13/16	¾	7⅞	9½	Sights
	7mm Rem. Mag.	3	24	44½	13½	9/16	13/16	¾	7⅞	9½	B + R
	30-06 Spgfld.	5	24	44½	13½	9/16	13/16	¾	7⅞	10	Sights
	30-06 Spgfld.	5	24	44½	13½	9/16	13/16	¾	7⅞	10	B + R
	300 H&H Mag.	3	24	44½	13½	9/16	13/16	¾	7⅞	10	Sights
	300 H&H Mag.	3	24	44½	13½	9/16	13/16	¾	7⅞	10	B + R
	300 Win. Mag.	3	24	44½	13½	9/16	13/16	¾	7⅞	10	Sights
	300 Win. Mag.	3	24	44½	13½	9/16	13/16	¾	7⅞	10	B + R
	300 Weath. Mag.	3	24	44½	13½	9/16	13/16	¾	7⅞	10	B + R
	338 Win. Mag.	3	24	44½	13½	9/16	13/16	¾	7⅞	10	Sights
	338 Win. Mag.	3	24	44½	13½	9/16	13/16	¾	7⅞	10	B + R
70 WALNUT SPORTER DBM	270 Win.	3	24	44½	13½	9/16	13/16	7⅞	10		
Detachable Box Magazine	7mm Rem. Mag.	3	24	44½	13½	9/16	13/16	¾	7⅞	9½	B + R
	30-06 Spfld.	3	24	44½	13½	9/16	13/16	¾	7⅞	10	B + R
	300 Win. Mag.	3	24	44½	13½	9/16	13/16	¾	7⅞	10	B + R
70 SUPER EXPRESS	375 H&H Mag.	3	24	44½	13½	9/16	1 5/16	¾	8½	12	Sights
WALNUT MAGNUM	458 Win. Mag.	3	22	42½	13½	9/16	1 5/16	¾	8½	14	Sights

(A) For additional capacity, add one round in chamber when ready to fire. Drops are measured from center line of bore. B + R—Bases and Rings included. Right-hand twist.

WINCHESTER BOLT ACTION RIFLES

WINCHESTER RANGER®
BOLT ACTION CENTERFIRE RIFLE
$427.00

The Ranger Bolt Action Rifle comes with an American hardwood stock, a wear-resistant satin walnut finish, ramp bead-post front sight, steel barrel, hinged steel magazine floorplate, three-position safety and engine-turned, anti-bind bolt. The receiver is drilled and tapped for scope mounting; accuracy is enhanced by thermoplastic bedding of the receiver. Barrel and receiver are brushed and blued.

WINCHESTER RANGER®
YOUTH BOLT ACTION CARBINE
$443.00

This carbine offers dependable bolt action performance combined with a scaled-down design to fit the younger, smaller shooter. It features anti-bind bolt design, jeweled bolt, three-position safety, contoured recoil pad, ramped bead front sight, semi-buckhorn folding leaf rear sight, hinged steel magazine floorplate, and sling swivels. Receiver is drilled and tapped for scope mounting. Stock is of American hardwood with protective satin walnut finish. Pistol grip, length of pull, overall length, and comb are all tailored to youth dimensions (see table).

RANGER & YOUTH RIFLE SPECIFICATIONS

Model	Caliber	Magazine Capacity (A)	Barrel Length	Overall Length	Nominal Length Of Pull	Nominal Drop At Comb	Heel	MC	Nominal Weight (Lbs.)	Rate of Twist 1 Turn in	Bases & Rings Sights
RANGER BOLT ACTIONS	223 Rem.	6	22"	42"	13½"	9/16"	7/8"	—	6¾	12"	Sights
	243 Win.	5	22	42"	13½	9/16	7/8	—	6¾	10"	Sights
	270 Win.	5	22	42½	13½	9/16	7/8	—	6¾	10	Sights
	30-06 Spgfld.	5	22	42½	13½	9/16	7/8	—	6¾	10	Sights
RANGE YOUTH/LADIES BOLT ACTION	243 Win.	5	22	41	12½	3/4	1	—	6½	10	Sights
	308 Win.	5	22	41	12½	3/4	1	—	6½	12	Sights
70 RANGER New	223 Rem.	6	22	42	13½	9/16	7/8	—	6¾	12	Sights
	243 Win.	5	22	42	13½	9/16	7/8	—	6¾	10	Sights
	270 Win.	5	22	42½	13½	9/16	7/8	—	6¾	10	Sights
	30-06 Spfld.	5	22	41½	13½	9/16	7/8	—	6¾	10	Sights
70 RANGER LADIES/ YOUTH	243 Win.	5	22	41	12½	3/4	1	—	6½	10	Sights
	308 Win.	5	22	41	12½	3/4	1	—	6½	12	Sights

(A) For additional capacity, and one round in chamber when ready to fire. Drops are measured from center line of bore. Rate of twist is right-hand.

WINCHESTER LEVER ACTION CARBINES & RIFLES

MODEL 94 STANDARD WALNUT RIFLE

and forearm have a protective stain finish with precise-cut wraparound checkering. It has a 20-inch barrel with hooded blade front sight and semi-buckhorn rear sight. **Calibers:** 30-30 Win., 32 Win. Special and 7-30 Waters.

Prices:
30-30 Win., checkered **$352.00**
30-30 Win., 7-30 Waters, 32 Win. Special **325.00**

The top choice for lever-action styling and craftsmanship. Metal surfaces are highly polished and blued. American walnut stock

MODEL 94 WALNUT TRAPPER CARBINE

44 S&W Special). **Calibers:** 30-30 Winchester, 357 Mag., 45 Colt, and 44 Rem. Mag./44 S&W Special.

Prices:
30-30 Winchester **$325.00**
357 Mag., 45 Colt, 44 Rem. Mag./44 S&W
Special **344.00**

With 16-inch short-barrel lever action and straight forward styling. Compact and fast-handling in dense cover, it has a magazine capacity of five shots (9 in 45 Colt or 44 Rem. Mag./

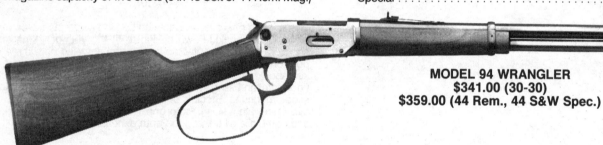

MODEL 94 WRANGLER
$341.00 (30-30)
$359.00 (44 Rem., 44 S&W Spec.)

MODEL 94 SPECIFICATIONS

Model	Caliber	Magazine Capacity (A)	Barrel Length	Overall Length	Nominal Length Of Pull	Nominal Drop At Comb	Nominal Drop At Heel	Nominal Weight (Lbs.)	Rate of Twist 1 Turn in	Rings Sights
94 CHECKERED WALNUT	30 30 Win.	6	20"	37³/₄"	13"	1¹/₈"	1⁷/₈"	6¹/₂	12"	Rifle
94 STANDARD WALNUT	30-30 Win.	6	20	37³/₄	13	1¹/₈	1⁷/₈	6¹/₂	12	Rifle
	32 Win.	6	20	37³/₄	13	1¹/₈	1⁷/₈	6¹/₂	12	Rifle
	7-30 Waters	6	20	37³/₄	13	1¹/₈	1⁷/₈	6¹/₂	9.9	Rifle
94 TRAPPER CARBINE WALNUT	30-30 Win.	5	16	33³/₄	13	1¹/₈	1⁷/₈	6¹/₈	12	Rifle
	357 Mag.	9	16	33³/₄	13¹/₂	1¹/₈	1⁷/₈	6	16	Rifle
	44 Rem. Mag.	9	16	33³/₄	13	1¹/₈	1⁷/₈			
	44 S&W Spec.							6	38	Rifle
	45 Colt	9	16	33³/₄	13	1¹/₈	1⁷/₈	6	38	Rifle
94 TRAPPER WALNUT	30-30 Win.	5	16	33³/₄	13¹/₂	1¹/₈	1⁷/₈	6¹/₈	12	Rifle
	44 Rem. Mag. 44 S&W Spec.	9	16	33³/₄	13¹/₂	1¹/₈	1⁷/₈	6	38	Rifle
	357 Mag.	9	16	33³/₄	13¹/₂	1¹/₈	1⁷/₈	6	16	Rifle
	45 Colt	9	16	33³/₄	13¹/₂	1¹/₈	1⁷/₈	6	38	Rifle
94 WRANGLER WALNUT	30-30 Win.	5	16	33³/₄	13¹/₂	1¹/₈	1⁷/₈	6¹/₈	12	Rifle
LARGE LOOP	44 Rem. Mag. 44 S&W Spec.	9	16	33³/₄	13¹/₂	1¹/₈	1⁷/₈	6	12	Rifle

(A) for additional capacity, add one round in chamber when ready to fire. Drops are measured from center line of bore. Rate of twist is right-hand.

WINCHESTER LEVER ACTION RIFLES

MODEL 94 RANGER
$287.00 ($338.00 with Scope)

Model 94 Ranger is an economical version of the Model 94. Lever action is smooth and reliable. In 30-30 Winchester, the rapid-firing six-shot magazine capacity provides two more shots than most centerfire hunting rifles.

MODEL 94 BIG BORE WALNUT
$352.00

Winchester's powerful 307 and 356 hunting calibers combined with maximum lever-action power and angled ejection provide hunters with improved performance and economy.

MODEL 94 WIN-TUFF RIFLE
$352.00

Includes all features and specifications of standard Model 94 plus tough laminated hardwood styled for the brush-gunning hunter who wants good concealment and a carbine that can stand up to all kinds of weather.

MODEL 94 SPECIFICATIONS

Model	Caliber	Magazine Capacity (A)	Barrel Length	Overall Length	Nominal Length Of Pull	Nominal Drop At Comb	Heel	Nominal Weight (Lbs.)	Rate of Twist 1 Turn in	Sights
94 WIN-TUFF	30-30 Win.	6	20″	37³/₄″	13″	1¹/₈″	1⁷/₈″	6¹/₂	12″	Rifle
94 BIG BORE WALNUT	307 Win.	6	20	37¹/₄	13	1¹/₈	1⁷/₈	6¹/₂	12	Rifle
	356 Win.	6	20	37³/₄	13	1¹/₈	1⁷/₈	6¹/₂	12	Rifle
RANGER	30-30 Win.	6	20	37³/₄	13¹/₂	1¹/₈	1⁷/₈	6¹/₂	12	Rifle
Scope 4 × 32 and see-through mounts	30-30 Win.	6	20	37³/₄	13¹/₂	1¹/₈	1⁷/₈	6¹/₂	12	R/S

(A) For additional capacity, add one round in chamber when ready to fire. Drops are measured from center line of bore. R/S-Rifle sights and Bushnell® Sportview™ scope with mounts. Rate of twist is right-hand.

WINCHESTER LEVER ACTION RIFLES

MODEL 9422 LEVER-ACTION RIMFIRE RIFLES

These Model 9422 rimfire rifles combine classic 94 styling and handling in ultra-modern lever action 22s of superb craftsmanship. Handling and shooting characteristics are superior because of their carbine-like size.

Positive lever action and bolt design ensure feeding and chambering from any shooting position. The bolt face is T-slotted to guide the cartridge with complete control from magazine to chamber. A color-coded magazine follower shows when the brass magazine tube is empty. Receivers are grooved for scope mounting. Other functional features include exposed hammer with half-cock safety, hooded bead front sight, semi-buckhorn rear sight and side ejection of spent cartridges.

Stock and forearm are American walnut with checkering, high-luster finish, and straight-grip design. Internal parts are carefully finished for smoothness of action.

MODEL 9422 WALNUT

Considered one of the world's finest production sporting arms, this lever action rimfire (shown above) holds 21 Short, 17 Long or 15 Long Rifle cartridges.

Model 9422 Walnut Magnum gives exceptional accuracy at longer ranges than conventional 22 rifles. It is designed specifically for the 22 Winchester Magnum Rimfire cartridge and holds 11 cartridges.

Model 9422 Win-Cam Magnum features laminated non-glare, green-shaded stock and forearm. American hardwood stock is bonded to withstand all weather and climates. **Model 9422 Win-Tuff** is also available to ensure resistance to changes in weather conditions, or exposure to water and hard knocks.

SPECIFICATIONS

Model	Caliber	Magazine Capacity	Barrel Length	Overall Length	Nominal Length Of Pull	Nominal Drop At Comb	Heel	Nominal Weight (Lbs.)	Rate of Twist 1 Turn in	Sights	Prices
9422 WALNUT	22 S, L, LR	21S,17L,15LR	20½"	37⅛"	13½"	1⅛"	1⅞"	6¼	16"	Rifle	$367.00
	22WMR Mag.	11	20½	37⅛	13½	1⅛	1⅞	6¼	16	Rifle	381.00
9422 WIN-TUFF	22 S, L, LR	21S,17L,15LR	20½"	37⅛"	13½"	1⅛"	1⅞"	6¼	16"	Rifle	367.00
	22WMR Mag.	11	20½	37⅛	13½	1⅛	1⅞	6¼	16	Rifle	381.00
9422 WIN-CAM	22WMR Mag.	11	20½"	37⅛"	13½"	1⅛"	1⅞"	6¼	16"	Rifle	381.00

WMR-Winchester Magnum Rimfire. S-Short, L-Long, LR-Long Rifle. Drops are measured from center line of bore.

WINSLOW RIFLES

SPECIFICATIONS

Stock: Choice of two stock models. **The Plainsmaster** offers pinpoint accuracy in open country with full curl pistol grip and flat forearm. **The Bushmaster** offers lighter weight for bush country; slender pistol with palm swell; beavertail forend for light hand comfort. Both styles are of hand-rubbed black walnut. Length of pull—13½ inches; plainsmaster ⅜ inch castoff; Bushmaster ³⁄₁₆ inch castoff; all rifles are drilled and tapped to incorporate the use of telescopic sights; rifles with receiver or open sights are available on special order; all rifles are equipped with quick detachable sling swivel studs and white-line recoil pad. All Winslow stocks incorporate a slight castoff to deflect recoil, minimizing flinch and muzzle jump. **Magazine:** Staggered box type, four shot. (Blind in the stock has no floorplate). **Action:** Mauser Mark X Action. **Overall length:** 43″ (Standard Model); 45″ (Magnum); all Winslow rifles have company name and serial number and grade engraved on the action

and caliber engraved on barrel. **Barrel:** Douglas barrel premium grade, chrome moly-type steel; all barrels, 20 caliber through 35 caliber, have six lands and grooves; barrels larger than 35 caliber have eight lands and grooves. All barrels are finished to (.2 to .4) micro inches inside the lands and grooves. **Total weight** (without scope): 7 to 7½ lbs. with 24″ barrel in standard calibers 243, 308, 270, etc; 8 to 9 lbs. with 26″ barrel in Magnum calibers 264 Win., 300 Wby., 458 Win., etc. Winslow rifles are made in the following calibers:

Standard cartridges: 22-250, 243 Win., 244 Rem., 257 Roberts, 308 Win., 30-06, 280 Rem., 270 Win., 25-06, 284 Win., 358 Win., and 7mm (7×57).

Magnum cartridges: 300 Weatherby, 300 Win., 338 Win., 358 Norma, 375 H.H., 458 Win., 257 Weatherby, 264 Win., 270 Weatherby, 7mm Weatherby, 7mm Rem., 300 H.H., 308 Norma.

Left-handed models available in most calibers.

WINSLOW BASIC RIFLE

The Basic Rifle, available in the Bushmaster stock, features one ivory diamond inlay in a rose-wood grip cap and ivory trademark in bottom of forearm. Grade 'A' walnut jeweled bolt and follower. **Price: $1750.00 and up.** With **Plainsmaster stock: $100.00** extra. **Left-hand model: $1850.00 and up.**

WINSLOW VARMINT

This 17-caliber rifle is available with Bushmaster stock or Plainsmaster stock, which is a miniature of the original with high roll-over cheekpiece and a round leading edge on the forearm, modified spoon billed pistol grip. Available in 17/222, 17/222 Mag. 17/233, 222 Rem. and 223. Regent grade shown. With **Bushmaster stock: $1750.00 and up.** With **Plainsmaster stock: $100.00** extra. **Left-hand model: $1850.00 and up.**

ANTONIO ZOLI RIFLES

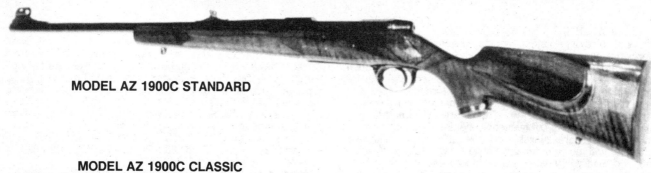

MODEL AZ 1900C STANDARD

MODEL AZ 1900C CLASSIC
$1199.95

This bolt-action rifle features a blued finish, jeweled and polished bolt body, and blued receiver (drilled and tapped for scope mounts). Also, a double safety bolt lock release permits the user to clear the chamber and unload the gun without taking the firearm off safe. For specifications, see the table below.

Also available: **MODEL AZ 1900DL** with photo-engraved receiver and floorplate. **Price: $1275.00**

MODEL AZ 1900C SPECIFICATIONS

	Standard calibers	Magnum calibers
Barrel length	21″	24″
Overall length	41³/₄″	44″
Length of pull	13¹/₂″	13¹/₂″
Sights	Furnished not mounted barrel drilled and tapped	
Stock	Hand rubbed finely checkered Turkish circassian walnut	
Materials	Barrel: hardened-high tensile chrome molybdenum steel-polished blued. Action: same as barrel	
Calibers and rate of twist	Standard: 243 W - 6.5 × 55mm - 270 W-308 Win. 30.06 Magnum: 7mm. Rem. Mag - 300 Win. Mag.	
Magazine capacity	5	
Nominal weight	7¹/₄″	7⁵/₇″

MANUFACTURER DOES NOT FURNISH SUGGESTED RETAIL PRICES; ABOVE PRICES ARE FOR COMPARATIVE PURPOSES ONLY

Shotguns

For addresses and phone numbers of manufacturers and distributors included in this section, turn to *DIRECTORY OF MANUFACTURERS AND SUPPLIERS* at the back of the book.

AMERICAN ARMS

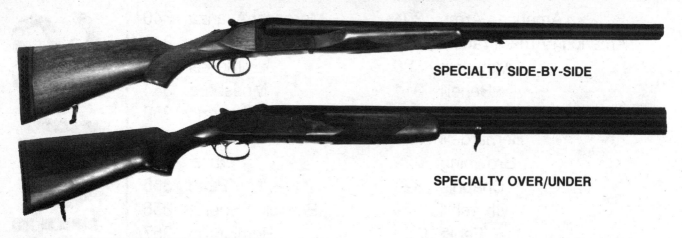

SPECIALTY SIDE-BY-SIDE

SPECIALTY OVER/UNDER

MODEL	GAUGE	BBL LGTH.	CHAMBER	CHOKES	AVG. WGT.	PRICES
WT/OU	10	26″	3 1/2″	CT-2	9 lbs. 10 oz.	**$859.00**
WS/OU	12	28″	3 1/2″	CT-3	7 lbs. 2 oz.	659.00
TS/SS	10	26″	3 1/2″	CT-2	10 lbs. 13 oz.	599.00
TS/SS	12	26″	3 1/2″	CT-3	7 lbs. 6 oz.	599.00
WS/SS	10	32″	3 1/2″	SF/SF	11 lbs. 3 oz.	599.00

CT-3 = Choke tubes IC/M/F
SF = Steel Full Choke
ASE = Auto selective ejector
Drop at Comb = 1 1/8″

CT-2 = Choke tubes F/F
SST = Single Selective Trigger

Drop at Heel = 2 0/8″

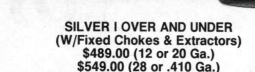

SILVER I OVER AND UNDER
(W/Fixed Chokes & Extractors)
$489.00 (12 or 20 Ga.)
$549.00 (28 or .410 Ga.)

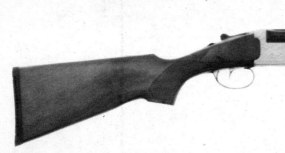

SILVER II
(W/Choke Tubes & Automatic Selective Ejectors)
$629.00 (12 & 20 Ga.)
$999.00 (28 & .410 Ga.)

SPECIFICATIONS
Gauges: 12, 20, 28 or .410
Chambers: 3″ (2³/₄″ in 28 ga.)
Barrel lengths: 26″, choked IC/M (all gauges); 28″, choked M/F (12 and 20 ga.)
Trigger: Single selective
Weight: 6 lbs. 15 oz. (12 ga.); 6 lbs. 10 oz. (20 ga.); 5 lbs. 14 oz. (28 ga.); 6 lbs. 6 oz. (.410 ga.)

Stock: Hand-checkered, walnut, pistol-grip stock and forend
Length of pull: 14¹/₈″
Drop at comb: 1³/₈″
Drop at heel: 2³/₈″
Features: Fitted recoil pad; ¹/₄″ vent rib; manual thumb safety; scroll-engraved, precision-made boxlocks; one-piece, steel-forged receiver; locking cross bolt; monobloc chrome-lined barrels; extractors

AMERICAN ARMS

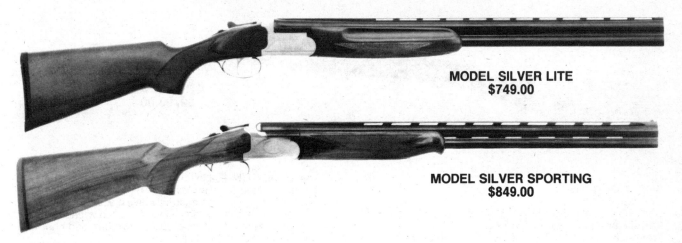

MODEL SILVER LITE
$749.00

MODEL SILVER SPORTING
$849.00

SPECIFICATIONS

MODEL	GAUGE	BBL. LENGTH	CHAMBER	CHOKES	AVG. WEIGHT
SILVER I	12	26"–28"	3"	IC/M-M/F	6 lbs. 15 oz.
	20	26"–28"	3"	IC/M-M/F	6 lbs. 12 oz.
	28	26"	2 3/4"	IC/M	5 lbs. 14 oz.
	.410	26"	3"	IC/M	6 lbs. 6 oz.
SILVER II	12	26"–28"	3"	CT-3	6 lbs. 15 oz.
	20	26"	3"	CT-3	6 lbs. 12 oz.
	28	26"	2 3/4"	IC/M	5 lbs. 14 oz.
	.410	26"	3"	IC/M	6 lbs. 6 oz.
	28/.410 Set	26"	2 3/4"–3"	IC/M	6 lbs. 6 oz.
SILVER LITE	12	26"	2 3/4"	CT-3	6 lbs. 5 oz.
	20	26"	2 3/4"	CT-3	6 lbs. 1 oz.
SPORTING	12	28"	2 3/4"	CTS	7 lbs. 6 oz.

CT-3 Choke Tubes IC/M/F   CT-4 Choke Tubes SK/IC/M/F   Cast Off = 3/8"   CTS = SK/SK/IC/M
SILVER I: Pull = 14 1/8"; Drop at Comb = 1 3/8"; Drop at Heel = 2 3/8"
SILVER II: Pull = 14 1/8"; Drop at Comb = 1 3/8"; Drop at Heel = 2 3/8"
SILVER LITE: Pull = 14 1/8"; Drop at Comb = 1 1/2"; Drop at Heel = 2 1/2"
SILVER SPORTING: Pull = 14 3/8"; Drop at Comb = 1 1/2"; Drop at Heel = 2 3/8"

BASQUE SERIES

BRITTANY
$689.00

SPECIFICATIONS
Gauges: 12, 20
Chamber: 3"
Barrel length: 26"
Weight: 6 lbs. 7 ozs. (20 ga.); 6 lbs. 15 oz. (12 ga.)
Chokes: Tubes IC/M/F

Features: Engraved case-colored frame; single selective trigger with top tang selector; automatic selective ejectors; manual safety; hard chrome-lined barrels; walnut English-style straight stock and semi-beavertail forearm w/cut checkering and oil-rubbed finish; ventilated rubber recoil pad; and choke tubes with key

AMERICAN ARMS

BASQUE SERIES

GRULLA #2
$2798.00

SPECIFICATIONS
Gauges: 12, 20, 28, .410
Chambers: 2³/₄″ (12 & 28 ga.); 3″ (20 & .410 ga.)
Barrel length: 26″ (28″ also in 12 ga.)
Weight: 6 lbs. 4 oz. (12 ga.); 5 lbs. 11 oz. (20 & 28 ga.); 5 lbs. 13 oz. (.410)

Chokes: IC/M (M/F also in 12 ga.)
Features: Hand-fitted and finished high-grade classic double; double triggers; automatic selective ejectors; fixed chokes; concave rib; case-colored sidelock action w/engraving; English-style straight stock; splinter forearm and checkered butt of oil rubbed walnut
Also available in sets (20 & 28 or 28 & .410): **$3658.00**

GENTRY SIDE-BY-SIDE
$559.00 (12 or 20 Ga.)
$599.00 (28 or .410 Ga.)

Features boxlocks with engraved English-style scrollwork on side plates; one-piece, steel-forged receiver; chrome barrels; manual thumb safety; independent floating firing pin.

SPECIFICATIONS
Gauges: 12, 16, 20, 28, .410
Chambers: 3″ (except 28 gauge, 2³/₄″)
Barrel lengths: 26″, choked IC/M (all gauges); 28″, choked M/F (12, 16 and 20 gauges)

Weight: 6 lbs. 15 oz. (12 ga.); 6 lbs. 7 oz. (20 and .410 ga.); 6 lbs. 5 oz. (28 ga.)
Drop at comb: 1³/₈″
Drop at heel: 2³/₈″
Other features: Fitted recoil pad; flat matted rib; walnut pistol-grip stock and beavertail forend with hand-checkering; gold front sight bead

DERBY SIDE-BY-SIDE
$929.00

Features functioning side locks with English-style hand engraving on side plates; one-piece, steel-forged receiver; chrome barrels; automatic safety

SPECIFICATIONS
Gauges: 12 and 20
Chambers: 3″
Barrel lengths: 26″, choked IC/M (all gauges); 28″, choked M/F (12 and 20 gauges)
Weight: 6 lbs. 12 oz. (12 ga.); 6 lbs. (20 ga.)

Sights: Gold bead front sight
Stock: Walnut and splinter forend with hand-checkering
Length of pull: 14¹/₈″
Drop at comb: 1³/₈″
Drop at heel: 2³/₈″
Features: Walnut straight stock and splinter forearm; auto selective ejectors; fixed chokes; single non-selective trigger; frame and sidelocks finished with antique silver and machine engraving.

AMERICAN ARMS/FRANCHI SHOTGUNS

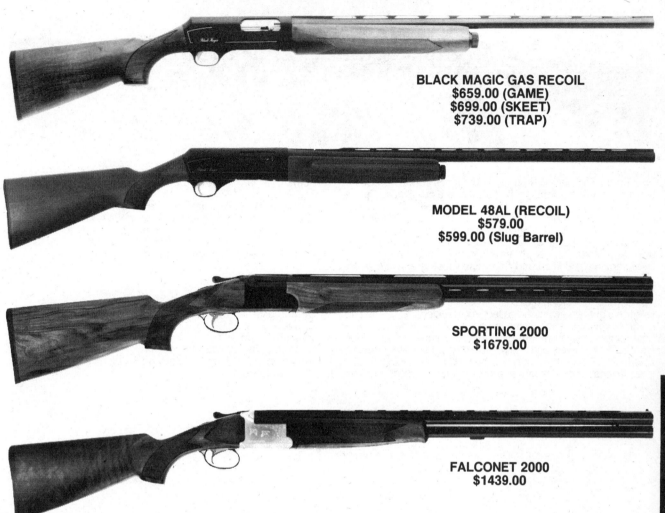

BLACK MAGIC GAS RECOIL
$659.00 (GAME)
$699.00 (SKEET)
$739.00 (TRAP)

MODEL 48AL (RECOIL)
$579.00
$599.00 (Slug Barrel)

SPORTING 2000
$1679.00

FALCONET 2000
$1439.00

SHOTGUNS

SPECIFICATIONS

Model	Ga.	Action Type	Barrel Length	Chamber	Choke*	Length of Pull	Drop at Comb	Drop at Heel	Nominal weight (lbs.)
Game	12	SA	26″ or 28″	3″	FC	14 1/4″	1 1/2″	2 3/8″	7
Trap	12	SA	30″	2 3/4″	FC	14 1/2″	1 1/4″	1 5/8″	7 1/2
Skeet	12	SA	26″	2 3/4″	SK	14 1/2″	1 1/2″	2 1/4″	7 1/4
48 AL	12/20	SA	24,″ 26,″ 28″	2 3/4″	FC	14 1/4″	1 1/2″	2 3/8″	5 1/2–6 1/2
Sporting 2000	12	O/U	28″	2 3/4″	SK/FC	14 1/4″	1 1/2″	2 3/8″	7
Falconet 2000	12	O/U	26″	2 3/4″	FC	14 1/4″	1 1/2″	2 3/8″	6

*FC = Franchokes (IC-M-F)

AMERICAN ARMS/FRANCHI SHOTGUNS

FRANCHI SPAS-12
$589.00

This Franchi 12-gauge shotgun is designed for law enforcement and personal defense. It operates as a pump action and/or semiautomatic action (a manual action selector switch is located at the bottom of the forearm). The barrel features a muzzle protector and is made of chrome-moly steel with a hard-chromed bore and matte finish. A rifle-type aperture rear sight and blade front sight are standard, along with cylinder bore choking (modified and full choke tubes are available as accessories). The muzzle is threaded externally for mounting the SPAS-12 choke tubes (SPAS-12 and standard Franchi tubes are *not* interchangeable; 2¾" only). The receiver/frame is lightweight alloy with non-reflective anodized finish. The fire control system is easily removable for maintenance with two push pins; a magazine cut-off button is located on the right side of the receiver, and the primary crossbolt safety button is in front of the trigger guard. A secondary "tactical" safety lever is located on the left side of the trigger guard, and the bolt/carrier latch release button is on the left side of the receiver.

The SPAS-12 operates as a recoil-operated semiautomatic and/or pump action. The operating mode is easily selected by pressing the selector button located on the underside of the forearm. The SPAS-12 is designed to shoot 2¾" shells only. Two safety systems are standard.

SPECIFICATIONS
Gauge: 12; 2¾" chamber
Capacity: 7 rounds
Choke: Cylinder bore
Barrel length: 21½"
Overall length: 41"
Weight: 8 lbs. 12 oz.
Stock: Nylon full-length stock with full pistol grip and serrated nylon forearm

ARMSPORT SHOTGUNS

MODELS 1050/1053
SIDE-BY-SIDE DOUBLE BARREL
ITALIAN SHOTGUNS
$785.00

Chambered for 3" magnum with hard chrome-lined barrels, these shotguns feature center ribs, fluorescent front sights, Italian boxlock actions and gloss finish stocks and forends. Also antique silver finish receivers engraved with bird scenes. Model 1050 is 12 gauge with 28" barrel with Modified & Full choke. Model 1053 is 20 gauge with 26" barrel with Imp. & Modified choke.
Also available: **MODEL 1054** (.410 ga.) and **MODEL 1055** (28 ga.) w/26" barrels: **$860.00**

ARMSPORT SHOTGUNS

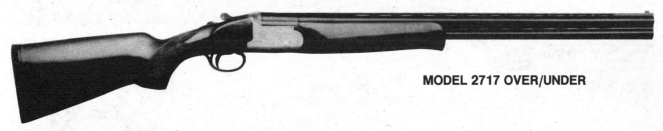

MODEL 2717 OVER/UNDER

"SENATOR" SERIES
O/U DOUBLE TRIGGER WITH EXTRACTORS
From $650.00 to $1295.00

The Armsport over/unders with double triggers are lightweight, well balanced and are chambered for 3″ Mag. shells. The special grade steel barrels are chrome-lined, with both an upper vent rib and lateral vent rib. The fine grain walnut stock has a palm swell pistol grip and both the stock and schnabel-type forend have a deep, sure-grip checkering. The beautifully engraved antique silver receiver is engineered from the finest gun steel. The double trigger instantly allows the shooter his barrel choice.

Available in:
Model 2697 10 Ga. 28″ w/3 chokes
Model 2698 10 Ga. 32″ w/3 chokes
Model 2702 12 Ga. 28″ O/U 3″ Mag. 2 Trig. Ext. Mod. & Full
Model 2704 20 Ga. 26″ O/U 3″ Mag. 2 Trig. Ext. Imp. & Mod.
Model 2705 .410 Ga. 26″ O/U 3″ Mag. 2 Triggers Ext. Imp. & Mod.
Model 2707 28 Ga. 26″ O/U 2 Trigger Full & Full
Also available:
Single Selective Trigger Models 2708, 2717, 2719, 2720, 2725. $735.00 to $800.00
Single Selective Trigger Models 2727, 2729, 2741 & 2743 w/auto ejectors and wide rib. $810.00 to $830.00

MODELS 2699 and 2700
10 GAUGE OVER & UNDER GOOSE GUN
$1175.00

This 10 gauge 3½″ "Fowler" Magnum Boss-type action O/U Goose gun has two bottom locking lugs on its OM8 steel barrels attached to an antiqued silver finished action. Three Canada geese scenes are engraved on the two sides and bottom of the receiver. The hard chrome-lined barrels have an extra wide 12mm top vent rib with a fluorescent front sight and a brass mid-bead sight. Both the 32″ barrels choked full and the 28″ barrels choked Imp. and Mod. will shoot steel BB's effectively. The walnut stock with rubber recoil pad and matching forend are hand-checkered.

ARMSPORT SHOTGUNS

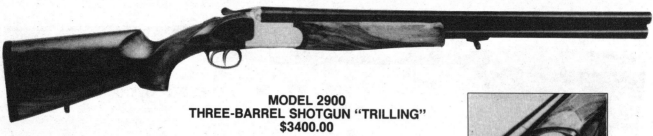

MODEL 2900
THREE-BARREL SHOTGUN "TRILLING"
$3400.00

The only three-barrel shotgun being manufactured, Model 2900 features 28″ barrels (12 gauge) lined and chambered for 3″ magnum shells choked improved, modified and full. The front trigger fires the top two barrels and the rear trigger fires the bottom barrel. Made on a boss type action from special steel, the shotgun frame has two bottom locking lugs. The select grain walnut palm swell pistol grip stock and forend has a rubber recoil pad, high gloss finish and checkering.

MODEL 2900
TRI-BARREL

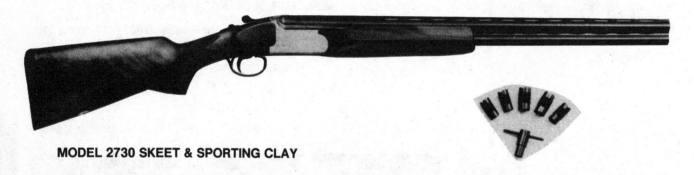

MODEL 2730 SKEET & SPORTING CLAY

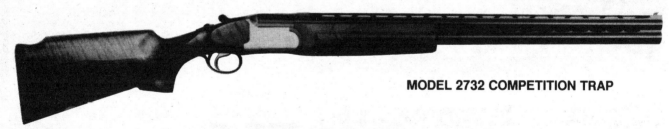

MODEL 2732 COMPETITION TRAP

OVER/UNDER SPORTING CLAY & SKEET GUNS
SINGLE SELECTIVE TRIGGER
WITH AUTO EJECTORS
$900.00 to $2000.00

Designed specifically for sporting clay shooting, this series has all the features demanded for sporting, including 5 interchangeable chokes. Each shotgun features chrome-lined barrels with 12mm ventilated rib, an elongated fluorescent ramp front sight, and handsomely grained, hand-rubbed, oiled walnut stocks and forends.

Available in:
Model 2730 12 Ga. 28″ Skeet & Skeet w/5 chokes
Model 2731 20 Ga. 26″, Skeet & Skeet w/5 chokes
Model 2742 12 Ga. 28″, 5 Int. chokes
Model 2744 20 Ga. 26″, 5 Int. chokes
Model 2750 12 Ga. 28″, Side plates, 5 Int. chokes
Model 2751 20 Ga. 28″, Side plates, 5 Int. chokes
Model 2763 12 Ga. 30″ Sporting w/5 chokes by Ferlib
Model 2765 20 Ga. 26″ Sporting w/5 chokes by Ferlib

ARMSPORT SHOTGUNS

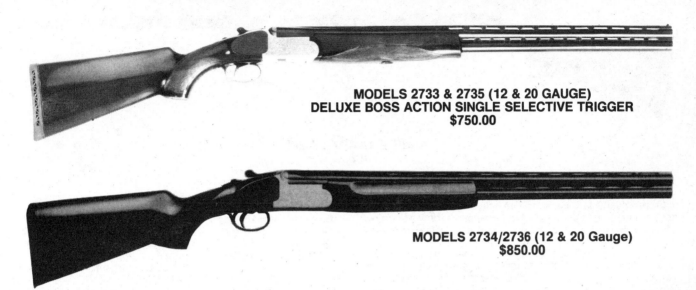

MODELS 2733 & 2735 (12 & 20 GAUGE)
DELUXE BOSS ACTION SINGLE SELECTIVE TRIGGER
$750.00

MODELS 2734/2736 (12 & 20 Gauge)
$850.00

BENELLI SHOTGUNS

MODEL M1 SUPER 90 SERIES

MODEL M1 SUPER 90 DEFENSE
$749.00 (w/Pistol Grip)
$797.00 (w/Ghost-Ring Sighting System)

MODEL M1 SUPER 90 SLUG
$699.00 ($749.00 w/Ghost-Ring Sighting System)

MODEL M1 SUPER 90 FIELD
$799.00

BENELLI SHOTGUNS

SUPER BLACK EAGLE (26″ Barrel)

SUPER BLACK EAGLE
$1059.00

Benelli's new Super Black Eagle shotgun offers the advantage of owning one 12-gauge auto that fires every type of 12-gauge currently available. It has the same balance, sighting plane and fast-swinging characteristics whether practicing on the sporting clays course with light target loads or touching off a 3¹/₂″ magnum steel load at a high-flying goose.

The Super Black Eagle also features a specially strengthened steel upper receiver mated to the barrel so as to endure the toughest shotgunning. The alloy lower receiver keeps the overall weight low, making this model as well balanced and point-able as possible. Distinctive high-gloss or satin walnut stocks and a choice of dull finish or blued metal add up to a universal gun for all shotgun hunting and sports.

SPECIFICATIONS

Chamber: 3¹/₂″ (accepts 3″ and 2³/₄″)
Capacity: 2 shells (3¹/₂″) or 3 shells (2³/₄″ or 3″)
Barrel length: 26″ or 28″ (24″ slug barrel also available)
Overall length: 47⁵/₈″ or 49⁵/₈″
Weight: 7 lbs. 3 oz. (26″); 7 lbs. 5 oz. (28″)
Choke: Screw-in; Skeet, IC, Modified, Imp. Mod., Full
Stock: Satin walnut (28″) with drop adjustment kit; high-gloss walnut (26″) with drop adjustment kit
Finish: Matte black finish on receiver, barrel and bolt (28″); blued finish on receiver and barrel (26″) with bolt mirror polished
Features: Montefeltro rotating bolt with dual locking lugs

SPECIFICATIONS BENELLI SHOTGUNS

	Gauge (Chamber)	Operation	Magazine Capacity*	Barrel Length	Overall Length	Weight (in lbs.)	Choke	Finish	Stock	Sights
Super Black Eagle (28)	12 (3¹/₂ in.)	semi-auto inertia recoil	3	28 in.	49⁵/₈ in.	7.3	S, IC, M, IM, F**	matte	satin walnut	bead
Super Black Eagle (26)	12 (3¹/₂ in.)	semi-auto inertia recoil	3	26 in.	47⁵/₈ in.	7.1	S, IC, M, IM, F**	matte or blued	satin or gloss walnut	bead
Super Black Eagle Custom Slug	12 (3¹/₂ in.)	semi-auto inertia recoil	3	24 in.	45¹/₂ in.	7.6	rifled barrel	blued	gloss walnut	scope mount base
Black Eagle Competition	12 (3 in.)	semi-auto inertia recoil	4	28 or 26 in.	49⁵/₈ in. or 47⁵/₈ in.	7.3/7	S, IC, M, IM, F**	blued	satin walnut	front. & mid rib bead
Montefeltro Super 90 (28/26)	12 (3 in.)	semi-auto inertia recoil	4	28 or 26in.	49¹/₂ or 47¹/₂in.	7.4/7	S, IC, M, IM, F**	blued	gloss walnut	bead
Montefeltro Super 90 (24/21)	12 (3 in.)	semi-auto inertia recoil	4	24 or 21 in.	45¹/₂ or 42¹/₂ in.	6.9/6.7	S, IC, M, IM, F**	blued	gloss walnut	bead
Montefeltro Left Hand	12 (3 in.)	semi-auto inertia recoil	4	28 or 26 in.	49¹/₂ or 47¹/₂ in.	7.4/7	S, IC, M, IM, F**	blued	gloss walnut	bead
Montefeltro Slug	12 (3 in.)	semi-auto inertia recoil	4	19³/₄ in.	41¹/₂ in.	7	Cylinder	blued	gloss walnut	rifle sights & scope mt. base
M1 Super 90 Field (28)	12 (3 in.)	semi-auto inertia recoil	3	28 in.	40¹/₂ in.	7.4	S, IC, M, IM, F**	matte	synthetic standard	bead
M1 Super 90 Field (26)	12 (3 in.)	semi-auto inertia recoil	3	26 in.	47¹/₂ in.	7.3	S, IC, M, IM, F**	matte	synthetic standard	bead
M1 Super 90 Field (24)	12 (3 in.)	semi-auto inertia recoil	3	24 in.	45¹/₂ in.	7.2	S, IC, M, IM, F**	matte	synthetic standard	bead
M1 Super 90 Field (21)	12 (3 in.)	semi-auto inertia recoil	3	21 in.	42¹/₂ in.	7	S, IC, M, IM, F**	matte	synthetic standard	bead
M1 Super 90 Slug	12 (3 in.)	semi-auto inertia recoil	7	19³/₄ in.	41in.	6.7	Cylinder	matte	synthetic standard	rifle or ghost ring
M1 Super 90 Defense	12 (3 in.)	semi-auto inertia recoil	7	19³/₄ in.	41in.	7.1	Cylinder	matte	synthetic pistol grip	rifle or ghost ring
M1 Super 90 Entry	12 (3 in.)	semi-auto inertia recoil	5	14 in.	35¹/₂ in.	6.7	Cylinder	matte	synthetic pistol grip or standard	rifle
M3 Super 90 Pistol Grip Stock	12 (3 in.)	semi-auto/pump inertia recoil	7	19³/₄ in.	41in.	7.9	Cylinder	matte	synthetic pistol grip	rifle or ghost ring
M3 Super 90 Folding Stock	12 (3 in.)	semi-auto/pump inertia recoil	7	19³/₄ in.	41in. 31in. (folded)	7.6	Cylinder	matte	folding tubular steel	rifle
M3 Super 90 Standard Stock	12 (3 in.)	semi-auto/pump inertia recoil	7	19³/₄ in.	41in.	7.2	Cylinder	matte	synthetic standard	rifle or ghost ring

*Magazine capacity given for 2³/₄ inch shells   **Skeet, Improved Cylinder, Modified, Improved Modified, Full

BENELLI SHOTGUNS

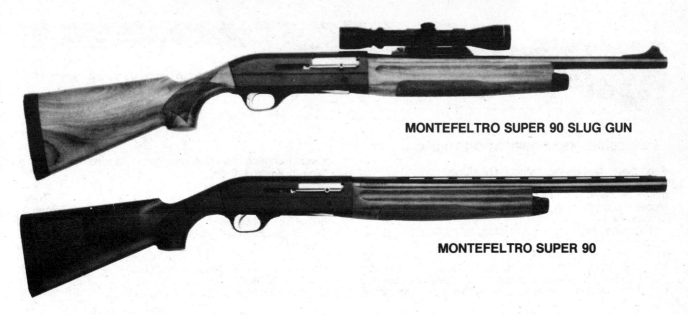

MONTEFELTRO SUPER 90 SLUG GUN

MONTEFELTRO SUPER 90

MONTEFELTRO SUPER 90
$799.00 ($849.00 Left Hand)

The Montefeltro Super 90 combines the fast firing characteristics of the M1 Super 90 with the look of a classic sporting shotgun. The heart of this Benelli remains the Montefeltro rotating bolt system, a rugged and simple inertia recoil design that functions with all types of 3″ and 2¾″ loads. A drop adjustment kit allows the stock to be custom-fitted to any shooter. See table for specifications.

Also available:
MONTEFELTRO SUPER 90 SLUG GUN w/24″ barrel, gloss finish stock, and scope mount. **Price:** **$799.00**
MONTEFELTRO SUPER 90 with 21″ or 24″ vent. rib and gloss finish stock. **Price:** **$799.00**

BLACK EAGLE COMPETITION

BLACK EAGLE COMPETITION
$1059.00

Benelli's new Black Eagle Competition shotgun combines the best technical features of the Montefeltro Super 90 and the classic design of the old SL 80 Series. It comes standard with a specially designed two-piece receiver of steel and aluminum, adding to its reliability and resistance to wear. A premium high-gloss walnut stock and gold-plated trigger are included, along with a Montefeltro rotating bolt. The Black Eagle Competition has no complex cylinders and pistons to maintain. Features include etched receiver, competition stock and mid-rib bead.

BERETTA SHOTGUNS

SERIES 682 COMPETITION TRAP O/U

SERIES 682 COMPETITION TRAP O/U

Available in Competition Mono, Over/Under or Mono Trap Over/Under Combo Set, the 12-gauge 682X trap guns boast hand-checkered walnut stock and forend with International or Monte Carlo left- or right-hand stock and choice of 3 stock dimensions.

Features: Adjustable gold-plated, single selective sliding trigger for precise length of pull fit; fluorescent competition front sight; step-up top rib; non-reflective black matte finish; low profile improved boxlock action; manual safety with barrel selector; 2³/₄″ chambers; auto ejector; competition recoil pad butt plate; light hand-engraving; stock with silver oval for initials;

silver inscription inlaid on trigger guard; handsome fitted case.
Weight: Approx. 8 lbs.

Barrel length/Choke	Prices
30″ Imp. Mod./Full (Silver)	$2495.00
30″ or 32″ Mobilchoke® (Black or Silver)	2570.00
Top Single 32″ or 34″ Mobilchoke®	2650.00
Pigeon (Silver)	2760.00
Unsingle	2650.00
Combo.: 30″ or 32″ Mobilchoke® (Top)	3400.00
30″ IM/F (Top)	3340.00
32″ Mobilchoke® (Mono)	3400.00

682 COMPETITION SKEET O/U
26″ SK/SK $2520.00
28″ SK/SK $2915.00
4-Barrel Set (28″) $5860.00

This skeet gun sports hand-checkered premium walnut stock, forged and hardened receiver, manual safety with trigger selector, auto ejector, stock with silver oval for initials, silver inlaid on trigger guard. Price includes fitted case.
Gauges: 12, 20, 28, .410
Action: Low profile hard chrome-plated boxlock

Trigger: Single adjustable sliding trigger
Barrels: 26″ or 28″ rust blued barrels with 2³/₄″ chambers
Stock dimensions: Length of pull 14³/₈″; drop at comb 1 ¹/₂″; drop at heel 2¹/₃″
Sights: Fluorescent front and metal middle bead
Weight: Approx. 8 lbs.

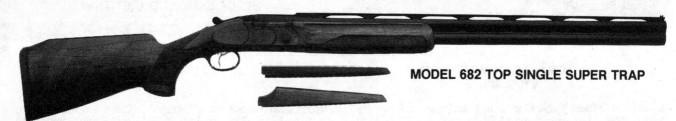

MODEL 682 TOP SINGLE SUPER TRAP

MODEL 682 SUPER TRAP

Beretta's 12 gauge over/under shotgun features a revolutionary adjustable stock. Comb is adjustable with interchangeable comb height adjustments. Length of pull is also adjustable with interchangeable butt pad spacers. Also features ported barrels and tapered step rib, satin-finished receiver and adjustable trigger.

Barrel lengths: 30″, 32″, 34″; chamber 2³/₄″
Chokes: Choice of Mobilchoke®, IM/F
Prices:
Model 682 Super Trap O/U (Mobilchoke®) $2885.00
Model 682 Top Single Super Trap (32″ barrel) . . 3060.00
Model 682 Top Combo Super Trap 3790.00
  Same as above w/o Mobilchoke® 3865.00

BERETTA SHOTGUNS

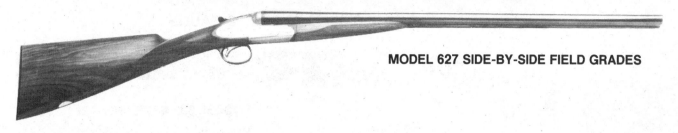

MODEL 627 SIDE-BY-SIDE FIELD GRADES

These good-looking field models feature low profile solid box-lock design, hand-fitted stocks and forends of handsome European walnut with deep diamond hand-checkering, tang-mounted safety/barrel selectors, single-selective trigger and metal bead sight. 12 gauge barrels are chambered 3″. **Model 627EL** boasts scoll-engraved side plates. **Model 627EELL** features game-scene engraving.

Model 627EL Field $3270.00
12 ga., 26″ Mobilchoke®
12 ga., 28″ Mobilchoke®

Model 627EELL $5405.00
12 ga., 28″ Mobilchoke®
12 ga., 26″ Mobilchoke®

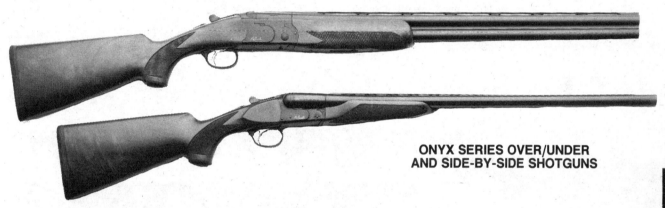

ONYX SERIES OVER/UNDER AND SIDE-BY-SIDE SHOTGUNS

The **Model 626 Onyx** has a full-figured American walnut stock, lustrous black semi-matte finish on the barrels and receiver, and front and center sighting beads on a vent rib.

SPECIFICATIONS
Gauges: 12, 20
Chambers: 3″ or 3½″

Barrel lengths: 26″ and 28″
Chokes: Mobilchoke® screw-in system
Weight: 6 lbs. 10 oz. (12 ga.); 6 lbs. (20 ga.)
Stock: American walnut with recoil pad (English stock available)
Features: Automatic ejectors; matte black finish on barrels and receiver to reduce glare
Price: $1355.00 to $1870.00

MODEL ASE 90

Features drop-out trigger group assembly for ease in cleaning, inspection, or in-the-field replacement. Also has wide ventilating top and side rib, hard-chromed bores, and a strong competition-style receiver in coin-silver finish and gold inlay with P. Beretta initials.
Gauge: 12
Barrel lengths: 28″ (Pigeon, Skeet, Sporting Clays); 30″ (Trap and Sporting Clays)

Chokes: IM/F Trap or MCT (Trap); MC4 (Sporting Clays); SK/SK (Skeet); IM/F (Pigeon)
Prices:
Model ASE 90 (Pigeon, Trap, Skeet) **$8070.00**
Model ASE 90 (Sporting Clays) **8140.00**

BERETTA SHOTGUNS

SPORTING CLAY SHOTGUNS 12 AND 20 GAUGE

MODEL 682 SPORTING

MODELS 682/686/687 SPORTING CLAYS

This competition-style shotgun for sporting clays features 28″ or 30″ barrels with four flush-mounted screw-in choke tubes (Full, Modified, Improved Cylinder and Skeet), plus hand-checkered stock and forend of fine walnut, 2³/₄″ chambers and adjustable trigger. **Super Sport** model features tapered rib, schnable forend. **Model 686 Onyx Sporting** has classic black finish on receiver to reduce glare.

Prices:

682 Sporting	$2605.00
682 Super Sport	2760.00
682 Sporting Combo	3470.00
686 Sporting	1940.00
686 Onyx Sporting	1940.00
686 Sporting Combo	2605.00
687 Sporting	2560.00
687 Sporting Combo	3410.00
687EELL Sporting	4705.00
Special English Court (Model 686)	2015.00
Model 687	2630.00

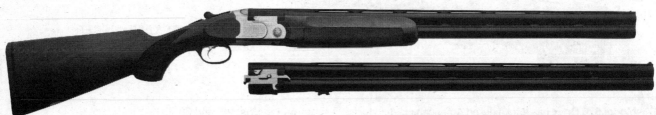

MODEL 686 SPORTING COMBO

MODELS 686/687 SPORTING COMBO

Beretta's 12 gauge over/under features interchangeable 28″ and 30″ barrels for versatility in competition at different courses with short and long passing shots. **Chamber:** 3″. **Mobilchoke®** **screw-in tube system.**

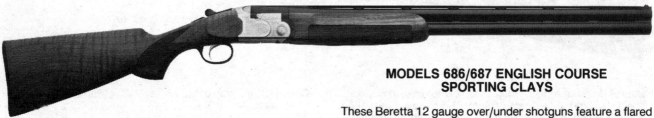

MODEL 686 ENGLISH COURSE SPORTING CLAY

MODELS 686/687 ENGLISH COURSE SPORTING CLAYS

These Beretta 12 gauge over/under shotguns feature a flared top rib that widens from 10 to 12.5mm at the muzzle and has a 2.5mm groove cut into the rib. **Model 686** includes scroll engraving. **Barrel length:** 28″. **Chamber:** 2³/₄″. **Choke:** Mobil-choke® screw-in choke tube system.

BERETTA SHOTGUNS

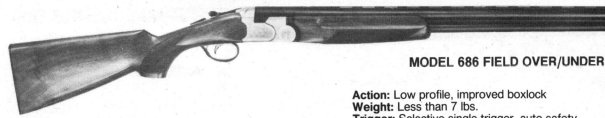

MODEL 686 FIELD OVER/UNDER

Gauge: 28
Barrels/chokes: 26″ and 28″ with Mobilchoke® screw-in choke tubes

Action: Low profile, improved boxlock
Weight: Less than 7 lbs.
Trigger: Selective single trigger, auto safety
Extractors: Auto ejectors
Stock: Choice walnut, hand-checkered and hand-finished with a tough gloss finish
Price: $1355.00

MODEL 686E

This new 12 or 20 gauge over/under field gun features scroll engraving on sideplates, European walnut stock and forend, hard-chromed bores and Mobilchoke® system of interchangeable choke tubes.
Price: $2200.00

Also available:
Model 686 Silver with highly polished silver receiver, traditional blued finish barrels, and rubber recoil pad, plus Mobilchoke®
Price: $1385.00

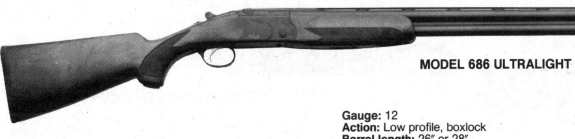

MODEL 686 ULTRALIGHT

This new 12 gauge over/under field gun features the payload of a 12-gauge gun in a 20-gauge weight (approx. 5 lbs. 13 oz.). Chambered for 2³/₄″, the Ultralight has a matte black finish on its receiver with a gold inlay of the P. Beretta signature.

Gauge: 12
Action: Low profile, boxlock
Barrel length: 26″ or 28″
Trigger: Single, selective gold trigger
Safety: Automatic
Stock: Walnut, hand-checkered
Price: $1525.00

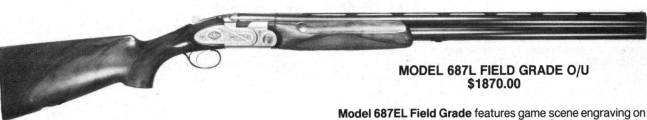

MODEL 687L FIELD GRADE O/U
$1870.00

The **687L** features Mobilchoke® in 12 and 20 gauge; strong boxlock action handsomely tooled with floral hand-engraved decorative side plates, finest quality walnut stock accented with silver monogram plate, selective auto ejectors and fitted case.

Model 687EL Field Grade features game scene engraving on receiver with gold highlights. Available in 12, 20 gauge (28 ga. and .410 in small frame).
Barrels/chokes: 26″ and 28″ with Mobilchoke®
Action: Low-profile improved boxlock
Weight: 7 lbs. 2 oz.
Trigger: Single selective with manual safety
Extractors: Auto ejectors

BERETTA SHOTGUNS

MODEL 1201F

This All-Weather semiautomatic shotgun features an adjustable space-age technopolymer stock and forend with recoil pad. Lightweight, it sports a unique weather-resistant matte black finish to reduce glare, resist corrosion and aid in heat dispersion; short recoil action for light and heavy loads. **Gauge:** 12. **Chamber:** 3″. **Barrel lengths:** 24″, 26″ and 28″. **Choke:** Mobilchoke® (Full, Modified). **Weight:** 7.4 lbs.
Price: $625.00

Also available:
Model 1200 Riot (Law Enforcement) with 20″ barrel (2³/₄″ or 3″ shells) and Improved Cylinder choke (7-round capacity). $660.00

MODEL 687EELL (not shown)
$4625.00

In 12, 20 or 28 ga., this model features the Modilchoke® choke system, a special premium walnut, custom-fitted stock and exquisitely engraved sideplate with game-scene motifs.
Also available:
Model 687EELL Combo (20 and 28 ga.) $5130.00
Model 687EL (12, 20, 28, .410; 26″ or 28″ bbl.) . . 3180.00
Model 687EL Small Frame 3320.00

PREMIUM GRADE SHOTGUN SERIES

These hand-crafted over/under and side-by-side shotguns feature custom engraved or game scenes, casehardened, gold-inlay, scroll or floral patterns, all available on receivers. Sidelock action. Stocks are of select European walnut, hand-finished and hand-checkered. Also available in Competition Skeet, Trap, Sporting Clays and Custom Sidelock Side-by-Side models. Barrels are constructed of Boehler high-nickel antinit steel. **Gauges:** 12, 20, 28, .410. **Chamber:** 2¹/₂″ or 3″.

Prices:
SO5 Competition (Sporting Clays, Skeet,
  Trap) $12,300.00
SO6 O/U Competition (Sporting Clays, Skeet,
  Trap) 16,600.00
SO6 EELL Custom Sidelock (12 gauge only) . . . 27,300.00
SO9 Custom Sidelock (12, 20, 28, .410 ga.) . . . 29,250.00
452 Custom Sidelock Side/Side (12 ga.) 22,470.00
452 EELL Custom Sidelock Side/Side
  (12 ga.) 30,680.00
Extra barrels and leather cases available: each . . 4,000.00

BERETTA SHOTGUNS

MODEL 390 FIELD

This new gas-operated semiautomatic field gun has an innovative gas system that handles a variety of loads. A self-regulating valve automatically adjusts gas pressure to handle anything from 2½" target loads to heavy 3" magnums. Matte finish models for turkey/waterfowl are available.

Gauge: 12
Barrel lengths: 24", 26", 28", 30"
Weight: 7 lbs.
Sights: Ventilated rib with front bead
Action: Locked breech, gas-operated
Safety: Crossbolt (reversible)
Price: $775.00

MODEL 303 YOUTH GUN

MODEL 303 SEMIAUTOMATIC

This unique gas-operated autoloader features Mobilchoke® screw-in choke tubes and a magazine cut-off that allows shooters to hand-feed a lighter or heavier load into the breech without emptying the magazine. Disassembly takes one minute.

MODEL 303 GENERAL SPECIFICATIONS

Gauge: 12 or 20
Barrel lengths: 22", 24", 26", 28", 30", 32"
Weight: 7 lbs. (12 gauge) and 6 lbs. (20 gauge)
Safety: Crossbolt
Action: Locked breech, gas-operated
Sights: Vent rib with front metal bead
Length of pull: 14⅞"
Capacity: Plugged to 2 rounds

303 YOUTH SPECIFICATIONS
Gauge: 20 (2¾" or 3" chamber)
Barrel length: 24"
Chokes: Mobilchoke® screw-in chokes
Length of pull: 13½"

MODEL 303 PRICES:
Upland	$ 735.00
Field (English)	735.00
Youth	735.00
Skeet	735.00
Trap	735.00
With Mobilchoke® F, IM, M	775.00
Sporting Clays	835.00
Super Skeet	1160.00
Super Trap	1210.00

MODEL 303 COMPETITION TRAP (not shown)
$685.00   ($725.00 w/Mobilchoke®)

The Beretta A303 Competition guns are versions of the proven A303 semiautomatic. Their gas-operated systems lessen recoil; other features include wide floating vent rib with fluorescent front and mid-rib bead sights. The A303 also comes with hand-checkered stock and forend of select European walnut, plus gold-plated trigger.

Gauge: 12
Barrel lengths: 26" and 28" (Skeet); 30" and 32" (Trap); 28" (Sporting)
Chamber: 2¾"
Sight: Ventilated rib with fluorescent front bead, metal middle bead
Action: Semiautomatic, locked breech, gas-operated
Safety: Crossbolt
Ejector: Auto
Trigger: Gold-plated
Stock: Select walnut
Weight: 8 lbs.
Buttplate: Special trap recoil pad

BERNARDELLI SHOTGUNS

Bernardelli shotguns are the creation of the Italian firm of Vincenzo Bernardelli, known for its fine quality firearms and commitment to excellence for more than a century. Most of the long arms featured below can be built with a variety of options, customized for the discriminating sportsman. With the exceptions indicated for each gun respectively, options include choice of barrel lengths and chokes; pistol or straight English grip stock; single selective or non-selective trigger; long tang trigger guard; checkered butt; beavertail forend; hand-cut rib; automatic safety; custom stock dimensions; standard or English recoil pad; extra set of barrels; choice of luggage gun case.

MODEL 112 EM
$1798.00 (Single Trigger)

Features ejectors, English stock and splinter forend. **Barrel length:** 26³/₄″ (3″ chamber). **Choke:** Improved Cylinder and Improved Modified. **Safety:** Manual. **Weight:** 6¹/₂ lbs.
Price (with ejector and multi-choke): $1971.00

BRESCIA SIDE-BY-SIDE
$2482.00

Available in 12, 16, or 20 gauge, the Brescia side-by-side features Greener or Purdey locks, small engravings, hardened marbled mounting, chrome-lined barrels, finely grained stock. Prices on request.

HEMINGWAY DELUXE
SIDE-BY-SIDE LIGHTWEIGHT

An elegant side-by-side suitable for upland bird hunting, the Hemingway features 25¹/₂-inch barrels without monobloc, choked Skeet 1/Skeet 2, automatic ejectors, special rib with white bead front sight, hinged front trigger, engraved woodcock hunting scenes, long-type trigger guard and splinter forend, hand-checkered walnut woods, metal shield for initials. Special steel frame and barrels. Available in 12, 20 and 28 gauge. **Weight:** 6¹/₄ lbs.
Prices:

W/Ejectors.	$2172.00
W/Single trigger.	2253.00
Deluxe w/ejectors & sideplates.	2482.00
Deluxe w/single trigger	2563.00

BERNARDELLI SHOTGUNS

HOLLAND & HOLLAND TYPE SIDELOCK SIDE-BY-SIDE

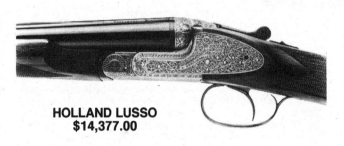

HOLLAND LUSSO
$14,377.00

HOLLAND V.B. LISCIO
$10,757.00

These 12-gauge Holland & Holland style sidelock side-by-sides feature sidelocks with double safety levers, reinforced breech, three round Purdey locks, automatic ejectors, right trigger folding, striker retaining plates, best-quality walnut stock and finely chiselled high-grade engravings. The eight shotguns in this series differ only in the amount and intricacy of engravings. Prices range from **$10,757.00** to **$57,922.00** (with gold engravings).

SIDE-BY-SIDE ROMA SERIES WITH SIDEPLATES

ROMA 6E

ROMA 6E (With Ejectors)
$2482.00

Available in 12, 16, 20 and 28 gauge, the Roma Series is Bernardelli's premier boxlock and most popular model. These side-by-side shotguns feature Anson & Deeley action with Purdey-style locks, sideplated and coin-finished receivers with elaborate scroll engravings covering 100% of the action, precision-bored barrels made of superior chromium steel, single or double triggers (articulated front trigger), English stocks of oiled walnut and forends with fine, hand-cut checkering. Prices range from **$2000.00** to **$2500.00**.

SHOTGUNS

BROWNING AUTOMATIC SHOTGUNS

AUTO-5 STALKER

AUTO-5

The Browning Auto-5 Shotgun is offered in an unusually wide variety of models and specifications. The Browning 12-gauge 3-inch Magnum accepts up to and including the 3-inch, 1^7/$_8$ ounce, 12-gauge Magnum load, which contains only ^{1}/$_8$ ounce of shot less than the maximum 3^1/$_2$-inch 10-gauge load. The 2^3/$_4$-inch Magnums and 2^3/$_4$-inch high velocity shells may be used with equal pattern efficiency. Standard features include a special shock absorber and a hunting-style recoil pad. The Auto-5 is also available with the Invector screw-in choke system.

Browning also offers the 20 gauge in a 3-inch Magnum model. This powerful, light heavyweight offers maximum versatility to 20-gauge advocates. It handles the 20-gauge, 2^3/$_4$-inch high velocity and Magnums, but it literally thrives on the 3-inch, 1^1/$_4$-ounce load which delivers real 12-gauge performance in a 20-gauge package.

The 12-gauge Auto-5, chambered for regular 2^3/$_4$-inch shells, handles all 12-gauge, 2^3/$_4$-inch shells, from the very lightest 1 ounce field load to the heavy 1^1/$_2$-ounce Magnums. The Browning 20-gauge Auto-5 is lightweight and a top performer for the upland hunter. Yet, with 2^3/$_4$-inch high velocity or 2^3/$_4$-inch Magnums, it does a fine job in the duck blind. 24-inch barrels are available as an accessory.

Prices:
HUNTING MODELS

Light 12, Sweet 16 and Light 20 gauge, Invector . .	**$719.95**
Light 12 Buck Special	**724.95**
3″ Magnum 12 and Magnum 20 gauge, Invector . . .	**742.95**
3″ Magnum 12 ga., Buck Special.	**747.95**
Stalker Light 12, vent rib, Invector	**719.95**
In Magnum 12	**742.95**

BT-99
SINGLE SHOT TRAP SPECIAL

SPECIFICATIONS
Receiver: Machined steel, tastefully hand-engraved and richly blued
Barrel: Choice of 32″ or 34″ lengths; Invector-Plus choke tube system; back-bored barrel; chambered for 12 gauge, 2^3/$_4$″ shells only; choke tubes supplied (Full, Imp. Mod. and Mod.)
Trigger: Gold-plated, crisp, positive, pull approximately 3^1/$_2$ lbs.
Stock and forearm: Select French walnut, hand-rubbed finish, sharp 20-line hand-checkering; Monte Carlo or conventional stock available; full pistol grip; length of pull 14^3/$_8$″; drop at comb 1^3/$_8$″; drop at heel 2″; full beavertail forearm

Safety: No manual safety, a feature preferred by trap shooters
Sights: Ivory front and center sight beads
Rib: High post, ventilated, full floating, matted, ^{11}/$_{32}$″ wide
Recoil pad: Deluxe, contoured trap style; recoil reducer system
Weight: 8 lbs. with 32″ barrel; 8 lbs. 3 oz. with 34″ barrel
Automatic ejection: Fired shell ejected automatically on opening action, unfired shell elevated from chamber for convenient removal
Price:
Grade I Competition, Invector-Plus (32″/ 34″ bbl.) **$1200.00**

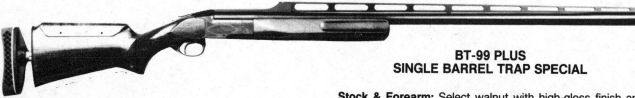

BT-99 PLUS
SINGLE BARREL TRAP SPECIAL

SPECIFICATIONS
Gauge: 12 (2^3/$_4$″ shells only)
Barrel length: 34″ (.745 over bore; barrel porting optional)
Weight: 8 lbs. 12 oz.
Choke: Invector Plus system (Invector Plus Full, Imp. Mod., and Modified tubes and wrench included)
Rib: High post, ventilated, tapered, target rib; matted sight plane

Stock & Forearm: Select walnut with high-gloss finish and cut checkering; Monte Carlo stock; modified beavertail forearm; stock fully adjustable for length of pull (14-14^1/$_2$″), drop at comb (2^1/$_2$-2″) and drop at Monte Carlo (2^3/$_8$-1^1/$_8$″)
Prices:

Model BT-99 Plus	**$1780.00**
Without ported barrels	**1765.00**
Also available:	
Model BT-99 Micro with 30″ barrel	**1780.00**
Without ported barrel	**1765.00**

BROWNING SHOTGUNS

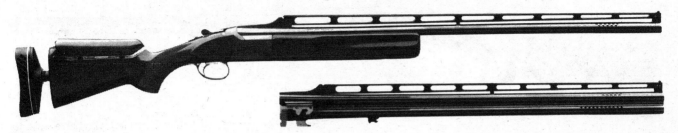

CITORI PLUS COMBO TRAP O/U

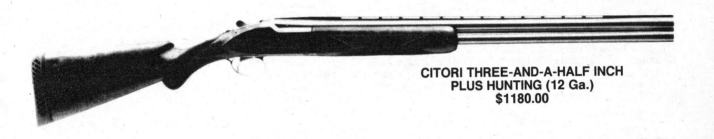

**CITORI THREE-AND-A-HALF INCH
PLUS HUNTING (12 Ga.)
$1180.00**

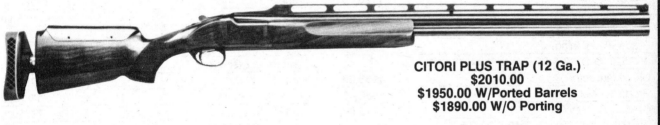

**CITORI PLUS TRAP (12 Ga.)
$2010.00
$1950.00 W/Ported Barrels
$1890.00 W/O Porting**

CITORI PLUS COMBO TRAP O/U

Browning's new Citori Plus Combo is two trap guns in one—a single barrel trap gun for singles and an over/under trap gun for doubles. It features Browning's recoil reducer system, fully adjustable stock dimension, back-bored barrels, optional barrel porting, ventilated side ribs, and the Invector-Plus choke tube system.

SPECIFICATIONS
Gauge: 12; 2³/₄″ chamber
Barrel lengths: 30″ and 32″
Chokes: Invector-Plus
Overall length: 47¹/₄″ (30″ barrel); 49¹/₄″ (32″ barrel)

Weight: 9 lbs. 5 oz. (30″ barrel); 9 lbs. 7 oz. (32″ barrel)
Stock: Monte Carlo style comb w/recoil reducer system, fully adjustable for drop, trap-style recoil pad, cast and length of pull; modified beavertail forearm; stock and forearm are select walnut with high-gloss finish and cut-checkering
Features: Back-bored barrel; blued steel receiver with engraved rosette scroll design; automatic ejectors; barrel selector in top tang safety; gold-colored trigger; manual top tang safety
Price:
W/fitted luggage case for gun and extra barrel . . . **$3,275.00**

(See following page for Citori prices and specifications.)

BROWNING SHOTGUNS

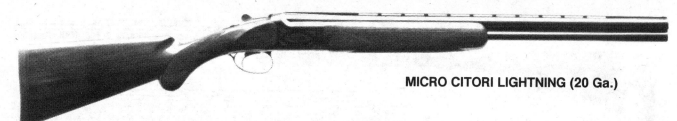

MICRO CITORI LIGHTNING (20 Ga.)

FIELD GRADE

Gauges: 12, 20, 28 and .410 gauge

Barrels: 24″, 26″, 28″, or 30″ in 12 gauge; 28″ in 16 gauge; 24″, 26″, or 28″ in 20 gauge; ventilated rib with matted sighting plane; medium raised German nickel-silver sight bead; 26″ or 28″ in 28 gauge; 26″ or 28″ in .410 gauge

Overall length: All gauges 41″ with 24″ barrels; 43″ with 26″ barrels; 45″ with 28″ barrels; 47″ with 30″ barrels

Chokes: Mod.-Full, Invector in 30″ barrels; choice of Invector, Mod.-Full or Imp. Cyl.-Mod. in 28″ and 26″ barrels

Trigger: Single selective; gold-plated, fast and crisp

Chamber: All 20-gauge Field models and all 12-gauge Field models accept all 3″ Magnum loads as well as 2³/₄″ loads; 16 and 28-gauge accepts 2³/₄″ loads; .410-gauge accepts 2¹/₂″, 3″, or 3″ Mag. loads

Safety: Manual thumb safety; combined with barrel selector mechanism

Automatic ejectors: Fired shells thrown out of gun; unfired shells are elevated for easy removal

Approximate Weight:

	12 gauge	16 gauge	20 gauge
24″ barrels	6 lbs. 9 oz.		5 lbs. 12 oz.
26″ barrels	7 lbs. 9 oz.		6 lbs. 11 oz.
28″ barrels	7 lbs. 11 oz.	7 lbs.	6 lbs. 13 oz.
30″ barrels	7 lbs. 13 oz		

Stock and forearm: Dense walnut; skillfully checkered; full pistol grip; hunting Beavertail forearm; field-type recoil pad installed on 12 gauge models.

	12 gauge	20 gauge
Length of pull	14¹/₄″	14¹/₄″
Drop at comb	1⁵/₈″	1¹/₂″
Drop at heel	2¹/₂″	2³/₈″

CITORI HUNTING, LIGHTNING, SUPERLIGHT & UPLAND SPECIAL MODELS

HUNTING & LIGHTNING 28 GA., .410 BORE	PRICES
Grade I Hunting	$1100.00
Grade I Lightning	1145.00
Grade III Lightning	1830.00
Grade VI Lightning	2560.00
SUPERLIGHT 12 & 20 GA. (UPLAND SPECIAL)	
Grade I Invector	1155.00
Grade III Invector	1680.00
Grade VI Invector	2415.00
HUNTING & LIGHTNING 12 & 20 GA.	
Grade I Invector	1100.00
Grade I Lightning Invector	1140.00
Grade 1 Micro Model, 20 ga.	1170.00
Gran Lightning Invector 12 & 20 ga.	1560.00
Grade III Invector	1645.00
Grade III Lightning Invector	1675.00
Grade VI Invector	2360.00
Grade VI Lightning Invector	2400.00

SUPERLIGHT 28 GAUGE & .410 BORE	PRICES
Grade I	$1160.00
Grade III	1845.00
Grade VI	2575.00
TRAP MODELS (High Post Target Rib)	
Standard 12 Gauge	
Grade I Invector*	1250.00
Grade III Invector*	1785.00
Grade VI Invector*	2520.00
SKEET MODELS (High Post Target Rib)	
Standard 12 and 20 Gauge	
Grade I Invector*	1250.00
Grade III Invector*	1785.00
Grade VI Invector*	2520.00
Standard 28 Gauge and .410 Bore	
Grade I	1250.00
Grade III	1785.00
Grade VI	2520.00

4-BARREL SKEET SET

12 gauge with one removable forearm and four sets of barrels, 12, 20, 28 and .410 gauges, high post target rib.
(Furnished with fitted luggage case for gun and extra barrels)

Grade 1	$4160.00
Grade III	4780.00
Grade VI	5355.00

3-BARREL SKEET SET

20 gauge with one removable forearm and three sets of barrels, 20, 28 and .410 bore.

Grade 1	$2890.00
Grade III	3360.00
Grade VI	4125.00

* Invector-Plus Ported Barrel option: **$65 add'l** (Grade I); **$35 add'l** (Grades III & VI)

BROWNING SHOTGUNS

BPS PUMP SHOTGUNS

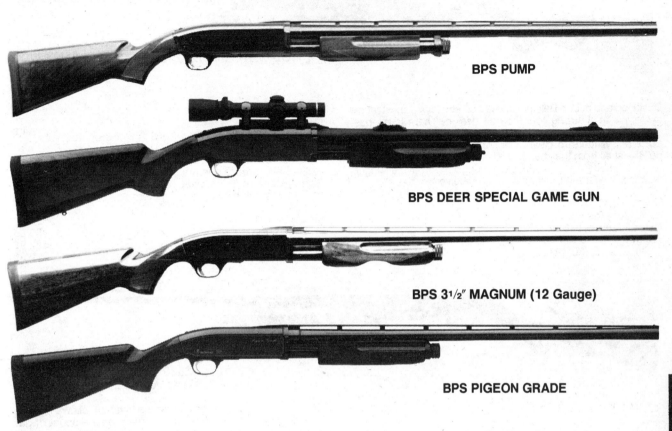

BPS PUMP

BPS DEER SPECIAL GAME GUN

BPS 3½″ MAGNUM (12 Gauge)

BPS PIGEON GRADE

Gauges: 10, 12 and 20

Barrels: Choice of 22″, 26″, 28″, 30″ or 32″ lengths with high-post ventilated rib; Hunting model has German nickel sight bead

Action: Pump action with double-action bars; bottom loading and ejection; serrated slide release located at rear of trigger guard

Choke: Invector only

Trigger: Crisp and positive; let-off at 4½ lbs.

Chamber: 3″ chamber in Hunting models accepts all 2¾″, 2¾″ Magnum and 3″ Magnum shells; target models 2¾″ shells only

Safety: Convenient knurled-thumb, top-receiver safety; slide forward to shoot

Approximate weight: 7 lbs. 12 oz. with 28″ barrel

Overall length: 42¾″ with 22″ barrel; 46¾″ with 26″ barrel; 48¾″ with 28″ barrel; 50¾″ with 30″ barrel

Stock and forearm: Select walnut, weather-resistant finish, sharp 18-line checkering; full pistol grip; semi-beavertail forearm with finger grooves; length of pull 14¼″; drop at comb 1½″; drop at heel 2½″

Prices*:

Invector Hunting, 12 and 20 ga., V.R.	**$442.95**
Invector Hunting, 10 ga.	584.95
Invector PLUS Hunting & Stalker	584.95
Upland Special, 22″ barrel with Invector, 12 and 20 ga., V.R.	442.95
Invector Stalker, 12 ga. only	442.95
Buck Special, 12 ga. only	448.95
Buck Special, 10 ga. & 3½″ 12 ga.	589.95
BPS Youth & Ladies, 20 ga. only	442.95
BPS 3½″ Magnum	584.95
Pigeon Grade, 12 ga. only	599.95
Deer Special Game Gun	489.95
Turkey Special Game Gun	469.95

* Incl. engraved receiver on 12 and 20 ga. only

BROWNING SHOTGUNS

MODEL A-500R 12 GAUGE SEMIAUTOMATIC

Designed and built in Belgium, the A-500 employs a short recoil system with a strong four-lug bolt design. There is no gas system to collect powder residues or grime, and no pistons, ports or cylinders to clean. Only one extractor is needed to pull the shell from the chamber. The stock has no drilled holes to accommodate action springs, making it that much stronger (especially where it bolts against the receiver).

SPECIFICATIONS
Barrel lengths: 26″, 28″ and 30″
Overall lengths: 45½″, 47½″ and 49½″
Weight: 7 lbs. 3 oz. (26″ barrel); 7 lbs. 5 oz. (28″ barrel) and 7 lbs. 7 oz. (30″ barrel)

Chamber: 3″
Choke: Invector
Stock dimensions: length of pull 14¼″; drop at comb 1½″; drop at heel 2½″
Safety: cross bolt, right or left hand
Action: short recoil operated with four lug rotary bolt
Barrel/receiver finish: deep high polish blued finish; receiver lightly engraved with scroll pattern
Prices:
Model A-500 . . . . $559.95
   Extra barrels 199.95
Buck Special 592.95
   Extra Buck Special barrel 232.95

MODEL A-500G GAS-OPERATED SHOTGUN
$639.95
$672.95 (Buck Special)

Browning's patented gas metering system allows reliable shooting with all loads and utilizes the proper amount of gas energy needed to operate the action. A unique gas regulation valve uses only enough gas to operate the action consistently.

SPECIFICATIONS

Gauge	Model	Chamber	Barrel Length	Overall Length	Average Weight	Chokes Available[1]
12	Hunting	3″	30″	51½″	8 lbs. 2 oz.	Invector
12	Hunting	3″	28″	49½″	8 lbs.	Invector
12	Hunting	3″	26″	47½″	7 lbs. 14 oz.	Invector
12	Buck Special	3″	24″	45½″	7 lbs. 12 oz.	Slug/buckshot

[1]All models are fitted with standard invector Choke Tube System: Full Choke installed; Modified, Improved Cylinder and wrench included. Improved Modified, Skeet and Cylinder choke tubes are available as accessories.

Additional features:
Safety: Crossbolt, right or left hand
Capacity: 4 rounds (2¾″) or 3 rounds (3″) with plug removed (with plug installed, 2 round in magazine, one in chamber)
Recoil pad: Ventilated style, standard
Stock and forearm: Select walnut, full pistol grip stock with gloss finish and cut checkering

Barrel and receiver finish: Deep, high polish blued finish; gold accents on receiver
Trigger: gold colored
Stock dimensions: Length of pull 14⅜″; drop at comb 1½″; drop at heel 2″
Action: Gas operated with 4-lug rotary bolt

BROWNING SHOTGUNS

SPORTING CLAYS MODELS

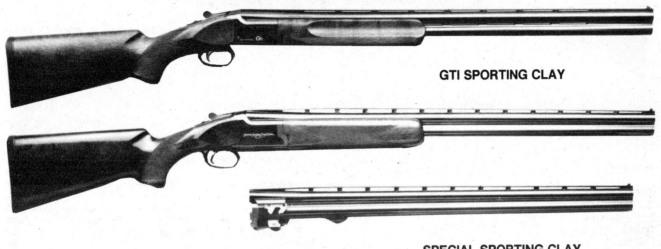

GTI SPORTING CLAY

SPECIAL SPORTING CLAY

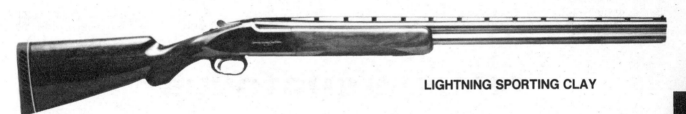

LIGHTNING SPORTING CLAY

Browning continues its line of Sporting Clays shotguns, including GTI, Special Sporting (with high post vent ribs), and Lightning Sporting models. All GTI models feature semi-pistol grips with slightly grooved semi-beavertail forearms and satin finish. The Special Sporting guns have full pistol grip stocks with palm swells, classic forearms, and high-gloss wood finish. All Lightning Sporting models feature rounded pistol grips with classic forearms and high-gloss wood finish.

Gauge: 12
Barrel lengths: 28″ & 30″ (GTI); 28″, 30″ & 32″ (Special Sporting); 30″ (Lightning)
Overall lengths: 45″ & 47″ (GTI); 45″, 47″ & 49″ (Special Sporting); 47″ (Lightning Sporting)

Weight: 8 lbs. & 8 lbs. 2 oz. (GTI); 8 lbs. 1 oz., 8 lbs. 3 oz. & 8 lbs. 5 oz. (Special Sporting); 8 lbs. 10 oz. (Lightning Sporting)
Chokes: Invector (GTI); IC/M (Special Sporting and Lightning Sporting)

Prices:
GTI, Invector PLUS w/ported barrels **$1350.00**
Grade I Special Sporting, Invector PLUS,
    ported barrels **1330.00**
Grade I Lightning Sporting, Invector PLUS,
    high rib, ported barrels **1330.00**
    Same as above w/low rib & ported barrel **1270.00**

BROWNING SHOTGUNS

**MODEL 42/12 LIMITED EDITION
PUMP SHOTGUN**

MODEL 42 GRADE V

After more than 75 years, the ageless Winchester Model 12, one of the most popular shotguns ever produced (over 2 million), is offered as part of Browning's Limited Edition Model 42/12 Program. It is available in 28 gauge and .410 bore.

SPECIFICATIONS
Gauges: 28 and .410
Barrel length: 26″
Overall length: 46″
Chamber: 3″
Choke: Full
Weight: 6 lbs. 4 oz.
Length of pull: 14″
Drop at heel: 2¹/₂″
Drop at comb: 1¹/₂″

Trigger: Approx. 4¹/₂ lbs. trigger pull
Capacity: 5 3-inch loads in magazine (w/plug removed), one in chamber; 2 loads in magazine (w/plug installed), one in chamber
Receiver: Grade I: deeply blued. Grade V: engraved with gold game scenes
Stock and forearm: Grade I: select walnut w/semi-gloss finish and cut checkering. Grade V: select high grade walnut with high gloss finish (both grades include steel grip cap)
Prices:
Grade I 28 ga. . . . . $ 771.95
Grade I .410 bore. (**Model 42**) 799.95
Grade V 28 ga. 1246.00
Grade V .410 bore (**Model 42**) 1360.00

CHAPUIS SHOTGUNS

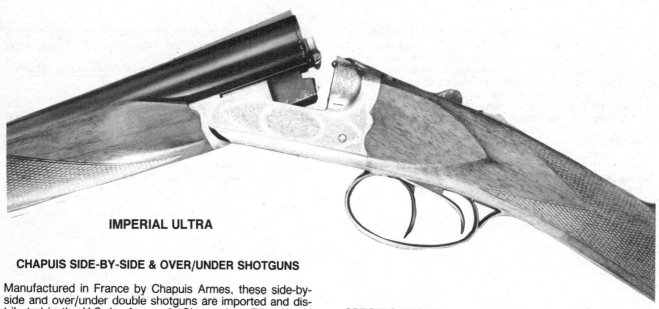

IMPERIAL ULTRA

CHAPUIS SIDE-BY-SIDE & OVER/UNDER SHOTGUNS

Manufactured in France by Chapuis Armes, these side-by-side and over/under double shotguns are imported and distributed in the U.S. by Armes de Chasse (see Directory of Manufacturers & Distributors for details). **Features:** These shotguns are boxlocks with long trigger guards (on most models), coin metal finish, automatic ejectors or extractors, barrels with double hooks, Blitz system boxlock actions, and choice of solid, ventilated or ultra light rib; plus deluxe French walnut stock, hand-cut checkering and oil finish.

SPECIFICATIONS
Gauges: 12, 16 and 20
Barrel lengths: 22″, 23.6″, 26.8″, 27.6″ & 31.5″
Weight: 5 to 8 lbs. (depending on gauge)
Stock: French walnut with pistol or English grips
Price:
Side-by-Side or **Over/Under** . . . . $4000.00–$5000.00

CHURCHILL SHOTGUNS

Durable gloss finish highlights the walnut pistol grip and finger-grooved forend of this new Churchill shotgun. Other features include hard chrome-lined bores, vent rib with matte finish and brass bead sight, cut-checkered stock and forend.

MONARCH OVER/UNDER
$519.95

SPECIFICATIONS
Gauges: 12 and 20; 3″ chamber
Chokes: IC/M and M/Full
Barrel lengths: 26″ and 28″
Weight: 6 lbs. 15 oz.
Additional features: Black rubber ventilated recoil pad; single selective trigger; manual top tang safety; shell extractor; polished blue luster on barrel, receiver and trigger

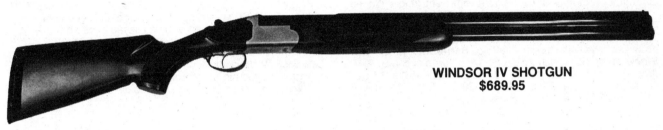

WINDSOR IV SHOTGUN
$689.95

Walnut stock with pistol grip features cut-checkering and black rubber ventilated recoil pad. Matching forend has finger grooves. Hard chrome-lined bores are suitable for steel shot. Vent rib has matte finish and brass bead sight. Gold trigger compliments blue luster finish. Antique silver receiver has full cover scroll engraving.

SPECIFICATIONS
Gauges: 12 and 20; 3″ chamber
Chokes: ICT
Barrel lengths: 26″ and 28″
Weight: 6 lbs. 15 oz.
Additional features: Automatic selective ejectors; single selective trigger

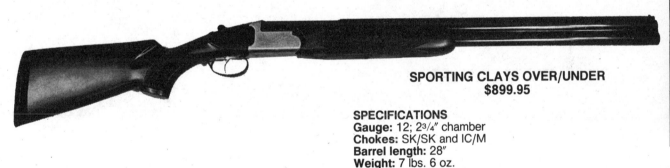

SPORTING CLAYS OVER/UNDER
$899.95

SPECIFICATIONS
Gauge: 12; 2¾″ chamber
Chokes: SK/SK and IC/M
Barrel length: 28″
Weight: 7 lbs. 6 oz.

AUTOMATIC SHOTGUNS
$549.95 (Standard) $569.95 (Turkey)
$189.95 (Extra Barrels/Modified Tubes)

SPECIFICATIONS
Gauge: 12
Chokes: ICT choke system
Barrel lengths: 24″ (Standard & Turkey); 26″ and 28″ (Standard only)

Stock: Hand-checkered walnut w/satin finish
Features: Magazine cut-off (shoots all loads interchangeably w/o alterations); non-glare finish; vent rib w/mid-bead; gold trigger

FERLIB SHOTGUNS

MODELS F. VI AND F. VII BOXLOCK SIDE-BY-SIDES

Hand-crafted by the small European artisan firm of the same name, Ferlib shotguns are high-quality, hand-fitted side-by-sides. With Anson & Deeley boxlock design, all Ferlib doubles are available in 12, 16, 20 and 28 gauge and .410 bore, with automatic ejectors, double triggers with front trigger hinged (non-selective single trigger is optional), hand-rubbed oil-finished straight grip stock with classic forearm (beavertail optional). Dovetail lump barrels have soft-luster blued finish; top rib is concave with file-cut matting. **Barrel length:** 25″-28″. **Stock dimensions:** Length of pull, 14½″; drop at comb, 1½″; drop at heel, 2¼. **Weight:** 12 ga., 6 lbs. 8 oz.—6 lbs. 14 oz.; 16 ga., 6 lbs. 4 oz.—6 lbs. 10 oz.; 20 ga., 5 lbs. 14 oz.—6 lbs. 4 oz.; 28 ga. and .410, 5 lbs. 6 oz.—5 lbs. 11 oz.

Model F. VI w/scalloped frame, border-line engraving, casehardened colors, select walnut stock . . . **$ 5600.00**
Model F. VII w/scalloped frame, full-coverage English scroll engraving, coin finish, select walnut stock **6600.00**
Model F. VII/SC w/scalloped frame, game scene with either bulino engraved or gold inlayed birds and scroll accents with coin finish, special walnut stock with extra figure and color **7300.00**
Model F. VII/Sideplate w/game scene engraving, gold inlayed birds and coin finish, special walnut stock, extra figure and color **11,800.00**

FRANCOTTE SHOTGUNS

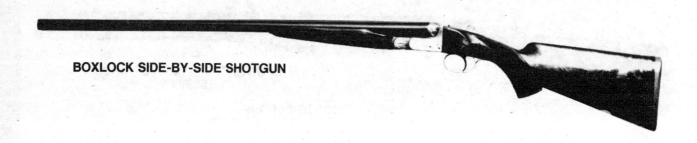

BOXLOCK SIDE-BY-SIDE SHOTGUN

There are no standard Francotte models, since every shotgun is custom made in Belgium to the purchaser's individual specifications. Features and options include Anson & Deeley boxlocks or Auguste Francotte system sidelocks. All guns have custom-fitted stocks. Available are exhibition-grade stocks as well as extensive engraving and gold inlays. U.S. agent for Auguste Francotte of Belgium is Armes de Chasse (see Directory of Manufacturers and Distributors).

SPECIFICATIONS
Gauges: 12, 16, 20, 28, .410; also 24 and 32

Chambers: 2½″, 2¾″ and 3″
Barrel length: to customer's specifications
Forend: to customer's specifications
Stock: Deluxe to exhibition grade; pistol, English or half-pistol grip
Prices:
Basic Boxlock **$16,000**
Basic Boxlock (28 & .410 ga.) **30,500**
Optional sideplates, add **1,700**
Basic Sidelock **27,500**
Basic Sidelock (28 & .410 ga.) **31,000**

GARBI SIDELOCK SHOTGUNS

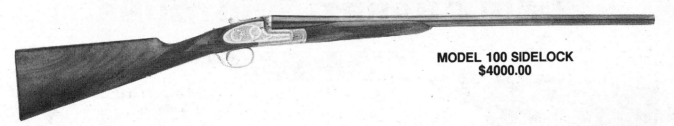

MODEL 100 SIDELOCK
$4000.00

Like this Model 100 shotgun, all Spanish-made Garbi models featured here are Holland & Holland pattern sidelock ejector guns with chopper lump (demibloc) barrels. They are built to English gun standards with regard to design, weight, balance and proportions, and all have the characteristic "feel" asso-

ciated with the best London guns. All of the models offer fine 24-line hand-checkering, with outstanding quality wood-to-metal and metal-to-metal fit. The Model 100 is available in 12, 16, 20 and 28 gauge and sports Purdey-style fine scroll and rosette engraving, partly done by machine.

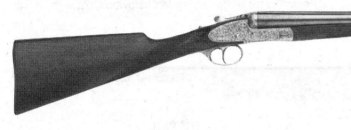

MODEL 200
$8500.00

Stock/forend: Straight grip stock with checkered butt (optional pistol grip); hand-rubbed oil finish; classic (splinter) forend (optional beavertail)

Weight: 12 ga. game, 6 lbs. 8 oz. to 6 lbs. 12 oz.; 12 ga. pigeon or wildfowl, 7 lbs.—7lbs. 8 oz.; 16 ga., 6 lbs. 4 oz. to 6 lbs. 10 oz.; 20 ga., 5 lbs. 15 oz.—6 lbs. 4 oz.; 28 ga., 5 lbs. 6 oz.—5 lbs. 10 oz.

Prices:

Model 101 . . . . **$4800.00**
Model 103A 6500.00
Model 120 . . . . 8400.00

MODELS 101, 103A and 120 (not shown)

Available in 12, 16, 20, and 28 gauge, the sidelocks are hand-crafted with hand-engraved receiver and select walnut straight grip stock.

SPECIFICATIONS
Barrels: 25″ to 30″ in 12 ga.; 25″ to 28″ in 16, 20 and 28 ga.; high-luster blued finish; smooth concave rib (optional Churchill or level, file-cut rib)

Action: Holland & Holland pattern sidelock; automatic ejectors; double triggers with front trigger hinged; case-hardened

Also available:

MODEL 200 in 12, 16, 20 or 28 gauge; features Holland pattern stock ejector double, heavy-duty locks, Continental-style floral and scroll engraving, walnut stock.

HARRINGTON & RICHARDSON SINGLE BARREL SHOTGUNS

TURKEY MAG
$159.95

SPECIFICATIONS
Gauge: 12 (3½″ chamber); Turkey Full choke
Barrel length: 24″
Overall length: 40″
Weight: 6 lbs.

Sights: Bead sights
Stock & forearm: American hardwood with recoil pad; swivel and studs
Finish: Mossy Oak camo coverage and sling

HARRINGTON & RICHARDSON
SINGLE BARREL SHOTGUNS

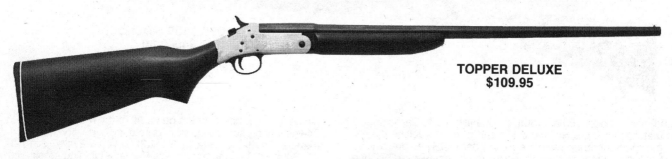

TOPPER DELUXE
$109.95

SPECIFICATIONS
Gauges: 12, 20 and .410 (3″ chamber)
Chokes: Modified (12 and 20 ga.); Full (.410 ga.)
Barrel lengths: 26″ and 28″

Weight: 5 to 6 lbs.
Action: Break-open; side lever release; automatic ejection
Stock: Full pistol grip; American hardwood; black finish with white buttplate spacer
Length of pull: 14½″

TOPPER JR.
$114.95

SPECIFICATIONS
Gauges: 20 and .410 (3″ chamber)
Chokes: Modified (20 ga.); Full (.410 ga.)
Barrel length: 22″

Weight: 5 to 6 lbs.
Stock: Full pistol grip; American hardwood; black finish; white line spacer; recoil pad
Finish: Satin nickel frame; blued barrel

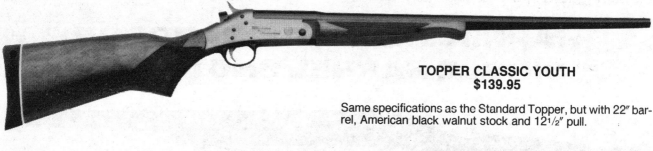

TOPPER CLASSIC YOUTH
$139.95

Same specifications as the Standard Topper, but with 22″ barrel, American black walnut stock and 12½″ pull.

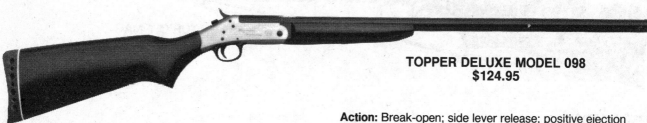

TOPPER DELUXE MODEL 098
$124.95

Action: Break-open; side lever release; positive ejection
Barrel length: 28″
Weight: 5 to 6 lbs.
Stock: American hardwood, black finish, full pistol grip stock with semi-beavertail forend; white line spacer; ventilated recoil pad
Finish: Satin nickel frame; blued barrel

SPECIFICATIONS
Gauge: 12 (3½″ chamber)
Chokes: Screw-in Modified (Full, Extra Full Turkey and Steel Shot also available)

ITHACA SHOTGUNS

FOR SPECIFICATIONS, SEE FOLLOWING PAGE

MODEL 87 FIELD GRADES

Made in much the same manner as 50 years ago, Ithaca's Model 37 pump (now designated as Model 87) features Roto-forged barrels hammered from 11″ round billets of steel, then triple-reamed, lapped and polished. The receivers are milled from a solid block of ordnance grade steel, and all internal parts—hammer, extractors, slides and carriers—are milled and individually fitted to each gun.

Prices:

Model 87 Supreme	$819.00
Model 87 Deluxe	495.00
Model 87 Field	458.00
Camoflage Field	524.00
Model 87 Deluxe Combo	549.00
Model 87 English	395.00
Model 87 Turkey Field Grade	420.00
Model 87 Turkey Field Camo	525.00

MODEL 87 DEERSLAYER

The first shotgun developed to handle rifled slugs successfully, Ithaca's Deerslayer shotgun remains first choice for many big-game hunters around the world. The Deerlayer's design results in an "undersized" cylinder bore—from the forcing cone all the way to the muzzle. This enables the slug to travel smoothly down the barrel with no gas leakage or slug rattle. The new Deerslayer II features the world's first production rifled barrel for shotguns; moreover, the Deerslayer's barrel is permanently screwed into the receiver for solid frame construction, which insures better accuracy to about 85 yards.

Prices:

Deluxe Deerslayer	$429.00
Field Grade Deerslayer	407.00
Basic Deerslayer	391.00
Monte Carlo Deerslayer	525.00
Basic Field Grade	427.00
Basic Field Grade Combo	459.00
With laminated wood	563.00

MODEL 87 FIELD TURKEY GUN
(Camo-seal Finish)

ITHACA SHOTGUNS

MODEL 87 DSPS 8-SHOT

SPECIFICATIONS: ITHACA MODEL 87 SHOTGUNS

Grade	Gauge	Barrel Length	Choke*	Chamber	Weight (lbs).	Grade	Gauge	Barrel Length	Choke*	Chamber	Weight (lbs.)
Supreme	12	30″	3 Tubes	3″	7	Basic Field/C	12	28″ & 20″	Mod Tube/DS	3″	7
Supreme	12	28″	3 Tubes	3″	7	Basic Field/C	12	28″ & 25″	Mod Tube/DS	3″	7
Supreme	12	26″	3 Tubes	3″	7	Basic Field/C	20	28″ & 20″	Mod Tube/DS	3″	6³/₄
Supreme	20	26″	3 Tubes	3″	6³/₄	Basic Field/C	12	28″ & 20″	Mod Tube/DSR	3″	7
Deluxe	12	30″	3 Tubes	3″	7	Basic Field/C	12	28″ & 25″	Mod Tube/DSR	3″	7
Deluxe	12	28″	3 Tubes	3″	7	Basic Field/C	20	28″& 20″	Mod Tube/DSR	3″	6³/₄
Deluxe	12	26″	3 Tubes	3″	7	Basic Field/C	20	28″ & 25″	Mod Tube/DSR	3″	6³/₄
Deluxe	20	26″	3 Tubes	3″	6³/₄	Turkey Gun Matte Blue	12	24″	Full Tube	3″	7
Field	12	30″	3 Tubes	3″	7	Turkey Gun Matte Blue	12	24″	Full Choke	3″	7
Field	12	28″	3 Tubes	3″	7	Turkey Gun Camo	12	24″	Full Tube	3″	7
Field	12	26″	3 Tubes	3″	7	Turkey Gun Camo	12	24″	Full Choke	3″	7
Field	20	26″	3 Tubes	3″	6³/₄	Hand Grip†	12	18¹/₂″	Cylinder	3″	5¹/₄
Camo Field	12	28″	3 Tubes	3″	7	Hand Grip	20	18¹/₂	Cylinder	3″	4¹/₂
Deluxe Deerslayer	12	20″	DS	3″	7	Hand Grip	20	18¹/₂″	Cylinder	3″	4¹/₂
Deluxe Deerslayer	12	25″	DS	3″	7	M&P†	12	20″	Cylinder	3″	7
Deluxe Deerslayer	20	20″	DS	3″	6³/₄	M&P	12	18¹/₂	Cylinder	3″	7
Deluxe Deerslayer	20	25″	DS	3″	6⁰/₄	DSPS†	12	20″	DS	3″	7
Deluxe Deerslayer	12	20″	DSR	3″	7	M&P 8 Shot	12	20″	Cylinder	3″	7
Deluxe Deerslayer	12	25″	DSR	3″	7	DSPS 8 Shot	12	20″	DS	3″	7
Deluxe Deerslayer	20	20″	DSR	3″	6³/₄	Custom Trap M5E Custom	12	32″	Full	2³/₄″	8¹/₂
Deluxe Deerslayer	20	25″	DSR	3″	6³/₄	Custom Trap M5E Custom	12	34″	Full	2³/₄″	8¹/₂
Field Deerslayer	12	20″	DS	3″	7	Custom Trap Dollar Grade	12	32″	Full	2³/₄″	8¹/₂
Field Deerslayer	12	25″	DS	3″	7	Custom Trap Dollar Grade	12	34″	Full	2³/₄″	8¹/₂
Field Deerslayer	20	20″	DS	3″	6³/₄	Combo Laminated	12	28″ & 20″	3 Tubes/DSR	3″	7
Field Deerslayer	20	25″	DS	3″	6³/₄	Combo Laminated	12	28″ & 25″	3 Tubes/DSR	3″	7
Basic Field Deerslayer	12	20″	DS	3″	7						
Basic Field Deerslayer	12	25″	DS II	3″	7						
Monte Carlo Deerslayer II	12	25″	DS II	3″	7						
English	20	24″	3 Tubes	3″	6³/₄						
English	20	26″	3 Tubes	3″	6³/₄						
Deluxe Combo	20	28″ & 20″	3 Tubes/DS	3″	6³/₄						
Deluxe Combo	12	28″ & 20″	3 Tubes/DS	3″	7						
Deluxe Combo	12	28″ & 20″	3 Tubes/DSR	3″	7						
Deluxe Combo	12	28″ & 25″	3 Tubes/DSR	3″	7						
Deluxe Combo	20	28″ & 20″	3 Tubes/DSR	3″	6³/₄						
Deluxe Combo	20	28″ & 25″	3 Tubes/DSR	3″	6³/₄						

* 3 tubes furnished are Improved Cylinder, Modified, and Full.
DS = Deer, Special Bore   DSR = Deer, Rifled Bore   DS II = Deer, Rifled Barrel
† Nickel plated models available (add $103.00)

KBI/KASSNAR SHOTGUNS

FIAS GRADE I OVER/UNDER
$619.00

Features: Single selective trigger; blued engraved receiver; ventilated rib; chrome-lined barrels; hinged floorplate for easy loading; positive non-slip thumb-type safety (locks the trigger but allows bolt to be opened safely for unloading and inspection of chamber; available with or without deluxe sights; rear sight adjustable for windage and elevation; swivel posts; recoil pad

SPECIFICATIONS
Gauges: 12, 20, 28, .410
Barrel lengths: 26″ (IC/M); 28″ (M/F, W/ICT)
Weight: 7½ lbs. (12 ga.); 6½ lbs. (20 ga.)
Stock: European walnut with checkered pistol grip and forend

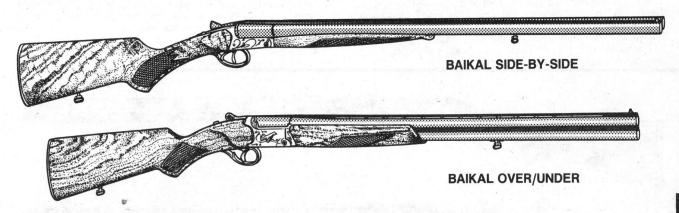

BAIKAL SIDE-BY-SIDE

BAIKAL OVER/UNDER

BAIKAL SHOTGUNS

Baikal shotguns are manufactured by Russian arms producers. The **Single Barrel** model has a chrome-lined barrel bore and chamber, non-auto safety and automatic ejector with external disengaging lever. Available in 12 or 20 gauge. Additional specifications are listed in the table below. . . . . **$ 89.00**

The **Side by Side** model also has chrome-lined barrels and chambers and comes with double triggers and extractors. 379.00
The **Over/Under** model features either double trigger and extractors or single selective trigger and auto ejectors. 399.00

Model	Article Number	Gauge	Barrel Length in.	Chamber in.	Chokes	Weight lb.
Single	GD1000	12	28	2¾″	F	6
Single	GD1019	12	28	2¾″	M	6
Single	GD1027	12	26	2¾″	IC	6
Single	GD1035	20	28	3″	F	5½
Single	GD1043	20	28	3″	M	5½
Single	GD1051	20	26	3″	IC	5½
Single	GD1078	410	26	3″	F	5½
Side/Side—DT	GE1006	12	28	2¾″	M/F	6¾
Side/Side—DT	GE1014	12	26	2¾″	IC/M	6¾
O/U—DT	GP1006	12	28	2¾″	M/F	7
O/U—DT	GP1014	12	26	2¾″	IC/M	7
O/U—SST	GP1065	12	28	2¾″	M/F	7
O/U—SST	GP1073	12	26	2¾″	IC/M	7

KRIEGHOFF SHOTGUNS

(See following page for additional Specifications and Prices)

MODEL K-80 SPORTING CLAY

MODEL K-80 TRAP, SKEET, SPORTING CLAY AND LIVE BIRD

Barrels: Made of Boehler steel; free-floating bottom barrel with adjustable point of impact; standard Trap and Live Pigeon ribs are tapered step; standard Skeet, Sporting Clay and International ribs are tapered or parallel flat.

Receivers: Hard satin-nickel finish; casehardened; blue finish available as special order

Triggers: Wide profile, single selective, position adjustable. Removable trigger option available (add'l **$1850.00**)

Weight: 8½ lbs. (Trap); 8 lbs. (Skeet)

Ejectors: Selective automatic

Sights: White pearl front bead and metal center bead

Stocks: Hand-checkered and epoxy-finished Select European walnut stock and forearm; quick-detachable palm swell stocks available in five different styles and dimensions

Safety: Push button safety located on top tang.

Also available:

SKEET SPECIAL (28″ and 30″ barrel; tapered flat rib; 2 choke tubes). **Price: $6250.00** (Standard)

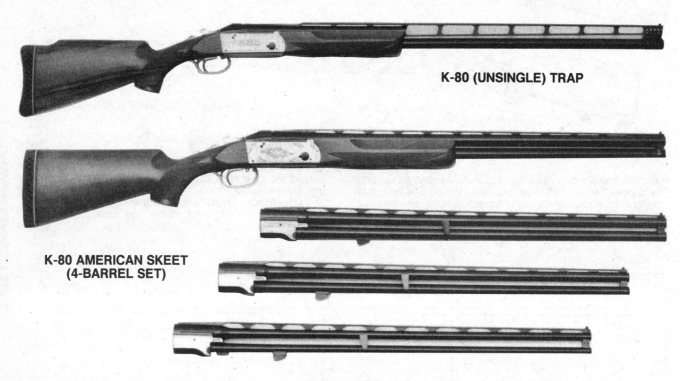

K-80 (UNSINGLE) TRAP

**K-80 AMERICAN SKEET
(4-BARREL SET)**

**MODEL ULM-P
O/U SIDELOCK LIVE BIRD GUN
$14,950.00**

SPECIFICATIONS

Gauge: 12

Chamber: 2¾″

Barrel: 28″ or 30″ long; tapered, ventilated rib

Choke: Top, Full; bottom, Imp. Mod.

Trigger action: Single trigger, non-selective bottom-top; hand-detachable sidelocks with coil springs; optional release trigger

Stock: Selected fancy English walnut, oil finish; length, 14⅜″; drop at comb, 1⅜″; optional custom-made stock

Forearm: Semi-beavertail

Engraving: Light scrollwork; optional engravings available

Weight: Approx. 8 lbs.

Also available in Skeet (28″) and Trap (30″) models

KRIEGHOFF SHOTGUNS

SPECIFICATIONS AND PRICES MODEL K-80 (see also preceding page)

Model	Description	Bbl Length	Choke	Standard	Bavaria	Danube	Gold Target	Extra Barrels
Trap	Over & Under	30"/32"	IM/F	$6145.00	$10,100.00	$12,450.00	$16,350.00	$2250.00
	Unsingle	32"/34"	Full	6695.00	10,600.00	12,995.00	16,900.00	2795.00
	Top Single	34" only	Full	6900.00	10,800.00	13,290.00	16,995.00	2995.00
	Combo (unsingle)	30" + 32" / 30" + 34"	IM/F+F	8850.00	12,950.00	15,445.00	19,500.00	
		32" + 34"	CT/CT + CT	9780.00	13,880.00	16,375.00	20,450.00	
Optional Features:* Screw-in chokes (O/U, Top or Unsingle) $380.00 Single factory release 350.00 Double factory release 575.00								
Skeet	4-Barrel Set	28"/12 ga.	Tula					2550.00
		28"/20 ga.	Skeet					2475.00
		28"/28 ga.	Skeet	13,400.00	16,995.00	19,250.00	24,675.00	2475.00
		28"/.410 ga.	Skeet					2475.00
	2-Barrel Set	28"/12 ga.	Tula	10,400.00	14,680.00	17,280.00	21,100.00	3850.00
	Lightweight	28" + 30"/12 ga.	Skeet	8600.00	12,750.00	15,150.00	19,200.00	2250.00
	Standardweight	28"/12 ga.	Tula	6175.00	10,400.00	12,500.00	16,450.00	2550.00
		28" + 30"/12 ga.	Skeet	5875.00	10,150.00	12,300.00	16,250.00	2250.00
	International	28"/12 ga.	Tula	6575.00	10,700.00	13,000.00	16,950.00	2550.00
Sporting Clays	Over/Under w/screw-in tubes (5)	28" + 30" + 32"/ 12 ga.	Tubes	6795.00	10,700.00	t13,100.00	17,000.00	2795.00
Pigeon	Live Bird	28" + 30" + 32"	IM/SF or CT/CT	6145.00	10,100.00	12,450.00	16,350.00	2250.00
Optional engravings: Super Scroll								990.00

* Choke tubes in single barrel (w/tubes): add **$335.00**. In O/U barrel (5 tubes) add **$490.00**.

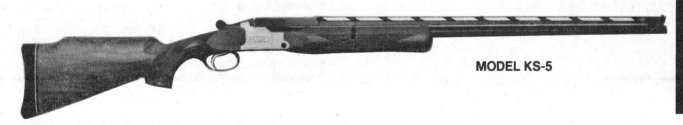

MODEL KS-5

The KS-5 is a single barrel trap gun with a ventilated, tapered and adjustable step rib, casehardened receiver in satin grey matte or blue, finished in electroless nickel. It features an adjustable point of impact by means of different optional fronthangers. Screw-in chokes and adjustable stock are optional. Trigger is adjustable externally for poundage.

SPECIFICATIONS
Gauge: 12
Chamber: 2³/₄"
Barrel length: 32" or 34"
Choke: Full; optional screw-in chokes
Rib: Tapered step; ventilated
Trigger: Weight of pull adjustable; optional release

Receiver: Casehardened; satin grey finished in electroless nickel; now available in blue
Grade: Standard; engraved models on special order
Weight: Approximately 8.6-8.8 lbs.
Case: Aluminum
Prices:
With full choke and case $3250.00
With screw-in choke and case 4000.00
Screw-in choke barrels 2070.00
Regular barrels 1690.00

Also available:
KS-5 SPECIAL. Same as **KS-5** except barrel has fully adjustable rib and stock. **Price: $4150.00**

LAURONA SHOTGUNS

MODEL 83 MG SUPER GAME
w/Twin-Single Triggers

MODEL 83 MG SUPER GAME
$1215.00

SPECIFICATIONS
Gauges: 12 and 20
Chamber: 2³/₄″ or 3″

Barrel lengths: 26″ or 28″ (20 ga.) and 28″ (12 ga.)
Chokes: Multichokes (screw-in)
Rib: ⁵/₁₆″
Frame finish: Old Silver
Weight: 6 lbs. 10 oz. (20 ga.); 7 lbs. (12 ga.)
Features: Non-rusting Black-chrome barrel finish; extra-long
forcing cones

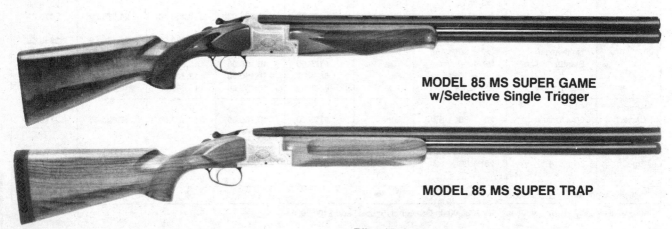

MODEL 85 MS SUPER GAME
w/Selective Single Trigger

MODEL 85 MS SUPER TRAP

MODEL 85 MS SUPER TRAP
$1390.00

SPECIFICATIONS
Gauge: 12
Chamber: 2³/₄″
Barrel length: 29″
Choke: Multichoke/Full

Rib: ¹/₂″ aluminum
Frame finish: Old silver
Weight: 7 lbs. 12 oz.

Also available:
MODEL 85 MS SUPER GAME **$1215.00**
12 or 20 gauge 2-barrel set **1630.00**
MODEL 85 MS SUPER PIGEON (12 ga.). Same specifications
as Super Trap model except **Barrel length:** 28″ and
Weight: 7 lbs. 4 oz. **Price:** **$1370.00**

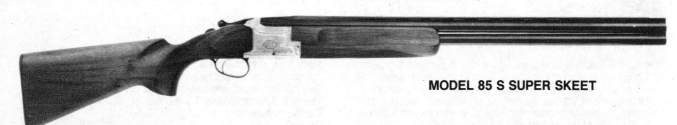

MODEL 85 S SUPER SKEET

MODEL 85 S SUPER SKEET
$1300.00

SPECIFICATIONS
Gauge: 12
Chamber: 2³/₄″

Barrel length: 28″
Choke: Skeet/Skeet
Rib: ¹/₂″ aluminum
Frame finish: Old silver
Weight: 7 lbs. 1 oz.
Features: Black-chrome barrel finish; extra-long forcing cones

LAURONA SHOTGUNS

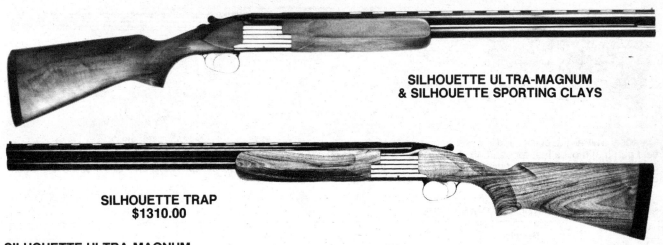

**SILHOUETTE ULTRA-MAGNUM
& SILHOUETTE SPORTING CLAYS**

**SILHOUETTE TRAP
$1310.00**

SILHOUETTE ULTRA-MAGNUM
$1265.00

SPECIFICATIONS (Game, Trap & Sporting Clay Models)
Gauge: 12
Chamber: 3 1/2″ Magnum
Barrel length: 28″
Choke: Multichoke
Rib: 7/16″ steel
Weight: 7 lbs. 12 oz.

Note: All Laurona shotguns have extra-long forcing cones and 5-year warranty on rust-proof black-chrome finish. Optional 20 gauge barrels (26″ or 28″) with multichoke 3″ Magnum **($425.00 to $500.00).**

SILHOUETTE SPORTING CLAYS
$1250.00

SPECIFICATIONS
Gauge: 12
Chamber: 2 3/4″ and 3″
Weight: 8 lbs. (7 lbs. 15 oz. in Trap; 7 lbs. 12 oz. in Sporting Clays)
Ejectors: Automatic selective ejectors
Rib: 7/16 steel
Finish: Black-chrome
Stock: Full pistol grip

SHOTGUNS

MARLIN SHOTGUNS

**MARLIN MODEL 55
GOOSE GUN
$267.00**

High-flying ducks and geese are the Goose Gun's specialty. The Marlin Goose Gun has an extra-long 36-inch full-choked barrel and Magnum capability, making it the perfect choice for tough shots at wary waterfowl. It also features a quick-loading 2-shot clip magazine, a convenient leather carrying strap and a quality ventilated recoil pad.

SPECIFICATIONS
Gauge: 12; 2 3/4″ Magnum, 3″ Magnum or 2 3/4″ regular shells
Choke: Full
Capacity: 2-shot clip magazine
Action: Bolt action; positive thumb safety; red cocking indicator
Stock: Walnut-finish hardwood with pistol grip and ventilated recoil pad; swivel studs; tough Mar-Shield® finish
Barrel length: 36″
Sights: Bead front sight and U-groove rear sight
Overall length: 56 3/4″
Weight: About 8 lbs.

MAROCCHI AVANZA SHOTGUNS

Marocchi's ultralight, quick handling over and under is an ideal field gun that moves fast for sporting clays as well. It houses a strong boxlock action fitted with a single selective trigger. Barrel cycling is controlled mechanically and features automatic selective extractors and ejectors, plus unbreakable firing pins. The barrels, chambered for 3″, are made of chrome steel with highly polished bores. Both top and filler ribs have modern wide ventilated styling.

SPECIFICATIONS MAROCCHI AVANZA O/U

Gauge	Barrel Length	Chokes	Overall Length	Weight	Prices
12	28″	M & F	44¹/₂″	6 lbs. 9 oz.	$725.00
12	28″	IC & M & F Interchokes	44¹/₂″	6 lbs. 13 oz.	769.00
12	26″	IC & M	42¹/₂″	6 lbs. 6 oz.	725.00
12	26″	IC & M & F Interchokes	42¹/₂″	6 lbs. 9 oz.	769.00
20	28″	M & F	44¹/₂″	6 lbs. 8 oz.	768.00
20	28″	IM & M & F Interchokes	44¹/₂″	6 lbs. 12 oz.	814.00
20	26″	IC & M	42¹/₂″	6 lbs. 5 oz.	768.00
20	26″	IC & M & F Interchokes	42¹/₂″	6 lbs. 8 oz.	814.00

Features: Single selective trigger (5¹/₂ lb. pull); stock is select walnut with cut checkering; ribs are top and middle ventilated; 3″ chambers; mechanism is lightweight, all steel with Mono-Block boxlock, automechanical barrel cycling, selective automatic, ejectors/extractors, automatic safety

AVANZA SPORTING CLAYS MODEL
$839.00

SPECIFICATIONS
Gauge: 12 (3″ chamber)
Barrel length: 28″
Choke: Interchangeable tubes in IC & Modified
Weight: 7 lbs.
Sights: Ventilated rib, front and mid beads
Trigger pull: 5¹/₂ lbs.

Stock: Checkered select walnut, beavertail forend
Features: Chrome steel double barrel over/under with highly polished bores; all steel mono block boxlock action; automatic safety; single selective trigger adjustable for length of pull without tools; automechanical barrel cycling; selective automatic ejectors/extractors; unbreakable firing pins

MAVERICK PUMP ACTION SHOTGUNS

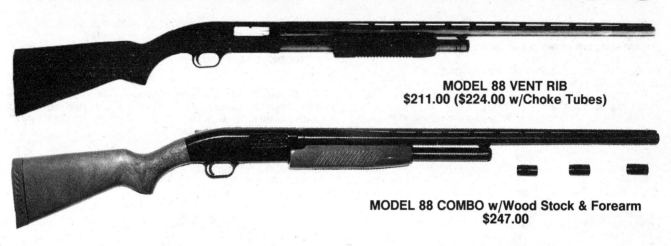

MODEL 88 VENT RIB
$211.00 ($224.00 w/Choke Tubes)

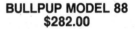

MODEL 88 COMBO w/Wood Stock & Forearm
$247.00

SPECIFICATIONS
Gauge: 12
Chamber: 2³/₄″ or 3″
Capacity: 6 shots (2³/₄″); 5 shots (3″)
Barrel length: 28″ Modified; 30″ Full
Overall length: 48″ (w/28″ barrel)
Weight: 7¹/₄ lbs. (w/28″ barrel)
Features: Rubber recoil pad; positive crossbolt safety; interchangeable barrels without tools; durable black synthetic

stock and matching forend; high strength aluminum alloy receiver; steel-to-steel lockup between hardened barrel extension and bolt lock
Also available:
MODEL 88 PLAIN **$193.00**
 W/24″ barrel & rifle sights, cyl. bore choke **211.00**
MODEL 88 COMBO w/18¹/₂″ & 28″ bbl. **218.00**
 W/vent rib **235.00**

BULLPUP MODEL 88
$282.00

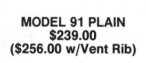

SPECIFICATIONS
Gauge: 12; 2³/₄″ or 3″ chamber
Choke: Cylinder bore barrel
Barrel length: 18¹/₂″
Overall length: 26¹/₂″
Weight: 9¹/₂ lbs.
Sight: Open
Features: Same as Model 88

MODEL 91 PLAIN
$239.00
($256.00 w/Vent Rib)

SPECIFICATIONS
Gauge: 12; 2³/₄″, 3″ or 3¹/₂″ chamber
Choke: Choke tube
Barrel length: 28″
Overall length: 48″
Weight: 7.7 lbs.
Features: Synthetic stock and forend; thick rubber recoil pad; positive crossbolt safety design; Maverick Cablelock

MERKEL OVER/UNDER SHOTGUNS

Merkel over-and-unders are the first hunting guns with barrels arranged one above the other, and they have since proved to be able competitors of the side-by-side gun. Merkel superiority lies in the following details:
- Available in 12, 16, 20 and .410 gauges
- Lightweight (5³/₄ to 6³/₄ lbs.)
- The high, narrow forend protects the shooter's hand from the barrel in hot or cold climates.
- The forend is narrow and therefore lies snugly in the hand to permit easy and positive swinging.

- The slim barrel line provides an unobstructed field of view and thus permits rapid aiming and shooting.
- The over-and-under barrel arrangement reduces recoil error; the recoil merely pushes the muzzle up vertically.

All Merkel shotguns are manufactured by Jagd und Sportwaffen GmbH, Suhl, Thuringia, Germany; imported, distributed and retailed in the U.S. by Armes de Chasse (see Directory of Manufacturers and Distributors).

MODEL 200E BOXLOCK

MODEL 201E BOXLOCK

MODEL 203E SIDELOCK

MERKEL OVER/UNDER SHOTGUN SPECIFICATIONS

Gauges: 12 and 20
Barrel lengths: 26″, 28″ and 30″
Weight: 5.5 to 7 lbs.
Stock: English or pistol grip in European walnut
Features: Models 200E and 201E are boxlocks; Model 203E is a sidelock. All models include three-piece forearm, automatic ejectors, Kersten double crossbolt lock, Blitz action and single selective triggers. Model 203E has Holland & Holland ejectors.
Prices:
Model 200E Boxlock (w/scroll engraved
  casehardened receiver) . . . . $ 2995.00
Model 201E Boxlock (w/hunting scenes) 3695.00
Model 203E Sidelock (w/hunting scenes) 7895.00

MERKEL SIDE-BY-SIDE SHOTGUNS

SPECIFICATIONS
Gauges: 12 and 20 (28 ga. and .410 in Models 47S and 147S)
Barrel lengths: 26″ and 28″ (25$^{1}/_{2}$″ in Models 47S and 147S)
Weight: 6 to 7 lbs.
Stock: English or pistol grip in European walnut
Features: Models 47E and 147E are boxlocks; Models 47S and 147S are sidelocks. All guns have cold hammer-forged barrels, double triggers, double lugs and Greener crossbolt locking systems and automatic ejectors.

Prices:
MODEL 8	**$ 995.00**
MODEL 47E (Holland & Holland ejectors)	1365.00
MODEL 147E (Engraved hunting scenes)	1695.00
MODEL 47S Sidelock	3595.00
In .410 & 28 ga. w/25$^{1}/_{2}$″ barrels	4590.00
MODEL 147S Sidelock	4495.00
In .410 & 28 ga. w/25$^{1}/_{2}$″ barrels	5490.00

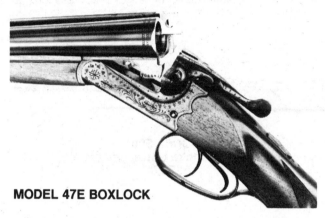

MODEL 47E BOXLOCK

MODEL 147E BOXLOCK

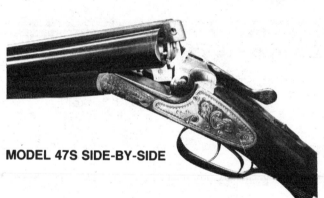

MODEL 47S SIDE-BY-SIDE

MODEL 147S

MOSSBERG PUMP SHOTGUNS

These slide-action Model 500's offer lightweight action and high tensile-strength alloys. They also feature the famous Mossberg "Safety on Top" and a full range of interchangeable barrels. Stocks are walnut-finished birch with rubber recoil pads with combs checkered pistol grip and forend. Cable locks are included with all Mossberg shotguns.

MODEL 500 SPECIFICATIONS

Action: Positive slide-action
Barrel: 12 or 20 gauge and .410 bore with free-floating vent. rib; ACCU-CHOKE interchangeable choke tubes; chambered for 2¾" standard and Magnum and 3" Magnum shells

Capacity: 6-shot (one less when using 3" Magnum shells); plug for 3-shot capacity included
Overall length: 48" with 28" barrel
Weight: 12 ga. 7½ lbs.; 20 ga. 6¾ lbs.; .410 bore 6½ lbs.; Slugster 6¾ lbs. (weight varies slightly due to wood density)
Receiver: Aluminum alloy, deep blue/black finish; ordnance steel bolt locks in barrel extension for solid "steel-to-steel" lockup
Safety: Top tang, thumb-operated; disconnecting trigger
Sights: Mid-point and front bead
Stock/forend: Walnut-finished American hardwood with checkering; rubber recoil pad
Standard stock dimensions: 14" length of pull; 2½" drop at heel; 1½" drop at comb

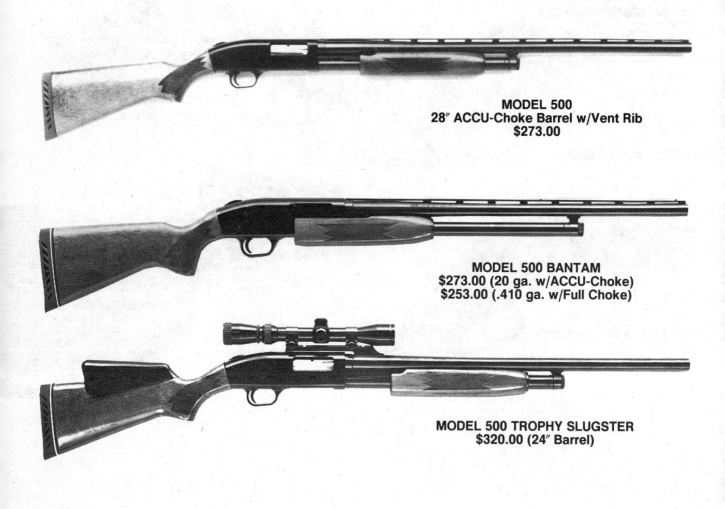

MODEL 500
28″ ACCU-Choke Barrel w/Vent Rib
$273.00

MODEL 500 BANTAM
$273.00 (20 ga. w/ACCU-Choke)
$253.00 (.410 ga. w/Full Choke)

MODEL 500 TROPHY SLUGSTER
$320.00 (24″ Barrel)

MOSSBERG PUMP SHOTGUNS

MODEL 500 MARINER
12 Gauge 6-Shot (18 1/2" Barrel)
w/Marinecoat™ Finish & Pistol Grip Kit

MARINER MODELS 500 & 590

All carbon steel parts of these 12 gauge shotguns are treated with MARINECOAT™ protective finish, a unique Teflon and metal coating. This finish makes each Mariner 500 shotgun resistant to salt spray and water damage by actually penetrating into the steel pores. All stock and forearms are made of a high-strength synthetic material rather than wood to provide extra durability with minimum maintenance. Mariners are available in a variety of 6- or 9-shot versions. Pistol grip kit and QD swivel post included.

SPECIFICATIONS
Gauge: 12
Chambers: 2 3/4" and 3"

Capacity: 6-shot model—5-shot (3" chamber) and 6-shot (2 3/4" chamber)
9-shot model—8-shot (3" chamber) and 9-shot (2 3/4" chamber)
Barrel lengths: 18 1/2" and 20"
Overall length: 40" w/20" barrel; 38 1/2" w/18 1/2" barrel
Weight: 6 1/2 lbs. w/18 1/2" barrel
Stock dimensions: 14" pull; 1 1/2" drop at comb; 2 1/2" drop at heel
Features: Double slide bars; twin extractors; dual shell latches; ambidextrous safety

Prices:
MODEL 500 MARINER 6-SHOT $336.00
MODEL 590 MARINER 9-SHOT 441.00

MODEL 590 MARINER
12 Gauge 9-Shot (20" Barrel)
w/Marinecoat™ Finish, Synthetic Stock
and Pistol Grip Kit

MOSSBERG PUMP SHOTGUNS

MODEL 500 OFM-CAMO

MODEL 500 CAMO
w/28″ ACCU-CHOKE Barrel

Same general specifications as standard Model 500, except all camo models have synthetic stock and forend, sling swivels, camo web strap, receiver drilled and tapped for scope mounting. Also available with 20″ and 24″ vent rib barrels.
Price: $293.00 ($346.00 w/Ghost Ring Sight)

MODEL 500 TURKEY/DEER CAMO COMBO

SPECIFICATIONS
Gauge: 12
Chamber: 3″
Barrel length: 20″ (ACCU-Choke w/one Extra Full choke tube) and 24″ Slugster barrel
Features: Synthetic forearm and buttstock; receiver drilled and tapped for scope mounting; quick disconnect posts and swivels, plus camo web sling, are supplied
Price: $334.00

MODEL HS410 HOME SECURITY

MODEL HS410 HOME SECURITY

SPECIFICATIONS
Gauge: .410
Chambers: 2¹/₂″ and 3″
Barrel length: 18¹/₂″
Weight: 6¹/₄ lbs.
Features: Synthetic stock, pistol grip forearm, spreader choke, rubber recoil pad, muzzle brake, cablelock, Home Security video tape, optional laser sight integral in forearm
Price: $308.00 ($561.00 w/optional Laser Sight)

MOSSBERG PUMP SHOTGUNS

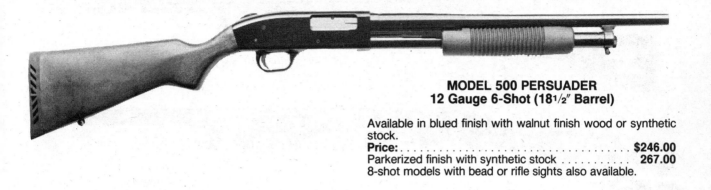

MODEL 500 PERSUADER
12 Gauge 6-Shot (18½″ Barrel)

Available in blued finish with walnut finish wood or synthetic stock.
Price:. **$246.00**
Parkerized finish with synthetic stock **267.00**
8-shot models with bead or rifle sights also available.

MODEL 500 PERSUADER
12 Gauge 8-Shot (20″ Barrel)

MODEL 590
INTIMIDATOR LASER SIGHT
9-Shot (20″ Barrel)

MODEL 500 SPECIAL PURPOSE

These slide-action shotguns are available in 6-, 8- or 9-shot versions, chambered for both 2¾-inch and 3-inch shells.

Six-shot models have 18½-inch barrel, overall length of 37¾ inches and a weight of 6¼ pounds with full buttstock. Eight-shot models have 20-inch barrels, overall length of 39¾ inches and weigh 6¾ pounds with full buttstock. Optional rifle sights available. Nine-shot 590 models have 20-inch barrels, overall length of 39¾ inches and weigh 7¼ pounds with full buttstock. Speedfeed stock available.

All models are available in choice of blued or parkerized finish. Lightweight aluminum alloy receiver with steel locking bolt into barrel extension affords solid "steel-to-steel" lockup. Heavy-duty rubber recoil pads come on all full stock models; sling swivels on all models. Pistol grip kit included on all 6- and 8-shot bead sight models. Optional integral laser sight forearm available with 4.8 milliwatt patented water/shock re sistant battery powered laser on 6 or 9 shot models, blue or Parkerized finish.

Prices:
MODEL 500 PERSUADER 6-SHOT (12 ga., 18½″)
Wood or synthetic stock, blued, bead sight	**$246.00**
Parkerized stock, blued, bead sight	**267.00**
Ghost Ring Sight, blued	**300.00**
Ghost Ring Sight, Parkerized	**348.00**

MODEL 500 PERSUADER 8-SHOT
Synthetic stock, blued	**246.00**
With rifle sight	**266.00**

MODEL 590 9-SHOT
Synthetic stock, blued	**305.00**
Speedfeed, blued	**319.00**
Synthetic, Parkerized	**349.00**
Speedfeed, Parkerized	**366.00**
Intimidator Laser Sight, blued	**555.00**
Intimidator Laser Sight, Parkerized	**601.00**
Ghost Ring Sight, blued	**359.00**
Ghost Ring Sight, Parkerized	**406.00**

MOSSBERG SHOTGUNS

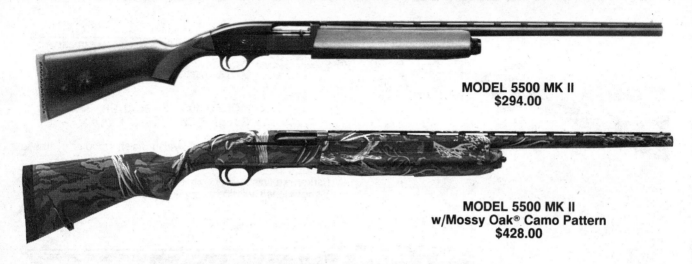

MODEL 5500 MK II
$294.00

MODEL 5500 MK II
w/Mossy Oak® Camo Pattern
$428.00

MODEL 5500 MKII

Mossberg's semiauto 12-gauge **Model 5500 MKII** is equipped for non-magnum 2³/₄″ 12-gauge loads only. A large gas port ensures reliable extraction and ejection with even the lightest target or field loads. The 28″ non-magnum barrel is ideal for close cover upland hunting and comes equipped with one Modified ACCU-Choke tube.

The **Model 5500 MKII Auto** has a full 5-shot capacity and features a high-strength aluminum alloy receiver for good balance and fast handling in the field. The positive tang safety is located in the top rear of the receiver for easy operation by right- or left-handed shooters. Also available with a 28″ magnum barrel.

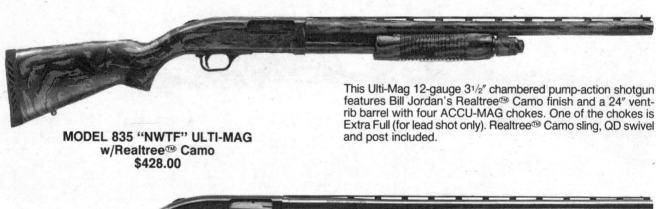

MODEL 835 "NWTF" ULTI-MAG
w/Realtree™ Camo
$428.00

This Ulti-Mag 12-gauge 3¹/₂″ chambered pump-action shotgun features Bill Jordan's Realtree™ Camo finish and a 24″ vent-rib barrel with four ACCU-MAG chokes. One of the chokes is Extra Full (for lead shot only). Realtree™ Camo sling, QD swivel and post included.

MODEL 835 REGAL ULTI-MAG
$373.00 (Blued)

The world's first shotgun chambered specifically for Federal Cartridge's 3¹/₂″ 12 gauge Magnum shotshell, the **Ulti-Mag** fires all standard 12 gauge 2³/₄″ and 3″ field and target loads as well. Designed for waterfowlers who need a shotshell capable of delivering larger payloads of steel shot, the high-velocity (1300+ fps) load provides a 23 percent or more increase in steel shot capacity compared to conventional 12 gauge 3″ Magnums.

The **Ulti-Mag** also features a "backbored" barrel that reduces recoil and improves patterns. With the ACCU-MAG choke tube system, stainless steel tubes fit flush with the muzzle to handle high-velocity steel shot loads with efficiency. Capacity is five shots with 3″ or 3¹/₂″ shells, and six shots with 2³/₄″ shells. Other features include an ambidextrous safety, solid "steel-to-steel" lockup, high-strength aluminum alloy receivers with anodized finish, and walnut dual-comb stock.

MOSSBERG SHOTGUNS

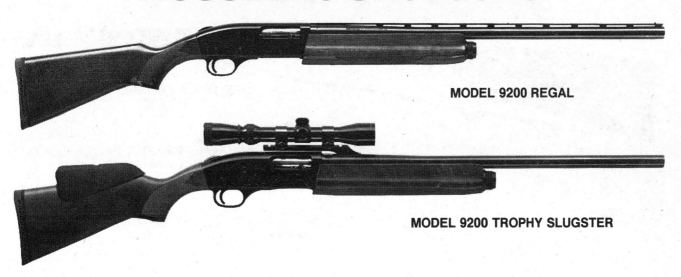

MODEL 9200 REGAL

MODEL 9200 TROPHY SLUGSTER

MODEL 9200

This new semiautomatic fires any sequence of 12 gauge loads from 2¼″ field to 3″ magnums. No barrels to change, no buttons to push, no adjustments to make. The 9200 has a gas regulating system that instantly compensates for varied pressures developed by a wide range of shotshell loads. For example, when firing light field loads, the system remains closed, with all available gases used to cycle the action.

SPECIFICATIONS
Gauge: 12
Capacity: 5 rounds (2¾″ chamber)
Chokes: ACCU-Choke (Rifled bore in 24″ Trophy Slugster model)

Barrel lengths: 24″ and 28″
Overall length: 44″ (24″ barrel) and 48″ (28″ barrel)
Weight: 7.3 lbs. (24″ barrel); 7.7 lbs. (28″ barrel)
Stock: Walnut finish
Finish: Blued
Prices:
MODEL 9200 ACCU-Choke $373.00
MODEL 9200 Rifled Bore 393.00
MODEL 9200 Combo w/Trophy Scope Base 441.00
MODEL 9200 Combo w/Rifled Bore 432.00

MUZZLELOADING CONVERSION BARRELS

Mossberg's new Muzzleloading Conversion Barrels enable shooters to convert their Mossberg Model 500 pump shotguns into muzzleloaders in minutes. Both 3½-pound barrels accept No. 209 shotshell primer, which is in direct line with the powder. The 24-inch barrel has a fast 1:26″ twist, while front and rear slugster sights make aiming fast and easy. Barrels are removable and can be submerged in water for cleaning.
Price: $172.00

NEW ENGLAND FIREARMS

NWTF TURKEY SPECIAL
$199.95

SPECIFICATIONS
Gauge: 10 (3½″ chamber)
Chokes: Screw-in chokes (Turkey Full Choke provided; Extra Full and steel shot choke available)
Barrel length: 24″
Overall length: 40″
Weight: 9¼ lbs.
Sights: Bead sights; drilled and tapped for scope mounting
Stock: American hardwood; Mossy Oak camo finish; full pistol grip; swivel and studs
Length of pull: 14½″

TURKEY & GOOSE GUN
$149.95
($159.00 w/Camo Paint, Swivels & Sling)

SPECIFICATIONS
Gauge: 10 (3½″ chamber)
Choke: Full
Barrel length: 28″
Overall length: 44″
Weight: 9½ lbs.
Sights: Bead sights
Length of pull: 14½″
Stock: American hardwood; walnut or camo finish; full pistol grip; ventilated recoil pad

TRACKER II RIFLED SLUG GUN
$129.95

SPECIFICATIONS
Gauges: 12 and 20 (3″ chamber)
Choke: Rifled Bore
Barrel length: 24″
Overall length: 40″
Weight: 6 lbs.
Sights: Adjustable rifle sights
Length of pull: 14½″
Stock: American hardwood; walnut or camo finish; full pistol grip; recoil pad; sling swivel studs
Also available:
TRACKER SLUG GUN w/Cylinder Bore: **$124.95**

PARKER REPRODUCTIONS

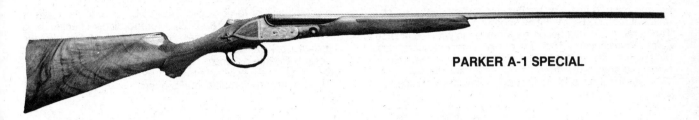

PARKER A-1 SPECIAL

Recognized by the shooting fraternity as the finest American shotgun ever produced, the Parker A-1 Special is again available. Exquisite engraving and rare presentation-grade French walnut distinguish the A-1 Special from any other shotguns in the world. Currently offered in 12 and 20 gauge, each gun is custom-fitted in its own oak and leather trunk case. Two models are offered: Hand Engraved and Custom Engraved. Also available in D Grade.

Standard features: Automatic safety, selective ejectors, skeleton steel butt plate, splinter forend, engraved snap caps, fitted leather trunk case, canvas and leather case cover, chrome barrel interiors, hand-checkering. The A-1 Special also features a 24k gold initial plate or pistol cap, 32 lines-per-inch checkering, selected wood and fine hand-engraving. Choose from single or double trigger, English or pistol grip stock (all models). Options include beavertail forend, additional barrels.

Prices:
A-1 SPECIAL Two-barrel set $11,200.00
A-1 SPECIAL CUSTOM ENGRAVED . . . . . from 10,500.00
D-GRADE
One barrel set 3,370.00
Two sets of barrels 4,200.00

SPECIFICATIONS

Gauge	Barrel Length	Chokes	Chambers	Drop At Comb	Drop At Heel	Length of Pull	Nominal Weight	Overall Length
12	26	Skeet I & II or IC/M	$2^3/_1$	$1^3/_8$	$2^3/_{16}$	$14^1/_2$	$6^3/_4$	$42^5/_8$
12	28	IC/M or M/F	$2^3/_4$ & 3	$1^3/_8$	$2^3/_{16}$	$14^1/_8$	$6^3/_4$	$44^5/_8$
12	28	IC/M	3	$1^3/_8$	$2^3/_{16}$	$14^1/_8$	7+	$44^5/_8$
20	26	Skeet I & II or IC/M	$2^3/_4$	$1^3/_8$	$2^3/_{16}$	$14^3/_8$	$6^1/_2$	$42^3/_8$
20	28	M/F	3	$1^3/_8$	$2^3/_{16}$	$14^3/_8$	$6^1/_2$	$44^5/_8$

PERAZZI SHOTGUNS

For the past 20 years or so, Perazzi has concentrated solely on manufacturing competition shotguns for the world market. Today the name has become synonymous with excellence in competitive shooting. The heart of the Perazzi line is the classic over/under, whose barrels are soldered into a monobloc that holds the shell extractors. At the sides are the two locking lugs that link the barrels to the action, which is machined from a solid block of forged steel. Barrels come with flat, step or raised ventilated rib. The walnut forend, finely checkered, is available with schnabel, beavertail or English styling, and the walnut stock can be of standard, Monte Carlo, Skeet or English design. Double or single non-selective or selective triggers. Sideplates and receiver are masterfully engraved and transform these guns into veritable works of art.

GAME MODEL MX20C

GAME MODELS MX12, MX12C, MX20, & MX20C

SPECIFICATIONS
Gauges: 12 (MX12 & MX12C); 20 (MX20 & MX20C); 28 & .410 (MX20)
Chambers: 2³/₄″ (MX20 & MX20C also avail. in 3″)
Barrel lengths: 26″ (except MX12C) and 27″ (MX12 & MX12C only)
Chokes: Mod./Full (MX12 & MX20); Chokes (MX12C & MX20C)
Trigger group: Non-detachable with coil springs and selective trigger

Stock: Interchangeable and custom made
Forend: Schnabel
Weight: 7 lbs. 4 oz. (MX12 & MX12C); 6 lbs. 6 oz. (MX20 & MX20C)
Prices:
Standard Grade . . . . $ 7,000.00- 7,730.00
SC3 Grade 11,950.00-13,080.00
SCO Grade 20,400.00-21,280.00

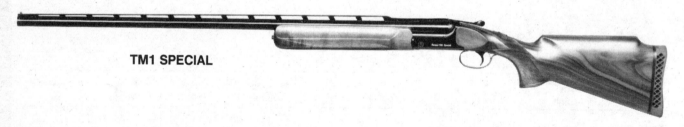

TM1 SPECIAL

TMX SPECIAL

AMERICAN TRAP SINGLE BARREL MODELS TM1 SPECIAL & TMX SPECIAL

SPECIFICATIONS
Gauge: 12
Chamber: 2³/₄″
Barrel lengths: 32″ and 34″
Choke: Full
Trigger group: Detachable and interchangeable with coil springs

Stock: Interchangeable and custom made
Forend: Beavertail
Weight: 8 lbs. 6 oz.
Prices: (Standard Grade)
TM1 SPECIAL $5500.00
TMX SPECIAL 5700.00

PERAZZI SHOTGUNS

MODEL DB81 SPECIAL

AMERICAN TRAP STANDARD COMBO SET MODELS MX8 SPECIAL COMBO, MX3 SPECIAL COMBO, GRAND AMERICAN 88 SPECIAL COMBO & DB81 SPECIAL COMBO

SPECIFICATIONS
Gauge: 12
Chamber: 2³/₄″
Barrel lengths: 29¹/₂″ and 31¹/₂″ (O/U); 32″ and 34″ (single barrel)
Chokes: Mod./Full (O/U); Full (single barrel)
Trigger group: Detachable and interchangeable with flat "V" springs
Stock: Interchangeable and custom made
Forend: Beavertail

Weight: 8 lbs. 6 oz.
Prices:
Standard Grade (MX Special, MX8 Special, Grand American 88 Special, DB81 Special) .... $ 8,850.00-10,450.00
SC3 Grade 13,750.00-16,150.00
SCO Grade 22,700.00-25,400.00
Gold Grade 25,150.00-28,150.00

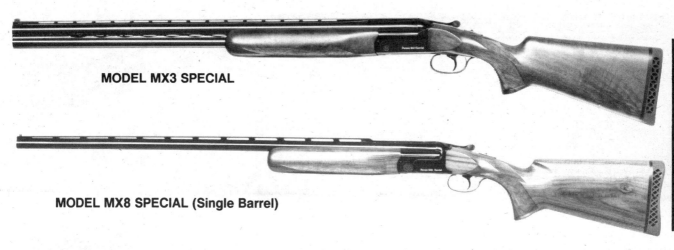

MODEL MX3 SPECIAL

MODEL MX8 SPECIAL (Single Barrel)

AMERICAN TRAP SINGLE BARREL MODELS MX3 SPECIAL, MX8 SPECIAL & GRAND AMERICAN 88 SPECIAL

SPECIFICATIONS
Gauge: 12
Chamber: 2³/₄″
Barrel lengths: 32″ and 34″
Choke: Full
Trigger group: Detachable and interchangeable with flat "V" springs
Stock: Interchangeable and custom made
Forend: Beavertail
Weight: 8 lbs. 6 oz.

Prices:
Standard Grade .... $ 5,500.00- 7,300.00
SC3 Grade 10,550.00-12,300.00
SCO Grade 16,200.00-20,550.00
Gold Grade 18,050.00-22,650.00
Also available:
SCO & Gold Grade Sideplates 31,350.00-31,650.00
Extra & Extra Gold Grades 57,400.00-62,300.00

PERAZZI SHOTGUNS

MX3 SPECIAL SPORTING

OLYMPIC TRAP OVER/UNDER MODELS
MX8-MX8 SPECIAL, MX3 SPECIAL &
GRAND AMERICAN 88 SPECIAL

SPECIFICATIONS
Gauge: 12
Chamber: 2³/₄″
Barrel lengths: 29¹/₂″ and 31¹/₂″ (Grand American 29¹/₂″ only)
Chokes: Imp./Mod. and X Full
Trigger group: Detachable & interchangeable with flat "V" springs
Stock: Interchangeable and custom made
Forend: Beavertail
Weight: 8 lbs. 4¹/₂ oz. (MX8); 8 lbs. 6 oz. (MX3 & Grand American)

Prices:
Model MX8	$7000.00-23,000.00
Model MX8 Special	7400.00-23,400.00
Model MX3 Special	6500.00-21,050.00
Grand American 88 Special	7400.00-23,400.00

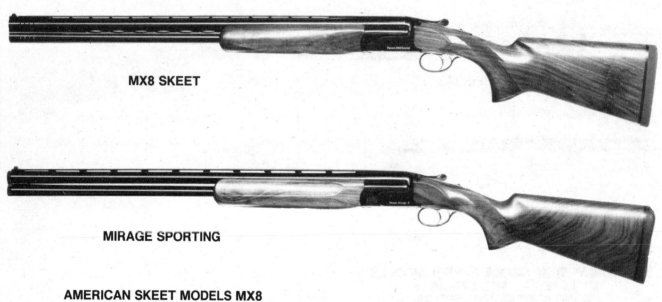

MX8 SKEET

MIRAGE SPORTING

AMERICAN SKEET MODELS MX8
& MIRAGE SPECIAL

SPECIFICATIONS
Gauge: 12
Chamber: 2³/₄″
Barrel length: 27⁵/₈″
Choke: Skeet/Skeet
Trigger group: Detachable and interchangeable with flat "V" springs
Stock: Interchangeable and custom made
Forend: Beavertail

Weight: 7 lbs. 15 oz.
Prices:
Standard Grade	$ 6,500.00-16,800.00
SC3 Grade	10,850.00-25,100.00
SCO Grade	18,650.00-33,650.00
Gold Grade	21,050.00-36,350.00

PIOTTI SHOTGUNS

One of Italy's top gunmakers, Piotti limits its production to a small number of hand-crafted, best-quality double-barreled shotguns whose shaping, checkering, stock, action and barrel work meets or exceeds the standards achieved in London prior to WWII. The Italian engravings are the finest ever and are becoming recognized as an art form in themselves.

All of the sidelock models exhibit the same overall design, materials and standards of workmanship; they differ only in the quality of the wood, shaping and sculpturing of the action, type of engraving and gold inlay work and other details. The Model Piuma differs from the other shotguns only in its Anson & Deeley boxlock design.

SPECIFICATIONS
Gauges: 10, 12, 16, 20, 28, .410
Chokes: As ordered
Barrels: 12 ga., 25″ to 30″; other gauges, 25″ to 28″; chopper lump (demi-bloc) barrels with soft-luster blued finish; level, file-cut rib or optional concave or ventilated rib
Action: Boxlock, Anson & Deeley; Sidelock, Holland & Holland pattern; both have automatic ejectors, double triggers with front trigger hinged (non-selective single trigger optional), coin finish or optional color case-hardening
Stock: Hand-rubbed oil finish (or optional satin luster) on straight grip stock with checkered butt (pistol grip optional)
Forend: Classic (splinter); optional beavertail
Weight: Ranges from 4 lbs. 15 oz. (.410 ga.) to 8 lbs. (12 ga.)

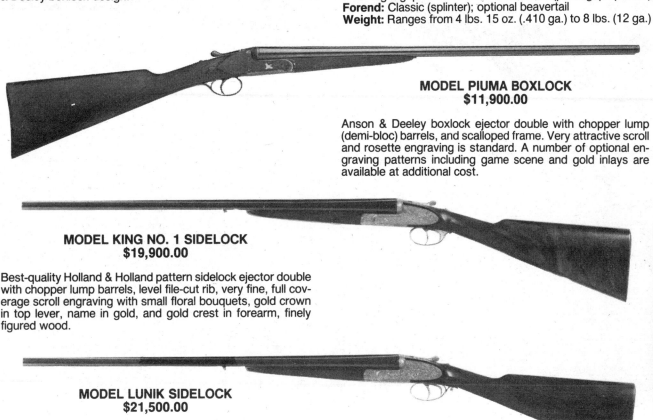

MODEL PIUMA BOXLOCK
$11,900.00

Anson & Deeley boxlock ejector double with chopper lump (demi-bloc) barrels, and scalloped frame. Very attractive scroll and rosette engraving is standard. A number of optional engraving patterns including game scene and gold inlays are available at additional cost.

MODEL KING NO. 1 SIDELOCK
$19,900.00

Best-quality Holland & Holland pattern sidelock ejector double with chopper lump barrels, level file-cut rib, very fine, full coverage scroll engraving with small floral bouquets, gold crown in top lever, name in gold, and gold crest in forearm, finely figured wood.

MODEL LUNIK SIDELOCK
$21,500.00

Best-quality Holland & Holland pattern sidelock ejector double with chopper lump (demi-bloc) barrels, level, filecut rib, Renaissance-style, large scroll engraving in relief, gold crown in top lever, gold name, and gold crest in forearm, finely figured wood.

MODEL KING EXTRA (With Gold)
$30,000.00

Best-quality Holland & Holland pattern sidelock ejector double with chopper lump barrels, level filecut rib, choice of either bulino game scene engraving or game scene engraving with gold inlays, engraved and signed by a master engraver, exhibition grade wood.

PRECISION SPORTS SHOTGUNS

"600" SERIES DOUBLE BARREL SHOTGUNS

Superbly crafted by the Spanish gunmaking firm of Ignacio Ugartechea, the "600" Series doubles are offered in either extractor or ejector configurations. All models boast stocks of hand-checkered walnut, actions and parts machined from ordnance steel, standard auto safety, forged barrels, deep lustrous bluing and English scroll design engraving. **American** (A) models: Single non-selective trigger, pistol grip, beavertail forend, butt plate, raised matted rib. **English** (E) models: Double triggers, straight grip, splinter forend, checkered butt, concave rib; XXV models have Churchill-type rib. **Chokes:** Imp. Cyl./Mod.; Mod./Full. **Weight:** 12 ga., 6¾-7 lbs.; 20 ga. 5¾ lbs.-6 lbs.; 28 and .410 ga., 5¼-5½ lbs. 3″ chambers on 20 and .410 ga.; 2¾ chambers on others. Bi-Gauge models have two sets of barrels, one set in each gauge.

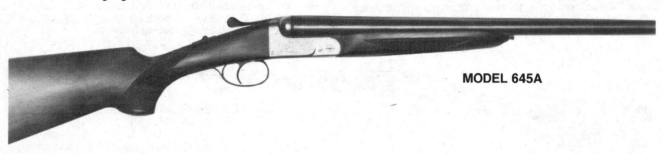

MODEL 645A

SIDE-BY-SIDE "600" SERIES SHOTGUNS

Model	Gauges	Action	Barrel Length	Price
640E (English)	12, 16, 20	Boxlock Ex.	26″, 28″	$ 849.95
640E (English)	28, .410	Boxlock Ex.	26″ (.410), 27″ (28 ga.)	939.95
640A (American)	12, 16, 20	Boxlock Ex.	26″, 28″	969.95
640A (American)	28, .410	Boxlock Ex.	26″ (.410), 27″ (28 ga.)	1079.95
640M "Big Ten", "Turkey Gun", "Goose Gun"	10 (3½″ Mag.)	Boxlock Ex.	26″, 30″, 32″	999.95
640 "Slug Gun"	12	Boxlock Ex.	25″	1119.95
645E (Bi-Gauge)	20/28	Boxlock Ej.	26″	1619.95
645E (English)	12, 16, 20	Boxlock Ej.	26″, 28″	1089.95
645E (English)	28, .410	Boxlock Ej.	26″ (.410), 27″ (28 ga.)	1149.95
645A (American)	12, 16, 20	Boxlock Ej.	26″, 28″	1199.95
645A (American)	28, .410	Boxlock Ej.	26″ (.410), 27″ (28 ga.)	1309.95
645A (Bi-Gauge)	20/28	Boxlock Ej.	27″	1749.95
645E-XXV (English)	12, 16, 20	Boxlock Ej.	25″	1099.95
645E-XXV (English)	28, .410	Boxlock Ej.	25″	1199.95
650E (English)**	12	Boxlock Ex.	28″	919.95
650A (American)	12	Boxlock Ex.	28″	1039.95
655E (English)	12	Boxlock Ej.	28″	1149.95
655A (American)	12	Boxlock Ej.	28″	1259.95

* Ex.=Extractor; Ej.=Ejector; ** Custom order only

BILL HANUS BIRDGUNS
$1269.95 ($1399.00 in 28 Ga.)

Gauges: 16, 20 and 28. **Barrel length:** 26″. **Choke:** Skeet 1/Skeet 2. **Features:** Straight stock; ejectors; boxlock; single non-selective trigger; case-colored receiver; Churchill rib.

REMINGTON PUMP SHOTGUNS

MODEL 870 EXPRESS (20 GA.)

MODEL 870 EXPRESS (12 & 20 GA.)
$264.00

Model 870 Express features the same action as the Wingmaster and is available with 3″ chamber and 26″ or 28″ vent-rib barrel. It has a hardwood stock with low-luster finish and solid butt pad. Choke is Modified REM Choke tube and wrench. **Overall length:** 48½″. **Weight:** 7¼ lbs.

MODEL 870 EXPRESS TURKEY GUN
$277.00

The **Model 870 Express Turkey Gun** boasts all the same features as the Model 870 Express, except has 21″ vent rib barrel and Turkey Extra-Full REM Choke. Also available in .410 bore w/25″ Full Choke barrel: **$289.00**

MODEL 870 EXPRESS DEER GUN
W/Rifle Sights
$260.00

This 12 gauge pump-action deer gun is for hunters who prefer open sights. Features a 20″ barrel, quick-reading iron sights, fixed Imp. Cyl. choke and Monte Carlo stock.

MODEL 870 EXPRESS COMBO (not shown)
$359.00

The **Model 870 Express** in 12 and 20 gauge offers all the features of the standard Model 870, including twin-action bars, quick-changing barrels, REM Choke plus low-luster, checkered hardwood stock and no-shine finish on barrel and receiver. The Model 870 Combo is packaged with an extra 20″ deer barrel, fitted with rifle sights and fixed, Improved Cylinder choke (additional REM chokes can be added for special applications). The 3-inch chamber handles all 2¾″ and 3″ shells without adjustment.

REMINGTON PUMP SHOTGUNS

MODEL 870 EXPRESS DEER GUN
W/Cantilever Scope Mount & Rings
$333.00

The no-nonsense choice for whitetail hunting features a 20″ barrel for maneuverability and the sighting advantages of a Monte Carlo stock and barrel-mounted scope. Comes with Rifles and Imp. Cyl. REM Choke tubes designed for slugs or buckshot.

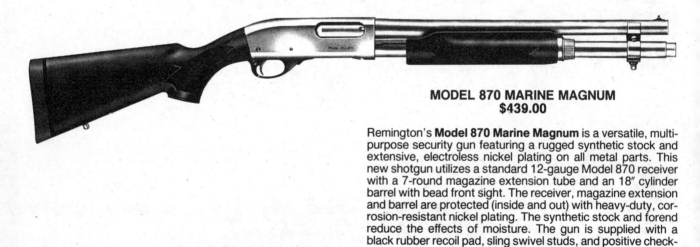

MODEL 870 MARINE MAGNUM
$439.00

Remington's **Model 870 Marine Magnum** is a versatile, multi-purpose security gun featuring a rugged synthetic stock and extensive, electroless nickel plating on all metal parts. This new shotgun utilizes a standard 12-gauge Model 870 receiver with a 7-round magazine extension tube and an 18″ cylinder barrel with bead front sight. The receiver, magazine extension and barrel are protected (inside and out) with heavy-duty, corrosion-resistant nickel plating. The synthetic stock and forend reduce the effects of moisture. The gun is supplied with a black rubber recoil pad, sling swivel studs, and positive checkering on both pistol grip and forend.

MODEL 870 EXPRESS SMALL GAUGE
$289.00

This new shotgun is designed for shooters who want the light weight and maneuverability of a .410 or 20-gauge with the concealment advantages of the non-reflective metal and wood finish of Remington's Express line. The .410 comes with a 25″ Full Choke barrel, and the 20-gauge is available with a 26″ or 28″ REM Choke barrel with Modified REM Choke tube.

REMINGTON PUMP SHOTGUNS

MODEL 870 EXPRESS "YOUTH" GUN
20 Gauge Lightweight
$264.00

The Model 870 Express "Youth" Gun has been specially designed for youths and smaller-sized adults. It's a 20-gauge lightweight with a 1-inch shorter stock and 21-inch barrel. Yet it is still all 870, complete with REM Choke and ventilated rib barrel. **Barrel length:** 21″. **Stock Dimensions:** Length of pull 12½″ (including recoil pad); drop at heel; 2½″ drop at comb 1⅝″. **Overall length:** 40″. **Average Weight:** 6 lbs. **Choke:** REM Choke-Mod.

MODEL 870 SPS
$359.00

Remington's Special Purpose Synthetic model comes with a synthetic stock, 26″ or 28″ vent rib barrels and REM Choke tubes. Black sling furnished.

MODEL 870 SPS-CAMO
$673.00

This new Mossy Oak Bottomland™ Camo version of Model 11-87 and Model 870 Special Purpose Synthetic shotguns features a durable camo finish and synthetic stocks that are immune to the effects of ice, snow and mud. Available with 26″ or 28″ vent rib barrels with twin bead sights and Imp. Cyl., Modified, and full REM Choke tubes.

MODEL 870 SPST TURKEY
$372.00

Same as the Model 870 SPS above, except with a 21″ vent rib turkey barrel and Extra-Full REM Choke tube.

REMINGTON PUMP SHOTGUNS

MODEL 870 "TC" TRAP (12 Gauge Only)
$613.00 ($628.00 w/Monte Carlo Stock)

The **870 "TC"** is a trap version of Model 870 that features REM Choke and a high step-up ventilated rib. REM chokes include regular full, extra full and super full. **Stock:** Redesigned stock and forend of select American walnut with cut-checkering and satin finish; length of pull 14³/₈"; drop at heel 1⁷/₈"; drop at comb 1³/₈". **Weight:** 8 lbs. **Barrel length:** 30". **Overall length:** 51".

MODEL 870 WINGMASTER
12 Gauge, Light Contour Barrel
$460.00 ($519.00 Left Hand)

This restyled **870 "Wingmaster"** pump has cut-checkering on its satin-finished American walnut stock and forend for confident handling, even in wet weather. Also available in Hi-Gloss finish. An ivory bead "Bradley"-type front sight is included. Rifle is available with 26", 28" and 30" barrel with REM Choke and handles 3" and 2³/₄" shells interchangeably. **Overall length:** 46¹/₂ (26" barrel), 48¹/₂" (28" barrel), 50¹/₂ (30" barrel). **Weight:** 7¹/₄ lbs. (w/26" barrel).

MODEL 870 BRUSHMASTER DEER GUN
$439.00 ($495.00 Left Hand)

The **Model 870 Wingmaster Deer Gun** is made to handle rifled slugs and buck shot. It features a 20-inch barrel with 3-inch chamber and fully adjustable rifle-type sights. Stock fitted with rubber recoil pad and white-line spacer. Also available in standard model, but with lacquer finish, no checkering, recoil pad, grip cap; special handy short forend. **Choke:** Imp. Cyl. **Weight:** 6¹/₄ lbs.

MODEL 870 WINGMASTER
20 Gauge Lightweight
$451.00

This is the pump action designed for the upland game hunter who wants enough power to stop fast flying game birds but light enough to be comfortable for all-day hunting. The 20-gauge Lightweight handles all 20-gauge 2³/₄" and 3" shells. REM choke and ventilated rib. **Stock:** American walnut stock and forend. Satin or Hi-Gloss finish. **Barrel lengths:** 26" and 28". **Average weight:** 6 lbs.

REMINGTON PUMP SHOTGUNS

MODEL 870 SPECIAL FIELD
12 and 20 Gauge
$450.00

The **Model 870 "Special Field"** shotgun combines the traditional, straight-stock styling of years past with features never before available on a Remington pump. Its 21-inch vent rib barrel, slimmed and shortened forend, straight, cut-checkered stock offers upland hunters a quick, fast-pointing shotgun. The "Special Field" is chambered for 3-inch shells and will also handle all 2¾-inch shells interchangeably. Barrels will not interchange with standard 870 barrels. **Overall length:** 41½". **Weight:** 7 lbs. (12 ga.); 6 lbs. (20 ga.).

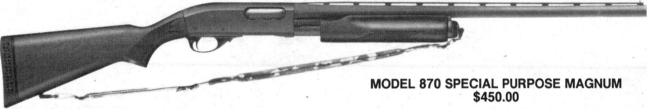

MODEL 870 SPECIAL PURPOSE MAGNUM
$450.00

Available in 12 gauge Magnum with 3-inch Mag. chamber, the **Model 870 SP (Special Purpose) Magnum** pump gun has been designed with waterfowlers and turkey hunters in mind. For concealment, all metal surfaces have been finished in non-glare, non-reflective Parkerized black. And all wood surfaces have been given a dull, non-reflective oil finish with a slightly rough feel for firmer grip. For ease of carrying, the SP Mag. Pump comes factory-equipped with a camo-patterned padded sling, attached at both ends by quick-detachable sling swivels. More than 2 inches wide at the shoulder, the sling is made of durable Du Pont nylon "Cordura." **Barrel:** 26" or 28" chrome-lined barrel bore; ventilated rib. **Choke:** Full. **Stock:** Supplied with dark-colored recoil pad and black line spacers. **Overall length:** 46½" with 26" barrel; 48½" with 28" barrel. **Weight:** Approx. 7¼ lbs.

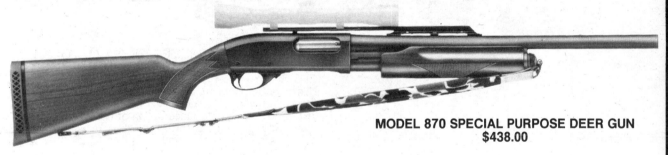

MODEL 870 SPECIAL PURPOSE DEER GUN
$438.00

Gauge: 12. **Choke:** Imp. Cyl. Equipped with rifle sights, recoil pad. **Barrel length:** 20". **Overall length:** 40½." **Average weight:** 7 lbs.

Also available with cantilever barrel for scope mounting and Extra Full Turkey choke. **Price:** $496.00.

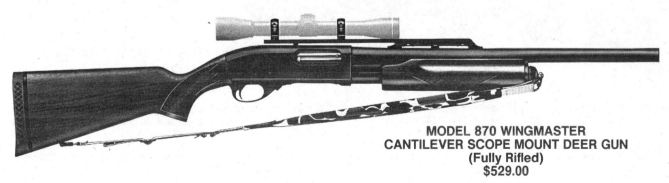

MODEL 870 WINGMASTER
CANTILEVER SCOPE MOUNT DEER GUN
(Fully Rifled)
$529.00

REMINGTON SHOTGUNS

MODEL 11-87 "PREMIER" AUTOLOADER
Light Contour Barrel
$607.00 ($665.00 Left Hand)

Remington's redesigned 12-gauge **Model 11-87 Premier Autoloader** features new, light-contour barrels that reduce both barrel weight and overall weight (more than 8 ounces). The shotgun has a standard 3-inch chamber and handles all 12-gauge shells interchangeably—from 2¾″ field loads to 3″ magnums. The gun's interchangeable REM choke system in- cludes Improved Cylinder, Modified and Full chokes. Select American walnut stocks with fine-line, cut-checkering in satin or high-gloss finish are standard. Right-hand models are available in 26″, 28″ and 30″ barrels (left-hand models are 28″ only). A two-barrel gun case is supplied.

MODEL 11-87 PREMIER TRAP (12 Gauge)
$669.00 ($735.00 Left Hand)
$684.00 (w/Monte Carlo Stock; add $67 for LH)

A 30″ trap barrel offers trap shooters a REM Choke system with three interchangeable choke constrictions: trap full, trap extra full, and trap super full.

MODEL 11-87 PREMIER SKEET (12 Gauge)
$661.00 ($726.00 Left Hand)

This model features American walnut wood and distinctive cut checkering with satin finish, plus new two-piece butt plate. REM Choke system includes option of two skeet chokes— skeet and improved skeet. Trap and skeet guns are designed for 12-gauge target loads and are set to handle 2¾″ shells only. **Barrel length: 26″.**

MODEL 11-87 PREMIER SPORTING CLAYS
$718.00

Remington's new **Model 11-87 Premier Sporting Clays** features a target-grade, American walnut competition stock with a length of pull that is 3/16″ longer and 1/4″ higher at the heel. The tops of the receiver, barrel and rib have a non-reflective matte finish. The rib is medium high with a stainless mid-bead and ivory front bead. The barrel (26″ or 28″) has a lengthened forcing cone to generate greater pattern uniformity; and there are 5 REM choke tubes—Skeet, Improved Skeet, Improved Cylinder, Modified and Full. All sporting clays choke tubes have a knurled end extending .45″ beyond the muzzle for fast field changes. Both the toe and heel of the butt pad are rounded.

REMINGTON SHOTGUNS

MODEL 11-87 SPS (Special Purpose Synthetic)
12 Gauge Autoloader, 3″ Chamber with
Synthetic Stock and REM Chokes
26″ or 28″ Vent Rib Barrels
$605.00

MODEL 11-87 SPST TURKEY GUN
12 Gauge Autoloader, 3″ Chamber with
21″ Barrel and Synthetic Stock
Extra-Full REM Choke Turkey Tube
$618.00

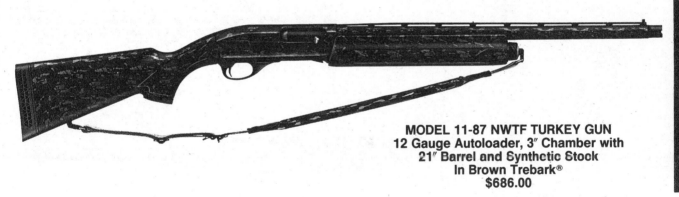

MODEL 11-87 NWTF TURKEY GUN
12 Gauge Autoloader, 3″ Chamber with
21″ Barrel and Synthetic Stock
In Brown Trebark®
$686.00

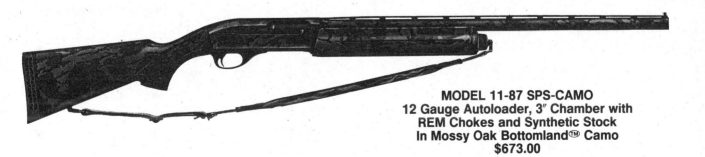

MODEL 11-87 SPS-CAMO
12 Gauge Autoloader, 3″ Chamber with
REM Chokes and Synthetic Stock
In Mossy Oak Bottomland™ Camo
$673.00

REMINGTON SHOTGUNS

MODEL 11-87 "PREMIER" DEER GUN
With Cantilever Scope Mount and
Interchangeable Rifled and Imp. Cyl. REM Chokes
Or Fully Rifled Barrel
$647.00

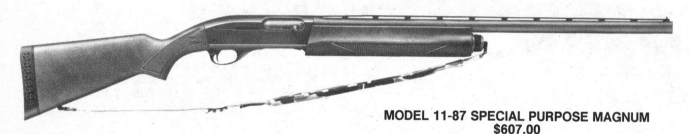

MODEL 11-87 SPECIAL PURPOSE MAGNUM
$607.00

Features non-reflective wood and metal finish for all types of hunting where concealment is critical. Exposed metal surfaces of both barrel and receiver are Parkerized; bolt and carrier have non-glare blackened coloring. **Barrel lengths:** 26" and 28". **Chamber:** 3". **Choke:** REM Choke.

MODEL 11-87 SP DEER GUN
w/Cantilever Scope Mount

MODEL 11-87 SPECIAL PURPOSE DEER GUN
3" Magnum
$587.00

Features same finish as other SP models plus a padded, camostyle carrying sling of Cordura nylon with Q.D. sling swivels. Barrel is 21" with rifle sights and rifled and IC choke (handles all 2³/₄" and 3" rifled slug and buckshot loads as well as high-velocity field and magnum loads; does not function with light 2³/₄" field loads).

Also available with cantilever barrel and rings for scope mount. Includes interchangeable rifled and IC "REM" chokes. **Price: $638.00**

REMINGTON AUTOLOADING SHOTGUNS

MODEL 1100 AUTOLOADING SHOTGUNS

The Remington Model 1100 is a 5-shot gas-operated auto-loading shotgun with a gas metering system designed to reduce recoil effect. This design enables the shooter to use all 2³/₄-inch standard velocity "Express" and 2³/₄-inch Magnum loads without any gun adjustments. Barrels, within gauge and versions, are interchangeable. The 1100 is made in gauges of 12, Lightweight 20, 28 and .410. All 12 and 20 gauge versions include REM Choke; interchangeable choke tubes in 26" and 28" (12 gauge only) barrels. The solid-steel receiver features decorative scroll work. Stocks come with fine-line checkering in a fleur-de-lis design combined with American walnut and a scratch-resistant finish. Features include white-diamond inlay in pistol-grip cap, white-line spacers, full beavertail forend, fluted-comb cuts, chrome-plated bolt and metal bead front sight. Made in U.S.A.

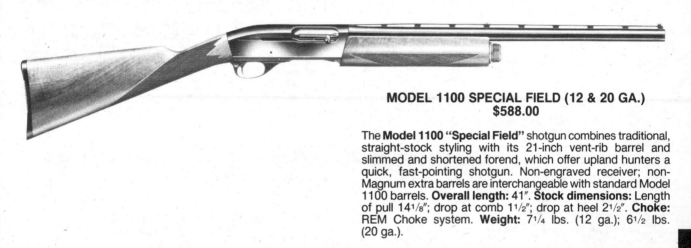

MODEL 1100 SPECIAL FIELD (12 & 20 GA.)
$588.00

The **Model 1100 "Special Field"** shotgun combines traditional, straight-stock styling with its 21-inch vent-rib barrel and slimmed and shortened forend, which offer upland hunters a quick, fast-pointing shotgun. Non-engraved receiver; non-Magnum extra barrels are interchangeable with standard Model 1100 barrels. **Overall length:** 41". **Stock dimensions:** Length of pull 14¹/₈"; drop at comb 1¹/₂"; drop at heel 2¹/₂". **Choke:** REM Choke system. **Weight:** 7¹/₄ lbs. (12 ga.); 6¹/₂ lbs. (20 ga.).

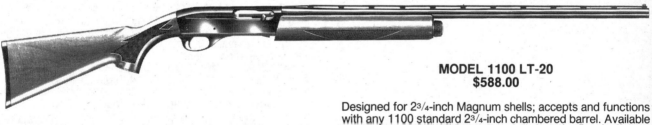

MODEL 1100 LT-20
$588.00

Designed for 2³/₄-inch Magnum shells; accepts and functions with any 1100 standard 2³/₄-inch chambered barrel. Available in 20 gauge, 26" or 28" ventilated rib barrels. **Stock dimensions:** 14" long including pad; 1¹/₂" drop at comb; furnished with recoil pad. Satin or Hi-Gloss finish. **Weight:** About 7 lbs. Also available: 3" Magnum (28" and satin finish only).

MODEL 1100 LT-20 DEER GUN
Lightweight 20 Gauge
$531.00

Features 20-inch (LT-20 gauge) barrels, Improved Cylinder choke. Rifle sights adjustable for windage and elevation. Recoil pad. Choked for both rifled slugs and buck shot. **Weight:** 6¹/₂ lbs. **Overall length:** 40".

REMINGTON AUTOLOADING SHOTGUNS

MODEL 1100 TOURNAMENT SKEET
$669.00

The world's winningest skeet gun, with high-grade positive cut-checkering on selected American walnut stock and forend. The LT-20, 28 and .410 gauge Model 1100 Tournament Skeet guns have a higher vent rib to match the sight picture of the 12-gauge model. A true "matched set," with all the reliability, superb balance, and low recoil sensation that make it the choice of over 50% of the entrants in the world skeet shooting championships. **Barrel lengths:** 25″ (28 ga. & .410 bore) and 26″. **Chokes:** REM Choke (20 ga.) and Skeet choke (28 and .410 ga.). **Weight:** 6³/₄ lbs. (20 ga.), 6¹/₂ lbs. (28 ga.), 7¹/₄ lbs. (.410 ga.).

MODEL 1100 AUTOLOADER
28 and .410 Gauge
$632.00

The Remington Model 1100 Autoloading shotguns in 28 and .410 gauges are scaled-down models of the 12-gauge version. Built on their own receivers and frames, these small gauge shotguns are available in full (.410 only) and modified chokes with ventilated rib barrels.

SPECIFICATIONS. Type: Gas-operated. **Capacity:** 5-shot with 28 ga. shells; 4-shot with 3″ .410 ga. shells; 3-shot plug furnished. **Barrel:** 25″ of special Remington ordnance steel; extra barrels interchangeable within gauge. **Chamber:** 3″ in .410, 2³/₄″ in 28 ga. **Overall length:** 45″. **Safety:** Convenient cross-bolt type. **Receiver:** Made from solid steel, top matted, scroll work on bolt and both sides of receiver. **Stock dimensions:** Walnut; 14″ long; 2¹/₂″ drop at heel; 1¹/₂″ drop at comb. **Average weight:** 6¹/₂ lbs. (28 ga.); 7 lbs. (.410).

MODEL 1100 LT-20 YOUTH GUN
Lightweight, 20 Gauge Only
$575.00

The Model 1100 LT-20 Youth Gun autoloading shotgun features a shorter barrel (21″) and stock. **Overall length:** 39¹/₂″. **Weight:** 6¹/₂ lbs.

REMINGTON SHOTGUNS

SP-10 MAGNUM SHOTGUN
$933.00

Remington's **SP-10 Magnum** is the only gas-operated semi-automatic 10 gauge shotgun made today. Engineered to shoot steel shot, the SP-10 delivers up to 34 percent more pellets to the target than standard 12 gauge shotgun and steel shot combinations. This autoloader features a non-corrosive, stainless steel gas system, in which the cylinder moves—not the piston. This reduces felt recoil energy by spreading the recoil over a longer period of time. The SP-10 has a $3/8''$ vent rib with middle and front sights for a better sight plane. It is also designed to appear virtually invisible to the sharp eyes of waterfowl. The American walnut stock and forend have a protective, low-gloss satin finish that reduces glare, and positive

deep-cut checkering for a sure grip. The receiver and barrel have a matte finish, and the stainless steel breech bolt features a non-reflective finish. Remington's new autoloader also has a brown vented recoil pad and a padded camo sling of Cordura nylon for easy carrying. The receiver is machined from a solid billet of ordnance steel for total integral strength. The SP-10 vented gas system reduces powder residue buildup and makes cleaning easier.

Gauge: 10. **Barrel lengths & choke:** 26″ REM Choke and 30″ REM Choke. **Overall length:** $51^{1}/_{2}''$ (30″ barrel) and $47^{1}/_{2}''$ (26″ barrel). **Weight:** $11^{1}/_{4}$ lbs. (30″ barrel) and 11 lbs. (26″ barrel).

MODEL SP-10 MAGNUM COMBO
10 Gauge Autoloader with REM Chokes
Extra 22″ Barrel with Rifle Sights and
Extra-Full Turkey Choke Tube
$1066.00

MODEL 90-T SINGLE BARREL TRAP GUN
$2995.00

Remington's **Model 90-T Single Barrel Trap** features a top-lever release and internal, full-width, horizontal bolt lockup. Barrels are overbored, with elongated forcing cones, and are available in 30″, 32″ and 34″ lengths (an optional, heavier 34″ barrel can also be ordered). Shooters can choose barrels with either fixed chokes or Remington's interchangeable Trap Choke system. A medium-high, tapered, ventilated rib includes a white, Bradley-type front bead and stainless steel center

bead. Choice of stocks includes Monte Carlo style with $1^{3}/_{8}''$, $1^{1}/_{2}''$ or $1^{1}/_{4}''$ drop at comb, or a conventional straight stock with $1^{1}/_{2}''$ drop. Standard length of pull is $14^{3}/_{8}''$. Stocks and modified beavertail forends are made from semi-fancy American walnut. Wood finish is low-lustre satin with positive, deep-cut checkering 20 lines to the inch. All stocks come with black, vented-rubber recoil pads. **Weight:** Approx. $8^{3}/_{4}$ lbs.

ROTTWEIL SHOTGUNS

ROTTWEIL PARAGON

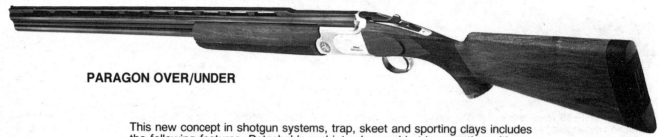

PARAGON OVER/UNDER

This new concept in shotgun systems, trap, skeet and sporting clays includes the following features: Detachable and interchangeable trigger action with superimposed hammers • Safety action on trigger and sears • Spring-loaded self-adjusting wedges • Ejector can be turned on and off at will • Top lever convertible for right- and left-handed shooters • Interchangeable firing pins (without disassembly) • Length and weight of barrels selected depending on application (see below) • Module system: Fully interchangeable receiver, barrels, stocks trigger action and forends • Select walnut stocks

Barrel lengths:

Field & Skeet	27½″	Sporting	28½″
American Skeet	28″	Trap	29″ & 30″
Parcours	28³/₈″	American Trap Single	32″ & 34″

Price: $5,200.00 to $7,200.00

PARAGON
(Close-up Open)

RUGER SHOTGUNS

RED LABEL OVER/UNDER SHOTGUN
$1157.50 (Incl. Screw-in Chokes)
See Specifications table below for
Models KRL-1226, -1227, -2029, -2030

Hardened chrome molybdenum, other alloy steels and music wire coil springs are used throughout. Features single-selective mechanical trigger, selective automatic ejectors, automatic top safety, standard brass bead front sight. Free-floating vent rib with serrated top surface to reduce glare. Stock and semi-beavertail forearm are shaped from American walnut with hand-cut checkering (20 lines per inch). Pistol grip cap and rubber recoil pad are standard, and all wood surfaces are polished and beautifully finished. Stainless steel receiver. Available in 12 or 20 gauge with 3″ chambers.

SCREW-IN CHOKE INSERTS (not shown)

Designed especially for the popular 12 gauge "Red Label" over/under shotgun. Easily installed with a key wrench packaged with each shotgun. Choke fits flush with the muzzle. Every shotgun is equipped with a Full, Modified, Improved Cylinder and two Skeet screw-in chokes. The muzzle edge of the chokes has been slotted for quick identification in or out of the barrels. Full choke has 3 slots; Modified has 2 slots, and Improved Cylinder has 1 slot (Skeet has no slots).

ENGLISH FIELD OVER/UNDER
$1157.00 (w/Screw-in Chokes)
See Specifications table below for
Models KRLS-1226, -1227, -2029, -2030

SPORTING CLAYS OVER/UNDER
$1285.00 (w/Screw-in Chokes)
See Specifications table below for Model KRLS-1236

SPECIFICATIONS OVER & UNDER SHOTGUNS WITH SCREW-IN CHOKES

Catalog Number	Gauge	Chamber	Choke*	Barrel Length	Overall Length	Length Pull	Drop Comb	Drop Heel	**Sights	Approx. Wt. (lbs.)	Type Stock
KRL-1226	12	3″	F,M,IC,S†	26″	43″	14 1/8″	1 1/2″	2 1/2″	GBF	8	Pistol Grip
KRL-1227	12	3″	F,M,IC,S†	28″	45″	14 1/8″	1 1/2″	2 1/2″	GBF	8 1/4	Pistol Grip
KRLS-1226	12	3″	F,M,IC,S†	26″	43″	14 1/8″	1 1/2″	2 1/2″	GBF	7 1/2	Straight
KRLS-1227	12	3″	F,M,IC,S†	28″	45″	14 1/8″	1 1/2″	2 1/2″	GBF	8	Straight
KRLS-1236	12	3″	M,IC,S†	30″	47″	14 1/8″	1 1/2″	2 1/2″	GBF/GBM	7 3/4	Pistol Grip
KRL-2029	20	3″	F,M,IC,S†	26″	43″	14 1/8″	1 1/2″	2 1/2″	GBF	7 1/4	Pistol Grip
KRL-2030	20	3″	F,M,IC,S†	28″	45″	14 1/8″	1 1/2″	2 1/2″	GBF	7 1/2	Pistol Grip
KRLS-2029	20	3″	F,M,IC,S†	26″	43″	14 1/8″	1 1/2″	2 1/2″	GBF	7	Straight
KRLS-2030	20	3″	F,M,IC,S†	28″	45″	14 1/8″	1 1/2″	2 1/2″	GBF	7 1/4	Straight

*F-Full, M-Modified, IC-Improved Cylinder; S-Skeet; **GBF-Gold-Bead Front Sight, GBM-Gold-Bead Middle.
†Two skeet chokes standard with each shotgun. Sporting Clays shotgun has special chokes that are not interchangeable with other Red Label shotguns.

SAVAGE SHOTGUNS

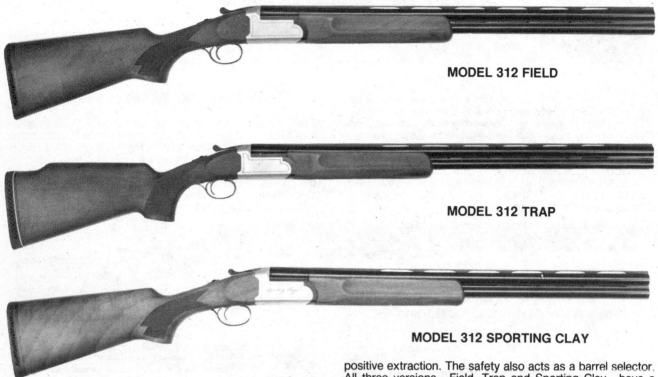

MODEL 312 FIELD

MODEL 312 TRAP

MODEL 312 SPORTING CLAY

MODEL 312 OVER & UNDERS

Savage's new Model 312 over/under shotguns feature select walnut stocks and fine cut checkering. The 312 also features internal hammers with an unbreakable coil mainspring and positive extraction. The safety also acts as a barrel selector. All three versions—Field, Trap and Sporting Clay—have a ventilated rib and ivory bead front sights. All specifications are listed in the table below.

Prices:

MODEL 312F (FIELD) **$700.00**
MODEL 312T (TRAP) 730.00
MODEL 312SC (SPORTING CLAY) 720.00

SPECIFICATIONS

Shotgun	Gauge	Chamber	Chokes	Barrel Length	O.A. Length	Pull	Avg. Wt. Lbs.	Stock
312 Field	12	2¾ & 3″	Full Mod IC with wrench	26″ or 28″	43″ or 45″	14″	7	Cut Checkered Walnut with Recoil Pad
312 Trap	12	2¾ & 3″	Full (2) Mod with wrench	30″	47″	14″	7¼	Cut Checkered Walnut Monte Carlo with Recoil Pad
312 Sporting Clays	12	2¾ & 3″	Full IC(2) Mod (2) #1 Skeet (1) #2 Skeet (1) with wrench	28″	45″	14″	7	Cut Checkered Walnut with Recoil Pad

Features: Ivory bead front sights, metal bead mid sight, internal hammers, positive extraction & manually operated top tang safety that acts as a barrel selector, (312 field has automatic safety feature.)

SKB SHOTGUNS

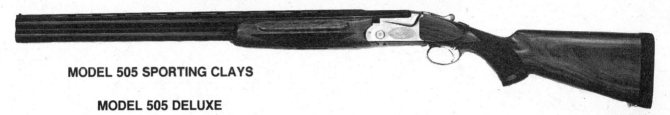

MODEL 505 SPORTING CLAYS

MODEL 505 DELUXE

SPECIFICATIONS
Gauges: 12 (2³/₄″ or 3″), 20 (3″), 28 (2³/₄″), .410 (3″)
Barrel lengths:
   12 gauge—26″, 28″, 30″, 32″, 34″ w/Inter-Choke tube
   20 or 28 gauge—26″ and 28″ w/Inter-Choke tube
   .410 gauge—26″ and 28″ w/Imp. Cyl., Mod./Mod. & Full
Overall length: 43 to 51³/₈″
Weight: 6.6 lbs. to 8¹/₂ lbs.
Sights: Metal front bead (Field Model); target sights on Trap, Skeet and Sporting Clay models
Stock: Hand-checkered walnut with high-gloss finish; target stocks available in standard or Monte Carlo

Features: Silver nitride receiver with game scene engraving; boxlock action; manual safety; automatic ejectors; single selective trigger; ventilated rib
Prices:
MODEL 505 DELUXE FIELD . . . . $ 995.00
MODEL 505 TWO BARREL FIELD SET 1495.00
MODEL 505 TRAP AND SKEET 995.00
MODEL 505 TWO BARREL TRAP COMBO 1395.00
MODEL 505 SPORTING CLAYS 1045.00
MODEL 505 SKEET SET (20, 28, .410 ga.) 2195.00

MODEL 605 SPORTING CLAYS

MODEL 605

Similar to Model 505 Deluxe, this model offers the following additional features: gold-plated trigger, semi-fancy American walnut stock, jeweled barrel block, and finely engraved scroll-work and game scenes on silver nitride receiver, top lever and trigger guard.

Prices:
MODEL 605 FIELD $1195.00
MODEL 605 TWO BARREL FIELD SET 1695.00
MODEL 605 TRAP AND SKEET 1195.00
MODEL 605 TWO BARREL TRAP COMBO 1595.00
MODEL 605 SPORTING CLAYS 1245.00
MODEL 605 SKEET SET (20, 28, .410 ga.) 2395.00

MODEL 885 FIELD

MODEL 885

Similar to Model 605. Additional features include intricately engraved scrollwork and game scenes on silver nitride receiver, side plates, top lever and trigger guard; select semi-fancy American walnut stock.

Prices:
MODEL 885 FIELD $1595.00
MODEL 885 TWO BARREL FIELD SET 2195.00
MODEL 885 TRAP AND SKEET 1595.00
MODEL 885 TWO BARREL TRAP COMBO 2195.00
MODEL 885 SPORTING CLAYS 1645.00
MODEL 885 SKEET SET (20, 28, .410 ga.) 2995.00

STOEGER (IGA) SHOTGUNS

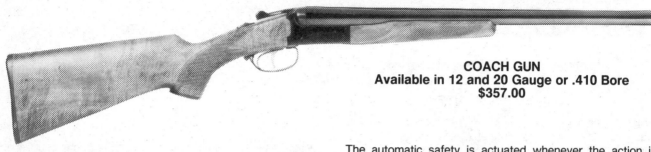

COACH GUN
Available in 12 and 20 Gauge or .410 Bore
$357.00

The **STOEGER CLASSIC SIDE-BY-SIDE COACH GUN** sports a 20-inch barrel. Lightning fast, it is the perfect shotgun for hunting upland game in dense brush or close quarters. This endurance-tested workhorse of a gun is designed from the ground up to give you years of trouble-free service. Two massive underlugs provide a super-safe, vise-tight locking system for lasting strength and durability. The mechanical extraction of spent shells and double-trigger mechanism assure reliability.

The automatic safety is actuated whenever the action is opened, whether or not the gun has been fired. The polish and blue is deep and rich, and the solid sighting rib is matte-finished for glare-free sighting. Chrome-moly steel barrels with micro-polished bores give dense, consistent patterns. The classic stock and forend are of durable hardwood . . . oil finished, hand-rubbed and hand-checkered.

Improved Cylinder/Modified choking and its short barrel make the Stoeger coach gun the ideal choice for hunting in close quarters, security and police work. 3-inch chambers.

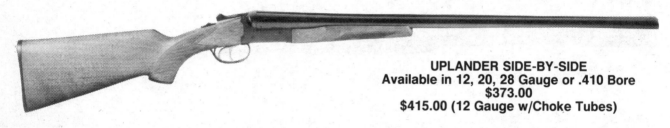

UPLANDER SIDE-BY-SIDE
Available in 12, 20, 28 Gauge or .410 Bore
$373.00
$415.00 (12 Gauge w/Choke Tubes)

The **STOEGER SIDE-BY-SIDE** is a rugged shotgun, endurance-tested and designed to give years of trouble-free service. A vise-tight, super-safe locking system is provided by two massive underlugs for lasting strength and durability. Two design features which make the Stoeger a standout for reliability are its positive mechanical extraction of spent shells and its traditional double-trigger mechanism. The safety is automatic

in that every time the action is opened, whether the gun has been fired or not, the safety is actuated. The polish and bluing are deep and rich. The solid sighting rib carries a machined-in matte finish for glare-free sighting. Barrels are of chrome-moly steel with micro-polished bores to give dense, consistent patterns. The stock and forend are of classic design in durable hardwood . . . oil finished, hand-rubbed and hand-checkered.

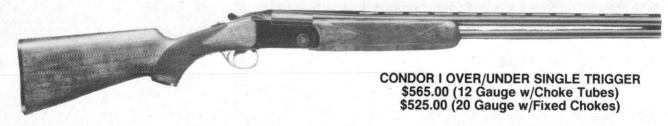

CONDOR I OVER/UNDER SINGLE TRIGGER
$565.00 (12 Gauge w/Choke Tubes)
$525.00 (20 Gauge w/Fixed Chokes)

The **STOEGER OVER/UNDER SINGLE TRIGGER** is a workhorse of a shotgun, designed for maximum dependability in heavy field use. The super-safe lock-up system makes use of a sliding underlug, the best system for over/under shotguns. A massive monobloc joins the barrel in a solid one-piece assembly at the breech end. Reliability is assured, thanks to the mechanical extraction system. Upon opening the breech, the spent shells are partially lifted from the chamber, allowing easy removal by hand. Stoeger barrels are of chrome-moly steel with micro-polished bores to give tight, consistent patterns. They are specifically formulated for use with steel shot where Federal migratory bird regulations require. Atop the barrel is

a sighting rib with an anti-glare surface. The buttstock and forend are of durable hardwood, hand-checkered and finished with an oil-based formula that takes dents and scratches in stride.

The Stoeger **Condor I** over/under shotgun is available in 12 gauge with 26- and 28-inch barrels with choke tubes and 3-inch chambers; 20 gauge with 26- and 28-inch barrels choked IC/M and Mod./Full, 3-inch chambers.

Also available: **Condor II O/U** in 12 gauge, double trigger, 26″ barrel IC/M or 28″ barrel M/F. **Price: $415.00**

STOEGER (IGA) SHOTGUNS

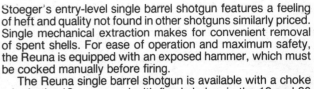

REUNA SINGLE BARREL
$112.00
$132.00 (w/Choke Tube)

NEW

Stoeger's entry-level single barrel shotgun features a feeling of heft and quality not found in other shotguns similarly priced. Single mechanical extraction makes for convenient removal of spent shells. For ease of operation and maximum safety, the Reuna is equipped with an exposed hammer, which must be cocked manually before firing.

The Reuna single barrel shotgun is available with a choke tube in the 12 gauge and with fixed chokes in the 12 and 20 gauge or .410 bore. Both the buttstock and semi-beavertail forearm are of durable Brazilian hardwood. The squared-off design of the firearm enhances stability and provides an additional gripping surface for greater comfort.

MODEL ERA 2000
$615.00

The **ERA 2000** was designed to provide maximum strength and safety in the lockup system. For additional rigidity, the system locks through the frame of the receiver, thus minimizing any barrel movement at the moment of discharge. The receiver has been styled to create a free-flowing look to the eye, while its lustrous deep bluing enhances the overall appearance.

The mechanical extraction system enables the spent shells to be partially lifted from the chamber for easy removal. The triggers operate mechanically and do not depend on inertia from recoil to activate for a second shot. The safety is manual.

Moly-chrome steel barrels, micro-polished to give tight, consistent patterns, are specifically formulated for use with steel shot. The ventilated rib has an anti-glare surface to minimize distortion.

The ERA 2000 stock and forend are constructed of oil-finished Brazilian hardwood. Hand-finished checkering provides for a sharp, sure gripping surface. Available in 12 gauge with 26" or 28" barrels (choke tubes). See table below for additional specifications.

STOEGER SHOTGUN SPECIFICATIONS

Model	Gauge	Chokes	Chamber	Barrel Length	Length of Pull	Drop at Comb	Drop at Heel	Approx. Average Weight	Safety	Extractors
Coach Gun Side-by-Side	12	IC&M	3"	20"	14 1/2"	1 1/2"	2 1/2"	6 1/2 lbs.	Automatic	Yes
	20	IC&M	3"	20"	14 1/2"	1 1/2"	2 1/2"	6 1/2 lbs.	Automatic	Yes
	.410	IC/M	3"	20"	14 1/2"	1 1/2"	2 1/2"	5 1/2 lbs.	Automatic	Yes
NEW Uplander Side-by-Side	12	Choke tubes	3"	26"/28"	14 1/2"	1 1/2"	2 1/2"	7 lbs.	Automatic	Yes
	12	M/F; IC&M	3"	26"/28"	14 1/2"	1 1/2"	2 1/2"	7 lbs.	Automatic	Yes
	20	M/F; IC&M	3"	26"/28"	14 1/2"	1 1/2"	2 1/2"	6 3/4 lbs.	Automatic	Yes
	28	IC/M	2 3/4"	26"	14 1/2"	1 1/2"	2 1/2"	6 1/4 lbs.	Automatic	Yes
	.410	F/F	3"	26"	14 1/2"	1 1/2"	2 1/2"	6 1/4 lbs.	Automatic	Yes
NEW Reuna Single Barrel	12	Choke tube	3"	28"	14 1/2"	1 1/2"	2 1/2"	6 1/4 lbs.	Manual	Yes
	12	F, IC	3"	26"/28"	14 1/2"	1 1/2"	2 1/2"	6 1/4 lbs.	Manual	Yes
	20	F	3"	26"	14 1/2"	1 1/2"	2 1/2"	6 1/2 lbs.	Manual	Yes
	.410	F	3"	26"	14 1/2"	1 1/2"	2 1/2"	5 1/8 lbs.	Manual	Yes
ERA 2000 Over/Under	12 **NEW**	Choke tubes	3"	26"/28"	14 1/2"	1 1/2"	2 1/2"	7 lbs.	Manual	Yes
Condor I Over/Under	12	Choke tubes	3"	26"/28"	14 1/2"	1 1/2"	2 1/2"	7 lbs.	Manual	Yes
	20	M/F IC/M	3"	26"/28"	14 1/2"	1 1/2"	2 1/2"	7 lbs.	Manual	Yes
Condor II* Over/Under	12	IC/M; M/F	3"	26"/28"	14 1/2"	1 1/2"	2 1/2"	7 lbs.	Manual	Yes

* Double trigger

TIKKA SHOTGUNS
(Formerly Valmet)

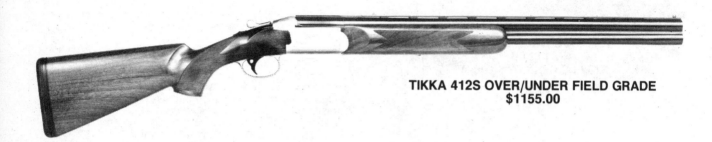

TIKKA 412S OVER/UNDER FIELD GRADE
$1155.00

Designed for the experienced hunter, Tikka's 412S represents the pride and skill of "Old World" European craftsmanship. The barrels are polished to a mirror finish and deeply blued. Select American walnut stock and forearm highlight fine, deep-cut checkering. Other features include:

Time-proven action: Designed to handle large centerfire calibers for more durability and reliability.

Mechanical trigger: Fires two shots as fast as you can pull the trigger. Does not rely on the inertia from the recoil of the first shot to set the trigger for the second. In the event of a faulty primer or light hit, inertia trigger shotguns cannot function on the second round.

Single selective trigger: Selector button is located on the trigger for fast, easy selection.

Large trigger guard opening: Designed for cold weather shooting; permits easy finger movement when wearing gloves.

American walnut stock and forearm: Add greatly to overall appearance.

Superior stock design: A palm swell provides additional hand comfort. Length and angle (pitch) can be adjusted for a perfect fit with addition of factory spacers. Fine, deep-cut checkering.

Palm-filling forearm: Rounded and tapered for comfort and smooth, true swing, plus fine, deep-cut checkering.

Automatic ejectors: Select and eject fired rounds. Raise unfired shells for safe removal.

Chrome-lined barrels: For more consistent patterns. Eliminates pitting and corrosion, extends barrel life even with steel shot.

Stainless steel choke tubes: Added strength over regular carbon and alloy materials. Easily handles steel shot. Recessed so as not to detract from appearance. Tight tolerances enable truer patterns and enhance choke versatility.

Sliding locking bolt: Secure lockup between receiver and barrels. Wears in, not loose.

Matte nickel receiver: Non-glare and more resistant to wear and corrosion.

Wide vent rib: Cross-file pattern reduces glare. Fluorescent front and middle beads.

Automatic safety: Goes to safe position automatically when gun is opened.

Cocking indicators: Allow shooter to determine (through sight or feel) which barrel has been fired.

Steel receiver: Forged and machined for durability.

Chamber: 3-inch on all models

Two-piece firing pin: For more durability

Versatility: Change from over/under shotgun to shotgun/rifle, trap, skeet or double rifle. Precision tolerances require only minor initial fitting.

SPECIFICATIONS
Gauge: 12
Chambers: 3"
Weight: 7¼ lbs. w/26" barrels; 7½ lbs. w/28" barrels
Barrel lengths/chokes:
26", 5 chokes (F, M, IM, IC & Skeet)
28", 5 chokes (F, M, IM, IC & Skeet)

SPORTING CLAYS SHOTGUN (not shown)
$1270.00

Designed to accommodate the specific requirements of the shooter in this, the fastest growing shooting sport in America today. The Sporting Clays shotgun features a specially designed American walnut stock with a double palm swell finished with a soft satin lacquer for maximum protection with minimum maintenance. Available in 12 gauge with a selection of 5 recessed choke tubes. Other features include a 3" chamber, manual safety, customized sporting clay recoil pad, single selective trigger, blued receiver and 28" barrel with ventilated side and top rib with two iridescent beads. In addition, the shotgun is furnished with an attractive carrying case.

Manufactured in Italy, Tikka is designed and crafted by Sako of Finland, which has enjoyed international acclaim for the manufacture of precision sporting firearms since 1918.

TIKKA SHOTGUNS
(Formerly Valmet)

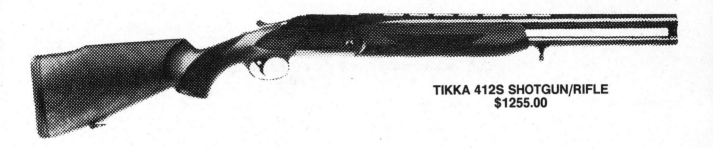

TIKKA 412S SHOTGUN/RIFLE
$1255.00

Tikka's unique 412S Shotgun/Rifle combination continues to be the most popular gun of its type in the U.S. Its features are identical to the 412S Field Grade over/under shotguns, including strong steel receiver, superior sliding locking mechanism with automatic safety, cocking indicators, mechanical triggers and two-piece firing pin. In addition, note the other features of this model—

Barrel regulation: Adjusts for windage simply by turning the screw on the muzzle. Elevation is adjustable by regulating the sliding wedge located between the barrels.

Compact: 24-inch barrels mounted on the low-profile receiver limit the overall length to 40 inches (about 5″ less than most bolt-action rifles with similar 24-inch barrels).

Single selective trigger: A barrel selector is located on the trigger for quick, easy selection. Double triggers are also available.

Choice of calibers: Choose from 222 or 308. Both are under the 12 gauge, 3″ chamber with Improved Modified choke.

Sighting options: The vent rib is cross-filed to reduce glare. The rear sight is flush-folding and permits rapid alignment with the large blade front sight. The rib is milled to accommodate Tikka's one-piece scope mount with 1″ rings. Scope mount is

of "quick release" design and can be removed without altering zero.

European walnut stock: Stocks are available with palm swell for greater control and comfort. Quick detachable sling swivel. Length or pitch adjustable with factory spacers. Semi-Monte Carlo design.

Interchangeability: Receiver will accommodate Tikka's over/under shotgun barrels and double-rifle barrels with minor initial fitting.

SPECIFICATIONS
Gauge/Caliber: 12/222 or 12/308
Chamber: 3″ with Improved Modified choke
Barrel length: 24″
Overall length: 40″
Weight: 8 lbs.
Stock: European walnut with semi-Monte Carlo design

Extra Barrel Sets:

Over/Under	$635.00
Shotgun/Rifle	720.00
Double Rifle	935.00

WEATHERBY SHOTGUNS

ATHENA GRADES IV & V OVER/UNDERS
$1950.00 to $2616.00

Receiver: The Athena receiver houses a strong, reliable box-lock action, yet it features side lock-type plates to carry through the fine floral engraving. The hinge pivots are made of a special high strength steel alloy. The locking system employs the time-tested Greener cross-bolt design. **Single selective trigger:** It is mechanically rather than recoil operated. This provides a fully automatic switchover, allowing the second barrel to be fired on a subsequent trigger pull, even in the event of a misfire. A flick of the trigger finger and the selector lever, located just in front of the trigger, is all the way to the left enabling you to fire the lower barrel first, or to the right for the upper barrel. The Athena trigger is selective as well. **Barrels:** The breech block is hand-fitted to the receiver, providing closest possible tolerances. Every Athena is equipped with a matted, ventilated rib and bead front sight. **Selective automatic ejectors:** The Athena contains ejectors that are fully automatic both in selection and action. **Slide safety:** The safety is the traditional slide type located conveniently on the upper tang on top of the pistol grip. **Stock:** Each stock is carved from specially selected Claro walnut, with fine line hand-checkering and high luster finish. Trap model has Monte Carlo stock only. *See* Athena and Orion table for additional information and specifications.

GRADE IV CHOKES
Fixed Choke
Field, .410 Gauge
Skeet, 12 or 20 Gauge
IMC Multi Choke
Field, 12, 20 or 28 Gauge
Trap, 12 Gauge
Trap, single barrel, 12 Gauge
Trap Combo, 12 Gauge

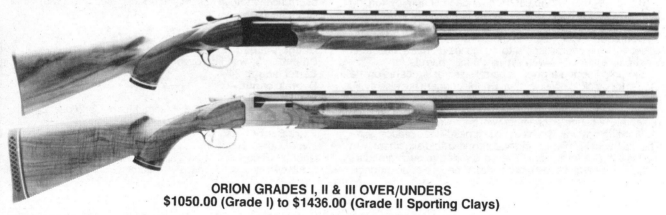

ORION GRADES I, II & III OVER/UNDERS
$1050.00 (Grade I) to $1436.00 (Grade II Sporting Clays)

For greater versatility, the Orion incorporates the integral multichoke (IMC) system. Available in Extra-full, Full, Modified, Improved Modified, Improved Cylinder and Skeet, the choke tubes fit flush with the muzzle without detracting from the beauty of the gun. Three tubes are furnished with each gun. The precision hand-fitted monobloc and receiver are machined from high-strength steel with a highly polished finish. The box-lock design uses the Greener cross-bolt locking system and special sears maintain hammer engagement. Pistol grip stock and forearm are carved of Claro walnut with hand-checkered diamond inlay pattern and high-gloss finish. Chrome moly steel barrels, and the receiver, are deeply blued. The Orion also features selective automatic ejectors, single selective trigger, front bead sight and ventilated rib. The trap model boasts a curved trap-style recoil pad and is available with Monte Carlo stock only. **Weight:** 12 ga. Field, 7½ lbs.; 20 ga. Field, 7½ lbs.; Trap, 8 lbs.

ORION CHOKES
Grade I
IMC Multi-Choke, Field, 12 or 20 Gauge
Grade II
Fixed Choke, Field, .410 Gauge
Fixed Choke, Skeet, 12 or 20 Gauge
IMC Multi Choke, Field, 12, 20 or 28 Gauge
IMC Multi Choke, Trap, 12 Gauge
Grade II Sporting Clays
12 Gauge only
Grade III
IMC Multi-choke, Field, 12 or 20 Gauge

WEATHERBY SHOTGUNS

ORION II SPORTING CLAYS
12 Gauge Over/Under
$1436.00
See table below for specifications

ATHENA & ORION OVER/UNDER SHOTGUN SPECIFICATIONS

Model	Chamber	Bbl Length	Chokes	Overall Length	Length Of Pull	Comb	Drop at Heel	MC	Bead Sights	Approx. Weight
IMC MULTI-CHOKE FIELD MODELS (12 GA., 20 GA.)										
Field	3"	26"	M/IC/Sk	43¼"	14¼"	1½"	2½"		Brilliant Front	6½-7½ lbs.
Field	3"	28"	F/M/IC	45¼"	14¼"	1½"	2½"		Brilliant Front	6½-7½ lbs.
Field (12 Ga. only)	3"¾	30"	F/M/F	47¼"	14¼"	1½"	2½"		Brilliant Front	7½-8 lbs.
FIXED CHOKE FIELD MODELS (28 GA., .410 GA.)										
28 Ga.	2¾	26"	M/IC	43¼"	14¼"	1½"	2½"		Brilliant Front	6½-7½ lbs.
28 Ga.	2¾"	28"	F/M	45¼"	14¼"	1½"	2½"		Brilliant Front	6½-7½ lbs.
.410	3"	26"	M/IC	43¼"	14¼"	1½"	2½"		Brilliant Front	6½-7½ lbs.
.410	3"	28"	F/M	45¼"	14¼"	1½"	2½"		Brilliant Ford	6½-7½ lbs.
IMC MULTI CHOKE TRAP MODELS (12 GA. only)**										
Trap	2¾"	30"	F/M/IM	47½"	14⅜"	1⅜"	2⅛"	1¾	White Fr/Mid Br	8-8½ lbs.
Trap	2¾"	32"	F/M/IM	49½"	14⅜"	1⅜"	2⅛"	1¾	White Fr/Mid Br	8-8½ lbs.
†Sgl Bbl Trap	2¾"	32"	F/M/IM	49½"	14⅜"	1⅜"	2⅛"	1¾ ·	White Fr/Mid Br	8-8½ lbs.
†Sgl Bbl Trap	2¾"	34"	F/M/IM	51½"	14⅜"	1⅜"	2⅛	1¾	White Fr/Mid Br	8½-9 lbs.

Single barrel trap available in combo set with 30" or 32" O/U barrels. † Available in Athena Model only.

Model	Chamber	Bbl Length	Chokes	Overall Length	Length Of Pull	Comb	Drop at Heel	MC	Bead Sights	Approx. Weight
FIXED CHOKE SKEET MODELS (12 GA., 28 GA., .410 GA.)										
12 Ga.	2¾"	26"	S/S	43½"	14¼"	1½"	2½"		White Fr/Mid Br	6½-7½ lbs.
12 Ga.	2¾"	28"	S/S	45¼"	14¼"	1½"	2½"		White Fr/Mid Br	6½-7½ lbs.
20 Ga.	2¾"	26"	S/S	43¼"	14¼"	1½"	2½"		White Fr/Mid Br	6½-7½ lbs.
28 Ga.	2¾"	26"	S/S	43¼"	14¼"	1½"	2½"		White Fr/Mid Br	6½-7½ lbs.
.410	3"	26"	S/S	43¼"	14¼"	1½"	2½"		White Fr/Mid Br	6½-7½ lbs.
ATHENA MASTER SKEET TUBE SET (12 GA. Shotgun with 20 GA., 28 GA, and .410 GA. tubes)										
12 Ga.	2¾"	28" & 26"	S/S	45¼"	14¼"	1½"	2½"		White Fr/Mid Br	7-8 lbs.
ORION II SPORTING CLAYS										
12 Ga.	2¾"	28" & 30"	IC/M/F	45¼" & 47¼"	14¼"	1½"	2¼"		White Fr/Mid Br	7½-8 lbs.

WINCHESTER SECURITY SHOTGUNS

This trio of tough 12-gauge shotguns provides backup strength for security and police work as well as all-around utility. The action is one of the fastest second-shot pumps made. It features a front-locking rotating bolt for strength and secure, single-unit lock-up into the barrel. Twin-action slide bars prevent binding.

All three guns are chambered for 3-inch shotshells. They handle 3-inch Magnum, 2³/₄-inch Magnum and standard 2³/₄-inch shotshells interchangeably. They have cross-bolt safety,

walnut-finished hardwood stock and forearm, black rubber butt pad and plain 18-inch barrel with Cylinder Bore choke. All are ultra-reliable and easy to handle.

Special chrome finishes on Police and Marine guns are actually triple-plated: first with copper for adherence, then with nickel for rust protection, and finally with chrome for a hard finish. This triple-plating assures durability and quality. Both guns have a forend cap with swivel to accommodate sling.

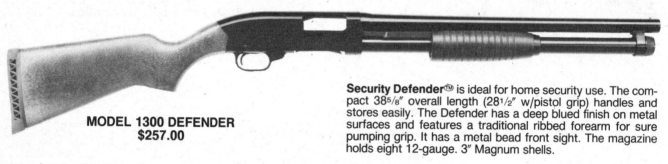

MODEL 1300 DEFENDER
$257.00

Security Defender® is ideal for home security use. The compact 38⁵/₈″ overall length (28¹/₂″ w/pistol grip) handles and stores easily. The Defender has a deep blued finish on metal surfaces and features a traditional ribbed forearm for sure pumping grip. It has a metal bead front sight. The magazine holds eight 12-gauge. 3″ Magnum shells.

Model	Symbol Number	Gauge	Chamber*	Shotshell Capacity	Choke	Barrel Length & Type	Overall Length	Nominal Weight (Lbs.)
1300 Defender Hardwood Stock	7665	12	3 Mag.	5	Cyl.	18″	38⁵/₈″	6¹/₂
1300 Defender Synthetic Stock Matte	7673	12	3 Mag.	5	Cyl.	18	38⁵/₈	6¹/₄
1300 Defender Synthetic Stock Matte	7681	20	3 Mag.	5	Cyl.	18	38⁵/₈	6

* Includes one shotshell in chamber when ready to fire. VR-Ventilated rib. Cyl-Cylinder Bore. W1M-Modified tube. Sights are metal beard front. Nominal drop at comb: 1³/₈″. Drop at heel: 2³/₄″.

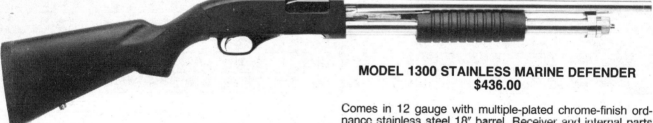

MODEL 1300 STAINLESS MARINE DEFENDER
$436.00

Comes in 12 gauge with multiple-plated chrome-finish ordnance stainless steel 18″ barrel. Receiver and internal parts are coated with Sandstrom 9A corrosion-inhibiting dry film lubricant. Stock and forend are made of corrosion and moisture-resistant material. **Capacity:** 7 shells (2³/₄″). **Sights:** Bead front (sling swivels incl.). Additional specifications same as Defender model described above.

Model	Symbol Number	Gauge	Chamber	Shotshell Capacity*	Choke	Barrel Length & Type	Overall Length	Nominal Length of Pull	Nominal Drop At Comb	Heel	Nominal Weight (Lbs.)	Sights
1300 Stainless Marine	7475	12	3″Mag.	7¹	Cyl.	18″	38⁵/₈	14″	1³/₈″	2³/₄″	7	MBF
1300 Pistol Grip	7483	12	3 Mag.	7¹	Cyl.	18	28⁵/₈	14	—	—	6	MBF

* Includes one shotshell in chamber when ready to fire. ¹ Subtract one shell capacity for 3″ shells. Cyl.-Cylinder Bare. MBF-Metal bead front.

WINCHESTER SHOTGUNS

MODEL 1300 PUMP DEER SLUG GUNS
$403.00

Winchester's Model 1300 Walnut Slug Hunter pump action shotgun features a rifled barrel with 8 lands and grooves, rifle-type sights, and a receiver that is factory-drilled and tapped for scope. Also available is a Model 1300 WinTuff Slug Hunter, featuring a Winchester Proof steel-rifled barrel with rifle-type sights. Model 1300 Walnut Slug Hunter has a smooth-bore barrel that comes with an extra long Sabot-rifled choke tube. Also included is an improved Cylinder Winchoke tube for traditional slug or buckshot shooting.

The Walnut models feature sculptured, cut-checkered forends, while the brown laminated WinTuff models have the traditional ribbed corn cob-style forend. All models have honey-comb recoil pad and a crossbolt safety. The lockup is a chrome molybdenum high-speed, four-slug rotary bolt and barrel extension system (lockup does not require use of the receiver top as part of the locking system). The Model 1300 receiver is made of lightweight, corrosion-resistant, space age alloy. Because the rotary lockup is concentric with the bore of the barrel, recoil forces are used to unlock the bolt and drive both bolt and forend rearward to help the shooter set up the next shot.

Also available:
Beavertail forend **Whitetail's Unlimited Model** . . . . **$449.00.**
Smooth-Bore model with IC and Rifled Sabot
Tubes . . . . **$437.00.**

MODEL 1300 WALNUT SLUG HUNTER (with Sabot Tube)

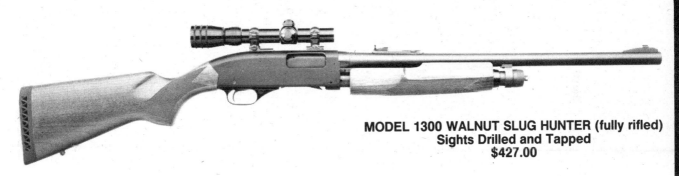

MODEL 1300 WALNUT SLUG HUNTER (fully rifled)
Sights Drilled and Tapped
$427.00

SPECIFICATIONS MODEL 1300—12 GAUGE

Model	Symbol Number	Chamber	Shotshell Capacity*	Choke	Barrel Length & Type	Overall Length	Nominal Weight (Lbs.)	Rate of Twist 1 Turn in	Sights
1300 Walnut	6204	3" Mag.	5	Cyl	22" Rifled	42³/₄	7	35"	Rifle
1300 Wintuff	6220	3 Mag.	5	Cyl	22 Rifled	42³/₄	7	35	Rifle
1300 Walnut Sabot Tube	6253	3 Mag.	5	W2	22 Smooth	42³/₄	7	—	Rifle
1300 Whitetail's Unlimited	6287	3 Mag.	5	Cyl	22 Rifled	42³/₄	7	35	Rifle

* Includes one shotshell in chamber when ready to fire. W2-Improved Cylinder and rifled Sabot choke tubes. Cyl-Cylinder bore. Drilled and Tapped-Bases included. Length of pull: 14". Drop at comb: 1¹/₂". Drop at heel: 2¹/₂".

SHOTGUNS

WINCHESTER SHOTGUNS

**MODEL 1300
PISTOL GRIP SLIDE-ACTION DEFENDER
$243.00**

Winchester Security shotguns are also available with high-strength pistol grip and forearm. The pistol grip features finger grooves and checkering for sure, fast handling. The shorter forearm is ribbed for positive grip and pumpability. Both pistol grip and forearm are high-impact-resistant ABS plastic with non-glare matte black finish. The Pistol Grip series is lighter in weight, compact, easily stored and fast handling.

**MODEL 1300 RANGER 12 GAUGE DEER COMBO
22″ Rifled w/Sights & 28″ Vent Rib Barrels
$375.00**

SPECIFICATIONS MODEL 1300 RANGER, RANGER DEER & LADIES/YOUTH

Model	Symbol Number	Gauge	Choke	Barrel Length & Type	Overall Length	Nominal Length of Pull	Nominal Weight (Lbs.)	Sights
1300 Ranger	6519	12	W3	28″ VR	48⅝″	14″	7¼	MBF
	6568	20	W3	28 VR	48⅝	14	7¼	MBF
	6592	12	W3	26 VR	46⅝	14	7	MBF
	6600	20	W3	26 VR	46⅝	14	7	MBF
1300 Ranger Deer Combo 12 ga. Extra Barrel	6618	12 12	Cyl W3	22 28 VR	42⅝	14	6½	Rifle MBF
1300 Ranger Deer Combo 20 ga. Extra Barrel	6667	20 20	Cyl W3	22 28 VR	42⅝	14	6½	Rifle MBF
1300 Ranger Deer Gun	6717	12	Cyl	22	42¾	14	6½	Rifle
	6766	20	Cyl	22	42⅝	14	6½	Rifle
	6782	12	Cyl	22 Rifled	48⅝	14	7¼	MBF
	6790	12	W2	22	42¾	14	6½	Rifle
1300 Walnut Ladies/Youth	6402	20	W3	22 VR	41⅝	13	6¼	MBF
1300 Ranger Ladies/Youth	7111	20	W3	22 VR	41⅝	13	6¼	MBF

All models have 3″ Mag. chambers and 5-shot shell capacity, including one shotshell in chamber when ready to fire. VR-Ventilated rib. Cyl.-Cylinder Bore, R-Rifled Barrel. MBF-Metal bead front. RT-Rifle type front and rear sights. Model 1300 and Ranger pump action shotguns have factory-installed plug which limits capacity to three shells. Ladies/Youth has factory-installed plug which limits capacity to one, two or three shells as desired. Extra barrels for Model 1300 and Ranger shotguns are available in 12 gauge, plain or ventilated rib, in a variety of barrel lengths and chokes; interchangeable with gauge. Winchoke sets with wrench come with gun as follows: W3W-Extra Full, Full, Modified tubes. W3-Full, Modified, Improved Cylinder tubes. W1M-Modified tube. W1F-Full tube. Nominal drop at comb: 1½″; nominal drop at heel: 2½″ (2⅜″-Ladies' models).

WINCHESTER SHOTGUNS

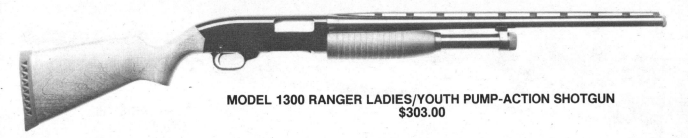

MODEL 1300 RANGER LADIES/YOUTH PUMP-ACTION SHOTGUN
$303.00

Gauge: 20 gauge only; 3″ chamber; 5-shot magazine. **Barrel:** 22″ barrel w/vent. rib; Winchoke (Full, Modified, Improved Cylinder). **Weight:** 6½ lbs. **Length:** 41⅝″. **Stock:** Walnut or American hardwood with ribbed forend. **Sights:** Metal bead front. **Features:** Cross-bolt safety; black rubber butt pad; twin-action slide bars; front-locking rotating bolt; removable segmented magazine plug to limit shotshell capacity for training purposes.

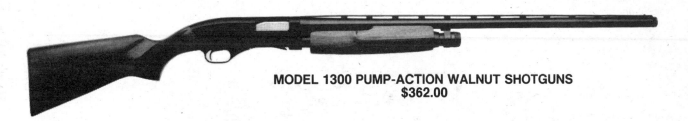

MODEL 1300 PUMP-ACTION WALNUT SHOTGUNS
$362.00

Whether hunting rabbits or pheasants with the 12 gauge, or going after doves or quail with the 20 gauge, Model 1300 Walnut with its beavertail forend is a versatile performer. This model features Winchester's Armor-Lock rotary-bolt lockup, which provides better balance, faster pointing and easier carrying. It also means that a new round is cycled into the chamber as fast as the pump can be operated. The trigger-blocking cross bolt safety is located at the front of the trigger guard. Single pin take-down provides easy field maintenance and cleaning. The floating ventilated rib assures consistent point-of-impact. The special ventilated rubber recoil pad on all 12 gauge models provides maximum recoil absorption.

Each barrel (22″ or 28″) is equipped with Winchoke Tubes, which extend ¼″ past the muzzle so that choice of choke tube can be identified easily; it also protects the muzzle of the barrel from getting crimped or accidentally damaged. All Winchester Model 1300 Walnut shotguns feature diamond point cut checkering. Stocks are American walnut with satin finish and diamond point cut checkering on the pistol grip.

SPECIFICATIONS MODEL 1300 WALNUT

Model	Symbol Number	Gauge	Chamber	Shotshell Capacity*	Choke	Barrel Length & Type	Overall Length	Nominal Drop At Heel	Nominal Weight (Lbs.)
1300 Walnut	6014	12	3 Mag.	5	W3	28 VR	48⅝	2½	7⅛
	6022	20	3 Mag.	5	W3	28 VR	48⅝	2½	7⅛
	6063	12	3 Mag.	5	W3	22 VR	42⅝	1½	6¾
	6071	12	3 Mag.	5	W3	26 VR	46⅝	1½	6¾
	6113	20	3 Mag.	5	W3	22 VR	42⅝	2½	6¾
	6121	20	3 Mag.	5	W3	26 VR	46⅝	2½	6¾

* Includes one shotshell in chamber when ready to fire. VR-Ventilated rib. Winchoke sets with wrench come with gun as follows: W3-Full, Modified, Improved Cylinder tubes. All models have 14″ nominal length of pull; 1½″ drop at comb. Sights are metal bead front.

SHOTGUNS

WINCHESTER SHOTGUNS

MODEL 1300—SERIES III
$436.00

U.S. Repeating Arms and the National Wild Turkey Federation announce their Gun of the Year (1992) designed for today's serious turkey hunters. Its WinCam camouflage stock and forearm are designed for strength, concealment and weather resistance. The green camo laminate stock with cut-checkering maintains a low profile in the woods, while the ribbed forearm ensures a secure grip. The receiver is roll-engraved on both sides with decorative turkey scenes. Dual action bars provide quiet, smooth, anti-bind operation. A trigger and hammer

blocking and cross-bolt safety are located at the front of the trigger guard. All Model 1300 receivers are machined from a single piece of high-strength alloy, reducing the overall weight and improving balance and handling.

Gauge: 12. **Capacity:** 5 shots. **Chamber:** 3″ Magnum. **Choke:** WinChoke tubes (Extra Full, Full and Modified), interchangeable. **Barrel length:** 22″. **Weight:** 6³/₈″. **Features:** Non-reflective matte finish; slip-resistant, camouflage sling w/quick release swivels; rifle sights.

MODEL 1300 TURKEY SHOTGUN
$414.00

Available in 12 gauge only, the Model 1300 Turkey gun comes equipped with a 22-inch ventilated rib barrel, which includes the Winchester Winchoke system with Extra Full, Full and Modified choke tubes and wrench. Its walnut stock and forearm have a special low-luster protective finish; the receiver, barrel and all exterior metal surfaces feature a non-glare matte finish. The receiver is roll engraved. The pistol grip has deep-cut checkering; the contoured forearm is ribbed for sure gripping

and has been modified for positioning and comfort. Other features include cross-bolt safety with red indicator blocks and metal bead sights. The 1300 Turkey Gun handles 3″ magnum, 2³/₄″ Magnum and 2³/₄″ standard shotshells interchangeably. See table below for complete specifications.

Also available:

National Wild Turkey Federation Model **$436.00**

SPECIFICATIONS: MODEL 1300 TURKEY

Model	Symbol Number	Gauge	Chamber	Shotshell Capacity*†	Choke	Barrel Length & Type	Overall Length	Nominal Length of Pull	Nominal Drop At Comb	Heel	Nominal Weight (Lbs.)	Sights
1300 NWTF Turkey Gun Wincam Series III	6311	12	3″Mag.	5	W3W	22″VR	42⁵/₈″	14″	1¹/₂″	2¹/₂″	6³/₈	MBF
1300 Turkey Gun Wincam	6295	12	3 Mag.	5	W3W	22 VR	42⁵/₈	14	1¹/₂	2¹/₂	6³/₈	MBF
1300 Ladies/Youth Turkey Gun	6378	20	3 Mag.	5	W3	22 VR	41⁵/₈	13	1¹/₂	2³/₈	6	MBF

* Includes one shotshell in chamber when ready to fire. VR-Ventilated rib. MBF-Metal bead front. Winchoke sets with wrench come with gun as follows: W3W-Extra Full, Full, Modified tubes. W3-Full, Modified, Improved Cylinder tubes.

† Includes one shotshell in chamber when ready to fire. VR-Floating ventilated rib. MBF-Metal bead front. Winchoke sets with wrench come with gun as follows: W3-Full, Modified, Improved Cylinder tubes.

WINCHESTER SHOTGUNS

MODEL 1400 SEMIAUTO SHOTGUNS

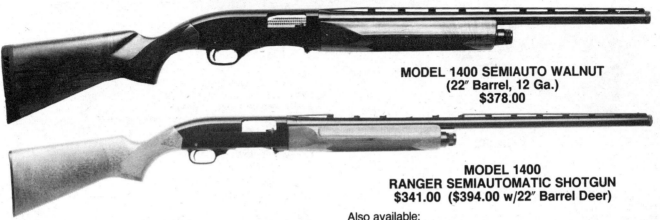

MODEL 1400 SEMIAUTO WALNUT
(22″ Barrel, 12 Ga.)
$378.00

MODEL 1400
RANGER SEMIAUTOMATIC SHOTGUN
$341.00 ($394.00 w/22″ Barrel Deer)

Also available:
Model 1400 Ranger Deer Combo with 28″ barrel
and Winchoke set **$333.00**
Model 1400 Rifled Deer 305.00
Model 1400 Ladies/Youth with shorter stock and
rearward forend 338.00
Model 1400 Ranger Deer Gun
12 ga., 22″ barrel 394.00
Model 1400 Semiauto Slug Gun 420.00

Gauge: 12 and 20; 2³/₄″ chamber; 3-shot magazine. **Barrel:** 28″ vent rib with Full, Modified and Improved Cylinder Winchoke tubes or 28″ plain barrel Modified. **Weight:** 7 to 7¹/₄ pounds. **Overall length:** 48⁵/₈″. **Stock:** Walnut-finished hardwood with cut-checkering. **Sights:** Metal bead front. **Features:** Crossbolt safety; front-locking rotating bolt; black serrated butt plate, gas-operated action. Also available in deer barrel.

SPECIFICATIONS MODEL 1400 SEMIAUTO

Model	Symbol Number	Gauge	Chamber	Shotshell Capacity*	Choke	Barrel Length & Type	Overall Length	Nominal Weight (Lbs.)	Sights
1400 Custom	7145	12	2³/₄″	3	W3	28″VR	48⁵/₈″	7³/₄	MBF
1400 Walnut	7152	12	2³/₄	3	W3	26 VR	46⁵/₈	7¹/₂	MBF
	7160	20	2³/₄	3	W3	26 VR	46⁵/₈	7¹/₂	MBF
	7186	12	2³/₄	3	W3	22 VR	42³/₄	7	MBF
	7194	20	2³/₄	3	W3	22 VR	42³/₄	7	MBF
	7202	12	2³/₄	3	W3	28 VR	48⁵/₈	7³/₄	MBF
	7236	20	2³/₄	3	W3	28 VR	48⁵/₈	7³/₄	MBF
1400 Walnut Sabot Tube	7244	12	2³/₄	3	W2	22 VR	42³/₄	7	MBF
1400 Ranger	7210	12	2³/₄	3	W3	28 VR	48⁵/₈	7³/₄	MBF
	7251	12	2³/₄	3	W3	26 VR	46⁵/₈	7¹/₂	MBF
	7269	20	2³/₄	3	W3	28 VR	48⁵/₈	7³/₄	MBF
	7285	12	2³/₄	3	W3	26 VR	46⁵/₈	7¹/₂	MBF
1400 Ranger Combo With Extra 28″ Barrel	7319	12 12	2³/₄ 2³/₄	3 3	Cyl W3	22 28 VR	42³/₄	7	RT MBF
1400 Ranger Deer	7368	12	2³/₄	3	Cyl	22	42³/₄	7	RT

* Includes one shotshell in chamber when ready to fire. VR-Ventilated rib. Cyl.-Cylinder Bore. MBF-Metal bead front. RT-Rifle type front and rear sights. Winchoke sets with wrench come with gun as follows: W1-Modified tube. W2 Improved Cylinder and rifled Sabot tubes. W3-Full, Modified, Improved Cylinder tubes. All models have 14″ nominal length of pull; 1¹/₂″ drop at comb; 2¹/₂″ drop at heel.

ANTONIO ZOLI SHOTGUNS

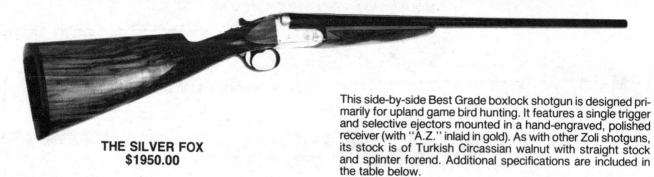

THE SILVER FOX
$1950.00

This side-by-side Best Grade boxlock shotgun is designed primarily for upland game bird hunting. It features a single trigger and selective ejectors mounted in a hand-engraved, polished receiver (with ''A.Z.'' inlaid in gold). As with other Zoli shotguns, its stock is of Turkish Circassian walnut with straight stock and splinter forend. Additional specifications are included in the table below.

SPECIFICATIONS

Gauge:	12–20*	Top rib:	Tapered from 25/64 to 15/64	Drop at heel:	1½″
Chamber	3″ Magnum	Finish:	Antiqued silver	Drop at comb:	2⁵⁄₁₆″
Barrel length:	26″–28″	Engraving:	By hand	Length of pull:	14½″
Chokes:	26″–IC/M 28″–M/F	Stock:	English	Total weight:	From 6.25 lbs. to 7.25 lbs.

* Available only in 26″.

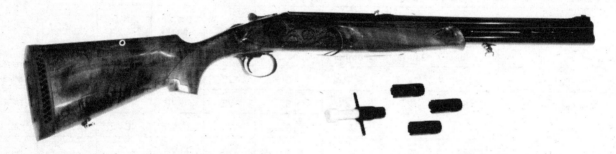

THE WOODSMAN
$1650.00

This over/under field shotgun features a special raised ''quarter-rib'' with pop-up rifle-type sights for use in hunting birds, deer, turkey, or large game, such as wild boar, in thick cover. The 23″ barrels with center ventilation are regulated to shoot rifled slugs at 55 yards and accept the interchangeable Zoli chokes with 5 tubes. Additional specifications are listed in the table below.
Also available:
WOODSMAN COMBO SET (2 barrels) **$2500.00**

SPECIFICATIONS

Gauge:	12	Finish:	Receiver photoengraved	Length of pull:	14½″
Chamber	3″ Magnum	Engraving:	Floral	Total weight:	6¾ lbs.
Barrel length:	23″	Stock:	Pistol grip	Regulated:	55 yds. with slugs
Chokes:	Screw-in Zoli-chokes (5)	Drop at heel:	1³⁄₈″		
Top rib:	Slug type	Drop at comb:	2⁵⁄₁₆″		

MANUFACTURER DOES NOT FURNISH SUGGESTED RETAIL PRICES; ABOVE PRICES ARE FOR COMPARATIVE PURPOSES ONLY.

ANTONIO ZOLI SHOTGUNS
Z90 TRAP GUN SERIES

Z90 MONO-TRAP GUN
$1900.00

This top/single barrel trap gun features a black competition receiver, ventilated raised rib barrels with two beads, gold-plated single selective trigger (adjustable to length of pull), and a polyurethane-type weatherproof finish stock of Turkish Circassian walnut, select grade, with Monte Carlo butt stock and rounded tip forend. For additional specifications see table below.

Z90 TRAP GUN
$1900.00

This Over/Under trap gun has the same features as the Mono-Trap model (see above) but with 2 barrels (29½" or 32").
Also available:
MODEL Z90 COMBO TRAP SET **$2850.00**

Z90 SKEET
$1900.00

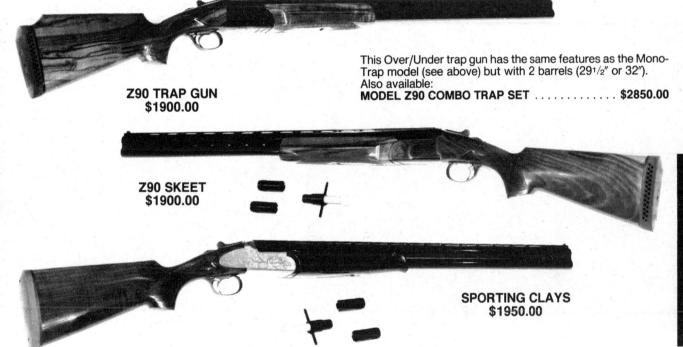

SPORTING CLAYS
$1950.00

Models	Gauge	BBL length	Chokes	Top rib	Stock	Action frame	Total weight
Z90-Trap	12	29½"–32"	Screw-in Zoli chokes	7/16"	Pistol deluxe walnut	Black	8½ lbs.
Z90-Skeet	12	28"	Screw-in Zoli chokes	7/16"	Pistol deluxe walnut	Black	7¾ lbs.
Z90-Mono trap	12	32"–34"	Screw-in Zoli chokes	7/16"	Pistol deluxe walnut	Black	8½ lbs.
Z90-Sporting	12	28"	Screw-in Zoli chokes	Tapered	Pistol deluxe walnut	Antique silver side plated	7⅓ lbs.

MANUFACTURER DOES NOT FURNISH SUGGESTED RETAIL PRICES; ABOVE PRICES ARE FOR COMPARATIVE PURPOSES ONLY.

Black Powder

For addresses and phone numbers of manufacturers and distributors included in this section, turn to *DIRECTORY OF MANUFACTURERS AND SUPPLIERS* at the back of the book.

AMERICAN ARMS

MODEL HAWKEYE
$279.00   ($419.00 Stainless)

The new Hawkeye muzzleloader combines the traditional "cap-'n-ball" side hammer with the user-friendly features of the modern bolt-action rifle, including dual safety systems, striker fired in-line ignition system, and a contemporary designed stock fitted with a rubber recoil pad. Rifling is a fast 1 in 28".

SPECIFICATIONS
Calibers: 50 and 54
Barrel length: 22" round, tapered

Overall length: 41½"
Weight: 6¾ lbs.
Receiver: Blued or stainless steel
Action: Adjustable trigger; side-mounted ambidextrous bolt handle
Sights: Ramp blade type with bead front; ramp-type rear adjustable for windage and elevation; both sights removable; receiver drilled and tapped for Weaver No. 61 bases

ARMSPORT

MODEL 5145
COLT 1847 WALKER
$295.00

The largest of all Colt revolvers, this true copy of the original weighs 4½ lbs., making it also the most powerful (and only) revolver made at the time. **Caliber:** 44.

MODEL 5152
ENGRAVED REMINGTON
GOLD & NICKEL-PLATED 44 CALIBER
$320.00

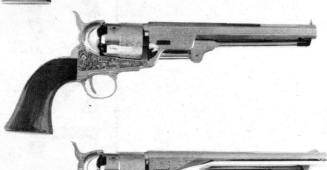

MODEL 5153
ENGRAVED COLT ARMY 44 CALIBER
$320.00

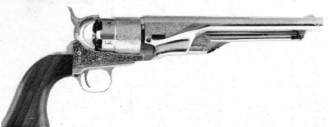

MODEL 5154
ENGRAVED COLT NAVY 36 CALIBER
$320.00

ARMSPORT

REPLICA REVOLVERS

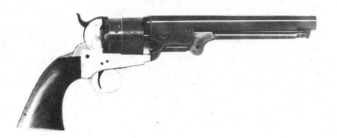

MODEL 5133
COLT 1851 NAVY "REB"

A modern replica of a Confederate percussion revolver, this has a polished brass frame, rifled blued barrel and polished walnut grips. **Price: $149.00** (Kit: **$130.00**)

MODEL 5138
REMINGTON ARMY STAINLESS STEEL

This stainless-steel version of the 44-caliber Remington New Army Revolver is made for the shooter who seeks the best. Its stainless steel frame assures lasting good looks and durability. **Price: $385.00**

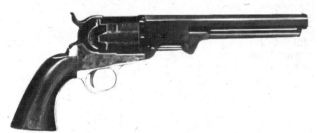

MODEL 5136
COLT 1851 NAVY STEEL

This authentic reproduction of the Colt Navy Revolver in 36 or 44 caliber, which helped shape the history of America, features a rifled barrel, casehardened steel frame, engraved cylinder, polished brass trigger guard and walnut grips. **Price: $185.00** (Kit: **$190.00**)

MODEL 5139
COLT 1860 ARMY

This authentic 44-caliber reproduction offers the same balance and ease of handling for fast shooting as the original 1860 Army model. **Price: $215.00** (Kit: **$190.00**)

MODEL 5120
NEW REMINGTON ARMY
STEEL REVOLVER

One of the most accurate cap-and-ball revolvers of the 1860's. Its rugged steel frame and top strap made this 44 caliber the favorite of all percussion cap revolvers. **Price: $210.00** (Kit: **$190.00**)
With brass frame: **$130.00**

MODEL 5140
COLT 1860 ARMY

Same as the Model 5139 Colt Army replica, but with brightly polished brass frame. **Price: $149.00** (Kit: **$130.00**)

CVA REVOLVERS

**1858 REMINGTON ARMY
STEEL FRAME REVOLVER**

1858 REMINGTON ARMY REVOLVER
Brass Frame: $169.95
Steel Frame: 224.95
Kit—Brass only: 145.95

**1858 REMINGTON TARGET MODEL
$234.95**

Caliber: 44
Cylinder: 6-shot
Barrel length: 8″ octagonal
Overall length: 13″
Weight: 38 oz.
Sights: Blade front; adjustable target
Grip: Two-piece walnut

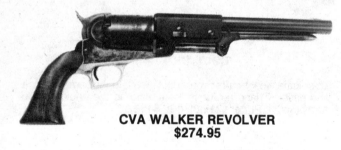

**CVA WALKER REVOLVER
$274.95**

Caliber: 44
Barrel: 9″ rounded with hinged-style loading lever
Cylinder: 6-shot engraved
Overall length: 15½″
Weight: 72 oz.
Grip: One-piece walnut
Front sight: Blade
Finish: Solid brass trigger guard

**NEW MODEL POCKET REMINGTON
Finished $125.95**

Caliber: 31 percussion
Barrel length: 4″ octagonal
Cylinder: 5 shots
Overall length: 7½″
Sights: Post in front; groove in frame in rear
Weight: 15 oz.
Finish: Solid brass frame

CVA REVOLVERS

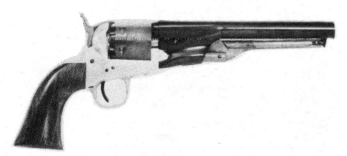

1861 NAVY BRASS-FRAMED REVOLVER
Finished $139.95
Steel Frame (44 Cal.) $229.95
Kit $124.95

Calibers: 36 and 44
Barrel length: 7¹/₂″ rounded; creeping style
Weight: 44 oz.
Cylinder: 6-shot, engraved
Sights: Blade front; hammer notch rear
Finish: Solid brass frame, trigger guard and backstrap; blued barrel and cylinder
Grip: One-piece walnut

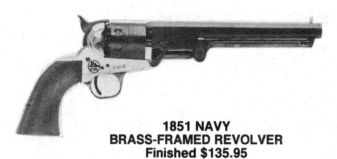

**1851 NAVY
BRASS-FRAMED REVOLVER**
Finished $135.95

Caliber: 36
Barrel length: 7¹/₂″ octagonal; hinged-style loading lever
Overall length: 13″
Weight: 44 oz.
Cylinder: 6-shot, engraved
Sights: Post front; hammer notch rear
Grip: One-piece walnut
Finish: Solid brass frame, trigger guard and backtrap; blued barrel and cylinder; color casehardened loading lever and hammer

SHERIFF'S MODEL REVOLVER
Brass Frame $149.95

Caliber: 36
Barrel length: 5¹/₂″ (rounded w/creeping-style loading lever)
Overall length: 11¹/₂″
Weight: 40¹/₂ oz.
Cylinder: 6-shot semi-fluted
Grip: One-piece walnut
Sight: Hammer notch in rear
Finish: Solid brass frame, trigger guard and backstrap

Also available: **Engraved Nickel Plated Model** (with matching flask) **$211.95**

1860 ARMY REVOLVER
$229.95 (Steel Frame Only)

Caliber: 44
Barrel length: 8″ rounded; creeping-style loading lever
Overall length: 13″
Weight: 44 oz.
Cylinder: 6-shot, engraved and rebated
Sights: Blade front; hammer notch rear
Grip: One-piece walnut
Finish: Solid brass trigger guard; blued barrel and cylinder with color casehardened loading lever, hammer and frame

CVA REVOLVERS

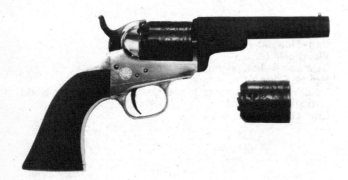

WELLS FARGO MODEL
Brass Frame $125.95

Caliber: 31
Capacity: 5-shot cylinder (engraved)
Barrel length: 4″ octagonal
Overall length: 9″
Weight: 28 oz. (w/extra cylinder)
Sights: Post front; hammer notch rear
Grip: One-piece walnut

POCKET POLICE
Brass Frame $135.95

Caliber: 36
Capacity: 5-shot cylinder
Barrel length: 5½″ octagonal, with creeping-style loading lever
Overall length: 10½″
Weight: 26 oz.
Sights: Post front; hammer notch rear

THIRD MODEL DRAGOON
Steel Frame $229.95

Caliber: 44
Cylinder: 6-shot engraved
Barrel length: 7½″ rounded with hinged-style loading lever
Overall length: 14″
Weight: 66 oz.
Sights: Blade front; hammer notch rear
Grip: One-piece walnut

REMINGTON BISON
$239.95

Caliber: 44
Cylinder: 6-shot
Barrel length: 10¼″ octagonal
Overall length: 18″
Weight: 48 oz.
Sights: Fixed blade front; screw adjustable target rear
Grip: Two-piece walnut
Finish: Solid brass frame

CVA PISTOLS

KENTUCKY PISTOL
Finished $149.95
Percussion Kit $89.95

Caliber: 50 percussion
Barrel: 10¼", rifled, octagonal
Overall length: 15½"
Weight: 40 oz.
Finish: Blued barrel, brass hardware
Sights: Brass blade front; fixed open rear
Stock: Select hardwood
Ignition: Engraved, color casehardened percussion lock, screw adjustable sear engagement
Accessories: Brass-tipped, hardwood ramrod; stainless steel nipple or flash hole liner

PHILADELPHIA DERRINGER
Finished $89.95
Kit $75.95

Caliber: 45 percussion
Barrel: 3¼" rifled, octagonal
Overall length: 7⅛"
Weight: 16 oz.
Finish: Brass hardware; blued barrel
Stock: Select hardwood
Ignition: Color casehardened and engraved, coil-spring back-action lock
Accessories: Stainless steel nipple

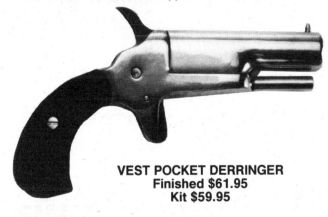

VEST POCKET DERRINGER
Finished $61.95
Kit $59.95

Caliber: 31
Barrel length: 2½" (single shot) brass
Overall length: 5"
Weight: 16 oz.
Grip: Two-piece walnut
Frame: Brass

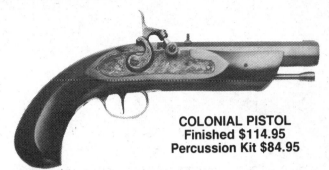

COLONIAL PISTOL
Finished $114.95
Percussion Kit $84.95

Caliber: 45 percussion
Barrel: 6¾", rifled, octagon
Overall length: 12¾"
Weight: 31 oz.
Finish: Casehardened lock; blued barrel; brass hardware
Sights: Dovetail rear; brass blade front
Stock: Select hardwood
Ignition: Engraved, color casehardened lock
Accessories: Steel ramrod, stainless steel nipple; kits available for percussion and flintlock

HAWKEN PISTOL
Finished $164.95
Kit $104.95

Caliber: 50 percussion
Barrel length: 9¾", octagonal
Overall length: 16½"
Weight: 50 oz.
Trigger: Early-style brass
Sights: Beaded steel blade front; fully adjustable rear (click adj. screw settings lock into position)
Stock: Select hardwood
Finish: Solid brass wedge plate, nose cap, ramrod thimbles, trigger guard and grip cap

SIBER TARGET PISTOL
$439.95

Caliber: 45 percussion
Barrel length: 10½", octagonal
Overall length: 16½"
Weight: 38 oz.
Sights: Blade front; rear adjustable for elevation
Stock: Fancy European walnut
Trigger: Adjustable single-set trigger with rear over-lateral limiting screw
Finish: Polished steel barrel, lock plate, hammer and trigger

CVA RIFLES

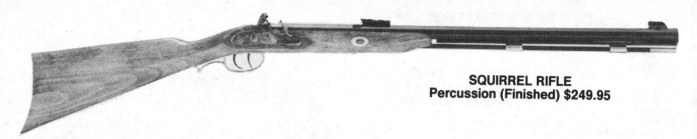

SQUIRREL RIFLE
Percussion (Finished) $249.95

Ignition: Color case-hardened and engraved lockplate; bridle, fly, screw-adjustable sear engagement; authentic V-type mainspring
Caliber: 36 percussion
Stock: Select hardwood
Barrel: 25″ octagonal; ⁷/₈″ across flats; hooked breech for easy take down and cleaning; rifling, one turn in 48″; 8 lands, deep grooves; blued steel
Overall length: 40³/₄″
Weight: 6 lbs.

Trigger: Double set with adj. trigger pull (will fire set or unset)
Front sight: Dovetail, beaded blade
Rear sight: Fully adjustable, open hunting-style dovetail
Finish: Solid brass butt plate, trigger guard, wedge plates and thimbles
Accessories: Stainless steel nipple or flash hole liner; aluminum ramrod with brass tips, cleaning jag
Also available:
SQUIRREL RIFLE HUNTING COMBO KIT (36 and 50 caliber percussion): **$249.95**

BUSHWACKER RIFLE
$159.95

SPECIFICATIONS
Caliber: 50
Barrel length: 26″ blued octagonal
Overall length: 40″
Weight: 7¹/₂ lbs.

Sights: Brass blade front; fixed open semi-buckhorn rear
Stock: Walnut stained select hardwood with rounded nose
Trigger: Single trigger with oversized trigger guard
Features: Blued steel wedge plates; ramrod thimbles; blackened trigger guard and black plastic butt plate

ST. LOUIS HAWKEN RIFLE

Calibers: 50, 54 and 58 percussion or flintlock
Barrel: 28″ octagonal ¹⁵/₁₆″ across flats; hooked breech; rifling one turn in 66″, 8 lands and deep grooves
Overall length: 44″
Weight: 8 lbs.
Sights: Dovetail, beaded blade (front); adjustable open hunting-style dovetail (rear)
Stock: Select hardwood with beavertail cheekpiece

Triggers: Double set; fully adjustable trigger pull
Finish: Solid brass wedge plates, nose cap, ramrod thimbles, trigger guard and patch box

Prices:
50 Caliber Flintlock **$239.95**
50 Caliber Percussion **229.95**
50 Caliber Percussion, Left Hand **239.95**

CVA RIFLES

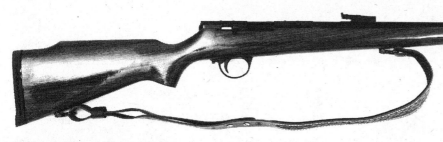

APOLLO 90 PERCUSSION RIFLE
$379.95 (Standard Grade)
$439.95 (Laminated Stock)

Calibers: 50 and 54 percussion
Barrel length: 27″ round, tapered, one-piece; chrome bore
Overall length: 45″
Weight: 7½ lbs.
Trigger: Box-type with hooking tumbler automatic trigger safety system (Premier Grade)
Sights: Front, ramp-mounted brass bead with hood to fit ³/₈″ dovetails; rear, Hunting-style full click adjustable for windage and elevation to fit ³/₈″ dovetail; drilled and tapped for scope

Stock: Walnut, Monte Carlo-style comb with flutes; fully formed beavertail cheekpiece, pistol-grip handle (Standard Grade); laminated stock (50 cal. only)
Accessories: Stainless steel nipple; fiberglass ramrod with cleaning jag; black ABS trigger guard; sling swivel studs
Also available:
LAMINATED STOCK MODEL (50 cal. only) **$439.95**
APOLLO 90 CARBINE (50 cal. only) 379.95

APOLLO 90 SHADOW RIFLE
$299.95

Weight: 9½ lbs.
Sights: Ramp mounted brass bead with hood front; fully click adjustable rear
Stock: Black, textured epoxicoat hardwood with Monte Carlo fluted combo and fully formed cheekpiece and pistol grip
Trigger: Box style with hooking tumbler; auto safety system
Features: Ventilated rubber recoil pad; molded black oversized trigger guards; bottom screw attachment and blued thimble

SPECIFICATIONS
Caliber: 50 and 54
Barrel length: 27″ blued round taper with octagonal one-piece receiver, drilled and tapped
Overall length: 45″

APPOLO SPORTER
$255.95

Sights: Steel beaded blued blade front; adjustable hunting style rear
Stock: Hardwood with pistol grip
Trigger: Box style with hooking tumbler; auto safety system
Features: Butt plate and blued thimble; stainless percussion bolt; barrel and action formed from one piece of steel; in-line ignition

SPECIFICATIONS
Caliber: 50
Barrel length: 25″ blued round taper with octagonal one-piece receiver, drilled and tapped
Overall length: 43″
Weight: 8½ lbs.

FRONTIER HUNTER CARBINE
$249.95

Caliber: 50
Barrel length: 24″, blued, octagonal

Overall length: 40″
Weight: 7½ lbs.
Sights: Beaded steel blade front; hunting-style rear, fully click adjustable for windage and elevation
Stock: Select hardwood with straight grip; solid rubber recoil pad
Triggers: Single
Finish: Black trigger guard and wedge plate

CVA RIFLES

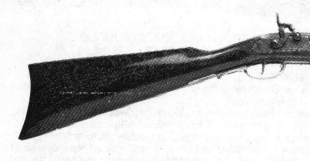

PENNSYLVANIA LONG RIFLE
Percussion (Finished) $459.95
Flintlock $459.95

Caliber: 50 percussion or flintlock
Stock: Select walnut
Barrel: 40″ octagonal, 7/8″ across flats; rifling 8 lands, deep grooves
Overall length: 55 3/4″
Weight: 8 lbs.
Trigger: Double set (will fire set or unset)
Rear sight: Fixed semi-buckhorn, dovetail
Finish: Brass butt plate, patchbox, trigger guard, thimbles and nose cap
Ignition: Color casehardened and engraved lockplate; bridle, fly, screw-adjustable sear engagement; authentic V-type mainspring
Accessories: Color casehardened nipple or flash hole liner; hardwood ramrod and brass tips

FRONTIER CARBINE
Finished $195.95
Kit $129.95

Caliber: 50 percussion
Barrel length: 24″ octagonal (15/16″ across flats)
Rifling: 1 turn in 48″ (8 lands and deep grooves)
Overall length: 40″
Weight: 6 lbs. 9 oz.
Sights: Brass blade front; fully adjustable rear
Trigger: Early-style brass with tension spring
Stock: Select hardwood
Finish: Solid brass butt plate, trigger guard wedge plate, nose cap and thimble
Accessories: Stainless steel nipple, hardwood ramrod with brass tips and cleaning jag

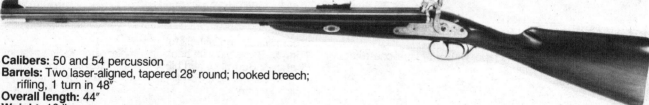

Calibers: 50 and 54 percussion
Barrels: Two laser-aligned, tapered 28″ round; hooked breech; rifling, 1 turn in 48″
Overall length: 44″
Weight: 10 lbs.
Locks: Plate is color hardened and engraved; includes bridle, fly, screw-adjustable sear engagement
Triggers: Double, color casehardened
Sights: Fully adjustable for windage and elevation, hunting style (rear); dovetail, beaded blade (front)
Stock: Select hardwood
Finish: Polished steel wedge plates; color casehardened locks, hammers, triggers and trigger guard; engraved locks, hammers and tang

EXPRESS DOUBLE BARREL RIFLE
Finished $489.95

CVA RIFLES

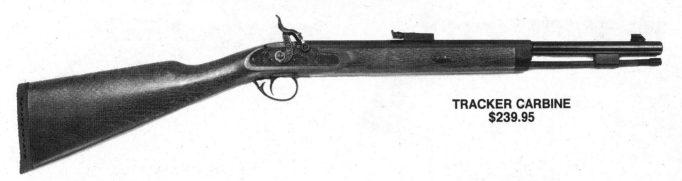

TRACKER CARBINE
$239.95

SPECIFICATIONS
Caliber: 50
Barrel length: 21″ blued half round, half octagonal
Overall length: 37″
Weight: 6½ lbs.
Sights: Steel beaded blued blade front; fully click adjustable rear

Stock: Matte finish with straight grip
Lock: Hawken style with bridle and fly, color casehardened
Trigger: Single trigger integral with trigger guard
Features: Ventilated rubber recoil pad; molded black oversized trigger guard and blued wedge plates and thimbles; drilled and tapped for scope mount

PLAINSMAN RIFLE
$149.95

Caliber: 50 percussion
Barrel length: 26″ octagonal (15/16″ across flats)
Overall length: 40″
Weight: 6 lbs. 9 oz.
Sights: Brass blade front; fixed open rear

Trigger: Single trigger with large trigger guard
Stock: Select hardwood
Finish: Black trigger guard, wedge plate and thimble
Accessories: Color casehardened nipple, hardwood ramrod with brass tip and cleaning jag

STALKER RIFLE/CARBINE
$210.95

Calibers: 50 and 54 percussion
Barrel length: 28″ octagonal (Rifle); 24″ (Carbine)
Overall length: 40″ (Carbine); 44″ (Rifle)
Weight: 7½ lbs.
Sights: Steel beaded blade front; hunting-style rear, fully click adjustable for windage and elevation (click adjustable screw settings lock into position); drilled and tapped for scope

Trigger: Single trigger with oversized trigger guard
Stock: Select hardwood with pistol grip and rubber recoil pad
Finish: Blackened trigger guard; blued thimble, wedge and wedge plate
Accessories: Color casehardened nipple, hardwood ramrod with brass tips and cleaning jag

DIXIE

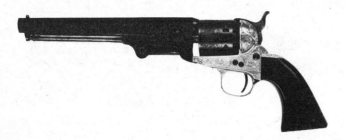

DIXIE NAVY REVOLVER
Plain Model $95.00
Engraved Model $139.95
Kit $84.95

This 36-caliber revolver was a favorite of the officers of the Civil War. Although called a Navy type, it is somewhat mis-named since many more of the Army personnel used it. Made in Italy; uses .376 mold or ball to fit and number 11 caps. Blued steel barrel and cylinder with brass frame.

SPILLER & BURR 36 CALIBER
BRASS FRAME REVOLVER
$125.00   Kit $95.00

The 36-caliber octagonal barrel on this revolver is 7 inches long. The six-shot cylinder chambers mike .378, and the hammer engages a slot between the nipples on the cylinder as an added safety device. It has a solid brass trigger guard and frame with backstrap cast integral with the frame, two-piece walnut grips and Whitney-type casehardened loading lever.

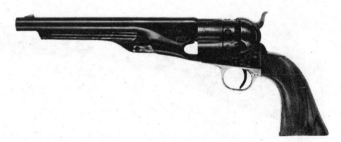

REMINGTON 44 ARMY REVOLVER
$145.00

All steel external surfaces finished bright blue, including 8″ octagonal barrel (hammer is casehardened). Polished brass guard and two-piece walnut grips are standard.

DIXIE 1860 ARMY REVOLVER
$149.95

The Dixie 1860 Army has a half-fluted cylinder and its chamber diameter is .447. Use .451 round ball mold to fit this 8-inch barrel revolver. Cut for shoulder stock.

"WYATT EARP" REVOLVER (Not shown)
$130.00

This 44-caliber revolver has a 12-inch octagon rifled barrel and rebated cylinder. Highly polished brass frame, backstrap and trigger guard. The barrel and cylinder have a deep blue luster finish. Hammer, trigger, and loading lever are case-hardened. Walnut grips. Recommended ball size is .451.

DIXIE

RHO200 WALKER REVOLVER
$215.00   Kit $179.95

This 4¹/₂-pound, 44-caliber pistol is the largest ever made. Steel backstrap; guard is brass with Walker-type rounded-to-frame walnut grips; all other parts are blued. Chambers measure .445 and take a .450 ball slightly smaller than the originals.

RHO301 THIRD MODEL DRAGOON
$199.95

This engraved-cylinder, 4¹/₂-pounder is a reproduction of the last model of Colt's 44 caliber "horse" revolvers. Barrel measures 7³/₈ inches, ¹/₈ inch shorter than the original; color casehardened steel frame, one-piece walnut grips. Recommended ball size: .454.

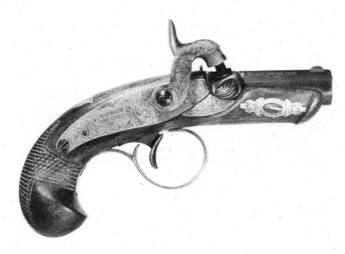

DSB-58 SCREW BARREL DERRINGER
(Not shown)
$89.00   Kit $74.95

Overall length: 6¹/₂". Unique loading system; sheath trigger, color case-hardened frame, trigger and center-mounted hammer; European walnut, one-piece, "bag"-type grip. Uses #11 percussion caps.

LINCOLN DERRINGER
$285.00   Kit $89.95

This 41-caliber, 2-inch browned barrel gun has 8 lands and 8 grooves and will shoot a .400 patch ball.

DIXIE BRASS-FRAMED "HIDEOUT" DERRINGER
(Not shown)
Plain $69.95   Engraved $95.50
Kit $53.95

This small handgun sports a brass frame and walnut grips, and fires a .395 round ball.

FHO201 FRENCH CHARLEVILLE FLINT PISTOL
(Not shown)
$189.95

Reproduction of the Model 1777 Cavalry, Revolutionary War-era pistol. Has reversed frizzen spring; forend and lock housing are all in one; casehardened, round-faced, double-throated hammer; walnut stock; casehardened frizzen and trigger; shoots .680 round ball loaded with about 40 grains FFg black powder.

ABILENE DERRINGER (Not shown)
$81.50   Kit $51.95

An all-steel version of Dixie's brass-framed derringers. The 2¹/₂-inch, 41-caliber barrel is finished in a deep blue black; frame and hammer are case-hardened. Bore is rifled with 6 lands and grooves. Uses a tightly patched .395 round ball and 15 or 20 grains of FFFg powder. Walnut grips. Comes with wood presentation case.

BLACK POWDER

DIXIE

LePAGE PERCUSSION DUELING PISTOL
$259.95

This percussion pistol features a blued 10″ octagonal barrel with 12 lands and grooves. The 45-caliber sidearm has a brass-bladed front sight with open rear sight dovetailed into the barrel. Trigger guard and butt cap are polished silver plating. Right side of barrel is stamped "LePage á Paris." Double-set triggers are single screw adjustable. **Overall length:** 16″. **Weight:** 2¹/₂ lbs.

PEDERSOLI ENGLISH DUELING PISTOL
(Not shown)
$265.00

This reproduction of an English percussion dueling pistol, created by Charles Moore of London, features a European walnut halfstock with oil finish and checkered grip. The 45-caliber octagonal barrel is 11″ with 12 grooves and a twist of 1 in 15″. Nose cap and thimble are silver. Barrel is blued; lock and trigger guard are color casehardened.

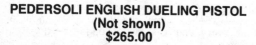

PEDERSOLI MANG TARGET PISTOL
(Not shown)
$545.00

Designed specifically for the precision target shooter, this 38-caliber pistol has a 10⁷/₁₆″ octagonal barrel with 7 lands and grooves. Twist is 1 in 15″. Blade front sight is dovetailed into the barrel, and rear sight is mounted on the breech-plug tang, adjustable for windage. **Overall length:** 17¹/₄″. **Weight:** 2¹/₂ lbs.

QUEEN ANNE PISTOL
$166.50
Kit $149.95

Named for the Queen of England (1702-1714), this flintlock pistol has a 7¹/₂″ barrel that tapers from rear to front with a cannon-shaped muzzle. The brass trigger guard is fluted and the brass butt on the walnut stock features a grotesque mask worked into it. **Overall length:** 13″. **Weight:** 2¹/₄ lbs.

DIXIE PENNSYLVANIA PISTOL (Not shown)
Percussion $144.95   Kit $109.95
Flintlock $149.95   Kit $115.00

Available in 44-caliber percussion or flintlock. The bright luster blued barrel measures 10 inches long; rifled, ⁷/₈-inch octagonal and takes .430 ball; barrel is held in place with a steel wedge and tang screw; brass front and rear sights. The brass trigger guard, thimbles, nose cap, wedge plates and side plates are highly polished. Locks are fine quality with early styling. Plates measure 4³/₄ inches × ⁷/₈ inch. Percussion hammer is engraved and both plates are left in the white. The flint is an excellent style lock with the gooseneck hammer having an early wide thumb piece. The stock is walnut stained and has a wide bird's-head-type grip.

DIXIE

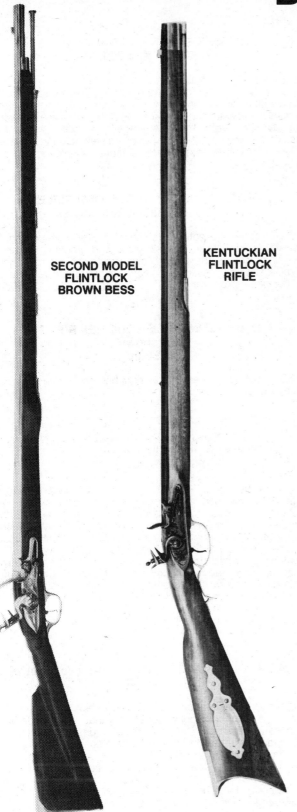

SECOND MODEL FLINTLOCK BROWN BESS

KENTUCKIAN FLINTLOCK RIFLE

SECOND MODEL BROWN BESS MUSKET
$530.00

This 75-caliber Brown Bess has a 41¾-inch smoothbore barrel that takes a .730 round ball. In keeping with the traditional musket, it has brass furniture on a walnut-stained stock. The lock is marked "Tower" and has the crown with the "GR" underneath. Barrel, lock and ramrod are left bright.
Kit: **$400.00**

THE KENTUCKIAN RIFLE
Flintlock $259.95
Percussion $249.95

This 45-caliber rifle, in flintlock or percussion, has a 33½-inch blued octagonal barrel that is ¹³/₁₆ inch across the flats. The bore is rifled with 6 lands and grooves of equal width and about .006 inch deep. Land-to-land diameter is .453 with groove-to-groove diameter of .465. Ball size ranges from .445 to .448. The rifle has a brass blade front sight and a steel open rear sight. The Kentuckian is furnished with brass butt plate, trigger guard, patch box, side plate, thimbles and nose cap plus case-hardened and engraved lock plate. Highly polished and finely finished stock in European walnut. **Overall length:** 48″. **Weight:** Approx. 6¼ lbs.

DIXIE DOUBLE BARREL MAGNUM
MUZZLE LOADING SHOTGUN (Not shown)

A full 12-gauge, high-quality, double-barreled percussion shotgun with 30-inch browned barrels. Will take the plastic shot cups for better patterns. Bores are choked modified and full. Lock, barrel tang and trigger are case-hardened in a light gray color and are nicely engraved.
12 Gauge $399.00
12 Gauge Kit 350.00
10 Gauge Magnum (double barrel—right-hand = cyl. bore, left-hand = Mod.) 425.00
10 Gauge Magnum Kit 375.00

DIXIE

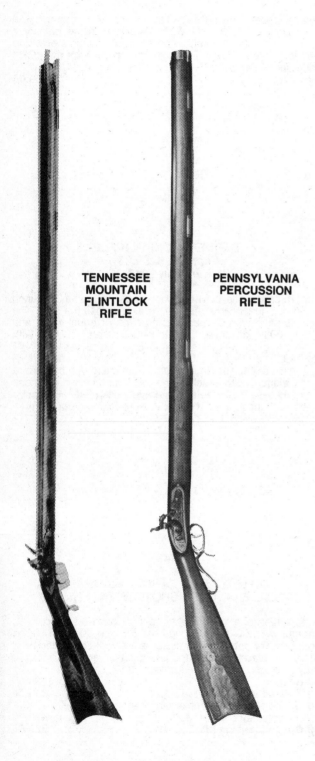

TENNESSEE
MOUNTAIN
FLINTLOCK
RIFLE

PENNSYLVANIA
PERCUSSION
RIFLE

HAWKEN RIFLE (Not shown)
$250.00   Kit $220.00

Blued barrel is $^{15}/_{16}$″ across the flats and 30″ in length with a twist of 1 in 64″. Stock is of walnut with a steel crescent buttplate, halfstock with brass nosecap. Double set triggers, front action lock and adjustable rear sight. Ramrod is equipped with jag. **Overall length:** 46$^{1}/_{2}$″. Average actual **weight:** about 8 lbs., depending on the caliber; shipping weight is 10 lbs. Available in either finished gun or kit. **Calibers:** 45, 50, and 54.

DIXIE TENNESSEE MOUNTAIN RIFLE
$450.00 Percussion or Flintlock

This 50-caliber rifle features double-set triggers with adjustable set screw, bore rifled with six lands and grooves, barrel of $^{15}/_{16}$ inch across the flats, brown finish and cherry stock. **Overall length:** 41$^{1}/_{2}$ inches. Right- and left-hand versions in flint or percussion. **Kit:** **$360.00**

DIXIE TENNESSEE SQUIRREL RIFLE
(Not shown)
$450.00

In 32-caliber flint or percussion, right hand only, cherry stock. Kit available: **$360.00**

PENNSYLVANIA RIFLE
Percussion or Flintlock $395.00
Kit (Flint or Perc.) $345.00

A lightweight at just 8 pounds, the 41$^{1}/_{2}$-inch blued rifle barrel is fitted with an open buckhorn rear sight and front blade. The walnut one-piece stock is stained a medium darkness that contrasts with the polished brass butt plate, toe plate, patchbox, side plate, trigger guard, thimbles and nose cap. Featuring double-set triggers, the rifle can be fired by pulling only the front trigger, which has a normal trigger pull of four to five pounds; or the rear trigger can first be pulled to set a spring-loaded mechanism that greatly reduces the amount of pull needed for the front trigger to kick off the sear in the lock. The land-to-land measurement of the bore is an exact .450 and the recommended ball size is .445. **Overall length:** 51$^{1}/_{2}$″.

PEDERSOLI WAADTLANDER RIFLE (Not shown)
$1295.00

This authentic re-creation of a Swiss muzzleloading target rifle features a heavy octagonal barrel (31″) that has 7 lands and grooves. **Caliber:** 45. Rate of twist is 1 turn in 48″. Double-set triggers are multi-lever type and are easily removable for adjustment. Sights are fitted post front and tang-mounted Swiss-type diopter rear. Walnut stock, color casehardened hardware, classic buttplate and curved trigger guard complete this reproduction. The original was made between 1839 and 1860 by Marc Bristlen, Morges, Switzerland.

DIXIE

MISSISSIPPI RIFLE
$430.00

Commonly called the U.S. Rifle Model 1841, this Italian-made replica is rifled in a 58 caliber to use a round ball or a Minie ball; 3 grooves and regulation sights; solid brass furniture; casehardened lock.

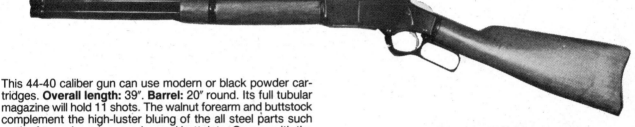

This 44-40 caliber gun can use modern or black powder cartridges. **Overall length:** 39″. **Barrel:** 20″ round. Its full tubular magazine will hold 11 shots. The walnut forearm and buttstock complement the high-luster bluing of the all steel parts such as the frame, barrel, magazine and buttplate. Comes with the trap door in the butt for the cleaning rod; leaf rear sight and blade front sight. This carbine is marked "Model 1873" on the tang and caliber "44-40" on the brass carrier block.

WINCHESTER '73 CARBINE
$875.00
ENGRAVED WINCHESTER '73 RIFLE
$995.00

1863 SPRINGFIELD CIVIL WAR MUSKET
$475.00   Kit $330.00

An exact copy of the Model 1863 Springfield, which was the last of the regulation muzzleloading rifles. The barrel on this .58 caliber gun measures 40 inches. The action and all metal furniture is finished bright. The oil-finished walnut-stain stock is 53 inches long. **Overall length:** 56 inches. **Weight:** 9½ lbs.

TRYON CREEDMOOR RIFLE (Not shown)
$575.00

This Tryon rifle features a high-quality back-action lock, double-set triggers, steel buttplate, patchbox, toe plate and curved trigger guard. **Caliber:** 45. **Barrel:** 32¾″, octagonal, with 1 twist in 20.87″. **Sights:** Hooded post front fitted with replaceable inserts; rear is tang-mounted and adjustable for windage and elevation.

DIXIE

U.S. MODEL 1861 SPRINGFIELD PERCUSSION RIFLE-MUSKET
$450.00   Kit $420.00

An exact re-creation of an original rifle produced by Springfield National Armory, Dixie's Model 1861 Springfield .58-caliber rifle features a 40″ round, tapered barrel with three barrel bands. Sling swivels are attached to the trigger guard bow and middle barrel band. The ramrod has a trumpet-shaped head with swell; sights are standard military rear and bayonet-attachment lug front. The percussion lock is marked "1861" on the rear of the lockplate with an eagle motif and "U.S. Springfield" in front of the hammer. "U.S." is stamped on top of buttplate. All furniture is "National Armory Bright." **Overall length:** 55¹³/₁₆″. **Weight:** 8 lbs.

1862 THREE-BAND ENFIELD RIFLED MUSKET
$485.00

One of the finest reproduction percussion guns available, the 1862 Enfield was widely used during the Civil War in its original version. This rifle follows the lines of the original almost exactly. The .58 caliber musket features a 39-inch barrel and walnut stock. Three steel barrel bands and the barrel itself are blued; the lock plate and hammer are case colored and the remainder of the furniture is highly polished brass. The lock is marked, "London Armory Co." **Weight:** 10½ lbs. **Overall length:** 55 inches.

U.S. MODEL 1816 FLINTLOCK MUSKET
$695.00

The U.S. Model 1816 Flintlock Musket was made by Harpers Ferry and Springfield Arsenals from 1816 until 1864. It had the highest production of any U.S. flintlock musket and, after conversion to percussion, saw service in the Civil War. It has a .69 caliber, 42″ smoothbore barrel held by three barrel bands with springs. All metal parts are finished in "National Armory Bright." The lockplate has a brass pan and is marked "Harpers Ferry" vertically behind the hammer, with an American eagle placed in front of the hammer. The bayonet lug is on top of the barrel and the steel ramrod has a button-shaped head. Sling swivels are mounted on the trigger guard and middle barrel band. **Overall length:** 56½″. **Weight:** 9¾ lbs.

1858 TWO-BAND ENFIELD RIFLE
$425.00

This 33-inch barrel version of the British Enfield is an exact copy of similar rifles used during the Civil War. The .58 caliber rifle sports a European walnut stock, deep blue-black finish on the barrel, bands, breech-plug tang and bayonet mount. The percussion lock is color casehardened and the rest of the furniture is brightly polished brass.

EMF REVOLVERS

SHERIFF'S MODEL 1851

SHERIFF'S MODEL 1851 REVOLVER
$140.00 (Brass) $172.00 (Steel)

SPECIFICATIONS
Caliber: 36 Percussion
Ball diameter: .376 round or conical, pure lead
Barrel length: 5″
Overall length: 10½″
Weight: 39 oz.
Sights: V-notch groove in hammer (rear); truncated cone in front
Percussion cap size: #11

MODEL 1860 ARMY REVOLVER
$145.00 (Brass) $200.00 (Steel)

SPECIFICATIONS
Caliber: 44 Percussion
Barrel length: 8″
Overall length: 13⅝″
Weight: 41 oz.
Frame: Casehardened
Finish: High-luster blue with walnut grips
Also available as a **cased set** with steel frame, wood case, flask and mold: **$375.00**

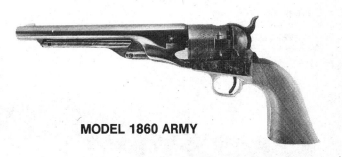

MODEL 1860 ARMY

SECOND MODEL 44 DRAGOON
$275.00

SPECIFICATIONS
Caliber: 44
Barrel length: 7½″ (round)
Overall length: 14″
Weight: 4 lbs.
Finish: Steel casehardened frame

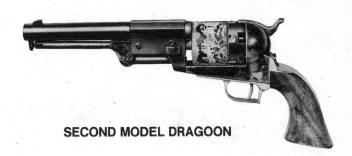

SECOND MODEL DRAGOON

MODEL 1862 POLICE REVOLVER
$200.00   ($150.00 Brass)

SPECIFICATIONS
Caliber: 36 Percussion
Capacity: 5-shot
Barrel length: 6½″
Also available as a steel **cased set:** **$294.00**

MODEL 1862 POLICE

EUROARMS OF AMERICA

COOK & BROTHER CONFEDERATE CARBINE
Model 2300: $504.00

Classic re-creation of the rare 1861, New Orleans-made Artillery Carbine. The lockplate is marked "Cook & Brother N.O. 1861" and is stamped with a Confederate flag at the rear of the hammer.

Caliber: 58
Barrel length: 24"
Overall length: 40⅓"
Weight: 7½ lbs.

Sights: Fixed blade front and adjustable dovetailed rear
Ramrod: Steel
Finish: Barrel is antique brown; butt plate, trigger guard, barrel bands, sling swivels and nose cap are polished brass; stock is walnut
Recommended ball sizes: .575 r.b., .577 Minie and .580 maxi; uses musket caps
Also available:
MODEL 2301 COOK & BROTHER FIELD (33" Barrel). **Price $549.60**

J.P. MURRAY CARBINE
MODEL 2315: $495.95

Replica of an extremely rare CSA Cavalry Carbine based on an 1841 design of parts and lock.

Caliber: 58 percussion
Barrel length: 23"
Features: Brass barrel bands and butt plate; oversized trigger guard; sling swivels

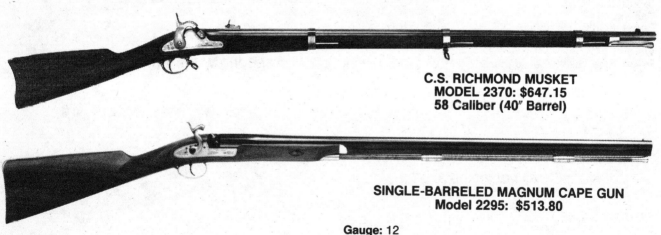

C.S. RICHMOND MUSKET
MODEL 2370: $647.15
58 Caliber (40" Barrel)

SINGLE-BARRELED MAGNUM CAPE GUN
Model 2295: $513.80

Gauge: 12
Barrel: 32", open choke
Overall length: 47½"
Weight: 7½ lbs.
Stock: English style; European walnut with satin oil finish; moderate recoil, even with relatively heavy powder charges
Finish: Barrel, underrib, thimbles, nose cap, trigger guard and butt plate are deep, rich blue

Euroarms of America offers a beautiful reproduction of a classic English-styled single-barreled shotgun. The lock is left in the white and displays a scroll engraving, as does the bow of the trigger guard. Uses #11 percussion caps and recommended wads are felt over powder and cardboard over shot.

EUROARMS OF AMERICA

LONDON ARMORY COMPANY
2-BAND RIFLE MUSKET
Model 2270: $531.75

Caliber: 58
Barrel length: 33", blued and rifled
Overall length: 49"
Weight: 8½ to 8¾ lbs., depending on wood density
Stock: One-piece walnut; polished "bright" brass butt plate, trigger guard and nose cap; blued barrel bands
Sights: Inverted 'V' front sight; Enfield folding ladder rear
Ramrod: Steel

LONDON ARMORY COMPANY
ENFIELD MUSKETOON
Model 2280: $495.95

Caliber: 58; Minie ball
Barrel length: 24"; round high-luster blued barrel
Overall length: 40½"
Weight: 7 to 7½ lbs., depending on density of wood
Stock: Seasoned walnut stock with sling swivels
Ramrod: Steel
Ignition: Heavy-duty percussion lock
Sights: Graduated military-leaf sight
Furniture: Brass trigger guard, nose cap and butt plate; blued barrel bands, lock plate, and swivels

LONDON ARMORY COMPANY
3-BAND ENFIELD RIFLED MUSKET
Model 2260: $565.85

Caliber: 58
Barrel length: 39", blued and rifled
Overall length: 54"
Weight: 9½ to 9¾ lbs., depending on wood density
Stock: One-piece walnut; polished "bright" brass butt plate, trigger guard and nose cap; blued barrel bands
Ramrod: Steel; threaded end for accessories
Sights: Traditional Enfield folding ladder rear sight; inverted 'V' front sight
Also available: **MODEL 2261** with White Barrel. **Price:** $593.45

BLACK POWDER

EUROARMS OF AMERICA

1803 HARPERS FERRY FLINTLOCK RIFLE
Model 2305: $650.40

Caliber: 54 Flintlock
Barrel length: 33", octagonal
Features: Walnut half stock with cheekpiece; browned barrel

1841 MISSISSIPPI RIFLE
Model 2310: $569.00

Caliber: 58 percussion
Barrel length: 33", octagonal
Features: Walnut stock; brass barrel bands and buttplate; sling swivels

1863 ZOUAVE RIFLE (2-Barrel Bands)
Model 2255: $582.25 (Range Grade)
Model 2250: $422.75 (Field Grade)

Caliber: 58 percussion
Barrel length: 33", octagonal
Overall length: 48½"
Weight: 9½ to 9¾ lbs.
Sights: U.S. Military 3-leaf rear; blade front
Features: Two brass barrel bands; brass buttplate and nose cap; sling swivels

1861 SPRINGFIELD RIFLE
Model 2360: $647.25

Caliber: 58
Barrel length: 40"
Features: 3 barrel bands

EUROARMS OF AMERICA

MODEL 1005

ROGERS & SPENCER ARMY REVOLVER
Model 1006 (Target): $291.00

Caliber: 44; takes .451 round or conical lead balls; #11 per-
cussion cap
Weight: 47 oz.
Barrel length: 7¹/₂″
Overall length: 13³/₄″
Finish: High gloss blue; flared walnut grip; solid frame design;
precision-rifled barrel
Sights: Rear fully adjustable for windage and elevation; ramp
front sight

ROGERS & SPENCER REVOLVER
Model 1007, London Gray (not shown)
$299.25

Revolver is the same as Model 1005, except for London Gray
finish, which is heat treated and buffed for rust resistance;
same recommended ball size and percussion caps.

Also available: **MODEL 1008 ENGRAVED**
Price: $349.60

ROGERS & SPENCER REVOLVER
Model 1005: $276.40

Caliber: 44 Percussion; #11 percussion cap
Barrel length: 7¹/₂″
Sights: Integral rear sight notch groove in frame; brass trun-
cated cone front sight
Overall length: 13³/₄″
Weight: 47 oz.
Finish: High gloss blue; flared walnut grip; solid frame design;
precision-rifled barrel
Recommended ball diameter: .451 round or conical, pure
lead

MODEL 1006

REMINGTON 1858
NEW MODEL ARMY ENGRAVED (not shown)
Model 1040: $334.95

Classical 19th-century style scroll engraving on this 1858
Remington New Model revolver.

Caliber: 44 Percussion; #11 cap
Barrel length: 8″
Overall length: 14³/₄″
Weight: 41 oz.
Sights: Integral rear sight notch groove in frame; blade front
sight
Recommended ball diameter: .451 round or conical, pure
lead

REMINGTON 1858
NEW MODEL ARMY REVOLVER
Model 1020: $260.25

This model is equipped with blued steel frame, brass trigger
guard in 44 caliber.

Weight: 40 oz.
Barrel length: 8″
Overall length: 14³/₄″
Finish: Deep luster blue rifled barrel; polished walnut stock;
brass trigger guard.
MODEL 1010: Same as Model 1020, except with 6¹/₂″ barrel
and in 36 caliber: **$260.25**

MODEL 1010
(36 Cal. w/6¹/₂″ barrel)

EUROARMS OF AMERICA

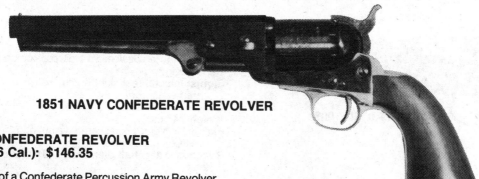

1851 NAVY CONFEDERATE REVOLVER

1851 NAVY CONFEDERATE REVOLVER
Model 1050 (36 Cal.): $146.35

A modern replica of a Confederate Percussion Army Revolver. Polished brass frame, rifled high-luster blued, octagonal barrel and polished walnut grips.

Weight: 40 oz.
Barrel length: 7½"
Overall length: 13"
Finish: Brass frame, backstrap and trigger guard; blued rifled barrel; casehardened hammer and loading lever; engraved cylinder with naval battle scene

1851 NAVY (Not shown)
Model 1120: $190.25

Calibers: .36 or 44 percussion, #11 cap
Barrel length: 7½", octagonal barrel, precision rifled
Overall length: 13"
Weight: 42 oz.
Finish: Blued barrel and frame; backstrap and trigger guard are polished brass; walnut grips.

GONIC ARMS

SPECIFICATIONS
Calibers: 30, 38, 44, 45, 50 and 54
Barrel lengths: 26" (Rifle); 24" (Carbine)
Overall length: 43" (Rifle); 41" (Carbine)
Weight: 6½ lbs. (Rifle); 6 lbs. (Carbine)
Sights: Bead front; open rear (adjustable for windage and elevation); drilled and tapped for scope bases
Stock: American walnut (grey or brown laminated stock optional)

MODEL GA-87 RIFLE/CARBINE
$493.38 Standard
$526.06 Deluxe
$336.33 Kit

Length of pull: 14"
Trigger: Single stage (4-lb. pull)
Mechanism type: Closed-breech muzzleloader
Features: Ambidextrous safety; non-glare satin finish; newly designed loading system; all-weather performance guaranteed; faster lock time
Also available:
Brown or Grey Laminated Stock Models: $538.38 (Standard)

MODEL GA-90 16" PISTOL BARREL ASSEMBLY
Calibers 30, 38, 44, 45
$186.25 (#11 Ignition System)

LYMAN

DEERSTALKER RIFLE
Percussion $339.95
Flintlock $359.95

Lyman's Deerstalker rifle incorporates many features most desired by muzzleloading hunters, including the following: higher comb for better sighting plane • non-glare hardware • 24″ octagonal barrel • casehardened side plate • Q.D. sling swivels • Lyman sight package (37MA beaded front; fully adjustable fold-down 16A rear) • walnut stock with 1/2″ black recoil pad • single trigger. Left-hand models available. **Calibers:** 50 and 54, flintlock or percussion. **Weight:** 7 1/2 lbs.

DEERSTALKER CARBINE
Percussion $349.95
Flintlock $374.95

This carbine version of the famous Deerstalker Hunting Rifle is now available in 50 caliber percussion or flintlock and features a precision-rifled "stepped octagon" barrel with a 1 in 24″ twist for optimum performance with conical projectiles. The specially designed Lyman sight package features a fully adjustable Lyman 16A fold-down in the rear. The front sight is Lyman's 37MA white bead on an 18 ramp. Each rifle comes complete with a darkened nylon ramrod and modern sling and swivels set. Left-hand models available. **Weight:** 6 3/4 lbs.

GREAT PLAINS RIFLE
Percussion $399.95   (Kit $324.95)
Flintlock $429.95   (Kit $354.95)

The Great Plains Rifle has a 32-inch deep-grooved barrel and 1 in 66-inch twist to shoot patched round balls. Blued steel furniture including the thick steel wedge plates and steel toe plate; correct lock and hammer styling with coil spring dependability; and a walnut stock without a patch box. A Hawken-style trigger guard protects double-set triggers. Steel front sight and authentic buckhorn styling in an adjustable rear sight. A fixed primitive rear sight is also included. **Calibers:** 50 and 54.

LYMAN TRADE RIFLE
Percussion $309.95   (Kit $249.95)
Flintlock $339.95   (Kit $284.95)

The Lyman Trade Rifle features a 28-inch octagonal barrel, rifled one turn at 48 inches, designed to fire both patched round balls and the popular maxistyle conical bullets. Polished brass furniture with blued finish on steel parts; walnut stock; hook breech; single spring-loaded trigger; coil-spring percussion lock; fixed steel sights; adjustable rear sight for elevation also included. Steel barrel rib and ramrod ferrrule. **Caliber:** 50 or 54 percussion and flint. **Overall length:** 45″.

MITCHELL ARMS REVOLVERS

1851 COLT NAVY "WILD BILL HICKOK" MODEL

SPECIFICATIONS
Calibers: 36 and 44
Barrel length: 7$\frac{1}{2}$" (brass or steel)
Frame: Polished solid brass or color case steel
Grips: Walnut
Price: $199.00

1860 COLT ARMY MODEL

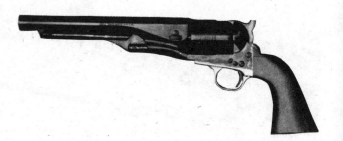

SPECIFICATIONS
Caliber: 44
Barrel length: 7$\frac{1}{2}$" (round rebated cylinder)
Weight: 2 lbs. 11 oz.
Frame: Steel
Grips: Walnut
Features: Detachable shoulder stock (optional)
Price: $199.00

Also available:
1861 COLT NAVY (36 or 44 cal.) **$199.00**
'51 NAVY SHERIFF'S MODEL (36 or 44 cal.) **199.00**

GENERAL CUSTER'S REMINGTON NEW MODEL ARMY

SPECIFICATIONS
Calibers: 36 and 44
Barrel length: 8"
Frame: Blued steel
Grips: Walnut
Features: Progressive rifling; brass trigger guard
Price: $199.00

REMINGTON "TEXAS" MODEL

SPECIFICATIONS
Calibers: 36 and 44
Barrel length: 8" octagonal; blued steel
Frame: Bright brass
Grips: Walnut
Price: $199.00

MODERN MUZZLE LOADING

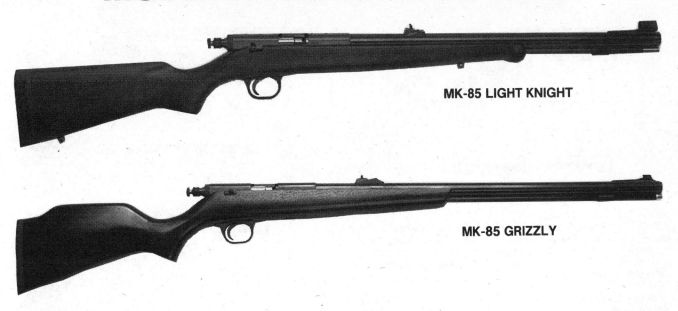

MK-85 LIGHT KNIGHT

MK-85 GRIZZLY

MK-85 LIGHT KNIGHT RIFLE

The MK-85 muzzleloading rifles (designed by William A. "Tony" Knight of Schuyler County, Missouri) are handcrafted, lightweight rifles capable of 1½-inch groups at 100 yards. They feature a one-piece, in-line bolt assembly, patented double safety system, Timney featherweight deluxe trigger system, recoil pad, and Lothar Walther barrels (1 in 32″ twist in 50 and 54 caliber; 1 in 17″ twist in 45 caliber).

SPECIFICATIONS
Calibers: 50 and 54
Barrel lengths: 20″ and 24″
Weight: 7 lbs.
Sights: Adjustable high-visibility open sights
Stock: Classic walnut, laminated, or composite

Features: Swivel studs installed; LS&B Perfect Memory nylon ramrod; combo tool; flush valve; hex keys, and more.
Prices:

MK-85 HUNTER (Walnut)	**$529.95**
MK-85 STALKER (Laminated)	579.95
MK-85 PREDATOR (Stainless)	649.95
MK-85 LIGHT KNIGHT (Walnut)	499.95
With Black Composite Stock	519.95
MK-85 GRAND AMERICAN (Blued barrel	
Shadow brown or black)	995.95
In Stainless Steel	1095.95
MK-85 PLB GRIZZLY (Autumn Brown, Black	
Composite or Shadow Black)	649.95
In Stainless Steel	749.95

BK-92 BLACK KNIGHT

MODEL BK-92 BLACK KNIGHT
$319.99

SPECIFICATIONS
Calibers: 50 and 54
Barrel length: 24″ (tapered non-glare w/open breech system)
Sights: Adjustable; tapped and drilled for scope mount
Stock: Black synthetic coated (see also below)

Features: Patented double safety system; in-line ignition system; 1 in 28″ twist; stainless steel breech plug; adjustable trigger; ½″ recoil pad; Knight precision loading ramrod; Monte Carlo stock
Also available:

With Hardwood stock	**$329.99**
With Composite stock	349.99

NAVY ARMS REVOLVERS

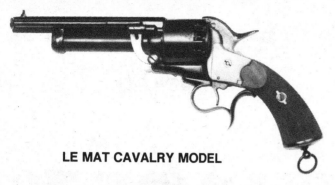

LE MAT CAVALRY MODEL

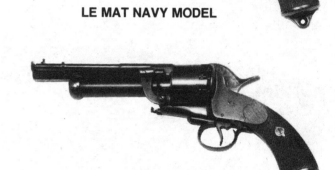

LE MAT NAVY MODEL

LE MAT ARMY MODEL

LE MAT REVOLVERS

Once the official sidearm of many Confederate cavalry officers, this 9 shot .44 caliber revolver with a central single shot barrel of approx. 65 caliber gave the cavalry man 10 shots to use against the enemy. **Barrel length:** 7⅝″. **Overall length:** 14″. **Weight:** 3 lbs. 7 oz.

Cavalry Model $595.00
Navy Model 595.00
Army Model 595.00

1862 POLICE

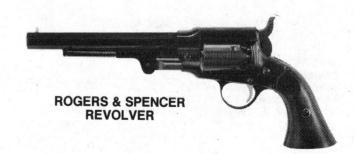

COLT WALKER 1847

1862 POLICE MODEL

This is the last gun manufactured by the Colt Plant in the percussion era. It encompassed all the modifications of each gun starting from the early Paterson to the 1861 Navy. It was favored by the New York Poolice Dept. for many years. One-half fluted and rebated cylinder, 36 cal., 5 shot, .375 dia. ball, 18 grains of black powder, brass trigger guard and backstrap. Casehardened frame, loading lever and hammer—balance blue. **Barrel length:** 5½″.

1862 Police $275.00
Law and Order Set 350.00

COLT WALKER 1847

The 1847 Walker replica comes in 44 caliber with a 9-inch barrel. **Weight:** 4 lbs. 8 oz. Well suited for the collector as well as the black powder shooter. Features include: rolled cylinder scene; blued and casehardened finish; and brass guard. Proof tested.

Colt Walker 1847 . . . . $250.00
Single Cased Set 375.00

ROGERS & SPENCER REVOLVER

This revolver features a six-shot cylinder, octagonal barrel, hinged-type loading lever assembly, two-piece walnut grips, blued finish and case-hardened hammer and lever. **Caliber:** 44. **Barrel length:** 7½″. **Overall length:** 13¾″. **Weight:** 3 lbs.

Rogers & Spencer $225.00
  With satin finish 250.00

ROGERS & SPENCER REVOLVER

NAVY ARMS REVOLVERS

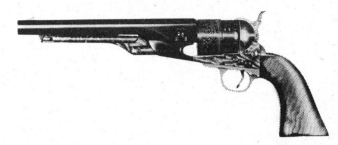

REB MODEL 1860

A modern replica of the confederate Griswold & Gunnison percussion Army revolver. Rendered with a polished brass frame and a rifled steel barrel finished in a high-luster blue with genuine walnut grips. All Army Model 60's are completely proof-tested by the Italian government to the most exacting standards. **Calibers:** 36 and 44. **Barrel length:** 7¼″. **Overall length:** 13″. **Weight:** 2 lbs. 10 oz.-11 oz. **Finish:** Brass frame, backstrap and trigger guard, round barrel, hinged rammer on the 44 cal. rebated cylinder.

Reb Model 1860	$100.00
Single Cased Set	195.00
Double Cased Set	310.00
Kit	80.00

1860 ARMY

These guns from the Colt line are 44 caliber and all six-shot. The cylinder was authentically roll engraved with a polished brass trigger guard and steel strap cut for shoulder stock. The frame, loading lever and hammer are finished in high-luster color case-hardening. Walnut grips. **Weight:** 2 lbs. 9 oz. **Barrel length:** 8″. **Overall length:** 13⅝″. **Caliber:** 44. **Finish:** Brass trigger guard, steel back strap, round barrel, creeping lever, rebated cylinder, engraved Navy scene. Frame cut for s/stock (4 screws).

1860 Army	$150.00
Single Cased Set	250.00
Double Cased Set	400.00
Kit	130.00

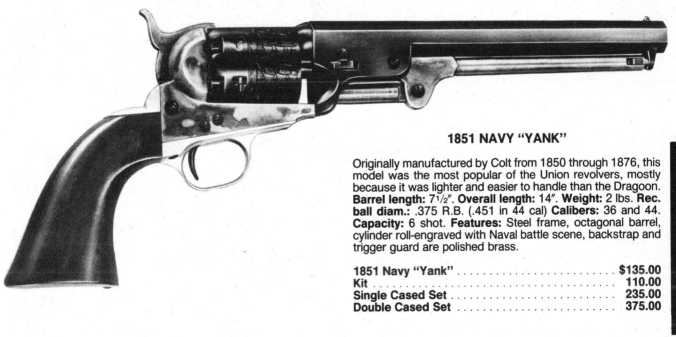

1851 NAVY "YANK"

Originally manufactured by Colt from 1850 through 1876, this model was the most popular of the Union revolvers, mostly because it was lighter and easier to handle than the Dragoon. **Barrel length:** 7½″. **Overall length:** 14″. **Weight:** 2 lbs. **Rec. ball diam.:** .375 R.B. (.451 in 44 cal) **Calibers:** 36 and 44. **Capacity:** 6 shot. **Features:** Steel frame, octagonal barrel, cylinder roll-engraved with Naval battle scene, backstrap and trigger guard are polished brass.

1851 Navy "Yank"	$135.00
Kit	110.00
Single Cased Set	235.00
Double Cased Set	375.00

BLACK POWDER

NAVY ARMS REVOLVERS

STAINLESS STEEL 1858 REMINGTON

Exactly like the standard 1858 Remington except that every part with the exception of the grips and trigger guard is manufactured from corrosion-resistant stainless steel. This gun has all the style and feel of its ancestor with all of the conveniences of stainless steel. **Caliber: 44.**

1858 Remington Stainless **$240.00**

TARGET MODEL REMINGTON REVOLVER

With its top strap solid frame, the Remington Percussion Revolver is considered the magnum of Civil War revolvers and is ideally suited to the heavy 44-caliber charges. Based on the Army Model, the target gun has target sights for controlled accuracy. Ruggedly built from modern steel and proof tested.

Remington Percussion Revolver **$185.00**

REMINGTON
NEW MODEL ARMY REVOLVER

REMINGTON NEW MODEL ARMY REVOLVER

This rugged, dependable, battle-proven Civil War veteran with its top strap and rugged frame was considered the magnum of C.W. revolvers, ideally suited for the heavy 44 charges. Blued finish. **Caliber: 44. Barrel length: 8″. Overall length:** 14¼″. **Weight: 2 lbs. 8 oz.**

Remington Army Revolver	**$145.00**
Single cased set	240.00
Double cased set	390.00
Kit	125.00

DELUXE 1858 REMINGTON-STYLE 44 CALIBER
(not shown)

Built to the exact dimensions and weight of the original Remington 44, this model features an 8″ barrel with progressive rifling, adjustable front sight for windage, all-steel construction with walnut stocks and silver-plated trigger guard. Steel is highly polished and finished in rich charcoal blue. **Barrel length:** 8″. **Overall length:** 14¼″. **Weight: 2 lbs. 14 oz.**

Deluxe 1858 Remington-Style 44 Cal. **$350.00**

ARMY 60 SHERIFF'S MODEL
(not shown)

A shortened version of the Army Model 60 Revolver. The Sheriff's model version became popular because the shortened barrel was fast out of the leather. This is actually the original snub nose, the predecessor of the detective specials or belly guns designed for quick-draw use. **Calibers: 36 and 44.**

Army 60 Sheriff's Model	**$100.00**
Kit	80.00

NAVY ARMS PISTOLS

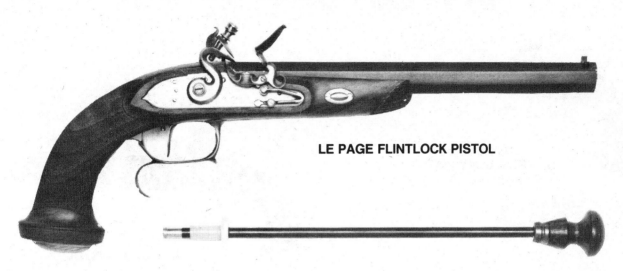

LE PAGE FLINTLOCK PISTOL

LE PAGE FLINTLOCK PISTOL
(44 Caliber)

The Le Page pistol is a beautifully hand-crafted reproduction featuring hand-checkered walnut stock with hinged buttcap and carved motif of a shell at the forward portion of the stock. Single-set trigger and highly polished steel lock and furniture together with a brown finished rifled barrel make this a highly desirable target pistol. **Barrel length:** 10½″. **Overall length:** 17″. **Weight:** 2 lbs. 2 oz.

Le Page Flintlock (rifled or smoothbore) **$550.00**

LE PAGE PERCUSSION PISTOL
(44 Caliber)

The tapered octagonal rifled barrel is in the traditional style with 7 lands and grooves. Fully adjustable single-set trigger. Engraved overall with traditional scrollwork. The European walnut stock is in the Boutet style. Spur-style trigger guard. Fully adjustable elevating rear sight. Dovetailed front sight adjustable for windage. **Barrel length:** 9″. **Overall length:** 15″. **Weight:** 2 lbs. 2 oz. **Rec. ball diameter:** 424 R.B.

Le Page Percussion **$475.00**

CASED LE PAGE PISTOL SETS

The case is French-fitted and the accessories are the finest quality to match.

Double Cased Flintlock Set **$1430.00**
French-fitted double-cased set comprising two Le Page pistols, turn screw, nipple key, oil bottle, cleaning brushes, leather covered flask and loading rod.

Double Cased Percussion Set **$1290.00**

Single Cased Flintlock Set **$760.00**
French-fitted single-cased set comprising one Le Page pistol, turn screw, nipple key, oil bottle, cleaning brushes, leather covered flask and loading rod.

Single Cased Percussion Set **$685.00**

BLACK POWDER

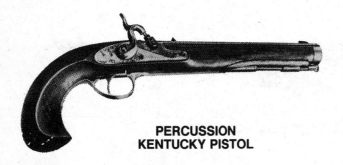

**PERCUSSION
KENTUCKY PISTOL**

**FLINTLOCK
KENTUCKY PISTOL**

KENTUCKY PISTOLS

The Kentucky Pistol is truly a historical American gun. It was carried during the Revolution by the Minutemen and was the sidearm of "Andy" Jackson in the Battle of New Orleans. Navy Arms Company has conducted extensive research to manufacture a pistol truly representative of its kind, with the balance and handle of the original for which it became famous.

Prices:

Flintlock	**$205.00**
Single Cased Flintlock Set	300.00
Double Cased Flintlock Set	515.00
Percussion	195.00
Single Cased Percussion Set	290.00
Double Cased Percussion Set	495.00

**HARPERS FERRY
FLINTLOCK PISTOL**

HARPERS FERRY PISTOLS

Of all the early American martial pistols, Harpers Ferry is one of the best known and was carried by both the Army and the Navy. Navy Arms Company has authentically reproduced the Harper's Ferry to the finest detail, providing a well-balanced and well-made pistol. **Weight:** 2 lbs. 9 oz. **Barrel length:** 10″. **Overall length:** 16″. **Caliber:** 58 smoothbore. **Finish:** Walnut stock; casehardened lock; brass-mounted browned barrel.

Harpers Ferry **$265.00**

NAVY ARMS RIFLES

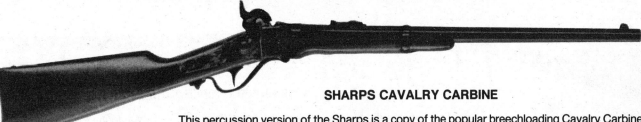

SHARPS CAVALRY CARBINE

This percussion version of the Sharps is a copy of the popular breechloading Cavalry Carbine of the Civil War. It features a bar and saddle ring on left side of the stock. **Caliber:** 54. **Barrel length:** 22″. **Overall length:** 39″. **Weight:** 7³/₄ lbs. **Sights:** Blade front; military ladder rear. **Stock:** Walnut.

Sharps Cavalry Carbine **$650.00**

1816 M.T. WICKHAM MUSKET

This version of the French 1777 Charleville musket was chosen by the U.S. Army in 1816 to replace the 1808 Springfield. Manufactured in Philadelphia by M.T. Wickham, it was one of the last contract models. **Caliber:** 69. **Barrel length:** 44¹/₂″. **Overall length:** 56¹/₄″. **Weight:** 10 lbs. **Sights:** Brass blade front. **Stock:** European walnut. **Feature:** Brass flashpan.

1816 M.T. Wickham Musket **$690.00**

MORTIMER FLINTLOCK RIFLE

This big-bore flintlock rifle, a former Gold Medal winner in the International Black Powder World Shoot, features a checkered stock (with cheekpiece), sling swivels, waterproof pan, roller frizzen and external safety. **Caliber:** 54. **Barrel length:** 36″. **Overall length:** 53″. **Weight:** 9 lbs. **Sights:** Blade front; notch rear. **Stock:** Walnut.

Mortimer Flintlock Rifle **$690.00**
   12 gauge drop-in barrel **285.00**

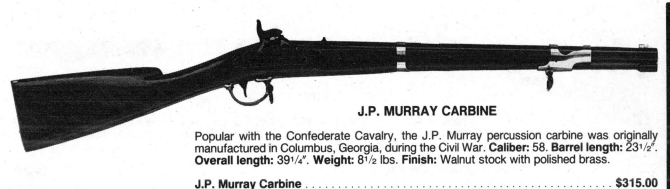

J.P. MURRAY CARBINE

Popular with the Confederate Cavalry, the J.P. Murray percussion carbine was originally manufactured in Columbus, Georgia, during the Civil War. **Caliber:** 58. **Barrel length:** 23¹/₂″. **Overall length:** 39¹/₄″. **Weight:** 8¹/₂ lbs. **Finish:** Walnut stock with polished brass.

J.P. Murray Carbine **$315.00**

BLACK POWDER

NAVY ARMS RIFLES

1853 ENFIELD RIFLE MUSKET

The Enfield Rifle Musket marked the zenith in design and manufacture of the military percussion rifle and this perfection has been reproduced by Navy Arms Company. This and other Enfield muzzleloaders were the most coveted rifles of the Civil War, treasured by Union and Confederate troops alike for their fine quality and deadly accuracy. **Caliber:** 58. **Barrel length:** 39″. **Weight:** 10 lbs. 6 oz. **Overall length:** 55″. **Sights:** Fixed front; graduated rear. **Stock:** Seasoned walnut with solid brass furniture.

1853 Enfield Rifle Musket **$410.00**

1858 ENFIELD RIFLE

In the late 1850s the British Admiralty, after extensive experiments, settled on a pattern rifle with a 5-groove barrel of heavy construction, sighted to 1100 yards, designated the Naval rifle, Pattern 1858. **Caliber:** 58. **Barrel length:** 33″. **Weight:** 9 lbs. 10 oz. **Overall length:** 48.5″. **Sights:** Fixed front; graduated rear. **Stock:** Seasoned walnut with solid brass furniture.

1858 Enfield Rifle **$360.00**

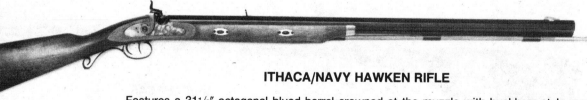

1861 ENFIELD MUSKETOON

The 1861 Enfield Musketoon was the favorite long arm of the Confederate Cavalry. **Caliber:** 58. **Barrel length:** 24″. **Weight:** 7 lbs. 8 oz. **Overall length:** 40.25″. **Sights:** Fixed front; graduated rear. **Stock:** Seasoned walnut with solid brass furniture.

1861 Enfield Musketoon **$325.00**
Kit **285.00**

ITHACA/NAVY HAWKEN RIFLE

Features a 31½″ octagonal blued barrel crowned at the muzzle with buckhorn-style rear sight, blade front sight. Color casehardened percussion lock is fitted on walnut stock. Furniture is all steel and blued (except for nose cap and escutcheons). Available in 50 caliber only.

Ithaca/Navy Hawken Rifle **$400.00**
Kit **360.00**

NAVY ARMS RIFLES

MISSISSIPPI RIFLE MODEL 1841

The historic percussion lock weapon that gained its name as a result of its performance in the hands of Jefferson Davis' Mississippi Regiment during the heroic stand at the Battle of Buena Vista. Also known as the "Yager" (a misspelling of the German Jaeger), this was one of the first percussion rifles adopted by Army Ordnance. The Mississippi is handsomely furnished in brass, including patch box for tools and spare parts. **Weight:** 9¹/₂ lbs. **Barrel length:** 32¹/₂″. **Overall length:** 48¹/₂″. **Calibers:** 54 and 58. **Finish:** Walnut finish stock, brass mounted.

Mississippi Rifle Model 1841 . . . . **$440.00**

RIGBY-STYLE TARGET RIFLE

This affordable reproduction of the famed Rigby Target Rifle of the 1880s features a 32-inch blued barrel, target front sight with micrometer adjustment, fully adjustable vernier rear sight (adjustable up to 1000 yards), hand-checkered walnut stock color casehardened breech plug, hammer lock plate, and escutcheons. This .451 caliber gun comes with loading accessories, including bullet starter and sizer and special ramrod.

Rigby-Style Target Rifle **$645.00**

1861 SPRINGFIELD RIFLE

One of the most popular Union rifles of the Civil War, the 1861 used the 1855-style hammer. The lockplate on this replica is marked "1861, U.S. Springfield." **Caliber:** 58. **Barrel length:** 40″. **Overall length:** 56″. **Weight:** 10 lbs. **Finish:** Walnut stock with polished metal lock and stock fitting.

1861 Springfield Rifle **$550.00**

1863 SPRINGFIELD RIFLE

An authentically reproduced replica of one of America's most historical firearms, the 1863 Springfield rifle features a full-size, three-band musket and precision-rifled barrel. **Caliber:** 58. **Barrel length:** 40″. **Overall length:** 56″. **Weight:** 9¹/₂ lbs. **Finish:** Walnut stock with polished metal lock and stock fittings. Casehardened lock available upon request.

1863 Springfield Rifle **$550.00**
Springfield Kit **450.00**

BLACK POWDER

NAVY ARMS

PENNSYLVANIA LONG RIFLE

This new version of the Pennsylvania Rifle is an authentic reproduction of the original model. Its classic lines are accented by the long, browned octagon barrel and polished lock plate. **Caliber:** 32 or 45 (flint or percussion. **Barrel length:** 40½". **Overall length:** 56½". **Weight:** 7½ lbs. **Sights:** Blade front; adjustable Buckhorn rear. **Stock:** Walnut.

Pennsylvania Long Rifle (Flint) **$410.00**
   Percussion **395.00**

JAPANESE MATCHLOCK

A favorite weapon of the Samurai warrior, the Matchlock was first introduced to Japan by the early traders from Portugal. It is now a recognized competition arm in the International Black Powder Championships. **Caliber:** 50. **Barrel length:** 41". **Overall length:** 54¼". **Weight:** 8½ lbs. **Sights:** Open.

Japanese Matchlock **$495.00**

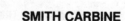

SMITH CARBINE

The Smith Carbine was considered one of the finest breechloading carbines of the Civil War period. The hinged breech action allowed fast reloading for cavalry units. Available in either the **Cavalry Model** (with saddle ring and bar) or **Artillery Model** (with sling swivels). **Caliber:** 50. **Barrel length:** 21½". **Overall length:** 39". **Weight:** 7¾ lbs. **Sights:** Brass blade front; folding ladder rear. **Stock:** American walnut.

Smith Carbine **$600.00**

BROWN BESS MUSKET

Used extensively in the French and Indian War, the Brown Bess Musket proved itself in the American Revolution as well. This fine replica of the ''Second Model'' is marked ''Grice'' on the lock plate. **Caliber:** 75. **Barrel length:** 42". **Overall length:** 59". **Weight:** 9½ lbs. **Sights:** Lug front. **Stock:** Walnut.

Brown Bess Musket **$550.00**

BROWN BESS CARBINE (not shown)

Caliber: 75. **Barrel length:** 30". **Overall length:** 47". **Weight:** 7¾ lbs. **Price:** **$550.00**
Also available: **Economy Brown Bess** **490.00**

NAVY ARMS RIFLES

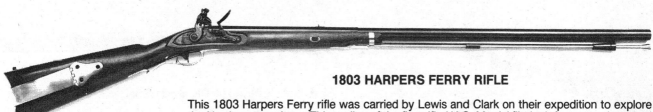

1803 HARPERS FERRY RIFLE

This 1803 Harpers Ferry rifle was carried by Lewis and Clark on their expedition to explore the Northwest territory. This replica of the first rifled U.S. Martial flintlock features a browned barrel, casehardened lock and a brass patch box. **Caliber:** 54. **Barrel length:** 35″. **Overall length:** 50½″. **Weight:** 8½ lbs.

1803 Harpers Ferry Rifle **$495.00**

1862 C.S. RICHMOND RIFLE

This model was manufactured by the Confederacy at the Richmond Armory utilizing 1855 Rifle Musket parts captured from the Harpers Ferry Arsenal. This replica features the unusual 1855 lockplate, stamped "1862 C.S. Richmond, V.A." **Caliber:** 58. **Barrel length:** 40″. **Overall length:** 56″. **Weight:** 10 lbs. **Finish:** Walnut stock with polished metal lock and stock fittings.

1862 C.S. Richmond Rifle **$550.00**

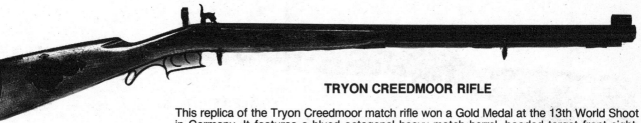

TRYON CREEDMOOR RIFLE

This replica of the Tryon Creedmoor match rifle won a Gold Medal at the 13th World Shoot in Germany. It features a blued octagonal heavy match barrel, hooded target front sight, adjustable Vernier tang sight, double-set triggers, sling swivels and a walnut stock. **Caliber:** 451. **Barrel length:** 33″. **Overall length:** 48¼″. **Weight:** 9½ lbs.

Tryon Creedmoor Rifle **$680.00**

MODEL 1860 BRASS TELESCOPIC SIGHT

First used by snipers during the Civil War, this telescopic sight later became popular with hunters and target shooters in the late 19th century. It is available in the standard 32½″ length (shown mounted on a NO. 2 Creedmoor rifle) and a new compact 18″ version. Coated optics, 4 power. Mounts included.

Standard Model **$125.00**
Compact Model **130.00**

NAVY ARMS SHOTGUNS

MORTIMER FLINTLOCK SHOTGUN

This replica of the Mortimer Shotgun features a browned barrel, casehardened furniture, sling swivels and checkered walnut stock. The lock contains waterproof pan, roller frizzen and external safety. **Gauge:** 12. **Barrel length:** 36″. **Overall length:** 53″. **Weight:** 7 lbs.

Mortimer Flintlock Shotgun **$670.00**

STEEL SHOT MAGNUM SHOTGUN

This shotgun, designed for the hunter who must use steel shot, features engraved polished lock plates, English-style checkered walnut stock (with cheekpiece) and chrome-lined barrels. **Gauge:** 10. **Barrel length:** 28″. **Overall length:** 45½″. **Weight:** 7 lbs. 9 oz. **Choke:** Cylinder/ Cylinder.

Steel Shot Magnum Shotgun **$510.00**

FOWLER SHOTGUN

A traditional side-by-side percussion field gun, this fowler model features blued barrels and English-style straight stock design. It also sports a hooked breech, engraved and color casehardened locks, double triggers and checkered walnut stock. **Gauge:** 12. **Chokes:** Cylinder/ Cylinder. **Barrel length:** 28″. **Overall length:** 44½″. **Weight:** 7½ lbs.

Fowler Shotgun **$325.00**

T & T SHOTGUN

This Turkey and Trap side-by-side percussion shotgun, choked full/full, features a genuine walnut stock with checkered wrist and oil finish, color casehardened locks and blued barrels. **Gauge:** 12. **Barrel length:** 28″. **Overall length:** 44″. **Weight:** 7½ lbs.

T & T Shotgun **$480.00**

PARKER-HALE RIFLES

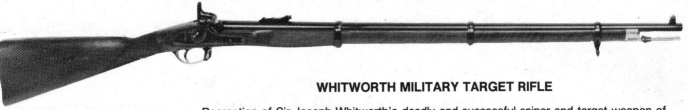

WHITWORTH MILITARY TARGET RIFLE

Recreation of Sir Joseph Whitworth's deadly and successful sniper and target weapon of the mid-1800s. Devised with a hexagonal bore with a pitch of 1 turn in 20 inches. Barrel is cold-forged from ordnance steel, reducing the build-up of black powder fouling. Globe front sight; open military target rifle rear sight has interchangeable blades of different heights. Walnut stock is hand-checkered. Manufactured by the Gibbs Rifle Company. **Caliber:** 451. **Barrel length:** 36″. **Weight:** 9½ lbs.

Whitworth Military Target Rifle **$815.00**

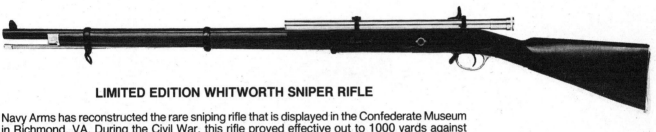

LIMITED EDITION WHITWORTH SNIPER RIFLE

Navy Arms has reconstructed the rare sniping rifle that is displayed in the Confederate Museum in Richmond, VA. During the Civil War, this rifle proved effective out to 1000 yards against Union troops. The scope mount has been altered slightly to permit offhand shooting, but it is virtually identical to the original. Manufactured by the Gibbs Rifle Company. **Caliber:** 451. **Barrel length:** 36″. **Overall length:** 52½″. **Weight:** 11 lbs.

Limited Edition Whitworth Rifle **$995.00**

VOLUNTEER RIFLE

Originally designed by Irish gunmaker William John Rigby, this relatively small-caliber rifle was issued to volunteer regiments during the 1860s. Today it is rifled by the cold-forged method, making one turn in 20 inches. Sights are adjustable: globe front and ladder-type rear with interchangeable leaves; hand-checkered walnut stock. Manufactured by the Gibbs Rifle Company. **Caliber:** 451. **Barrel length:** 32″. **Weight:** 9½ lbs.

Volunteer Rifle **$750.00**
    Same as above with 3-band barrel 815.00

Other Parker-Hale muskets available:
2-BAND MUSKET MODEL 1858
Caliber: 577. **Barrel length:** 33″. **Overall length:** 48½″. **Wt.:** 8½ lbs. **$550.00**
MUSKETOON MODEL 1861
Caliber: 577. Barrel length: 24″. **Overall length:** 40¼″. **Wt.:** 7½ lbs. 450.00
3-BAND MUSKET MODEL 1853
Caliber: 577. **Barrel length:** 39″. **Overall length:** 55″. **Wt.:** 9 lbs. 585.00

BLACK POWDER

PARKER-HALE RIFLES

1853 ENFIELD RIFLE

Commonly known as the 3-band Enfield, this is a high-quality replica of the 1853 Enfield rifle musket that was manufactured between 1853 and 1863 by various British contractors. Manufactured today by the Gibbs Rifle Company. **Caliber:** 577. **Barrel length:** 39″. **Overall length:** 55″. **Weight:** 9 lbs. **Rate of twist:** 1:48″; 3-groove barrel.

1853 Enfield Rifle $585.00

1858 ENFIELD RIFLE

One of the most accurate military rifles of the percussion era, the 1858 two-band Enfield was developed for the British Admiralty in the late 1850s. This replica of the Enfield Naval Pattern rifle has won many blackpowder national and world championships. Manufactured by the Gibbs Rifle Company. **Caliber:** 577. **Barrel length:** 33″. **Overall length:** 48 1/2″. **Weight:** 8 1/2 lbs. **Rate of twist:** 1:48″, 5-groove barrel.

1858 Enfield Rifle $550.00

1861 ENFIELD MUSKETOON

The British 1861 Musketoon was very popular with Confederate Cavalry and Artillery units. This reproduction, like all the Parker-Hale replicas, is constructed using the original 130-year-old gauges for authentic reference. Manufactured by the Gibbs Rifle Company. **Caliber:** 577. **Barrel length:** 24″. **Overall length:** 40 1/4″. **Weight:** 7 1/2 lbs. **Rate of twist:** 1:48″; 5-groove barrel.

1861 Enfield Musketoon $450.00

SHILOH SHARPS

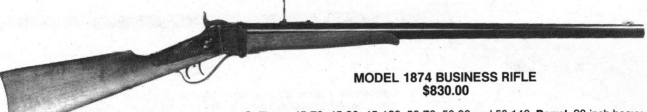

MODEL 1874 BUSINESS RIFLE
$830.00

Calibers: 45-70, 45-90, 45-120, 50-70, 50-90 and 50-140. **Barrel:** 28-inch heavy-tapered round; dark blue. Double-set triggers adjustable set. **Sights:** Blade front, and sporting rear with leaf. Buttstock is straight grip rifle butt plate, forend sporting schnabel style. Receiver group and butt plate case-colored; wood is American walnut oil-finished. **Weight:** 9 lbs. 8 oz.
Also available:
MODEL 1874 SADDLE RIFLE w/26″ tapered octagonal barrel **$895.00**

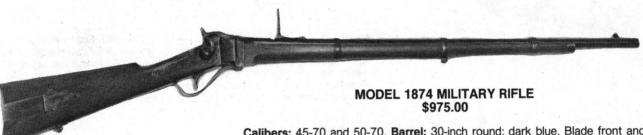

MODEL 1874 MILITARY RIFLE
$975.00

Calibers: 45-70 and 50-70. **Barrel:** 30-inch round; dark blue. Blade front and Lawrence-style sights. Military-style forend with 3 barrel bands and 1¼-inch swivels. Receiver group, butt plate and barrel bands case-colored. Wood is oil finished. **Weight:** 8 lbs. 2 oz.
Also available:
1874 MILITARY CARBINE w/22″ round barrel. **Weight:** 7 lbs. 8 oz. . **$835.00**

SHARPS RIFLE CARTRIDGE AVAILABILITY TABLE

MODEL	30–40	38–55	38–56	40–50 1¹¹⁄₁₆ B.N.	40–70 2¹⁄₁₀ B.N.	40–70 2¼ B.N.	40–70 ST	40–90 ST	40–90 2⅝ B.N.	44–77 B.N.	40–90 B.N.	45–70 2¹⁄₁₀ ST	45–90 2⁴⁄₁₀ ST	45–100 2⁶⁄₁₀ ST	45–110 2⅞ ST	45–120 3¼ ST	50–70 1¾ ST	50–100 2½ ST	40–65 WIN
Long Range Express	X	X	X	X	X	X	X	X	X	X	X	X	X	X	X	X	X	X	X
No. 1 Sporting Rifle	X	X	X	X	X	X	X	X	X	X	X	X	X	X	X	X	X	X	X
No. 3 Sporting Rifle	X	X	X	X	X	X	X	X	X	X	X	X	X	X	X	X	X	X	X
Business Rifle	X	X	X	X	X	X	X	X	X	X	X	X	X	X		X	X	X	X
Carbine, Civ.	X	X	X	X	X	X						X	X				X	X	
1874 Military Rifle	X	X	X	X	X	X						X	X				X	X	
1874 Saddle Rifle	X	X	X	X	X	X	X	X	X	X		X	X				X	X	
1874 Military Carbine	X	X	X	X	X	X						X	X				X	X	
Montana Roughrider	X	X	X	X	X	X	X	X	X	X	X	X	X	X	X	X	X	X	X
Shiloh Jaeger	X	X	X	X	X	X													X
Hartford Model Rifle	X	X	X	X	X	X	X	X	X	X	X	X	X	X	X	X	X	X	X

B.N.-Bottleneck   ST-Straight

SHILOH SHARPS

MODEL 1863 SPORTING RIFLE
$840.00

Caliber: 54. **Barrel:** 30″ tapered octagonal. Blade front sight, sporting rear with elevation leaf; double-set triggers with adjustable set; curved trigger plate, pistol grip buttstock with steel butt plate, schnabel-style forend; optional Tang sight. **Weight:** 9 lbs.
Also available:
MODEL 1863 PERCUSSION MILITARY RIFLE $940.00
   Add **$85.00** for Patchbox
MODEL 1863 PERCUSSION MILITARY CARBINE 860.00

MODEL 1874 SPORTING RIFLE NO. 1
$940.00

Calibers: 45-70, 45-90, 45-120, 50-70, 50-90 and 50-140. Features 28-inch or 30-inch tapered octagon barrel. Double-set triggers with adjustable set, blade front sight, sporting rear with elevation leaf and sporting tang sight adjustable for elevation and windage. Buttstock is pistol grip, shotgun butt, sporting forend style. Receiver group and butt plate case colored. Barrel is high finish blue-black; wood is American walnut oil finish. **Weight:** 10 lbs.

MODEL 1874 SPORTING RIFLE NO. 3
$840.00

Calibers: 45-70, 45-90, 45-120, 50-70, 50-90 and 50-140. **Barrel:** 30-inch tapered octagonal; with high finish blue-black. Double-set triggers with adjustable set, blade front sight, sporting rear with elevation leaf and sporting tang sight adjustable for elevation and windage. Buttstock is straight grip with rifle butt plate; trigger plate is curved and checkered to match pistol grip. Forend is sporting schnabel style. Receiver group and butt plate is case colored. Wood is American walnut oil-finished. **Weight:** 9 lbs. 8 oz.
Also available:
MODEL 1874 LONG RANGE EXPRESS $965.00
MODEL 1874 ROUGHRIDER 840.00
   With Semi-fancy Wood 920.00
MODEL 1874 "JAEGER" HUNTING RIFLE 895.00
HARTFORD MODEL 975.00

MODEL 1874 CARBINE "CIVILIAN"
$830.00

Calibers: 45-70 and 45-90. **Barrel:** 24-inch round; dark blue. Single trigger, blade front and sporting rear sight, buttstock straight grip, steel rifle butt plate, forend sporting schnabel style. Case-colored receiver group and butt plate; wood has oil finish. **Weight:** 8 lbs. 4 oz.

THOMPSON/CENTER

PENNSYLVANIA HUNTER

The 31″ barrel on this model is cut rifled (.010″ deep) with 1 turn in 66″ twist. Its outer contour is stepped from octagon to round. Sights are fully adjustable for both windage and elevation. Stocked with select American black walnut; metal hardware is blued steel. Features a hooked breech system and coil spring lock. **Caliber:** 50. **Overall length:** 48″. **Weight:** Approx. 7.6 lbs.

Pennsylvania Hunter Caplock **$320.00**
Pennsylvania Hunter Flintlock **335.00**

PENNSYLVANIA HUNTER CARBINE

Thompson/Center's new Pennsylvania Hunter Carbine is a 50-caliber carbine with 1:66″ twist and cut-rifling. It was designed specifically for the hunter who uses patched round balls only and hunts in thick cover or brush. The 21″ barrel is stepped from octagonal to round. **Overall length:** 38″. **Weight:** 6½ lbs. **Sights:** Fully adjustable open hunting-style rear with bead front. **Stock:** Select American walnut. **Trigger:** Single hunting-style trigger. **Lock:** Color cased, coil spring, with floral design.

Pennsylvania Hunter Carbine Caplock **$310.00**
Pennsylvania Hunter Carbine Flintlock **325.00**

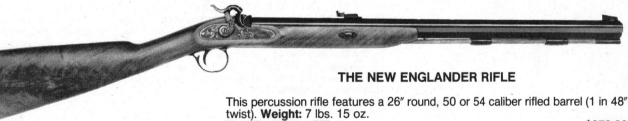

THE NEW ENGLANDER RIFLE

This percussion rifle features a 26″ round, 50 or 54 caliber rifled barrel (1 in 48″ twist). **Weight:** 7 lbs. 15 oz.

New Englander Rifle **$270.00**
    With Rynite stock (24″ barrel, right-hand only) **255.00**
Left-Hand Model **290.00**

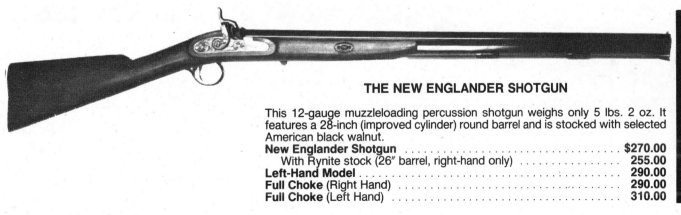

THE NEW ENGLANDER SHOTGUN

This 12-gauge muzzleloading percussion shotgun weighs only 5 lbs. 2 oz. It features a 28-inch (improved cylinder) round barrel and is stocked with selected American black walnut.

New Englander Shotgun **$270.00**
    With Rynite stock (26″ barrel, right-hand only) **255.00**
Left-Hand Model **290.00**
Full Choke (Right Hand) **290.00**
Full Choke (Left Hand) **310.00**

THOMPSON/CENTER

THE HAWKEN
45, 50 and 54 caliber

Similar to the famous Rocky Mountain rifles made during the early 1800's, the Hawken is intended for serious shooting. Button-rifled for ultimate precision, the Hawken is available in 45, 50 or 54 caliber, flintlock or percussion. It features a hooked breech, double-set triggers, first-grade American walnut stock, adjustable hunting sights, solid brass trim and color casehardened lock. Beautifully decorated. **Weight:** Approx. 8½ lbs.

Hawken Caplock 45, 50 or 54 caliber	**$375.00**
Hawken Flintlock 50 caliber	385.00
Kit: Caplock	275.00
Kit: Flintlock	295.00

WHITE MOUNTAIN CAPLOCK CARBINE

WHITE MOUNTAIN CARBINE

This hunter's rifle with single trigger features a wide trigger guard bow that allows the shooter to fire the rifle in cold weather without removing his gloves. Its stock is of select American black walnut finished off with a rifle-type rubber recoil pad, and equipped with swivel studs and quick detachable sling swivels. A soft leather hunting-style sling is included. The barrel is stepped from octagonal to round. **Calibers:** 45, 50 and 54 (Hawken or Renegade loads). **Barrel length:** 21″. **Overall length:** 38″. **Weight:** 6½ lbs. **Sights:** Open hunting (Patridge) style, fully adjustable. **Lock:** Heavy-duty coil springs; decorated with floral design and color-cased. **Breech:** Hooked breech system.

White Mountain Carbine–Caplock (right-hand only)	**$335.00**
White Mountain Carbine–Flintlock (right-hand only)	355.00

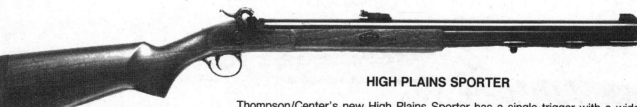

HIGH PLAINS SPORTER

Thompson/Center's new High Plains Sporter has a single trigger with a wide bow trigger guard and an intermediate barrel length of 24 inches, providing a longer sight radius than that of a carbine. The select American black walnut buttstock features a modern pistol grip, recoil pad and sling swivel studs. Two models are available: one with fully adjustable open hunting-style rear sight and the other with T/C's hunting-style tang peep sight. **Overall length:** 41″. **Weight:** 7 lbs. **Lock:** Heavy-duty coil springs; decorated with floral design and color cased.

High Plains Sporter (w/open hunting-style rear sight)	**$340.00**
High Plains Sporter (w/hunting-style tang peep sight)	345.00

THOMPSON/CENTER

THE RENEGADE

Available in 50 or 54 caliber percussion, the Renegade was designed to provide maximum accuracy and maximum shocking power. It is constructed of superior modern steel with investment cast parts fitted to an American walnut stock, featuring a precision-rifled (26-inch carbine-type) octagonal barrel, hooked-breech system, coil spring lock, double-set triggers, adjustable hunting sights and steel trim. **Weight:** Approx. 8 lbs.

Renegade Caplock 50 and 54 caliber $335.00
Renegade Caplock Left Hand 345.00
Renegade Caplock Kit (right-hand) 245.00
Renegade Caplock Kit (left-hand) 260.00
Renegade Flintlock 50 caliber (R.H. only) 345.00
Renegade Flintlock Kit (R.H. only) 260.00

RENEGADE SINGLE TRIGGER HUNTER
50 and 54 Caliber

This single trigger hunter model, fashioned after the double triggered Renegade, features a large bow in the shotgun-style trigger guard. This allows shooters to fire the rifle in cold weather without removing their gloves. The octagon barrel measures 26″ and the stock is made of select American walnut. **Weight:** About 8 pounds.

Renegade Hunter $310.00

BIG BOAR CAPLOCK RIFLE

This new large 58 caliber caplock rifle is designed for the muzzleloading hunter who prefers larger game. The rifle features a 26″ octagonal barrel, rubber recoil pad, leather sling with QD sling swivels, and an adjustable open-style hunting rear sight with bead front sight. Stock is American black walnut.

Big Boar Caplock $340.00

THOMPSON/CENTER

SCOUNT CARBINE

SCOUT CARBINE & PISTOL

Thompson/Center's new Scout Carbine & Pistol introduces a new "in-line ignition system" with a special vented breech plug that produces constant pressures from shot to shot, thereby improving accuracy. The patented trigger mechanism consists of only two moving parts—the trigger and the hammer—thus providing ease of operation and low maintenance. Both the carbine and pistol are available in 50 and 54 caliber. The carbine's 21″ barrel and the pistol's 12″ barrel are easily removable and readily interchangeable in either caliber. Their lines are reminiscent of the saddle guns and pistols of the "Old West," combining modern-day engineering with the flavor of the past. Both are suitable for left-hand shooters.

Scout Carbine **$395.00**
Scout Pistol **315.00**

TRADITIONS

PIONEER PISTOL
$169.00   ($119.00 Kit)

SPECIFICATIONS
Caliber: 45 Percussion
Barrel length: 9⅝″ octagonal with tenon; ¹³/₁₆″ across flats, rifled 1 in 18″; hooked breech
Overall length: 15″
Weight: 2¼ lbs.
Sights: Blade front; fixed rear
Trigger: Single
Stock: Beech
Lock: V-type mainspring
Features: German silver furniture; blackened hardware

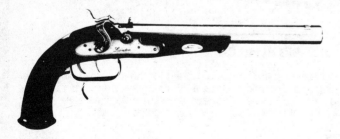

TRAPPER PISTOL
$170.00 (Percussion) $130.00 (Kit)

SPECIFICATIONS
Calibers: 45 and 50
Barrel length: 9¾″; octagonal (⅞″ across flats) with tenon
Overall length: 16″
Weight: 2¾ lbs.
Stock: Beech
Lock: Adjustable sear engagement with fly and bridle
Triggers: Double set, will fire set and unset
Sights: Primitive-style adjustable rear; brass blade front
Furniture: Solid brass; blued steel on assembled pistol

WILLIAM PARKER PISTOL
$252.00

SPECIFICATIONS
Calibers: 45 and 50 percussion
Barrel length: 10⅜″ octagonal (¹⁵/₁₆″ across flats, rifled one turn in 18″)
Overall length: 17½″
Weight: 2½ lbs.
Sights: Brass blade front; fixed rear
Stock: Walnut, checkered at wrist
Triggers: Double set; will fire set and unset
Lock: Adjustable sear engagement with fly and bridle; V-type mainspring
Features: Brass percussion cap guard; polished hardware, brass inlays and separate ramrod

TRADITIONS

FRONTIER SCOUT
$239.00 (Percussion)

SPECIFICATIONS
Calibers: 36, 45 and 50
Barrel length: 24″ (36 caliber); 26″ (45 and 50 caliber); octagonal ($7/8$″ across flats) with tenon; rifled 1:48″ (36 cal.) and 1:66″ (45 and 50 cal.); hooked breech
Overall length: $39^{1/8}$″ (36 caliber); $41^{1/8}$″ (45 and 50 caliber)
Weight: 6 lbs.
Length of pull: $12^{1/4}$″
Sights: Primitive, adjustable rear, brass blade front
Stock: Beech
Lock: Adjustable sear engagement with fly and bridle
Furniture: Solid brass, blued steel

HUNTER RIFLE
$424.00 (Percussion)

SPECIFICATIONS
Calibers: 50 and 54
Barrel length: $28^{1/4}$″; octagonal (1″ across flats) with 2 tenons; hooked breech, rifled 1:48″ (50 cal.) and 1:66″ (54 cal.)
Overall length: 46″
Weight: 8 lbs.
Lock: Adjustable sear engagement with fly and bridle
Stock: Walnut with contoured beavertail cheekpiece
Sights: Beaded blade front; hunting-style rear adjustable for windage and elevation
Furniture: Black-chromed brass with German silver wedge plates and stock ornaments

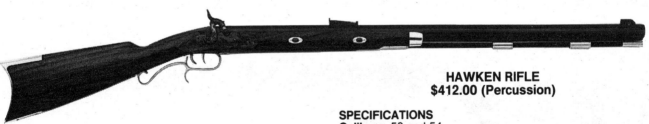

HAWKEN RIFLE
$412.00 (Percussion)

SPECIFICATIONS
Calibers: 50 and 54
Barrel length: $32^{1/4}$″; octagonal (1″ across flats w/2 tenons)
Overall length: 50″
Weight: 9 lbs.
Lock: Adjustable sear engagement with fly and bridle
Stock: Walnut, beavertail cheekpiece
Triggers: Double set; will fire set and unset
Sights: Beaded blade front; hunting-style rear adjustable for windage and elevation
Furniture: Solid brass, blued steel

BLACK POWDER

TRADITIONS

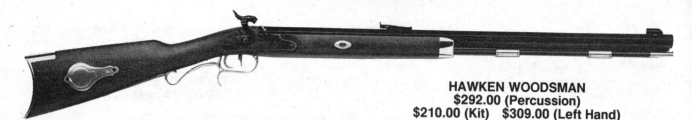

HAWKEN WOODSMAN
$292.00 (Percussion)
$210.00 (Kit) $309.00 (Left Hand)

SPECIFICATIONS
Calibers: 50 and 54
Barrel length: 28″ (octagonal); hooked breech; rifled 1 turn in 66″ (1 turn in 48″ optional)
Overall length: 45³/₄″
Weight: 7 lbs.

Triggers: Double set; will fire set or unset
Lock: Adjustable sear engagement with fly and bridle
Stock: Beech
Sights: Beaded blade front; hunting-style rear, fully screw adjustable for windage and elevation
Furniture: Solid brass, blued steel

PENNSYLVANIA RIFLE
$495.00 (Flintlock)
$467.00 (Percussion)

SPECIFICATIONS
Calibers: 45 and 50
Barrel length: 40¹/₄″; octagonal (⁷/₈″ across flats) with 3 tenons; rifled 1 turn in 66″
Overall length: 57¹/₂″

Weight: 9 lbs.
Lock: Adjustable sear engagement with fly and bridle
Stock: Walnut, beavertail style
Triggers: Double set; will fire set and unset
Sights: Primitive-style adjustable rear; brass blade front
Furniture: Solid brass, blued steel

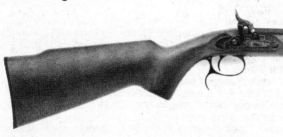

PIONEER RIFLE & CARBINE (not shown)
$227.00

SPECIFICATIONS
Calibers: 50 and 54 percussion (rifle only)
Barrel length: Carbine—24″ (1:32″); Rifle—27¹/₄″ (1:48″ or 1:66″), octagonal w/tenon
Overall length: 40³/₄″ (Carbine); 44″ (Rifle)

Weight: 5¹/₂ lbs. (Carbine); 7 lbs. (Rifle)
Trigger: Sear adjustable
Stock: Beech
Sights: Buckhorn rear with elevation ramp, adjustable for windage and elevation; German silver blade front
Lock: Adjustable sear engagement; V-type mainspring
Features: Blackened hardware; German silver furniture

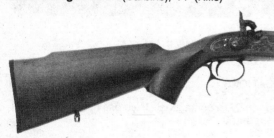

TROPHY RIFLE
$424.00

SPECIFICATIONS
Calibers: 50 and 54
Barrel length: 27¹/₄″ octagonal-to-round with tenon (rifled 1 turn in 48″ or 66″)
Overall length: 44³/₄″

Weight: 7 lbs.
Lock: Adjustable sear engagement with bridle, claw mainspring
Trigger: Sear adjustable
Stock: Walnut with cheekpiece
Sights: Hunting-style rear, click adjustable for windage and elevation; Patridge-style blade front
Features: Sling swivel, fiberglass ramrod, blackened furniture

TRADITIONS

FRONTIER RIFLE
$274.00 (Flintlock–50 Cal. only)
$254.00 (Percussion)
$179.00 (Kit–50 Cal. Percussion)

Sights: Beaded blade front; hunting-style rear, adjustable for windage and elevation
Furniture: Solid brass, blued steel

Also available:
FRONTIER CARBINE with 24″ barrel (1:66″ or 1:32″ twist), 40½″ overall length; weight 6½ lbs.; percussion only in 50 caliber.
Price: **$254.00**

SPECIFICATIONS
Calibers: 45 and 50
Barrel length: 28″ octagonal (15/16″ across flats) with tenon; hooked breech, rifled 1 turn in 66″ (1 turn in 48″ optional)
Overall length: 44¾″
Weight: 8 lbs.
Lock: Adjustable sear engagement with fly and bridle
Triggers: Double set; will fire set and unset
Stock: Beech

BUCKSKINNER CARBINE
$297.00 (Flintlock and Left Hand)
$280.00 (Percussion)
$327.00 (Laminated Stock)

Weight: 6 lbs.
Sights: Hunting style, click adjustable rear; beaded blade front with white dot
Trigger: Single
Features: Blackened furniture; German silver ornamentation; belting leather sling and sling swivels

SPECIFICATIONS
Caliber: 50
Barrel length: 21″ octagonal-to-round with tenon; 15/16″ across flats
Overall length: 36¼″

A. UBERTI

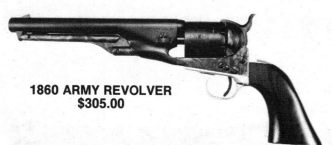

1860 ARMY REVOLVER
$305.00

SPECIFICATIONS
Caliber: 44
Barrel length: 8″ (round, tapered)
Overall length: 13¾″
Weight: 2.65 lbs.
Frame: One-piece, color casehardened steel
Trigger guard: Brass
Cylinder: 6 shots (engraved)
Grip: One-piece walnut

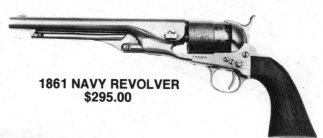

1861 NAVY REVOLVER
$295.00

SPECIFICATIONS
Caliber: 36
Capacity: 6 shots
Barrel length: 7½″
Overall length: 13″
Weight: 2.75 lbs.
Grip: One-piece walnut
Frame: Color casehardened steel

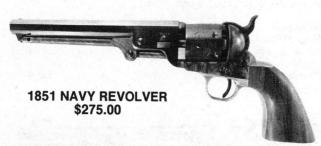

1851 NAVY REVOLVER
$275.00

SPECIFICATIONS
Caliber: 36
Barrel length: 7½″ (octagonal, tapered)
Cylinder: 6 shots (engraved)
Overall length: 13″
Weight: 2¾ lbs.
Frame: Color casehardened steel
Backstrap and trigger guard: Brass
Grip: One-piece walnut

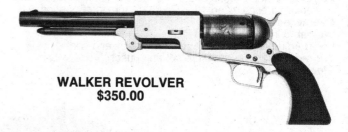

WALKER REVOLVER
$350.00

SPECIFICATIONS
Caliber: 44
Barrel length: 9″ (round in front of lug)
Overall length: 15¾″
Weight: 4.41 lbs.
Frame: Color casehardened steel
Backsstrap: Steel
Cylinder: 6 shots (engraved with "Fighting Dragoons" scene)
Grip: One-piece walnut

SPECIFICATIONS
Caliber: 44
Capacity: 6 shots
Barrel length: 7½″ round forward of lug
Overall length: 13½″
Weight: 4 lbs.
Frame: Color casehardened steel
Grip: One-piece walnut
Also available:
2nd Model Dragoon w/square cylinder bolt shot . . $315.00
3rd Model Dragoon w/loading lever latch, steel
   backstrap, cut for shoulder stock 320.00

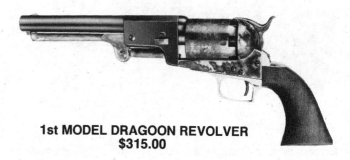

1st MODEL DRAGOON REVOLVER
$315.00

A. UBERTI

1858 REMINGTON TARGET MODEL

1858 Remington 44 Revolver (7⅞″ barrel, open sights) **$269.00**
    With stainless steel and open sights **365.00**
    Target Model, black finish **315.00**
    Target Model, stainless steel **399.00**
Also available:
1858 New Navy (36 cal.) **269.00**

PATERSON REVOLVER
$380.00
($425.00 w/Lever)

Manufactured at paterson, New Jersey, by the Patent Arms Manufacturing Company from 1836 to 1842, these were the first revolving pistols created by Samuel Colt. All early Patersons featured a 5-shot cylinder, roll-engraved with one or two scenes, octagon barrel and folding trigger that extends when the hammer is cocked.

SPECIFICATIONS
Caliber: 36
Capacity: 5 shots (engraved cylinder)
Barrel length: 7½″ octagonal
Overall length: 11½″
Weight: 2.552 lbs.
Frame: Color casehardened steel
Grip: One-piece walnut

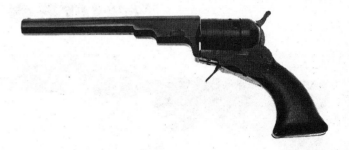

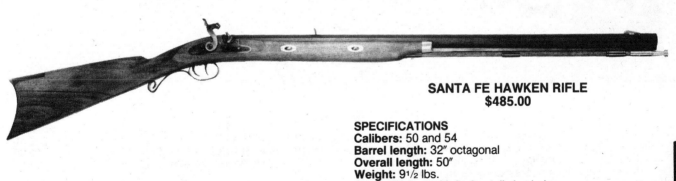

SANTA FE HAWKEN RIFLE
$485.00

SPECIFICATIONS
Calibers: 50 and 54
Barrel length: 32″ octagonal
Overall length: 50″
Weight: 9½ lbs.
Stock: Walnut with beavertail cheekpiece
Features: Brown finish; double-set trigger; color casehardened lockplate; German silver wedge plates

ULTRA LIGHT ARMS

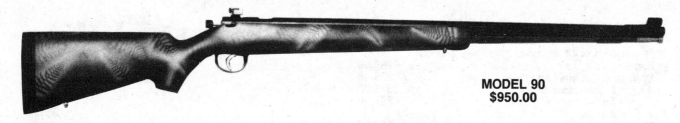

MODEL 90
$950.00

This muzzleloader comes with a 28″ button-rifled barrel (1 in 48″ twist) and 13½″ length of pull. Fast ignition with in-line action and fully adjustable Timney trigger create consistent shots. Available in 45 or 50 caliber, each rifle has a Kevlar/

Graphite stock and Williams sights, plus integral side safety. Recoil pad, sling swivels and a hard case are included. **Overall length:** 6 lbs.

WHITE SYSTEMS

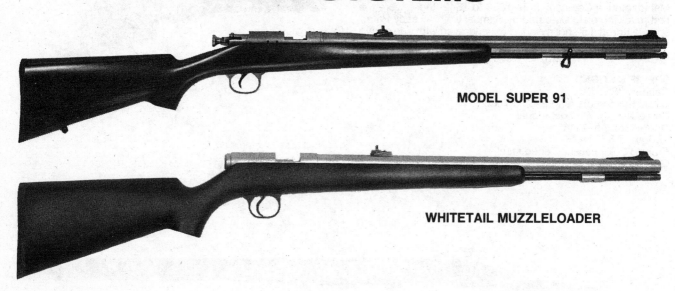

MODEL SUPER 91

WHITETAIL MUZZLELOADER

WHITE MODEL SUPER 91

This new muzzleloading system has the following features: Ordnance grade stainless steel construction • Fast twist, shallow groove rifling • Stainless steel nipple and breech plug • Side swing safety (locks the striker, not just the trigger) • Classic stock configuration (fits right- or left-handed shooters • Fast second shot and easy access to nipple from either side for quick capping • Fully adjustable trigger

SPECIFICATIONS
Calibers: .410, .451, .504
Barrel length: 24″
Sights: Fully adjustable Williams sights

Prices:
MODEL SUPER 91 Walnut	**$675.00**
MODEL SUPER 91 KIT Walnut	622.00
MODEL SUPER 91 Black Laminate	712.00
With Black Fibercomposite	712.00

Also available:
WHITETAIL MUZZLELOADING RIFLE. Calibers: .410, .451, .504, 54. Shoots Superslugs, sabots and Supertechs. **Barrel length:** 20″ Carbine. Hardwood or composite stock. Insta-fire ignition. Adjustable trigger and sights. G Series action.
In Hardwood	**$325.00**
Stainless steel w/composite stock	437.00

Sights & Scopes

For addresses and phone numbers of manufacturers and distributors included in this section, turn to *DIRECTORY OF MANUFACTURERS AND SUPPLIERS* at the back of the book.

AIMPOINT SIGHTS

AIMPOINT 5000 SIGHT
$319.95

The first sight with a true 30mm field of view, Aimpoint's 5000 allows the shooter to find the target quickly. With its patented lens system, this sight needs no parallax—the shooter does not have to center the red dot. The 5000 is available in two reticle patterns: regular 3-minute dot for precision shooting, or the Mag Dot (10 minutes) for speed shooting on pistols or on shotguns for turkey, deer and waterfowl. Each 5000 comes with 30mm rings, extension tube, lithium battery, polarizing filter and lens covers.

SPECIFICATIONS
System: Parallax free
Optical: Anti-reflex coated lenses
Adjustment: 1 click = 1/4-inch at 100 yards
Length: 5½″
Weight: 5.8 oz.
Objective diameter: 36mm
Mounting system: 30mm rings
Magnification: 1X
Material: Anodized aluminum; blue or stainless finish
Diameter of dot: 3″ at 100 yds. or Mag Dot reticle, 10″ at 100 yds.

AIMPOINT 2 POWER ELECTRONIC SIGHT
$299.95

Aimpoint has developed a fixed low power electronic sight with a floating red dot and is the only red dot sight with built-in magnification. Shooters now have the speed and accuracy of a red dot sight combined with the range of a low power scope.

SPECIFICATIONS
System: Parallax free
Optical: Anti-reflex coated lens
Adjustment: clock = 1/4″ at 100 yards
Length: 8½″
Weight: 8.3 oz.
Objective diameter: 42mm
Diameter of dot: 1½″ at 100 yards
Mounting system: 1″ rings
Magnification: 2X
Material: Anodized aluminum; blue finish

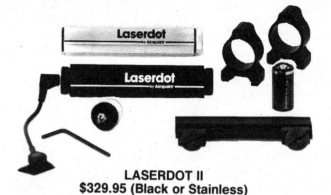

LASERDOT II
$329.95 (Black or Stainless)

SPECIFICATIONS
Length: 4″
Weight: 4.06 oz.
Diameter: 1″
Switch pad: 5.5″ long cable and pressure switch (optional toggle switch available)
Material: 6061T aluminum
Finish: Black or stainless
Output beam: Wavelength 670 nm; Class IIIa limit; output aperture approx. 1/4″ (6mm); beam divergence 0.5 Rad
Batteries: 1 X 3v Lithium
Battery life: Up to 15 hours continuous
Environmental: 0-30 C. operating 0-95% rh.; will withstand 2 meter drop; one meter immersion proof

SERIES 3000 LONG
$229.95 (Black or Stainless)

SERIES 3000 LONG SPECIFICATIONS
Weight: 5.85 oz.
Length: 6⅞″
Magnification: 1X
Scope Attachment: 3X
Battery Choices: Lithium CR 1/3 N, 2L76, DL 1/3 N, Mercury (2) MP 675 or SP 675, Silver Oxide (2) D 375 H, Alkaline (2) LR 44
Material: Anodized Aluminum, Blue or Stainless Finish
Mounting: 1″ Rings (Medium or High)

SERIES 3000 SHORT
$229.95 (Black or Stainless)
(not shown)

SERIES 3000 SHORT SPECIFICATIONS
Weight: 5.15 oz.
Length: 5½″
Magnification: 1X
Battery Choices: Lithium CR 1/3 N, 2L76, DL 1/3 N, Mercury (2) MP 675 or SP 675, Silver Oxide (2) D 375 H, Alkaline (2) LR 44
Material: Anodized Aluminum, Blue or Stainless Finish
Mounting: 1″ Rings

BAUSCH & LOMB SCOPES

2.5-10x (40mm)

3-9x (40mm)

BALVAR RIFLESCOPES SPECIFICATIONS

Model	Special Features	Actual Magnifi-cation	Obj. Lens Aperture (mm)	Field of View at 100 yds. (ft.)	Weight (oz.)	Length (in.)	Eye Relief (in.)	Exit pupil (mm)	Click Value at 100 yds. (in.)	Adjust Range at 100 yds. (in.)	Selections
64-6244	Semi-turret target adjustments. Matte finish sunshades.	6x-24x	40	18@6x 4.5@24x	20.9	16.8	3.3	6.7@6x 1.7@24x	.125	±13	Varmint, target and silhouette long range capability with all steel target adjustments for pin-point accuracy. Parallax focus adjustments.
64-2540	Adj. obj.	2.5x-10x	40	43.5@2.5x 11.2@10x	16.4	13.7	3.3	16@2.5x 4@10x	.25	±50	All purpose hunting scope with 4 times zoom range for close-in brush and long range shooting, parallax focus adjustment
64-2548	Matte finish Adj. obj.										
64-0394	Matte finish	3x-9x	40	36@3x 12@9x	16.5	13	3.2	13.3@3x 4.4@9x	t.25	±30	All purpose variable excellent for use at any range. Extra brightness for low light conditions. Large exit pupil for quick sighting.
64-1563		1.5x-6x	32	70@1.5x 18@6x	12.7	11.5	3.3	21.3@1.5x 5.3@6x	.25	±50	Compact wide angle for close-in and brush hunting. Maximum brightness and extra large exit pupil for quick sighting. Versatile four times zoom ratio.
64-1598	Matte finish										

Model 64 Balvar Riflescope

6-24x40mm $719.95	1.5-6x32mm $583.95
3-9x40mm 570.95	2.5-10x40mm 652.95

BAUSCH & LOMB SCOPES

SCOPE-CHIEF RIFLESCOPES

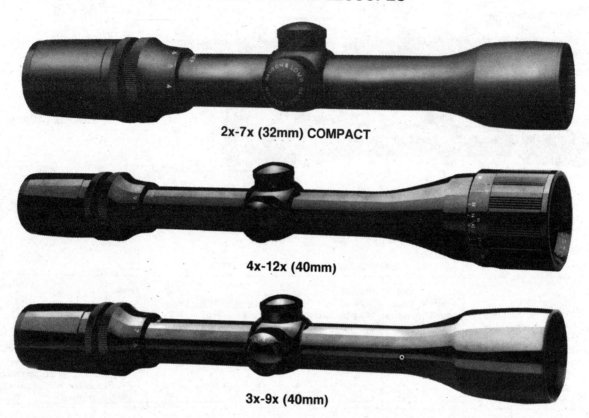

2x-7x (32mm) COMPACT

4x-12x (40mm)

3x-9x (40mm)

BAUSCH & LOMB SCOPE-CHIEF RIFLESCOPES SPECIFICATIONS

Model	Prices & Special Features	Actual Magnification	Obj. Lens Aperture (mm)	Field of View at 100 yds. (ft.)	Weight (oz.)	Length (in.)	Eye Relief (in.)	Exit Pupil (mm)	Click Value at 100 yds. (in.)	Adjust Range at 100 yds. (in.)	Selection
63-4124	**$397.95** Adjustable objective	4x-12x	40	29@4x 10@12x	15.4	13.5	3.2	10@4x 3.3@12x	.25	±40	Medium to long-range variable makes superb choice for varmint or big game shooting. Parallax focus adjustment
63-3940	**$354.95**	3x-9x	40	39@3x 13@9x	13.9	12.6	3.3	13.3@3x 4.4@9x	.25	±45	For the full range of hunting. From varmint to big game. Tops in versatility.
63-3948	Matte **$367.95**										
63-2732	**$343.95**	2x-7x	32	49.7@2x 14.2@7x	12.7	11.2	3.3	16@2x 4.5@7x	.25	±25	Compact variable for close-in-brush or medium range shooting.
63-1545	**$335.95**	1.5x-4.5x	32	69.9@1.5x 23.3@4.5	10	9.6	3.3	21@1.5x 7.1@4.5x	.25	±25	Low power variable for close-in-brush at medium range shooting.
63-1548	Matte **$349.95**										
63-0440	**$306.95**	4x	40	37.3	12	12.3	3	10	.25	±30	All purpose riflescope.

BEEMAN SCOPES

BEEMAN SS-1

BEEMAN SS-2 W/FIREARM

SS-1 AND SS-2 SERIES

Beeman SS-1 and SS-2 short scopes are extra compact and rugged, due largely to breakthroughs in optical engineering and computer programming of lens formulas. Less than 7 inches long, both scopes pack 11 lenses that actually gather light for bigger, brighter targets than "projected spot" targets. Scope body and built-in mounts are milled as a single unit from a solid block of hi-tensile aircraft aluminum.

BEEMAN SS-2

SS-1 Series	**$198.50**
SS-2 Series	265.00

BEEMAN SS-2L "SKYLITE" RIFLESCOPE

Features a brightly illuminated reticle powered by daylight and even moonlight (no batteries necessary). In addition to standard black reticle, supplementary color filters are available for different lighting and shooting situations. Filter options include: white (for silhouette or target); red (for twilight and general purpose); yellow (for haze, fog and low light); green (for bright light and snow). A small electrical illuminator is also available for use in total darkness.

Beeman SS-2L w/color reticle, 3x	**$298.50**
Beeman SS-2L w/color reticle, 4x	329.95
Lamp	29.95
Filter Kit (green or yellow)	18.95

BEEMAN SS-3

SS-3 SERIES

Offers 1.5-4x zoom power for greater flexibility. Glare-free black matte finish is anodized into metal for deep sheen and extra toughness. Instant action dial around front of scope dials away parallax error and dials in perfect focus from 10 feet to infinity. Scope measures only 5³/₄ inches in length and weighs only 8.5 ounces. **SS-3 Series** **$279.95**

BURRIS SCOPES

SIGNATURE SERIES 3X-12X PLEX

The Signature Series features a computer-designed optical system, using the most advanced optical glass available. All models have Hi-Lume (multi-coated) lenses for maximum light transmission. Also features full-field wide angle field-of-view sight picture. The 6X-24X and 3X-12X models feature Burris' patented **Light Collector.**

Prices:

2½X-10X Plex	**$514.95**
2½X-10X Plex Safari	532.95
2½X-10X Plex Silver Safari	541.95
3X-12X Plex	571.95
3X-12X Plex-Safari	587.95
3X-9X Plex	455.95
3X-9X Plex-Safari	472.95
3X-9X Plex Silver Safari	483.95
1½-6X Plex	384.95
1½-6X Plex-Safari	401.95

6X-24X SIGNATURE
w/LIGHT COLLECTOR

6X Plex	**$340.95**
6X Plex-Safari	353.95
4X Plex	325.95
4X Plex-Safari	341.95
6X-24X Plex	600.95
6X-24X 2"-.5" Dot	613.95
6X-24X 2"-.5" Dot Silhouette	636.95
6X-24X Fine Flex Silhouette	622.95

GUNSITE SCOUT SCOPE

Made for hunters who need a seven to 14-inch eye relief to mount just in front of the ejection port opening, allowing hunters to shoot with both eyes open. The 15-foot field of view and 2¾X magnification are ideal for brush guns and handgunners who use the "two-handed hold."

1½X Plex XER	**$184.95**
1½X Plex XER Safari Finish	199.95
1½X German 3 Post XER	202.95
2¾X German 3 Post XER	224.95
2¾X Plex XER	192.95
2¾X Plex XER Safari Finish	204.95

12X FULLFIELD SILHOUETTE

FULLFIELD SCOPES
Fixed Power with Hi-Lume Lenses

1½X Plex	**$223.95**
2½X Plex	233.95
4X Plex	249.95
4X Plex, Safari Finish	258.95
4X Post Crosshair	258.95
4X 3." Dot	262.95
6X Plex	266.95
6X Plex, Safari Finish	279.95
6X 2." Dot	280.95
10X Plex	307.95
10X Fine Plex	307.95
10X ½" Dot	324.95
10X Fine Plex Silhouette	335.95
10X ½" Dot Silhouette	345.95
12X Plex	336.95
12X Fine Plex	336.95
12X ½" Dot	352.95
12X Fine Plex Silhouette	362.95
12X ½" Dot Silhouette	376.95

3X-9X RAC SCOPE
with AUTOMATIC RANGE FINDER &
HI-LUME LENSES

When the crosshair is zeroed at 200 yards (or 1.8" high at 100 yards), it will remain zeroed at 200 yards regardless of the power ring setting. The Range Reticle automatically moves to zero at ranges up to 500 yards as power is increased to fit the target between the stadia range wires. No need to adjust the elevation knob; bullet drop compensation is automatic.

3X-9X RAC CHP Safari Finish	**$371.95**
3X-9X RAC Crosshair Dot	356.95
3X-9X RAC Crosshair Plex	356.95

4X-12X FULLFIELD ARC SCOPE
with AUTOMATIC RANGEFINDER RETICLE

3X-9X Fullfield ARC Crosshair (Dot or Plex)	**$356.95**
3X-9X ARC Crosshair Plex	356.95
4X-12X ARC Crosshair F.P. or Dot	428.95

BURRIS SCOPES

4X-12X FULLFIELD VARIABLE POWER

The ideal scope for long-range varmint hunting and testing hand loads. Can also be used for big-game hunting. Features crisp resolution, accurate parallax settings and a big field of view. Friction-type parallax settings from 50 yards to infinity with positive stop to prevent overturning. Fully sealed to withstand the worst field conditions and designed to deliver years of excellent service.

4X-12X FULLFIELD

Plex	$406 95
Fine Plex	406.95
2"–.7" Dot	429.95

6X-18X FULLFIELD VARIABLE POWER

This versatile, high-magnification, variable scope can be used for hunting, testing hand loads or shooting bench rest. It features excellent optics, a precise parallax adjustment from 50 yards to infinity, accurate internal adjustments and a rugged, reliable mechanical design that will give years of dependable service. Fully sealed against moisture and dust.

6X-18X FULLFIELD

Plex	$422.95
Fine Plex	422.95
2"–.7" Dot	436.95
2"–.7" Dot Silhouette	445.95
Fine Plex Silhouette	462.95

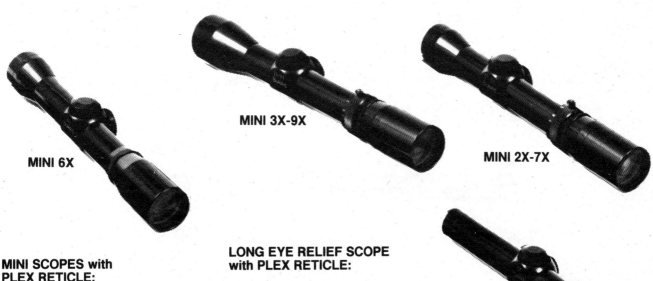

MINI 6X

MINI 3X-9X

MINI 2X-7X

3X LER

MINI SCOPES with PLEX RETICLE:

Mini 4X Plex	$201.95
Mini 4X Plex P.A. Airgun	231.95
Mini 4X Plex P.A.	231.95
Mini 4X Plex, Silver Safari	231.95
Mini 6X Plex	221.95
Mini 6X-2" Dot P.A. Airgun	265.95
Mini 6X Plex P.A. Airgun	245.95
Mini 6X Plex P.A.	245.95
Mini 6X 2" Dot P.A.	256.95
Mini 6X HBR Plex P.A.	276.95
Mini 6X HBR .375 Dot	288.95
6X HBR .375 Dot P.A. Silver Safari	319.95
6X HBR FCH P.A.	276.95
6X HBR FCH P.A. Silver Safari	306.95
Mini 2X-7X Plex	273.95
Mini 3X-9X Plex	281.95
Mini 3X-9X Plex Safari	292.95
Mini 3X-9X Plex Silver Safari	309.95
Mini 4X-12X Plex	372.95
Mini 4X-12X Fine Plex Silhouette	377.95
Mini 4X-12X 1.2-.4 Dot Silhouette	391.95

LONG EYE RELIEF SCOPE with PLEX RETICLE:

1½X-4X LER Plex	$308.95
1½X-4X LER 3."-1." Dot	343.95
1½X-4X LER Plex, Silver Safari	336.95
2½X-7X LER Plex	303.95
2½X-7X LER Plex P.A.	330.95
2½X-7X LER Plex P.A. Silver Safari	354.95
2½X-7X Plex Silver Safari	325.95
3X-9X LER Plex	341.95
3X-9X LER Plex P.A.	369.95
3X-9X LER Plex, Silver Safari	365.95
1X LER Plex	190.95
1X LER 5" Dot	202.95
2X LER Plex	193.95
2X LER Plex P.A.	231.95
2X LER Plex, Silver Safari	223.95
3X LER Plex	212.95
3X LER Plex P.A.	245.95
4X LER Plex	219.95
4X LER Plex P.A.	256.95
4X LER Dot P.A.	272.95
4X LER Plex P.A. Silver Safari	279.95
5X LER Plex	238.95
5X LER Plex P.A.	273.95

INTERMEDIATE EYE RELIEF (IER) SCOPES

7X IER Plex	$244.95
7X IER 2." Dot	258.95
7X IER Plex P.A.	278.95
7X IER 2." Dot P.A.	292.95
7X IER Plex P.A. Silver Safari	301.95
10X IER Plex	301.95
10X IER ½" Dot	320.95
10X IER Plex P.A.	330.95

BUSHNELL RIFLESCOPES

BANNER STANDARD CENTERFIRE RIFLESCOPES

Model	Special Feature	Actual Magnifi-cation	Obj. Lens Apert. (mm)	Field of View at 100 yds. (ft.)	Weight (oz.)	Length (oz.)	Eye Relief (in.)	Exit Pupil (mm)	Click Value at 100 yds. (in.)	Adjust. range at 100 yds. (in.)	Selection
71-3956		3X-9X	56	39@3X 12.5@9X	17.3	13.8	3.5	18.7@3X 6.2@9X	.25	±20	All purpose variable w/ maximum brightness.
71-6102	BDC, WA	3X-9X	40	39@3X 13@9X	13.1	12	3.3	13.3@3X 4.4@9X	.25	±30	All purpose variable, excellent for use from close to long range.
71-1643		6X	40	19	10.9	13.4	3.1	6.7	.25	±60	For open country.
71-3403	BDC	4X	32	37.3	8.9	11.8	3.1	8	.25	±30	Gen. purpose. Lightwt.
71-2520		2.5X	20	44	7.8	10	3.6	8	.25	±50	Shotgun use.

3X-9X (56mm) $314.95
3X-9X (40mm) Wide Angle, BDC 162.95

6X (40mm) $194.95
2.5X (20mm) Shotgun Scope 105.95
10X (40mm) Target 263.95

BANNER 3-9X (56mm) CENTERFIRE RIFLESCOPE

SPORTVIEW RIFLESCOPE SPECIFICATIONS Prices: $17.95 (Rimfire) to $157.95

Model	Special Features	Actual Magnifi-cation	Obj. Lens Aperature (mm)	Field of View at 100 yds. (ft.)	Weight (oz.)	Length (in.)	Eye Relief (in.)	Exit Pupil (mm)	Click Value at 100 yds. (in.)	Adjust Range at 100 yds. (in.)	Selection
74-0412	Adjustable objective	4X–12X	40	29 @ 4X 10 @ 12X	14.6	13.2	3.2	10 @ 4X 3.3 @ 2X	.25	±25	Long range.
74-3938	Wide angle	3X–9X	38	41.5 @ 3X 13.6 @ 9X	11.9	12.5	3	12.7 @ 3X 4.2 @ 9X	.25	±30	Excellent for use at any range.
74-4389	Wide angle	4X	38	34	11.3	12.6	3	9.5	.25	±25	General purpose. Wide angle.
74-1393		3X–9X	32	40 @ 3X 13 @ 9X	10	11.75	3.5	10.7 @ 3X 3.6 @ 9X	.25	±25	All purpose, variable.
74-1545		1.5X–4.5X	20	69 @1.5X 24.5 @ 4.5X	8.6	10.7	3	13.3 @ 1.5X 4.7 @ 4.5X	.25	±35	Low power variable ideal for close-in brush or medium range shooting.
74-1403		4X	32	30	9.5	11.75	4	8	.25	±30	General purpose.
74-3720	³⁄₄″ Rimfire	3X–7X	20	26 @ 3X 12 @ 7X	5.7	11.7	2.5	6.7 @ 3X 2.9 @ 7X	Friction	±30	All purpose variable.

BUSHNELL TROPHY RIFLESCOPES

4X-12X (40mm) TROPHY WIDE ANGLE
$318.95

Also available:
1.75X-5X (32mm) Trophy Wide Angle Shotgun
Scope $240.95
2X-6X (32mm) Trophy Handgun Scope. 261.95
2X-6X (32mm) Trophy Handgun Scope (Silver) 274.95
2X-7X (32mm) Trophy Wide Angle 237.95

2X (32mm) Trophy Handgun Scope $210.95
2X (32mm) Trophy Handgun Scope (Silver) 224.95
3X-9X (40mm) Trophy Wide Angle 226.95
4X (40mm) Trophy Wide Angle 173.95
4X-12X (40mm) Trophy Wide Angle 327.95
6X-18X (40mm) Trophy Wide Angle Air Rifle
Scope 370.95

Model	Special Feature	Actual Magnifi-cation	Obj. Lens Apert. (mm)	Field of View at 100 yds. (ft.)	Weight (oz.)	Length (in.)	Eye Relief (in.)	Exit Pupil (mm)	Click Value at 100 yds. (in.)	Adjust. range at 100 yds. (in.)	Selection
				TROPHY HANDGUN SCOPES							
73-2632		2X-6X	32	16.7@2X 5.8@6X	10.9	9.1	9-26	16@2X 5.3@6X	.25	±50	Versatile all-purpose 4 time zoom range for close-in brush and long range shooting.
73-2632S	Silver										
73-0232		2X	32	18.5	7.5	8.7	9-26	16	.25	±50	Designed for target and short to medium range hunting. Magnum recoil resistant.
73-0232S	Silver										
				TROPHY SHOTGUN RIFLESCOPE							
73-1500	Wide Angle	1.7X-5X	32	73@1.5X 24.5@5X	10.9	10.8	3.5	18.3@1.75X 6.4@5X	.25	±50	Shotgun, black powder, or centerfire close-in brush hunting.
				TROPHY RIFLESCOPES							
73-4124	Wide Angle w/ adj. obj.	4X-12X	40	30@4X 10.1@12X	16.2	12.5	3	10@4X 3.3@12X	.25	±30	Medium to long range variable for varmint & big game. Parallax adjust.
73-3940	Wide Angle	3X-9X	40	40@3X 13.4@9X	13.1	12	3	13.3@3X 4.4@9X	.25	±35	All-purpose variable, excellent for use from close to long range. Circular view provides a definite advantage over "TV screen"-type scopes for running game—uphill or down.
73-2732	Wide Angle	2X-7X	32	60@2X 18@7X	11.6	10	3	16@2X 4.6@7X	.25	±50	Compact variable for close-in brush & medium range shooting.
73-0440	Wide Angle	4X	40	34	12.2	12.6	3	10	.25	±35	General purpose—wide angle field of view.

INTERAIMS ELECTRONIC RED DOT SIGHTS

The following superior features are incorporated into each model including the MONO TUBE:

—5 YEAR WARRANTY—

- Sharp Red Dot
- Lightweight
- Compact
- Wide Field of View
- Parallaxfree
- True 1 X for Unlimited Eye Relief
- Nitrogen Filled Tube

- Waterproof • Moisture Proof • Shockproof
- Rugged Aluminum Body
- Easy 1″ and 30mm Ring Mounting
- Manually Adjustable Light Intensity

- Windage and Elevation Adjustments
- Dielectrical Coated Lenses
- Battery—Polarized Filter—Extension Tube—Protective Rubber Eye Piece—All included

1″ MODEL

ONE V
$139.95

MONOTUBE CONSTRUCTIONS ONE V

Weight	Length	Battery	Finish
3.9 oz.	4½″	(1) 3 V Lithium	Black Satin Nickel

ONE V 30
$149.95

MONOTUBE CONSTRUCTIONS ONE V 30

Weight	Length	Battery	Finish
5.5 oz.	5.4″	(1) 3 V Lithium DL 2032	Black or Satin Chrome

LEUPOLD RIFLE SCOPES

VARI-X III LINE

The Vari-X III scopes feature a power-changing system that is similar to the sophisticated lens systems in today's finest cameras. Some of the Improvements include an extremely accurate internal control system and a sharp, superb-contrast sight picture. All lenses are coated with **Multicoat 4**. Reticles are the same apparent size throughout power range, stay centered during elevation/windage adjustments. Eyepieces are adjustable and fog-free.

VARI-X III 1.5X5

VARI-X III 1.5X5
Here's a fine selection of hunting powers for ranges varying from very short to those at which big game is normally taken. The exceptional field at 1.5X lets you get on a fast-moving animal quickly. With the generous magnification at 5X, you can hunt medium and big game around the world at all but the longest ranges. **$464.30**. In black matte finish: **$485.70**

Also available:
VARI-X III 1.75X32mm: $482.10 ($503.60 w/matte finish**)**

VARI-X III 2.5X8

VARI-X III 2.5X8
This is an excellent range of powers for almost any kind of game, inlcuding varmints. In fact, it possibly is the best all-around variable going today. The top magnification provides plenty of resolution for practically any situation. **$500.00**. In matte finish: **$521.40**

VARI-X III 3.5X10

VARI-X III 3.5X10
The extra power range makes these scopes the optimum choice for year-around big game and varmint hunting. The adjustable objective model, with its precise focusing at any range beyond 50 yards, also is an excellent choice for some forms of target shooting. **$517.90**. With matte finish: **$539.30**. With adjustable objective: **$576.80**. With silver: **$539.30**

VARI-X III 3.5X10–50mm
Leupold announces its first hunting scope designed specifically for low-light situations. The 3.5X10–50mm scope, featuring lenses coated with Multicoat 4, is ideal for twilight hunting (especially whitetail deer) because of its efficient light transmission. The new scope delivers maximum available light through its large 50mm objective lens, which translates into an exit pupil that transmits all the light the human eye can handle in typical low-light circumstances, even at the highest magnification: **$610.70**. With matte finish: **$632.10**

Also available:
VARI-X III 3.5X10-50mm Adj. Objective: $648.20. With matte finish: **$669.60**

VARI-X III 3.5X10–50mm

VARI-X III 6.5X20 (Adj. Objective)
This scope has the widest range of power settings in our variable line, with magnifications that are especially useful to hunters of all types of varmints. In addition, it can be used for any kind of big game hunting where higher magnifications are an aid: **$607.10**. With matte finish: **$628.60**

**VARI-X III 6.5X20
(With Adjustable Objective)**

LEUPOLD SCOPES

THE COMPACT SCOPE LINE

The introduction of the Leupold Compacts has coincided with the increasing popularity of the new featherweight rifles. Leupold Compact scopes give a more balanced appearance atop these new scaled-down rifles and offer generous eye relief, magnification and field of view, yet are smaller inside and out. Fog-free.

2.5X COMPACT

2.5X COMPACT (Duplex or Heavy Duplex)
The 2.5X Compact is only 8½ inches long and weighs just 7.4 ounces. **$260.70**

4X COMPACT & 4X RF SPECIAL

4X COMPACT
The 4X Compact is over an inch shorter than the standard 4X. The 4X RF Special is focused to 75 yards and has a Duplex reticle with finer crosshairs. **$278.60.** Also available: **M8-4X COMPACT RF SPECIAL: $278.60**

2X7 COMPACT

2X7 COMPACT
Two ounces lighter and a whole inch shorter than its full-size counterpart, this 2X7 is one of the world's most compact variable power scopes. It's the perfect hunting scope for today's trend toward smaller and lighter rifles. **$355.40.** Also available: **RF Special $355.40**

3X9 COMPACT

3X9 COMPACT
The 3X9 Compact is a full-blown variable that's 3½ ounces lighter and 1.3 inches shorter than a standard 3X9. Also available in flat black, matte finish. **$369.60**

Also available: **3X9 COMPACT SILVER $391.10**

3X9 COMPACT SILVER

SHOTGUN SCOPES (not shown)

Leupold shotgun scopes are parallax-adjusted to deliver precise focusing at 75 yards (as opposed to 150 yards usually prescribed for rifle scopes). Each scope features a special Heavy Duplex reticle that is more effective against heavy, brushy backgrounds.

Prices:

2X Extended Eye Relief Model	**$257.10**
Vari-X II 1X4 Model	337.50
4X Model	300.00
Vari-X III 2X7 Model	378.60

LEUPOLD SCOPES

HANDGUN SCOPES

M8-2X EER
With an optimum eye relief of 12-24 inches, the 2X EER is an excellent choice for most handguns. It is equally favorable for carbines and other rifles with top ejection that calls for forward mounting of the scope. Available in black anodized or silver finish to match stainless steel and nickel-plated handguns. **$233.90**. In silver: **$255.40**. In matte finish: **$225.40**

M8-4X EER
Only 8.4 inches long and 7.6 ounces. Optimum eye relief 12-24 inches. Available in black anodized or silver finish to match stainless steel and nickel-plated handguns. **$296.40**. In silver: **$317.90**. In matte finish: **$317.90**

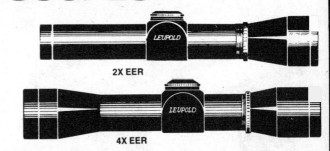

2X EER

4X EER

Also available:
VARI-X 2.5X8 EER w/MULTICOAT 4: **$482.10** (**$503.60** w/ Dot). In Silver: **$503.60** (**$525.00** w/Dot)

FIXED-POWER SCOPES

M8-4X
The all-time favorite is the 4X, which delivers a widely used magnification and a generous field of view. **$278.60**. Also available in new flat black, matte finish. **$300.00**. With CPC reticle or Dot: **$300.00**

4X

M8-6X
Gaining popularity fast among fixed power scopes is the 6X, which can extend the range for big game hunting and double, in some cases, as a varmint scope. **$296.40**. CPC reticle or Dot: **$317.90**

6X

M8-6X42mm W/Multicoat 4
Large 42mm objective lens features increased light gathering capability and a 7mm exit pupil. Great for varmint shooting at night. Duplex or Heavy Duplex: **$369.60**. In matte finish: **$391.10**

6X42mm

VARMINT SCOPES

M8-8X (Adj. Obj.)
A true varmint scope, the 8X has the sharp resolution, contrast and accuracy that also make it effective for some types of target shooting. Adjustable objective permits precise, parallax-free focusing. **$400.00**. CPC reticle or Dot: **$421.40**

8X

M8-12X VARMINT (Adj. Obj.) Target Dot Scopes w/ Multicoat 4: $453.60

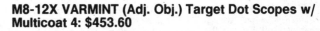

12X

8X-12X STANDARD (Adj. Obj. W/Multicoat 4)
Superlative optical qualities, outstanding resolution and magnification make the 12X a natural for the varmint shooter. Adjustable objective is standard for parallax-free focusing. **$408.90**. CPC reticle or Dot: **$430.40**

VARI-X III 3.5X10 VARMINT (Adj. Obj.) Target Dot w/Multicoat 4: $621.40

VARI-X III 6.5X20 VARMINT (Adj. Obj.) Target Dot w/Multicoat 4: $651.80

MILLETT SIGHTS

FLUSH-MOUNT SLING SWIVELS

Millett's flush-mount redesigned Pachmayr sling swivels are quick detachable and beautifully styled in heat treated nickel steel. The sling swivel loop has been redesigned to guide the sling into the loop, eliminating twisitng and fraying on edges of sling. Millett flush-mount bases are much easier to install than the old Pachmayr design, with no threading and an easy to use step drill.

Flush-Mount Swivels (pair)	SS00001	$15.65
Loops Only	SS00002	8.70
Installation Drill	SS00003	16.75

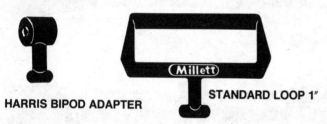

HARRIS BIPOD ADAPTER   **STANDARD LOOP 1″**

FLUSH-MOUNT HARRIS BIPOD ADAPTER

Millett's flush-mount sling swivels have a simple-to-use adapter for the Harris bipod, that detaches quickly so the loop can then be installed in the bipod loop receptacle. Will also fit Pachmayr flush-mount bases.

| Harris Bipod Adapter | SS00004 | $8.70 |

DUAL-CRIMP INSTALLATION TOOL KIT

The Dual-Crimp System is a new revolutionary way of installing front sights on autos. Now it is not necessary to heliarc or silver solder to get a good secure job. Dual-Crimp has a two-post, hollow rivet design that works very much like an aircraft rivet and withstands the heavy abuse of hardball ammo. Your choice of four styles and nine heights. Dual-Crimp is the quick and easy system for professionals. Requires a drill press.

Dual-Crimp Tool Set, Complete	$142.95
Application Tool	76.95
Reverse counterbore (solid carbide)	36.85
3/16″ Drill (solid carbide)	17.05
Drill Jig	21.95
Complete Tool Kit (Stake-On)	87.95

3-DOT SYSTEM SIGHTS

Millett announces 3-Dot System sights for a wide variety of popular handguns.

3-Dot System Front and Rear Sight Selection Chart (partial listing only)

DUAL-CRIMP® FRONTS (White Dot) **$15.25**

DC 18500	.185 Height
DC 20004	.200 Height
DC 22512	.225 Height
DC31216	.312 Height
DC34020	.340 Height
DC36024	.360 Height

WIDE STAKE-ON FRONTS (White Dot) **$15.25**
(for Colt pistols only, after June 1988)

WS18504	.185 Height
WS20008	.200 Height
WS31220	.312 Height

SPECIAL-APPLICATION PISTOL FRONTS **$15.25**

GL00006	Glock 17, 17L & 19
RP85009	Ruger-P-85
RS22015	Ruger Std. Auto (Fixed Model)
SP22567	Sig Sauer P225/226, Dovetail
SW40513	S&W 3rd Generation, Dovetail
SW46913	S&W 3rd Generation, Dovetail
BE00010	Beretta Accurizer

AUTOPISTOL REAR SIGHTS **$52.95**

BE00003	Beretta
BA00008	Browning Hi-Power, Adjustable
BF00008	Browning Hi-Power, Fixed
CA00008	Colt-Hi-Profile
CC00008	Colt Custom Combat Lo-Profile
GC00008	Colt Gold Cup
RP85008	Ruger P-85
RS22003	Ruger Std. Auto
SP22005	Sig P220, 225, 226
SW40504	Smith & Wesson, _ALL_ Factory Adjustable (incl. 2nd & 3rd Generation)*
SW46904	Smith & Wesson, _ALL_ Factory Fixed (incl. 2nd & 3rd Generation)*

* 2nd Generation use DC Fronts; 3rd Generation use Dovetail Fronts

MILLETT SIGHTS

REVOLVER SIGHTS

COLT REVOLVER
The Series 100 Adjustable Sight System offers today's discriminating Colt owner the finest quality replacement sight available. 12 crisp click stops for each turn of adjustment, delivers 5/8″ of adjustment per click at 100 yards with a 6″ barrel. Easy to install, using factory front sight. Guaranteed to give your Colt that custom look.

For Colt Python, Trooper, Diamond Back, and new Frontier single action army.

Rear Only (White Outline)	CR00001	**$46.95**
Rear Only (Target Blade)	CR00002	46.95
Rear Only (Silhouette)	CR00003	46.95

Colt owners will really appreciate the high visibility feature of Colt front sights. Easy to install—just drill 2 holes in the new sight and pin on. All steel. Your choice of blaze orange or white bar. Fits 4″, 6″ & 8″ barrels only.

Colt Python & Anaconda (White or Orange Bar)	FB00007-8	**$12.95**
Diamond Back, King Cobra, Peacemaker	FB00015-16	12.95

SMITH & WESSON
The Series 100 Adjustable Sight System for Smith & Wesson revolvers provides the sight picture and crisp click adjustments desired by the discriminating shooter. 1/2″ of adjustment per click, at 100 yards on elevation, and 5/8″ on windage, with a 6″ barrel. Can be installed in a few minutes, using factory front sight.

K&N frames manufactured prior to 1974 did not standardize on front screw hole location, so the front hole must be drilled and counterbored on these sights.

Smith & Wesson N Frame:
N.312—Model 25-5, all bbl., 27-3½″ & 5″, 28-4″ & 6″
N.360—Model 25, 27, 29, 57, & 629-4, 6 & 6½″ bbl.
N.410—Model 27, 29, 57, 629 with 8⅜″ bbl.

Smith & Wesson K&L Frame:
K.312—Models 14, 15, 18, 48-4″, & 53
K&L360—Models 16, 17, 19, 48-6″, 8⅜″, 66, 686, 586

Smith & Wesson K&L-Frame		
Rear Only .312 (White Outline)	SK00001	**$46.95**
Rear Only .312 (Target Blade)	SK00002	46.95
Rear Only .360 (White Outline)	SK00003	46.95
Rear Only .360 (Target Blade)	SK00004	46.95
Rear Only .410 (White Outline)	SK00005	46.95
Rear Only .410 (Target Blade)	SK00006	46.95
Smith & Wesson K&N Old Style		
Rear Only .312 (White Outline)	KN00001	**$46.95**
Rear Only .312 (Target Blade)	KN00002	46.95
Rear Only .360 (White Outline)	KN00003	46.95
Rear Only .360 (Target Blade)	KN00004	46.95
Rear Only .410 (White Outline)	KN00005	46.95
Rear Only .410 (Target Blade)	KN00006	46.95
Smith & Wesson N-Frame		
Rear Only .312 (White Outline)	SN00001	**$46.95**
Rear Only .312 (Target Blade)	SN00002	46.95
Rear Only .360 (White Outline)	SN00003	46.95
Rear Only .360 (Target Blade)	SN00001	46.95
Rear Only .410 (White Outline)	SN00005	46.95
Rear Only .410 (Target Blade)	KN00006	46.95

RUGER
The high visibility white outline sight picture and precision click adjustments of the Series 100 Adjustable Sight System will greatly improve the accuracy and fast sighting capability of your Ruger. 3/4″ per click at 100 yard for elevation, 5/8″ per click for windage, with 6″ barrel. Can be easily installed, using factory front sight or all-steel replacement front sight which is a major improvement over the factory front. Visibility is greatly increased for fast sighting. Easy to install by drilling one hole in the new front sight.

The Red Hawk all-steel replacement front sight is highly visible and easy to pickup under all lighting conditions. Very easy to install. Fits the factory replacement system.

SERIES 100 Ruger Double Action Revolver Sights	
Rear Sight (fits all adjustable models)	**$46.95**
Front Sight (Security Six, Police Six, Speed Six)	12.95
Front Sight (Redhawk)	15.25

SERIES 100 Ruger Single Action Revolver Sights	
Rear Sight (Black Hawk Standard & Super; Bisley Large Frame, Single-Six	**$46.95**
Front Sight (Millett Replacement sights not available for Ruger single action revolvers).	

TAURUS	
Rear, .360 White Outline	**$46.95**
Rear, .360 Target Blade	46.95

DAN WESSON
This sight is exactly what every Dan Wesson owner has been looking for. The Series 100 Adjustable Sight System provides 12 crisp click stops for each turn of adjustment, with 5/8″ per click for windage, with a 6″ barrel. Can be easily installed, using the factory front or new Millett high visibility front sights.

Choice of white outline or target blade.

Rear Only (White Outline)	DW00001	**$46.95**
Rear Only (Target Blade)	DW00002	46.95
Rear Only (White Outline) 44 Mag.	DW00003	46.95
Rear Only (Target Blade) 44 Mag.	DW00004	46.95

If you want super-fast sighting capability for your Dan Wesson, the new Millett blaze orange or white bar front is the answer. Easy to install. Fits factory quick-change system. All steel, no plastic. Available in both heights.

Dan Wesson .44 Mag (White Bar) (high)	FB00009	**$12.95**
Dan Wesson .44 Mag (Orange Bar) (high)	FB00010	12.95
Dan Wesson 22 Caliber (White Bar) (low)	FB00011	12.95
Dan Wesson 22 Caliber (Orange Bar) (low)	FB00012	12.95

MILLETT SIGHTS

The Millett Steel One- and Two-Piece Turn-In and Angle-Loc® (Weaver style) Bases fit a variety of long guns—as well as the Thompson Contender and Remington XP-100.

MILLETT ONE-PIECE BASES: $23.95

Order #	Model/Description
	BROWNING A-BOLT *NEW*
BB00000	A-Bolt Browning (Long Action-Right Hand)/Turn-in
BB00001	A-Bolt Browning (Long Action-Left Hand)/Turn-in
BB00002	A-Bolt Browning (Long Action-Right Hand)/Angle-Loc™
BB00003	A-Bolt Browning (Long Action-Left Hand)/Angle-Loc™
BB00006	A-Bolt Browning (Short Action-Right Hand)/Turn-In
BB00007	A-Bolt Browning (Short Action-Left Hand)/Turn-In
BB00008	A-Bolt Browning (Short Action-Right Hand)/Angle-Loc™
BB00009	A-Bolt Browning (Short Action-Left Hand)/Angle-Loc™
	BROWNING BAR/BLR *NEW*
BB00010	Browning BAR/BLR (Long Action-Right Hand)/Turn-In
BB00011	Browning BAR/BLR (Long Action-Right Hand)/Angle-Loc™
	INTERARMS *NEW*
MI00001	MK X, FN, 98 Mauser Interarms (Right Hand)/Turn-In
MI00002	MK X, FN, 98 Mauser Interarms (Right Hand)/Angle-Loc™
	MARLIN *NEW*
MB00005	Marlin 336 (Long Action-Right Hand)/Turn-In
MB00006	Marlin 336 (Long Action-Right Hand)/Angle-Loc™
	REMINGTON *NEW*
RB00004	Rem 600/Rem 7 (Short Action-Right Hand)/Turn in
RB00005	Rem 600/Rem 7 (Short Action-Right Hand)/Angle-Loc™
SB70002	Rem 700 (Short Action-Right Hand)/Turn-In
SB70003	Rem 700 (Short Action-Left Hand)/Turn-In
SB70004	Rem 700 (Short Action-Right Hand)/Angle-Loc™
SB70005	Rem 700 (Short Action-Left Hand)/Angle-Loc™
SB70006	Rem 700 (Long Action-Right Hand)/Turn-In
SB70007	Rem 700 (Long Action-Left Hand)/Turn-In
SB70008	Rem 700 (Long Action-Right Hand)/Angle-Loc™
SB70009	Rem 700 (Long Action-Left Hand)/Angle-Loc™
XP00001	Rem XP-100 (Short Action-Right Hand)/Turn-In
XP00002	Rem XP-100 (Short Action-Right Hand)/Angle-Loc™
RB00002	Rem 7400/7600 (Long Action-Right Hand)/Turn-In
RB00003	Rem 7400/7600 (Long Action-Right Hand)/Angle-Loc™
	SAVAGE *NEW*
SB00005	Savage 110 (Long Action-Right Hand)/Turn-In
SB00006	Savage 110 (Long Action-Left Hand)/Turn-In
SB00007	Savage 110 (Long Action-Right Hand)/Angle-Loc™
SB00008	Savage 110 (Long Action-Left Hand)/Angle-Loc™
	THOMPSON CONTENDER *NEW*
TC00001	Thompson Contender (Blue)/Turn-In
TC00002	Thompson Contender (Nickel)/Turn-In
TC00003	Thompson Contender (Blue)/Angle-Loc™
TC00004	Thompson Contender (Nickel)/Angle-Loc™
	WINCHESTER *NEW*
WB70001	Winchester 70 (Short Action-Right Hand)/Turn-In
WB70002	Winchester 70 (Short Action-Right Hand)/Angle-Loc™
WB70004	Win 70-Magnum/Std (Long Action-Right Hand)/Turn-In
WB00005	Win 70-Magnum/Std (Long Action-Right Hand)/Angle-Loc™

TWO-PIECE BASES

Order #	Model/Description	Price
SB70001	700 Series	$23.95
FN00002	Interarms Mark X, FN Series	23.95
WB70003	70 Series	23.95
BB00004	Browning BLR, BAR	23.95
BB00005	Browning A-Bolt	23.95
BB00905	Browning A-Bolt (Nickel Finish)	27.95
RB00006	Remington 7400/7600/4/6	23.95
MB00007	Marlin 336	23.95
WB00008	Winchester 94, Angle-Eject	23.95
SB00009	Savage 110	23.95
SB00909	Savage 110 (Nickel Finish)	27.95

MILLETT SCOPE MOUNTS FOR HANDGUNS

Colt Python/Trooper/Diamondback/Peacekeeper (smooth rings) $32.95
    With smooth nickel finish 40.95
Dan Wesson (calibers up thru 357; smooth rings, 2-ring set) 32.95
    With smooth nickel finish 40.95
    41/44 Magnum, smooth rings only (3-ring set) 49.35
    With smooth nickel finish 61.35
Ruger Redhawk (also Ranch Rifle, #1, #3; smooth rings) 29.65
    With smooth nickel finish 40.95
Ruger Super Redhawk (also M77; front & rear) 40.95
    Smooth rings (front & rear, set) 29.65
Smith & Wesson K- and N-Frame smooth rings 32.95
    Same as above w/nickel finish 40.95

SHOTGUN SCOPE MOUNTS
Remington 870 & 1100 (Smooth rings only) $26.95

MILLETT AUTO PISTOL SIGHTS

| | COLT | COLT GOLD CUP | MARK II HI-PROFILE |

RUGER STANDARD AUTO

The Ruger Standard Auto Combo provides a highly visible sight picture even under low light conditions. The blaze orange or white bar front sight allows the shooter to get on target fast. Great for target use or plinking. Uses Factory Front Sight on adjustable model guns when using Millett target rear only. All other installations use Millett Front Sight. Easy to install.

Rear Only (White Outline)	$52.95
Rear Only (Silhouette Target Blade)	52.95
Rear Only (Target Blade)	52.95
Front Only (White), Fixed Model	15.25
Front Only (Orange), Fixed Model	15.25
Front Only (Serrated Ramp), Fixed Model	15.25
Front Only (Target-Adjustable Model/White Bar)	15.25
Front Only (Target-Adjustable Model/Orange Bar)	15.25
Front Only Bull Barrel (White or Orange Ramp)	16.75

RUGER P85

Rear (White Outline)	$52.95
Rear (Target Blade)	52.95
Front (White Ramp)	15.25
Front (Orange Ramp)	15.25
Front (Serrated Ramp)	15.25

TAURUS PT92

Rear (White Outline, use Beretta Front)	$52.95
Rear (Target Blade, use Beretta Front)	52.95
Front (White Bar)	23.95
Front (Orange Bar)	23.95
Front (Serrated Ramp)	23.95

AMT HARDBALLER

Rear (White Outline, use .185 DC Front)	$46.95
Rear (Target Blade, use .185 DC Front)	46.95

HECKLER & KOCH (P7 ONLY)

Rear (White Outline)	$32.95
Front (White Ramp)	15.25
Front (Blaze Orange Ramp)	15.25

COLT

Colt Gold Cup Marksman Speed Rear Only (Target .410 Blade)	$46.95
Custom Combat Low Profile Marksman Speed Rear Only (Target .410 Blade)	52.95
Colt Government & Commander (High Profile) Marksman Speed Rear Only (Target .410 Blade) CA00018	52.95
Colt Gold Cup Rear (use DC or WS 200 Frt)	46.95
Colt Mark II Low-Profile Rear Only (DC 200 Front)	32.95

COLT WIDE STAKE FRONT SIGHTS (POST 6/88)

.185 WS White Bar	$15.25
.185 WS Orange Bar	$15.25
.185 WS Serrated Ramp	$15.25
.185 WS White Dot	$15.25
.200 WS White Bar	$15.25
.200 WS Orange Bare with Skirt	$15.25
.200 WS Serrated Ramp with Skirt	$15.25
.200 WS White Dot with Skirt	$15.25
.312 WS White Bar with Skirt	$15.25
.312 WS Orange Bar with Skirt	$15.25
.312 WS Serrated Ramp with Skirt	$15.25
.312 WS White Dot with Skirt	$15.25

SIG/SAUER P-220, P-225, P-226

Now Sig Pistol owners can obtain a Series-100 adjustable sight system for their guns. Precision click adjustment for windage and elevation makes it easy to zero when using different loads. The high visibility features assures fast sight acquisition when under the poorest light conditions. Made of high quality heat treated nickel steel and built to last. Extremely easy to install on P-225 and P-226. The P-220 and Browning BDA 45 require the Dual-Crimp front sight installation.

Sig P220-25-26 Rear Only (White)*	SP22003	52.95
Sig P220-25-26 Rear Only (Target)*	SP22004	52.95
Sig P225-0 (White) Dovetail Front*	SP22565	15.25
Sig P225-6 (Orange) Dovetail Front*	SP22566	15.25

The Sig P220 Uses .360 Dual-Crimp Front Sight. The Sig P225-6 Uses a Dovetail Mount Front Sight

NIKON SCOPES

PISTOL SCOPES

Key Features:
- Edge to edge sharpness for precise detection of camouflaged game
- Super multicoating and blackened internal metal parts provide extreme reduction of flare and image ghost-out
- Aluminum alloy one-piece 1″ tube provides lightweight but rugged construction (fully tested on Magnum calibers)
- ¼ MOA windage/elevation adjustment

- Extended eye relief
- Nitrogen gas filled and 0-ring sealed for water and fogproofing
- Black Lustre or satin silver finish

Prices:

2×20 EER	$218.00
1.5-4.5×24 EER	361.00

2×20 EER PISTOL SCOPE

1.5-4.5×24 EER PISTOL SCOPE

1.5-4.5×20 RIFLESCOPE

RIFLESCOPES

Key Features: Essentially the same as the **Pistol Scopes** (above). Available in black lustre and black matte finishes.

Prices:

4×40	$275.00
1.5-4.5×20	361.00
2-7×32	398.00
3-9×40	404.00
4-12×40 AO	526.00
6.5-20×44 AO	609.00
3.5-10×50	609.00
4-12×50	665.00

4-12×40 AO RIFLESCOPE

6.5-20×44 AO RIFLESCOPE

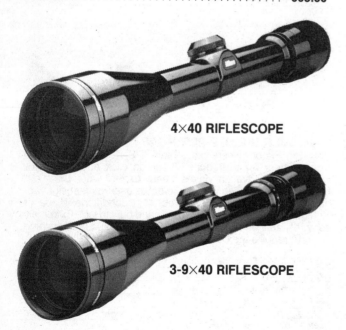

4×40 RIFLESCOPE

3-9×40 RIFLESCOPE

3.5-10×50 RIFLESCOPE

4-12×50 AO RIFLESCOPE

PENTAX SCOPES

FIXED POWER

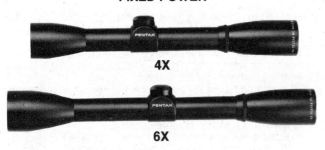

4X

6X

VARIABLE POWER

3X-9X

2X-7X

MINI 3X-9X

FIXED POWER RIFLESCOPES

Magnification: 4X
Field of view: 35'
Eye relief: 3.25"
Diameter: 1"
Weight: 12.2 oz.
Length: 11.6"
Prices: $280.00 (Glossy)
    300.00 (ProFinish)

Magnification: 6X
Field of view: 20'
Eye relief: 3.25"
Diameter: 1"
Weight: 13½ oz.
Length: 13.4"
Prices: $310.00 (Glossy)
    330.00 (ProFinish)

VARIABLE POWER RIFLESCOPES

Magnification: 1.5X-5X
Field of view: 66'-25'
Eye relief: 3"-3¼"
Diameter: 1"
Weight: 13 oz.
Length: 11"
Price: $330.00 (ProFinish)
    310.00 (Glossy)
    365.00 (Satin Chrome)

Magnification: 3X-9X
Field of view: 33'-13½'
Eye relief: 3"-3¼"
Diameter: 1"
Weight: 15 oz.
Length: 13"
Prices: $380.00 (Glossy)
    400.00 (ProFinish)
    420.00 (Satin Chrome)

Magnification: 2X-7X
Field of view: 42.5'-17'
Eye relief: 3"-3¼"
Diameter: 1"
Weight: 14 oz.
Length: 12"
Prices: $360.00 (Glossy)
    380.00 (ProFinish)
    400.00 (Satin Chrome)

Magnification: Mini 3X-9X
Field of view: 26½'-10½'
Eye relief: 3¼"
Diameter: 1"
Weight: 13 oz.
Length: 10.4"
Prices: $320.00 (Mini Glossy)
    340.00 (Mini ProFinish)

Also available:
4X-12X (Mini Glossy): **$410.00 ($430.00** ProFinish**)**
6X-12X (Glossy): **$460.00 ($500.00** ProFinish**)**
6X-12X Silhouette: $500.00

2X-8X LIGHTSEEKER

LIGHTSEEKER 3X-9X RIFLE SCOPE

Field of view: 36-14'
Eye relief: 3"
Diameter: 1"
Weight: 15 oz.
Length: 12.7"
Prices: $520.00 (Glossy)
    550.00 (ProFinish)
    550.00 (Satin)

Also available:
2X-8X (Glossy): **$450.00**
2X-8X (ProFinish): **$460.00**
2X-8X (Satin Chrome): **$480.00**

PISTOL SCOPES

Magnification: 2X
Field of view: 21'
Eye relief: 10"-24"
Diameter: 1"
Weight: 6.8 oz.
Length: 8¼"
Prices: $240.00 (Glossy)
    260.00 (Chrome-Matte)

Also available:
1.5X-4X (Glossy): **$360.00**
1.5X-4X (Satin Chrome): **$390.00**
2.5X-7X (Glossy): **$380.00**
2.5X-7X (Chrome-Matte): **$400.00**

Magnification: 1.5X-4X
Field of view: 16'-11'
Eye relief: 11"-25"/11"-18"
Diameter: 1"
Weight: 11 oz.
Length: 10"
Prices: $360.00 (Glossy)
    390.00 (Chrome-Matte)

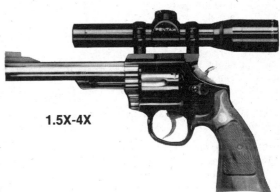

1.5X-4X

REDFIELD SCOPES

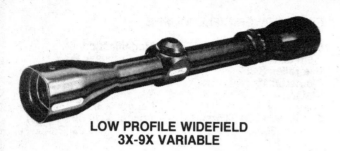

**LOW PROFILE WIDEFIELD
3X-9X VARIABLE**

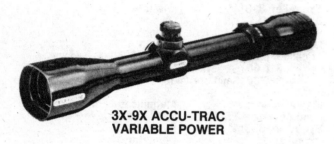

**3X-9X ACCU-TRAC
VARIABLE POWER**

LOW PROFILE WIDEFIELD

In heavy cover, game may jump out of the brush 10 feet away or appear in a clearing several hundred yards off, either standing or on the move.

The Widefield®, with 25% more field of view than conventional scopes, lets you spot game quicker, stay with it and see other animals that might be missed.

The patented Low Profile design means a low mounting on the receiver, allowing you to keep your cheek tight on the stock for a more natural and accurate shooting stance, especially when swinging on running game.

The one-piece, fog-proof tube is machined with high tensile strength aluminum alloy and is anodized to a lustrous finish that's rust-free and virtually scratch-proof. Available in 7 models.

WIDEFIELD LOW PROFILE SCOPES

1³/₄X-5X Low Profile Variable Power
113806 1³/₄X-5X 4 Plex $340.95
2X-7X Low Profile Variable Power
111806 2X-7X 4 Plex 350.95
2X-7X Low Profile Accu-Trac Variable Power
111810 2X-7X 4 Plex AT 415.95
3X-9X Low Profile Variable Power
112806 3X-9X 4 Plex 389.95
3X-9X Low Profile Accu-Trac Variable Power
112810 3X-9X 4 Plex AT 452.95
2³/₄X Low Profile Fixed Power
141807 2³/₄X 4 Plex 247.95
4X Low Profile Fixed Power
143806 4X 4 Plex 279.95
6X Low Profile Fixed Power
146806 6X 4 Plex 300.95
3X-9X Low Profile RealTree Camo 407.95

GOLDEN FIVE STAR SCOPES

This series of seven scopes incorporates the latest variable and fixed power scope features, including multi-coated and magnum recoil-resistant optical system, plus maximum light-gathering ability. Positive quarter-minute click adjustments for ease of sighting and optimum accuracy. Anodized finish provides scratch-resistant surface.

Golden Five Star Scopes:
4X Fixed Power $224.95
6X Fixed Power 244.95
1X-4X Variable Power 276.95
2X-7X Variable Power 289.95
3X-9X Variable Power 310.95
3X-9X Nickel Plated Variable Power 329.95
3X-9X Accu-Trac Variable Power 355.95
4X-12X Variable Power (Adj. Objective) 396.95
4X-12X Accu-Trac (AO) 440.95
6X-18X Variable Power (Adj. Objective) 419.95
6X-18X Accu-Trac Variable Power (Adj. Obj.) 465.95

50mm Golden Five Star Scopes:
3X-9X 50mm Five Star Variable
116500 4 Plex $376.95
3X-9X 50mm Five Star RealTree Camo
116505 4 Plex 395.95
3X-9X 50mm Five Star Matte Finish
116508 4 Plex Matte 386.95

3X-9X NICKEL PLATED GOLDEN FIVE STAR SCOPE

50mm GOLDEN FIVE STAR SCOPE

REDFIELD SCOPES

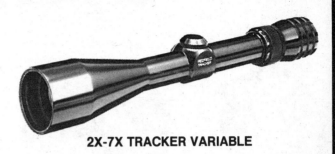

2X-7X TRACKER VARIABLE

THE TRACKER

The Tracker series brings you a superior combination of price and value. It provides the same superb quality, precision and strength of construction found in all Redfield scopes, but at an easily affordable price. Features include the tough, one-piece tube, machined and hand-fitted internal parts, excellent optical quality and traditional Redfield styling.

TRACKER SCOPES:
2X-7X Tracker Variable Power
122300 2X-7X 4 Plex $207.95
3X-9X Tracker Variable Power
123300 3X-9X 4 Plex 233.95
3X-9X Tracker RealTree Camo
123305 4 Plex 252.95
4X Tracker Fixed Power
135300 4X 4 Plex 162.95
4X 40mm Tracker RealTree Camo
135305 4 Plex 187.95
6X Tracker Fixed Power
135600 6X 4 Plex 182.95
Matte Finish
122308 2X-7X 4 Plex 222.95
123308 3X-9X 4 Plex 243.95
135608 6X 4 Plex 190.95
135308 4X 32mm 172.95

6X TRACKER SCOPE FIXED

4X 40mm TRACKER SCOPES

REALTREE CAMO SCOPES

New rifle scope models featuring the popular RealTree camouflage pattern have joined Redfield's Illuminator, Low-Profile Widefield and Tracker lines. Also available with 1X-4X shotgun scope.

SAKO SCOPE MOUNTS

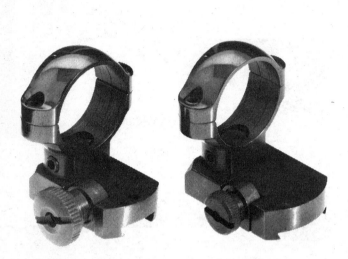

SCOPE MOUNTS

These new Sako scope mounts are lighter, yet stronger than ever. Tempered steel allows the paring of every last gram of unnecessary weight without sacrificing strength. Like the original mount, these rings clamp directly to the tapered dovetails on Sako rifles, thus eliminating the need for separate bases. Grooves inside the rings preclude scope slippage even under the recoil of the heaviest calibers. Nicely streamlined and finished In a rich blue-black to complement any Sako rifle.

Price: Low, medium, or high (1") **$67.00**
       Medium or high (30mm) **81.00**

"ORIGINAL" SCOPE MOUNTS

Sako's "Original" scope mounts are designed and engineered to exacting specifications, which is traditional to all Sako products. The dovetail mounting system provides for a secure and stable system that is virtually immovable. Unique to this Sako mount is a synthetic insert that provides maximum protection against possible scope damage. It also affords additional rigidity by compressing itself around the scope. Manufactured in Finland.

Prices: 1" Medium & High (Short, Medium
   & Long Action) **$125.00**
       30mm Medium & High (Short, Medium
   & Long Action) **140.00**

SCHMIDT & BENDER RIFLE SCOPES

**2¹/₂-10×56 VARIABLE POWER
     SCOPE**
**$1090.00 ($1130.00 w/Glass
Reticle)**

**1¹/₂-6×42 VARIABLE POWER
     SCOPE**
$860.00 ($895.00 w/Glass Reticle)

**4-12×42 VARIABLE POWER
     SCOPE**
$1010.00

**1¹/₄-4×20 VARIABLE POWER
     SCOPE**
$830.00 ($860.00 w/Glass Reticle)

SIMMONS SCOPES

44 MAG RIFLESCOPES

MODEL 1045

MODEL 1043
2-7×44mm

Field of view: 56'-16'
Eye relief: 3.3"
Length: 11.8"
Weight: 13 oz.
Price: $256.95

MODEL 1044
3-10×44mm

Field of view: 38'-12'
Eye relief: 3"
Length: 12.8"
Weight: 16.9 oz.
Price: $268.95

MODEL 1045
4-12×44mm

Field of view: 27'-9'
Eye relief: 3"
Length: 12.8"
Weight: 19.5 oz.
Price: $280.95

PROHUNTER RIFLESCOPES

MODEL 7710

MODEL 7710
3-9×40mm Wide Angle Riflescope

Field of view: 40'-15' at 100 yards
Eye relief: 3"
Length: 12.6"
Weight: 11.6 oz.
Features: Triplex reticle; silver finish
Price: $144.95 ($142.95 in black matte
or black polish**)**

MODELS 7711/7712

Also available:
2-7X32 Black Matte or Black Polish **$131.95**
4-12X40 Black Polish **$168.95**
6-18X40 (adj. obj. Black) **$168.95**

RIFLESCOPE ALLOY RINGS

Low 1" Set **Model 1401** $11.95
Medium 1" Set **Model 1403** 11.95
High 1" Set **Model 1404** 11.95
1" See-Thru Set **Model 1405** 13.95
1" Rings for 22 Grooved Receiver **Model 1406** 11.95
1" Rings extention for Compact Scopes
    Model 1409 . . . . 20.95

#1401

#1406

#1403

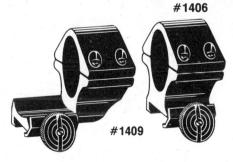

#1409

SIMMONS SCOPES

DEERFIELD RIFLESCOPES

MODEL 21006
4×32mm

Field of view: 28' at 100 yards
Eye relief: 4"
Length: 12"
Weight: 9.1 oz.
MOA click adjustment: 1/4 minute
Price: $74.95

MODEL 21010
3-9×32mm

Field of view: 38'-12' at 100 yards
Eye relief: 3.4"-2.9"
Length: 12"
Weight: 9.8 oz.
MOA click adjustment: 1/4 minute
Price: $91.95

MODEL 21029
3-9×40mm

Field of view: 32'-11' at 100 yards
Eye relief: 3.4"-2.9"
Length: 12.6"
Weight: 12.3 oz.
MOA click adjustment: 1/4 minute
Price: $104.95

MODEL 21031
4-12×40mm (Adj. Obj.)

Field of view: 30'-11' at 100 yards
Eye relief: 3"-2.8"
Length: 13.9"
Weight: 14.6 oz.
MOA click adjustment: 1/4 minute
Feature: Fully coated lens system
Price: $104.95

MODEL 21005
2.5×20mm Shotgun Scope

Field of view: 29' at 100 yards
Eye relief: 4.6"
Length: 7.1"
Weight: 7.2 oz.
MOA click adjustment: 1/4 minute
Finish: Matte black
Feature: Fully coated lens system
Price: $85.95

MODEL 7790
4X32 Shotgun Scope

Field of view: 16'
Eye relief: 5.5"
Length: 8.8"
Weight: 9.2 oz.
Finish: Matte black
Price: $117.95

SHOTGUN SCOPE MODEL 21005

MODEL 21006

MODEL 21010

MODEL 21029

MODEL 21031

SIMMONS SCOPES

WHITETAIL CLASSIC RIFLESCOPES

Simmons' new Whitetail Classic Series features fully coated lenses and glare-proof BlackGranite finish. Its Mono-Tube construction means that front bell and tube and saddle and rear tube are all turned from one piece of aircraft aluminum.

This system eliminates 3 to 5 joints found in most other scopes in use today. The Whitetail Classic is therefore up to 400 times stronger than comparably priced scopes.

MODEL WTC10
4×32mm

Field of view: 35'
Eye relief: 4″
Length: 12″
Weight: 11.0 oz.
Price: $134.95

MODEL WTC10

MODEL WTC11
1.5-5×20mm

Field of view: 80'-23.5'
Eye relief: 3.5″
Length: 9¹/₂″
Weight: 9.9 oz.
Price: $169.95

MODEL WTC11

MODEL WTC12
2.5-8×36mm

Field of view: 48'-14.8'
Eye relief: 3″
Length: 12.8″
Weight: 12.9 oz.
Price: $185.95

MODEL WTC12

MODEL WTC13
3.5-10×40mm

Field of view: 35'-12'
Eye relief: 3″
Length: 12.8″
Weight: 16.9 oz.
Price: $204.95

MODEL WTC13

MODEL WTC14
2-10×44mm

Field of view: 50'-11'
Eye relief: 3″
Length: 12.8″
Weight: 16.9 oz.
Price: $256.95

MODEL WTC14

MODEL WT03

MODEL WTC15
3.5-10×50 Black Granite

Field of view: NA
Eye relief: NA
Length: NA
Weight: NA
Price: $336.95

MODEL WTC23
3.5-10×40

Field of view: 34'-11.5'
Eye relief: 3.2″
Length: 12.4″
Weight: 12.8 oz.
Price: $216.95

MODEL WTC33
3.5-10×40 Silver

Same specifications as Model WTC23
Price: $218.95

SIMMONS SCOPES

GOLD MEDAL SILHOUETTE SERIES

Simmons Gold Medal Silhouette Riflescopes are made of state-of-the-art drive train and erector tube design, a new windage and elevation indexing mechanism, camera-quality 100% multicoated lenses, and a super smooth objective focusing device. High silhouette-type windage and elevation turrets house 1/8 minute click adjustments. The scopes have a black matte finish and crosshair reticle and are fogproof, waterproof and shockproof.

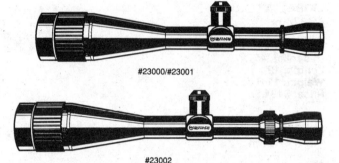

#23000/#23001

#23002

MODEL #23000
12×44mm

Field of view: 8.7′
Eye relief: 3.17″
Length: 14.5″
Weight: 18.3 oz.
Feature: Truplex Reticle, 100% Multi-Coat Lens system, black matte finish, obj. focus
Price: $616.95

MODEL #23001
24×44mm

Field of view: 4.3′
Eye relief: 3″
Length: 14.5″
Weight: 18.3 oz.
Feature: Truplex reticle, 100% Multi-Coat Lens System, black matte finish, obj. focus
Price: $627.95

MODEL #23002
6-20×44mm

Field of view: 17.4′-5.4′
Eye relief: 3″
Length: 14.5″
Weight: 18.3 oz.
Feature: Truplex reticle, 100% Multi-Coat Lens System, black matte finish, obj. focus
Price: $680.95

GOLD MEDAL HANDGUN SERIES

Simmons gold medal handgun scopes offer longer eye relief, no tunnel vision, light weight, high resolution, non-critical head alignment, compact size, and durability to withstand the heavy recoil of today's powerful handguns. Available in black and silver finishes, all have fully multicoated lenses and a Truplex reticle. Additional models on following page.

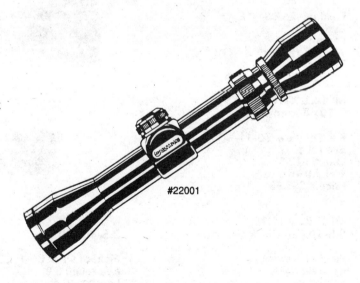

#22001

MODEL #22001
2.5-7×28mm

Field of view: 9.7′-4.0′
Eye relief: 8.9″-19.4″
Length: 9.2″
Weight: 9 oz.
Feature: Truplex reticle, 100% Multi-Coat Lens System, black polished finish.
Price: $324.95

MODEL #22002
2.5-7×28mm

Field of view: 9.7′-4.0′
Eye relief: 8.9″-19.4″
Length: 9.2″
Weight: 9 oz.
Feature: Truplex reticle, 100% Multi-Coat Lens System, black polished finish.
Price: $326.95

SWAROVSKI

TRADITIONAL RIFLESCOPES

These fine Austrian-made sights feature brilliant optics with high-quality lens coating and optimal sighting under poor light and weather conditions. The Nova ocular system with telescope recoil damping reduces the danger of injury, especially with shots aimed in an upward direction. The main tube is selectable in steel or light metal construction. Because of Nova's centered reticle, the aiming mark remains in the center of the field of view regardless of corrections of the impact point. See **Specifications** table on the following page.

VARIABLE POWER

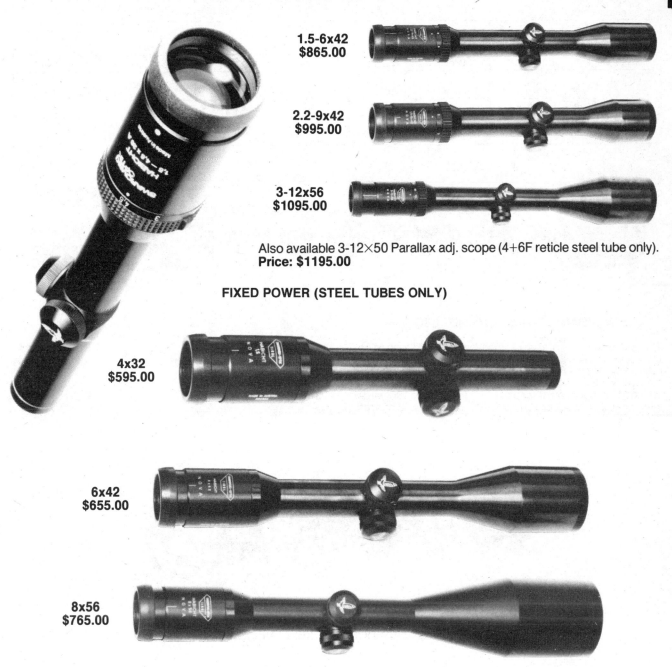

1.5-6x42
$865.00

2.2-9x42
$995.00

3-12x56
$1095.00

Also available 3-12×50 Parallax adj. scope (4+6F reticle steel tube only).
Price: $1195.00

FIXED POWER (STEEL TUBES ONLY)

4x32
$595.00

6x42
$655.00

8x56
$765.00

SWAROVSKI

SPECIFICATIONS TRADITIONAL RIFLESCOPES

Telescopic Sights	4x32	6x42	8x56	1.5-6x42	2.2-9x42	3-12x56
Magnification	4x	6x	8x	1.5-6x	2.2-9x	3-12x
Max. effective objective dia.	32mm	42mm	56mm	42mm	42mm	56mm
Exit pupil dia.	8mm	7mm	7mm	14.3-7mm	14.3-4.7mm	14.3-4.7mm
Field of view at 100m	10m	7m	5.2m	18.5-6.5m	12-4.5m	9-3.3m
Twilight effective factor (DIN 58388)	11.3	15.9	21.1	4.2-15.9	6.2-19.4	8.5-25.9
Intermediary tube dia. Steel-Standard	26mm	26mm	26mm	30mm	30mm	30mm
Objective tube dia.	38mm	48mm	62mm	48mm	48mm	62mm
Ocular tube dia.	40mm	40mm	40mm	40mm	40mm	40mm
Scope length	290mm	322mm	370mm	322mm	342mm	391mm
Weight Steel	430g	500g	660g	570g	580g	710g
(approx.) Light metal with rail	NA	NA	NA	480g	470g	540g
A change of the impact point per click in mm/100m	7	6	4	9	6	4

AMERICAN LIGHTWEIGHT RIFLESCOPE

This model features precision ground, coated and aligned optics sealed in a special aluminum alloy tube to withstand heavy recoil. Eye relief is 85mm and the recoiling eyepiece protects the eye. Positive click adjustments for elevation and windage change the impact point (approx. 1/4") per click at 100 yards, with parallax also set at 100 yards. Weight is only 13 ounces.

Prices:
1.5-4.5x20 with duplex reticle $565.00
4x32 with duplex reticle 465.00
6x36 with duplex reticle 500.00
3-9x36 with duplex reticle 600.00

1.5-4.5x20
LOW MAGNIFICATION VARIABLE RIFLESCOPE

TASCO SCOPES

WORLD CLASS WIDE ANGLE® RIFLESCOPES

MODEL WA1.35×20

Features:
- 25% larger field of view
- Exceptional optics
- Fully coated for maximum light transmission
- Waterproof, shockproof, fogproof
- Non-removable eye bell
- Free haze filter lens caps
- TASCO's unique World Class Lifetime Warranty

This member of Tasco's World Class Wide Angle line offers a wide field of view—115 feet at 1X and 31 feet at 3.5X—and quick sighting without depending on a critical view. The scope is ideal for hunting deer and dangerous game, especially in close quarters or in heavily wooded and poorly lit areas. Other features include 1/2-minute positive click stops, fully coated lenses (including Supercon process), nonremovable eyebell and windage/elevation screws. Length is 9¾", with 1" diameter tube. Weight is 10.5 ounces.

WORLD CLASS WIDE ANGLE VARIABLE ZOOM RIFLESCOPES

Model No.	Description	Reticle	Price
WA13.5×20	1X-3.5X Zoom (20mm)	Wide Angle 30/30	$183.00
WA39X40TV	3X-9X (40mm)	Wide Angle 30/30	159.00
WA4×40	4X (40mm)	Wide Angle 30/30	128.00
WA6×40	6X (40mm)	Wide Angle 30/30	134.00
WA1.755×20	1.75X-5X Zoom (20mm)	Wide Angle 30/30	206.00
WA27×32	2X-7X Zoom (32mm)	Wide Angle 30/30	165.00
WA39×40	3X-9X Zoom (40mm)	Wide Angle 30/30	159.00
CW28×32 COMPACT	2X-8X (32mm)	Wide Angle 30/30	171.00
CW4×32 LE COMPACT	4X (32mm)	Wide Angle 30/30	147.00
		Wide Angle 30/30	
ER39×40WA	3X-9X 40m Electronic Reticle	Electronic Red	368.00

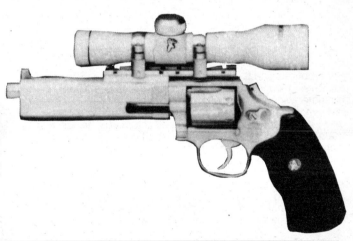

WORLD CLASS 1″ PISTOL SCOPES

Built to withstand the most punishing recoil, these scopes feature a 1″ tube that provides long eye relief to accommodate all shooting styles safely, along with fully coated optics for a bright, clear image and shot-after-shot durability. The 2×22 model is recommended for target shooting, while the 4×28 model and 1.25X-4X28 are used for hunting as well. All are fully waterproof, fogproof, shockproof and include haze filter caps.

SPECIFICATIONS

Model	Power	Objective Diameter	Finish	Reticle	Field of View @ 100 Yds	Eye Relief	Tube Diam.	Scope Length	Scope Weight	Prices
PWC2X22	2X	22mm	Blk Gloss	30/30	25′	11″–20″	1″	8.75″	7.3 oz.	$147.00
PWC2X22MA	2X	22mm	Matte Alum.	30/30	25′	11″–20″	1″	8.75″	7.3 oz.	147.00
PWC4X28	4X	28mm	Blk Gloss	30/30	8′	12″–19″	1″	9.45″	7.9 oz.	190.00
PWC4X28MA	4X	28mm	Matte Alum.	30/30	8′	12″–19″	1″	9.45″	7.9 oz.	190.00
P1.254X28	1.25X-4X	28mm	Blk Gloss	30/30	23′-9′	15″-23″	1″	9.25″	8.2 oz.	220.00
P1.254X28MA	1.25X-4X	28mm	Matte Alum.	30/30	23′-9′	15″-23″	1″	9.25″	8.2 oz.	220.00

TASCO SCOPES

RIMFIRE RIFLESCOPE
FOR 22's WITH 22 RING MOUNTS

MODEL RF4×15
$14.95

SPECIFICATIONS

Model	Power	Objective Diameter	Finish	Reticle	Field of View @ 100 yards	Eye Relief	Tube Diam.	Scope Length	Scope Weight	Price
RF4X15	4	15mm	Black	Cross Hair	21'	2½"	¾"	11"	4 oz.	**$13.00**
RF4X32	4	32mm	Black	30/30	31'	3"	1"	12¼"	12.6 oz.	70.00
RF4X20DS	4	20mm	Dull Satin	Cross Hair	20'	2½"	¾"	10½"	3.8 oz.	22.00
RF37X20	3-7	20mm	Black	30/30	24'-11'	2½"	¾"	11½"	5.7 oz.	39.00
P1.5X15	1.5	15mm	Black	Cross Hair	22½'	9½"–20¾"	¾"	8¾"	3.25 oz.	30.00

TRAJECTORY RANGE FINDING RIFLESCOPE

All Tasco TR Scopes have fully coated optics, Opti-Centered® stadia reticle, ¼-minute positive click stops and haze filter caps. All are fogproof, shockproof, waterproof and anodized.

Model No.	Description	Reticle	Price
TR39X40WA	3X-9X Zoom (40mm) Wide Angle	30/30 RF	$196.00
TR416X40	4X-16X Zoom (40mm)	30/30 RF	208.00
TR624X40	6X-24X Zoom (40mm)	30/30 RF	257.00

WORLD CLASS TS® SCOPES

For silhouette and target shooting, Tasco's TS® scopes adjust for varying long-range targets, with ⅛-minute Positrac® micrometer windage and elevation adjustments. All TS® scopes are waterproof, fog-proof, shockproof, fully Supercon-coated, and include screw-in metal lens protectors. All include two metal mirage deflection and sunshade hoods, five and eight inches in length, which can be used separately or together to eliminate image distortion resulting from excessive barrel temperatures or to shade the objective lens from direct sunlight. All include a focusing objective for precise parallax correction and extra-large 44mm objective lenses for extra brightness at high magnifications. Each scope is available in a choice of two reticle patterns: ¾-minute dot (A) and fine crosshair (B).

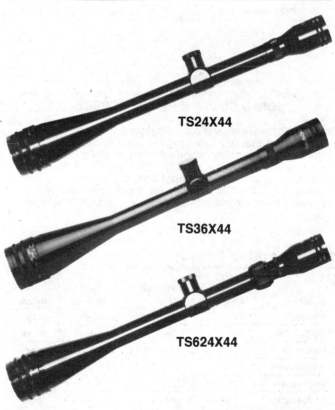

TS24X44

TS36X44

TS624X44

Model No.	Description	Price
TS24X44	24X (44mm)	$344.00
TS36X44	36X (44mm)	368.00
TS624X44	6X-24X Zoom (44mm)	408.00
TS832X44	8X-32X (44mm)	440.00
World Class TR®		
TR39X40WA	3X-9X (40mm)	196.00

TASCO RIFLE SCOPES

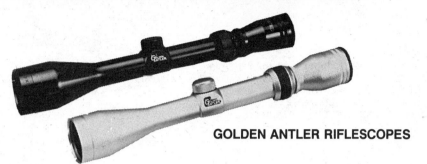

GOLDEN ANTLER RIFLESCOPES

GOLDEN ANTLER™ RIFLESCOPES

Model	Power	Objective Diameter	Finish	Reticle	Field of View @ 100 Yds.	Eye Relief	Tube Diam.	Scope Length	Scope Weight	Prices
GA4X32TV	4X	32mm	Black Gloss	30/30TV	32′	3″	1″	13″	12.7 oz.	$ 62.00
GA4X40TV	4X	40mm	Black Gloss	30/30TV	32′	3″	1″	12″	12.5 oz.	77.00
GA2.510X44TV	2.5X-10X	44mm	Black Gloss	30/30TV	35′-9′	3.5″	1″	12.5″	14.4 oz.	171.00
GA39X32TV	3X-9X	32mm	Black Gloss	30/30TV	39′-13′	3″	1″	13.25″	12.2 oz.	80.00
GA39X32MA	3X-9X	32mm	Matte Aluminum	30/30TV	39′-13′	3″	1″	13.25″	12.2 oz.	80.00
GA39X40TV	3X-9X	40mm	Black Gloss	30/30TV	39′-13′	3″	1″	12.5″	13 oz.	106.00
GA39X40MA	3X-9X	40mm	Matte Aluminum	30/30TV	39′-13′	3″	1″	12.5″	13 oz.	106.00

SILVER ANTLER™ RIFLESCOPES

Model	Power	Objective Diameter	Finish	Reticle	Field of View @ 100 Yds.	Eye Relief	Tube Diam.	Scope Length	Scope Weight	Prices
SA2.5X32	2.5X	32mm	Black Gloss	30/30	42′	3.25″	1″	11″	10 oz.	67.00
SA4X32	4X	32mm	Black Gloss	30/30	32′	3″	1″	12″	12.5 oz.	62.00
SA4X40	4X	40mm	Black Gloss	30/30	32′	3″	1″	12″	12.5 oz.	77.00
SA39X32	3X-9X	32mm	Black Gloss	30/30	39′-13′	3″	1″	12″	11 oz.	80.00
SA39X32MA	3X-9X	32mm	Matte Aluminum	30/30	39′-13′	3″	1″	12″	11 oz.	80.00
SA39X40	3X-9X	40mm	Black Gloss	30/30	39′-13′	3″	1″	12.5″	13 oz.	106.00
SA39X40MA	3X-9X	40mm	Matte Aluminum	30/30	39′-13′	3″	1″	12.5″	13 oz.	106.00
SA2.51OX44	2.5X-10X	44mm	Black Gloss	30/30	35′-9′	3.5″	1″	12.5″	14.4 oz.	171.00

TASCO SCOPES

WORLD CLASS PLUS RIFLESCOPES

Large 44mm objective lenses—the same optics used in the Tasco Titan series—gather 21% more light than standard 40mm scopes, making them well suited for hunters who prefer the dusk and dawn hours. Fully coated optical glass with Super-Con® coating reduces internal reflections. All World Class Plus scopes are waterproof, fogproof and shockproof. **Length:** 12.75″.

SPECIFICATIONS

Model	Power	Objective Diameter	Finish	Reticle	Field of View @ 100 Yds.	Eye Relief	Tube Diam.	Scope Length	Scope Weight	Prices
WCP4X44	4X	44mm	Black Gloss	30/30	32′	3 1/4″	1″	12.75″	13.5 oz.	**$248.00**
WCP6X44	6X	44mm	Black Gloss	30/30	21′	3 1/4″	1″	12.75″	13.6 oz.	**248.00**
WCP39X44	3X-9X	4mm	Black Gloss	30/30	39′-14′	3 1/2″	1″	12.75″	15.8 oz.	**296.00**
DWCP39X44	3X-9X	44mm	Black Matte	30/30	39′-14′	3 1/2″	1″	12.75″	15.8 oz.	**296.00**
WCP3.510X50	3.5X-10X	50mm	Black Gloss	30/30	30′-10.5′	3 3/4″	1″	13″	17.1 oz.	**440.00**
DWCP3.510X50	3.5X-10X	50mm	Black Matte	30/30	30′-10.5′	3 3/4″	1″	13″	17.1 oz.	**440.00**

RUBBER ARMORED SCOPES

Extra padding helps these rugged scopes stand up to rough handling. Custom-fitting rings are included. Scopes feature:
- Fully coated optics
- Windage and elevation controls
- Waterproofing, fogproofing, shockproofing
- 1/4-minute positive click stops
- Opti-centered 30/30 rangefinding reticle
- Haze filter caps

Model	Power	Objective Diameter	Finish	Reticle	Field of View @ 100 Yards	Eye Relief	Tube Diam.	Scope Length	Scope Weight	Price
RC39X40 A,B	3-9	40mm	Green Rubber	30/30	35′-14′	3 1/4″	1″	12 5/8″	14.3 oz.	**176.00**

"A" fits standard dove tail base.
"B" fits 3/8″ grooved receivers—most 22 cal. and airguns.

MAG IV RIFLESCOPES (not shown)

MAG IV scopes yield four times magnification range in a standard size riflescope and one-third more zooming range than most variable scopes. Features include: Fully coated optics and large objective lens to keep target in low light . . . Non-removable eye bell. . . 1/4-minute positive click stops . . . Non-removable windage and elevation screws. . . Opticentered 30/30 rangefinding reticle . . . Waterproof, fogproof, shockproof.

SPECIFICATIONS

Model	Power	Objective Diameter	Finish	Reticle	Field of View @ 100 Yds.	Eye Relief	Tube Diam.	Scope Length	Scope Weight	Price
W312X40	3–12	40mm	Black	30/30	35′–9′	3 1/8″	1″	12 3/16″	12 oz.	**$147.00**
W416X40†	4–16	40mm	Black	30/30	26′–6′	3 1/8″	1″	14 1/8″	15.6 oz.	**183.00**
W624X40†	6–24	40mm	Black	30/30	17′–4′	3″	1″	15 3/8″	16.75 oz.	**232.00**

† Indicates focusing objective.

TASCO SCOPES

TITAN RIFLESCOPES

Tasco's Titan riflescope features image brightness and clarity, true multi-coating, strength and rigidity, lightweight aluminum with the strength of steel, and a 30mm tube diameter. It also includes fast focus, reticle center indicator, finger adjustable windage and elevation, titanium parts, special reticle design (located in the first image plane), and a 42mm objective lens. In addition, it offers one-piece body construction, individual serial number, special lubrication, extra wide field of view and maximum eye relief. Specifications and prices are listed below.

Model	Power	Objective Diameter	Finish	Reticle	Field of View @ 100 Yds.	Eye Relief	Tube Diam.	Scope Length	Scope Weight	Price
TT1.56X42	1.5X-6X	42mm	Black	Titan Quad	59'-20'	3.5"	30mm	12"	16.4 oz.	**$612.00**
TT156X42DS	1.5X-6X	42mm	Black Matte	Titan Quad	59'-20'	3.5"	30mm	12"	16.4 oz.	**612.00**
TT39X42DS	3X-9X	42mm	Black Matte	Titan Quad	37'-13'	5-4"	30mm	12.5"	16.8 oz.	**587.00**
TT39X42	3X-9X	42mm	Black	Titan Quad	37'-13'	5-4"	30mm	12.5"	16.8 oz.	**587.00**
TT312X52	3X-12X	52mm	Black	Titan Quad	28'-9'	3.5"	30mm	14"	19.9 oz.	**729.00**
TT312X52DS	3X-12X	52mm	Black Matte	Titan Quad	28'-9'	3.5"	30mm	14"	19.9 oz.	**729.00**

LASER POINT

After years of research, Tasco has created its newest LaserPoint model, the first compact to have a multi-mode red dot (one second continuous followed by one second pulsating), making it the fastest and easiest dot to locate on the target. A new index-guided diode designed with minimum astigmatism, maximum efficiency and battery life results in a much improved laser dot. Additional features include adjustable windage and elevation system, waterproofing and 22 optional mounts that require no gunsmithing.
Price: **$239.00**

THOMPSON/CENTER

T/C RECOIL PROOF SCOPES

Thompson/Center's line of Recoil Proof Pistol and Rifle Scopes features lighted duplex reticles, including models for pistols and rifles. The lighted duplex reticles include an off-on switch that acts as a rheostat, allowing the shooter to control the intensity of the lighted reticle. These help shooters achieve precise crosshair placement on game during prime hunting hours at dusk or dawn.

DUPLEX RETICLES

MODEL 8312
2.5X Compact Pistol Scope w/Rail Mount
$180.00

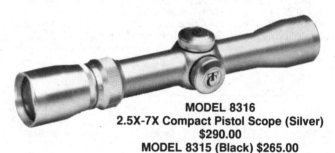

MODEL 8316
2.5X-7X Compact Pistol Scope (Silver)
$290.00
MODEL 8315 (Black) $265.00

MODEL 8317
2.5X-7X Compact Pistol Scope w/Rail
$275.00

Also available:
MODEL 8621. 1.5X-5X Compact Rifle Scope Std.
Ret. **$210.00**
MODEL 8623. 3X-9X Compact Riflescope Wide
Angle **230.00**
MODEL 8624. 4X Compact Riflescope Fixed
Power **175.00**

LIGHTED RETICLES

MODEL 8322
2.5X Compact Pistol Scope (Black)
$250.00
MODEL 8320 (w/Rail) $260.00

MODEL 8323
2.5X Compact Pistol Scope (Silver)
$260.00

MODEL 8327
2.5X-7X Compact Pistol Scope
$330.00 (w/Black Rail)
MODEL 8326 (Black) $320.00

Also available:
MODEL 8626. 3X-9X Compact Riflescope Wide
Angle **$310.00**
MODEL 8640. 4X Compact Riflescope w/Rail
Electra Dot **190.00**

WEATHERBY SUPREME SCOPES

WEATHERBY SUPREME SCOPES

As every hunter knows, one of the most difficult problems is keeping running game in the field of view of the scope. Once lost, precious seconds fade away trying to find the animal in the scope again. Too much time wasted means the ultimate frustration. No second shot. Or no shot at all. The Weatherby Wide Field helps you surmount the problem by increasing your field of view.

FEATURES:

Optical excellence—now protected with multicoated anti-glare coating. • Fog-free and waterproof construction. • Constantly self-centered reticles. • Non-magnifying reticle. • 1/4″ adjustments. • Quick variable power change. • Unique luminous reticle. • Neoprene eyepiece. • Binocular-type speed focusing. • Rugged score tube construction. Autocom point-blank system.

4 POWER

These are fixed-power scopes for big game and varmint hunting. Bright, clear image. Multicoated lenses for maximum luminosity under adverse conditions. 32-foot field of view at 100 yards.

3 TO 9 POWER

The most desirable variable for every kind of shooting from target to long-range big game. Outstanding light-gathering power. Fast, convenient focusing adjustment.

1 3/4 TO 5 POWER

A popular model for close-range hunting with large-bore rifles. Includes the Autocom system, which automatically compensates for trajectory and eliminates the need for range-finding without making elevation adjustments. Just aim and shoot!

Prices:
Fixed Power

4 × 44 . . . . $291.00

Variable Power

1.75-5 × 20 . . . . 281.00
2-7 × 34 . . . . 291.00
3-9 × 44 . . . . 341.00

SUPREME RIFLESCOPES SPECIFICATIONS

Item	1.75-5X20	2-7X34	4X44	3-9X44
Actual Magnification	1.7-5	2.1-6.83	3.9	3.15-8.98
Field of View @ 100 yards	66.6-21.4 ft.	59-16 ft.	32 ft.	36-13 ft.
Eye Relief (inches)	3.4	3.4	3.0	3.5
Exit Pupil dia. in mm	11.9-4	10-4.9	10	10-4.9
Clear Aperture of Objective	20mm	34mm	44mm	44mm
Twilight Factor	5.9-10	8.2-15.4	13.3	11.5-19.9
Tube Diameter	1″	1″	1″	1″
O.D. of Objective	1″	1.610″	2″	2″
O.D. of Ocular	1.635″	1.635″	1.635″	1.635″
Overall Length	10.7″	11.125″	12.5″	12.7″
Weight	11 oz.	10.4 oz.	11.6 oz.	11.6 oz.
Adjustment Graduations Major Divisions: Minor Divisions:	1 MOA 1/4 MOA	1 MOA 1/4 MOA	1 MOA 1/4 MOA	1 MOA 1/4 MOA
Maximum Adjustment (W&E)	60″	60″	60″	60″
Reticles Available	LUMIPLEX	LUMIPLEX	LUMIPLEX	LUMIPLEX

WEAVER SCOPES

MODEL V9
3x-9x38 Variable Hunting Scope
$141.09

MODEL V10
2x-10x38 Variable All-Purpose Scope
$149.84

MODEL V3
1x-3x20 Variable Hunting Scope
$130.75

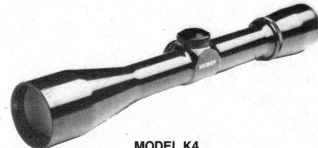

MODEL K4
4x38 Fixed Power Hunting Scope
$108.17

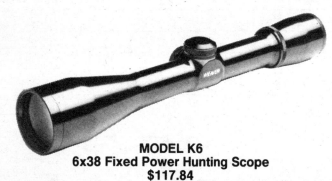

MODEL K6
6x38 Fixed Power Hunting Scope
$117.84

MODEL K2.5
2.5x20 Fixed Power Hunting Scope
$99.75

Also available:
MODEL KT 15. 15x42 Target Silhouette Scope. **$236.00**

WILLIAMS TWILIGHT SCOPES

1.5X-5X (and 2X-6X): $206.65

2½X: $146.25

4X: $152.90

3X-9X: $217.15

The "Twilight" series of scopes was introduced to accommodate those shooters who want a high-quality scope in the medium-priced field. The "Twilight" scopes are waterproof and shockproof, have coated lenses and are nitrogen-filled. Resolution is sharp and clear. All "Twilight" scopes have a highly polished, rich, black, hard anodized finish.

There are five models available: the 2½x, the 4x, the 1.5x-5x, the 2x-6x, and the 3x-9x. They are available in T-N-T reticle only (which stands for "thick and thin").

OPTICAL SPECIFICATIONS	2.5X	4X	1.5X-5X		2X-6X		3X-9X	
			At 1.5X	At 5X	At 2X	At 6X	At 3X	At 9X
Clear aperture of objective lens	20mm	32mm	20mm	Same	32mm	Same	40mm	Same
Clear aperture of ocular lens	32mm	32mm	32mm	Same	32mm	Same	32mm	Same
Exit Pupil	8mm	8mm	13.3mm	4mm	16mm	5.3mm	13.3mm	44.4mm
Relative Brightness	64	64	177	16	256	28	161.2	17.6
Field of view (degree of angle)	6°10'	5°30'	11°	4°	8°30'	3°10'	7°	2°20'
Field of view at 100 yards	32'	29'	57¾'	21'	45½'	16¾'	36½'	12¾'
Eye Relief	3.7"	3.6"	3.5"	3.5"	3"	3"	3.1"	2.9"
Parallax Correction (at)	50 yds.	100 yds.	100 yds.	Same	100 yds.	Same	100 yds.	Same
Lens Construction	9	9	10	Same	11	Same	11	Same
MECHANICAL SPECIFICATIONS								
Outside diameter of objective end . .	1.00"	1.525"	1.00"	Same	1.525"	Same	1.850"	1.850"
Outside diameter of ocular end	1.455"	1.455"	1.455"	Same	1.455"	Same	1.455"	Same
Ouside diameter of tube	1"	1"	1"	Same	1"	Same	1"	Same
Internal adjustment graduation	¼ min.	¼ min.	¼ min.	Same	¼ min.	Same	¼ min.	Same
Minimum internal adjustment	75 min.	75 min.	75 min.	Same	75 min.	Same	60 min.	Same
Finish			Glossy Hard Black Anodized					
Length	10"	11¾"	10¾"	Same	11½"	11½"	12¾"	12¾"
Weight	8½ oz.	9½ oz.	10 oz.	Same	11½ oz.	Same	13½ oz.	Same

WILLIAMS

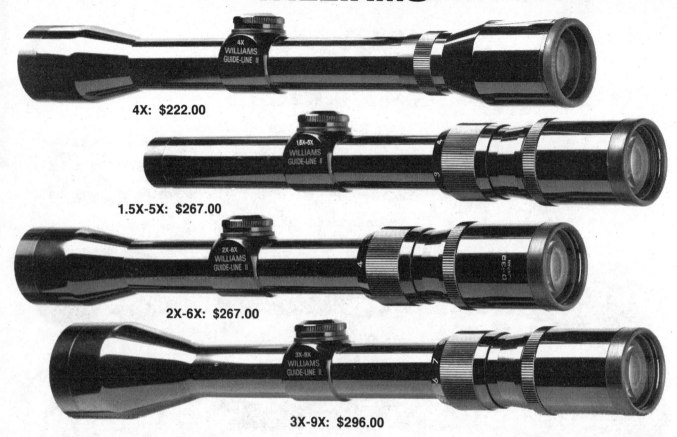

4X: $222.00

1.5X-5X: $267.00

2X-6X: $267.00

3X-9X: $296.00

GUIDELINE II SERIES

Patterned after the popular Twilight Series, Williams' new Guideline II Series features silent adjustment screws, streamlined adjustment caps and power adjustment rings. Fully multi-coated lenses ensure superior light gathering and brightness. Comes equipped with T-N-T reticle and a choice of matte or glossy black finish.

OPTICAL SPECIFICATIONS	4X	1.5X–5X		2X–6X		3X–9X	
		At 1.5X	At 5X	At 2X	At 6X	At 3X	At 9X
Clear aperture of objective lens	32mm	20mm	Same	32mm	Same	40mm	Same
Clear aperture of ocular lens	32mm	32mm	Same	32mm	Same	32mm	Same
Exit Pupil	8mm	13.3mm	4mm	16mm	5.3mm	13.3mm	44.4mm
Relative Brightness	64	177	16	256	28	161.2	17.6
Field of view (degree of angle)	5°30′	11°	4°	8°30′	3°10′	7°	2°20′
Field of view at 100 yards	29′	57¾′	21′	45½′	16¾′	36½′	12¾′
Eye Relief	3.6″	3.5″	3.5″	3″	3″	3.1″	2.9″
Parallax Correction (at)	100 yds.	100 yds.	Same	100 yds.	Same	100 yds.	Same
Lens Construction	9	10	Same	11	Same	11	Same
MECHANICAL SPECIFICATIONS							
Outside diameter of objective end . .	1.525″	1.00″	Same	1.525″	Same	1.850″	1.850″
Outside diameter of ocular end	1.455″	1.455″	Same	1.455″	Same	1.455″	Same
Outside diameter of tube	1″	1″	Same	1″	Same	1″	Same
Internal adjustment graduation	¼ min.	¼ min.	Same	¼ min.	Same	¼ min.	Same
Minimum internal adjustment	75 min.	75 min.	Same	75 min.	Same	60 min.	Same
Finish	Glossy Hard Black Anodized						
Length	11¾″	10¾″	Same	11½″	11½″	12¾″	12¾″
Weight	9½ oz.	10 oz.	Same	11½ oz.	Same	13½ oz.	Same

WILLIAMS

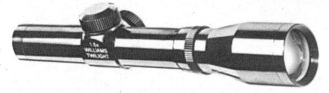

1.5X PISTOL & BOW SCOPE
$151.25

2X PISTOL & BOW SCOPE
$153.50

TWILIGHT SCOPES
FOR PISTOLS AND BOWS
WITH LONG EYE RELIEF

Built tough, compact and lightweight, the Twilight Scope was designed specifically for handgun hunters and precision target shooters. And for archers, these scopes offer the first practical scope-aiming device, including the new Wiliams bow scope mount, which opens up target and hunting possibilities never before available to the archer.

OPTICAL SPECIFICATIONS	1.5X20	2X20
Clear Aperture of Objective Lens	20mm	20mm
Clear Aperture of Ocular Lens	30mm	30mm
Exit Pupil	13.3mm	10mm
Relative Brightness	177	100
Field of View (Degree of Angle)	3°4'	3°20'
Field of View at 100 Yards	19 ft.	17½ ft.
Eye Relief	18"-25"	18"-25"
Parallax Correciton (at)	50 yds.	50 yds.
Lens Construction	6	6

MECHANICAL SPECIFICATIONS	1.5X20	2.20
Outside Diameter of Objective End	1"	1"
Outside Diameter of Ocular End	36.5mm	36.5mm
Outside Diameter of Tube	1"	1"
Internal Adjustment Graduation	1/4"	1/4"
Minimum Internal Adjustment	170"	162"
Finish	Glossy Hard Black Anodized	
Length	209mm	216mm
Weight	6.4 oz.	6.6 oz.

FP-T/C Scout Receiver Sight

The newest model to the Williams FP series of receiver sights, the FP-T/C Scout is an excellent addition to the Thompson/Center Scout rifle. It is easily installed. No drilling and tapping required. As with all FP receiver sights, the FP-T/C Scout is available with or without target knobs and 'Twilight' aperture. **Price: $53.25 ($63.25 w/Target Knobs)**

WGOS-Octagon

The Williams Guide Open Sight (WGOS) Octagon is an ideal sight for upgrading the rear sight on most octagon barreled muzzleloaders. It installs with two 6-48 screws and has the same hole spacing as most Thompson/Center muzzleloading rifles. By drilling and tapping, it can be installed on many other brands and models with 1" octagon barrels.

Height with 3/16" Blade ...... Adjustable from .350 to .450
Height with 1/4" Blade .... Adjustable from .412 to .512
Height with 5/16" Blade ...... Adjustable from .475 to .575
Height with 3/8" Blade .... Adjustable from .537 to .638
Price: $19.95

5D-94SE Reciever Sight

The new 5D-94SE Receiver Sight easily mounts to the Winchester 94 Side Eject carbines (except 'Big Bore' models). It fits the factory drilling and tapping on top of receiver and is fully adjustable for elevation and windage. The 5D-94SE is also available with the Williams 'Twilight' aperture. **Price: $29.95 ($31.60 w/Twilight Aperture)**

WILLIAMS RECEIVER SIGHTS

SLUGGER SIGHTS

SLUGGER SIGHTS

This new concept in front and rear sight combinations for ribbed shotgun barrels turns a shotgun into an accurate slug gun (ideal for turkey hunting). Fits 5/16″ or 1/4″ vent ribs. Installs in minutes (no drilling and tapping necessary). Made from tough aircraft aluminum. Fully adjustable rear sights for windage and elevation.

Price: **$34.95**

TARGET FP RECEIVER SIGHT (LOW)

TARGET FP RECEIVER SIGHTS

Available in High or Low sight line models, Target FP receiver sights with proper attaching bases can be attached to most 22-caliber target rifles and many sporter-type rifles as well. In most cases, the High models are recommended on target-type rifles with globe front sights. The Low models are for sporter-type rifles and are compatible with standard sights or the lowest globe-type front sights.

Price: **$72.00**
   Base only: 12.10

FP RECEIVER SIGHTS

Internal micrometer adjustments have positive internal locks. The FP model is made of an alloy with a tensile strength of 85,000 lbs., yet it weighs only 1½ oz. Target knobs are available on all models if desired. FP sights fit more than 100 different guns.

Prices:
FP RECEIVER SIGHT **$53.25**
   With "Twilight" Aperture 54.85
   With Target Knobs 63.25
   With Target Knobs & "Twilight" Aperture 64.85

FP RECEIVER SIGHT MODEL FP-RU77
(Ruger Model 77)

GUIDE RECEIVER SIGHTS
(not shown)

Features compact, low profile and positive windage and elevation locks. Lightweight, strong, and rustproof. These sights utilize dovetail or existing screws on top of receiver for installation. Made from an aluminum alloy that is stronger than many steels.

Prices:
GUIDE RECEIVER SIGHT **$29.95**
   With Twilight Aperture 31.60
   With 1/4″ "U" blade 27.55

ZEISS RIFLESCOPES

THE C-SERIES

The C-Series was designed by Zeiss specifically for the American hunter. It is based on space-age alloy tubes with integral objective and ocular bells, and an integral adjustment turret. This strong, rigid one-piece construction allows perfect lens alignment, micro-precise adjustments and structural integrity. Other features include quick focusing, a generous 3½″ of eye relief, rubber armoring, T-Star multi-layer coating, and parallax setting (free at 100 yards).

DIATAL-C 10×36T
$835.00

DIAVARI-C 3-9×36T
$975.00

DIATAL-C 6×32T
$715.00

DIATAL-C 4×32T
$680.00

DIAVARI-C 1.5-4.5×18T
$930.00

SPECIFICATIONS	4×32	6×32	10×36	3-9×36		C1.5-4.5×18	
Magnification	4X	6X	10X	3X	9X	1.5X	4.5X
Objective Diameter (mm)/(inch)	1.26″	1.26″	1.42″	1.42″		15.0/0.6	18.0/0.7
Exit Pupil	0.32″	0.21″	0.14″	0.39″	0.16″	10.0	4.0
Twilight Performance	11.3	13.9	19.0	8.5	18.0	4.2	9.0
Field of View at 100 yds.	30′	20′	12′	36′	13′	72′	27′
Eye Relief	3.5″	3.5″	3.5″	3.5″	3.5″	3.5″	
Maximum Interval Adjustment (elevation and windage (MOA)	80	80	50	50		10.5′ @ 100 yds.	
Click-Stop Adjustment 1 click = 1 interval (MOA)	¼	¼	¼	¼		.36″ @ 100 yds.	
Length	10.6″	10.6″	12.7″	11.2″		11.8″	
Weight approx. (ounces)	11.3	11.3	14.1	15.2		13.4	
Tube Diameter	1″	1″	1″	1″		1″	
Objective Tube Diameter	1.65″	1.65″	1.89″	1.73″		1″	
Eyepiece O.D.	1.67″	1.67″	1.67″	1.67″		1.8″	

ZEISS RIFLESCOPES

THE "Z" SERIES

These new Zeiss riflescopes feature a surface that is harder and more resistant to abrasion and mechanical damage than the multiple coatings or bluings. The black, silken matte finish suppresses reflections and prevents finger prints. All optical elements are provided with the Zeiss T multi-coating. The size of the reticles in the Diavari Z-types changes with the power set; therefore, the ratio of the reticle size to the target size always remains the same.

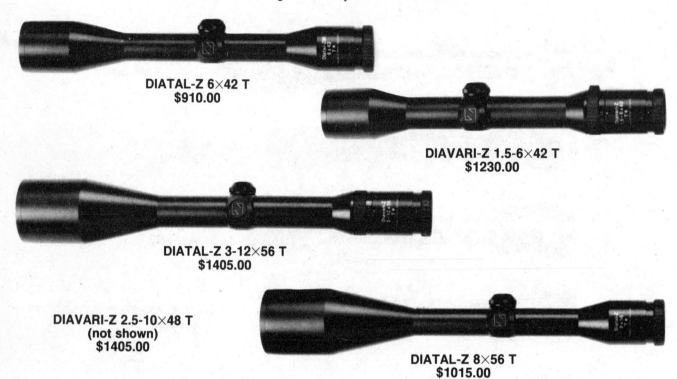

DIATAL-Z 6×42 T
$910.00

DIAVARI-Z 1.5-6×42 T
$1230.00

DIATAL-Z 3-12×56 T
$1405.00

DIAVARI-Z 2.5-10×48 T
(not shown)
$1405.00

DIATAL-Z 8×56 T
$1015.00

ZEISS RIFLESCOPES, ZM/Z-SERIES SPECIFICATIONS

Model	Diatal-ZM/Z 6×42 T*	Diavari-ZM/Z 1.5-6×42 T*	Diavari-ZM/Z 3-12×56 T*	Diatal-ZM/Z 8×56 T*	Diavari-ZM/Z 2.5-10×48 T
Magnification	6X	1.5X 6X	3X 12X	8X	2.5X-10X
Effective obj. diam. (mm, inch)	42/1.7	19.5/0.8 42/1.7	38/1.5 56/2.2	56/2.2	33/1.30 48/1.89
Diameter of exit pupil (mm)	7	13 7	12.7 4.7	7	13.2 4.8
Twilight factor	15.9	4.2 15.9	8.5 25.9	21.2	7.1 21.9
Field of view at 100 m (m)/ft. at 100 yds.	6.7/20.1	18/54.0 6.5/19.5	9.2/27.6 3.3/9.9	5/15.0	11.0/33.0 3.9/11.7
Approx. eye relief (cm, inch)	8/3.2	8/3.2	8/3.2	8/3.2	8/3.2
Click-stop adjustment 1 click = (cm at 100 m)/(inch at 100 yds.)	1/0.36	1/0.36	1/0.36	1/0.36	1/0.36
Max. adj. (elevation and windage) at 100 m (cm)/at 100 yds. (inch)	187	190	95	138	110/39.6
Center tube dia. (mm/inch)	25.4/1	30/1.18	30/1.18	25.4/1	30/1.18
Objective bell dia. (mm/inch)	48/1.9	48/1.9	62/2.44	62/2.44	54/2.13
Ocular bell dia. (mm/inch)	40/1.57	40/1.57	40/1.57	40/1.57	40/1.57
Length (mm/inch)	324/12.8	320/12.6	388/15.3	369/14.5	370/14.57
Approx. weight (ZM/Z) (g/ozs.)	35/400/15.3/14.1	586/562/20.7/19.8	765/731/27.0/25.8	550/520/19.4/18.3	715/680/25.2/24

Ammunition

For addresses and phone numbers of manufacturers and distributors included in this section, turn to *DIRECTORY OF MANUFACTURERS AND SUPPLIERS* at the back of the book.

FEDERAL AMMUNITION

The following pages include Federal's new lines of cartridges and shotshells for 1992-3. For a complete listing of all Federal ammunition, call or write the Federal Cartridge Company (see Directory of Manufacturers in the Reference section for address and phone number).

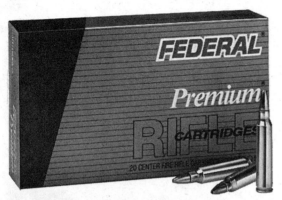

PREMIUM CARTRIDGES

A Sierra 40 grain hollow point bullet is featured in Federal's 223 Rem. Varmint load.

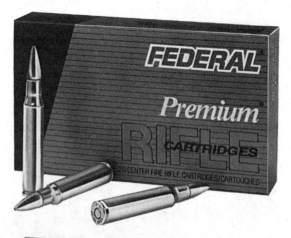

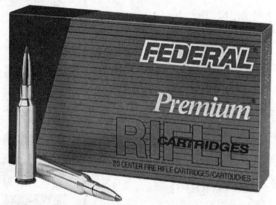

A 140 grain Nosler Partrition bullet has been added to Federal's 6.5 × 55 Swedish cartridge.

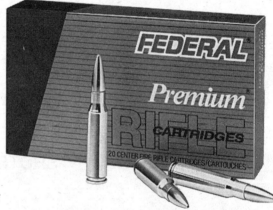

Federal's 30-06 Springfield and 308 Win. Match cartridges are teamed up with Sierra's Matchking 168 grain Boat-tail bullet.

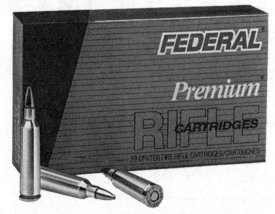

This varmint cartridge for the 22-250 Rem. delivers a muzzle velocity of 4000 feet per second.

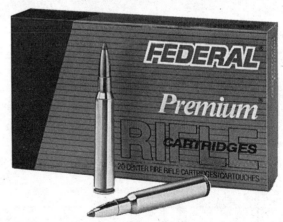

Federal's 7 × 64 Brenneke with a 160 grain Nosler Partition bullet has been added to the Premium line.

FEDERAL AMMUNITION

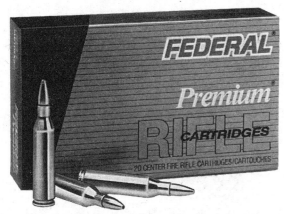

A Sierra 60 grain hollow point bullet is now available to all 243 Win. shooters.

CLASSIC CARTRIDGES
Federal introduces a 40 S&W cartridge with a 155 grain Hi-Shok jacketed hollow point bullet.

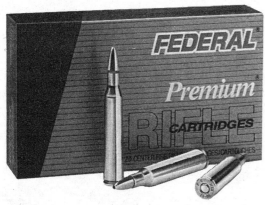

This 25-06 Rem. Varmint load features a Sierra 90 grain hollow point bullet.

A 230 grain Hi-Shok jacketed hollow point bullet complements Federal's 45 Auto cartridge.

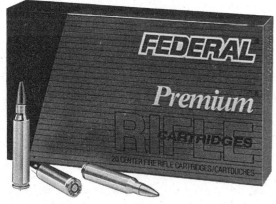

A 223 Rem. Match is now available with Sierra's Matchking 69 grain hollow point Boat-tail bullet.

This new 10mm auto cartridge offers a 155 grain Hi-Shok jacketed hollow point bullet (muzzle velocity: 1325 fps).

FEDERAL AMMUNITION

GOLD MEDAL CARTRIDGES
A higher velocity Special Handicap load is now offered in the Gold Medal line.

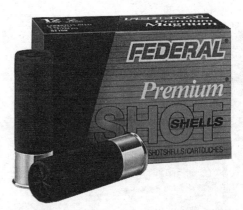

No. 5 copper-plated shot in a 12 gauge 3″ Premium shotshell is now available for turkey hunters.

AMERICAN EAGLE 22's
The American Eagle line now includes a 22 LR cartridge with a 40 grain lead bullet.

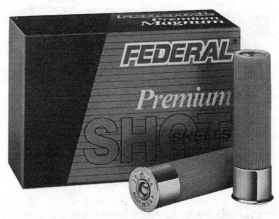

This 20 gauge 3″ Premium shotshell contains 1¼ oz. of copper-plated No. 6 shot.

SHOTSHELLS
The new 20 gauge American Eagle Heavy Game loads offer a choice of No. 6, 7½ or 8 shot.

A 12 gauge 3″ Premium slug load with copper-plated Sabot-style slug is new to the Premium line.

HORNADY AMMUNITION

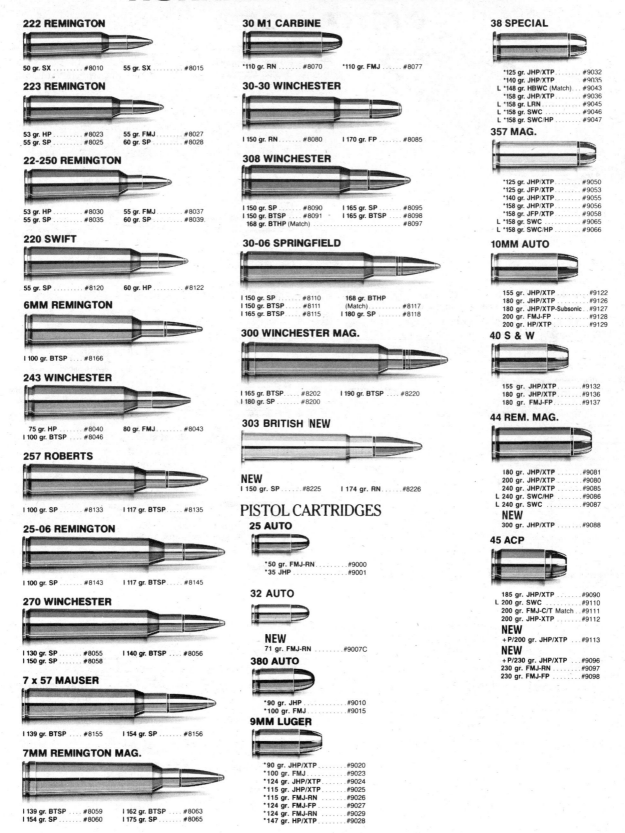

222 REMINGTON

50 gr. SX .... #8010   55 gr. SX .... #8015

223 REMINGTON

53 gr. HP .... #8023   55 gr. FMJ .... #8027
55 gr. SP .... #8025   60 gr. SP .... #8028

22-250 REMINGTON

53 gr. HP .... #8030   55 gr. FMJ .... #8037
55 gr. SP .... #8035   60 gr. SP .... #8039

220 SWIFT

55 gr. SP .... #8120   60 gr. HP .... #8122

6MM REMINGTON

I 100 gr. BTSP .... #8166

243 WINCHESTER

75 gr. HP .... #8040   80 gr. FMJ .... #8043
I 100 gr. BTSP .... #8046

257 ROBERTS

I 100 gr. SP ..... #8133   I 117 gr. BTSP .... #8135

25-06 REMINGTON

I 100 gr. SP ..... #8143   I 117 gr. BTSP .... #8145

270 WINCHESTER

I 130 gr. SP ..... #8055   I 140 gr. BTSP .... #8056
I 150 gr. SP ..... #8058

7 x 57 MAUSER

I 139 gr. BTSP .... #8155   I 154 gr. SP .... #8156

7MM REMINGTON MAG.

I 139 gr. BTSP .... #8059   I 162 gr. BTSP .... #8063
I 154 gr. SP ...... #8060   I 175 gr. SP ...... #8065

30 M1 CARBINE

*110 gr. RN ..... #8070   *110 gr. FMJ ..... #8077

30-30 WINCHESTER

I 150 gr. RN ...... #8080   I 170 gr. FP .... #8085

308 WINCHESTER

I 150 gr. SP ..... #8090   I 165 gr. SP ...... #8095
I 150 gr. BTSP ... #8091   I 165 gr. BTSP .... #8098
168 gr. BTHP (Match) .... #8097

30-06 SPRINGFIELD

I 150 gr. SP ..... #8110   168 gr. BTHP
I 150 gr. BTSP ... #8111   (Match) .... #8117
I 165 gr. BTSP ... #8115   I 180 gr. SP ..... #8118

300 WINCHESTER MAG.

I 165 gr. BTSP .... #8202   I 190 gr. BTSP .... #8220
I 180 gr. SP ...... #8200

303 BRITISH NEW

NEW
I 150 gr. SP ...... #8225   I 174 gr. RN ...... #8226

PISTOL CARTRIDGES

25 AUTO

*50 gr. FMJ-RN .... #9000
*35 JHP .... #9001

32 AUTO

NEW
71 gr. FMJ-RN .... #9007C

380 AUTO

*90 gr. JHP .... #9010
*100 gr. FMJ .... #9015

9MM LUGER

*90 gr. JHP/XTP .... #9020
*100 gr. FMJ .... #9023
*124 gr. JHP/XTP ...... #9024
*115 gr. JHP/XTP ...... #9025
*115 gr. FMJ-RN ...... #9026
*124 gr. FMJ-FP ...... #9027
*124 gr. FMJ-RN ...... #9029
*147 gr. HP/XTP ...... #9028

38 SPECIAL

*125 gr. JHP/XTP ... #9032
*140 gr. JHP/XTP ... #9035
L *148 gr. HBWC (Match) ... #9043
*158 gr. JHP/XTP ... #9036
L *158 gr. LRN .... #9045
L *158 gr. SWC .... #9046
L *158 gr. SWC/HP .... #9047

357 MAG.

*125 gr. JHP/XTP ...... #9050
*125 gr. JFP/XTP ...... #9053
*140 gr. JHP/XTP ...... #9055
*158 gr. JHP/XTP ...... #9056
*158 gr. JFP/XTP ...... #9058
L *158 gr. SWC .... #9065
L *158 gr. SWC/HP ...... #9066

10MM AUTO

155 gr. JHP/XTP ...... #9122
180 gr. JHP/XTP ...... #9126
180 gr. JHP/XTP-Subsonic ... #9127
200 gr. FMJ-FP .... #9128
200 gr. HP/XTP .... #9129

40 S & W

155 gr. JHP/XTP ...... #9132
180 gr. JHP/XTP ...... #9136
180 gr. FMJ-FP .... #9137

44 REM. MAG.

180 gr. JHP/XTP ...... #9081
200 gr. JHP/XTP ...... #9080
240 gr. JHP/XTP ...... #9085
L 240 gr. SWC/HP ...... #9086
L 240 gr. SWC .... #9087
NEW
300 gr. JHP/XTP ...... #9088

45 ACP

185 gr. JHP/XTP ...... #9090
L 200 gr. SWC .... #9110
200 gr. FMJ-C/T Match .. #9111
200 gr. JHP-XTP ...... #9112
NEW
+ P/200 gr. JHP/XTP ... #9113
NEW
+ P/230 gr. JHP/XTP ... #9096
230 gr. FMJ-RN .... #9097
230 gr. FMJ-FP .... #9098

REMINGTON CENTERFIRE RIFLE CARTRIDGES

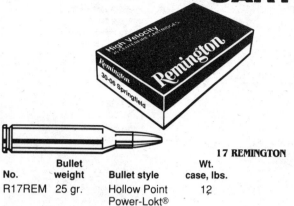

17 REMINGTON

No.	Bullet weight	Bullet style	Wt. case, lbs.
R17REM	25 gr.	Hollow Point Power-Lokt®	12

20 IN A BOX, 500 IN A CASE.

22 HORNET

No.	Bullet weight	Bullet style	Wt. case, lbs.
R22HN1	45 gr.	Pointed Soft Point	9
R22HN2	45 gr.	Hollow Point	9

20 IN A BOX, 500 IN A CASE.

220 SWIFT

No.	Bullet weight	Bullet style	Wt. case, lbs.
R22051†	50 gr.	Pointed Soft Point	10

222 REMINGTON

No.	Bullet weight	Bullet style	Wt. case, lbs.
R222R1	50 gr.	Pointed Soft Point	14
R222R4	50 gr.	Hollow Point Power-Lokt®	14

20 IN A BOX, 500 IN A CASE.

222 REMINGTON MAGNUM

No.	Bullet weight	Bullet style	Wt. case, lbs.
R222M1	55 gr.	Pointed Soft Point	15

20 IN A BOX, 500 IN A CASE.

22-250 REMINGTON

No.	Bullet weight	Bullet style	Wt. case, lbs.
R22501	55 gr.	Pointed Soft Point	21
R22502	55 gr.	Hollow Point Power-Lokt®	21

20 IN A BOX, 500 IN A CASE.

†New for 1992

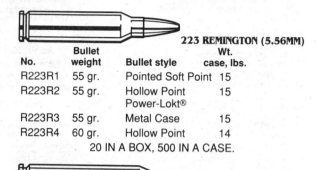

223 REMINGTON (5.56MM)

No.	Bullet weight	Bullet style	Wt. case, lbs.
R223R1	55 gr.	Pointed Soft Point	15
R223R2	55 gr.	Hollow Point Power-Lokt®	15
R223R3	55 gr.	Metal Case	15
R223R4	60 gr.	Hollow Point	14

20 IN A BOX, 500 IN A CASE.

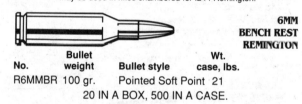

6MM REMINGTON

No.	Bullet weight	Bullet style	Wt. case, lbs.
R6MM1*	80 gr.	Pointed Soft Point	26
R6MM2*	80 gr.	Hollow Point Power-Lokt®	26
R6MM4	100 gr.	Pointed Soft Point Core-Lokt®	26
ER6MMRA†	105 gr.	Extended Range	27

20 IN A BOX, 500 IN A CASE.

*May be used in rifles chambered for .244 Remington.

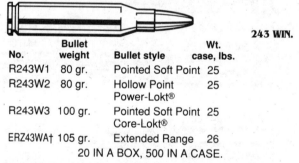

6MM BENCH REST REMINGTON

No.	Bullet weight	Bullet style	Wt. case, lbs.
R6MMBR	100 gr.	Pointed Soft Point	21

20 IN A BOX, 500 IN A CASE.

243 WIN.

No.	Bullet weight	Bullet style	Wt. case, lbs.
R243W1	80 gr.	Pointed Soft Point	25
R243W2	80 gr.	Hollow Point Power-Lokt®	25
R243W3	100 gr.	Pointed Soft Point Core-Lokt®	25
ERZ43WA†	105 gr.	Extended Range	26

20 IN A BOX, 500 IN A CASE.

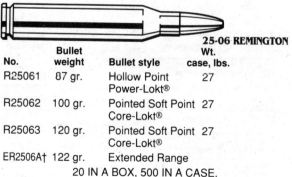

25-06 REMINGTON

No.	Bullet weight	Bullet style	Wt. case, lbs.
R25061	87 gr.	Hollow Point Power-Lokt®	27
R25062	100 gr.	Pointed Soft Point Core-Lokt®	27
R25063	120 gr.	Pointed Soft Point Core-Lokt®	27
ER2506A†	122 gr.	Extended Range	

20 IN A BOX, 500 IN A CASE.

REMINGTON CENTERFIRE RIFLE CARTRIDGES

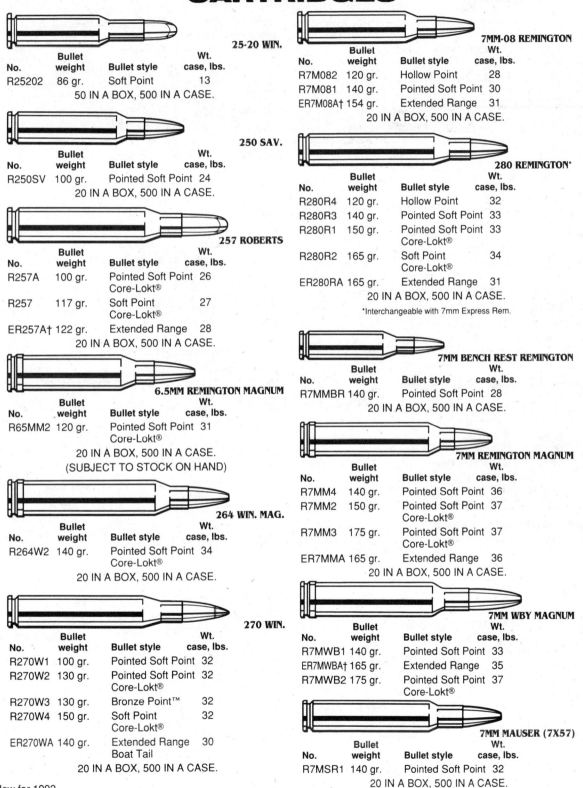

25-20 WIN.

No.	Bullet weight	Bullet style	Wt. case, lbs.
R25202	86 gr.	Soft Point	13

50 IN A BOX, 500 IN A CASE.

250 SAV.

No.	Bullet weight	Bullet style	Wt. case, lbs.
R250SV	100 gr.	Pointed Soft Point	24

20 IN A BOX, 500 IN A CASE.

257 ROBERTS

No.	Bullet weight	Bullet style	Wt. case, lbs.
R257A	100 gr.	Pointed Soft Point Core-Lokt®	26
R257	117 gr.	Soft Point Core-Lokt®	27
ER257A†	122 gr.	Extended Range	28

20 IN A BOX, 500 IN A CASE.

6.5MM REMINGTON MAGNUM

No.	Bullet weight	Bullet style	Wt. case, lbs.
R65MM2	120 gr.	Pointed Soft Point Core-Lokt®	31

20 IN A BOX, 500 IN A CASE.
(SUBJECT TO STOCK ON HAND)

264 WIN. MAG.

No.	Bullet weight	Bullet style	Wt. case, lbs.
R264W2	140 gr.	Pointed Soft Point Core-Lokt®	34

20 IN A BOX, 500 IN A CASE.

270 WIN.

No.	Bullet weight	Bullet style	Wt. case, lbs.
R270W1	100 gr.	Pointed Soft Point	32
R270W2	130 gr.	Pointed Soft Point Core-Lokt®	32
R270W3	130 gr.	Bronze Point™	32
R270W4	150 gr.	Soft Point Core-Lokt®	32
ER270WA	140 gr.	Extended Range Boat Tail	30

20 IN A BOX, 500 IN A CASE.

†New for 1992

7MM-08 REMINGTON

No.	Bullet weight	Bullet style	Wt. case, lbs.
R7M082	120 gr.	Hollow Point	28
R7M081	140 gr.	Pointed Soft Point	30
ER7M08A†	154 gr.	Extended Range	31

20 IN A BOX, 500 IN A CASE.

280 REMINGTON*

No.	Bullet weight	Bullet style	Wt. case, lbs.
R280R4	120 gr.	Hollow Point	32
R280R3	140 gr.	Pointed Soft Point	33
R280R1	150 gr.	Pointed Soft Point Core-Lokt®	33
R280R2	165 gr.	Soft Point Core-Lokt®	34
ER280RA	165 gr.	Extended Range	31

20 IN A BOX, 500 IN A CASE.

*Interchangeable with 7mm Express Rem.

7MM BENCH REST REMINGTON

No.	Bullet weight	Bullet style	Wt. case, lbs.
R7MMBR	140 gr.	Pointed Soft Point	28

20 IN A BOX, 500 IN A CASE.

7MM REMINGTON MAGNUM

No.	Bullet weight	Bullet style	Wt. case, lbs.
R7MM4	140 gr.	Pointed Soft Point	36
R7MM2	150 gr.	Pointed Soft Point Core-Lokt®	37
R7MM3	175 gr.	Pointed Soft Point Core-Lokt®	37
ER7MMA	165 gr.	Extended Range	36

20 IN A BOX, 500 IN A CASE.

7MM WBY MAGNUM

No.	Bullet weight	Bullet style	Wt. case, lbs.
R7MWB1	140 gr.	Pointed Soft Point	33
ER7MWBA†	165 gr.	Extended Range	35
R7MWB2	175 gr.	Pointed Soft Point Core-Lokt®	37

7MM MAUSER (7X57)

No.	Bullet weight	Bullet style	Wt. case, lbs.
R7MSR1	140 gr.	Pointed Soft Point	32

20 IN A BOX, 500 IN A CASE.

REMINGTON CENTERFIRE RIFLE CARTRIDGES

30 CARBINE

No.	Bullet weight	Bullet style	Wt. case, lbs.
R30CAR	110 gr.	Soft Point	15

50 IN A BOX, 500 IN A CASE.

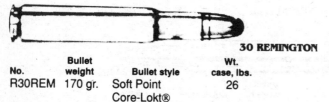

30 REMINGTON

No.	Bullet weight	Bullet style	Wt. case, lbs.
R30REM	170 gr.	Soft Point Core-Lokt®	26

20 IN A BOX, 500 IN A CASE.

30-30 WIN.

No.	Bullet weight	Bullet style	Wt. case, lbs.
R30301	150 gr.	Soft Point, Core-Lokt®	27
R30302	170 gr.	Soft Point, Core-Lokt®	27
R30303	170 gr.	Hollow Point, Core-Lokt®	27

20 IN A BOX, 500 IN A CASE.

30-40 KRAG

No.	Bullet weight	Bullet style	Wt. case, lbs.
R30402	180 gr.	Pointed Soft Point Core-Lokt®	32

20 IN A BOX, 500 IN A CASE.

30-30 "ACCELERATOR"

No.	Bullet weight	Bullet style	Wt. case, lbs.
R3030A	180 gr.	Pointed Soft Point Core-Lokt®	32

20 IN A BOX, 500 IN A CASE.

30-06 "ACCELERATOR"

No.	Bullet weight	Bullet style	Wt. case, lbs.
R30069	55 gr.	Pointed Soft Point	26

20 IN A BOX, 500 IN A CASE.

30-06 SPFD.

No.	Bullet weight	Bullet style	Wt. case, lbs.
R30061	125 gr.	Pointed Soft Point	35
R30062	150 gr.	Pointed Soft Point Core-Lokt®	35
R30063	150 gr.	Bronze Point™	35
R3006B	165 gr.	Pointed Soft Point Core-Lokt®	35
R30064	180 gr.	Soft Point Core-Lokt®	35
R30065	180 gr.	Pointed Soft Point Core-Lokt®	35
R30066	180 gr.	Bronze Point™	35
R30067	220 gr.	Soft Point Core-Lokt®	35
R3006C	168 gr.	Boat Tail Hollow Point (Match)	31
ER3006A†	152 gr.	Extended Range	30
ER3006B†	165 gr.	Extended Range Boat Tail	31
ER3006C†	178 gr.	Extended Range	32

20 IN A BOX, 500 IN A CASE.

300 SAV.

No.	Bullet weight	Bullet style	Wt. case, lbs.
R30SV2	150 gr.	Pointed Soft Point Core-Lokt®	29
R30SV3	180 gr.	Soft Point Core-Lokt®	29

20 IN A BOX, 500 IN A CASE.

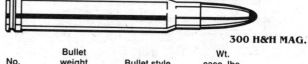

300 H&H MAG.

No.	Bullet weight	Bullet style	Wt. case, lbs.
R300HH	180 gr.	Pointed Soft Point Core-Lokt®	39

20 IN A BOX, 500 IN A CASE.

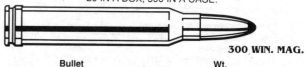

300 WIN. MAG.

No.	Bullet weight	Bullet style	Wt. case, lbs.
R300W1	150 gr.	Pointed Soft Point Core-Lokt®	39
R300W2	180 gr.	Pointed Soft Point Core-Lokt®	39
ER300WA†	178 gr.	Extended Range	38
ER300WB†	190 gr.	Extended Range Boat Tail	39

20 IN A BOX, 500 IN A CASE.

REMINGTON CENTERFIRE RIFLE CARTRIDGES

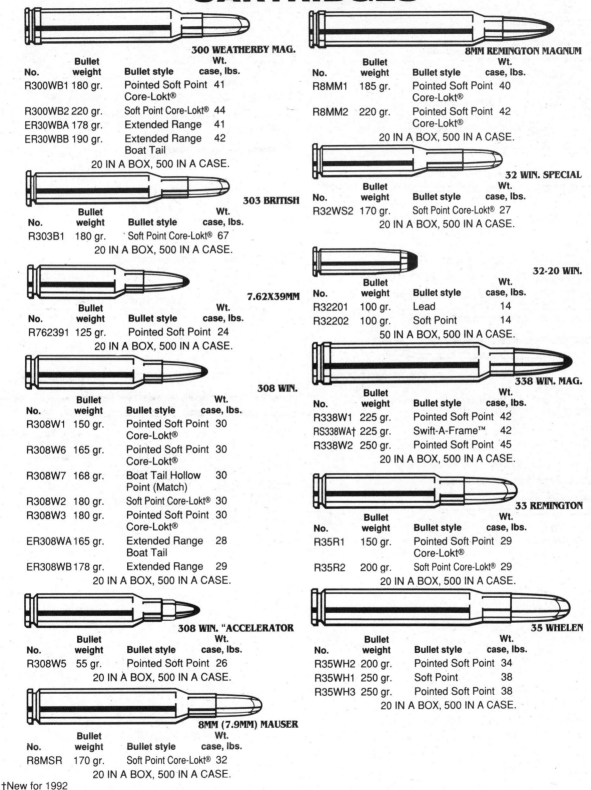

300 WEATHERBY MAG.

No.	Bullet weight	Bullet style	Wt. case, lbs.
R300WB1	180 gr.	Pointed Soft Point Core-Lokt®	41
R300WB2	220 gr.	Soft Point Core-Lokt®	44
ER30WBA	178 gr.	Extended Range	41
ER30WBB	190 gr.	Extended Range Boat Tail	42

20 IN A BOX, 500 IN A CASE.

303 BRITISH

No.	Bullet weight	Bullet style	Wt. case, lbs.
R303B1	180 gr.	Soft Point Core-Lokt®	67

20 IN A BOX, 500 IN A CASE.

7.62X39MM

No.	Bullet weight	Bullet style	Wt. case, lbs.
R762391	125 gr.	Pointed Soft Point	24

20 IN A BOX, 500 IN A CASE.

308 WIN.

No.	Bullet weight	Bullet style	Wt. case, lbs.
R308W1	150 gr.	Pointed Soft Point Core-Lokt®	30
R308W6	165 gr.	Pointed Soft Point Core-Lokt®	30
R308W7	168 gr.	Boat Tail Hollow Point (Match)	30
R308W2	180 gr.	Soft Point Core-Lokt®	30
R308W3	180 gr.	Pointed Soft Point Core-Lokt®	30
ER308WA	165 gr.	Extended Range Boat Tail	28
ER308WB	178 gr.	Extended Range	29

20 IN A BOX, 500 IN A CASE.

308 WIN. "ACCELERATOR

No.	Bullet weight	Bullet style	Wt. case, lbs.
R308W5	55 gr.	Pointed Soft Point	26

20 IN A BOX, 500 IN A CASE.

8MM (7.9MM) MAUSER

No.	Bullet weight	Bullet style	Wt. case, lbs.
R8MSR	170 gr.	Soft Point Core-Lokt®	32

20 IN A BOX, 500 IN A CASE.

†New for 1992

8MM REMINGTON MAGNUM

No.	Bullet weight	Bullet style	Wt. case, lbs.
R8MM1	185 gr.	Pointed Soft Point Core-Lokt®	40
R8MM2	220 gr.	Pointed Soft Point Core-Lokt®	42

20 IN A BOX, 500 IN A CASE.

32 WIN. SPECIAL

No.	Bullet weight	Bullet style	Wt. case, lbs.
R32WS2	170 gr.	Soft Point Core-Lokt®	27

20 IN A BOX, 500 IN A CASE.

32-20 WIN.

No.	Bullet weight	Bullet style	Wt. case, lbs.
R32201	100 gr.	Lead	14
R32202	100 gr.	Soft Point	14

50 IN A BOX, 500 IN A CASE.

338 WIN. MAG.

No.	Bullet weight	Bullet style	Wt. case, lbs.
R338W1	225 gr.	Pointed Soft Point	42
RS338WA†	225 gr.	Swift-A-Frame™	42
R338W2	250 gr.	Pointed Soft Point	45

20 IN A BOX, 500 IN A CASE.

33 REMINGTON

No.	Bullet weight	Bullet style	Wt. case, lbs.
R35R1	150 gr.	Pointed Soft Point Core-Lokt®	29
R35R2	200 gr.	Soft Point Core-Lokt®	29

20 IN A BOX, 500 IN A CASE.

35 WHELEN

No.	Bullet weight	Bullet style	Wt. case, lbs.
R35WH2	200 gr.	Pointed Soft Point	34
R35WH1	250 gr.	Soft Point	38
R35WH3	250 gr.	Pointed Soft Point	38

20 IN A BOX, 500 IN A CASE.

REMINGTON CENTERFIRE RIFLE CARTRIDGES

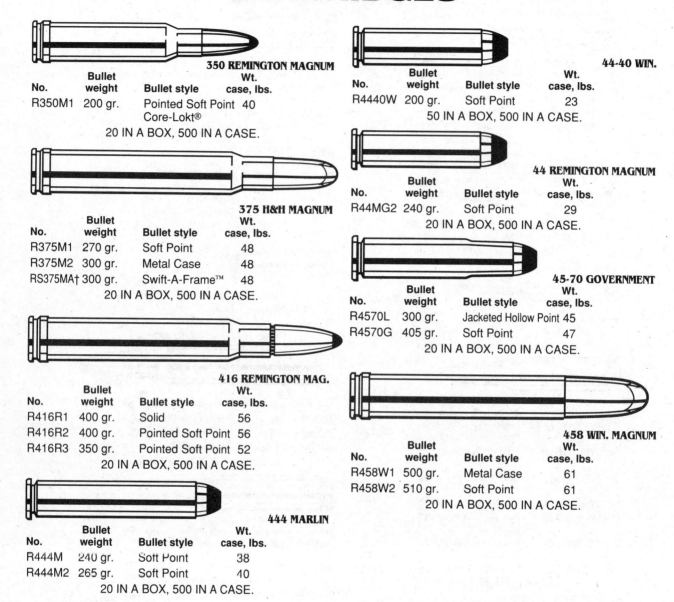

350 REMINGTON MAGNUM

No.	Bullet weight	Bullet style	Wt. case, lbs.
R350M1	200 gr.	Pointed Soft Point Core-Lokt®	40

20 IN A BOX, 500 IN A CASE.

375 H&H MAGNUM

No.	Bullet weight	Bullet style	Wt. case, lbs.
R375M1	270 gr.	Soft Point	48
R375M2	300 gr.	Metal Case	48
RS375MA†	300 gr.	Swift-A-Frame™	48

20 IN A BOX, 500 IN A CASE.

416 REMINGTON MAG.

No.	Bullet weight	Bullet style	Wt. case, lbs.
R416R1	400 gr.	Solid	56
R416R2	400 gr.	Pointed Soft Point	56
R416R3	350 gr.	Pointed Soft Point	52

20 IN A BOX, 500 IN A CASE.

444 MARLIN

No.	Bullet weight	Bullet style	Wt. case, lbs.
R444M	240 gr.	Soft Point	38
R444M2	265 gr.	Soft Point	40

20 IN A BOX, 500 IN A CASE.

44-40 WIN.

No.	Bullet weight	Bullet style	Wt. case, lbs.
R4440W	200 gr.	Soft Point	23

50 IN A BOX, 500 IN A CASE.

44 REMINGTON MAGNUM

No.	Bullet weight	Bullet style	Wt. case, lbs.
R44MG2	240 gr.	Soft Point	29

20 IN A BOX, 500 IN A CASE.

45-70 GOVERNMENT

No.	Bullet weight	Bullet style	Wt. case, lbs.
R4570L	300 gr.	Jacketed Hollow Point	45
R4570G	405 gr.	Soft Point	47

20 IN A BOX, 500 IN A CASE.

458 WIN. MAGNUM

No.	Bullet weight	Bullet style	Wt. case, lbs.
R458W1	500 gr.	Metal Case	61
R458W2	510 gr.	Soft Point	61

20 IN A BOX, 500 IN A CASE.

†New for 1992

REMINGTON CENTERFIRE PISTOL
AND REVOLVER CARTRIDGES
WITH KLEANBORE® PRIMING

221 REMINGTON "FIRE BALL"

No.	Bullet weight	Bullet style	Wt. case, lbs.
R221F	50 gr.	Pointed Soft Point	12

20 IN A BOX, 500 IN A CASE.

25 (6.35MM) AUTO. PISTOL

No.	Bullet weight	Bullet style	Wt. case, lbs.
R25AP	50 gr.	Metal Case	7

50 IN A BOX, 500 IN A CASE.

32 S&W

No.	Bullet weight	Bullet style	Wt. case, lbs.
R32SW	88 gr.	Lead	11

50 IN A BOX, 500 IN A CASE.

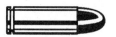

32 S&W LONG

No.	Bullet weight	Bullet style	Wt. case, lbs.
R32SWL	98 gr.	Lead	12

50 IN A BOX, 500 IN A CASE.

32 (7.65MM) AUTO. PISTOL

No.	Bullet weight	Bullet style	Wt. case, lbs.
R32AP	71 gr.	Metal Case	9

50 IN A BOX, 500 IN A CASE.

357 MAGNUM

No.	Bullet weight	Bullet style	Wt. case, lbs.
R357M7	110 gr.	Semi-Jacketed Hollow Point	16
R357M1	125 gr.	Semi-Jacketed Hollow Point	17
R357M8	125 gr.	Semi-Jacketed Soft Point	17
R357M9	140 gr.	Semi-Jacketed Hollow Point	18
R357M2	158 gr.	Semi-Jacketed Hollow Point	19
R357M3	158 gr.	Soft Point	19
R357M5	158 gr.	Lead	19
R357M6	158 gr.	Lead (Brass Case)	20
R357M10	180 gr.	Semi-Jacketed Hollow Point	22
R357M11	140 gr.	Semi-Jacketed Hollow Point (Med. Vel.)	16
R357MB	140 gr.	Multi-Ball	18

50 IN A BOX, 500 IN A CASE.

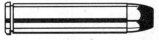

357 REMINGTON MAXIMUM

No.	Bullet weight	Bullet style	Wt. case, lbs.
357MX1	158 gr.	Semi-Jacketed Hollow Point	29

20 IN A BOX, 500 IN A CASE.

9MM LUGER AUTO. PISTOL

No.	Bullet weight	Bullet style	Wt. case, lbs.
R9MM5	88 gr.	Jacketed Hollow Point	20
R9MM1	115 gr.	Jacketed Hollow Point	22
R9MM3	115 gr.	Metal Case	22
R9MM2	124 gr.	Metal Case	23
R9MM6	115 gr.	Jacketed Hollow Point (+P)	13
R9MM7	140 gr.	JHP (Practice)	15
R9MM8†	147 gr.	JHP	16

50 IN A BOX, 500 IN A CASE.

(+P) Ammunition with (+P) on the case headstamp is loaded to higher pressure. Use only in firearms designated for this cartridge and so recommended by the gun manufacturer.

REMINGTON CENTERFIRE PISTOL AND REVOLVER CARTRIDGES

380 AUTO. PISTOL

No.	Bullet weight	Bullet style	Wt. case, lbs.
R380A1	88 gr.	Jacketed Hollow Point	12
R380AP	95 gr.	Metal Case	12

50 IN A BOX, 500 IN A CASE.

38 AUTO. COLT PISTOL

Adapted only for 38 Colt Sporting, Military and Pocket Model Automatic Pistols.

No.	Bullet weight	Bullet style	Wt. case, lbs.
R38ACP	130 gr.	Metal Case	16

50 IN A BOX, 500 IN A CASE.
(Subject to stock on hand)

38 SUPER AUTO. COLT PISTOL

Adapted only for 38 Colt Super and Colt Commander Automatic Pistols.

No.	Bullet weight	Bullet style	Wt. case, lbs.
R38SU1	115 gr.	Jacketed Hollow Point (+P)	14

50 IN A BOX, 500 IN A CASE.

38 S&W

No.	Bullet weight	Bullet style	Wt. case, lbs.
R38SW	146 gr.	Lead	16

50 IN A BOX, 500 IN A CASE.

40 S&W

No.	Bullet weight	Bullet style	Wt. case, lbs.
R40SW1	155 gr.	Jacketed Hollow Point	18
R40SW2	180 gr.	Jacketed Hollow Point	20

38 SPECIAL

No.	Bullet weight	Bullet style	Wt. case, lbs.
R38S1	95 gr.	Semi-Jacketed Hollow Point (+P)	13
R38S10	110 gr.	Semi-Jacketed Hollow Point (+P)	13
R38S16†	110 gr.	Semi-Jacketed Hollow Point	13
R38S2	125 gr.	Semi-Jacketed Hollow Point (+P)	17
R38S13	125 gr.	Semi-Jacket Soft Point (+P)	17
R38S3	148 gr.	Targetmaster Lead Wadcutter, brass case	17
R38S4	158 gr.	Targetmaster Lead Round Nose	18
R38S5	158 gr.	Lead	18
R38S6	158 gr.	Lead Semi-Wadcutter	18
R38S14	158 gr.	Lead Semi-Wadcutter (+P)	18
R38S7	158 gr.	Metal Point	18
R38S12	158 gr.	Lead Hollow Point (+P)	18
R38SMB	140 gr.	Multi-Ball	17

50 IN A BOX, 500 IN A CASE.

38 SHORT COLT

No.	Bullet weight	Bullet style	Wt. case, lbs.
R38SC	125 gr.	Lead	14

10MM AUTO.

No.	Bullet weight	Bullet style	Wt. case, lbs.
R10MM2	200 gr.	Metal Case	24
R10MM3	180 gr.	JHP (950 FPS)	22
R10MM4	180 gr.	JHP (HIGH VEL)	22

50 IN A BOX, 500 IN A CASE.

(+P) Ammunition with (+P) on the case headstamp is loaded to higher pressure. Use only in firearms designated for this cartridge and so recommended by the gun manufacturer.

†New for 1992

REMINGTON CENTERFIRE PISTOL AND REVOLVER CARTRIDGES

WITH KLEANBORE® PRIMING

41 REMINGTON MAGNUM

No.	Bullet weight	Bullet style	Wt. case, lbs.
R41MG3	170 gr.	Semi-Jacketed Hollow Point	24
R41MG1	210 gr.	Soft Point	26
R41MG2	210 gr.	Lead	26

50 IN A BOX, 500 IN A CASE.

44 S&W SPECIAL

No.	Bullet weight	Bullet style	Wt. case, lbs.
R44SW1	200 gr.	Lead Semi-Wadcutter	22
R44SW	246 gr.	Lead	25

50 IN A BOX, 500 IN A CASE.

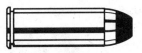

44 REMINGTON MAGNUM

No.	Bullet weight	Bullet style	Wt. case, lbs.
R44MG5	180 gr.	Semi-Jacketed Hollow Point	29
R44MG1	310 gr.	Semi-Jacketed Hollow Point	27
R44MG1	240 gr.	Lead, Gas-Check	29
R44MG4	240 gr.	Lead	29
R44MG2	240 gr.	Soft Point	29
R44MG3	240 gr.	Semi-Jacketed Hollow Point	29

20 IN A BOX, 500 IN A CASE.

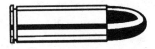

45 COLT

No.	Bullet weight	Bullet style	Wt. case, lbs.
R45C1	225 gr.	Lead Semi-Wadcutter	24
R45C	250 gr.	Lead	26

50 IN A BOX, 500 IN A CASE.

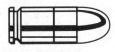

45 AUTO.

No.	Bullet weight	Bullet style	Wt. case, lbs.
R45AP1	185 gr.	Targetmaster Metal Case Wadcutter	11
R45AP2	185 gr.	Jacketed Hollow Point	11
R45AP4	230 gr.	Metal Case	13
R45AP6	185 gr.	Jacketed Hollow Point (+P)	21

50 IN A BOX, 500 IN A CASE

..45 AUTO. SHOT CARTRIDGE

No.	Bullet style	Wt. case, lbs.
R45AP5	650 Pellets — No. 12 Shot	18

20 IN A BOX, 500 IN A CASE.

REMINGTON CENTERFIRE BLANK

No.	Caliber	No. in case	Wt. case, lbs.
R32BLNK	32 S&W	500	4
R38SWBL	38 S&W	500	7
R38BLNK	38 Special	500	7

50 IN A BOX.

(+P) Ammunition with (+P) on the case headstamp is loaded to higher pressure. Use only in firearms designated for this cartridge and so recommended by the gun manufacturer.

REMINGTON RIMFIRE CARTRIDGES

"HIGH VELOCITY" CARTRIDGES WITH "GOLDEN" BULLETS

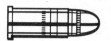

22 SHORT

No.	Bullet weight and style	Wt. case, lbs.
1022	29 gr., Lead	29

50 IN A BOX, 5,000 IN A CASE.

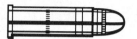

22 LONG

No.	Bullet weight and style	Wt. case, lbs.
1322	29 gr., Lead	31

50 IN A BOX, 5,000 IN A CASE.

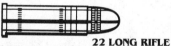

22 LONG RIFLE

No.	Bullet weight and style	Wt. case, lbs.
1522	40 gr., Lead	40
1622	36 gr., Lead, Hollow Point	38

50 IN A BOX, 5,000 IN A CASE.

100 PACK

No.	Bullet weight and style	Wt. case, lbs.
1500	40 gr., Lead	40
1600	36 gr., Lead, Hollow Point	38

100 IN A BOX, 5,000 IN A CASE.

"TARGET" STANDARD VELOCITY CARTRIDGES

22 SHORT

No.	Bullet weight and style	Wt. case, lbs.
5522	29 gr., Lead	29

50 IN A BOX, 5,000 IN A CASE.

22 LONG RIFLE

No.	Bullet weight and style	Wt. case, lbs.
6122	40 gr., Lead	40

50 IN A BOX, 5,000 IN A CASE.

100 PACK

No.	Bullet weight and style	Wt. case, lbs.
6100	40 gr., Lead	40

100 IN A BOX, 5,000 IN A CASE.

22 BOX OF BULLETS

No.	Bullet weight and style	Wt. case, lbs.
1522-BX	40 gr., Lead	37

CBee™ CARTRIDGES LOW NOISE LEVEL

Velocity of 720 f.p.s.; the quietness of an airgun, the impact of a .22 bullet.

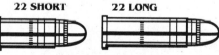

22 SHORT   22 LONG

No.	Bullet weight and style	Wt. case, lbs.
CB-22S Short	30 gr., Lead	29
CB-22L Long	30 gr., Lead	30

50 IN A BOX, 5,000 IN A CASE.

YELLOW JACKET® CARTRIDGES HYPER-VELOCITY

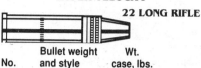

22 LONG RIFLE

No.	Bullet weight and style	Wt. case, lbs.
1722	33 gr., Truncated Cone, Hollow Point	36

50 IN A BOX, 5,000 IN A CASE.

"VIPER" CARTRIDGES HYPER-VELOCITY

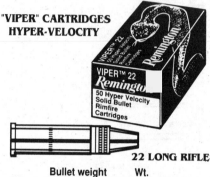

22 LONG RIFLE

No.	Bullet weight and style	Wt. case, lbs.
1922	36 gr., Truncated Cone, Solid Point, Copper Plated	38

50 IN A BOX, 5,000 IN A CASE.

"THUNDERBOLT" CARTRIDGES HI-SPEED

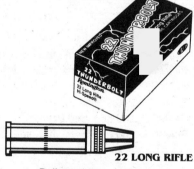

22 LONG RIFLE

No.	Bullet weight and style	Wt. case, lbs.
TB22A	36 gr., Truncated Cone, Solid Point	40

50 IN A BOX, 5,000 IN A CASE.

REMINGTON SHOTGUN SHELLS

REMINGTON PREMIER™ TARGET LOADS

	No.	Gauge	Length shell, in.	Powder equiv. drams	Size, oz.	Size shot	Wt. case, lbs.	Per box
PREMIER™ TARGET LOADS	RTL12L•	12	2 3/4	2 3/4	1 1/8	7 1/2, 8, 8 1/2, 9	27	
	RTL12M•	12	2 3/4	3	1 1/8	7 1/2, 8, 9	27	
	RTL20	20	2 3/4	2 1/2	7/8	9	41	
"REMLITE" PREMIER™ TARGET LOAD	LRTL12•	12	2 3/4	—	1 1/8	7 1/2, 8, 9	27	
DUPLEX® PREMIER™ TARGET LOAD	MRTL12L•	12	2 3/4	2 3/4	1 1/8	7 1/2X8	27	
	MRTL12M•			3	1 1/8	7 1/2X8	27	
DUPLEX® SPORTING CLAYS	SC12L	12	2 3/4	2 3/4	1 1/8	7 1/2 X 8	27	
SKEET LOADS	SP28	28	2 3/4	2	3/4	9	37	
	SP410	410	2 1/2	Max.	1/2	9	22	
PREMIER™ PIGEON LOADS	RTL12P•	12	2 3/4	3 1/4	1 1/4	7 1/2, 8	27	
	RTL12PN•	12	2 3/4	3 1/4	1 1/4	7 1/2, 8 (nickel)	27	
PREMIER™ INTERNATIONAL TARGET LOADS	RIT12 •	12	2 3/4	—	28 gm (1 oz.)	7 1/2, 8, 9	54	
	RIT12N •	12	2 3/4	—	28 gm (1 oz.)	7 1/2, 8 (nickel)	54	

25 IN A BOX, 500 IN A CASE • 25 IN A BOX, 250 PER CASE

	No.	Gauge	Length shell, in.	Powder equiv. drams	Size, oz.	Size shot	Wt. case, lbs.	Per box
GAME LOAD	GL12	12	2 3/4	3 1/4	1	6, 7 1/2, 8	24	
	GL16	16	2 3/4	2 1/2	1	6, 7 1/2, 8	24	
	GL20	20	2 3/4	2 1/2	7/8	6, 7 1/2, 8	16	
HEAVY GAME LOAD	HGL12	12	2 3/4	3 3/4	1 1/4	4, 6, 7 1/2	30	
	HGL16	16	2 3/4	3 1/4	1 1/8	4, 6, 7 1/2	27	
	HGL20	20	2 3/4	2 3/4	1	4, 6, 7 1/2	24	

25 IN A BOX, 250 IN A CASE

REMINGTON SHOTGUN SHELLS

REMINGTON PREMIER® MAGNUM BUCKSHOT WITH EXTRA HARD NICKEL PLATED SHOT

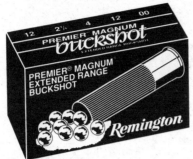

Nickel plated extra-hard buckshot and granulated polyethylene filler for reduced deformation and improved pattern.

	No.	Gauge	Shell length, in.	Powder drams equiv.	Shot size	Pellets	Case wt., lbs.	Per box
PREMIER®	PR12SNBK	12	2 3/4	4	00	12	29	
MAGNUM	PR12SNBK	12	2 3/4	4	4	34	31	
EXTENDED	PR12HNBK	12	3	4	000	10	40	
RANGE	PR12HNBK	12	3	4	00	15	40	
BUCKSHOT	PR12HNBK	12	3	Max.	1	24	40	
WITH NICKEL	PR12HNBK	12	3	4	4	41	42	
PLATED SHOT								

10 IN A BOX, 250 RDS. PER CASE.

REMINGTON EXPRESS® BUCKSHOT LOADS AND "SLUGGER" RIFLED SLUGS

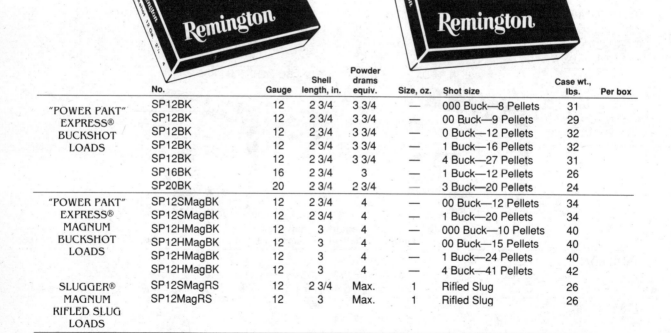

	No.	Gauge	Shell length, in.	Powder drams equiv.	Size, oz.	Shot size	Case wt., lbs.	Per box
"POWER PAKT"	SP12BK	12	2 3/4	3 3/4	—	000 Buck—8 Pellets	31	
EXPRESS®	SP12BK	12	2 3/4	3 3/4	—	00 Buck—9 Pellets	29	
BUCKSHOT	SP12BK	12	2 3/4	3 3/4	—	0 Buck—12 Pellets	32	
LOADS	SP12BK	12	2 3/4	3 3/4	—	1 Buck—16 Pellets	32	
	SP12BK	12	2 3/4	3 3/4	—	4 Buck—27 Pellets	31	
	SP16BK	16	2 3/4	3	—	1 Buck—12 Pellets	26	
	SP20BK	20	2 3/4	2 3/4	—	3 Buck—20 Pellets	24	
"POWER PAKT"	SP12SMagBK	12	2 3/4	4	—	00 Buck—12 Pellets	34	
EXPRESS®	SP12SMagBK	12	2 3/4	4	—	1 Buck—20 Pellets	34	
MAGNUM	SP12HMagBK	12	3	4	—	000 Buck—10 Pellets	40	
BUCKSHOT	SP12HMagBK	12	3	4	—	00 Buck—15 Pellets	40	
LOADS	SP12HMagBK	12	3	4	—	1 Buck—24 Pellets	40	
	SP12HMagBK	12	3	4	—	4 Buck—41 Pellets	42	
SLUGGER®	SP12SMagRS	12	2 3/4	Max.	1	Rifled Slug	26	
MAGNUM	SP12MagRS	12	3	Max.	1	Rifled Slug	26	
RIFLED SLUG								
LOADS								
SLUGGER®	SP12RS	12	2 3/4	Max.	1	Rifled Slug H.P.	26	
RIFLED SLUG	SP16RS	16	2 3/4	3	4/5	Rifled Slug H.P.	24	
LOADS	SP20RS	20	2 3/4	2 3/4	5/8	Rifled Slug H.P.	19	
	SP410RS	.410	2 1/2	Max.	1/5	Rifled Slug	8	

5 IN A BOX, 250 PER CASE

REMINGTON SHOTGUN SHELLS

REMINGTON NITRO MAGNUM® EXPRESS,® AND SHURSHOT® SHOTSHELLS

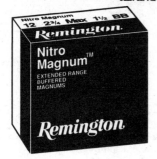

	No.	Gauge	Shell length, in.	Powder drams equiv.	Ounces of shot	Shot size	Wt. case, lbs.
NITRO	SP10HNM•	10	3 1/2	4 1/2	2 1/4	2, 4, 6	49
MAG®	SP12SNM•	12	2 3/4	Max.	1 1/2	2, 4, 6	34
EXTENDED	SP12NM•	12	3	4	1 5/8	2, 4, 6	35
RANGE	SP12HNM•	12	3	Max.	1 7/8	2, 4, 6	35
BUFFERED	SP20SNM•	20	2 3/4	Max.	1 1/8	4, 6	26
MAGNUMS	SP20HNM•	20	3	Max.	1 1/4	2, 4, 6, 7 1/2	30
EXPRESS®	SP10MAG•	10	3 1/2	Max.	2	BB, 2, 4	45
EXTRA LONG RANGE	SP12	12	2 3/4	3 3/4	1 1/4	BB, 2, 4, 5, 6, 7 1/2, 9	58
LOADS	SP16	16	2 3/4	3 1/4	1 1/8	4, 5, 6, 7 1/2, 9	52
	SP16CMAG	16	2 3/4	Max.	1 1/4	2, 4, 6	58
	SP20	20	2 3/4	2 3/4	1	4, 5, 6, 7 1/2, 9	47
	SP28	28	2 3/4	2 1/4	3/4	6, 7 1/2	36
	SP410	410	2 1/2	Max.	1/2	4, 6, 7 1/2	23
	SP4103	410	3	Max.	11/16	4, 5†, 6, 7 1/2, 9	31
SHURSHOT®	R12H	12	2 3/4	3 1/4	1 1/8	4, 5, 6, 9	51
FIELD	R12H250CS•	12	2 3/4	3 1/4	1 1/8	7 1/2, 8	29
LOADS	RP12H250CS•	12	2 3/4	3 1/4	1 1/4	6†, 7 1/2, 8	30
	R16H	16	2 3/4	2 3/4	1 1/8	4, 6, 7 1/2, 8, 9	51
	R20M	20	2 3/4	2 1/2	1	4, 5, 6, 9	45
	R20M250CS•	20	2 3/4	2 1/2	1	7 1/2, 8	23

25 IN A BOX, 500 IN A CASE. • 25 IN A BOX, 250 PER CASE

REMINGTON STEEL SHOT WATERFOWL LOADS

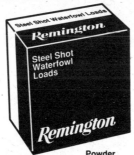

	No.	Gauge	Shell length, in.	Powder drams equiv.	Ounces of shot	Shot size	Wt. case, lbs.
STEEL SHOT	STL10MAG	10	3 1/2	Max.	1 3/4	T, BBB, BB, 1, 2, 3	48
WATERFOWL	STL12	12	2 3/4	Max.	1 1/8	BB, 1, 2, 3, 4, 6	28
LOADS	STL12SMAG	12	2 3/4	Max.	1 1/4	T, BBB, BB, 1, 2, 3, 4	30
	STL12MAG	12	3	Max.	1 1/4	BB, 1, 2, 3, 4, 6	30
	STL12HMAG	12	3	Max.	1 3/8	T, BBB, BB, 1, 2, 3, 4	32
	STL20HMAG	20	3	Max.	1	2, 3, 4, 6	23

25 IN A BOX, 250 PER CASE.

†New for 1992

WINCHESTER AMMUNITION
Super-X® Centerfire Rifle

WINCHESTER SYMBOL	CARTRIDGE
	218 Bee
X218B	46 gr. Hollow Point
	22 Hornet
X22H1	45 gr. Soft Point
X22H2	46 gr. Hollow Point
	22-250 Remington
X222501	55 gr. Pointed Soft Point
	222 Remington
X222R	50 gr. Pointed Soft Point
X222R1	55 gr. Full Metal Jacket
	223 Remington
X223RH	53 gr. Hollow Point
X223R	55 gr. Pointed Soft Point
X223R1	55 gr. Full Metal Jacket
X223R2	64 gr. Power Point
	225 Winchester
X2251	55 gr. Pointed Soft Point
	243 Winchester
X2431	80 gr. Pointed Soft Point
X2432	100 gr. Power Point
	6mm Remington
X6MMR1	80 gr. Pointed Soft Point
X6MMR2	100 gr. Power Point
	25-06 Remington
X25061	90 gr. Positive Expanding Point
X25062	120 gr. Positive Expanding Point
	25-20 Winchester
X25202	86 gr. Soft Point
	25-35 Winchester
X2535	117 gr. Soft Point
	250 Savage
X2503	100 gr. Silvertip

WINCHESTER SYMBOL	CARTRIDGE
	257 Roberts +P
X257P2	100 gr. Silvertip
X257P3	117 gr. Power Point
	264 Winchester Magnum
X2642	140 gr. Power Point
	270 Winchester
X2701	100 gr. Pointed Soft Point
X2705	130 gr. Power Point
X2703	130 gr. Silvertip
X2704	150 gr. Power Point
	280 Remington
X280R	140 gr. Power Point
	284 Winchester
X2842	150 gr. Power Point
	7mm Mauser (7x57)
X7MM1	145 gr. Power Point
	30-06 Springfield
X30062	125 gr. Pointed Soft Point
X30061	150 gr. Power Point
X30063	150 gr. Silvertip
X30065	165 gr. Soft Point
X30064	180 gr. Power Point
X30066	180 gr. Silvertip
X30069	220 gr. Silvertip
	7mm Remington Magnum
X7MMR1	150 gr. Power Point
X7MMR2	175 gr. Power Point
	7.62 x 39mm Russian
X76239	123 gr. Pointed Soft Point
	30 Carbine
X30M1	110 gr. Hollow Soft Point
X30M2	110 gr. Full Metal Jacket

WINCHESTER AMMUNITION
Super-X® Centerfire Rifle

WINCHESTER SYMBOL	CARTRIDGE
	30-30 Winchester
X30301	150 gr. Hollow Point
X30306	150 gr. Power Point
X30302	150 gr. Silvertip
X30303	170 gr. Power Point
X30304	170 gr. Silvertip
	30-40 Krag
X30401	180 gr. Power Point
	300 Winchester Magnum
X30WM1	150 gr. Power Point
X30WM2	180 gr. Power Point
X30WM3	220 gr. Silvertip
	300 H & H Magnum
X300H2	180 gr. Silvertip
	300 Savage
X3001	150 gr. Power Point
X3003	150 gr. Silvertip
X3004	180 gr. Power Point
	303 Savage
X3032	190 gr. Silvertip
	303 British
X303B1	180 gr. Power Point
	307 Winchester
+ X3075	150 gr. Power Point
X3076	180 gr. Power Point
	308 Winchester
X3085	150 gr. Power Point
X3082	150 gr. Silvertip
X3086	180 gr. Power Point
X3083	180 gr. Silvertip
	32 Winchester Special
X32WS2	170 gr. Power Point
X32WS3	170 gr. Silvertip
	32-20 Winchester
X32201	100 gr. Lead

WINCHESTER SYMBOL	CARTRIDGE
	8mm Mauser (8x57)
X8MM	170 gr. Power Point
	338 Winchester Magnum
X3381	200 gr. Power Point
X3383	225 gr. Soft Point
	35 Remington
X35R1	200 gr. Power Point
X35R3	200 gr. Silvertip
	356 Winchester
X3561	200 gr. Power Point
X3563	250 gr. Power Point
	357 Magnum
X3574P	158 gr. Jacketed Hollow Point
X3575P	158 gr. Jacketed Soft Point
	358 Winchester
X3581	200 gr. Silvertip
	375 Winchester
X375W	200 gr. Power Point
X375W1	250 gr. Power Point
	375 H & H Magnum
X375H1	270 gr. Power Point
X375H2	300 gr. Silvertip
X375H3	300 gr. Full Metal Jacket
	38-40 Winchester
X3840	180 gr. Soft Point
	38-55 Winchester
X3855	255 gr. Soft Point
	44 Remington Magnum
X44MSTHP2	210 gr. Silvertip Hollow Point
X44MHSP2	240 gr. Hollow Soft Point
	44-40 Winchester
X4440	200 gr. Soft Point
	45-70 Government
X4570H	300 gr. Jacketed Hollow Point
	458 Winchester Magnum
X4580	500 gr. Full Metal Jacket
X4581	510 gr. Soft Point

WINCHESTER AMMUNITION

Super-X Rimfire

WINCHESTER SYMBOL	CARTRIDGE	BULLET TYPE	WT. GRS.
Super-X High Velocity Cartridges - Copperplated Bullets			
X22S	22 Short	LRN	29
X22LR	22 Long Rifle	LRN	40
X22LR1	22 Long Rifle	LRN	40
X22LRH	22 Long Rifle	LHP	37
X22LRH1	22 Long Rifle	LHP	37
Super-X 22 Winchester Magnum Cartridge			
X22WMR	22 Win. Mag.	JHP	40
X22MR1	22 Win. Mag.	FMC	40
Winchester Super Silhouette Cartridge			
XS22LR1	22 Long Rifle	LTC	42
Winchester Standard Velocity Cartridge			
XT22LR	22 Long Rifle Target	LRN	40
Other Winchester Rimfire Cartridges			
X22LRS	22 Long Rifle, Shot	#12 Shot	25
22BL	22 Short Blank	Black Powder	-
WW22CBS2	22 Short CB	LRN	29

International Rimfire

WINCHESTER SYMBOL	CARTRIDGE	BULLET TYPE	WT. GRS.
SS22LRH	22 Long Rifle Hyper Velocity	HP	34
AUS22LR	22 Long Rifle High Velocity	SHP	40
W22SUB	Subsonic 22 Long Rifle	HP	40
PP22LRH	22 Long Rifle High Velocity	HP	40

Promotional Rimfire

WINCHESTER SYMBOL	CARTRIDGE	BULLET TYPE	WT. GRS.
WW22LR	22 Long Rifle	LRN	40
WW22LRW	22 Long Rifle (Shrinkwrap)	LRN	40

Supreme®

Centerfire Rifle Cartridges

WINCHESTER SYMBOL	CARTRIDGE
S22250R52	**Supreme 22-250 Remington** 52 gr. Hollow Point Boattail
S243W100	**Supreme 243 Winchester** 100 gr. Soft Point Boattail
S270W140	**Supreme 270 Winchester** 140 gr. Silvertip Boattail
S280R160	**Supreme 280 Remington** 160 gr. Silvertip Boattail
S7MAG S7MMRM160	**Supreme 7mm Remington Magnum** 139 gr. Soft Point Boattail 160 gr. Silvertip Boattail
S3030W150	**Supreme 30-30 Winchester** 150 gr. Silvertip
S308W150 S308W180	**Supreme 308 Winchester** 150 gr. Silvertip Boattail 180 gr. Silvertip Boattail
S3006S165 S3006S180	**Supreme 30-06 Springfield** 165 gr. Silvertip Boattail 180 Gr. Silvertip Boattail
S300WM190	**Supreme 300 Winchester Magnum** 190 gr. Silvertip Boattail

Black Talon™
Centerfire Pistol Cartridges

WINCHESTER SYMBOL	CARTRIDGE
▷ S9MM **NEW**	**Supreme 9mm Luger** 147 gr. Supreme Expansion Talon
▷ S40SW **NEW**	**Supreme 40 Smith & Wesson** 180 gr. Supreme Expansion Talon
▷ S10MM **NEW**	**Supreme 10mm Auto** 200 gr. Supreme Expansion Talon
▷ S45A **NEW**	**Supreme 45 Automatic** 230 gr. Supreme Expansion Talon

WINCHESTER AMMUNITION
Super-X® Centerfire Pistol/Revolver Cartridges

Subsonic™

WINCHESTER SYMBOL	CARTRIDGE
▷ XSUB38S **NEW**	**38 Special** 147 gr. Jacketed Hollow Point
▷ XSUB9MM **NEW**	**9mm** 147 gr. Jacketed Hollow Point
▷ XSUB40SW **NEW**	**40 Smith & Wesson** 180 gr. Jacketed Hollow Point
▷ XSUB10MM **NEW**	**10mm Automatic** 180 gr. Jacketed Hollow Point
▷ XSUB45A **NEW**	**45 Automatic** 230 gr. Jacketed Hollow Point

Silvertip®

WINCHESTER SYMBOL	CARTRIDGE
X32ASHP	**32 Automatic** 60 gr. Silvertip Hollow Point
X380ASHP	**380 Automatic** 85 gr. Silvertip Hollow Point
X38S9HP	**38 Special** 110 gr. Silvertip Hollow Point
X38SSHP X38S8HP	**38 Special +P** 95 gr. Silvertip Hollow Point 125 gr. Silvertip Hollow Point
X9MMSHP X9MMST147	**9mm Luger (Parabellum)** 115 gr. Silvertip Hollow Point 147 gr. Silvertip Hollow Point
X357SHP	**357 Magnum** 145 gr. Silvertip Hollow Point
X38ASHP	**38 Super Automatic +P** *(For use in 38 Super Automatic Pistols ONLY)* 125 gr. Silvertip Hollow Point
X40SWSTHP	**40 Smith & Wesson** 155 gr. Silvertip Hollow Point
X10MMSTHP	**10mm Automatic** 175 gr. Silvertip Hollow Point
X41MSTHP2	**41 Remington Magnum** 175 gr. Silvertip Hollow Point
X44STHPS2	**44 Smith & Wesson Special** 200 gr. Silvertip Hollow Point
X44MSTHP2	**44 Remington Magnum** 210 gr. Silvertip Hollow Point
X45ASHP2	**45 Automatic** 185 gr. Silvertip Hollow Point
X45CSHP2	**45 Colt** 225 gr. Silvertip Hollow Point

Super Match™

WINCHESTER SYMBOL	CARTRIDGE
X38SMRP	**38 Special Match** 148 gr. Lead Mid-Range (clean cutting)
X9MMTCM	**9mm** 147 gr. Full Metal Jacket Truncated Cone
X40SWTCM	**40 Smith & Wesson** 155 gr. Full Metal Jacket Truncated Cone
X10MMTCM	**10mm Automatic** 155 gr. Full Metal Jacket Truncated Cone
X45AWCP	**45 Automatic** 185 gr. Full Metal Jacket Semi-Wad Cutter

Super-X

WINCHESTER SYMBOL	CARTRIDGE
X25AXP X25AP	**25 Automatic** 45 gr. Expanding Point 50 gr. Full Metal Jacket
X30LP	**30 Luger (7.65mm)** 93 gr. Full Metal Jacket
X30M1 X30M2	**30 Carbine** 110 gr. Hollow Soft Point 110 gr. Full Metal Jacket
X32SWP	**32 Smith & Wesson** 85 gr. Lead Round Nose
X32SWLP	**32 Smith & Wesson Long** 98 gr. Lead Round Nose
X32SCP	**32 Short Colt** 80 gr. Lead Round Nose
X32AP	**32 Automatic** 71 gr. Full Metal Jacket
X38SWP	**38 Smith & Wesson** 145 gr. Lead Round Nose
X380AP	**380 Automatic** 95 gr. Full Metal Jacket
X38S1P X38WCPSV	**38 Special** 158 gr. Lead Round Nose 158 gr. Lead Semi-Wad Cutter
X38S6PH X38S7PH X38SPD X38WCP	**38 Special +P** 110 gr. Jacketed Hollow Point 125 gr. Jacketed Hollow Point 158 gr. Lead Hollow Point Semi-Wad Cutter 158 gr. Lead Semi-Wad Cutter
X9LP	**9mm Luger (Parabellum)** 115 gr. Full Metal Jacket
X38A1P	**38 Super Automatic +P** *(For use in 38 Super Automatic Pistols ONLY)* 130 gr. Full Metal Jacket
X3573P X3576P X3571P X3574P X3575P	**357 Magnum** 110 gr. Jacketed Hollow Point 125 gr. Jacketed Hollow Point 158 gr. Lead Semi-Wad Cutter (Lubaloy) 158 gr. Jacketed Hollow Point 158 gr. Jacketed Soft Point
X41MP X41MJSP2 X41MHP2	**41 Remington Magnum** 210 gr. Lead Semi-Wad Cutter 210 gr. Jacketed Soft Point 210 gr. Jacketed Hollow Point
X44SP	**44 Smith & Wesson Special** 246 gr. Lead Round Nose
+ X44MWCP X44MHSP2	**44 Remington Magnum** 240 gr. Lead Semi-Wad Cutter (Med. Vel.) 240 gr. Hollow Soft Point
X45A1P2	**45 Automatic** 230 gr. Full Metal Jacket
X45CP2	**45 Colt** 255 gr. Lead Round Nose
X45WM2	**45 Winchester Magnum** *(Not for arms chambered for standard 45 Auto)* 230 gr. Full Metal Jacket

Blanks

WINCHESTER SYMBOL	CARTRIDGE
32BL2P	**32 Smith & Wesson** Black Powder
38SBLP	**38 Special** Smokeless Powder

WINCHESTER AMMUNITION
Super-X® Shotshells

Game Loads

WINCHESTER SYMBOL	GAUGE	LENGTH INCHES	DRAM EQUIV.	Oz. SHOT	SHOT SIZES
Super-X Game Loads - High Brass					
X12	12	2¾	3¾	1¼	2,4,5,6,7½,9
X16H	16	2¾	3¼	1⅛	4,6,7½
X20	20	2¾	2¾	1	4,5,6,7½,9
X28	28	2¾	2¼	¾	6,7½
X28H	28	2¾	Max	1	6,7½,8
X41	410	2½	Max	½	4,6,7½
X413	410	3	Max	11/16	4,6,7½

WINCHESTER SYMBOL	GAUGE	LENGTH INCHES	DRAM EQUIV.	Oz. SHOT	SHOT SIZES
Super-X Game Loads - Low Brass					
XLH12	12	2¾	3¼	1¼	6,7½,8
XL12	12	2¾	3¼	1⅛	6,7½,8,9
XL16	16	2¾	2¾	1⅛	6,7½,8
XL20	20	2¾	2½	1	6,7½,8,9

WINCHESTER SYMBOL	GAUGE	LENGTH INCHES	DRAM EQUIV.	Oz. SHOT	SHOT SIZES
Double X Magnum Game Loads - Copperplated, Buffered Shot					
X103XC	10	3½	4½	2¼	BB,2,4
X123XC	12	3	4	1⅞	BB,2,4,6
X12MXC	12	3	4	1⅝	2,4,5,6
X12XC	12	2¾	3¾	1½	BB,2,4,5,6
X16XC	16	2¾	3¼	1¼	4,6
X203XC	20	3	3	1¼	2,4,6
X20XC	20	2¾	2¾	1⅛	4,6,7½

WINCHESTER SYMBOL	GAUGE	LENGTH INCHES	DRAM EQUIV.	Oz. SHOT	SHOT SIZES
Double X Magnum Turkey Loads - Copperplated, Buffered Shot					
X103XCT	10	3½	4½	2¼	6
XXT12L NEW	12	3½	Max	2¼	4,6
X123MXCT	12	3	Max	2	4,5,6
X12HXCT	12	2¾	Max	1⅝	4,5,6

Slug Loads

WINCHESTER SYMBOL	GAUGE	LENGTH INCHES	DRAM EQUIV.	OZ.	TYPE
Super-X Slug Loads					
XRS12	12	2¾	Max	1	Sabot Slug
XRS123	12	3	Max	1	Sabot Slug
X12RS15	12	2¾	Max	1	Rifled Slug
X16RS5	16	2¾	Max	⅘	Rifled Slug
XRS20	20	2¾	Max	⅝	Sabot Slug
X20RSM5	20	2¾	Max	¾	Rifled Slug
X41RS5	410	2½	Max	⅕	Rifled Slug

Waterfowl Loads

WINCHESTER SYMBOL	GAUGE	LENGTH INCHES	DRAM EQUIV.	Oz. SHOT	SHOT SIZES
Super Steel Non-Toxic Loads					
W12SD	12	2¾	Max	1	2,4,6
A X12SSL	12	2¾	Max	1⅛	1,2,3,4,5,6
X16SS	16	2¾	Max	⅞	2,4
X20SSL	20	2¾	Max	¾	4,6
Super Steel Non-Toxic Magnum Loads					
X10SSM	10	3½	Mag	1¾	BB,1,2
XS1235SSM	12	3½	Mag	19/16	1
X12SSM	12	3	Mag	1⅜	BB,1,2,3,4
X123SSM	12	3	Mag	1¼	BB,1,2,3,4,5
B X12SSF	12	2¾	Mag	1¼	BB,1,2,3,4,5,6
C X20SSM	20	3	Mag	1	2,3,4,5,6
Super Steel Non-Toxic Copperplated Magnum Loads					
XS10C	10	3½	Mag	1⅝	F,T,BBB
XS10CF25	10	3½	Mag	1⅝	F
XS10CT25	10	3½	Mag	1⅝	T
XS10CBBB25	10	3½	Mag	1⅝	BBB
XS1235	12	3½	Mag	19/16	F,T,BBB
XS12	12	2¾	Mag	1⅛	T,BBB
XS12T25	12	2¾	Mag	1⅛	T
XS12BBB25	12	2¾	Mag	1⅛	BBB
XS123	12	3	Mag	1¼	F,T,BBB
XS123F25	12	3	Mag	1¼	F
XS123T25	12	3	Mag	1¼	T
XS123BBB25	12	3	Mag	1¼	BBB

Buckshot Loads

WINCHESTER SYMBOL	GAUGE	LENGTH INCHES	# PELLETS	SHOT SIZES
Super-X Buckshot Loads with Buffered Shot				
▷ XB12L00 NEW	12	3½	18 Pellets	00 Buck
XB1231	12	3	24 Pellets	1 Buck
XB12300	12	3	15 Pellets	00 Buck
X12000B5	12	2¾	8 Pellets	000 Buck
X12RB	12	2¾	9 Pellets	00 Buck
X12RB5	12	2¾	9 Pellets	00 Buck
X120B5	12	2¾	12 Pellets	0 Buck
X121B5	12	2¾	16 Pellets	1 Buck
X124B5	12	2¾	27 Pellets	4 Buck
X16B5	16	2¾	12 Pellets	1 Buck
X20B5	20	2¾	20 Pellets	3 Buck
Double X Buckshot Loads - Copperplated, Buffered Shot				
+ X10C4B	10	3½	54 Pellets	4 Buck
▷ X10C00B NEW	10	3½	18 Pellets	00 Buck
X123C000B	12	3	10 Pellets	000 Buck
X12XC3B5	12	3	15 Pellets	00 Buck
X12XC0B5	12	2¾	12 Pellets	00 Buck
X12C1B	12	2¾	20 Pellets	1 Buck
X12XCMB5	12	3	41 Pellets	4 Buck
X12XC4B5	12	2¾	34 Pellets	4 Buck
X203C3B	20	3	24 Pellets	3 Buck

CENTERFIRE PISTOL & REVOLVER BALLISTICS

CENTERFIRE RIFLE BALLISTICS

Ballistics

FEDERAL BALLISTICS

CLASSIC® CENTERFIRE RIFLE BALLISTICS (Approximate) Usage Key: ①=Varmints, predators, small game ②=Medium game ③=Large, heavy game ④=Dangerous game

USAGE	FEDERAL LOAD NO.	CALIBER	BULLET WGT. GRAINS	BULLET WGT. GRAMS	BULLET STYLE**	FACTORY PRIMER NO.	VEL. MUZZLE	100 YDS.	200 YDS.	300 YDS.	400 YDS.	500 YDS.	EN. MUZZLE	100 YDS.	200 YDS.	300 YDS.	400 YDS.	500 YDS.
①	222A	222 Rem. (5.56x43mm)	50	3.24	Hi-Shok Soft Point	205	3140	2600	2120	1700	1350	1110	1095	750	500	320	200	135
⑤	222B		55	3.56	Hi-Shok FMJ Boat-tail	205	3020	2740	2480	2230	1990	1780	1115	915	750	610	485	385
①	223A	223 Rem. (5.56x45mm)	55	3.56	Hi-Shok Soft Point	205	3240	2750	2300	1910	1550	1270	1280	920	650	445	295	195
⑤	223B		55	3.56	Hi-Shok FMJ Boat-tail	205	3240	2950	2670	2410	2170	1940	1280	1060	875	710	575	460
①	22250A	22-250 Rem.	55	3.56	Hi-Shok Soft Point	210	3680	3140	2660	2220	1830	1490	1655	1200	860	605	410	270
①	243A	243 Win. (6.16x51mm)	80	5.18	Hi-Shok Soft Point	210	3350	2960	2590	2260	1950	1670	1995	1550	1195	905	675	495
②	243B		100	6.48	Hi-Shok Soft Point	210	2960	2700	2450	2220	1990	1790	1945	1615	1330	1090	880	710
①	6A	6mm Rem.	80	5.18	Hi-Shok Soft Point	210	3470	3060	2690	2350	2040	1750	2140	1665	1290	980	735	540
②	6B		100	6.48	Hi-Shok Soft Point	210	3100	2830	2570	2330	2100	1890	2135	1775	1470	1205	985	790
②	2506B	25-06 Rem.	117	7.58	Hi-Shok Soft Point	210	2990	2730	2480	2250	2030	1830	2320	1985	1645	1350	1100	885
②	270A	270 Win.	130	8.42	Hi-Shok Soft Point	210	3060	2800	2560	2330	2110	1900	2700	2265	1890	1565	1285	1045
②	270B		150	9.72	Hi-Shok Soft Point RN	210	2850	2500	2180	1890	1620	1390	2705	2085	1585	1185	870	640
②	7A	7mm Mauser (7x57mm Mauser)	175	11.34	Hi-Shok Soft Point RN	210	2440	2140	1860	1600	1380	1200	2315	1775	1340	1000	740	565
②	7B		140	9.07	Hi-Shok Soft Point	210	2660	2450	2260	2070	1890	1730	2200	1865	1585	1330	1110	930
②	280B	280 Rem.	150	9.72	Hi-Shok Soft Point	210	2890	2670	2460	2260	2060	1880	2780	2370	2015	1695	1420	1180
②	7RA	7mm Rem. Magnum	150	9.72	Hi-Shok Soft Point	215	3110	2830	2570	2320	2090	1870	3220	2670	2200	1790	1450	1160
③	7RB		175	11.34	Hi-Shok Soft Point	215	2860	2650	2440	2240	2060	1880	3180	2720	2310	1960	1640	1370
①	30CA	30 Carbine (7.62x33mm)	110	7.13	Hi-Shok Soft Point RN	205	1990	1570	1240	1040	920	840	965	600	375	260	210	175
②	76239B	7.62x39mm Soviet	123	7.97	Hi-Shok Soft Point	210	2300	2030	1780	1550	1350	1200	1445	1125	860	655	500	395
②	3030A	30-30 Win.	150	9.72	Hi-Shok Soft Point FN	210	2390	2020	1680	1400	1180	1040	1900	1355	945	650	460	355
②	3030B		170	11.01	Hi-Shok Soft Point RN	210	2200	1900	1620	1380	1190	1060	1830	1355	990	720	535	425
①	3030C		125	8.10	Hi-Shok Hollow Point	210	2570	2090	1660	1320	1080	960	1830	1210	770	480	320	260
②	300A	300 Savage	150	9.72	Hi-Shok Soft Point	210	2630	2350	2100	1850	1630	1430	2305	1845	1460	1145	885	685
②	300B		180	11.66	Hi-Shok Soft Point	210	2350	2140	1940	1750	1570	1410	2205	1825	1495	1215	985	800
②	308A	308 Win. (7.62x51mm)	150	9.72	Hi-Shok Soft Point	210	2820	2530	2260	2010	1770	1560	2650	2140	1705	1345	1050	810
②	308B		180	11.66	Hi-Shok Soft Point	210	2620	2390	2180	1970	1780	1600	2745	2290	1895	1555	1270	1030
②	3006A	30-06 Springfield (7.62x63mm)	150	9.72	Hi-Shok Soft Point	210	2910	2620	2340	2080	1840	1620	2820	2280	1825	1445	1130	875
③	3006B		180	11.66	Hi-Shok Soft Point	210	2700	2470	2250	2040	1850	1660	2915	2435	2025	1665	1360	1105
①	3006C		125	8.10	Hi-Shok Soft Point	210	3140	2780	2450	2140	1850	1600	2735	2145	1660	1270	955	705
③	3006H		220	14.25	Hi-Shok Soft Point RN	210	2410	2130	1870	1630	1420	1250	2835	2215	1705	1300	985	760
③	3006J		180	11.66	Hi-Shok Soft Point RN	210	2700	2350	2020	1730	1470	1250	2915	2200	1630	1190	860	620
③	300WB	300 Win. Magnum	180	11.66	Hi-Shok Soft Point	215	2960	2750	2540	2340	2160	1980	3500	3010	2580	2195	1860	1565
②	303A	303 British	180	11.66	Hi-Shok Soft Point	210	2460	2230	2020	1820	1630	1460	2420	1995	1625	1315	1060	850
②	303B		150	9.72	Hi-Shok Soft Point	210	2690	2440	2210	1980	1780	1590	2400	1980	1620	1310	1055	840
②	32A	32 Win. Special	170	11.01	Hi-Shok Soft Point	210	2250	1920	1630	1370	1180	1040	1910	1395	1000	710	520	410
②	*8A	8mm Mauser (8x57mm JS Mauser)	170	11.01	Hi-Shok Soft Point	210	2360	1970	1620	1330	1120	1000	2100	1465	995	670	475	375
③	338C	338 Win. Magnum	225	14.58	Hi-Shok Soft Point	215	2780	2570	2370	2180	2000	1830	3860	3305	2815	2380	2000	1670
②	357G	357 Magnum	180	11.66	Hi-Shok Hollow Point	100	1550	1160	980	860	770	680	960	535	385	295	235	185
②	35A	35 Rem.	200	12.96	Hi-Shok Soft Point	210	2080	1700	1380	1140	1000	910	1920	1280	840	575	445	370
③	375A	375 H&H Magnum	270	17.50	Hi-Shok Soft Point	215	2690	2420	2170	1920	1700	1500	4340	3510	2810	2220	1740	1355
④	375B		300	19.44	Hi-Shok Soft Point	215	2530	2270	2020	1790	1580	1400	4265	3425	2720	2135	1665	1295
②	44A	44 Rem. Magnum	240	15.55	Hi-Shok Hollow Point	150	1760	1380	1090	950	860	790	1650	1015	640	485	395	330
②	4570A	45-70 Government	300	19.44	Hi-Shok Hollow Point	210	1880	1650	1430	1240	1110	1010	2355	1815	1355	1015	810	680

* Only for use in barrels intended for .323 inch diameter bullets. Do not use in 8x57mm J Commission Rifles (M1888) or in sporting or other military arms of .318 inch bore diameter.
**RN=Round Nose FN=Flat Nose FMJ=Full Metal Jacket HP=Hollow Point

FEDERAL BALLISTICS

| WIND DRIFT IN INCHES 10 MPH CROSSWIND | | | | | HEIGHT OF BULLET TRAJECTORY IN INCHES ABOVE OR BELOW LINE OF SIGHT IF ZEROED AT ⊕ YARDS. SIGHTS 1.5 INCHES ABOVE BORE LINE. | | | | | | | | | | TEST BARREL LENGTH INCHES | FEDERAL LOAD NO. |
| | | | | | AVERAGE RANGE | | | | LONG RANGE | | | | | | | |
100 YDS.	200 YDS.	300 YDS.	400 YDS.	500 YDS.	50 YDS.	100 YDS.	200 YDS.	300 YDS.	50 YDS.	100 YDS.	200 YDS.	300 YDS.	400 YDS.	500 YDS.		
1.7	7.3	18.3	36.4	63.1	−0.2	⊕	−3.7	−15.3	+0.7	+1.9	⊕	−9.7	−31.6	−71.3	24	222A
0.9	3.4	8.5	16.8	26.3	−0.2	⊕	−3.1	−12.0	+0.6	+1.6	⊕	−7.3	−21.5	−44.6	24	222B
1.4	6.1	15.0	29.4	50.8	−0.3	⊕	−3.2	−12.9	+0.5	+1.6	⊕	−8.2	−26.1	−58.3	24	223A
0.8	3.3	7.8	14.5	24.0	−0.3	⊕	−2.5	−9.9	+0.3	+1.3	⊕	−6.1	−18.3	−37.8	24	223B
1.2	5.2	12.5	24.4	42.0	−0.4	⊕	−2.1	−9.1	+0.1	+1.0	⊕	−6.0	−19.1	−42.6	24	22250A
1.0	4.3	10.4	19.8	33.3	−0.3	⊕	−2.5	−10.2	+0.3	+1.3	⊕	−6.4	−19.7	−42.2	24	243A
0.9	3.6	8.4	15.7	25.8	−0.2	⊕	−3.3	−12.4	+0.6	+1.6	⊕	−7.5	−22.0	−45.4	24	243B
1.0	4.1	9.9	18.8	31.6	−0.3	⊕	−2.2	−9.3	+0.2	+1.1	⊕	−5.9	−18.2	−39.0	24	6A
0.8	3.3	7.9	14.7	24.1	−0.3	⊕	−2.9	−11.0	+0.5	+1.4	⊕	−6.7	−19.8	−40.6	24	6B
0.8	3.4	8.1	15.1	24.9	−0.2	⊕	−3.2	−12.0	+0.6	+1.6	⊕	−7.2	−21.4	−44.0	24	2506B
0.8	3.2	7.6	14.2	23.3	−0.2	⊕	−2.9	−11.2	+0.5	+1.5	⊕	−6.8	−20.0	−41.1	24	270A
1.2	5.3	12.8	24.5	41.3	−0.1	⊕	−4.1	−15.5	+0.9	+2.0	⊕	−9.4	−28.6	−61.0	24	270B
1.5	6.2	15.0	28.7	47.8	−0.1	⊕	−6.2	−22.6	+1.6	+3.1	⊕	−13.3	−40.1	−84.6	24	7A
1.3	3.2	8.2	15.4	23.4	−0.1	⊕	−4.3	−15.4	+1.0	+2.1	⊕	−9.0	−26.1	−52.9	24	7B
0.7	3.1	7.2	13.4	21.9	−0.2	⊕	−3.4	−12.6	+0.7	+1.7	⊕	−7.5	−21.8	−44.3	24	280B
0.8	3.4	8.1	15.1	24.9	−0.3	⊕	−2.9	−11.0	+0.5	+1.4	⊕	−6.7	−19.9	−41.0	24	7RA
0.7	3.1	7.2	13.3	21.7	−0.2	⊕	−3.5	−12.8	+0.7	+1.7	⊕	−7.6	−22.1	−44.9	24	7RB
3.4	15.0	35.5	63.2	96.7	+0.6	⊕	−12.8	−46.9	+3.9	+6.4	⊕	−27.7	−81.8	−167.8	18	30CA
1.5	6.4	15.2	28.7	47.3	+0.2	⊕	−7.0	−25.1	+1.9	+3.5	⊕	−14.5	−43.4	−90.6	20	76239B
2.0	8.5	20.9	40.1	66.1	+0.2	⊕	−7.2	−26.7	+1.9	+3.6	⊕	−15.9	−49.1	−104.5	24	3030A
1.9	8.0	19.4	36.7	59.8	+0.3	⊕	−8.3	−29.8	+2.4	+4.1	⊕	−17.4	−52.4	−109.4	24	3030B
2.2	10.1	25.4	49.4	81.6	+0.1	⊕	−6.6	−26.0	+1.7	+3.3	⊕	−16.0	−50.9	−109.5	24	3030C
1.1	4.8	11.6	21.9	36.3	0	⊕	−4.8	−17.6	+1.2	+2.4	⊕	−10.4	−30.9	−64.4	24	300A
1.1	4.6	10.9	20.3	33.3	+0.1	⊕	−6.1	−21.6	+1.7	+3.1	⊕	−12.4	−36.1	−73.8	24	300B
1.0	4.4	10.4	19.7	32.7	−0.1	⊕	−3.9	−14.7	+0.8	+2.0	⊕	−8.8	−26.3	−54.8	24	308A
0.9	3.9	9.2	17.2	28.3	−0.1	⊕	−4.6	−16.5	+1.1	+2.3	⊕	−9.7	−28.3	−57.8	24	308B
1.0	4.2	9.9	18.7	31.2	−0.2	⊕	−3.6	−13.6	+0.7	+1.8	⊕	−8.2	−24.4	−50.9	24	3006A
0.9	3.7	8.8	16.5	27.1	−0.1	⊕	−4.2	−15.3	+1.0	+2.1	⊕	−9.0	−26.4	−54.0	24	3006B
1.1	4.5	10.8	20.5	34.4	−0.3	⊕	−3.0	−11.9	+0.5	+1.5	⊕	−7.3	−22.3	−47.5	24	3006C
1.4	6.0	14.3	27.2	45.0	−0.1	⊕	−6.2	−22.4	+1.7	+3.1	⊕	−13.1	−39.3	−82.2	24	3006H
1.5	6.4	15.7	30.4	51.2	−0.1	⊕	−4.9	−18.3	+1.1	+2.4	⊕	−11.0	−33.6	−71.9	24	3006J
0.7	2.8	6.6	12.3	20.0	−0.2	⊕	−3.1	−11.7	+0.6	+1.6	⊕	−7.0	−20.3	−41.1	24	300WB
1.1	4.5	10.6	19.9	32.7	0	⊕	−5.5	−19.6	+1.4	+2.8	⊕	−11.3	−33.2	−68.1	24	303A
1.0	4.1	9.6	18.1	29.9	−0.1	⊕	−4.4	−15.9	+1.0	+2.2	⊕	−9.4	−27.6	−56.8	24	303B
1.9	8.4	20.3	38.6	63.0	+0.3	⊕	−8.0	−29.2	+2.3	+4.0	⊕	−17.2	−52.3	−109.8	24	32A
2.1	9.3	22.9	43.9	71.7	+0.2	⊕	−7.6	−28.5	+2.1	+3.8	⊕	−17.1	−52.9	−111.9	24	8A
0.8	3.1	7.3	13.6	22.2	−0.1	⊕	−3.8	−13.7	+0.8	+1.9	⊕	−8.1	−23.5	−47.5	24	338C
5.8	21.7	45.2	76.1	NA	⊕	−3.4	−29.7	−88.2	+1.7	⊕	−22.8	−77.9	−173.8	−321.4	18	357G
2.7	12.0	29.0	53.3	83.3	+0.5	⊕	−10.7	−39.3	+3.2	+5.4	⊕	−23.3	−70.0	−144.0	24	35A
1.1	4.5	10.8	20.3	33.7	−0.4	⊕	−5.5	−18.4	+1.0	+2.4	⊕	−10.9	−33.3	−71.2	24	375A
1.2	5.0	11.9	22.4	37.1	+0.5	⊕	−6.3	−21.2	+1.3	+2.6	⊕	−11.2	−33.3	−69.1	24	375B
4.2	17.8	39.8	68.3	102.5	⊕	−2.2	−21.7	−67.2	+1.1	⊕	−17.4	−60.7	−136.0	−250.2	20	44A
1.7	7.6	18.6	35.7	NA	⊕	−1.3	−14.1	−43.7	+0.7	⊕	−11.5	−39.7	−89.1	−163.1	24	4570A

These trajectory tables were calculated by computer using the best available data for each load. Trajectories are representative of the nominal behavior of each load at standard conditions (59°F temperature; barometric pressure of 29.53 inches; altitude at sea level). Shooters are cautioned that actual trajectories may differ due to variations in altitude, atmospheric conditions, guns, sights, and ammunition.

FEDERAL BALLISTICS

PREMIUM® HUNTING RIFLE BALLISTICS (Approximate) Usage Key: ①=Varmints, predators, small game ②=Medium game ③=Large, heavy game ④=Dangerous game

USAGE	FEDERAL LOAD NO.	CALIBER	BULLET WGT. IN GRAINS	BULLET WGT. IN GRAMS	BULLET STYLE**	FACTORY PRIMER NO.	VELOCITY IN FEET PER SECOND (TO NEAREST 10 FEET) MUZZLE	100 YDS.	200 YDS.	300 YDS.	400 YDS.	500 YDS.	ENERGY IN FOOT/POUNDS (TO NEAREST 5 FOOT/POUNDS) MUZZLE	100 YDS.	200 YDS.	300 YDS.	400 YDS.	500 YDS.
①	P223E	223 Rem. (5.56x45mm)	55	3.56	Boat-tail HP	205	3240	2770	2340	1950	1610	1330	1280	935	670	465	315	215
①	P22250B	22-250 Rem.	55	3.56	Boat-tail HP	210	3680	3280	2920	2590	2280	1990	1655	1315	1040	815	630	480
②	P243C	243 Win. (6.16x51mm)	100	6.48	Boat-tail SP	210	2960	2760	2570	2380	2210	2040	1950	1690	1460	1260	1080	925
①	P243D	243 Win. (6.16x51mm)	85	5.50	Boat-tail SP	210	3320	3070	2830	2600	2380	2180	2080	1770	1510	1280	1070	890
②	P243E	243 Win. (6.16x51mm)	100	6.48	Nosler Partition***	210	2960	2730	2510	2300	2100	1910	1945	1650	1395	1170	975	805
②	P6C	6mm Rem.	100	6.48	Nosler Partition	210	3100	2830	2570	2330	2100	1890	2135	1775	1470	1205	985	790
②NEW	P257B	257 Roberts (High-Velocity + P)	120	7.77	Nosler Partition	210	2780	2560	2360	2160	1970	1790	2060	1750	1480	1240	1030	855
②	P2506C	25-06 Rem.	117	7.58	Boat-tail SP	210	2990	2770	2570	2370	2190	2000	2320	2000	1715	1465	1240	1045
②NEW	P6555A*	6.5x55 Swedish	140	9.07	Nosler Partition	210	2850	2640	2440	2250	2070	1890	2525	2170	1855	1575	1330	1115
②	P270C	270 Win.	150	9.72	Boat-tail SP	210	2850	2660	2480	2300	2130	1970	2705	2355	2040	1760	1510	1290
②	P270D	270 Win.	130	8.42	Boat-tail SP	210	3060	2830	2620	2410	2220	2030	2700	2320	1980	1680	1420	1190
②	P270E	270 Win.	150	9.72	Nosler Partition	210	2850	2590	2340	2100	1880	1670	2705	2225	1815	1470	1175	930
②NEW	P730A	7-30 Waters	120	7.77	Boat-tail SP	210	2700	2300	1930	1600	1330	1140	1940	1405	990	685	470	345
②	P7C	7mm Mauser (7x57mm Mauser)	140	9.07	Nosler Partition	210	2660	2450	2260	2070	1890	1730	2200	1865	1585	1330	1110	930
②NEW	P764A*	7x64 Brenneke	160	10.37	Nosler Partition	210	2850	2669	2495	2327	2166	2012	2885	2530	2211	1924	1667	1438
②	P280A	280 Rem.	150	9.72	Nosler Partition	210	2890	2620	2370	2140	1910	1710	2780	2295	1875	1520	1215	970
②	P7RD	7mm Rem. Magnum	150	9.72	Boat-tail SP	215	3110	2920	2750	2580	2410	2250	3220	2850	2510	2210	1930	1690
③	P7RE	7mm Rem. Magnum	165	10.69	Boat-tail SP	215	2950	2800	2650	2510	2370	2230	3190	2865	2570	2300	2050	1825
③	P7RF	7mm Rem. Magnum	160	10.37	Nosler Partition	215	2950	2770	2590	2420	2250	2090	3090	2715	2375	2075	1800	1555
③	P7RG	7mm Rem. Magnum	140	9.07	Nosler Partition	215	3150	2930	2710	2510	2320	2130	3085	2660	2290	1960	1670	1415
②	P3030D	30-30 Win.	170	11.01	Nosler Partition	210	2200	1900	1620	1380	1190	1060	1830	1355	990	720	535	425
②	P308C	308 Win. (7.62x51mm)	165	10.69	Boat-tail SP	210	2700	2520	2330	2160	1990	1830	2670	2310	1990	1700	1450	1230
③	P308E	308 Win. (7.62x51mm)	180	11.66	Nosler Partition	210	2620	2430	2240	2060	1890	1730	2745	2355	2005	1700	1430	1200
②	P3006D	30-06 Spring. (7.62x63mm)	165	10.69	Boat-tail SP	210	2800	2610	2420	2240	2070	1910	2870	2490	2150	1840	1580	1340
③	P3006F	30-06 Spring. (7.62x63mm)	180	11.66	Nosler Partition	210	2700	2500	2320	2140	1970	1810	2910	2510	2150	1830	1550	1350
②	P3006G	30-06 Spring. (7.62x63mm)	150	9.72	Boat-tail SP	210	2910	2690	2480	2270	2070	1880	2820	2420	2040	1710	1430	1180
③	P3006L	30-06 Spring. (7.62x63mm)	180	11.66	Nosler Partition	210	2700	2540	2380	2220	2080	1930	2915	2570	2260	1975	1720	1495
③	P300HA	300 H&H Magnum	180	11.66	Nosler Partition	215	2880	2620	2380	2150	1930	1730	3315	2750	2260	1840	1480	1190
③	P300WC	300 Win. Magnum	200	12.96	Boat-tail SP	215	2830	2680	2530	2380	2240	2110	3560	3180	2830	2520	2230	1970
③	P300WD2	300 Win. Magnum	180	11.66	Nosler Partition	215	2960	2700	2450	2210	1990	1780	3500	2905	2395	1955	1585	1270
③	P338A2	338 Win. Magnum	210	13.60	Nosler Partition	215	2830	2590	2370	2160	1960	1770	3735	3140	2620	2170	1785	1455
③	P338B2	338 Win. Magnum	250	16.20	Nosler Partition	215	2660	2400	2150	1910	1690	1500	3925	3185	2555	2055	1590	1245
③	P375C	375 H&H Magnum	250	16.20	Boat-tail SP	215	2750	2520	2290	2080	1880	1690	4200	3510	2910	2395	1950	1580
④	P375D	375 H&H Magnum	300	19.44	Solid	215	2530	2170	1840	1550	1310	1140	4265	3140	2260	1605	1140	860
④	P375F	375 H&H Magnum	300	19.44	Nosler Partition	215	2530	2320	2120	1930	1750	1590	4265	3585	2995	2475	2040	1675
③	P458A	458 Win. Magnum	350	22.68	Soft Point	215	2470	1990	1570	1250	1060	950	4740	3065	1915	1205	870	705
④	P458B	458 Win. Magnum	510	33.04	Soft Point	215	2090	1820	1570	1360	1190	1080	4945	3730	2790	2080	1605	1320
④	P458C	458 Win. Magnum	500	32.40	Solid	215	2090	1870	1670	1480	1320	1190	4850	3880	3085	2440	1945	1585
④	P416A	416 Rigby	410	26.57	Weldcore SP	215	2370	2110	1870	1640	1440	1280	5115	4050	3165	2455	1895	1485
④	P416B	416 Rigby	410	26.57	Solid	215	2370	2110	1870	1640	1440	1280	5115	4050	3165	2455	1895	1485
④	P470A	470 Nitro Express	500	32.40	Weldcore SP	215	2150	1890	1650	1440	1270	1140	5130	3965	3040	2310	1790	1435
④	P470B	470 Nitro Express	500	32.40	Woodleigh Solid	215	2150	1890	1650	1440	1270	1140	5130	3965	3040	2310	1790	1435

*Available 3/92.

**HP = Hollow Point SP = Soft Point

***"Nosler" and "Partition" are registered trademarks of Nosler Bullets, Inc.

+P ammunition is loaded to a higher pressure. Use only in firearms so recommended by the gun manufacturer.

PREMIUM® VARMINT RIFLE BALLISTICS (Approximate)

USAGE	FEDERAL LOAD NO.	CALIBER	BULLET WGT. IN GRAINS	GRAMS	BULLET STYLE	FACTORY PRIMER NO.	VELOCITY IN FEET PER SECOND (TO NEAREST 10 FEET) MUZZLE	100 YDS.	200 YDS.	300 YDS.	400 YDS.	500 YDS.	ENERGY IN FOOT/POUNDS (TO NEAREST 5 FOOT/POUNDS) MUZZLE	100 YDS.	200 YDS.	300 YDS.	400 YDS.	500 YDS.
①NEW	P223V	223 Rem. (5.56x45mm)	40	2.59	Hollow Point Varmint	205	3650	3010	2450	1950	1530	1210	1185	805	535	340	205	130
①NEW	P22250V	22-250 Rem.	40	2.59	Hollow Point Varmint	210	4000	3320	2720	2200	1740	1360	1420	980	660	430	265	165
①NEW	P243V	243 Win. (6.16x51mm)	60	3.89	Hollow Point Varmint	210	3600	3110	2660	2260	1890	1560	1725	1285	945	680	475	325
①NEW	P2506V	25-06 Rem.	90	5.83	Hollow Point Varmint	210	3440	3040	2680	2340	2030	1750	2365	1850	1435	1100	825	610

PREMIUM® MATCH RIFLE BALLISTICS (Approximate)

USAGE	FEDERAL LOAD NO.	CALIBER	BULLET WGT. GRAINS	GRAMS	BULLET STYLE	FACTORY PRIMER NO.	VELOCITY IN FEET PER SECOND (TO NEAREST 10 FEET) MUZZLE	100 YDS.	200 YDS.	300 YDS.	400 YDS.	500 YDS.	600 YDS.	700 YDS.	800 YDS.	900 YDS.	1000 YDS.	ENERGY IN FOOT/POUNDS MUZZLE	100 YDS.
⑤NEW	P223M	223 Rem. (5.56 x 45mm)	69	4.47	Boat-tail HP Match	205M	3000	2720	2460	2210	1980	1760	1560	1390	1240	1130	1060	1380	1135
⑤NEW	P308M	308 Win. (7.62 x 51mm)	168	10.88	Boat-tail HP Match	210M	2600	2420	2240	2070	1910	1760	1610	1480	1360	1260	1170	2520	2180
⑤NEW	P3006M	30-06 Springfield (7.62 x 63mm)	168	10.88	Boat-tail HP Match	210M	2700	2510	2330	2150	1990	1830	1680	1540	1410	1300	1210	2720	2350

⑤ = Target shooting, training, practice

WIND DRIFT IN INCHES 10 MPH CROSSWIND					HEIGHT OF BULLET TRAJECTORY IN INCHES ABOVE OR BELOW LINE OF SIGHT IF ZEROED AT ⊕ YARDS. SIGHTS 1.5 INCHES ABOVE BORE LINE.										TEST BARREL LENGTH INCHES	FEDERAL LOAD NO.
					AVERAGE RANGE				LONG RANGE							
100 YDS.	200 YDS.	300 YDS.	400 YDS.	500 YDS.	50 YDS.	100 YDS.	200 YDS.	300 YDS.	50 YDS.	100 YDS.	200 YDS.	300 YDS.	400 YDS.	500 YDS.		
1.3	5.8	14.2	27.7	47.6	−0.3	⊕	−2.7	−10.8	+0.4	+1.4	⊕	−6.7	−20.5	−43.4	24	P223E
0.8	3.6	8.4	15.8	26.3	−0.4	⊕	−1.7	−7.6	0	+0.9	⊕	−5.0	−15.1	−32.0	24	P22250B
0.6	2.6	6.1	11.3	18.4	−0.2	⊕	−3.1	−11.4	+0.6	+1.5	⊕	−6.8	−19.8	−39.9	24	P243C
0.7	2.7	6.3	11.6	18.8	−0.3	⊕	−2.2	−8.8	+0.2	+1.1	⊕	−5.5	−16.1	−32.8	24	P243D
0.7	3.1	7.3	13.5	22.1	−0.2	⊕	−3.2	−11.9	+0.6	+1.6	⊕	−7.1	−20.9	−42.5	24	P243E
0.8	3.3	7.9	14.7	24.1	−0.3	⊕	−2.9	−11.0	+0.5	+1.4	⊕	−6.7	−19.8	−39.0	24	P6C
0.8	3.3	7.7	14.3	23.5	−0.1	⊕	−3.8	−14.0	+0.8	+1.9	⊕	−8.2	−24.0	−48.9	24	P257B
0.7	2.8	6.5	12.0	19.6	−0.2	⊕	−3.0	−11.4	+0.5	+1.5	⊕	−6.8	−19.9	−40.4	24	P2506C
0.8	3.0	7.0	13.0	20.9	−0.2	⊕	−3.5	−12.8	+0.7	+1.7	⊕	−7.6	−22.1	−44.5	24	P6555A
0.7	2.7	6.3	11.6	18.9	−0.2	⊕	−3.4	−12.5	+0.7	+1.7	⊕	−7.4	−21.4	−43.0	24	P270C
0.7	2.8	6.6	12.1	19.7	−0.2	⊕	−2.8	−10.7	+0.5	+1.4	⊕	−6.5	−19.0	−38.5	24	P270D
0.9	3.9	9.2	17.3	28.5	−0.2	⊕	−3.7	−13.8	+0.8	+1.9	⊕	−8.3	−24.4	−50.5	24	P270E
1.6	7.2	17.7	34.5	58.1	0	⊕	−5.2	−19.8	+1.2	+2.6	⊕	−12.0	−37.6	−81.7	24	P730A
1.3	3.2	8.2	15.4	23.4	−0.1	⊕	−4.3	−15.4	+1.0	+2.1	⊕	−9.0	−26.1	−52.9	24	P7C
0.7	2.6	5.9	11.0	17.7	−0.2	⊕	−3.4	−12.3	+0.7	+1.7	⊕	−7.2	−21.0	−42.0	24	P764A
0.9	3.8	9.0	16.8	27.8	−0.2	⊕	−3.6	−13.4	+0.7	+1.8	⊕	−8.0	−23.8	−49.2	24	P280A
0.5	2.2	5.1	9.3	15.0	−0.3	⊕	−2.6	−9.8	+0.4	+1.3	⊕	−5.9	−17.0	−34.2	24	P7RD
0.5	2.0	4.6	8.4	13.5	−0.2	⊕	−3.0	−10.9	+0.5	+1.5	⊕	−6.4	−18.4	−36.6	24	P7RE
0.6	2.5	5.6	10.4	16.9	−0.2	⊕	−3.1	−11.3	+0.6	+1.5	⊕	−6.7	−19.4	−39.0	24	P7RF
0.6	2.6	6.0	11.1	18.2	−0.3	⊕	−2.6	−9.9	+0.4	+1.3	⊕	−6.0	−17.5	−35.6	24	P7RG
0.9	8.0	19.4	36.7	59.8	−0.3	⊕	−8.3	−29.8	+2.4	+4.1	⊕	−17.4	−52.4	−109.4	24	P3030D
0.7	3.0	7.0	13.0	21.1	−0.1	⊕	−4.0	−14.4	+0.9	+2.0	⊕	−8.4	−24.3	−49.0	24	P308C
0.8	3.3	7.7	14.3	23.3	−0.1	⊕	−4.4	−15.8	+1.0	+2.2	⊕	−9.2	−26.5	−53.6	24	P308E
0.7	2.8	6.6	12.3	19.9	−0.2	⊕	−3.6	−13.2	+0.8	+1.8	⊕	−7.8	−22.4	−45.2	24	P3006D
0.7	3.0	7.3	13.4	27.7	−0.1	⊕	−4.0	−14.6	+0.9	+2.0	⊕	−8.6	−24.6	−49.6	24	P3006F
0.7	3.0	7.1	13.4	22.0	−0.2	⊕	−3.3	−12.4	+0.6	+1.7	⊕	−7.4	−21.5	−43.7	24	P3006G
0.6	2.6	6.0	11.0	17.8	−0.1	⊕	−3.9	−13.9	+0.9	+1.9	⊕	−8.1	−23.1	−46.1	24	P3006L
0.9	3.7	8.8	16.3	27.1	−0.3	⊕	−3.5	−13.3	+0.7	+1.8	⊕	−8.0	−23.4	−48.6	24	P300HA
0.5	2.2	5.0	9.2	14.9	−0.2	⊕	−3.4	−12.2	+0.7	+1.7	⊕	−7.1	−20.4	−40.5	24	P300WC
0.9	3.5	8.4	15.8	25.9	−0.2	⊕	−3.3	−12.4	+0.6	+1.6	⊕	−7.5	−22.1	−45.4	24	P300WD2
0.9	3.4	8.2	15.2	24.9	−0.2	⊕	−3.6	−13.6	+0.8	+1.8	⊕	−8.1	−23.6	−48.3	24	P338A2
1.1	4.5	10.8	20.3	33.6	−0.1	⊕	−4.6	−16.7	+1.1	+2.3	⊕	−9.8	−29.1	−60.2	24	P338B2
0.9	3.7	8.7	16.3	26.7	−0.1	⊕	−4.0	−14.7	+0.9	+2.0	⊕	−8.7	−25.4	−52.1	24	P375C
1.7	7.2	17.6	33.9	56.5	⊕	−1.1	−9.1	−27.5	+0.5	⊕	−7.0	−24.2	−55.8	−106.5	24	P375D
0.9	3.9	9.1	17.0	27.8	0	⊕	−5.0	−17.7	+1.2	+2.5	⊕	−10.3	−29.9	−60.8	24	P375F
2.5	11.0	27.6	52.6	83.9	⊕	−1.5	−11.0	−34.9	+0.1	⊕	−7.5	−29.1	−71.1	−138.0	24	P458A
1.9	7.9	18.9	35.3	56.8	⊕	−1.8	−13.7	−39.7	+0.4	⊕	−9.1	−32.3	−73.9	−138.0	24	P458B
1.5	6.1	14.5	26.9	43.7	⊕	−1.7	−12.9	−36.7	+0.4	⊕	−8.5	−29.5	−66.2	−122.0	24	P458C
1.3	5.7	13.6	25.6	42.3	⊕	−1.2	−9.8	−28.5	+0.6	⊕	−7.4	−24.8	−55.0	−101.6	24	P416A
1.3	5.7	13.6	25.6	42.3	⊕	−1.2	−9.8	−28.5	+0.6	⊕	−7.4	−24.8	−55.0	−101.6	24	P416B
1.6	7.0	16.6	31.1	50.6	⊕	−1.6	−12.6	−36.2	+0.8	⊕	−9.3	−31.3	−69.7	−128.6	24	P470A
1.6	7.0	16.6	31.1	50.6	⊕	−1.6	−12.6	−36.2	+0.8	⊕	−9.3	−31.3	−69.7	−128.6	24	P470B

These trajectory tables were calculated by computer using the best available data for each load. Trajectories are representative of the nominal behavior of each load at standard conditions (59°F temperature; barometric pressure of 29.53 inches; altitude at sea level). Shooters are cautioned that actual trajectories may differ due to variations in altitude, atmospheric conditions, guns, sights, and ammunition.

WIND DRIFT IN INCHES 10 MPH CROSSWIND					HEIGHT OF BULLET TRAJECTORY IN INCHES ABOVE OR BELOW LINE OF SIGHT IF ZEROED AT ⊕ YARDS. SIGHTS 1.5 INCHES ABOVE BORE LINE.										TEST BARREL LENGTH INCHES	FEDERAL LOAD NO.
					AVERAGE RANGE				LONG RANGE							
100 YDS.	200 YDS.	300 YDS.	400 YDS.	500 YDS.	50 YDS.	100 YDS.	200 YDS.	300 YDS.	50 YDS.	100 YDS.	200 YDS.	300 YDS.	400 YDS.	500 YDS.		
1.5	6.5	16.1	32.3	56.9	−0.4	⊕	−2.4	−10.7	+0.2	+1.2	⊕	−7.1	−23.4	−54.2	24	P223V
1.3	5.7	14.0	27.9	49.2	−0.4	⊕	−1.7	−8.1	0	+0.8	⊕	−5.6	−18.4	−42.8	24	P22250V
1.1	4.8	11.7	22.6	38.7	−0.4	⊕	−2.1	−9.2	+0.2	+1.1	⊕	−6.0	−18.9	−41.6	24	P243V
1.0	4.1	9.8	18.7	31.3	−0.3	⊕	−2.3	−9.4	+0.2	+1.1	⊕	−6.0	−18.3	−39.2	24	P2506V

ENERGY IN FOOT/POUNDS (TO NEAREST 5 FOOT/POUNDS)									WIND DRIFT IN INCHES 10 MPH CROSSWIND										HEIGHT OF BULLET TRAJECTORY IN INCHES ABOVE OR BELOW LINE OF SIGHT IF ZEROED AT ⊕ YARDS. SIGHTS 1.5 INCHES ABOVE BORE LINE.									
200 YDS.	300 YDS.	400 YDS.	500 YDS.	600 YDS.	700 YDS.	800 YDS.	900 YDS.	1000 YDS.	100 YDS.	200 YDS.	300 YDS.	400 YDS.	500 YDS.	600 YDS.	700 YDS.	800 YDS.	900 YDS.	1000 YDS.	100 YDS.	200 YDS.	300 YDS.	400 YDS.	500 YDS.	600 YDS.	700 YDS.	800 YDS.	900 YDS.	1000 YDS.
925	750	600	475	375	295	235	195	170	0.9	3.7	8.7	16.3	27.0	41.3	59.5	82.2	109.2	140.0	+1.6	⊕	−7.4	−21.9	−45.3	−79.8	−128.7	−194.1	−280.2	−388.7
1870	1600	1355	1150	970	815	690	590	510	0.8	3.1	7.4	13.6	22.2	33.3	47.1	64.1	84.2	107.5	+17.5	+30.5	+36.6	+34.5	+22.9	⊕	−36.1	−87.8	−157.5	−247.4
2025	1730	1470	1245	1050	880	740	630	540	0.7	3.0	7.0	13.0	21.2	31.8	45.1	61.5	81.0	103.6	+16.1	+28.1	+33.8	+31.9	+21.1	⊕	−33.4	−81.3	−146.0	−230.1

FEDERAL BALLISTICS

CLASSIC® AUTOMATIC PISTOL BALLISTICS (Approximate)

Usage Key: [1]=Varmints, predators, small game [2]=Medium game [3]=Self defense [4]=Target shooting, training, practice

USAGE	FEDERAL LOAD NO.	CALIBER	BULLET WGT. IN GRAINS	GRAMS	BULLET STYLE**	FACTORY PRIMER NO.	VELOCITY IN FEET PER SECOND					ENERGY IN FOOT/POUNDS					MID-RANGE TRAJECTORY				TEST BARREL LENGTH INCHES
							MUZZLE	25 YDS.	50 YDS.	75 YDS.	100 YDS.	MUZZLE	25 YDS.	50 YDS.	75 YDS.	100 YDS.	25 YDS.	50 YDS.	75 YDS.	100 YDS.	
[3],[4]	25AP	25 Auto (6.35mm Browning)	50	3.24	Full Metal Jacket	100	760	750	730	720	700	65	60	59	55	55	0.5	1.9	4.5	8.1	2
[3],[4]	32AP	32 Auto (7.65mm Browning)	71	4.60	Full Metal Jacket	100	905	880	855	830	810	129	20	115	110	105	0.3	1.4	3.2	5.9	4
[3],[4]	380AP	380 Auto (9x17mm Short)	95	6.15	Full Metal Jacket	100	955	910	865	830	790	190	175	160	145	130	0.3	1.3	3.1	5.9	3¾
[3]	380BP	380 Auto (9x17mm Short)	90	5.83	Hi-Shok JHP	100	1000	940	890	840	800	200	175	160	140	130	0.3	1.2	2.9	5.5	3¾
[3],[4]	9AP	9mm Luger (9x19mm Parabellum)	124	8.03	Full Metal Jacket	100	1120	1070	1030	990	960	345	315	290	270	255	0.2	0.9	2.2	4.1	4
[3]	9BP	9mm Luger (9x19mm Parabellum)	115	7.45	Hi-Shok JHP	100	1160	1100	1060	1020	990	345	310	285	270	250	0.2	0.9	2.1	3.8	4
[3]	40SWA	40 S&W	180	11.06	Hi-Shok JHP	100	985	955	930	905	885	390	365	345	330	315	0.3	1.2	2.8	5.0	4
[3] NEW	40SWB	40 S&W	155	10.04	Hi-Shok JHP	100	1140	1080	1030	990	950	445	400	365	335	315	0.2	0.9	2.2	4.1	4
[3]	10C	10mm Auto	180	11.06	Hi-Shok JHP	150	1030	995	970	945	920	425	400	375	355	340	0.3	1.1	2.5	4.7	5
[3] NEW	10E	10mm Auto	155	10.04	Hi-Shok JHP	150	1325	1225	1140	1075	1025	605	515	450	400	360	0.2	0.7	1.8	3.3	5
[3]	45A	45 Auto	230	14.90	Full Metal Jacket	150	850	830	810	790	770	370	350	335	320	305	0.4	1.6	3.6	6.6	5
[4]	45C	45 Auto	185	11.99	Hi-Shok JHP	150	950	920	900	880	860	370	350	335	315	300	0.3	1.3	2.9	5.3	5
[3] NEW	45D*	45 Auto	230	14.90	Hi-Shok JHP	150	850	830	810	790	770	370	350	335	320	300	0.4	1.6	3.7	6.7	5

*Available 3/92.

CLASSIC® REVOLVER BALLISTICS (Approximate)

USAGE	FEDERAL LOAD NO.	CALIBER	BULLET WGT. GRAINS	GRAMS	BULLET STYLE**	FACTORY PRIMER NO.	VELOCITY IN FEET PER SECOND					ENERGY IN FOOT/POUNDS					MID-RANGE TRAJECTORY				TEST BARREL LENGTH INCHES
							MUZZLE	25 YDS.	50 YDS.	75 YDS.	100 YDS.	MUZZLE	25 YDS.	50 YDS.	75 YDS.	100 YDS.	25 YDS.	50 YDS.	75 YDS.	100 YDS.	
[4]	32LA	32 S&W Long	98	6.35	Lead Wadcutter	100	780	700	630	560	500	130	105	85	70	55	0.5	2.2	5.6	11.1	4
[4]	32LB	32 S&W Long	98	6.35	Lead Round Nose	100	705	690	670	650	640	115	105	98	95	90	0.6	2.3	5.3	9.6	4
[3]	32HRA	32 H&R Magnum	95	6.15	Lead Semi-Wadcutter	100	1030	1000	940	930	900	225	210	190	185	170	0.3	1.1	2.5	4.7	4½
[3]	32HRB	32 H&R Magnum	85	5.50	Hi-Shok JHP	100	1100	1050	1020	970	930	230	210	195	175	165	0.2	1.0	2.3	4.3	4½
[4]	38B	38 Special	158	10.23	Lead Round Nose	100	755	740	723	710	690	200	190	183	175	170	0.5	2.0	4.6	8.3	4-V
[3],[4]	38C	38 Special	158	10.23	Lead Semi-Wadcutter	100	755	740	723	710	690	200	190	183	175	170	0.5	2.0	4.6	8.3	4-V
[1],[3]	38E	38 Special (High Velocity +P)	125	8.10	Hi-Shok JHP	100	945	920	898	880	860	248	235	224	215	205	0.3	1.3	2.9	5.4	4-V
[1],[3]	38F	38 Special (High Velocity +P)	110	7.13	Hi-Shok JHP	100	995	960	926	900	870	242	225	210	195	185	0.3	1.2	2.7	5.0	4-V
[3],[4]	38G	38 Special (High Velocity +P)	158	10.23	Semi-Wadcutter HP	100	890	870	855	840	820	278	265	257	245	235	0.3	1.4	3.3	5.9	4-V
[3],[4]	38H	38 Special (High Velocity +P)	158	10.23	Lead Semi-Wadcutter	100	890	870	855	840	820	270	265	257	245	235	0.3	1.4	3.3	5.9	4-V
[1],[3]	38J	38 Special (High Velocity +P)	125	8.10	Hi-Shok JSP	100	945	920	898	880	860	248	235	224	215	205	0.3	1.3	2.9	5.4	4-V
[2],[3]	357A	357 Magnum	158	10.23	Hi-Shok JSP	100	1235	1160	1104	1060	1020	535	475	428	395	365	0.2	0.8	1.9	3.5	4-V
[1],[3]	357B	357 Magnum	125	8.10	Hi-Shok JHP	100	1450	1350	1240	1160	1100	583	495	427	370	335	0.1	0.6	1.5	2.8	4-V
[4]	357C	357 Magnum	158	10.23	Lead Semi-Wadcutter	100	1235	1160	1104	1060	1020	535	475	428	395	365	0.2	0.8	1.9	3.5	4-V
[1],[3]	357D	357 Magnum	110	7.13	Hi-Shok JHP	100	1295	1180	1094	1040	990	410	340	292	260	235	0.2	0.8	1.9	3.5	4-V
[2],[3]	357E	357 Magnum	158	10.23	Hi-Shok JHP	100	1235	1160	1104	1060	1020	535	475	428	395	365	0.2	0.8	1.9	3.5	4-V
[2]	357G	357 Magnum	180	11.66	Hi-Shok JHP	100	1090	1030	980	930	890	475	425	385	350	320	0.2	1.0	2.4	4.5	4-V
[1],[3]	41A	41 Rem. Magnum	210	13.60	Hi-Shok JHP	150	1300	1210	1130	1070	1030	790	680	595	540	495	0.2	0.7	1.8	3.3	4-V
[1],[3]	44SA	44 S&W Special	200	12.96	Semi-Wadcutter HP	150	900	860	830	800	770	360	330	305	285	260	0.3	1.4	3.4	6.3	6½-V
[2],[3]	44A	44 Rem. Magnum	240	15.55	Hi-Shok JHP	150	1180	1130	1081	1050	1010	741	675	623	580	550	0.2	0.9	2.0	3.7	6½-V
[1],[2]	44B*	44 Rem. Magnum	180	11.66	Hi-Shok JHP	150	1610	1480	1365	1270	1180	1035	875	750	640	555	0.1	0.5	1.2	2.3	6½-V
[1],[3]	45LCA	45 Colt	225	14.58	Semi-Wadcutter HP	150	900	880	860	840	820	405	385	369	355	340	0.3	1.4	3.2	5.8	5½

+P ammunition is loaded to a higher pressure. Use only in firearms so recommended by the gun manufacturer. "V" indicates vented barrel to simulate service conditions.
*Also available in 20-round box (A44R20).

MATCH PISTOL AND REVOLVER BALLISTICS (Approximate)

USAGE	FEDERAL LOAD NO.	CALIBER	BULLET WGT. IN GRAINS	GRAMS	BULLET STYLE**	FACTORY PRIMER NO.	VELOCITY IN FEET PER SECOND					ENERGY IN FOOT/POUNDS					MID-RANGE TRAJECTORY				TEST BARREL LENGTH INCHES
							MUZZLE	25 YDS.	50 YDS.	75 YDS.	100 YDS.	MUZZLE	25 YDS.	50 YDS.	75 YDS.	100 YDS.	25 YDS.	50 YDS.	75 YDS.	100 YDS.	
[4]	9MP	9mm Luger (9x19mm Parabellum)	124	8.03	FMJ-SWC Match	100	1120	1070	1030	990	960	345	315	290	270	255	0.2	0.9	2.2	4.1	4
[4]	38A	38 Special	148	9.59	Lead Wadcutter Match	100	710	670	634	600	560	166	150	132	115	105	0.6	2.4	5.7	10.8	4-V
[4]	44D	44 Rem. Magnum	250	16.20	MC Profile Match*	150	1180	1140	1100	1070	1040	775	715	670	630	600	0.2	0.8	1.9	3.6	6½-V
[4]	45A	45 Auto	230	14.90	FMJ-Match	150	850	830	810	790	770	370	350	335	320	305	0.4	1.6	3.6	6.6	5
[4]	45B	45 Auto	185	11.99	FMJ-SWC Match	150	775	730	695	660	620	247	220	200	175	160	0.5	2.0	4.8	9.0	5

*MC Profile Match = Metal Case Profile Match
**JHP = Jacketed Hollow Point   HP = Hollow Point   JSP = Jacketed Soft Point   FMJ = Full Metal Jacket   SWC = Semi-Wadcutter

FEDERAL BALLISTICS

NYCLAD® PISTOL AND REVOLVER BALLISTICS (Approximate)

Usage Key: ①=Varmints, predators, small game ②=Medium game ③=Self defense ④=Target shooting, training, practice

USAGE	FEDERAL LOAD NO.	CALIBER	BULLET WGT. IN GRAINS	GRAMS	BULLET STYLE*	FACTORY PRIMER NO.	VELOCITY IN FEET PER SECOND MUZZLE	25 YDS.	50 YDS.	75 YDS.	100 YDS.	ENERGY IN FOOT/POUNDS MUZZLE	25 YDS.	50 YDS.	75 YDS.	100 YDS.	MID-RANGE TRAJECTORY 25 YDS.	50 YDS.	75 YDS.	100 YDS.	TEST BARREL LENGTH INCHES
①	P9BP	9mm Luger (9x19mm Parabellum)	124	8.03	Nyclad Hollow Point	100	1120	1070	1030	990	960	345	315	290	270	255	0.2	0.9	2.2	4.1	4
④	P38B	38 Special	158	10.23	Nyclad Round Nose	100	755	740	723	710	690	200	190	183	175	170	0.5	2.0	4.6	8.3	4-V
①,③	P38G	38 Special (High Velocity +P)	158	10.23	Nyclad SWC-HP	100	890	870	855	840	820	270	265	257	245	235	0.3	1.4	3.3	5.9	4-V
③	P38M	38 Special	125	8.10	Nyclad Hollow Point	100	825	780	730	690	650	190	170	150	130	115	0.4	1.8	4.3	8.1	2-V
①,③	P38N	38 Special (High Velocity +P)	125	8.10	Nyclad Hollow Point	100	945	920	898	880	860	248	235	224	215	205	0.3	1.3	2.9	5.4	4-V
②,③	P357E	357 Magnum	158	10.23	Nyclad SWC-HP	100	1235	1160	1104	1060	1020	535	475	428	395	365	0.2	0.8	1.9	3.5	4-V

HYDRA-SHOK® PISTOL AND REVOLVER BALLISTICS (Approximate)

USAGE	FEDERAL LOAD NO.	CALIBER	BULLET WGT. IN GRAINS	GRAMS	BULLET STYLE*	FACTORY PRIMER NO.	VELOCITY IN FEET PER SECOND MUZZLE	25 YDS.	50 YDS.	75 YDS.	100 YDS.	ENERGY IN FOOT/POUNDS MUZZLE	25 YDS.	50 YDS.	75 YDS.	100 YDS.	MID-RANGE TRAJECTORY 25 YDS.	50 YDS.	75 YDS.	100 YDS.	TEST BARREL LENGTH INCHES
③	P380HS1	380 Auto (9x17mm Short)	90	5.83	Hydra-Shok HP	100	1000	940	890	840	800	200	175	160	140	130	0.3	1.2	2.9	5.5	3¾
③	P9HS1	9mm Luger (9x19mm Parabellum)	124	8.03	Hydra-Shok HP	100	1120	1070	1030	990	960	345	315	290	270	255	0.2	0.9	2.2	4.1	4
③	P9HS2	9mm Luger (9x19mm Parabellum)	147	9.52	Hydra-Shok HP	100	975	940	910	885	860	310	290	270	255	240	0.3	1.2	2.9	5.3	4
③	P40HS1	40 S&W	180	11.06	Hydra-Shok HP	100	985	955	930	910	890	390	365	345	330	315	0.3	1.2	2.8	5.0	4
③	P10HS1	10mm Auto	180	11.06	Hydra-Shok HP	150	1030	995	970	945	920	425	400	375	355	340	0.3	1.1	2.5	4.7	5
③	P45HS1	45 Auto	230	14.90	Hydra-Shok HP	150	850	830	810	790	770	370	350	335	320	305	0.4	1.6	3.6	6.6	5
③	P38HS1	38 Special (High Velocity +P)	129	8.36	Hydra-Shok HP	100	945	930	910	890	870	255	245	235	225	215	0.3	1.3	2.9	5.3	4-V
③	P357HS1	357 Magnum	158	10.23	Hydra-Shok HP	100	1235	1160	1104	1060	1020	535	475	428	395	365	0.2	0.8	1.9	3.5	4-V
③	P44HS1	44 Rem. Magnum	240	15.55	Hydra-Shok HP	150	1180	1130	1081	1050	1010	741	675	623	580	550	0.2	0.9	2.0	3.7	6½-V

+P ammunition is loaded to a higher pressure. Use only in firearms so recommended by the gun manufacturer.   "V" indicates vented barrel to simulate service conditions.
*HP = Hollow Point   SWC = Semi-Wadcutter

CLASSIC® 22 MAGNUM BALLISTICS (Approximate)

TYPE	FEDERAL LOAD NO.	CARTRIDGE PER BOX	CALIBER	BULLET WGT. IN GRAINS	BULLET STYLE*	VELOCITY IN FEET PER SECOND MUZZLE	50 YDS.	100 YDS.	150 YDS.	ENERGY IN FOOT/POUNDS MUZZLE	50 YDS.	100 YDS.	150 YDS.	WIND DRIFT IN INCHES 10 MPH CROSSWIND 50 YDS.	100 YDS.	150 YDS.	HEIGHT OF BULLET TRAJECTORY IN INCHES ABOVE OR BELOW LINE OF SIGHT IF ZEROED AT ⊕ YARDS. SIGHTS 1.5 INCHES ABOVE BORE LINE. 50 YDS.	100 YDS.	150 YDS.	50 YDS.	100 YDS.	150 YDS.
Magnum	757	50	22 Win. Magnum	50	Jacketed HP	1650	1450	1280	1150	300	235	180	145	1.1	4.5	10.3	⊕	−3.6	−12.5	+1.3	⊕	−6.5
Magnum	737	50	22 Win. Magnum	40	Full Metal Jacket	1910	1600	1330	1140	325	225	155	115	1.3	5.7	13.4	⊕	−2.9	−10.7	+1.0	⊕	−5.8

CLASSIC® 22 CARTRIDGE BALLISTICS (Approximate)

	TYPE	FEDERAL LOAD NO.	CARTRIDGE PER BOX	CALIBER	BULLET WGT. IN GRAINS	BULLET STYLE*	VELOCITY IN FEET PER SECOND MUZZLE	50 YDS.	100 YDS.	150 YDS.	ENERGY IN FOOT/POUNDS MUZZLE	50 YDS.	100 YDS.	150 YDS.	WIND DRIFT IN INCHES 10 MPH CROSSWIND 50 YDS.	100 YDS.	150 YDS.	HEIGHT OF BULLET TRAJECTORY IN INCHES ABOVE OR BELOW LINE OF SIGHT IF ZEROED AT ⊕ YARDS. SIGHTS 1.5 INCHES ABOVE BORE LINE. 50 YDS.	100 YDS.	150 YDS.	50 YDS.	100 YDS.	150 YDS.
Std. Vel.	Classic	711	50	22 Long Rifle	40	Solid	1150	1050	975	910	117	95	85	75	1.2	4.4	9.4	⊕	−7.3	−23.6	+3.2	⊕	−12.1
High Velocity	Classic	710	50	22 Long Rifle HV	40	Solid, Copper Plated	1255	1100	1015	940	140	110	92	80	1.5	5.5	11.4	⊕	−6.5	−21.0	+2.7	⊕	−10.8
	Classic	810	100	22 Long Rifle HV	40	Solid, Copper Plated	1255	1100	1015	940	140	110	92	80	1.5	5.5	11.4	⊕	−6.5	−21.0	+2.7	⊕	−10.8
	Classic	712	50	22 Long Rifle HV	38	HP Copper Plated	1280	1120	1020	950	138	105	88	75	1.6	5.8	12.1	⊕	−6.3	−20.6	+2.7	⊕	−10.6
Shot	Classic	716	50	22 Long Rifle Shot	25	No. 12 Lead Shot	—	—	—	—	—	—	—	—	—	—	—	—	—	—	—	—	—

These ballistic specifications were derived from test barrels 24 inches in length.   *HP = Hollow Point

Lightning™ Rimfire 22   (Approximate)

	TYPE	FEDERAL LOAD NO.	CARTRIDGE PER BOX	CALIBER	BULLET WGT. IN GRAINS	BULLET STYLE	VELOCITY IN FEET PER SECOND MUZZLE	50 YDS.	100 YDS.	150 YDS.	ENERGY IN FOOT/POUNDS MUZZLE	50 YDS.	100 YDS.	150 YDS.	WIND DRIFT IN INCHES 10 MPH CROSSWIND 50 YDS.	100 YDS.	150 YDS.	HEIGHT OF BULLET TRAJECTORY IN INCHES ABOVE OR BELOW LINE OF SIGHT IF ZEROED AT ⊕ YARDS. SIGHTS 1.5 INCHES ABOVE BORE LINE. 50 YDS.	100 YDS.	150 YDS.	50 YDS.	100 YDS.	150 YDS.
High Vel.	Lightning	510	50	22 Long Rifle HV	40	Solid	1255	1100	1015	940	140	110	92	80	1.5	5.5	11.4	⊕	-6.5	-21.0	+2.7	⊕	-10.8

REMINGTON BALLISTICS
CENTERFIRE RIFLE

REMINGTON BALLISTICS

CALIBER	REMINGTON Order No.	Wt.-Grs.	Style	Primer No.	Muzzle	100 Yds.	200 Yds.	300 Yds.	400 Yds.	500 Yds.
17 REM.	R17REM	25*	Hollow Point Power-Lokt®	7½	4040	3284	2644	2086	1606	1235
22 HORNET	R22HN1	45*	Pointed Soft Point	6½	2690	2042	1502	1128	948	840
	R22HN2	45	Hollow Point	6½	2690	2042	1502	1128	948	840
220 SWIFT	R220S1★	50*	Pointed Soft Point	9½	3780	3158	2617	2135	1710	1357
222 REM.	R222R1	50	Pointed Soft Point	7½	3140	2602	2123	1700	1350	1107
	R222R3	50*	Hollow Point Power-Lokt®	7½	3140	2635	2182	1777	1432	1172
222 REM. MAG.	R222M1	55*	Pointed Soft Point	7½	3240	2748	2305	1906	1556	1272
223 REM.	R223R1	55	Pointed Soft Point	7½	3240	2747	2304	1905	1554	1270
	R223R2	55*	Hollow Point Power-Lokt®	7½	3240	2773	2352	1969	1627	1341
	R223R3	55	Metal Case	7½	3240	2759	2326	1933	1587	1301
	R223R4	60	Hollow Point Match	7½	3100	2712	2355	2026	1726	1463
22-250 REM.	R22501	55*	Pointed Soft Point	9½	3680	3137	2656	2222	1832	1493
	R22502	55	Hollow Point Power-Lokt®	9½	3680	3209	2785	2400	2046	1725
243 WIN.	R243W1	80	Pointed Soft Point	9½	3350	2955	2593	2259	1951	1670
	R243W2	80*	Hollow Point Power-Lokt®	9½	3350	2955	2593	2259	1951	1670
	R243W3	100	Pointed Soft Point Core-Lokt®	9½	2960	2697	2449	2215	1993	1786
	ER243WA★	105	Extended Range	9½	2920	2689	2470	2261	2062	1874
6MM REM.	R6MM1	80‡	Pointed Soft Point	9½	3470	3064	2694	2352	2036	1747
	R6MM2§	80‡	Hollow Point Power-Lokt®	9½	3470	3064	2694	2352	2036	1747
	R6MM4	100*	Pointed Soft Point Core-Lokt®	9½	3100	2829	2573	2332	2104	1889
	ER6MMRA★	105	Extended Range	9½	3060	2822	2596	2381	2177	1982
6MM BR REM.	R6MMBR	100	Pointed Soft Point	7½	2550	2310	2083	1870	1671	1491
25-20 WIN.	R25202	86*	Soft Point	6½	1460	1194	1030	931	858	797
250 SAV.	R250SV	100*	Pointed Soft Point	9½	2820	2504	2210	1936	1684	1461
257 ROBERTS	R257	117	Soft Point Core-Lokt®	9½	2650	2291	1961	1663	1404	1199
	ER257A★	122	Extended Range	9½	2600	2331	2078	1842	1625	1431
25-06 REM.	R25062	100*	Pointed Soft Point Core-Lokt®	9½	3230	2893	2580	2287	2014	1762
	R25063	120	Pointed Soft Point Core-Lokt®	9½	2990	2730	2484	2252	2032	1825
	ER2506A★	122	Extended Range	9½	2930	2706	2492	2289	2095	1911
264 WIN. MAG.	R264W2	140*	Pointed Soft Point Core-Lokt®	9½M	3030	2782	2548	2326	2114	1914
270 WIN.	R270W1	100	Pointed Soft Point	9½	3320	2924	2561	2225	1916	1636
	R270W2	130*	Pointed Soft Point Core-Lokt®	9½	3060	2776	2510	2259	2022	1801
	R270W3	130	Bronze Point™	9½	3060	2802	2559	2329	2110	1904
	R270W4	150	Soft Point Core-Lokt®	9½	2850	2504	2183	1886	1618	1385
	ER270WA	140	Extended Range Boat Tail	9½	2960	2749	2548	2355	2171	1995
7MM BR REM.	R7MMBR	140*	Pointed Soft Point	7½	2215	2012	1821	1643	1481	1336
7MM MAUSER (7x57)	R7MSR1	140*	Pointed Soft Point	9½	2660	2435	2221	2018	1827	1648
7MM-08 REM.	R7M081	140	Pointed Soft Point	9½	2860	2625	2402	2189	1988	1798
	R7M083	120*	Hollow Point	9½	3000	2725	2467	2223	1992	1778
	ER7M08A★	154	Extended Range	9½	2715	2510	2315	2128	1950	1781
280 REM.†	R280R3	140	Pointed Soft Point	9½	3000	2758	2528	2309	2102	1905
	R280R1	150	Pointed Soft Point Core-Lokt®	9½	2890	2624	2373	2135	1912	1705
	R280R2	165	Soft Point Core-Lokt®	9½	2820	2510	2220	1950	1701	1479
	R280R4§	120*	Hollow Point	9½	3150	2866	2599	2348	2110	1887
	ER280RA	165	Extended Range	9½	2820	2623	2434	2253	2080	1915
7MM REM. MAG.	R7MM2	150	Pointed Soft Point Core-Lokt®	9½M	3110	2830	2568	2320	2085	1866
	R7MM3	175	Pointed Soft Point Core-Lokt®	9½M	2860	2645	2440	2244	2057	1879
	R7MM4	140*	Pointed Soft Point	9½M	3175	2923	2684	2458	2243	2039
	ER7MMA	165	Extended Range	9½M	2900	2699	2507	2324	2147	1979
7MM WBY. MAG.	R7MWB1	140	Pointed Soft Point	9½M	3225	2970	2729	2501	2283	2077
	R7MWB2	175	Pointed Soft Point Core-Lokt®	9½M	2910	2693	2486	2288	2098	1918
	ER7MWB4★	165	Extended Range	9½M	2950	2747	2553	2367	2189	2019
30 CARBINE	R30CAR	110*	Soft Point	6½	1990	1567	1236	1035	923	842
30 REM.	R30REM	170*	Soft Point Core-Lokt®	9½	2120	1822	1555	1328	1153	1036
30-30 WIN. ACCELERATOR®	R3030A	55*	Soft Point	9½	3400	2693	2085	1570	1187	986
30-30 WIN.	R30301	150*	Soft Point Core-Lokt®	9½	2390	1973	1605	1303	1095	974
	R30302	170	Soft Point Core-Lokt®	9½	2200	1895	1619	1381	1191	1061
	R30303	170	Hollow Point Core-Lokt®	9½	2200	1895	1619	1381	1191	1061
300 SAVAGE	R30SV3	180*	Soft Point Core-Lokt®	9½	2350	2025	1728	1467	1252	1098
	R30SV2	150	Pointed Soft Point Core-Lokt®	9½	2630	2354	2095	1853	1631	1432

★NEW FOR 1992. *Specifications are nominal. Ballistics figures established in test barrels. Individual rifles may* †280 Rem. and 7mm Express™ Rem. are interchangeable. ‡*Interchangeable in 244 Rem.* §*Subject to stock on hand.*

REMINGTON BALLISTICS
CENTERFIRE RIFLE

TRAJECTORY** 0.0 indicates yardage at which rifle was sighted in.

ENERGY FOOT-POUNDS — columns: Muzzle, 100, 200, 300, 400, 500 Yds.
SHORT RANGE — Bullet does not rise more than one inch above line of sight from muzzle to sighting-in range. Columns: 50, 100, 150, 200, 250, 300 Yds.
LONG RANGE — Bullet does not rise more than three inches above line of sight from muzzle to sighting-in range. Columns: 100, 150, 200, 250, 300, 400, 500 Yds.

Muzzle	100	200	300	400	500	50	100	150	200	250	300	100	150	200	250	300	400	500	Barrel
906	599	388	242	143	85	0.1	0.5	0.0	-1.5	-4.2	-8.5	2.1	2.5	1.9	0.0	-3.4	-17.0	-44.3	24"
723	417	225	127	90	70	0.3	0.0	-2.4	-7.7	-16.9	-31.3	1.6	0.0	-4.5	-12.8	-26.4	-75.6	-163.4	24"
723	417	225	127	90	70	0.3	0.0	-2.4	-7.7	-16.9	-31.3	1.6	0.0	-4.5	-12.8	-26.4	-75.6	-163.4	
1586	1107	760	506	325	204	0.2	0.5	0.0	-1.6	-4.4	-8.8	1.3	1.2	0.0	-2.5	-6.5	-20.7	-47.0	24"
1094	752	500	321	202	136	0.5	0.9	0.0	-2.5	-6.9	-13.7	2.2	1.9	0.0	-3.8	-10.0	-32.3	-73.8	24"
1094	771	529	351	228	152	0.5	0.9	0.0	-2.4	-6.6	-13.1	2.1	1.8	0.0	-3.6	-9.5	-30.2	-68.1	
1282	922	649	444	296	198	0.4	0.8	0.0	-2.2	-6.0	-11.8	1.9	1.6	0.0	-3.3	-8.5	-26.7	-59.5	24"
1282	921	648	443	295	197	0.4	0.8	0.0	-2.2	-6.0	-11.8	1.9	1.6	0.0	-3.3	-8.5	-26.7	-59.6	24"
1282	939	675	473	323	220	0.4	0.8	0.0	-2.1	-5.8	-11.4	1.8	1.6	0.0	-3.2	-8.2	-25.5	-56.0	
1282	929	660	456	307	207	0.4	0.8	0.0	-2.1	-5.9	-11.6	1.9	1.6	0.0	-3.2	-8.4	-26.2	-57.9	
1280	979	739	547	397	285	0.5	0.8	0.0	-2.2	-6.0	-11.5	1.9	1.6	0.0	-3.2	-8.3	-25.1	-53.6	
1654	1201	861	603	410	272	0.2	0.5	0.0	-1.6	-4.4	-8.7	2.3	2.6	1.9	0.0	-3.4	-15.9	-38.9	24"
1654	1257	947	703	511	363	0.2	0.5	0.0	-1.5	-4.1	-8.0	2.1	2.5	1.8	0.0	-3.1	-14.1	-33.4	
1993	1551	1194	906	676	495	0.3	0.7	0.0	-1.8	-4.9	-9.4	2.6	2.9	2.1	0.0	-3.6	-16.2	-37.9	24"
1993	1551	1194	906	676	495	0.3	0.7	0.0	-1.8	-4.9	-9.4	2.6	2.9	2.1	0.0	-3.6	-16.2	-37.9	
1945	1615	1332	1089	882	708	0.5	0.9	0.0	-2.2	-5.8	-11.0	1.9	1.6	0.0	-3.1	-7.8	-22.6	-46.3	
1988	1686	1422	1192	992	819	0.5	0.9	0.0	-2.2	-5.8	-11.0	2.0	1.6	0.0	-3.1	-7.7	-22.2	-44.8	
2139	1667	1289	982	736	542	0.3	0.6	0.0	-1.6	-4.5	-8.7	2.4	2.7	1.9	0.0	-3.3	-14.9	-35.0	24"
2139	1667	1289	982	736	542	0.3	0.6	0.0	-1.6	-4.5	-8.7	2.4	2.7	1.9	0.0	-3.3	-14.9	-35.0	
2133	1777	1470	1207	983	792	0.4	0.8	0.0	-1.9	-5.2	-9.9	1.7	1.5	0.0	-2.8	-7.0	-20.4	-41.7	
2183	1856	1571	1322	1105	916	0.4	0.8	0.0	-2.0	-5.2	-9.8	1.7	1.5	0.0	-2.7	-6.9	-20.0	-40.4	
1444	1185	963	776	620	494	0.3	0.0	-1.9	-5.6	-11.4	-19.3	2.8	2.3	0.0	-4.3	-10.9	-31.7	-65.1	15"
407	272	203	165	141	121	0.0	-4.1	-14.4	-31.8	-57.3	-92.0	0.0	-8.2	-23.5	-47.0	-79.6	-175.9	-319.4	24"
1765	1392	1084	832	630	474	0.2	0.0	-1.6	-4.7	-9.6	-16.5	2.3	2.0	0.0	-3.7	-9.5	-28.3	-59.5	24"
1824	1363	999	718	512	373	0.3	0.0	-1.9	-5.8	-11.9	-20.7	2.9	2.4	0.0	-4.7	-12.0	-36.7	-79.2	24"
1831	1472	1170	919	715	555	0.3	0.0	-1.9	-5.5	-11.2	-19.1	2.8	2.3	0.0	-4.3	-10.9	-32.0	-66.4	
2316	1858	1478	1161	901	689	0.4	0.7	0.0	-1.9	-5.0	-9.7	1.6	1.4	0.0	-2.7	-6.9	-20.5	-42.7	24"
2382	1985	1644	1351	1100	887	0.5	0.8	0.0	-2.1	-5.6	-10.7	1.9	1.6	0.0	-3.0	-7.5	-22.0	-44.8	
2325	1983	1683	1419	1189	989	0.5	0.9	0.0	-2.2	-5.7	-10.8	1.9	1.6	0.0	-3.0	-7.5	-21.7	-43.9	
2854	2406	2018	1682	1389	1139	0.5	0.8	0.0	-2.0	-5.4	-10.2	1.8	1.5	0.0	-2.9	-7.2	-20.8	-42.2	24"
2448	1898	1456	1099	815	594	0.3	0.7	0.0	-1.8	-5.0	-9.7	2.7	3.0	2.2	0.0	-3.7	-16.6	-39.1	24"
2702	2225	1818	1472	1180	936	0.5	0.8	0.0	-2.0	-5.5	-10.4	1.8	1.5	0.0	-2.9	-7.4	-21.6	-44.3	
2702	2267	1890	1565	1285	1046	0.4	0.8	0.0	-2.0	-5.3	-10.1	1.8	1.5	0.0	-2.8	-7.1	-20.6	-42.0	
2705	2087	1587	1185	872	639	0.7	1.0	0.0	-2.6	-7.1	-13.6	2.3	2.0	0.0	-3.8	-9.7	-29.2	-62.2	
2723	2349	2018	1724	1465	1237	0.5	0.8	0.0	-2.1	-5.5	-10.3	1.9	1.5	0.0	-2.9	-7.2	-20.7	-41.6	
1525	1259	1031	839	681	555	0.5	0.0	-2.7	-7.7	-15.4	-25.9	1.8	0.0	-4.1	-10.9	-20.6	-50.0	-95.2	15"
2199	1843	1533	1266	1037	844	0.2	0.0	-1.7	-5.0	-10.0	-17.0	2.5	2.0	0.0	-3.8	-9.6	-27.7	-56.3	24"
2542	2142	1793	1490	1228	1005	0.6	0.9	0.0	-2.3	-6.1	-11.6	2.1	1.7	0.0	-3.2	-8.1	-23.5	-47.7	24"
2398	1979	1621	1316	1058	842	0.5	0.8	0.0	-2.1	-5.7	-10.8	1.9	1.6	0.0	-3.0	-7.6	-22.3	-45.8	
2520	2155	1832	1548	1300	1085	0.7	1.0	0.0	-2.5	-6.7	-12.6	2.3	1.9	0.0	3.6	8.8	25.3	-51.0	
2797	2363	1986	1657	1373	1128	0.5	0.8	0.0	-2.1	-5.5	-10.4	1.8	1.5	0.0	-2.9	-7.3	-21.1	-42.9	24"
2781	2293	1875	1518	1217	968	0.6	0.9	0.0	-2.3	-6.2	-11.8	2.1	1.7	0.0	-3.3	-8.3	-24.2	-49.7	
2913	2308	1805	1393	1060	801	0.2	0.0	-1.5	-4.6	-9.5	-16.4	2.3	1.9	0.0	3.7	9.4	-28.1	-58.8	
2643	2188	1800	1468	1186	949	0.4	0.7	0.0	-1.9	-5.1	-9.7	2.8	3.0	2.2	0.0	-3.6	-15.7	-35.6	
2913	2520	2171	1860	1585	1343	0.6	0.9	0.0	-2.3	-6.1	-11.4	2.1	1.7	0.0	-3.2	-8.0	-22.8	-45.6	
3221	2667	2196	1792	1448	1160	0.4	0.8	0.0	-1.9	-5.2	-9.9	1.8	1.5	0.0	-2.8	-7.0	-20.5	-42.1	24"
3178	2718	2313	1956	1644	1372	0.6	0.9	0.0	-2.3	-6.0	-11.3	2.0	1.7	0.0	-3.2	-7.9	-22.7	-45.8	
3133	2655	2240	1878	1564	1292	0.4	0.7	0.0	-1.8	-4.8	-9.1	2.6	2.9	2.0	0.0	-3.4	-14.5	-32.6	
3081	2669	2303	1978	1689	1434	0.5	0.9	0.0	-2.1	-5.7	-10.7	1.9	1.6	0.0	-3.0	-7.5	-21.4	-42.9	
3233	2741	2315	1943	1621	1341	0.3	0.7	0.0	-1.7	-4.6	-8.8	2.5	2.8	2.0	0.0	-3.2	-14.0	-31.5	24"
3293	2818	2401	2033	1711	1430	0.5	0.9	0.0	-2.2	-5.7	-10.8	1.9	1.6	0.0	-3.0	-7.6	-21.8	-44.0	
3188	2765	2388	2053	1756	1493	0.5	0.8	0.0	-2.1	-5.5	-10.3	1.9	1.6	0.0	-2.9	-7.2	-20.6	-41.3	
967	600	373	262	208	173	0.9	0.0	-4.5	-13.5	-28.3	-49.9	0.0	-4.5	-13.5	-28.3	-49.9	-118.6	-228.2	20"
1696	1253	913	666	502	405	0.7	0.0	-3.3	-9.7	-19.6	-33.8	2.2	0.0	-5.3	-14.1	-27.2	-69.0	-136.9	24"
1412	886	521	301	172	119	0.4	0.8	0.0	-2.4	-6.7	-13.8	2.0	1.8	0.0	-3.8	-10.2	-35.0	-84.4	24"
1902	1296	858	565	399	316	0.5	0.0	-2.7	-8.2	-17.0	-30.0	1.8	0.0	-4.6	-12.5	-24.6	-65.3	-134.9	24"
1827	1355	989	720	535	425	0.6	0.0	-3.0	-8.9	-18.0	-31.1	2.0	0.0	-4.8	-13.0	-25.1	-63.6	-126.7	
1827	1355	989	720	535	425	0.6	0.0	-3.0	-8.9	-18.0	-31.1	2.0	0.0	-4.8	-13.0	-25.1	-63.6	-126.7	
2207	1639	1193	860	626	482	0.5	0.0	-2.6	-7.7	-15.6	-27.1	1.7	0.0	-4.2	-11.3	-21.9	-55.8	-112.0	24"
2303	1845	1462	1143	806	685	0.3	0.0	-1.8	-5.4	11.0	18.8	2.7	2.2	0.0	-4.2	-10.7	-31.5	-65.6	

vary from test-barrel specifications. *Illustrated (not shown actual size). **Inches above or below line of sight. Hold low for positive numbers, high for negative numbers.

REMINGTON BALLISTICS

CALIBER	REMINGTON Order No.	Wt.-Grs.	Style	Primer No.	Muzzle	100 Yds.	200 Yds.	300 Yds.	400 Yds.	500 Yds.
			BULLET				VELOCITY FEET PER SECOND				
30-40 KRAG	R30402	180*	Pointed Soft Point Core-Lokt®	9½	2430	2213	2007	1813	1632	1468
308 WIN. ACCELERATOR®	R308W5	55*	Pointed Soft Point	9½	3770	3215	2726	2286	1888	1541
308 WIN.	R308W1	150	Pointed Soft Point Core-Lokt®	9½	2820	2533	2263	2009	1774	1560
	R308W2	180	Soft Point Core-Lokt®	9½	2620	2274	1955	1666	1414	1212
	R308W3	180	Pointed Soft Point Core-Lokt®	9½	2620	2393	2178	1974	1782	1604
	R308W7	168*	Boat Tail H.P. Match	9½	2680	2493	2314	2143	1979	1823
	ER308WA	165	Extended Range Boat Tail	9½	2700	2497	2303	2117	1941	1773
	ER308WB	178	Extended Range	9½	2620	2415	2220	2034	1857	1691
30-06 ACCELERATOR	R30069	55*	Pointed Soft Point	9½	4080	3485	2965	2502	2083	1709
30-06 SPRINGFIELD	R30061	125	Pointed Soft Point	9½	3140	2780	2447	2138	1853	1595
	R30062	150	Pointed Soft Point Core-Lokt®	9½	2910	2617	2342	2083	1843	1622
	R30063	150	Bronze Point™	9½	2910	2656	2416	2189	1974	1773
	R3006B	165*	Pointed Soft Point Core-Lokt®	9½	2800	2534	2283	2047	1825	1621
	R30064	180	Soft Point Core-Lokt®	9½	2700	2348	2023	1727	1466	1251
	R30065	180	Pointed Soft Point Core-Lokt®	9½	2700	2469	2250	2042	1846	1663
	R30066	180	Bronze Point™	9½	2700	2485	2280	2084	1899	1725
	R30067	220	Soft Point Core-Lokt®	9½	2410	2130	1870	1632	1422	1246
	R3006C§	168	Boat Tail H.P. Match	9½	2710	2522	2346	2169	2003	1845
	ER3006A	152	Extended Range	9½	2910	2654	2413	2184	1968	1765
	ER3006B	165	Extended Range Boat Tail	9½	2800	2592	2394	2204	2023	1852
	ER3006C	178	Extended Range	9½	2720	2511	2311	2121	1939	1768
300 H&H MAG.	R300HH	180*	Pointed Soft Point Core-Lokt®	9½M	2880	2640	2412	2196	1990	1798
300 WIN. MAG.	R300W1	150	Pointed Soft Point Core-Lokt®	9½M	3290	2951	2636	2342	2068	1813
	R300W2	180*	Pointed Soft Point Core-Lokt®	9½M	2960	2745	2540	2344	2157	1979
	ER300WA	178	Extended Range	9½M	2980	2769	2568	2375	2191	2015
	ER300WB	190	Extended Range Boat Tail	9½M	2885	2691	2506	2327	2156	1993
300 WBY. MAG.	R300WB1	180	Pointed Soft Point Core-Lokt®	9½M	3120	2866	2627	2400	2184	1979
	R300WB2	220	Soft Point Core-Lokt®	9½M	2850	2541	2283	1984	1736	1512
	ER30WBA	178	Extended Range	9½M	3120	2902	2695	2497	2308	2126
	ER30WBB	190	Extended Range Boat Tail	9½M	3030	2830	2638	2455	2279	2110
303 BRITISH	R303B1	180*	Soft Point Core-Lokt®	9½	2460	2124	1817	1542	1311	1137
7.62x39MM	R762391	125	Pointed Soft Point	7½	2365	2062	1783	1533	1320	1154
32-20 WIN.	R32201	100	Lead	6½	1210	1021	913	834	769	712
	R32202	100*	Soft Point	6½	1210	1021	913	834	769	712
32 WIN. SPECIAL	R32WS2	170*	Soft Point Core-Lokt®	9½	2250	1921	1626	1372	1175	1044
8MM MAUSER	R8MSR	170*	Soft Point Core-Lokt®	9½	2360	1969	1622	1333	1123	997
8MM REM. MAG.	R8MM1	185*	Pointed Soft Point Core-Lokt®	9½M	3080	2761	2464	2186	1927	1688
	R8MM2§	220	Pointed Soft Point Core-Lokt®	9½M	2830	2581	2346	2123	1913	1716
338 WIN. MAG.	R338W1	225*	Pointed Soft Point	9½M	2780	2572	2374	2184	2003	1832
	R338W2	250	Pointed Soft Point	9½M	2660	2456	2261	2075	1898	1731
	RS338WA★	225	Swift A-Frame™ PSP	9½M	2785	2517	2266	2029	1808	1605
35 REM.	R35R1	150	Pointed Soft Point Core-Lokt®	9½	2300	1874	1506	1218	1039	934
	R35R2	200*	Soft Point Core-Lokt®	9½	2080	1698	1376	1140	1001	911
350 REM. MAG.	R350M1	200*	Pointed Soft Point Core-Lokt®	9½M	2710	2410	2130	1870	1631	1421
35 WHELEN	R35WH1	200	Pointed Soft Point	9½M	2675	2378	2100	1842	1606	1399
	R35WH2§	250*	Soft Point	9½M	2400	2066	1761	1492	1269	1107
	R35WH3	250	Pointed Soft Point	9½M	2400	2197	2005	1823	1652	1496
375 H&H MAG.	R375M1	270*	Soft Point	9½M	2690	2420	2166	1928	1707	1507
	RS375MA★	300	Swift A-Frame™ PSP	9½M	2530	2245	1979	1733	1512	1321
416 REM. MAG.	R416R1	400	Solid	9½M	2400	2042	1718	1436	1212	1062
	R416R2	400	Swift A-Frame™ PSP	9½M	2400	2175	1962	1763	1579	1414
	R416R3	350	Swift A-Frame™ PSP	9½M	2520	2270	2034	1814	1611	1429
44-40 WIN.	R4440W	200*	Soft Point	2½	1190	1006	900	822	756	699
44 REM. MAG.	R44MG2	240	Soft Point	2½	1760	1380	1114	970	878	806
	R44MG3	240	Semi-Jacketed Hollow Point	2½	1760	1380	1114	970	878	806
	R44MG6	210	Semi-Jacketed Hollow Point	2½	1920	1477	1155	982	880	802
444 MAR.	R444M	240	Soft Point	9½	2350	1815	1377	1087	941	846
45-70 GOVERNMENT	R4570G	405*	Soft Point	9½	1330	1168	1055	977	918	869
	R4570L	300	Jacketed Hollow Point	9½	1810	1497	1244	1073	969	895
458 WIN. MAG.	R458W1	500	Metal Case	9½M	2040	1823	1623	1442	1237	1161
	R458W2	510*	Soft Point	9½M	2040	1770	1527	1319	1157	1046

★NEW FOR 1992. *Specifications are nominal. Ballistics figures established in test barrels. Individual rifles may vary from test-barrel specifications.*

REMINGTON BALLISTICS
CENTERFIRE RIFLE

TRAJECTORY**   0.0 indicates yardage at which rifle was sighted in.

ENERGY FOOT-POUNDS						SHORT RANGE (Bullet does not rise more than one inch above line of sight from muzzle to sighting-in range.)						LONG RANGE (Bullet does not rise more than three inches above line of sight from muzzle to sighting-in range.)							BARREL LENGTH
Muzzle	100 Yds.	200 Yds.	300 Yds.	400 Yds.	500 Yds.	50 Yds.	100 Yds.	150 Yds.	200 Yds.	250 Yds.	300 Yds.	100 Yds.	150 Yds.	200 Yds.	250 Yds.	300 Yds.	400 Yds.	500 Yds.	
2360	1957	1610	1314	1064	861	0.4	0.0	-2.1	-6.2	-12.5	-21.1	1.4	0.0	-3.4	-8.9	-16.8	-40.9	-78.1	24"
1735	1262	907	638	435	290	0.2	0.5	0.0	-1.5	-4.2	-8.2	2.2	2.5	1.8	0.0	-3.2	-15.0	-36.7	24"
2648	2137	1705	1344	1048	810	0.2	0.0	-1.5	-4.5	-9.3	-15.9	2.3	1.9	0.0	-3.6	-9.1	-26.9	-55.7	
2743	2066	1527	1109	799	587	0.3	0.0	-2.0	-5.9	-12.1	-20.9	2.9	2.4	0.0	-4.7	-12.1	-36.9	-79.1	
2743	2288	1896	1557	1269	1028	0.2	0.0	-1.8	-5.2	-10.4	-17.7	2.6	2.1	0.0	-4.0	-9.9	-28.9	-58.8	24"
2678	2318	1998	1713	1460	1239	0.2	0.0	-1.6	-4.7	-9.4	-15.9	2.4	1.9	0.0	-3.5	-8.9	-25.3	-50.6	
2670	2284	1942	1642	1379	1152	0.2	0.0	-1.6	-4.7	-9.4	-16.0	2.3	1.9	0.0	-3.5	-8.9	-25.6	-51.5	
2713	2306	1948	1635	1363	1130	0.2	0.0	-1.7	-5.1	-10.2	-17.2	2.5	2.1	0.0	-3.8	-9.6	-27.6	-55.8	
2033	1483	1074	764	530	356	0.4	1.0	0.9	0.0	-1.9	-5.0	1.8	2.1	1.5	0.0	-2.7	-12.5	-30.5	24"
2736	2145	1662	1269	953	706	0.4	0.8	0.0	-2.1	-5.6	-10.7	1.8	1.5	0.0	-3.0	-7.7	-23.0	-48.5	
2820	2281	1827	1445	1131	876	0.6	0.9	0.0	-2.3	-6.3	-12.0	2.1	1.8	0.0	-3.3	-8.5	-25.0	-51.8	
2820	2349	1944	1596	1298	1047	0.6	0.9	0.0	-2.2	-6.0	-11.4	2.0	1.7	0.0	-3.2	-8.0	-23.3	-47.5	
2872	2352	1909	1534	1220	963	0.7	1.0	0.0	-2.5	-6.7	-12.7	2.3	1.9	0.0	-3.6	-9.0	-26.3	-54.1	
2913	2203	1635	1192	859	625	0.2	0.0	-1.8	-5.5	-11.2	-19.5	2.7	2.3	0.0	-4.4	-11.3	-34.4	-73.7	
2913	2436	2023	1666	1362	1105	0.2	0.0	-1.6	-4.8	-9.7	-16.5	2.4	2.0	0.0	-3.7	-9.3	-27.0	-54.9	24"
2913	2468	2077	1736	1441	1189	0.2	0.0	-1.6	-4.7	-9.6	-16.2	2.4	2.0	0.0	-3.6	-9.1	-26.2	-53.0	
2837	2216	1708	1301	988	758	0.4	0.0	-2.3	-6.8	-13.8	-23.6	1.5	0.0	-3.7	-9.9	-19.0	-47.4	-93.1	
2739	2372	2045	1754	1497	1270	0.7	1.0	0.0	-2.5	-6.6	-12.4	2.3	1.9	0.0	-3.5	-8.6	-24.7	-49.4	
2858	2378	1965	1610	1307	1052	0.6	0.9	0.0	-2.3	-6.0	-11.4	2.0	1.7	0.0	-3.2	-8.0	-23.3	-47.7	
2872	2462	2100	1780	1500	1256	0.6	1.0	0.0	-2.4	-6.2	-11.8	2.1	1.8	0.0	-3.3	-8.2	-23.6	-47.5	
2924	2491	2111	1777	1486	1235	0.7	1.0	0.0	-2.6	-6.7	-12.7	2.3	1.9	0.0	-3.5	-8.8	-25.4	-51.2	
3315	2785	2325	1927	1583	1292	0.6	0.9	0.0	-2.3	-6.0	-11.5	2.1	1.7	0.0	-3.2	-8.0	-23.3	-47.4	24"
3605	2900	2314	1827	1424	1095	0.3	0.7	0.0	-1.8	-4.8	-9.3	2.6	2.9	2.1	0.0	-3.5	-15.4	-35.5	
3501	3011	2578	2196	1859	1565	0.5	0.8	0.0	-2.1	-5.5	-10.4	1.9	1.6	0.0	-2.9	-7.3	-22.0	-41.9	24"
3509	3030	2606	2230	1897	1605	0.5	0.8	0.0	-2.0	-5.4	-10.2	1.8	1.5	0.0	-2.9	-7.1	-20.4	-40.9	
3511	3055	2648	2285	1961	1675	0.5	0.9	0.0	-2.2	-5.7	-10.7	1.9	1.6	0.0	-3.0	-7.5	-21.4	-42.9	
3890	3284	2758	2301	1905	1565	0.4	0.7	0.0	-1.9	-5.0	-9.5	2.7	3.0	2.1	0.0	-3.5	-15.2	-34.2	
3967	3155	2480	1922	1471	1117	0.6	1.0	0.0	-2.5	-6.7	-12.9	2.3	1.9	0.0	-3.6	-9.1	-27.2	-56.8	24"
3847	3329	2870	2464	2104	1787	0.4	0.7	0.0	-1.8	-4.8	-9.1	2.6	2.9	2.0	0.0	-3.3	-14.3	-31.8	
3873	3378	2936	2542	2190	1878	0.4	0.8	0.0	-1.9	-5.1	-9.6	1.7	1.4	0.0	-2.7	-6.7	-19.2	-38.4	
2418	1803	1319	950	687	517	0.4	0.0	-2.3	-6.9	-14.1	-24.4	1.5	0.0	-3.8	-10.2	-19.8	-50.5	-101.5	24"
1552	1180	882	652	483	370	0.4	0.0	-2.5	-7.3	-14.3	-25.7	1.7	0.0	-4.8	-10.8	-20.7	-52.3	-104.0	24"
325	231	185	154	131	113	0.0	-6.3	-20.9	-44.9	-79.3	-125.1	0.0	-11.5	-32.3	-63.8	-106.3	-230.3	-413.3	24"
325	231	185	154	131	113	0.0	-6.3	-20.9	-44.9	-79.3	-125.1	0.0	-11.5	-32.3	-63.6	-106.3	-230.3	-413.3	24"
1911	1393	998	710	521	411	0.6	0.0	-2.9	-8.6	-17.6	-30.5	1.9	0.0	-4.7	-12.7	-24.7	-63.2	-126.9	24"
2102	1463	993	671	476	375	0.5	0.0	-2.7	-8.2	-17.0	-29.8	1.8	0.0	-4.5	-12.4	-24.3	-63.8	-130.7	24"
3896	3131	2494	1963	1525	1170	0.5	0.8	0.0	-2.1	-5.6	-10.7	1.8	1.6	0.0	-3.0	-7.6	-22.5	-46.8	24"
3912	3254	2688	2201	1787	1438	0.6	1.0	0.0	-2.4	-6.4	-12.1	2.2	1.8	0.0	-3.4	-8.5	-24.7	-50.5	
3860	3305	2815	2383	2004	1676	0.6	1.0	0.0	-2.4	-6.3	-12.0	2.2	1.8	0.0	-3.3	-8.4	-24.0	-48.4	
3927	3348	2837	2389	1999	1663	0.2	0.0	-1.7	-4.9	-9.8	-16.6	2.4	2.0	0.0	-3.7	-9.3	-26.6	-53.6	24"
3871	3165	2565	2057	1633	1286	0.2	0.0	-1.5	-4.6	-9.4	-16.0	2.3	1.9	0.0	-3.6	-9.1	-26.7	-54.9	
1762	1169	755	494	359	291	0.6	0.0	-3.0	-9.2	-19.1	-33.9	2.0	0.0	-5.1	-14.1	-27.8	-74.0	-152.3	24"
1921	1280	841	577	445	369	0.8	0.0	-3.8	-11.3	-23.5	-41.2	2.5	0.0	-6.3	-17.1	-33.6	-87.7	-176.4	
3261	2579	2014	1553	1181	897	0.2	0.0	-1.7	-5.1	-10.4	-17.9	2.6	2.1	0.0	-4.0	-10.3	-30.5	-64.0	20"
3177	2510	1958	1506	1145	869	0.2	0.0	-1.8	-5.3	-10.8	-18.5	2.6	2.2	0.0	-4.2	-10.6	-31.5	-65.9	
3197	2369	1722	1235	893	680	0.4	0.0	-2.5	-7.3	-15.0	-26.0	1.6	0.0	-4.0	-10.9	-21.0	-53.8	-108.2	24"
3197	2680	2230	1844	1515	1242	0.4	0.0	-2.2	-6.3	-12.6	-21.3	1.4	0.0	-3.4	-9.0	-17.0	-41.0	-77.8	
4337	3510	2812	2228	1747	1361	0.2	0.0	-1.7	-5.1	-10.3	-17.6	2.5	2.1	0.0	-3.9	-9.9	-29.4	-60.7	24"
4262	3357	2608	2001	1523	1163	0.3	0.0	-2.0	-6.0	-12.3	-21.0	3.0	2.5	0.0	-4.7	-12.0	-35.6	-74.5	
5115	3702	2620	1832	1305	1001	0.4	0.0	-2.5	-7.5	-15.5	-27.0	1.7	0.0	-4.2	-11.3	-21.9	-56.7	-115.1	
5115	4201	3419	2760	2214	1775	0.4	0.0	-2.2	-6.5	-13.0	-22.0	1.5	0.0	-3.5	-9.3	-17.6	-42.9	-82.2	24"
4935	4004	3216	2557	2017	1587	0.3	0.0	-2.0	-5.9	-11.9	-20.2	2.9	2.4	0.0	-4.5	-11.4	-33.4	-68.7	
629	449	360	300	254	217	0.0	-6.5	-21.6	-46.3	-81.8	-129.1	0.0	-11.8	-33.3	-65.5	-109.5	-237.4	-426.2	24"
1650	1015	661	501	411	346	0.0	-2.7	-10.0	-23.0	-43.0	-71.2	0.0	-5.9	-17.6	-36.3	-63.1	-145.5	-273.0	
1650	1015	661	501	411	346	0.0	-2.7	-10.0	-23.0	-43.0	-71.2	0.0	-5.9	-17.6	-36.3	-63.1	-145.5	-273.0	20"
1719	1017	622	450	361	300	0.0	-2.2	-8.3	-19.7	-37.6	-63.2	0.0	-5.1	-15.4	-32.1	-56.7	-134.0	-256.2	
2942	1755	1010	630	472	381	0.6	0.0	-3.2	-9.9	-21.3	-38.5	2.1	0.0	-5.6	-15.9	-32.1	-87.8	-182.7	24"
1590	1227	1001	858	758	679	0.0	-4.7	-15.8	-34.0	-60.0	-94.5	0.0	-8.7	-24.6	-48.2	-80.3	-172.4	-305.9	24"
2182	1492	1031	767	625	533	0.0	-2.3	-8.5	-19.4	-35.9	-59.0	0.0	-5.0	-14.8	-30.1	-52.1	-119.5	—	
4620	3689	2924	2308	1839	1469	0.7	0.0	-3.3	-9.6	-19.2	-32.5	2.2	0.0	-5.2	-13.6	-25.8	-63.2	-121.7	24"
4712	3547	2640	1970	1516	1239	0.8	0.0	-3.5	-10.3	-20.8	-35.6	2.4	0.0	-5.6	-14.9	-28.5	-71.5	-140.4	24"

*Illustrated (not shown actual size). **Inches above or below line of sight. Hold low for positive numbers, high for negative numbers. §Subject to stock on hand.

REMINGTON BALLISTICS

PISTOL & REVOLVER

CALIBER	Order No.	Primer No.	Wt. Grs.	BULLET Style	VELOCITY (FPS) Muzzle	50 Yds.	100 Yds.	ENERGY (FT-LB) Muzzle	50 Yds.	100 Yds.	MID-RANGE TRAJECTORY 50 Yds.	100 Yds.	BARREL LENGTH
221 REM. FIREBALL*	R221F	7½	50*	Pointed Soft Point	2650	2380	2130	780	630	505	0.2"	0.8"	10
25 (6.35MM) AUTO. PISTOL	R25AP	1½	50*	Metal Case	760	707	659	64	56	48	2.0"	8.7"	2
6MM BR REM.	R6MMBR	7½	100*	Pointed Soft Point	Refer to page 30 for ballistics.								
7MM BR REM.	R7MMBR	7½	140*	Pointed Soft Point	Refer to page 30 for ballistics.								
32 S. & W.	R32SW	5½	88*	Lead	680	645	610	90	81	73	2.5"	10.5"	3
32 S. & W. LONG	R32SWL	1½	98*	Lead	705	670	635	115	98	88	2.3"	10.5"	4
32 (7.65MM) AUTO. PISTOL	R32AP	1½	71*	Metal Case	905	855	810	129	115	97	1.4"	5.8"	4
357 MAG. *Vented Barrel Ballistics*	R357M7	5½	110	Semi-Jacketed H.P.	1295	1094	975	410	292	232	0.8"	3.5"	4
	R357M1	5½	125	Semi-Jacketed H.P.	1450	1240	1090	583	427	330	0.6"	2.8"	4
	R357M2	5½	158	Semi-Jacketed H.P.	1235	1104	1015	535	428	361	0.8"	3.5"	4
	R357M3	5½	158	Soft Point	1235	1104	1015	535	428	361	0.8"	3.5"	4
	R357M5	5½	158	Semi-Wadcutter	1235	1104	1015	535	428	361	0.8"	3.5"	4
	R357M9	5½	140	Semi-Jacketed H.P.	1360	1195	1076	575	444	360	0.7"	3.0"	4
	R357M10	5½	180	Semi-Jacketed H.P.	1145	1053	985	524	443	388	0.9"	3.9"	8
	R357M11	5½	125*	Semi-Jacketed H.P. (Med. Vel.)	1220	1077	984	413	322	269	0.8"	3.7"	4
	R357MB	5½	140	"Multi-Ball"	1155	829	663	418	214	136	1.2"	6.4"	4
357 REM. MAXIMUM**	357MX1	7½	158*	Semi-Jacketed H.P.	1825	1588	1381	1168	885	669	0.4"	1.7"	10
9MM LUGER AUTO. PISTOL	R9MM1	1½	115	Jacketed H.P.	1155	1047	971	341	280	241	0.9"	3.9"	4
	R9MM2	1½	124	Metal Case	1110	1030	971	339	292	259	1.0"	4.1"	4
	R9MM3	1½	115*	Metal Case	1135	1041	973	329	277	242	0.9"	4.0"	4
	R9MM5	1½	88	Jacketed H.P.	1500	1191	1012	440	277	200	0.6"	3.1"	4
	R9MM6	1½	115	Jacketed H.P. (+P)‡	1250	1113	1019	399	316	265	0.8"	3.5"	4
	R9MM7	1½	140*	Semi-Jacketed H.P. (Practice)	935	889	849	272	246	224	1.3"	5.5"	4
	R9MM8	1½	147	Jacketed H.P. (Subsonic)	990	941	900	320	289	264	1.1"	4.9"	4
380 AUTO. PISTOL	R380AP	1½	95*	Metal Case	955	865	785	190	160	130	1.4"	5.9"	4
	R380A1	1½	88	Jacketed H.P.	990	920	868	191	165	146	1.2"	5.1"	4
38 AUTO. COLT PISTOL (A)	R38ACP$	1½	130*	Metal Case	1040	980	925	310	275	245	1.0"	4.7"	4
38 SUPER AUTO. COLT PISTOL (B)	R38SU1	1½	115	Jacketed H.P. (+P)‡	1300	1147	1041	431	336	277	0.7"	3.3"	5
38 S. & W.	R38SW	1½	146*	Lead	685	650	620	150	135	125	2.4"	10.0"	4

(continued on following page)

PISTOL & REVOLVER (cont)

CALIBER	Order No.	Primer No.	Wt. Grs.	BULLET Style	VELOCITY (FPS) Muzzle	50 Yds.	100 Yds.	ENERGY (FT-LB) Muzzle	50 Yds.	100 Yds.	MID-RANGE TRAJECTORY 50 Yds.	100 Yds.	BARREL LENGTH
38 SPECIAL *Vented Barrel Ballistics*	R38S1	1½	95	Semi-Jacketed H.P. (+P)‡	1175	1044	959	291	230	194	0.9"	3.9"	4
	R38S10	1½	110	Semi-Jacketed H.P. (+P)‡	995	926	871	242	210	185	1.2"	5.1"	4
	R38S16★	1½	110	Semi-Jacketed H.P.	950	890	840	220	194	172	1.4"	5.4"	4
	R38S2	1½	125*	Semi-Jacketed H.P. (+P)‡	945	898	858	248	224	204	1.3"	5.4"	4
	R38S3	1½	148	Targetmaster* Lead W.C. Match	710	634	566	166	132	105	2.4"	10.8"	4
	R38S4§	1½	158	Targetmaster Lead	755	723	692	200	183	168	2.0"	8.3"	4
	R38S5	1½	158	Lead (Round Nose)	755	723	692	200	183	168	2.0"	8.3"	4
	R38S14	1½	158	Semi-Wadcutter (+P)‡	890	855	823	278	257	238	1.4"	6.0"	4
	R38S6	1½	158	Semi-Wadcutter	755	723	692	200	183	168	2.0"	8.3"	4
	R38S12	1½	158	Lead H.P. (+P)‡	890	855	823	278	257	238	1.4"	6.0"	4
	R38SMB	1½	140*	"Multi-Ball"	830	731	506	216	130	80	2.0"	10.6"	4
38 SHORT COLT	R38SC	1½	125*	Lead	730	685	645	150	130	115	2.2"	9.4"	6
40 S. & W.	R40SW1	5½	155*	Jacketed H.P.	1140	1026	948	447	362	309	0.9"	4.1"	4
	R40SW2	5½	180	Jacketed H.P.	985	936	893	388	350	319	1.4"	5.0"	4
10MM AUTO.	R10MM2	2½	200	Metal Case	1160	1072	1007	597	510	450	0.9"	3.8"	5
	R10MM3	2½	180	Jacketed H. P. (Subsonic)	1055	997	951	445	397	361	1.0"	4.6"	5
	R10MM4	2½	180	Jacketed H. P. (High Vel.)	1240	1124	1037	618	504	430	0.8"	3.4"	5
41 REM. MAG. *Vented Barrel Ballistics*	R41MG1	2½	210	Soft Point	1300	1162	1062	788	630	526	0.7"	3.2"	4
	R41MG2	2½	210	Lead	965	898	842	434	376	331	1.3"	5.4"	4
	R41MG3	2½	170*	Semi-Jacketed H.P.	1420	1166	1014	761	513	388	0.7"	3.2"	4
44 REM. MAG. *Vented Barrel Ballistics*	R44MG5	2½	180	Semi-Jacketed H.P.	1610	1365	1175	1036	745	551	0.5"	2.3"	4
	R44MG1	2½	240	Lead Gas Check	1350	1186	1069	971	749	608	0.7"	3.1"	4
	R44MG2	2½	240*	Soft Point	1180	1081	1010	741	623	543	0.9"	3.7"	4
	R44MG3	2½	240	Semi-Jacketed H.P.	1180	1081	1010	741	623	543	0.9"	3.7"	4
	R44MG4	2½	240	Lead (Med. Vel.)	1000	947	902	533	477	433	1.1"	4.8"	6
	R44MG6	2½	210	Semi-Jacketed H.P.	1495	1312	1167	1042	803	634	0.6"	2.5"	6
44 S. & W. SPECIAL	R44SW	2½	246	Lead	755	725	695	310	285	265	2.0"	8.3"	6
	R44SW1	2½	200*	Semi-Wadcutter	1035	938	866	476	391	333	1.1"	4.9"	6
45 COLT	R45C	2½	250	Lead	860	820	780	410	375	340	1.6"	6.6"	5
	R45C1	2½	225*	Semi-Wadcutter (Keith)	960	890	832	460	395	346	1.3"	5.5"	5
45 AUTO.	R45AP1	2½	185	Targetmaster* Lead W.C. Match	770	707	650	244	205	174	2.0"	8.7"	5
	R45AP2	2½	185*	Jacketed H.P.	1000	939	889	411	362	324	1.1"	4.9"	5
	R45AP4	2½	230	Metal Case	835	800	767	356	326	300	1.6"	6.8"	5
	R45AP5	2½	Shot*	Shot				Number 12 shot.					
	R45AP6	2½	185	Jacketed H.P. (+P)‡	1140	1040	971	534	445	387	0.9"	4.0"	5
BLANK CARTRIDGES 38 S. & W.	R38SWBL§	1½	–	Blank	–	–	–	–	–	–	–	–	–
32 S. & W.	R32BLNK	5½	–	Blank	–	–	–	–	–	–	–	–	–
38 SPECIAL	R38BLNK	1½	–	Blank	–	–	–	–	–	–	–	–	–

★ *NEW FOR 1992.* * *Illustrated (not shown in actual size).* ** *Will not chamber in 357 Mag. or 38 Special handguns.* ‡ *Ammunition with (+P) on the case headstamp is loaded to higher pressure. Use only in firearms designated for this cartridge and so recommended by the gun manufacturer.* § *Subject to stock on hand.* (A) *Adapted only for 38 Colt sporting, military and pocket model automatic pistols. These pistols were discontinued after 1928.* (B) *Adapted only for 38 Colt Super and Colt Commander automatic pistols. Not for use in sporting, military and pocket models.*

WEATHERBY BALLISTICS

Cartridge	Weight Grains	Bullet Type	VELOCITY in Feet per Second						ENERGY in Foot-Pounds						PATH OF BULLET Above or below Line-of-sight of riflescopes mounted 1.5″ above bore				
			Muzzle	100 Yards	200 Yards	300 Yards	400 Yards	500 Yards	Muzzle	100 Yards	200 Yards	300 Yards	400 Yards	500 Yards	100 Yards	200 Yards	300 Yards	400 Yards	500 Yards
.224 WM	55	Pt-Ex	3650	3192	2780	2403	2057	1742	1627	1244	944	705	516	370	2.8	3.7	0.0	− 9.7	−27.7
.240 WM	87	Pt-Ex	3500	3202	2924	2663	2416	2183	2366	1980	1651	1369	1128	920	2.6	3.3	0.0	− 8.3	−22.5
	100	Pt-Ex	3395	3106	2835	2561	2340	2112	2559	2142	1785	1478	1215	990	2.9	3.6	0.0	− 8.8	−24.0
	100	Partition	3395	3126	2872	2633	2406	2190	2559	2169	1832	1539	1285	1065	2.8	3.5	0.0	− 8.5	−23.1
.257 WM	87	Pt-Ex	3825	3456	3118	2805	2513	2239	2826	2308	1878	1520	1220	969	2.1	2.9	0.0	− 7.3	−20.1
	100	Pt-Ex	3555	3237	2941	2665	2404	2159	2806	2326	1921	1576	1283	1035	2.6	3.3	0.0	− 8.2	−22.4
	100	*Partition®	3555	3270	3004	2753	2516	2290	2806	2374	2053	1683	1405	1165	2.5	3.2	0.0	− 7.8	−21.0
	120	Partition	3290	3032	2788	2557	2338	2129	2884	2448	2071	1742	1405	1165	3.0	3.8	0.0	− 9.1	−24.5
.270 WM	100	Pt-Ex	3760	3380	3033	2712	2412	2133	3139	2537	2042	1633	1292	1010	2.3	3.0	0.0	− 7.8	−21.6
	130	Pt-Ex	3375	3100	2842	2598	2367	2147	3287	2773	2330	1948	1616	1331	2.9	3.6	0.0	− 8.7	−23.7
	130	Partition	3375	3127	2893	2670	2458	2257	3287	2822	2415	2058	1714	1470	2.8	3.5	0.0	− 8.3	−22.4
	150	Pt-Ex	3245	3019	2803	2598	2402	2215	3507	3034	2617	2248	1922	1634	3.0	3.7	0.0	− 8.9	−23.8
	150	Partition	3245	3029	2823	2627	2439	2259	3507	3055	2655	2298	1981	1699	3.0	3.7	0.0	− 8.7	−23.3
7MM WM	139	Pt-Ex	3400	3138	2892	2658	2437	2226	3567	3039	2580	2181	1833	1529	2.7	3.5	0.0	− 8.4	−22.6
	140	Partition	3400	3160	2934	2719	2513	2317	3593	3105	2675	2297	1963	1669	2.7	3.4	0.0	− 8.1	−21.6
	154	Pt-Ex	3260	3022	2797	2583	2379	2184	3633	3123	2675	2281	1934	1630	3.0	3.7	0.0	− 9.0	−24.1
	160	Partition	3200	2991	2791	2600	2417	2241	3637	3177	2767	2401	2075	1784	3.1	3.8	0.0	− 8.9	−23.8
	175	Pt-Ex	3070	2879	2696	2520	2351	2188	3662	3220	2824	2467	2147	1861	3.4	4.1	0.0	− 9.6	−25.4
.300 WM	110	Pt-Ex	3900	3441	3028	2652	2305	1985	3714	2891	2239	1717	1297	962	2.2	3.0	0.0	− 8.0	−22.5
	150	Pt-Ex	3600	3297	3016	2751	2502	2266	4316	3621	3028	2520	2084	1709	2.4	3.1	0.0	− 7.7	−21.0
	150	Partition	3600	3319	3057	2809	2575	2353	4316	3669	3111	2628	2208	1843	2.4	3.0	0.0	− 7.5	−20.1
	165	Boat Tail	3450	3220	3003	2796	2598	2409	4360	3799	3303	2863	2473	2146	2.5	3.2	0.0	− 7.6	−20.4
	180	Pt-Ex	3300	3064	2841	2629	2426	2233	4352	3753	3226	2762	2352	1992	2.9	3.6	0.0	− 8.6	−23.2
	180	Partition	3300	3085	2881	2686	2499	2319	4352	3804	3317	2882	2495	2150	2.8	3.5	0.0	− 8.3	−22.3
	220	Rn-Ex	2905	2498	2125	1787	1491	1250	4122	3047	2206	1560	1085	763	5.3	6.6	0.0	−17.6	−51.3
.340 WM	200	Pt-Ex	3260	3011	2775	2552	2339	2137	4719	4025	3420	2892	2430	2027	3.1	3.8	0.0	− 9.1	−24.7
	210	Partition	3250	3000	2763	2539	2325	2122	4924	4195	3559	3004	2520	2098	3.1	3.8	0.0	− 9.2	−24.9
	250	Rn-Ex	3002	2672	2365	2079	1814	1574	5002	3963	3105	2399	1827	1375	1.7	0.0	− 7.9	−24.0	−50.7
	250	Partition	3002	2801	2609	2425	2248	2079	5002	4354	3777	3263	2805	2398	3.7	4.4	0.0	−10.3	−27.5
.378 WM	270	Pt-Ex	3180	2976	2781	2594	2415	2243	6062	5308	4635	4034	3496	3015	1.2	0.0	− 5.7	−16.6	−33.5
	300	Rn-Ex	2925	2576	2253	1953	1680	1439	5698	4419	3379	2540	1879	1380	1.8	0.0	− 2.8	− 6.4	−10.9
.416 WM	400	Swift A-F	2600	2364	2141	1930	1733	1552	6003	4965	4071	3309	2668	2139	2.4	0.0	−10.0	−29.3	−60.3
	400	Rn-Ex	2700	2390	2101	1834	1591	1379	6474	5073	3921	2986	2247	1688	2.3	0.0	−10.2	−30.9	−65.4
	400	**Mono Solid®	2700	2397	2115	1852	1613	1402	6474	5104	3971	3047	2310	1747	2.3	0.0	−10.1	−30.4	−64.3
.460 WM	500	RNSP	2700	2404	2128	1870	1634	1426	8092	6417	5025	3882	2965	2256	2.3	0.0	−10.0	−30.0	−63.2
	500	FMJ	2700	2425	2166	1924	1700	1497	8092	6527	5209	4109	3207	2488	2.2	0.0	− 9.7	−28.8	−60.0

LEGEND: Pt-Ex = Pointed-Expanding. Rn-Ex = Round nose-Expanding. FMJ = Full Metal Jacket.

WINCHESTER BALLISTICS

Super-X® Centerfire Pistol/Revolver Cartridges

Cartridge	Symbol	Bullet Wt. Grs.	Type	Velocity (fps) Muzzle	50 Yds.	100 Yds.	Energy (ft.-lbs.) Muzzle	50 Yds.	100 Yds.	Mid Range Traj. (In.) 50 Yds.	100 Yds.	Barrel Length Inches
25 Automatic	X25AXP	45	XP++	815	729	655	66	53	42	1.8	7.7	2
25 Automatic	X25AP	50	FMJ	760	707	659	64	56	48	2.0	8.7	2
30 Luger (7.65mm)	X30LP	93	FMJ	1220	1110	1040	305	255	225	0.9	3.5	4 1/2
30 Carbine #	X30M1	110	HSP	1790	1601	1430	783	626	500	0.4	1.7	10
30 Carbine #	X30M2	110	FMJ	1740	1552	1384	740	588	468	0.4	1.8	10
32 Smith & Wesson	X32SWP	85	Lead-RN	680	645	610	90	81	73	2.5	10.5	3
32 Smith & Wesson	X32SWLP	98	Lead-RN	705	670	635	115	98	88	2.3	10.5	4
32 Short Colt	X32SCP	80	Lead-RN	745	665	590	100	79	62	2.2	9.9	4
32 Automatic	X32ASHP	60	STHP	970	895	835	125	107	93	1.3	5.4	4
32 Automatic	X32AP	71	FMJ	905	855	810	129	115	97	1.4	5.8	4
38 Smith & Wesson	X38SWP	145	Lead-RN	685	650	620	150	135	125	2.4	10.0	4
380 Automatic	X380ASHP	85	STHP	1000	921	860	189	160	140	1.2	5.1	3 3/4
380 Automatic	X380AP	95	FMJ	955	865	785	190	160	130	1.4	5.9	3 3/4
38 Special	X38S9HP	110	STHP	945	894	850	218	195	176	1.3	5.4	4V
38 Special	X38S1P	158	Lead-RN	755	723	693	200	183	168	2.0	8.3	4V
38 Special	X38WCPSV	158	Lead-SWC	755	721	689	200	182	167	2.0	8.4	4V
38 Special + P	X38SSHP	95	STHP	1100	1002	932	255	212	183	1.0	4.3	4V
38 Special + P #	X38S6PH	110	JHP	995	926	871	242	210	185	1.2	5.1	4V
38 Special + P #	X38S7PH	125	JHP	945	898	858	248	224	204	1.3	5.4	4V
38 Special + P #	X38S8HP	125	STHP	945	898	858	248	224	204	1.3	5.4	4V
38 Special + P	X38SPD	158	Lead-SWCHP	890	855	823	278	257	238	1.4	6.0	4V
38 Special + P	X38WCP	158	Lead-SWC	890	855	823	278	257	238	1.4	6.0	4V
38 Special Match	X38SMRP	148	Lead-WC	710	634	566	166	132	105	2.4	10.8	4V
9mm Luger (Parabellum)	X9LP	115	FMJ	1155	1047	971	341	280	241	0.9	3.9	4
9mm Luger (Parabellum)	X9MMSHP	115	STHP	1225	1095	1007	383	306	259	0.8	3.6	4
9mm Subsonic	X9MMST147	147	STHP	1010	962	921	333	302	277	1.1	4.7	4
9mm Subsonic Match	X9MMTCM	147	FMJ-TCM	990	945	907	320	292	268	1.2	4.8	4
38 Super Automatic + P *	X38ASHP	125	STHP	1240	1130	1050	427	354	306	0.8	3.4	5
38 Super Automatic + P *	X38A1P	130	FMJ	1215	1099	1017	426	348	298	0.8	3.6	5
357 Magnum #	X3573P	110	JHP	1295	1095	975	410	292	232	0.8	3.5	4V
357 Magnum #	X3576P	125	JHP	1450	1240	1090	583	427	330	0.6	2.8	4V
357 Magnum #	X357SHP	145	STHP	1290	1155	1060	535	428	361	0.8	3.5	4V
357 Magnum	X3571P	158	Lead-SWC**	1235	1104	1015	535	428	361	0.8	3.5	4V
357 Magnum #	X3574P	158	JHP	1235	1104	1015	535	428	361	0.8	3.5	4V
357 Magnum #	X3575P	158	JSP	1235	1104	1015	535	428	361	0.8	3.5	4V
40 Smith & Wesson	X40SWSTHP	155	STHP	1205	1096	1018	500	414	357	0.8	3.6	4
40 Smith & Wesson Match	X40SWTCM	155	FMJ-TCM	1125	1046	986	436	377	335	0.9	3.9	4
40 Smith & Wesson	X40SW	180	JHP	990	936	891	392	350	317	1.2	4.9	5
10mm Automatic Match	X10MMTCM	155	FMJ-TCM	1125	1046	986	436	377	335	0.9	3.9	5 1/2
10mm Automatic	X10MMSTHP	175	STHP	1290	1141	1037	649	506	418	0.7	3.3	5 1/2
41 Remington Magnum #	X41MSTHP2	175	STHP	1250	1120	1029	607	488	412	0.8	3.4	4V
41 Remington Magnum	X41MP	210	Lead-SWC	965	898	842	434	376	331	1.3	5.4	4V
41 Remington Magnum #	X41MJSP2	210	JSP	1300	1162	1062	788	630	526	0.7	3.2	4V
41 Remington Magnum #	X41MHP2	210	JHP	1300	1162	1062	788	630	526	0.7	3.2	4V
44 Smith & Wesson Special #	X44STHPS2	200	STHP	900	860	822	360	328	300	1.4	5.9	6 1/2
44 Smith & Wesson Special	X44SP	246	Lead-RN	755	725	695	310	285	265	2.0	8.3	6 1/2
44 Remington Magnum	X44MSTHP2	210	STHP	1250	1106	1010	729	570	475	0.8	3.5	4V
44 Remington Magnum	X44MHSP2	240	HSP	1180	1081	1010	741	623	543	0.9	3.7	4V
44 Remington Magnum	X44MWCP	240	Lead-SWC	1000	937	885	533	468	417	1.2	4.9	6 1/2V
44 Remington Magnum (Gas Check)	X44MP	240	Lead-SWC	1350	1186	1069	971	749	608	0.7	3.1	4V
45 Automatic	X45ASHP2	185	STHP	1000	938	888	411	362	324	1.2	4.9	5
45 Automatic	X45A1P2	230	FMJ	835	800	767	356	326	300	1.6	6.8	5
45 Automatic Super-Match	X45AWCP	185	FMJ-SWC	770	707	650	244	205	174	2.0	8.7	5
45 Colt Silvertip #	X45CSHP2	225	STHP	920	877	839	423	384	352	1.4	5.6	5 1/2
45 Colt	X45CP2	255	Lead-RN	860	820	780	420	380	345	1.5	6.1	5 1/2
45 Winchester Magnum #	X45WM2	230	FMJ	1400	1232	1107	1001	775	636	0.6	2.8	5

(Not for Arms Chambered for Standard 45 Automatic)

FMJ-Full Metal Jacket
JHP-Jacketed Hollow Point
JSP-Jacketed Soft Point
RN-Round Nose
TCM-Truncated Cone-Match
XP-Expanding Point
WC-Wad Cutter
SWC-Semi Wad Cutter

HSP-Hollow Soft Point
STHP-Silvertip Hollow Point
HP-Hollow Point

**Lubaloy
*For use only in 38 Automatic Pistols.
#Acceptable for use in rifles also.

+P Ammunition with (+P) on the case head stamp is loaded to higher pressure. Use only in firearms designated for this cartridge and so recommended by the gun manufacturer.

V-Data is based on velocity obtained from 4" vented test barrels for revolver cartridges (38 Special, 357 Magnum, 41 Rem. Mag. and 44 Rem. Mag.)

Specifications are nominal. Test barrels are used to determine ballistics figures. Individual firearms may differ from test barrel statistics.

Specifications subject to change without notice.

WINCHESTER BALLISTICS
Super-X Centerfire Rifle Cartridges

Cartridge	Symbol	Game Selector Guide	CXP Guide Number	Bullet Wt. Grs.	Bullet Type	Barrel Length (In.)
218 Bee	X218B	V	1	46	HP	24
22 Hornet	X22H1	V	1	45	SP	24
22 Hornet	X22H2	V	1	46	HP	24
22-250 Remington	X222501	V	1	55	PSP	24
222 Remington	X222R	V	1	50	PSP	24
222 Remington	X222R1	V	-	55	FMJ	24
223 Remington	X223RH	V	1	53	HP	24
223 Remington	X223R	V	1	55	PSP	24
223 Remington	X223R1	V	-	55	FMJ	24
223 Remington	X223R2	D	2	64	PP	24
225 Winchester	X2251	V	1	55	PSP	24
243 Winchester	X2431	V	1	80	PSP	24
243 Winchester	X2432	D,O/P	2	100	PP	24
6mm Remington	X6MMR1	V	1	80	PSP	24
6mm Remington	X6MMR2	D,O/P	2	100	PP	24
25-06 Remington	X25061	V	1	90	PEP	24
25-06 Remington #	X25062	D,O/P	2	120	PEP	24
25-20 Winchester #	X25202	V	1	86	SP	24
25-35 Winchester	X2535	D	2	117	SP	24
250 Savage	X2503	D,O/P	2	100	ST	24
257 Roberts + P	X257P2	D,O/P	2	100	ST	24
257 Roberts + P	X257P3	D,O/P	2	117	PP	24
264 Winchester Mag.	X2642	D,O/P	2	140	PP	24
270 Winchester	X2701	V	1	100	PSP	24
270 Winchester	X2705	D,O/P	2	130	PP	24
270 Winchester	X2703	D,O/P	2	130	ST	24
270 Winchester	X2704	D,M	3	150	PP	24
280 Remington	X280R	D,O/P	2	140	PP	24
284 Winchester	X2842	D,O/P,M	3	150	PP	24
7mm Mauser (7x57)	X7MM1	D	2	145	PP	24
7mm Remington Mag.	X7MMR1	D,O/P,M	2	150	PP	24
7mm Remington Mag.	X7MMR2	D,O/P,M	3	175	PP	24
7.62 x 39	X76239	D,V	2	123	SP	20
30 Carbine #	X30M1	V	1	110	HSP	20
30 Carbine #	X30M2	V	-	110	FMJ	20
30-30 Winchester	X30301	D	2	150	IIP	24
30-30 Winchester	X30306	D	2	150	PP	24
30-30 Winchester	X30302	D	2	150	ST	24
30-30 Winchester	X30303	D	2	170	PP	24
30-30 Winchester	X30304	D	2	170	ST	24
30-06 Springfield	X30062	V	1	125	PSP	24
30-06 Springfield	X30061	D,O/P	2	150	PP	24
30-06 Springfield	X30063	D,O/P	2	150	ST	24
30-06 Springfield	X30065	D,O/P,M	2	165	SP	24
30-06 Springfield	X30064	D,O/P,M	2	180	PP	24
30-06 Springfield	X30066	D,O/P,M,L	3	180	ST	24
30-06 Springfield	X30069	M,L	3	220	ST	24

	CXP Class	Examples
V—Varmint	1	Prairie dog, coyote, woodchuck
D—Deer	2	Antelope, deer, black bear
O/P—Open or Plains	3	Elk, moose
M—Medium Game	3D	All game in category 3 plus large dangerous game (i.e. Kodiak bear)
L—Large Game	4	Cape Buffalo, elephant
XL—Extra Large Game		

Velocity in Feet Per Second (fps)						Energy in Foot Pounds (ft-lbs.)						Trajectory, Short Range Yards						Trajectory, Long Range Yards						
Muzzle	100	200	300	400	500	Muzzle	100	200	300	400	500	50	100	150	200	250	300	100	150	200	250	300	400	500
2760	2102	1550	1155	961	850	778	451	245	136	94	74	0.3	0	-2.3	-7.2	-15.8	-29.4	1.5	0	-4.2	-12.0	-24.8	-71.4	-155.6
2690	2042	1502	1128	948	840	723	417	225	127	90	70	0.3	0	-2.4	-7.7	-16.9	-31.3	1.6	0	-4.5	-12.8	-26.4	-75.6	-163.4
2690	2042	1502	1128	948	841	739	426	230	130	92	72	0.3	0	-2.4	-7.7	-16.9	-31.3	1.6	0	-4.5	-12.8	-26.4	-75.5	-163.3
3680	3137	2656	2222	1832	1493	1654	1201	861	603	410	272	0.2	0.5	0	-1.6	-4.4	-8.7	2.3	2.6	1.9	0	-3.4	-15.9	-38.9
3140	2602	2123	1700	1350	1107	1094	752	500	321	202	136	0.5	0.9	0	-2.5	-6.9	-13.7	2.2	1.9	0	-3.8	-10.0	-32.3	-73.8
3020	2675	2355	2057	1783	1537	1114	874	677	517	388	288	0.5	0.9	0	-2.2	-6.1	-11.7	2.0	1.7	0	-3.3	-8.3	-24.9	-52.5
3330	2882	2477	2106	1770	1475	1305	978	722	522	369	256	0.3	0.7	0	-1.9	-5.3	-10.3	1.7	1.4	0	-2.9	-7.4	-22.7	-49.1
3240	2747	2304	1905	1554	1270	1282	921	648	443	295	197	0.4	0.8	0	-2.2	-6.0	-11.8	1.9	1.6	0	-3.3	-8.5	-26.7	-59.6
3240	2877	2543	2232	1943	1679	1282	1011	790	608	461	344	0.4	0.7	0	-1.9	-5.1	-9.9	1.7	1.4	0	-2.8	-7.1	-21.2	-44.6
3020	2621	2256	1920	1619	1362	1296	977	723	524	373	264	0.6	0.9	0	-2.4	-6.5	-12.5	2.1	1.8	0	-3.5	-9.0	-27.4	-59.6
3570	3066	2616	2208	1838	1514	1556	1148	836	595	412	280	0.2	0.6	0	-1.7	-4.6	-9.0	2.4	2.8	2.0	0	-3.5	-16.3	-39.5
3350	2955	2593	2259	1951	1670	1993	1551	1194	906	676	495	0.3	0.7	0	-1.8	-4.9	-9.4	2.6	2.9	2.1	0	-3.6	-16.2	-37.9
2960	2697	2449	2215	1993	1786	1945	1615	1332	1089	882	708	0.5	0.9	0	-2.2	-5.8	-11.0	1.9	1.6	0	-3.1	-7.8	-22.6	-46.3
3470	3064	2694	2352	2036	1747	2139	1667	1289	982	736	542	0.3	0.6	0	-1.6	-4.5	-8.7	2.4	2.7	1.9	0	-3.3	-14.9	-35.0
3100	2829	2573	2332	2104	1889	2133	1777	1470	1207	983	792	0.4	0.8	0	-1.9	-5.2	-9.9	1.7	1.5	0	-2.8	-7.0	-20.4	-41.7
3440	3043	2680	2344	2034	1749	2364	1850	1435	1098	827	611	0.3	0.6	0	-1.7	-4.5	-8.8	2.4	2.7	2.0	0	-3.4	-15.0	-35.2
2990	2730	2484	2252	2032	1825	2382	1985	1644	1351	1100	887	0.5	0.8	0	-2.1	-5.6	-10.7	1.9	1.6	0	-3.0	-7.5	-22.0	-44.8
1460	1194	1030	931	858	798	407	272	203	165	141	122	0	-4.1	-14.4	-31.8	-57.3	-92.0	0	-8.2	-23.5	-47.0	-79.6	-175.9	-319.4
2230	1866	1545	1282	1097	984	1292	904	620	427	313	252	0.6	0	-3.1	-9.2	-19.0	-33.1	2.1	0	-5.1	-13.8	-27.0	-70.1	-142.0
2820	2467	2140	1839	1569	1339	1765	1351	1017	751	547	398	0.2	0	-1.6	-4.9	-10.0	-17.4	2.4	2.0	0	-3.9	-10.1	-30.5	-65.2
3000	2633	2295	1982	1697	1447	1998	1539	1169	872	639	465	0.5	0.9	0	-2.4	-4.9	-12.3	2.9	3.0	1.6	0	-6.4	-23.2	-51.2
2780	2411	2071	1761	1488	1263	2009	1511	1115	806	576	415	0.8	1.1	0	-2.9	-7.8	-15.1	2.6	2.2	0	-4.2	-10.8	-33.0	-70.0
3030	2782	2548	2326	2114	1914	2854	2406	2018	1682	1389	1139	0.5	0.8	0	-2.0	-5.4	-10.2	1.8	1.5	0	-2.9	-7.2	-20.8	-42.2
3430	3021	2649	2305	1988	1699	2612	2027	1557	1179	877	641	0.3	0.6	0	-1.7	-4.6	-9.0	2.5	2.8	2.0	0	-3.4	-15.5	-36.4
3060	2802	2559	2329	2110	1904	2702	2267	1890	1565	1285	1046	0.4	0.8	0	-2.0	-5.3	-10.1	1.8	1.5	0	-2.8	-7.1	-20.6	-42.0
3060	2776	2510	2259	2022	1801	2702	2225	1818	1472	1180	936	0.5	0.8	0	-2.0	-5.5	-10.4	1.8	1.5	0	-2.9	-7.4	-21.6	-44.3
2850	2585	2336	2100	1879	1673	2705	2226	1817	1468	1175	932	0.6	1.0	0	-2.4	-6.4	-12.2	2.2	1.8	0	-3.4	-8.6	-25.0	-51.4
3050	2705	2428	2167	1924	1698	2799	2274	1833	1461	1151	897	0.5	0.8	0.0	-2.2	-5.8	-11.1	1.9	1.6	0	-3.1	-7.8	-23.1	-47.8
2860	2595	2344	2108	1886	1680	2724	2243	1830	1480	1185	940	0.6	1.0	0	-2.4	-6.3	-12.1	2.1	1.8	0	-3.4	-8.5	-24.8	-51.0
2660	2413	2180	1959	1754	1564	2279	1875	1530	1236	990	788	0.2	0	-1.7	-5.1	-10.3	-17.5	1.1	0	-2.8	-7.4	-14.1	-34.4	-66.1
3110	2830	2568	2320	2085	1866	3221	2667	2196	1792	1448	1160	0.4	0.8	0	-1.9	-5.2	-9.9	1.7	1.5	0	-2.8	-7.0	-20.5	-42.1
2860	2645	2440	2244	2057	1879	3178	2718	2313	1956	1644	1372	0.6	0.9	0	-2.3	-6.0	-11.3	2.0	1.7	0	-3.2	-7.9	-22.7	-45.8
2365	2033	1731	1465	1248	1093	1527	1129	818	586	425	327	5	0	-2.6	-7.6	-15.4	-26.7	3.8	3.1	0	-6.0	-15.4	-46.3	-98.4
1990	1567	1236	1035	923	842	967	600	373	262	208	173	0.9	0	-4.5	-13.5	-28.3	-49.9	0	-4.5	-13.5	-28.3	-49.9	-118.6	-228.2
1990	1596	1278	1070	952	870	967	622	399	280	221	185	0.9	0	-4.3	-13.0	-26.9	-47.4	2.9	0	-7.2	-19.7	-38.7	-100.4	-200.5
2390	2018	1684	1398	1177	1036	1902	1356	944	651	461	357	0.5	0	-2.6	-7.7	-16.0	-27.9	1.7	0	-4.3	-11.6	-22.7	-59.1	-120.5
2390	2018	1684	1398	1177	1036	1902	1356	944	651	461	357	0.5	0	-2.6	-7.7	-16.0	-27.9	1.7	0	-4.3	-11.6	-22.7	-59.1	-120.5
2390	2018	1684	1398	1177	1036	1902	1356	944	651	461	357	0.5	0	-2.6	-7.7	-16.0	-27.9	1.7	0	-4.3	-11.6	-22.7	-59.1	-120.5
2200	1895	1619	1381	1191	1061	1827	1355	989	720	535	425	0.6	0	-3.0	-8.9	-18.0	-31.1	2.0	0	-4.8	-13.0	-25.1	-63.6	-126.7
2200	1895	1619	1381	1191	1061	1827	1355	989	720	535	425	0.6	0	-3.0	-8.9	-18.0	-31.1	2.0	0	-4.8	-13.0	-25.1	-63.6	-126.7
3140	2780	2447	2138	1853	1595	2736	2145	1662	1269	953	706	0.4	0.8	0	-2.1	-5.6	-10.7	1.8	1.5	0	-3.0	-7.7	-23.0	-48.5
2920	2580	2265	1972	1704	1466	2839	2217	1708	1295	967	716	0.6	1.0	0	-2.4	-6.6	-12.7	2.2	1.8	0	-3.5	-9.0	-27.0	-57.1
2910	2617	2342	2083	1843	1622	2820	2281	1827	1445	1131	876	0.6	0.9	0	-2.3	-6.3	-12.0	2.1	1.8	0	-3.3	-8.5	-25.0	-51.8
2800	2573	2357	2151	1956	1772	2873	2426	2036	1696	1402	1151	0.7	1.0	0	-2.5	-6.5	-12.2	2.2	1.9	0	-3.6	-8.4	-24.4	-49.6
2700	2348	2023	1727	1466	1251	2913	2203	1635	1192	859	625	0.2	0	-1.8	-5.5	-11.2	-19.5	2.7	2.3	0	-4.4	-11.3	-34.4	-73.7
2700	2469	2250	2042	1846	1663	2913	2436	2023	1666	1362	1105	0.2	0	-1.6	-4.8	-9.7	-16.5	2.4	2.0	0	-3.7	-9.3	-27.0	-54.9
2410	2192	1985	1791	1611	1448	2837	2347	1924	1567	1268	1024	0.4	0	-2.2	-6.4	-12.7	-21.6	1.5	0	-3.5	-9.1	-17.2	-41.8	-79.9

WINCHESTER BALLISTICS
Super-X Centerfire Rifle Cartridges

Cartridge	Symbol	Game Selector Guide	CXP Guide Number	Bullet Wt. Grs.	Bullet Type	Barrel Length (In.)
30-40 Krag	X30401	D	2	180	PP	24
300 Winchester Mag.	X30WM1	D,O/P	2	150	PP	24
300 Winchester Mag.	X30WM2	O/P,M,L	3	180	PP	24
300 Winchester Mag.	X30WM3	M,L,XL	3D	220	ST	24
300 H. & H. Magnum	X300H2	O/P,M,L	3	180	ST	24
300 Savage	X3001	D,O/P	2	150	PP	24
300 Savage	X3003	D,O/P	2	150	ST	24
300 Savage	X3004	D	2	180	PP	24
303 Savage	X3032	D	2	190	ST	24
303 British	X303B1	D	2	180	PP	24
307 Winchester	X3076	D,M	2	180	PP	24
308 Winchester	X3085	D,O/P	2	150	PP	24
308 Winchester	X3082	D,O/P	2	150	ST	24
308 Winchester	X3086	D,O/P,M	2	180	PP	24
308 Winchester	X3083	M,L	3	180	ST	24
32 Win Special	X32WS2	D	2	170	PP	24
32 Win Special	X32WS3	D	2	170	ST	24
32-20 Winchester #	X32201	V	1	100	Lead	24
8mm Mauser (8 x 57)	X8MM	D	2	170	PP	24
338 Winchester Mag.	X3381	D,O/P,M	3	200	PP	24
338 Winchester Mag.	X3383	M,L,XL	3D	225	SP	24
348 Winchester	Q3167	D,M	3	200	ST	24
35 Remington	X35R1	D	2	200	PP	24
35 Remington	X35R3	D	2	200	ST	24
356 Winchester	X3561	D,M	2	200	PP	24
356 Winchester	X3563	M,L	3	250	PP	24
357 Magnum	X3575P	V,D	2	158	JSP	20
358 Winchester	X3581	D,M	3	200	ST	24
375 Winchester	X375W	D,M	2	200	PP	24
375 Winchester	X375W1	D,M	2	250	PP	24
375 H. & H. Magnum	X375H1	M,L,XL	3D	270	PP	24
375 H. & H. Magnum	X375H2	M,L,XL	3D	300	ST	24
375 H. & H. Magnum	X375H3	XL	4	300	FMJ	24
38-40 Winchester #	X3840	D	2	180	SP	24
38-55 Winchester	X3855	D	2	255	SP	24
44 Remington Magnum #	X44MSTHP2	V,D	2	210	STHP	20
44 Remington Magnum #	X44MHSP2	D	2	240	HSP	20
44-40 Winchester #	X4440	D	2	200	SP	24
45-70 Government	X4570H	D,M	2	300	JHP	24
458 Winchester Magnum	X4580	XL	4	500	FMJ	24
458 Winchester Magnum	X4581	L,XL	3D	510	SP	24

WINCHESTER BALLISTICS

Velocity in Feet Per Second (fps)						Energy in Foot Pounds (ft-lbs.)						Trajectory, Short Range Yards						Trajectory, Long Range Yards						
Muzzle	100	200	300	400	500	Muzzle	100	200	300	400	500	50	100	150	200	250	300	100	150	200	250	300	400	500
2430	2099	1795	1525	1298	1128	2360	1761	1288	929	673	508	0.4	0	-2.4	-7.1	-14.5	-25.0	1.6	0	-3.9	-10.5	-20.3	-51.7	-103.9
3290	2951	2636	2342	2068	1813	3605	2900	2314	1827	1424	1095	0.3	0.7	0	-1.8	-4.8	-9.3	2.6	2.9	2.1	0	-3.5	-15.4	-35.5
2960	2745	2540	2344	2157	1979	3501	3011	2578	2196	1859	1565	0.5	0.8	0	-2.1	-5.5	-10.4	1.9	1.6	0	-2.9	-7.3	-20.9	-41.9
2680	2448	2228	2020	1823	1640	3508	2927	2424	1993	1623	1314	0.2	0	-1.7	-4.9	-9.9	-16.9	2.5	2.0	0	-3.8	-9.5	-27.5	-56.1
2880	2640	2412	2196	1991	1798	3315	2785	2325	1927	1584	1292	0.6	0.9	0	-2.3	-6.0	-11.5	2.1	1.7	0	-3.2	-8.0	-23.3	-47.4
2630	2311	2015	1743	1500	1295	2303	1779	1352	1012	749	558	0.3	0	-1.9	-5.7	-11.6	-19.9	2.8	2.3	0	-4.5	-11.5	-34.4	-73.0
2630	2354	2095	1853	1631	1434	2303	1845	1462	1143	886	685	0.3	0	-1.8	-5.4	-11.0	-18.8	2.7	2.2	0	-4.2	-10.7	-31.5	-65.5
2350	2025	1728	1467	1252	1098	2207	1639	1193	860	626	482	0.5	0	-2.6	-7.7	-15.6	-27.1	1.7	0	-4.2	-11.3	-21.9	-55.8	-112.0
1890	1612	1372	1183	1055	970	1507	1096	794	591	469	397	1.0	0	-4.3	-12.6	-25.5	-43.7	2.9	0	-6.8	-18.3	-35.1	-88.2	-172.5
2460	2233	2018	1816	1629	1459	2418	1993	1627	1318	1060	851	0.3	0	-2.1	-6.1	-12.2	-20.8	1.4	0	-3.3	-8.8	-16.6	-40.4	-77.4
2510	2179	1874	1599	1362	1177	2519	1898	1404	1022	742	554	0.3	0	-2.2	-6.5	-13.3	-22.9	1.5	0	-3.6	-9.6	-18.6	-47.1	-93.7
2820	2488	2179	1893	1633	1405	2648	2061	1581	1193	888	657	0.2	0	-1.6	-4.8	-9.8	-16.9	2.4	2.0	0	-3.8	-9.8	-29.3	-62.0
2820	2533	2263	2009	1774	1560	2648	2137	1705	1344	1048	810	0.2	0	-1.5	-4.5	-9.3	-15.9	2.3	1.9	0	-3.6	-9.1	-26.9	-55.7
2620	2274	1955	1666	1414	1212	2743	2066	1527	1109	799	587	0.3	0	-2.0	-5.9	-12.1	-20.9	2.9	2.4	0	-4.7	-12.1	-36.9	-79.1
2620	2393	2178	1974	1782	1604	2743	2288	1896	1557	1269	1028	0.2	0	-1.8	-5.2	-10.4	-17.7	2.6	2.1	0	-4.0	-9.9	-28.9	-58.8
2250	1870	1537	1267	1082	971	1911	1320	892	606	442	356	0.6	0	-3.1	-9.2	-19.0	-33.2	2.0	0	-5.1	-13.8	-27.1	-70.9	-144.3
2250	1870	1537	1267	1082	971	1911	1320	892	606	442	356	0.6	0	-3.1	-9.2	-19.0	-33.2	2.0	0	-5.1	-13.8	-27.1	-70.9	-144.3
1210	1021	913	834	769	712	325	231	185	154	131	113	0	-6.3	-20.9	-44.9	-79.3	-125.1	0	-11.5	-32.3	-63.6	-106.3	-230.3	-413.3
2360	1969	1622	1333	1123	997	2102	1463	993	671	476	375	0.5	0	-2.7	-8.2	-17.0	-29.8	1.8	0	-4.5	-12.4	-24.3	-63.8	-130.7
2960	2658	2375	2110	1862	1635	3890	3137	2505	1977	1539	1187	0.5	0.9	0	-2.3	-6.1	-11.6	2.0	1.7	0	-3.2	-8.2	-24.3	-50.4
2780	2572	2374	2184	2003	1832	3862	3306	2816	2384	2005	1677	1.2	1.3	0	-2.7	-7.1	-12.9	2.7	2.1	0	-3.6	-9.4	-25.0	-49.9
2520	2215	1931	1672	1443	1253	2820	2178	1656	1241	925	697	0.3	0	-2.1	-6.2	-12.7	-21.9	1.4	0	-3.4	-9.2	-17.7	-44.4	-87.9
2020	1646	1335	1114	985	901	1812	1203	791	551	431	360	0.9	0	-4.1	-12.1	-25.1	-43.9	2.7	0	-6.7	-18.3	-35.8	-92.8	-185.5
2020	1646	1335	1114	985	901	1812	1203	791	551	431	360	0.9	0	-4.1	-12.1	-25.1	-43.9	2.7	0	-6.7	-18.3	-35.8	-92.8	-185.5
2460	2114	1797	1517	1284	1113	2688	1985	1434	1022	732	550	0.4	0	-2.3	-7.0	-14.3	-24.7	1.6	0	-3.8	-10.4	-20.1	-51.2	-102.3
2160	1911	1682	1476	1299	1158	2591	2028	1571	1210	937	745	0.6	0	-3.0	-8.7	-17.4	-30.0	2.0	0	-4.7	-12.4	-23.7	-58.4	-112.9
1830	1427	1138	980	883	809	1175	715	454	337	274	229	0	-2.4	-9.1	-21.0	-39.2	-64.3	0	-5.5	-16.2	-33.1	-57.0	-128.3	-235.8
2490	2171	1876	1610	1379	1194	2753	2093	1563	1151	844	633	0.4	0	-2.2	-6.5	-13.3	-23.0	1.5	0	-3.6	-9.7	-18.6	-47.2	-94.1
2200	1841	1526	1268	1089	980	2150	1506	1034	714	527	427	0.6	0	-3.2	-9.5	-19.5	-33.8	2.1	0	-5.2	-14.1	-27.4	-70.1	-138.1
1900	1647	1424	1239	1103	1011	2005	1506	1126	852	676	568	0.9	0	-4.1	-12.0	-24.0	-40.9	2.7	0	-6.5	-17.2	-32.7	-80.6	-154.1
2690	2420	2166	1928	1707	1507	4337	3510	2812	2228	1747	1361	0.2	0	-1.7	-5.1	-10.3	-17.6	2.5	2.1	0	-3.9	-10.0	-29.4	-60.7
2530	2268	2022	1793	1583	1397	4263	3426	2723	2141	1669	1300	0.3	0	-2.0	-5.9	-11.9	-20.3	2.9	2.4	0	-4.5	-11.5	-33.8	-70.1
2530	2171	1843	1551	1307	1126	4263	3139	2262	1602	1138	844	0.3	0	-2.2	-6.5	-13.5	-23.4	1.5	0	-3.6	-9.8	-19.1	-49.1	-99.5
1160	999	901	827	764	710	538	399	324	273	233	201	0	-6.7	-22.2	-47.3	-83.2	-130.8	0	-12.1	-33.9	-66.4	-110.6	-238.3	-425.6
1320	1190	1091	1018	963	917	987	802	674	587	525	476	0	-4.7	-15.4	-32.7	-57.2	-89.3	0	-8.4	-23.4	-45.6	-75.2	-158.8	-277.4
1580	1198	993	879	795	725	1164	670	460	361	295	245	0	-3.7	-13.3	-29.8	-54.2	-87.3	0	-7.7	-22.4	-44.9	-76.1	-168.0	-305.8
1760	1362	1094	953	861	789	1650	988	638	484	395	332	0	-2.7	-10.2	-23.6	-44.2	-73.3	0	-6.1	-18.1	-37.4	-65.1	-150.3	-282.5
1190	1006	900	822	756	699	629	449	360	300	254	217	0	-6.5	-21.6	-46.3	-81.8	-129.1	0	-11.8	-33.3	-65.5	-109.5	-237.4	-426.2
1880	1650	1425	1235	1105	1010	2355	1815	1355	1015	810	680	0	-2.4	-8.2	-17.6	-31.4	-51.5	0	-4.6	-12.8	-25.4	-44.3	-95.5	—
2040	1823	1623	1442	1287	1161	4620	3689	2924	2308	1839	1496	0.7	0	-3.3	-9.6	-19.2	-32.5	2.2	0	-5.2	-13.6	-25.8	-63.2	-121.7
2040	1770	1527	1319	1157	1046	4712	3547	2640	1970	1516	1239	0.8	0	-3.5	-10.3	-20.8	-35.6	2.4	0	-5.6	-14.9	-28.5	-71.5	-140.4

Acceptable for use in pistols and revolvers also.

Reloading

For addresses and phone numbers of manufacturers and distributors included in this section, turn to *DIRECTORY OF MANUFACTURERS AND SUPPLIERS* at the back of the book.

HORNADY BULLETS
RIFLE

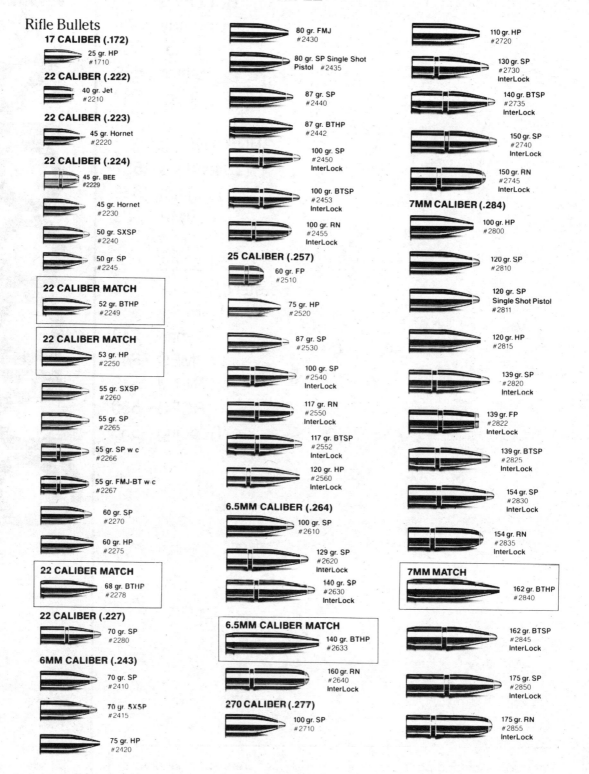

Rifle Bullets

17 CALIBER (.172)
25 gr. HP
#1710

22 CALIBER (.222)
40 gr. Jet
#2210

22 CALIBER (.223)
45 gr. Hornet
#2220

22 CALIBER (.224)
45 gr. BEE
#2229

45 gr. Hornet
#2230

50 gr. SXSP
#2240

50 gr. SP
#2245

22 CALIBER MATCH
52 gr. BTHP
#2249

22 CALIBER MATCH
53 gr. HP
#2250

55 gr. SXSP
#2260

55 gr. SP
#2265

55 gr. SP w c
#2266

55 gr. FMJ-BT w c
#2267

60 gr. SP
#2270

60 gr. HP
#2275

22 CALIBER MATCH
68 gr. BTHP
#2278

22 CALIBER (.227)
70 gr. SP
#2280

6MM CALIBER (.243)
70 gr. SP
#2410

70 gr. SXSP
#2415

75 gr. HP
#2420

80 gr. FMJ
#2430

80 gr. SP Single Shot
Pistol #2435

87 gr. SP
#2440

87 gr. BTHP
#2442

100 gr. SP
#2450
InterLock

100 gr. BTSP
#2453
InterLock

100 gr. RN
#2455
InterLock

25 CALIBER (.257)
60 gr. FP
#2510

75 gr. HP
#2520

87 gr. SP
#2530

100 gr. SP
#2540
InterLock

117 gr. RN
#2550
InterLock

117 gr. BTSP
#2552
InterLock

120 gr. HP
#2560
InterLock

6.5MM CALIBER (.264)
100 gr. SP
#2610

129 gr. SP
#2620
InterLock

140 gr. SP
#2630
InterLock

6.5MM CALIBER MATCH
140 gr. BTHP
#2633

160 gr. RN
#2640
InterLock

270 CALIBER (.277)
100 gr. SP
#2710

110 gr. HP
#2720

130 gr. SP
#2730
InterLock

140 gr. BTSP
#2735
InterLock

150 gr. SP
#2740
InterLock

150 gr. RN
#2745
InterLock

7MM CALIBER (.284)
100 gr. HP
#2800

120 gr. SP
#2810

120 gr. SP
Single Shot Pistol
#2811

120 gr. HP
#2815

139 gr. SP
#2820
InterLock

139 gr. FP
#2822
InterLock

139 gr. BTSP
#2825
InterLock

154 gr. SP
#2830
InterLock

154 gr. RN
#2835
InterLock

7MM MATCH
162 gr. BTHP
#2840

162 gr. BTSP
#2845
InterLock

175 gr. SP
#2850
InterLock

175 gr. RN
#2855
InterLock

HORNADY BULLETS
RIFLE

30 CALIBER (.308)

100 gr. SJ
#3005

110 gr. SP
#3010

110 gr. RN
#3015

110 gr. FMJ
#3017

130 gr. SP
#3020

130 gr. SP
Single Shot Pistol
#3021

150 gr. SP
#3031
InterLock

150 gr. BTSP
#3033
InterLock

150 gr. RN (30-30)
#3035
InterLock

150 gr. FMJ-BT
#3037

165 gr. SP
#3040
InterLock

165 gr. BTSP
#3045
InterLock

30 CALIBER NATIONAL MATCH

168 gr. BTHP
#3050

170 gr. FP (30-30)
#3060
InterLock

180 gr. SP
#3070
InterLock

180 gr. BTSP
#3072
InterLock

180 gr. RN
#3075
InterLock

30 CALIBER MATCH

190 gr. BTHP
#3080

190 gr. BTSP
#3085
InterLock

220 gr. RN
#3090
InterLock

7.62 x 39 (.311)

123 gr. SP
#3140

123 gr. FMJ
#3147

303 CAL. and 7.7 JAP (.312)

150 gr. SP
#3120
InterLock

174 gr. RN
#3130
InterLock

32 SPECIAL (.321)

170 gr. FP
#3210
InterLock

8MM CALIBER (.323)

125 gr. SP
#3230

150 gr. SP
#3232
InterLock

170 gr. RN
#3235
InterLock

220 gr. SP
#3238
InterLock

338 CALIBER (.338)

200 gr. SP
#3310
InterLock

200 gr. FP
(33 Win.)
#3315
InterLock

225 gr. SP
#3320
InterLock

250 gr. RN
#3330
InterLock

250 gr. SP
#3335
Interlock

---

348 CALIBER (.348)

200 gr. FP
#3410
InterLock

35 CALIBER (.358)

180 gr. SP
Single Shot Pistol
#3505

200 gr. SP
#3510
InterLock

200 gr. RN
#3515
InterLock

250 gr. SP
#3520
Interlock

250 gr. RN
#3525
InterLock

375 CALIBER (.375)

220 gr. FP
(375 Win.)
#3705
InterLock

*270 gr. SP
#3710
InterLock

*270 gr. RN
#3715
InterLock

*300 gr. RN
#3720
InterLock

300 gr. BTSP
#3725
Interlock

*300 gr. FMJ-RN
#3727

416 CALIBER (.416)

NEW
340 gr. BTSP
#4163

400 gr. FMJ
#4167

400 gr. RN
#4165
Interlock

44 CALIBER (.430)

*265 gr. FP
#4300
InterLock

HORNADY BULLETS
PISTOL

(Rifle Bullets Continued)

45 CALIBER (.458)

*300 gr. HP
#4500

*350 gr. RN
#4502
InterLock

*500 gr. RN
#4504
InterLock

*500 gr. FMJ-RN
#4507

NEW
750 gr. BTHP
#5165

Pistol Bullets

25 CALIBER (.251)

NEW
35 gr. HPXTP
#35450

50 gr. FMJ-RN
#3545

32 CALIBER (.311)

71 gr. FMJ-RN
#3200

32 CALIBER (.312)

85 gr. HP/XTP
#32050

NEW
100 gr. HP/XTP
#32070

9MM CALIBER (.355)

90 gr. HP/XTP
#35500

100 gr. FMJ
#3552

115 gr. HP/XTP
#35540

115 gr. FMJ-RN
#3555

124 gr. FMJ FP
#3556

124 gr. FMJ-RN
#3557

NEW
124 gr. HP XTP
#35571

147 gr. HP/XTP
#35580

147 gr. FMJ
#3559

38 CALIBER (.357)

110 gr. HP/XTP
#35700

125 gr. HP/XTP
#35710

125 gr. FP/XTP
#35730

140 gr. HP/XTP
#35740

158 gr. HP/XTP
#35750

158 gr. FP/XTP
#35780

160 gr. JTC-SIL
#3572

180 gr. JTC-SIL
#3577

NEW
180 gr. JHP/XTP
#35771

10MM CALIBER (.400)

155 gr. HP/XTP
#40000

180 gr. HP/XTP
#40040

180 gr. FMJ-FP
#40041

200 gr. FMJ-FP
#4007

200 gr. HP/XTP
#40060

41 CALIBER (.410)

210 gr. HP/XTP
#41000

---

210 gr. JTC-SIL
#4105

44 CALIBER (.430)

180 gr. HP/XTP
#44050

200 gr. HP/XTP
#44100

240 gr. HP/XTP
#44200

240 gr. JTC-SIL
#4425

300 gr. HP/XTP
#44280

45 CALIBER (.451)

185 gr. HP/XTP
#45100

45 CALIBER MATCH

185 gr. SWC
#4513

200 gr. HP/XTP
#45140

45 CALIBER MATCH

200 gr. FMJ-C/T
#4515

NEW
230 gr. JHP/XTP
#45160

230 gr. FMJ-RN
#4517

230 gr. FMJ-FP
#4518

45 CALIBER (.452)

250 gr. Long
Colt HP/XTP
#45200

---

300 gr. HP/XTP
#45230

Lead Pistol Bullets

32 CALIBER (.314)

90 gr. HBWC
#3252
*1002

90 gr. SWC
#3250
*1000

9MM CALIBER (.355)

124 gr. LRN
#3567
*1005

38 CALIBER (.358)

148 gr. BBWC
#3580
*1010

148 gr. HBWC
#3582
*1020

148 gr. DEWC
*1030

158 gr. RN
#3586
*1050

158 gr. SWC
#3588
*1040

158 gr. SWC/HP
*3589
*1042

10MM CALIBER (.400)

NEW
180 gr. SWC Lead
#1080

44 CALIBER (.430)

240 gr. SWC
#4430
*1110

240 gr. SWC/HP
#4431
*1111

45 CALIBER (.452)

200 gr. SWC
#4526
*1210

200 gr. L-C/T
#4528
*1220

230 gr. LRN
#4530
*1230

NOSLER BULLETS

Caliber/ Diameter	HANDGUN	Bullet Weight and Style	Sectional Density	Ballistic Coefficient	Part Number
9mm/ .355"		90 Gr. Hollow Point	.102	.086	42050
		115 Gr. Full Metal Jacket	.130	.103	42059
		115 Gr. Hollow Point 250 Quantity Bulk Pack	.130	.110	43009 44848
38/ .357"		125 Gr. Hollow Point 250 Quantity Bulk Pack	.140	.143	42055 44840
		150 Gr. Soft Point	.168	.153	42056
		150 Gr. IPSC 250 Quantity Bulk Pack	.168	.157	44839
		158 Gr. Hollow Point 250 Quantity Bulk Pack	.177	.182	42057 44841
		180 Gr. Silhouette (Non-Exp.)	.202	.210	42058
10mm/ .400"		NEW 135 Gr. Hollow Point	.121	.093	44838
		150 Gr. Hollow Point	.134	.106	44849
		170 Gr. Hollow Point	.152	.137	44844
		NEW 180 Gr. Hollow Point	.161	.147	44837
41/ .410"		210 Gr. Hollow Point	.178	.170	43012
44/ .429"		200 Gr. Hollow Point 250 Quantity Bulk Pack	.155	.151	42060 44846
		240 Gr. Soft Point	.186	.177	42068
		240 Gr. Hollow Point 250 Quantity Bulk Pack	.186	.173	42061 44842
		300 Gr. Hollow Point	.233	.206	42069
45/ .451"		185 Gr. Hollow Point 250 Quantity Bulk Pack	.130	.142	42062 44847
		230 Gr. Full Metal Jacket	.162	.183	42064

Caliber/ Diameter	HANDGUN	Bullet Weight and Style	Sectional Density	Ballistic Coefficient	Part Number
45 Colt/ .451"		250 Gr. Hollow Point	.176	.177	43013

Caliber/ Diameter	BALLISTIC TIP	Bullet Weight and Style	Sectional Density	Ballistic Coefficient	Part Number
22/ .224"		50 Gr. Spitzer (Orange Tip)	.142	.238	39522
		55 Gr. Spitzer (Orange Tip)	.157	.267	39526
6mm/ .243"		70 Gr. Spitzer (Purple Tip)	.169	.310	39532
		NEW 95 Gr. Spitzer (Purple Tip)	.230	.379	39534
25/ .257"		85 Gr. Spitzer (Blue Tip)	.183	.331	43004
		100 Gr. Spitzer (Blue Tip)	.216	.393	43005
6.5mm/ .264"		NEW 100 Gr. Spitzer (Brown Tip)	.205	.350	43008
		120 Gr. Spitzer (Brown Tip)	.246	.458	43007
270/ .277"		130 Gr. Spitzer (Yellow Tip)	.242	.433	39589
		140 Gr. Spitzer (Yellow Tip)	.261	.456	43983
		150 Gr. Spitzer (Yellow Tip)	.279	.496	39588
7mm/ .284"		NEW 120 Gr. Spitzer (Red Tip)	.213	.417	39550
		140 Gr. Spitzer (Red Tip)	.248	.485	39587
		150 Gr. Spitzer (Red Tip)	.266	.493	39586
30/ .308"		125 Gr. Spitzer (Green Tip)	.188	.366	43980
		150 Gr. Spitzer (Green Tip)	.226	.435	39585
		165 Gr. Spitzer (Green Tip)	.248	.475	39584
		180 Gr. Spitzer (Green Tip)	.271	.507	39583
338/ .338"		NEW 200 Gr. Spitzer (Maroon Tip)	.250	.414	39595

NOSLER BULLETS

PARTITION

Caliber/Diameter	Bullet Weight and Style	Sectional Density	Ballistic Coefficient	Part Number
270/.277"	130 Gr. Spitzer	.242	.416	16322
	150 Gr. Spitzer	.279	.465	16323
	160 Gr. Semi Spitzer	.298	.434	16324
7mm/.284"	140 Gr. Spitzer	.248	.434	16325
	150 Gr. Spitzer	.266	.456	16326
	160 Gr. Spitzer	.283	.475	16327
	175 Gr. Spitzer	.310	.519	35645
30/.308"	150 Gr. Spitzer	.226	.387	16329
	165 Gr. Spitzer	.248	.410	16330
	NEW 170 Gr. Round Nose	.256	.252	16333
	180 Gr. Spitzer	.271	.474	16331
	180 Gr. Protected Point	.271	.361	25396
	200 Gr. Spitzer	.301	.481	35626
	220 Gr. Semi Spitzer	.331	.351	16332
8mm/.323"	200 Gr. Spitzer	.274	.426	35277
338/.338"	210 Gr. Spitzer	.263	.400	16337
	225 Gr. Spitzer	.281	.454	16336
	250 Gr. Spitzer	.313	.473	35644

PARTITION

Caliber/Diameter	Bullet Weight and Style	Sectional Density	Ballistic Coefficient	Part Number
35/.358"	225 Gr. Spitzer	.251	.430	44800
	250 Gr. Spitzer	.279	.446	44801
375/.375"	NEW 260 Gr. Spitzer (Available mid-1992)	—	—	44850
	300 Gr. Spitzer	.305	.398	44845

SOLID BASE

Caliber/Diameter	Bullet Weight and Style	Sectional Density	Ballistic Coefficient	Part Number
22/.224"	45 Gr. Hornet	.128	.144	35487
	52 Gr. Hollow Point Match	.148	.224	25857
	55 Gr. Spitzer w/cannelure	.157	.261	16339
	60 Gr. Spitzer	.171	.266	30323
6mm/.243"	100 Gr. Spitzer	.242	.388	30390
25/.257"	120 Gr. Spitzer	.260	.446	30404
270/.277"	130 Gr. Spitzer	.242	.420	30394
7mm/.284"	140 Gr. Spitzer	.248	.461	29599
30/.308"	150 Gr. Spitzer	.226	.393	27583
	165 Gr. Spitzer	.248	.428	27585
	180 Gr. Spitzer	.271	.491	27587

SIERRA BULLETS

RIFLE

.22 Caliber Hornet (.223/5.66MM Diameter)
- 40 gr. Hornet Varminter #1100
- 45 gr. Hornet Varminter #1110

.22 Caliber Hornet (.224/5.69MM Diameter)
- 40 gr. Hornet Varminter #1200
- 45 gr. Hornet Varminter #1210

.22 Caliber (.224/5.69MM Diameter) High Velocity
- 40 gr. HP Varminter #1385
- 45 gr. SMP Varminter #1300
- 45 gr. SPT Varminter #1310
- 50 gr. SMP Varminter #1320
- 50 gr. SPT Varminter #1330
- 50 gr. Blitz Varminter #1340
- 52 gr. HPBT MatchKing #1410
- 53 gr. HP MatchKing #1400

- 55 gr. Blitz Varminter #1345
- 55 gr. SMP Varminter #1350
- 55 gr. FMJBT GameKing #1355
- 55 gr. SPT Varminter #1360
- 55 gr. SBT GameKing #1365
- 55 gr. HPBT GameKing #1390
- 60 gr. HP Varminter #1375
- 63 gr. SMP Varminter #1370
- 69 gr. HPBT MatchKing #1380

6MM .243 Caliber (.243/6.17MM Diameter)
- 60 gr. HP Varminter #1500
- 70 gr. HPBT MatchKing #1505
- 75 gr. HP Varminter #150
- 85 gr. SPT Varminter #1520
- 85 gr. HPBT GameKing #1530

- 90 gr. FMJBT GameKing #1535
- 100 gr. SPT Pro-Hunter #1540
- 100 gr. SMP Pro-Hunter #1550
- 100 gr. SBT GameKing #1560
- NEW 107 gr. HPBT MatchKing #1570

.25 Caliber (.257/6.53MM Diameter)
- 75 gr. HP Varminter #1600
- 87 gr. SPT Varminter #1610
- 90 gr. HPBT GameKing #1615
- 100 gr. SPT Pro-Hunter #1620
- 100 gr. SBT GameKing #1625
- 117 gr. SBT GameKing #1630
- 117 gr. SPT Pro-Hunter #1640
- 120 gr. HPBT GameKing #1650

6.5MM .264 Caliber (.264/6.71MM Diameter)
- 85 gr. HP Varminter #1700
- 100 gr. HP Varminter #1710
- 120 gr. SPT Pro-Hunter #1720
- 120 gr. HPBT MatchKing #1725
- 140 gr. SBT GameKing #1730
- 140 gr. HPBT MatchKing #1740

.270 Caliber (.277/7.04MM Diameter)
- 90 gr. HP Varminter #1800
- 110 gr. SPT Pro-Hunter #1810
- 130 gr. SBT GameKing #1820
- 130 gr. SPT Pro-Hunter #1830
- 140 gr. HPBT GameKing #1835
- 140 gr. SBT GameKing #1845
- 150 gr. SBT GameKing #1840
- 150 gr. RN Pro-Hunter #1850

SIERRA BULLETS

7MM .284 Caliber (.284/7.21MM Diameter)

- 100 gr. HP Varminter #1895
- 120 gr. SPT Pro-Hunter #1900
- 140 gr. SBT GameKing #1905
- 140 gr. SPT Pro-Hunter #1910
- 150 gr. SBT GameKing #1913
- 150 gr. HPBT MatchKing #1915
- 160 gr. SBT GameKing #1920
- 160 gr. HPBT GameKing #1925
- 168 gr. HPBT MatchKing #1930
- 170 gr. RN Pro-Hunter #1950
- 175 gr. SBT GameKing #1940

.30 (30-30) Caliber (.308/7.82MM Diameter)

- 125 gr. HP Pro-Hunter #2020
- 150 gr. FN Pro-Hunter #2000 POWER JACKET

.30 Caliber 7.62MM (.308/7.82MM Diameter)

- 170 gr. FN Pro-Hunter #2010 POWER JACKET
- 110 gr. RN Pro-Hunter #2100
- 110 gr. FMJ Pro-Hunter #2105
- 110 gr. HP Varminter #2110
- 125 gr. SPT Pro-Hunter #2120
- 150 gr. FMJBT GameKing #2115
- 150 gr. SPT Pro-Hunter #2130
- 150 gr. SBT GameKing #2125
- 150 gr. HPBT MatchKing #2190
- 150 gr. RN Pro-Hunter #2135
- 165 gr. SBT GameKing #2145
- 165 gr. HPBT GameKing #2140
- 155 gr. HPBT 1992 PALMA MatchKing #2155
- 168 gr. HPBT MatchKing #2200

- 180 gr. SPT Pro-Hunter #2150
- 180 gr. SBT GameKing #2160
- 180 gr. HPBT MatchKing #2220
- 180 gr. RN Pro-Hunter #2170
- 190 gr. HPBT MatchKing #2210
- 200 gr. SBT GameKing #2165
- 200 gr. HPBT MatchKing #2230
- 220 gr. HPBT MatchKing #2240
- 220 gr. RN Pro-Hunter #2180

.303 Caliber 7.7MM (.311/7.90MM Diameter)

- 150 gr. SPT Pro-Hunter #2300
- 180 gr. SPT Pro-Hunter #2310

8MM (.323/8.20MM Diameter)

- 150 gr. SPT Pro-Hunter #2400
- 175 gr. SPT Pro-Hunter #2410
- 220 gr. SBT GameKing #2420

.338 Caliber (.338/8.59MM Diameter)

- 250 gr. SBT GameKing #2600

.35 Caliber (.358/9.09MM Diameter)

- 200 gr. RN Pro-Hunter #2800
- 225 gr. SBT GameKing #2850

.375 Caliber (.375/9.53MM Diameter)

- 200 gr. FN Pro-Hunter #2900 POWER JACKET
- **NEW** 250 gr. SBT GameKing #2950
- 300 gr. SBT GameKing #3000

.45 Caliber (45.70) (.458/11.63MM Diameter)

- 300 gr. HP Pro-Hunter #8900

SIERRA BULLETS

HANDGUN
Single Shot Pistol Bullets

6MM .243 Dia. 80 gr. SPT Pro-Hunter #7150

7MM .284 Dia. 130 gr. SPT Pro-Hunter #7250

.30 cal. .308 Dia. 135 gr. SPT Pro-Hunter #7350

.25 Caliber (.251/6.38MM Diameter)

50 gr. FMJ Tournament Master #8000

.32 Caliber 7.65MM (.312/7.92MM Diameter)

71 gr. FMJ Tournament Master #8010

.32 Mag. .312/7.92MM Diameter

90 gr. JHC Sports Master #8030 POWER JACKET

9MM .355 Caliber (.355/9.02MM Diameter)

90 gr. JHP Sports Master #8100 POWER JACKET

95 gr. FMJ Tournament Master #8105

115 gr. JHP Sports Master #8110 POWER JACKET

115 gr. FMJ Tournament Master #8115

125 gr. FMJ Tournament Master #8120

130 gr. FMJ Tournament Master #8345

.38 Caliber (.357/9.07MM Diameter)

110 gr. JHC Blitz Sports Master #8300 POWER JACKET

125 gr. JSP Sports Master #8310

125 gr. JHC Sports Master #8320 POWER JACKET

140 gr. JHC Sports Master #8325 POWER JACKET

158 gr. JHC Sports Master #8360 POWER JACKET

158 gr. JSP Sports Master #8340

170 gr. JHC Sports Master #8365 POWER JACKET

170 gr. FMJ Match Tournament Master #8350

180 gr. FPJ Match Tournament Master #8370

10MM .400 Caliber (.400/10.16MM Diameter)

150 gr. JHP Sports Master #8430 POWER JACKET

180 gr. JHP Sports Master #8460 POWER JACKET

190 gr. FPJ Tournament Master #8480

.41 Caliber (.410/10.41MM Diameter)

170 gr. JHC Sports Master #8500 POWER JACKET

210 gr. JHC Sports Master #8520 POWER JACKET

220 gr. FPJ Match Tournament Master #8530

.44 Magnum (.4295/10.91MM Diameter)

180 gr. JHC Sports Master #8600 POWER JACKET

210 gr. JHC Sports Master #8620 POWER JACKET

220 gr. FPJ Match Tournament Master #8605

240 gr. JHC Sports Master #8610 POWER JACKET

250 gr. FPJ Match Tournament Master #8615

300 gr. JSP Sports Master #8630

.45 Caliber (.4515/11.47MM Diameter)

185 gr. JHP Sports Master #8800 POWER JACKET

185 gr. FPJ Match Tournament Master #8810

200 gr. FPJ Match Tournament Master #8825

230 gr. FMJ Match Tournament Master #8815

240 gr. JHC Sports Master #8820 POWER JACKET

SPEER RIFLE BULLETS

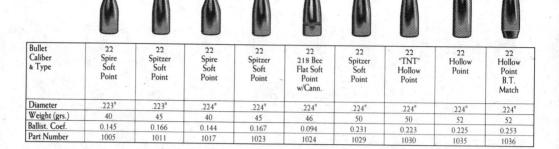

Bullet Caliber & Type	22 Spire Soft Point	22 Spitzer Soft Point	22 Spire Soft Point	22 Spitzer Soft Point	22 218 Bee Flat Soft Point w/Cann.	22 Spitzer Soft Point	22 "TNT" Hollow Point	22 Hollow Point	22 Hollow Point B.T. Match
Diameter	.223"	.223"	.224"	.224"	.224"	.224"	.224"	.224"	.224"
Weight (grs.)	40	45	40	45	46	50	50	52	52
Ballist. Coef.	0.145	0.166	0.144	0.167	0.094	0.231	0.223	0.225	0.253
Part Number	1005	1011	1017	1023	1024	1029	1030	1035	1036

Bullet Caliber & Type	6mm Spitzer Soft Point	25-20 Win. Flat Soft Point w/Cann.	25 Spitzer Soft Point	25 Spitzer Soft Point	25 Hollow Point	25 Spitzer Soft Point B.T.	25 Spitzer Soft Point B.T.	25 Spitzer Soft Point	6.5mm Spitzer Soft Point	6.5mm Spitzer Soft Point
Diameter	.243"	.257"	.257"	.257"	.257"	.257"	.257"	.257"	.263"	.263"
Weight	105	75	87	100	100	100	120	120	120	140
Ballist. Coef.	0.443	0.133	0.300	0.369	0.255	0.393	0.435	0.410	0.433	0.496
Part Number	1229	1237	1241	1405	1407	1408	1410	1411	1435	1441

Bullet Caliber & Type	7mm Spitzer Soft Point B.T.	7mm Spitzer Soft Point	7mm Mag-Tip™ Soft Point	7mm Mag-Tip™ Soft Point	30 Round Soft Point Plinker™	30 Hollow Point	30 Round Soft Point	30 Carbine Round FMJ	30 Spire Soft Point	30 Hollow Point	30 Flat Soft Point	30 Flat Soft Point	30 Round Soft Point
Diameter	.284"	.284"	.284"	.284"	.308"	.308"	.308"	.308"	.308"	.308"	.308"	.308"	.308"
Weight	160	160	160	175	100	110	110	110	110	130	130	150	150
Ballist. Coef.	0.556	0.502	0.354	0.385	0.124	0.136	0.144	0.179	0.273	0.263	0.248	0.268	0.266
Part Number	1634	1635	1637	1641	1805	1835	1845	1846	1855	2005	2007	2011	2017

Bullet Caliber & Type	30 Match Hollow Point B.T.	30 Spitzer Soft Point	303 Spitzer Soft Point w/Cann.	303 (7.62x39) FMJ w/Cann.	303 Spitzer Soft Point	303 Round Soft Point	32 Flat Soft Point	8mm Spitzer Soft Point	8mm Semi-Spitzer Soft Point	8mm Spitzer Soft Point	338 Spitzer Soft Point	338 Spitzer Soft Point B.T.	338 Semi-Spitzer Soft Point
Diameter	.308"	.308"	.311"	.311"	.311"	.311"	.321"	.323"	.323"	.323"	.338"	.338"	.338"
Weight	190	200	125	123	150	180	170	150	170	200	200	225	275
Ballist. Coef.	0.540	0.556	0.292	0.256	0.411	0.328	0.297	0.369	0.354	0.411	0.448	0.484	0.456
Part Number	2080	2211	2213	2214	2217	2223	2259	2277	2283	2285	2405	2406	2411

SPEER RIFLE BULLETS

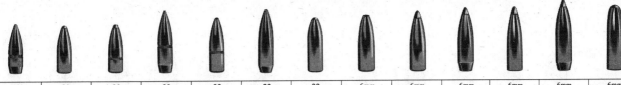

22 FMJ B.T. w/Cann.	22 Spitzer Soft Point	22 Spitzer S.P. w/Cann.	22 FMJ B.T. w/Cann.	22 Hollow Point w/Cann.	22 Hollow Point B.T. Match	22 Semi-Spitzer Soft Point	6mm Hollow Point	6mm Spitzer Soft Point	6mm Spitzer Soft Point B.T.	6mm Spitzer Soft Point	6mm Spitzer Soft Point B.T.	6mm Round Soft Point
.224"	.224"	.224"	.224"	.224"	.224"	.224"	.243"	.243"	.243"	.243"	.243"	.243"
55	55	55	62	62	68	70	75	80	85	90	100	105
0.269	0.255	0.241	0.307	0.251	0.299	0.214	0.234	0.365	0.404	0.385	0.430	0.207
1044	1047	1049	1050	1051	1052	1053	1205	1211	1213	1217	1220	1223

270 Hollow Point	270 Spitzer Soft Point	270 Spitzer Soft Point B.T.	270 Spitzer Soft Point	270 Spitzer Soft Point B.T.	270 Spitzer Soft Point	7mm Hollow Point	7mm Spitzer Soft Point	7mm Spitzer Soft Point	7mm Spitzer Soft Point B.T.	7mm Spitzer Soft Point B.T.	7mm Spitzer Soft Point	7mm Match Hollow Point B.T.
.277"	.277"	.277"	.277"	.277"	.277"	.284"	.284"	.284"	.284"	.284"	.284"	.284"
100	100	130	130	150	150	115	120	130	130	145	145	145
0.225	0.319	0.449	0.408	0.496	0.481	0.257	0.386	0.394	0.411	0.502	0.457	0.465
1447	1453	1458	1459	1604	1605	1617	1620	1623	1624	1628	1629	1631

30 FMJ B.T. w/Cann.	30 Spitzer Soft Point B.T.	30 Spitzer Soft Point	30 Mag-Tip™ Soft Point	30 Round Soft Point	30 Spitzer Soft Point B.T.	30 Spitzer Soft Point	30 Match Hollow Point B.T.	30 Flat Soft Point	30 Round Soft Point	30 Spitzer Soft Point B.T.	30 Spitzer Soft Point	30 Mag-Tip™ Soft Point
.308"	.308"	.308"	.308"	.308"	.308"	.308"	.308"	.308"	.308"	.308"	.308"	.308"
150	150	150	150	165	165	165	168	170	180	180	180	180
0.425	0.423	0.389	0.301	0.274	0.477	0.433	0.480	0.304	0.304	0.540	0.483	0.352
2018	2022	2023	2025	2029	2034	2035	2040	2041	2047	2052	2053	2059

35 Flat Soft Point	35 Flat Soft Point	35 Spitzer Soft Point	9.3mm Semi-Spitzer Soft Point	375 Semi-Spitzer Soft Point	375 Spitzer Soft Point B.T.	45 Flat Soft Point	45 Flat Soft Point	50 BMG FMJ
.358"	.358"	.358"	.366"	.375"	.375"	.458"	.458"	.510"
180	220	250	270	235	270	350	400	647
0.245	0.316	0.446	0.361	0.317	0.429	0.232	0.214	0.701
2435	2439	2453	2459	2471	2472	2478***	2479	2491

SPEER BULLETS

Handgun Bullets Jacketed

Caliber & Type	25 TMJ	32 JHP	9mm JHP	9mm TMJ	9mm JHP	9mm TMJ	9mm JHP	9mm HP	9mm SP	9mm TMJ	9mm TMJ	9mm HP
Diameter	.251"	.312"	.355"	.355"	.355"	.355"	.355"	.355"	.355"	.355"	.355"	.355"
Weight (grs.)	50	100	88	95	100	115	115	115	124	124	147	147
Ballist. Coef.	0.110	0.167	0.095	0.131	0.111	0.177	0.118	0.099	0.115	0.114	0.208	0.190
Part Number	3982	3981	4000	4001	3983	3995*	3996	4003	3997	4004	4006	3990

Caliber & Type	40/10mm TMJ	40/10mm TMJ	41 AE HP	41 JHP-SWC	41 JSP-SWC	41 TMJ-Sil.	44 Mag. JHP	44 JHP-SWC	44 JSP-SWC	44 Mag.JHP	44 Mag.JSP	44 TMJ-Sil.
Diameter	.400"	.400"	.410"	.410"	.410"	.410"	.429"	.429"	.429"	.429"	.429"	.429"
Weight (grs.)	180	200	180	200	220	210	200	225	240	240	240	240
Ballist. Coef.	0.143	0.208	0.138	0.113	0.137	0.216	0.122	0.146	0.157	0.165	0.164	0.206
Part Number	4402	4403	4404	4405	4417	4420	4425	4435	4447	4453	4457	4459

Handgun Bullets Lead

Caliber & Type	32 HB-WC	9mm RN	38 BB-WC	38 HB-WC	38 SWC	38 HP-SWC	38 RN	44 SWC	45 SWC
Diameter	.314"	.356"	.358"	.358"	.358"	.358"	.358"	.430"	.452"
Weight (grs.)	98	125	148	148	158	158	158	240	200
Part Number	4600*	4601*	4605*	4617*	4623*	4627*	4647	4660*	4677*

SPEER BULLETS

38 JHP	38 JSP	38 JHP	38 TMJ	38 JHP	38 JHP-SWC	38 TMJ	38 JHP	38 JSP	38 JSP-SWC	38 TMJ-Sil.	38 TMJ-Sil.	40/10mm HP
.357"	.357"	.357"	.357"	.357"	.357"	.357"	.357"	.357"	.357"	.357"	.357"	.400"
110	125	125	125	140	146	158	158	158	160	180	200	180
0.122	0.140	0.135	0.146	0.152	0.159	0.173	0.158	0.150	0.170	0.230	0.236	0.188
4007	4011	4013	4015	4203	4205	4207	4211	4217	4223	4229	4231	4401

44 Mag. SP	45 TMJ-Match	45 TMJ-Match	45 JHP	45 Mag. JHP	45 TMJ	45 Mag. JHP	45 SP	50 AE HP
.429"	.451"	.451"	.451"	.451"	.451"	.451"	.451"	.500"
300	185	200	200	225	230	260	300	325
0.213	0.090	0.129	0.138	0.169	0.153	0.183	0.199	0.149
4463	4473	4475	4477	4479	4480	4481	4485	4495

45 RN	45 SWC
.452"	.452"
230	250
4690*	4683*

Plastic Indoor Ammo

		Bullets	Cases
No. Per Box		50	50
Part No.	38 Cal.	8510	8515
	44 Cal.	8520	8525
	45 Cal.	8530	See Note

Note: Shown are 38 bullet and 38 case. 45 bullet is used with regular brass case.

Lead Balls

	Wt. (Grs.)	Diam.	Part No.		Wt. (Grs.)	Diam.	Part No.
Some 36 Pistols & Rifles	64	.350"	5110	44 Percussion Revolving Carb.	141	.454"	5135
36 Sheriffs Revolver 36 Leech & Rigdon Revolver 36 Navy Revolver	80	.375"	5113	Ruger New Old Army	144	.457"	5137
45 Hawken 45 Kentucky 45 Percussion Pistols	120	.433"	5127	50 Thompson Center Hawken	177	.490"	5139
45 Thompson Center Rifle Senecca Hawken	128	.440"	5129	50 Douglas 50 Sharon 50 Morse Navy	182	.495"	5140
45 Kentucky (F&P) 45 Mountain 45 Springfield 45 Yorkshire	133	.445"	5131	54 Thompson Center Renegade	224	.530"	5142
45 Michigan Carbine 45 Morse Navy 45 Huntsman				54 Douglas 54 Sharon 54 Mountain	230	.535"	5150
44 Revolvers 44 Percussion Revolving Carb. 44 Ballister Revolver	138	.451"	5133	58 Harpers Ferry Pistol 58 Morse Navy	278	.570"	5180

SPEER BIG GAME BULLETS

GRAND SLAM

Bullet Caliber & Type	6mm GS Soft Point	25 GS Soft Point	270 GS Soft Point	270 GS Soft Point	7mm GS Soft Point	7mm GS Soft Point	7mm GS Soft Point	30 GS Soft Point	30 GS Soft Point
Diameter	.243"	.257"	.277"	.277"	.284"	.284"	.284"	.308"	.308"
Weight (grs.)	100	120	130	150	145	160	175	150	165
Ballist. Coef.	0.351	0.328	0.345	0.385	0.327	0.387	0.465	0.305	0.393
Part Number	1222	1415	1465	1608	1632	1638	1643	2026	2038

AFRICAN GLAND SLAM

Bullet Caliber & Type	30 GS Soft Point	338 GS Soft Point	35 GS Soft Point	375 GS Soft Point
Diameter	.308"	.338"	.358"	375"
Weight (grs.)	180	250	250	285
Ballist. Coef.	0.416	0.431	0.335	0.354
Part Number	2063	2408	2455	2473

Bullet Caliber & Type	338 AGS Tungsten Solid	375 AGS Tungsten Solid	416 AGS Soft Point	416 AGS Tungsten Solid	45 AGS Soft Point	45 AGS Tungsten Solid
Diameter	338"	.375"	.416"	.416"	.458"	.458"
Weight (grs.)	275	300	400	400	500	500
Ballist. Coef.	0.291	0.258	0.381	0.262	0.285	0.277
Part Number	2414	2474	2475	2476	2485	2486

HERCULES SMOKELESS SPORTING POWDERS

Twelve types of Hercules smokeless sporting powders are available to the handloader. These have been selected from the wide range of powders produced for factory loading to provide at least one type that can be used efficiently and economically for each type of ammunition. These include:

BULLSEYE® A high-energy, quick-burning powder especially designed for pistol and revolver. The most popular powder for .38 special target loads. Can also be used for 12 gauge-1 oz. shotshell target loads.

RED DOT® The preferred powder for light-to-medium shotshells; specifically designed for 12-gauge target loads. Can also be used for handgun loads.

GREEN DOT® Designed for 12-gauge medium shotshell loads. Outstanding in 20-gauge skeet loads.

UNIQUE® Has an unusually broad application from light to heavy shotshell loads. As a handgun powder, it is our most versatile, giving excellent performance in many light to medium-heavy loads.

HERCO® A long-established powder for high velocity shotshell loads. Designed for heavy and magnum 10-, 12-, 16- and 20-gauge loads. Can also be used in high-performance handgun loads.

BLUE DOT® Designed for use in magnum shotshell loads, 10-, 12-, 16-, 20- and 28-gauge. Also provides top performance with clean burning in many magnum handgun loads.

HERCULES 2400® For use in small-capacity rifle cartridges and .410-Bore shotshell loads. Can also be used for large-caliber magnum handgun cartridges.

RELODER® SERIES Designed for use in center-fire rifle cartridges. Reloder 7, 12, 15, 19 and 22 provide the right powder for the right use. From small capacity to magnum loads. All of them deliver high velocity, clean burn, round-to-round consistency, and economy.

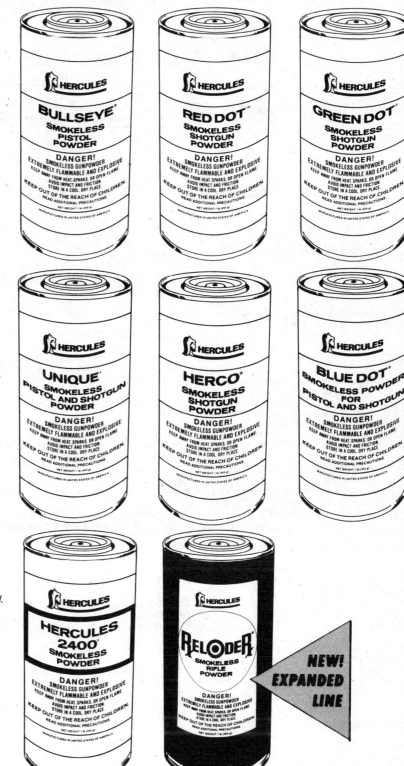

PACKAGING

POWDER	1-LB CANISTERS	4-LB CANISTERS	5-LB CANISTERS	8-LB KEG
Bullseye	●			●
Red Dot	●	●		●
Green Dot	●	●		●
Unique	●	●		●
Herco	●	●		●
Blue Dot	●		●	
Hercules 2400	●	●		●
Reloder Series	●		●	

HODGDON SMOKELESS POWDER

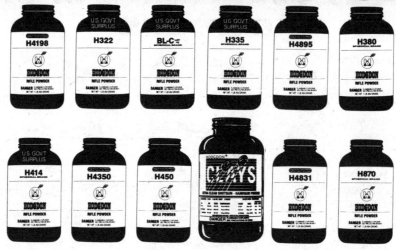

RIFLE POWDER

H4198

H4198 was developed especially for small and medium capacity cartridges.

H322

Any extruded bench rest powder which has proved to be capable of producing fine accuracy in the 22 and 308 bench rest guns. This powder fills the gap between H4198 and BL-C(2). Performs best in small to medium capacity cases.

SPHERICAL BL-C®, Lot No. 2

A highly popular favorite of the bench rest shooters. Best performance is in the 222, and in other cases smaller than 30/06.

SPHERICAL H335®

Similar to BL-C(2), H335 is popular for its performance in medium capacity cases, especially in 222 and 308 Winchester.

H4895®

4895 may well be considered the most versatile of all propellants. It gives desirable performance in almost all cases from 222 Rem. to 458 Win. Reduced loads, to as low as ³/₅ of maximum, still give target accuracy.

SPHERICAL H380®

This number fills a gap between 4320 and 4350. It is excellent in 22/250, 220 Swift, the 6mm's, 257 and 30/06.

SPHERICAL H414®

In many popular medium to medium-large calibers, pressure velocity relationship is better.

SPHERICAL H870®

Very slow burning rate adaptable to overbore capacity Magnum cases such as 257, 264, 270 and 300 Mags with heavy bullets.

H4350

This powder gives superb accuracy at optimum velocity for many large capacity metallic rifle cartridges.

H450

This slow-burning spherical powder is similar to H4831. It is recommended especially for 25-06, 7mm Mag., 30-06, 270 and 300 Win. and Wby. Mag.

H4831®

The most popular of all powders. Outstanding performance with medium and heavy bullets in the 6mm's, 25/06, 270 and Magnum calibers.

H1000 EXTRUDED POWDER

Fills the gap between H4831 and H870. Works especially well in overbore capacity cartridges (1,000-yard shooters take note).

SHOTGUN AND PISTOL POWDER

HP38

A fast pistol powder for most pistol loading. Especially recommended for mid-range 38 specials.

CLAYS

A new powder developed for 12 gauge clay target shooters. Also performs well in many handgun applications, including .38 Special, .40 S&W and 45 ACP. Perfect for 1¹/₈ and 1 oz. loads.

HS-6 and HS-7

HS-6 and HS-7 for Magnum field loads are unsurpassed, since they do not pack in the measure. They deliver uniform charges and are dense to allow sufficient wad column for best patterns.

H110

A spherical powder made especially for the 30 M1 carbine. H110 also does very well in 357, 44 Spec., 44 Mag. or .410 ga. shotshell. Magnum primers are recommended for consistent ignition.

H4227

An extruded powder similar to H110, it is the fastest burning in Hodgdon's line. Recommended for the 22 Hornet and some specialized loading in the 45/70 caliber. Also excellent in magnum pistol and .410 shotgun.

IMR SMOKELESS POWDERS

SHOTSHELL POWDER

Hi-Skor 700-X Double-Base Shotshell Powder. Specifically designed for today's 12-gauge components. Developed to give optimum ballistics at minimum charge weight (which means more reloads per pounds of powder). 700-X is dense, easy to load, clean to handle and loads uniformly.

PB Shotshell Powder. Produces exceptional 20 and 28-gauge skeet reloads; preferred by many in 12-gauge target loads, it gives 3-dram equivalent velocity at relatively low chamber pressures.

Hi-Skor 800-X Shotshell Powder. An excellent powder for 12-gauge field loads and 20 and 28-gauge loads.

SR-4756 Powder. Great all-around powder for target and field loads.

SR-7625. A fast-growing favorite for reloading target as well as light and heavy field loads in 4 gauges. Excellent velocity-chamber pressure.

IMR-4227 Powder. Can be used effectively for reloading .410-gauge shotshell ammunition.

RIFLE POWDER

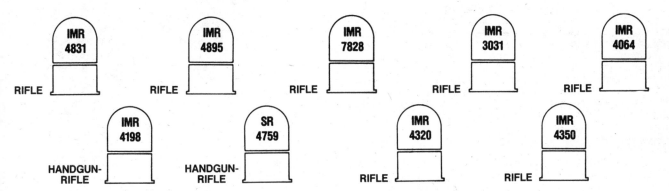

IMR-3031 Rifle Powder. Specifically recommended for medium-capacity cartridges.

IMR-4064 Rifle Powder. Has exceptionally uniform burning qualities when used in medium and large-capacity cartridges.

IMR-4198. Made the Remington 222 cartridge famous. Developed for small and medium-capacity cartridges.

IMR-4227 Rifle Powder. Fastest burning of the IMR Series. Specifically designed for the 22 Hornet class of cartridges.

SR-4759. Brought back by shooter demand. Available for cast bullet loads.

IMR-4320. Recommended for high-velocity cartridges.

IMR-4350 Rifle Powder. Gives unusually uniform results when loaded in Magnum cartridges.

IMR-4831. Produced as a canister-grade handloading powder. Packaged in 1 lb. canister, 8 lb. caddy and 20 lb. kegs.

IMR-4895 Rifle Powder. The time-tested standard for caliber 30 military ammunition; slightly faster than IMR-4320. Loads uniformly in all powder measures. One of the country's favorite powder.

IMR-7828 Rifle Powder. The slowest burning DuPont IMR canister powder, intended for large-capacity and magnum-type cases with heavy bullets.

PISTOL POWDER

PB Powder. Another powder for reloading a wide variety of centerfire handgun ammunition.

IMR-4227 Powder. Can be used effectively for reloading Magnum handgun ammunition.

Hi-Skor 700-X Powder. The same qualities that make it a superior powder contribute to its excellent performance in all the popular handguns.

Hi-Skor 800-X Powder. Good powder for heavier bullet handgun calibers.

SR-7625 Powder. For reloading a wide variety of centerfire handgun ammunition.

SR-4756. Clean burning with uniform performance. Can be used in a variety of handgun calibers.

FORSTER/BONANZA RELOADING TOOLS

CO-AX® BENCH REST® RIFLE DIES

Bench Rest Rifle Dies are glass hard for long wear and minimum friction. Interiors are polished mirror smooth. Special attention is given to headspace, tapers and diameters so that brass will not be overworked when resized. Sizing die has an elevated expander button which is drawn through the neck of the case at the moment of the greatest mechanical advantage of the press. Since most of the case neck is still in the die when expanding begins, better alignment of case and neck is obtained.

Bench Rest® Seating Die is of the chamber type. The bullet is held in alignment in a close-fitting channel. The case is held in a tight-fitting chamber. Both bullet and case are held in alignment while the bullet is being seated. Cross-bolt lock ring included at no charge.

Bench Rest® Die Set	$55.60
Full Length Sizer	25.80
Bench Rest Seating Die	30.90

PRIMER SEATER
with "E-Z-Just" Shellholder

The Bonanza Primer Seater is designed so that primers are seated Co-Axially (primer in line with primer pocket). Mechanical leverage allows primers to be seated fully without crushing. With the addition of one extra set of Disc Shell Holders and one extra Primer Unit, all modern cases, rim or rimless, from 222 up to 458 Magnum, can be primed. Shell holders are easily adjusted to any case by rotating to contact rim or cannelure of the case.

Primer Seater	$53.50
Primer Tube	4.00

PRIMER SEATER

CO-AX® INDICATOR

Bullets will not leave a rifle barrel at a uniform angle unless they are started uniformly. The Co-Ax Indicator provides a reading of how closely the axis of the bullet corresponds to the axis of the cartridge case. The Indicator features a spring-loaded plunger to hold cartridges against a recessed, adjustable rod while the cartridge is supported in a "V" block. To operate, simply rotate the cartridge with the fingers; the degree of misalignment is transferred to an indicator which measures in one-thousandths.

Price: Without dial $44.50
Indicator Dial 54.60

HORNADY

APEX-91 SHOTSHELL RELOADER

This new and versatile shotshell reloader has all the features of a progressive press along with the control, accuracy, easy operation and low price tag of a single-stage loader. You can load one shell at a time or seven shells at once, turning out a fully loaded shell with every pull of the handle. Other features include: extra-large shot hopper, short linkage arm, automatic dual-action crimp die, swing-out wad guide, and extra-long shot and powder feed tubes.

Apex-91 Shotshell Reloader (Automatic)
In 12 and 20 gauge	$375.00
In 28 and .410 gauge	414.00
Basic Die Set in 12 and 20 gauge	140.00
Basic Die Set in 28 and .410 gauge	179.50

Apex-91 Shotshell Reloader (Basic)
In 12 and 20 gauge	142.00
In 28 and .410 gauge	159.00
Automatic Die Set in 12 and 20 ga.	60.00
Automatic Die Set in 28 and .410 ga.	77.00

00-7 PRESS

- "Power-Pac" linkage multiplies lever-to-arm power.
- Frame of press angled 30° to one side, making the "O" area of press totally accessible.
- More mounting area for rock-solid attachment to bench.
- Special strontium-alloy frame provides greater stress resistance. Won't spring under high pressures needed for full-length resizing.

00-7 Press (does not include dies or shell holder)	$115.00
00-7 Automatic Primer Feed (complete with large and small primer tubes)	19.95

THE 00-7 PRESS PACKAGE
A reloading press complete with dies and shell holder

Expanded and improved to include Automatic Primer Feed. It sets you up to load many calibers and includes choice of a basic 00-7 complete with: • Set of New Dimension Dies • Primer catcher • Removable head shell holder • Positive Priming System • Automatic Primer Feed.

00-7 Package with Series I & II Dies (14 lbs.)	$163.00
00-7 Package Series II Titanium Nitride (15 lbs.)	177.00
00-7 Kit with Series I & II Dies	335.00
00-7 Kit with Titanium Nitride Dies	350.00

THE HANDLOADER'S ACCESSORY PACK I

Here's everything you need in one money-saving pack. It includes: • Deluxe powder measure • Powder scale • Two non-static powder funnels • Universal loading block • Primer turning plate • Case lube • Chamfering and deburring tool • 3 case neck brushes • Large and small primer pocket cleaners • Accessory handle. Plus one copy of the *Hornady Handbook of Cartridge Reloading*.

Handloader's Accessory Pack I No. 030300	$180.00

HORNADY

TRIMMER PACKAGE

Combines Hornady's Case Trimmer with the new Metric Caliper and Steel Dial Caliper, which measures case and bullet lengths plus inside/outside diameters. Made from machined steel, the caliper provides extremely accurate measurements with an easy-to-read large dial gauge.

Trimmer Package **$165.15**
    With Micrometer **214.60**

NEW DIMENSION RELOADING DIES

Features an Elliptical Expander that minimizes friction and reduces case neck stretch, plus the need for a tapered expander for "necking up" to the next larger caliber. Other recent design changes include a hardened steel decap pin that will not break, bend or crack even when depriming stubborn military cases. A bullet seater alignment sleeve guides the bullet and case neck into the die for in-line benchhrest alignment. All New Dimension Reloading Dies include: collar and collar lock to center expander precisely; one-piece expander spindle with tapered bottom for easy cartridge insertion; wrench flats on die body, Sure-Loc™ lock rings and collar lock for easy tightening; and built-in crimper.

New Dimension Reloading Dies:
Series I Two-die Rifle Set **$25.00**
Series I Three-die Rifle Set **27.00**
Series II Three-die Pistol Set (w/Titanium Nitride) **38.00**
Series III Two-die Rifle Set **31.75**
Series IV Custom Die Set **54.00**

PRO-JECTOR PRESS PACKAGE

- Includes Pro-Jector Press, set of New Dimension dies, automatic primer feed, brass kicker, primer catcher, shell plate, and automatic primer shut-off
- Just place case in shell plate, start bullet, pull lever and drop powder. Automatic rotation of shell plate prepares next round.
- Fast inexpensive changeover requires only shell plate and set of standard 7/8 × 14 threaded dies.
- Primes automatically.
- Power-Pac Linkage assures high-volume production even when full-length sizing.
- Uses standard powder measures and dies.

Series I & II **$393.75**
Seriess II Titanium Nitride Dies **407.00**
Extra Shell Plates **22.50**
Pro-Jector Kit with Serles I & II Dies **567.00**
Kit Series II with Titanium Nitride Dics **580.00**

MODEL 366 AUTO SHOTSHELL RELOADER

The 366 Auto features full-length resizing with each stroke, automatic primer feed, swing-out wad guide, three-stage crimping featuring Taper-Loc for factory tapered crimp, automatic advance to the next station and automatic ejection. The turntable holds 8 shells for 8 operations with each stroke. The primer tube filler is fast. The automatic charge bar loads shot and powder. Right- or left-hand operation; Interchangeable charge bushings, die sets and Magnum dies and crimp starters for 6 point, 8 point and paper crimps.

Model 366 Auto Shotshell Reloader:
12, 20, 28 gauge or .410 bore **$475.00**
Model 366 Auto Die Set **94.50**
Auto Advance **46.60**
Swing-out Wad Guide & Shell Drop Combo **115.00**

LYMAN BULLET SIZING EQUIPMENT

MAG 20 ELECTRIC FURNACE

The MAG 20 is a new furnace offering several advantages to cast bullet enthusiasts. It features a steel crucible of 20-pound capacity and incorporates a proven bottom-pour valve system and a fully adjustable mould guide. The improved design of the MAG 20 makes it equally convenient to use the bottom-pour valve, or a ladle. A new heating coil design reduces the likelihood of pour spout "freeze." Heat is controlled from "Off" to nominally 825° F by a calibrated thermostat which automatically increases temperature output when alloy is added to the crucible. A pre-heat shelf for moulds is attached to the back of the crucible. Availalbe for 100 V and 200 V systems.

Price: 110 V **$259.95**
220 V **260.00**

BULLET MAKING EQUIPMENT

Deburring Tool
Lyman's deburring tool can be used for chamfering or deburring of cases up to 45 caliber. For precise bullet seating, use the pointed end of the tool to bevel the inside of new or trimmed cases. To remove burrs left by trimming, place the other end of the deburring tool over the mouth of the case and twist. The tool's centering pin will keep the case aligned . . **$13.50**

Mould Handles
These large hardwood handles are available in three sizes single-, double- and four-cavity.
Single-cavity handles (for small block, black powder and specialty moulds; 12 oz.) **$21.95**
Double-cavity handles (for two-cavity and large-block single-cavity moulds; 12 oz.) **21.95**
Four-cavity handles (1 lb.) **24.95**

Rifle Moulds
All Lyman rifle moulds are available in double cavity only, except those moulds where the size of the bullet necessitates a single cavity (12 oz.) **$48.95**

Hollow-Point Bullet Moulds
Hollow-point moulds are cut in single-cavity blocks only and require single-cavity handles (9 oz.) **$48.95**

Shotgun Slug Moulds
Available in 12 or 20 gauge; do not require rifling. Moulds are single cavity only, cut on the larger double-cavity block and require double-cavity handles (14 oz.) **$49.95**

Pistols Moulds
Cover all popular calibers and bullet designs in double-cavity blocks and, on a limited basis, four-cavity blocks.
Double-cavity mould block **$48.95**
Four-cavity mould block **79.95**

Lead Casting Dipper
Dipper with cast-iron head. The spout is shaped for easy, accurate pouring that prevents air pockets in the finished bullet **$11.95**

Gas Checks
Gas checks are gilding metal caps which fit to the base of cast bullets. These caps protect the bullet base from the burning effect of hot powder gases and permit higher velocities. Easily seated during the bullet sizing operation. Only Lyman gas checks should be used with Lyman cast bullets.

22 through 35 caliber (per 1000) **$23.95**
375 through 45 caliber (per 1000) **27.95**
Gas check seater **7.95**

Lead Pot
The cast-iron pot allows the bullet caster to use any source of heat. Pot capacity is about 8 pounds of alloy and the flat bottom prevents tipping **$13.00**

Universal Decapping Die
Covers all calibers .22 through .45 (except .378 and .460 Weatherby). Can be used before cases are cleaned or lubricated. Requires no adjustment when changing calibers; fits all popular makes of $7/8 \times 14$ presses, single station or progressive, and is packaged with 10 replacement pins   **$10.95**

UNIVERSAL CARBIDE FOUR-DIE SET

Lyman's new 4-die carbide sets allow simultaneous neck expanding and powder charging. They feature specially designed hollow expanding plugs that utilize Lyman's 2-step neck-expansion system, while allowing powder to flow through the die into the cartridge case after expanding. Includes taper crimp die. All popular pistol calibers. **$47.95**

LYMAN RELOADING TOOLS

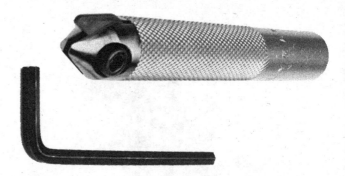

"INSIDE/OUTSIDE" DEBURRING TOOL

This unique new tool features an adjustable cutting blade that adapts easily to any rifle or pistol case from 22 caliber to 45 caliber with a simple hex wrench adjustment. Inside deburring is completed by a conical internal section with slotted cutting edges, thus providing uniform inside and outside deburring in one simple operation. The deburring tool is mounted on an anodized aluminum handle that is machine-knurled for a sure grip.

Deburring Tool **$17.95**

MAG TUMBLER

This new Mag Tumbler features an industrial strength motor and large 14-inch bowl design. With a working capacity of 2¾ gallons, it cleans more than 1,500 pistol cases in each cycle. The Mag Tumbler is also suitable for light industrial use in deburring and polishing metal parts. Available in 110V or 220V, with standard on/off switch.

Mag Tumbler **$299.95**

TUBBY TUMBLER

This popular tumbler now features a clear plastic "see thru" lid that fits on the outside of the vibrating tub. The Tubby has a polishing action that cleans more than 100 pistol cases in less than two hours. The built-in handle allows easy dumping of cases and media. An adjustable tab also allows the user to change the tumbling speed for standard or fast action.

Tubby Tumbler **$79.95**

MUZZLELOADERS' CASTING KIT

Designed especially to meet the needs of blackpowder shooters, this new kit features Lyman's combination round ball and maxi ball mould blocks. It also contains a combination double cavity mould, mould handle, mini-mag furnace, lead dipper, bullet lube, a user's manual and a cast bullet guide. Kits are available in 45, 50 and 54 caliber.

Muzzleloaders' Casting Kit **$89.95**

LYMAN RELOADING TOOLS

FOR RIFLE OR PISTOL CARTRIDGES

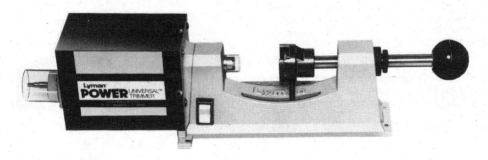

POWER CASE TRIMMER

The new Lyman Power Trimmer is powered by a fan-cooled electric motor designed to withstand the severe demands of case trimming. The unit, which features the Universal™ Chuckhead, allows cases to be positioned for trimming or removed with fingertip ease. The Power Trimmer package includes Nine Pilot Multi-Pack. In addition to two cutter heads, a pair of wire end brushes for cleaning primer pockets are included. Other features include safety guards, on-off rocker switch, heavy cast base with receptacles for nine pilots, and bolt holes for mounting on a work bench. Available for 110 V or 220 V systems.

Prices: 110 V Model **$199.95**
        220 V Model **210.00**

ACCULINE OUTSIDE NECK TURNER
(not shown)

To obtain perfectly concentric case necks, Lyman's Outside Neck Turner assures reloaders of uniform neck wall thickness and outside neck diameter. The unit fits Lyman's Universal Trimmer and AccuTrimmer. In use, each case is run over a mandrel, which centers the case for the turning operation. The cutter is carefully adjusted to remove a minimum amount of brass. Rate of feed is adjustable and a mechanical stop controls length of cut. Mandrels are available for calibers from .17 to .375; cutter blade can be adjusted for any diameter from .195″ to .405″.

Outside Neck Turner w/extra blade, 6 mandrels . . . **$28.95**
Outside Neck Turner only **19.95**
Individual Mandrels **4.00**

STARTER KIT

Includes "Orange Crusher" Press, loading block, case lube kit, primer tray, Model 500 scale, powder funnel and Lyman Reloading Handbook.

Starter Kit **$189.95**

LYMAN "ORANGE CRUSHER" RELOADING PRESS

The only press for rifle or pistol cartridges that offers the advantage of powerful compound leverage combined with a true magnum press opening. A unique handle design transfers power easily where you want it to the center of the ram. A 4½-inch press opening accommodates even the largest cartridges.

"Orange Crusher" Press:
With Priming Arm and Catcher **$109.95**

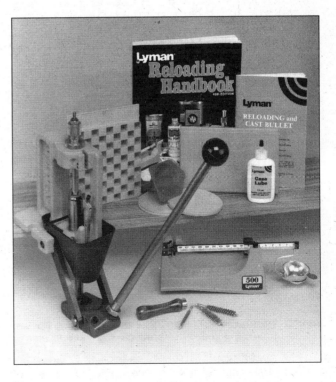

STARTER KIT

LYMAN RELOADING TOOLS

T-MAG TURRET RELOADING PRESS

With the T-Mag you can mount up to six different reloading dies on our turret. This means you can have all your dies set up, precisely mounted, locked in and ready to reload at all times. The T-Mag works with all $7/8 \times 14$ dies. The T-Mag turret with its quick-disconnect release system is held in rock-solid alignment by a $3/4$-inch steel stud.

Also featured is Lyman's Orange Crusher compound leverage system. It has a longer handle with a ball-type knob that mounts easily for right- or left-handed operation.

T-Mag Press w/Priming Arm & Catcher **$144.95**
    Extra Turret Head **19.95**

Also available:
EXPERT KIT that includes T-MAG Press, Universal Case Trimmer and pilot Multi-Pak, Model 500 powder scale and Model 50 powder measure, plus accessories. Available in calibers 9mm Luger, 38/357, 44 Mag., 45 ACP and 30-06 . . . . **$399.95**

ELECTRONIC SCALE MODEL LE: 1000

Accurate to $1/10$ grain, Lyman's new LE: 1000 measures up to 1000 grains of powder and easily converts to the gram mode for metric measurements. The push-botton automatic calibration feature eliminates the need for calibrating with a screwdriver. The scale works off a single 9V battery or AC power adaptor (included with each scale). Its compact design allows the LE: 1000 to be carried to the field easily. A sculpted carrying case is optional. 110 Volt or 220 Volt.

Model LE: 1000 Electronic Scale **$339.60**

PISTOL ACCUMEASURE

Lyman's Pistol AccuMeasure uses changeable brass rotors pre-drilled to drop precise charges of ball and flake pistol propellants (the tool is not intended for use with long grain IMR-type powders). Most of the rotors are drilled with two cavities for maximum accuracy and consistency. The brass operating handle, which can be shifted for left or right hand operation, can be removed. The Pistol AccuMeasure can be mounted on all turret and single station presses; it can also be hand held with no loss of accuracy.

Pistol AccuMeasure **$22.00**
    With 3-rotor starter kit **32.95**

Also available:
AMMO HANDLER KIT that includes every tool (except reloading press) needed to produce high-quality ammunition **$174.95**
ROTOR SELECTION SET including 8 dual-cavity rotors and 4 single-cavity units. Enables reloaders to throw a variety of charges for all pistol calibers through 45 . . . . **$49.95**

MEC SHOTSHELL RELOADERS

MODEL 600 JR. MARK 5
$151.81

MODEL 8567 GRABBER
$428.28

This single-stage reloader features a cam-action crimp die to ensure that each shell returns to its original condition. MEC's 600 Jr. Mark 5 can load 8 to 10 boxes per hour and can be updated with the 285 CA primer feed. Press is adjustable for 3″ shells. Die sets are available in all gauges at **$54.90.**

This reloader features 12 different operations at all 6 stations, producing finished shells with each stroke of the handle. It includes a fully automatic primer feed and Auto-Cycle charging, plus MEC's exclusive 3-stage crimp. The "Power Ring" resizer ensures consistent, accurately sized shells without interrupting the reloading sequence. Simply put in the wads and shell casings, then remove the loaded shells with each pull of the handle. Optional kits to load 3″ shells and steel shot make this reloader tops in its field. Resizes high and low base shells. Available in 12, 16, 20, 28 gauge and .410 bore. No die sets are available.

MODEL 650
$298.54

MODEL 8120 SIZEMASTER
$228.75

This reloader works on 6 shells at once. A reloaded shell is completed with every stroke. The MEC 650 does not resize except as a separate operation. Automatic Primer feed is standard. Simply fill it with a full box of primers and it will do the rest. Reloader has 3 crimping stations: the first one starts the crimp, the second closes the crimp, and the third places a taper on the shell. Available in 12, 16, 20 and 28 gauge and .410 bore. No die sets are available.

Sizemaster's "Power Ring" collet resizer returns each base to factory specifications. This new generation resizing station handles brass or steel heads, both high and low base. An 8-fingered collet squeezes the base back to original dimensions, then opens up to release the shell easily. The E-Z Prime auto primer feed is standard equipment. Press is adjustable for 3″ shells and is available in 12, 16, 20, 28 gauge and .410 bore. Die sets are available at: **$85.26 ($100.00** in 10 ga.).

MEC RELOADING

MEC 8462 SPINDEX STAR CRIMP HEADS
(not shown)

Dual purpose 6 & 8 fold Spindex Kit in 12, 16 and 20 gauge. **$4.65**
In 10, 28 gauge and .410 bore 4.08

Additional MEC Accessories:
301L 13X BH & Cap Assy. **$3.99**
8300 Wad Finger Ptlc. 1.24
8042 Magnum Container 5.68
15CA E-Z Pak Accy. 6.99

E-Z PRIME "S"

E-Z PRIME "S" AND "V"
AUTOMATIC PRIMER FEEDS

From carton to shell with security, these primer feeds provide safe, convenient primer positioning and increase rate of production. Reduce bench clutter, allowing more free area for wads and shells.

- Primers transfer directly from carton to reloader, tubes and tube fillers
- Positive mechanical feed (not dependent upon agitation of press)
- Visible supply
- Automatic. Eliminate hand motion
- Less susceptible to damage
- Adapt to all domestic and most foreign primers with adjustment of the cover
- May be purchased separately to replace tube-type primer feed or to update your present reloader

E-Z Prime "S" (for Super 600, 650) or
E-Z Prime "V" (for 600 Jr. Mark V & VersaMEC) . . . **$37.07**

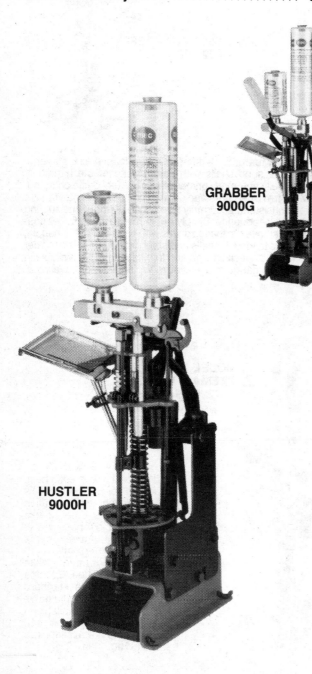

**GRABBER
9000G**

**HUSTLER
9000H**

MEC 9000 SERIES SHOTSHELL RELOADER

MEC's new 9000 Series features automatic indexing and finished shell ejection for quicker and easier reloading. The factory set speed provides uniform movement through every reloading stage. Dropping the primer into the reprime station no longer requires operator "feel." The reloader requires only a minimal adjustment from low to high brass domestic shells, any one of which can be removed for inspection from any station.

MEC 9000H Hustler **$1256.26**
MEC 9000G Grabber 520.00

MTM

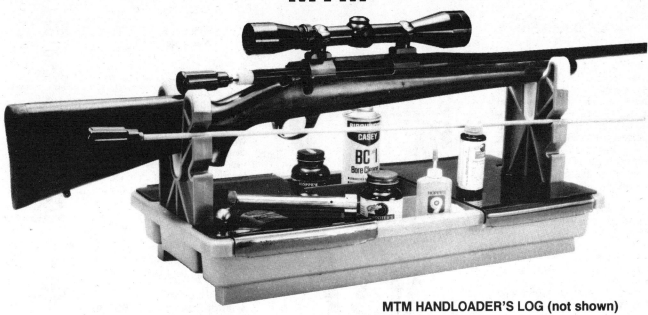

PORTABLE RIFLE MAINTENANCE CENTER

Holds rifles and shotguns for easy cleaning and maintenance (can also be used as a shooting rest). Features gun forks with built-in cleaning rod holders; sliding see-through dust covers; tough polypropylene material; fits conveniently on top of Case-Gard A-760.

Price: $29.15

50 ROUND HANDGUN AMMO BOXES

Designed with the shooter in mind, these 50-round ammo boxes feature a new "Step Design" on the partitions inside (for "E-Z" ammo extraction). The specially grooved lid is designed to match up with the feet on the bottom so that they nest into each other. Each box is supplied with its own label for recording custom loads.

Price: $1.20

MTM HANDLOADER'S LOG (not shown)

Space is provided for 1,000 entries covering date, range, group size or score, components, and conditions. Book is heavy-duty vinyl, reinforced 3-ring binder.

HL-74 . . . . **$9.50**
HL-50 (incl. 50 extra log sheets) **3.95**

CASE-GARD 100 AMMO CARRIER
FOR SKEET AND TRAP (not shown)

The MTM™ Case-Gard® 100-round shotshell case carries 100 rounds in 2 trays; or 50 rounds plus 2 boxes of factory ammo; or 50 rounds plus sandwiches and insulated liquid container; or 50 round with room left for fired hulls. Features include:
- Recessed top handle for easy storage.
- High-impact material supports 300 pounds, and will not warp, split, expand or contract.
- Dustproof and rainproof.
- Living hinge guaranteed 3 years.
- Available in deep forest green.

S-100-12 (12 gauge) **$16.00**
S-100-20 (20 gauge) **16.00**

FUNNELS

MTM Benchrest Funnel Set is designed specifically for the bench-rest shooter. One fits 222 and 243 cases only; the other 7mm and 308 cases. Both can be used with pharmaceutical vials popular with bench-rest competitors for storage of pre-weighed charges. Funnel design prevents their rolling off the bench.

MTM Universal Funnel fits all calibers from 222 to 45.
UF-1 . . . . **$2.87**

Patented MTM Adapt 5-in-1 Funnel Kit includes funnel, adapters for 17 Rem., 222 Rem. and 30 through 45. Long drop tube facilitates loading of maximum charges: 222 to 45.
AF-5 . . . . **$4.14**

RCBS RELOADING TOOLS

ROCK CHUCKER "COMBO"

The Rock Chucker Press, with patented RCBS compound leverage system, delivers up to 200% more leverage than most presses for heavy-duty reloading of even the largest rifle and pistol cases. Rugged, Block "O" Frame prevents press from springing out of alignment even under the most strenuous operations. It case-forms as easily as most presses full-length size; it full-length sizes and makes bullets with equal ease. Shell holders snap into sturdy, all-purpose shell holder ram. Non-slip handle with convenient grip. Operates on downstroke for increased leverage. Standard 7/8-inch×14 thread.

Rock Chucker Press
(Less dies) **$140.90**

PRIMER POCKET SWAGER COMBO

For fast, precision removal of primer pocket crimp from military cases. Leaves primer pocket perfectly rounded and with correct dimensions for seating of American Boxer-type primers. Will not leave oval-shaped primer pocket that reaming produces. Swager Head Assemblies furnished for large and small primer pockets no need to buy a complete unit for each primer size. For use with all presses with standard 7/8-inch×14 top thread, except RCBS "A-3" Press. The RCBS "A-2" Press requires the optional Case Stripper Washer.

**Primer Pocket
Swager Combo** **$24.80**

ROCK CHUCKER MASTER RELOADING KIT

For reloaders who want the best equipment, the Rock Chucker Master Reloading Kit includes all the tools and accessories needed. Included are the following: • Rock Chucker Press • RCBS 505 Reloading Scale • Speer Reloading Manual #11 • Uniflow Powder Measure • RCBS Rotary Case Trimmer-2 • deburring tool • case loading block • Primer Tray-2 • Automatic Primer Feed Combo • powder funnel • case lube pad • case neck brushes • fold-up hex ket set.

Rock Chucker Master Reloading Kit **$374.72**

PRIMER POCKET BRUSH COMBO

A slight twist of this tool thoroughly cleans residue out of primer pockets. Interchangeable stainless steel brushes for large and small primer pockets attach easily to accessory handle.

Primer Pocket Brush Combo **$12.94**

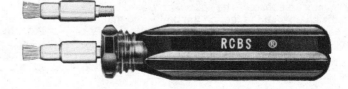

RCBS RELOADING TOOLS

RELOADER SPECIAL-5

This RCBS Reloader Special-5 Press is the ideal setup to get started reloading your own rifle and pistol ammo from 12 gauge shotshells and the largest Magnums down to 22 Hornets. This press develops ample leverage and pressure to perform all reloading tasks including: (1) resizing cases their full length; (2) forming cases from one caliber into another; (3) making bullets. Rugged Block "O" Frame, designed by RCBS, prevents press from springing out of alignment even under tons of pressure. Frame is offset 30° for unobstructed front access, and is made of 48,000 psi aluminum alloy. Compound leverage system allows you to swage bullets, full-length resize cases, form 30-06 cases into other calibers. Counter-balanced handle prevents accidental drop. Extra-long ram-bearing surface minimizes wobble and side play. Standard 7/8-inch-14 thread accepts all popular dies and reloading accessories.

Reloader Special-5
(Less dies) **$109.72**

**RELOADER
SPECIAL-5**

RELOADING SCALE
MODEL 5-0-5

This 511-grain capacity scale has a three-poise system with widely spaced, deep beam notches to keep them in place. Two smaller poises on right side adjust from 0.1 to 10 grains, larger one on left side adjusts in full 10-grain steps. The first scale to use magnetic dampening to eliminate beam oscillation, the 5-0-5 also has a sturdy die-cast base with large leveling legs for stability. Self-aligning agate bearings support the hardened steel beam pivots for a guaranteed sensitivity to 0.1 grains.

Model 5-0-5 . . . . **$79.50**

AMMOMASTER

AMMOMASTER RELOADING
SYSTEM

The AmmoMaster offers the handloader the freedom to configure a press to his particular needs and preferences. It covers the complete spectrum of reloading, from single stage through fully automatic progressive reloading, from .32 Auto to .50 caliber. The **AmmoMaster Auto** has all the features of a five-station press.

AmmoMaster **$189.74**
AmmoMaster Auto **432.48**

**AMMOMASTER
AUTO**

RELOADING SCALE
MODEL 10-10

Up to 1010 Grain Capacity
Normal capacity is 510 grains, which can be increased, without loss in sensitivity, by attaching the included extra weight.

Features include micrometer poise for quick, precise weighing, special approach-to-weight indicator, easy-to-read graduations, magnetic dampener, agate bearings, anti-tip pan, and dustproof lid snaps on to cover scale for storage. Sensitivity is guaranteed to 0.1 grains.

Model 10-10 Scale **$122.50**

RCBS RELOADING TOOLS

ELECTRONIC SCALE

This new RCBS Electronic Scale brings solid state electronic accuracy and convenience to handloaders. The LCD digital readings are ideal for weighing bullets and cases. The balance gives readings in grains, from zero to 500. The tare feature allows direct reading of the sample's weight with or without using the scale pan. The scale can be used on the range, operating on 8 AA batteries (approx. 50 hours).

Electronic Scale **$395.00**

POWDER CHECKER

Operates on a free-moving rod for simple, mechanical operation with nothing to break. Standard $7/8 \times 14$ die body can be used in any progressive loader that takes standard dies. Black oxide finish provides corrosion resistance with good color contrast for visibility.

Powder Checker **$24.38**

UPM MICROMETER ADJUSTMENT SCREW

Handloaders who want the convenience of a micrometer adjustment on their Uniflow Powder Measure can now add that feature to their powder measure. The RCBS Micrometer Adjustment Screw fits any Uniflow Powder Measure equipped with a large cylinder. It is easily installed by removing the standard metering screw, lock ring and bushing, which are replaced by the micrometer unit. Handloaders may then record the micrometer reading for a specific charge of a given powder and return to that setting at a later date when the same charge is used again.

UPM Micrometer Adjustment Screw **$34.98**

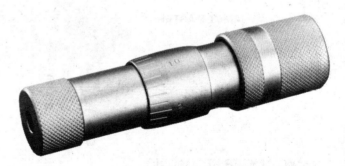

PRECISION MIC

This "Precisioneered Cartridge Micrometer" provides micrometer readings of case heads to shoulder lengths, improving accuracy by allowing the best possible fit of cartridge to chamber. By allowing comparison of the chamber to SAAMI specifications, it alerts the handloader to a long chamber or excess headspace situation. It also ensures accurate adjustment of seater die to provide optimum seating depth. Available in 19 popular calibers.

Precision MIC **$39.22**

REDDING RELOADING TOOLS

MODEL 721
"THE BOSS" PRESS

This "O" type reloading press features a rigid cast iron frame whose 36° offset provides the best visibility and access of comparable presses. Its "Smart" primer arm moves in and out of position automatically with ram travel. The priming arm is positioned at the bottom of ram travel for lowest leverage and best feel. Model 721 accepts all standard 7/8-14 threaded dies and universal shell holders.

Model 721 "The Boss" **$102.50**
    With Shellholder and 10A Dies **132.00**

Also available:
Boss Pro-Pak Deluxe Reloading Kit. Includes Boss Reloading Press, #2 Powder and Bullet Scale, Powder Trickler, Reloading Dies, and more **$261.50**

ULTRAMAG MODEL 700

Unlike other reloading presses that connect the linkage to the lower half of the press, the Ultramag's compound leverage system is connected at the top of the press frame. This allows the reloader to develop tons of pressure without the usual concern about press frame deflection. Huge frame opening will handle 50 × 3 1/4-inch Sharps with ease.

No. 700 Press, complete **$229.50**
No. 700K Kit, includes shell holder and one set of dies **259.00**

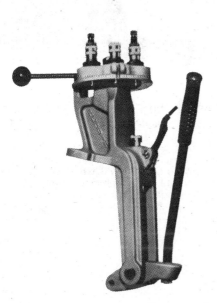

METALLIC TURRET RELOADING PRESS
MODEL 25

Extremely rugged, ideal for production reloading. No need to move shell, just rotate turret head to positive alignment. Ram accepts any standard snap-in shell holder. Includes primer arm for seating both small and large primers.

No. 25 Press, complete **$239.00**
No. 25K Kit, includes press, shell holder, and one set of dies **269.00**

REDDING RELOADING TOOLS

MASTER POWDER MEASURE MODEL 3

Universal- or pistol-metering chambers interchange in seconds. Measures charges from ¹/₂ to 100 grains. Unit is fitted with lock ring for fast dump with large "clear" plastic reservoir. "See-thru" drop tube accepts all calibers from 22 to 600. Precision-fitted rotating drum is critically honed to prevent powder escape. Knife-edged powder chamber shears coarse-grained powders with ease, ensuring accurate charges.

No. 3 Master Powder Measure
(specify Universal- or Pistol-
Metering chamber) . . . . **$ 89.50**
No. 3K Kit Form, includes both
Universal and Pistol
chambers **109.50**
**No. 3-12 Universal or Pistol
chamber** **22.00**

MATCH GRADE POWDER MEASURE MODEL 3BR

Designed for the most demanding reloaders—bench rest, silhouette and varmint shooters. The Model 3BR is unmatched for its precision and repeatability. Its special features include a powder baffle and zero backlash micrometer.

No. 3BR with Universal or Pistol
Metering Chamber **$109.50**
No. 3 BRK includes both metering chambers **139.50**
No. 3-30 Benchrest metering chambers (fit only 3BR) . . . **32.00**

COMPETITION MODEL BR-30 POWDER MEASURE (not shown)

This powder measure features a new drum and micrometer that limit the overall charging range from a low of 10 grains (depending on powder density) to a maximum of approx. 50 grains. For serious competitive shooters whose loading requirements are between 10 and 50 grains, this is the measure to choose. The diameter of Model 3BR's metering cavity has been reduced, and the metering plunger on the new model has a unique hemispherical or cup shape, creating a powder cavity that resembles the bottom of a test tube. The result: irregular powder setting is alleviated and charge-to-charge uniformity is enhanced.

Competition Model BR-30 Powder Measure **$129.50**

MASTER CASE TRIMMER MODEL 1400

This unit features a universal collet that accepts all rifle and pistol cases. The frame is solid cast iron with storage holes in the base for extra pilots. Both coarse and fine adjustments are provided for case length.

The case-neck cleaning brush and primer pocket cleaners attached to the frame of this tool make it a very handy addition to the reloading bench. Trimmer comes complete with:
• New speed cutter shaft
• Six pilots (22, 6mm, 25, 270, 7mm and 30 cal.)
• Universal collet
• Two neck cleaning brushes (22 thru 30 cal.)
• Two primer pocket cleaners (large and small)

No. 1400 Master Case Trimmer complete **$74.50**
No. 1500 Pilots **3.00**

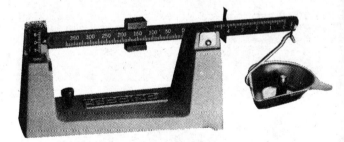

STANDARD POWDER AND BULLET SCALE MODEL RS-1

For the beginner or veteran reloader. Only two counterpoises need to be moved to obtain the full capacity range of ¹/₁₀ grain to 380 grains. Clearly graduated with white numerals and lines on a black background. Total capacity of this scale is 380 grains. An over-and-under plate graduate in 10th grains allows checking of variations in powder charges or bullets without further adjustments.

Model No. RS-1 . . . . **$51.00**

Also available: **Master Powder & Bullet Scale.** Same as standard model, but includes a magnetic dampened beam swing for extra fast readings. 505-grain capacity **$64.50**

Reference

THE SHOOTER'S BOOKSHELF

An up-to-date listing of recently published book titles of special interest to shooters and gun enthusiasts. Most of these books can be found at your local library, bookstore, or gunshop. If not available, contact the publisher directly. For a complete listing of in-print titles covering all subjects of interest to shooters, turn to the *Subject Guide to Books in Print,* which is updated annually and is available at most public libraries. Each of the following entries includes date of publication, number of pages, publisher and retail price along with the title and author.

AMMUNITION
Ammunition Handbook, 1991. Gordon Press. lib. bdg. $79.95

ARCHERY
Combs, Roger. **Archer's Digest,** 5th ed. (Illus.). 256 p. 1991. DBI. pap. $14.95

ARMS & ARMOR
Brenner, Eliot. **Desert Storm: The Weapons of War.** 1991. Crown. pap. $9.00

Foss, Christopher F., ed. **Jane's Armour & Artillery 1991–1992.** (Illus). 900 p. Janes Info Group. $170.00

Kimmel, Jay. **Savage-Stevens Arms: Collectors Edition.** (Illus.). 230 p. 1990. Corey-Stevens Pub. pap. $24.95

Wright, James D., et al. **Under the Gun: Weapons, Crime & Violence in America.** 362 p. 1986. Aldine de Gruyten. pap. $20.95

BALLISTICS
Pejsa, Arthur. **Modern Practical Ballistics,** 2d ed. (Illus.). 224 p. 1991. Kenwood Pub. $17.95

BLACK POWDER
Roberts, Ned H. **The Muzzle-loading Cap Lock Rifle.** 216 p. 1991. Wolfe. $30.00

CARTRIDGES
Big Bore Rifles & Cartridges. (Illus.). 360 p. 1990. Wolfe Pub. $26.00

Stowers, Roger. **Gibbs on Rifles & Cartridges.** 1990. 64 p. Wolfe Pub. $14.95

Wildcat Cartridges (from Handloader Mag.). 125 p. 1992. Wolfe Pub. pap. $16.95

DECOYS
Barber, Joel. **Wild Fowl Decoys,** 2d ed. (Illus.). 151 p. repr. of 1934 ed. Derrydale Press. $39.95

DEER HUNTING (see also Hunting)
Warren, Michael. **Deer Dad: A Hunter's Guide.** 200 p. 1991. Ledero Press. pap. $13.95

FIREARMS
Fadala, Sam. **Great Shooters of the World.** (Illus.). 288 p. 1990. Stoeger Pub. pap. $18.95

Grennell, Dean A. **Handgun Digest,** 2d ed. (Illus.). 256 p. 1991. pap. $15.95

Jarrett, William, ed. **Shooter's Bible 1993.** (Illus.). 576 p. 1992. Stoeger Pub. pap. $18.95

Lewis, Jack, ed. **Handguns 1992,** 4th ed. (Illus.). 320 p. 1991. DBI. pap. $16.95

Lewis, Jack, ed. **Gun Digest Book of Modern Gun Values,** 8th ed. 528 p. 1991. DBI. pap. $18.95

Magnum School Inc., Staff. **Firearms: A Complete Guide for Their Proper Use & Care.** (Illus.). 103 p. 1990. Magnum School. Price not set.

Medlin, Eugene & Doane, Colin. **The French Modele 1935 Pistols: 32s with a French Accent.** (Illus.). 288 p. 1990. BFH. $40.00

Murtz, Harold A., ed. **Guns Illustrated, 1992.** 24th ed. 320 p. 1991. DBI. pap. $16.95

O'Connor, Jack. **Jack O'Connor's Gun Book** (new ed.). 208 p. 1992. Wolfe Pub. $26.00

Quigley, Paxton. **Armed & Female: 12 Million American Women Own Guns, Should You?** 1990. St. Martins. pap. $4.50

van Zwoll, Wayne. **America's Great Gunmakers.** (Illus.). 288 p. 1992. Stoeger Pub. pap. $16.95

Warner, Ken, ed. **Gun Digest 1992.** (Illus.). 496 p. 1991. DBI. pap. $19.95

FIREARMS—CATALOGS
Brdik, Dan. **Standard Catalog of Firearms.** (Illus.). 672 p. 1991. Krause Pub. pap. $24.95

Fjestad, Steven, **Blue Book of Gun Values,** 12th ed. (Illus.). 1024 p. 1991. Blue Book Pubns. pap. $19.95

FIREARMS—COLLECTORS & COLLECTING
Gun Trader's Guide, 15th ed. (Illus.). 528 p. 1992. Stoeger Pub. pap. $18.95

Benson, Ragnar. **Modern Weapons Caching: A Down-to-Earth Approach to Beating the Government Gun Grab.** (Illus.). 104 p. 1990. Paladin Press. pap. $14.00

FIREARMS—HISTORY
Gresham, Tom & Gresham, Grits. **Weatherby: The Man, the Gun, the Legend.** (Illus.). 256 p. 1991. Cane River AK. $22.95

Henderson, Halton. **Artistry in Single Action: The Dallas Six Gun.** ltd. ed. (Illus.). 125 p. 1989. Chama Press. $299.00

Keith, Elmer. **Sixguns** (replica edition). 308 p. 1992. Wolfe Pub. $34.95

Serven, James. **Colt Firearms** (facsimile ed.). 400 p. 1991. Wolfe Pub. $45.00

van Zwoll, Wayne. **America's Great Gunmakers.** (Illus.). 288 p. 1992. Stoeger Pub. $16.95

FIREARMS—JUVENILE

Barden, Renardo. **Gun Control.** (Illus.). 64 p. 1990. Rourke Corp. lib. bdg. $11.95

Landau, Elaine. **Armed America.** (Illus.). 128 p. 1991. Messner. pap. $5.95

FIREARMS—LAWS & REGULATIONS

Hayes, Marty. **The Gun Safety Handbook.** 48 p. 1992. Spec. Child. pap. $4.95

Kessinger, Roger A. **A Firearms Law.** 160 p. 1990. Kessinger Pub. pap. $24.95

Kleck, Gary. **Point Blank: Guns & Violence in America.** 128 p. 1991. Aldine de Gruyter. lib. bdg. $59.95

Nisbet, Lee, ed. **The Gun Control Debate: You Decide.** 341 p. 1990. Prometheus Books. pap. $16.95

O'Sullivan. Carol. **Gun Control: Distinguishing Between Fact & Opinion.** (Illus.). 32 p. 1990. Greenhaven. $8.95

GAME & GAME BIRDS (see also Hunting)

Kear, Janet. **Man & Wildfowl** (Illus.). 288 p. 1990. Acad. Pr. $39.95

Grooms, Steve. **Pheasant Hunter's Harvest.** 224 p. 1990. Lyons & Burford. $18.95

GAME COOKERY

Green, Delores & White, Connie. **Variety with Venison & Other Wild Game,** 2d ed. (Illus.). 85 p. 1989. Green & White Pub. pap. $8.95

Hemzo, K. **Ninety-Nine Game & Fish Dishes.** (Illus.). 64 p. 1987. Int'l Spec. Bks. $13.95

Manthel, George. **Wild & Famous Fish & Game Cookbook.** North Country. Write for info.

Steindler, Geraldine. **Game Cookbook.** New Rev. Ed. 1985. Stoeger Pub. Co. $14.95

GUNSMITHING

Kirkland, K. D. **America's Premier Gunmakers.** 1990. BDD Promo Bk. $29.98

HUNTING (see also Game & Game Birds, Deer Hunting)

Brook, Michael. **The Gameshooter's Pocket Guide.** (Illus.). 144 p. 1991. Trafalgar Sq. $24.95

Clancy, Gary & Nelson, Larry. **White-Tailed Deer.** 160 p.1991. Cy DeCosse. $18.95

Dorsey, Chris. **Grouse Hunter's Almanac.** (Illus.). 200 p. 1990. Voyageur Pr. $24.95

Elman, Robert, ed. **The Complete Book of Hunting: A Compilation of over 13,450 Catalog Entries with Prices & Annotations.** 1194 p. 1991. Scarecrow. $115.00

Holland, Anne. **A Practical Guide to Hunting.** (Illus.). 112 p. Trafalgar Sq. $29.95

Schneck, Marcus. **North American Hunters Handbook.** (Illus.). 176 p. 1991. Running Press. $29.95

Trense, Werner. **The Big Game of the World,** rev. ed. (Illus.). 420 p. 1989. ltd. ed. $270.00

Yajko, Doug. **Walk with the Eagles: Hunting North American Big Game.** (Illus.). 256 p. 1990. Roaring Co. $30.00

HUNTING DOGS

Jenkins, Len. **Gun Dog Training—Do it Yourself & Do it Right.** (Illus.). 250 p. 1991. CJ Pub. pap. $18.95

HUNTING WITH BOW AND ARROW

Pope, Saxton. **Hunting with the Bow & Arrow** (facsimile ed.). 250 p. 1991. Wolfe. $36.00

KNIVES

Page, Camille. **American Knives & Weapons, 1900–1990.** (Illus.). 60 p. Saifer. $20.00

Warner, Ken, ed. **Knives 1992,** 12th ed. (Illus.). 288 p. 1991. DBI. pap. $15.95

OUTDOOR LIFE

Auerbach, Paul S. **Medicine for the Outdoors: A Guide to Emergency Medical Procedures & First Aid,** rev. ed. 1991. Little. $27.95

PISTOLS

Kasler, Peter A. **Business Partners: The Best Pistol-Ammunition Combinations for Personal Defense.** (Illus.). 200 p. 1991. Paladin Press. $22.95

RIFLES (see also Firearms)

Big Bore Rifles & Cartridges. 1990. Wolfe Pub. Co.

Fadala, Sam. **Legendary Sporting Rifles.** (Illus.). 288 p. 1992. Stoeger Pub. pap. $16.95

Fadala, Sam. **The Book of the Twenty-two.** (Illus.) 1989. Stoeger Pub. Co. $16.95

Grant, James J. **Boys' Single-Shot Rifles** (facsimile ed.). 608 p. 1991. Wolfe. $36.00

Long, Duncan. **Combat Rifles of the Twenty-First Century: Futuristic Firearms for Tomorrow's Battlefields.** (Illus.). 88 p. 1990. Paladin Press. pap. $15.00

Newick, Glenn. **The Ultimate in Rifle Accuracy.** (Illus.). 210 p. 1990. Stoeger Pub. pap. $11.95

Stowers, Roger. **Gibbs On Rifles & Cartridges.** 1990. Wolfe Pub.

SHOTGUNS

U.S. Shotguns: Identification, Operation & Care. 1991. Gordon Press. lib. bdg. $69.95

SKEET & TRAP SHOOTING

Atwill, Lionel. **Sporting Clays: An Orvis Guide.** 1990. Atlantic Monthly Pr. $22.95

WILDLIFE CONSERVATION & PRESERVATION

Cadieux, Charles. **Wildlife Extinction.** (Illus.). 272 p. 1991. Stone Wall Pr. $24.95

Dunlap, Thomas R. **Saving America's Wildlife.** 238 p. 1991. Princeton U. Press. pap. $12.95

Reisner, Marc. **Game Wars: The Adventures of an Undercover Wildlife Agent.** 352 p. 1991. Viking Penguin. $19.95

WINCHESTER RIFLE

Scwing, Ned. **Winchester's Finest: The Model 21.** (Illus.). 360 p. 1991. Krause Pub. $49.95

Wilson, R. L. **Winchester: An American Legend.** 1991. Random. $64.50

DIRECTORY OF MANUFACTURERS AND SUPPLIERS

The following manufacturers, suppliers and distributors of firearms, ammunition, reloading equipment, sights, scopes and accessories all appear with their products in the catalog and/or "Manufacturers Showcase" sections of this edition of *Shooter's Bible*.

Action Arms, Ltd. (Brno rifles, Timber Wolf rifle, scopes)
P.O. Box 9573
Philadelphia, Pennsylvania 19124
(215) 744-0100

Aimpoint (sights, scopes, mounts)
203 Elden Street, Suite 302
Herndon, Virginia 22070
(703) 471-6828

American Arms (handguns, rifles, Franchi shotguns)
715 E. Armour Road
N. Kansas City, Missouri 64116
(816) 474-3161

American Derringer Corp. (handguns)
127 North Lacy Drive
Waco, Texas 76705
(817) 799-9111

American Military Arms Corp. (Iver Johnson pistols, rifles)
2202 Redmond Road
Jacksonville, Arkansas 72076
(501) 982-1633

Anschutz (handguns, rifles)
Available through Precision Sales International

Arcadia Machine & Tool Inc. (AMT handguns)
6226 Santos Diaz Street
Irwindale, California 91702
(818) 334-6629

Armes de Chasse (Chapuis and Francotte rifles and shotguns; AYA shotguns)
P.O. Box 827
Chadds Ford, Pennsylvania 19317
(215) 388-1146

Armsport, Inc. (shotguns, black powder)
3590 NW 49th Street, P.O. Box 523066
Miami, Florida 33142
(305) 635-7850

A-Square Company Inc. (rifles)
One Industrial Park
Bedford, Kentucky 40006
(502) 255-7456

Astra (handguns)
Available through Interarms

Auto-Ordnance Corp. (handgun, rifles)
Williams Lane
West Hurley, New York 12491
(914) 679-7225

AYA (shotguns)
Available through Armes de Chasse

Ballisti-Cast, Inc. (bullet molds, casting machines)
Box 383
Parshall, North Dakota 58770
(701) 862-3324

Bausch & Lomb (scopes)
See Bushnell (Division of)

Bedford Technologies, Inc. (gun safes)
P.O. Box 328
Miami, Oklahoma 74355
(800) 467-SAFE

Beeman Precision Arms, Inc. (imported handguns, rifles, scopes, mounts)
3440 Airway Drive
Santa Rosa, California 95403-2040
(707) 578-7900

Bell & Carlson, Inc. (rifle stocks)
509 North 5th
Atwood, Kansas 67730
(913) 626-3204

Benelli (shotguns)
Available through Heckler & Koch

Benjamin Air Rifle (airguns)
2600 Chickory Road
Racine, Wisconsin 53403
(414) 554-7900

Beretta U.S.A. Corp. (handguns, shotguns)
17601 Beretta Drive
Accokeek, Maryland 20607
(301) 283-2191

Bernardelli (handguns, shotguns)
Available through Magnum Research

Bersa (handguns)
Available through Eagle Imports Inc.

Blaser USA, Inc. (rifles)
c/o Autumn Sales, Inc.
1320 Lake Street
Fort Worth, Texas 76102
(817) 335-1634

Blount, Inc. (RCBS reloading equipment, Speer and CCI bullets, Weaver sights)
P.O. Box 856
Lewiston, Idaho 83501
(208) 746-2351

Bonanza (reloading tools)
See Forster Products

Briley Manufacturing Co. (screw-in chokes)
1085-Gessner, "B"
Houston, Texas 77055
(800) 331-5718

Brno (rifles)
Available through Action Arms

Ed Brown Products (handgun parts & accessories)
Route 2, Box 2922
Perry, Missouri 63462
(314) 565-3261

Browning (handguns, rifles, shotguns)
Route One
Morgan, Utah 84050
(801) 876-2711

Burris Company, Inc. (scopes, mounts)
331 East Eighth Street, P.O. Box 1747
Greeley, Colorado 80632
(303) 356-1670

Bushnell (scopes)
Division of Bausch & Lomb
300 North Lone Hill Avenue
San Dimas, California 91773
(714) 592-8000

Chapuis (shotguns)
Available through Armes de Chasse

Charter Arms Corp. (handguns)
430 Sniffens Lane
Stratford, Connecticut 06497
(203) 377-8080

Chinasports, Inc. (handguns and rifles)
2010 S. Balboa Ave.
Ontario, California 91761
(714) 923-1411

Choate Machine & tool Co. (gun stocks, grips)
P.O. Box 218
Bald Knob, Arkansas 72010
(501) 724-6193

Churchill (rifles, shotguns)
Available through Ellett Brothers, Inc.

Clifton Arms (custom rifles)
2326 Ingleside
Grand Prairie, Texas 75050
(214) 647-2500

Colt's Manufacturing Co., Inc. (handguns, rifles)
P.O. Box 1868
Hartford, Connecticut 06144-1868
(203) 236-6311

CVA (black powder guns)
5988 Peachtree Corners East
Norcross, Georgia 30071
(404) 449-4687

Daewoo (handguns)
Available through Davidson's

Dakota (handguns, rifles)
Available through E.M.F. Co., Inc.

Dakota Arms, Inc. (rifles)
HC 55, Box 326
Sturgis, South Dakota 57785
(605) 347-4686

Davidson's (Daewoo pistols)
2703 High Point Road
Greensboro, North Carolina 27403
800-367-4867

Davis Industries (handguns)
15150 Sierra Bonita Lane
Chino, California 91710
(714) 597-4726

Detonics (handguns)
See under New Detonics Manufacturing Corp.

Dixie Gun Works (black powder guns)
Reelfoot Avenue, P.O. Box 130
Union City, Tennessee 38261
(901) 885-0561

Dynamit Nobel/RWS (Diana rifles; Rottweil shotguns)
105 Stonehurst Court
Northvale, New Jersey 07647
(201) 767-1995

Eagle Arms Inc. (rifles)
131 East 22nd. Avenue, P.O. Box 457
Coal Valley, Illinois 61240
(309) 799-5619

Eagle Imports Inc. (Bersa handguns)
1907 Highway 35
Ocean, New Jersey 07712
(908) 531-8375

Ellett Brothers, Inc. (Churchill rifles, shotguns)
P.O. Box 128
Chapin, South Carolina 29036
(803) 345-3751

Emerging Technologies (Laser Aim sights)
P.O. Box 3548
Little Rock, Arkansas 72203
(501) 375-2227

E.M.F. Company, Inc. (Dakota handguns, black powder)
1900 East Warner Avenue 1-D
Santa Ana, California 92705
(714) 261-6611

Erma (handguns)
Available through Precision Sales

Euroarms of America Inc. (black powder guns)
1501 Lenoir Drive, P.O. Box 3277
Winchester, Virginia 22601
(703) 662-1863

Feather Industries, Inc. (rifles)
2300 Central Avenue, Unit K
Boulder, Colorado 80301
(303) 442-7021

Federal Cartridge Corporation (Federal/Norma ammunition, bullets, primers, cases)
900 Ehlen Drive
Anoka, Minnesota 55303-7503
(612) 422-2840

Ferlib (shotguns)
Available through W. L. Moore & Co.

Forster Products (Bonanza and Forster reloading)
82 East Lanark Avenue
Lanark, Illinois 61046
(815) 493-6360

Franchi (shotguns)
Available through American Arms

Francotte (rifles and shotguns)
Available through Armes de Chasse

Freedom Arms (handguns)
One Freedom Lane, P.O. Box 1776
Freedom, Wyoming 83120
(307) 883-2468

Galaxy Imports, Ltd., Inc. (Laurona shotguns)
P.O. Box 3361
Victoria, Texas 77903
(512) 573-GUNS

Garbi (shotguns)
Available through W. L. Moore & Co.

Gibbs Rifle Co. (rifles)
Cannon Hill Industrial Park
Hoffman Road
Martinsburg, West Virginia 25401
(304) 274-0458

Glaser Safety Slug, Inc. (ammunition and gun accessories)
P.O. Box 8223
Foster City, California 94404
(415) 345-7677

Glock, Inc. (handguns)
6000 Highlands Parkway
Smyrna, Georgia 30082
(404) 432-1202

Gonic Arms (black powder rifles)
134 Flagg Road
Gonic, New Hampshire 03867
(603) 332-8457

Carl Gustaf (rifles)
Available through Precision Sales Int'l

Grendel, Inc. (handguns)
P.O. Box 908
Rockledge, Florida 32955
(407) 636-1211

Gun South Inc. (Steyr, Steyr Mannlicher rifles)
108 Morrow Ave., P.O. Box 129
Trussville, Alabama 35173
(205) 655-8299

GunVault, Inc. (firearms containers)
200 Larkin Drive, Unit E
Wheeling, Illinois 60090
(708) 215-6606

Hammerli (handguns)
Available through Beeman Precision Arms

Harris Engineering Inc. (bipods and adapters)
Barlow, Kentucky 42024
(502) 334-3633

Heckler & Koch (handguns, rifles, Heym rifles, Benelli shotguns)
21480 Pacific Boulevard
Sterling, Virginia 22170-8903
(703) 450-1900

Hercules Inc. (powder)
Hercules Plaza
Wilmington, Delaware 19894
(302) 594-5000

Heym America, Inc. (rifles)
Available through Heckler & Koch

Hodgdon Powder Co., Inc. (gunpowder)
6231 Robinson, P.O. Box 2932
Shawnee Mission, Kansas 66201
(913) 362-9455

J.B. Holden Co. (mounts)
975 Arthur
Plymouth, Michigan 48170
(313) 455-4850

Hornady Manufacturing Company (reloading, ammunition)
P.O. Box 1848
Grand Island, Nebraska 68802-1848
(308) 382-1390

Howa (rifles)
Available through Interarms

IMR Powder Company (gunpowder)
R.D. 5, Box 247E
Plattsburgh, New York 12901
(518) 561-9530

Interarms (handguns, shotguns and rifles, including Astra, Howa, Mark X, Rossi, Star, Walther, Norinco, Whitworth)
10 Prince Street
Alexandria, Virginia 22314
(703) 548-1400

InterAims (sights)
Available through Stoeger Industries

Ithaca Gun (shotguns)
891 Route 34B
King Ferry, New York 13081
(315) 364-7182

Iver Johnson/AMAC (handguns, rifles)
Available through American Military Arms Corp.

Jarrett Rifles Inc. (custom rifles and accessories)
383 Brown Road
Jackson, South Carolina 29831
(803) 471-3616

K.B.I., Inc. (handguns, Kassnar shotguns, rifles, black powder, Omega shotguns)
P.O. Box 6346
Harrisburg, Pennsylvania 17112
(717) 540-8518

K.D.F. Inc. (rifles)
2485 Highway 46 North
Seguin, Texas 78155
(512) 379-8141

Krico (rifles)
Available through Beeman Precision Arms

Krieghoff International Inc. (rifles, shotguns)
337A Route 611, P.O. Box 549
Ottsville, Pennsylvania 18942
(215) 847-5173

Lakefield Arms Ltd. (rifles)
P.O. Box 129
Lakefield, Ontario K0L 2H0
Canada

L.A.R. Manufacturing, Inc. (Grizzly handguns)
4133 West Farm Road
West Jordan, Utah 84084
(801) 255-7106

Laurona (shotguns)
Available through Galaxy Imports

Leupold & Stevens, Inc. (scopes, mounts)
P.O. Box 688
Beaverton, Oregon 97075
(503) 646-9171

Llama (handguns)
Available through Stoeger Industries

Lyman Products Corp. (black powder guns, sights, reloading tools)
Route 147
Middlefield, Connecticut 06455
(203) 349-3421

M.O.A. Corp. (handguns)
175 Carr Drive
Brookville, Ohio 45309
(513) 833-5559

MTM Case Gard Co. (reloading tools)
3370 Obco Court
Dayton, Ohio 45414
(513) 890-7461

Magnum Research Inc. (Desert Eagle and Bernardelli handguns, Bernardelli shotguns)
7110 University Avenue N.E.
Minneapolis, Minnesota 55432
(612) 574-1868

Marble Arms Corp. (sights)
420 Industrial Park
Gladstone, Michigan 49837
(906) 428-3711

Mark X (rifles)
Available through Interarms

Marlin Firearms Company (rifles, shotguns)
100 Kenna Drive
North Haven, Connecticut 06473
(203) 239-5621

Marocchi (Avanza shotguns)
Available through Precision Sales

Mauser/Precision Imports, Inc. (Mauser rifles)
5040 Space Center Drive
San Antonio, Texas 78218
(512) 666-3033

Maverick Arms, Inc. (shotguns)
Industrial Blvd., P.O. Box 586
Eagle Pass, Texas 78853
(512) 773-9007

McMillan Gun Works (rifles)
302 W. Melinda Drive
Phoenix, Arizona 85027
(602) 582-9627

MEC Inc. (reloading tools)
℅ Mayville Engineering Co.
715 South Street
Mayville, Wisconsin 53050
(414) 387-4500

Merkel (shotguns)
Available through Gun South Inc.

Millett Sights (sights and mounts)
16131 Gothard Street
Huntington Beach, California 92647
(714) 842-5575

Mitchell Arms (handguns, black powder, rifles)
3400-1 West MacArthur Blvd.
Santa Ana, California 92704
(714) 957-5711

Modern Muzzle Loading Inc. (black powder guns)
P.O. Box 130, 234 Airport Rd.,
Centerville, Iowa 52544
(515) 856-2623

William L. Moore & Co. (Garbi, Ferlib and Piotti shotguns)
31360 Via Colinas, No. 109
Westlake Village, California 91361
(818) 889-4160

O.F. Mossberg & Sons, Inc. (shotguns)
7 Grasso Avenue
North Haven, Connecticut 06473
(203) 288-6491

Navy Arms Company, Inc. (handguns, black powder guns, replicas)
689 Bergen Boulevard
Ridgefield, New Jersey 07657
(201) 945-2500

New Detonics Manufacturing Corp. (handguns)
21438 North 7th Avenue
Phoenix, Arizona 85027
(602) 582-4867

New England Firearms Co., Inc. (handguns; Harrington & Richardson handguns and shotguns)
Industrial Rowe
Gardner, Massachusetts 01440
(617) 632-9393

Nikon Inc. (scopes)
1300 Walt Whitman Road
Melville, New York 11747
(516) 547-4200

Norinco (rifles)
Available through Interarms

Norma (ammunition, gunpowder, reloading cases)
Available through Federal Cartridge Corp.

North American Arms (handguns)
1800 North 300 West
P.O. Box 707
Spanish Fork, Utah 84660
(800) 821-5783

North American Shooting Systems/NASS (rifles)
P.O. Box 306
Osoyoos, British Columbia V0H 1V0
Canada
(604) 495-3131

Nosler Bullets, Inc. (bullets)
P.O. Box 671
Bend, Oregon 97709
(503) 382-3921

Olin/Winchester (ammunition, primers, cases)
427 North Shamrock
East Alton, Illinois 62024
(618) 258-2000

Pachmayr Ltd. (recoil pads, handgun grips, sights, swivels)
1875 South Mountain Avenue
Monrovia, California 91016
(818) 357-7771

Parker-Hale (rifles)
Available through Navy Arms

Parker Reproduction (shotguns)
124 River Road
Middlesex, New Jersey 08846
(908) 469-0100

Pentax (scopes)
35 Inverness Drive East
Englewood, Colorado 80112
(303) 799-8000

Perazzi U.S.A. (shotguns)
1207 S. Shamrock Ave.
Monrovia, California 91016
(818) 303-0068

Piotti (shotguns)
Available through W.L. Moore & Co.

Precision Sales International (Anschutz pistols and rifles, Carl Gustaf rifles, Marocchi shotguns; Erma pistols)
P.O. Box 1776
Westfield, Massachusetts 01086
(413) 562-5055

Precision Sports ("600 Series" shotguns)
P.O. Box 708
Cortland, New York 13045
(607) 756-2851

Quality Firearms (QFI) (handguns)
4541 Northwest 133 Street
Opa Locka, Florida 33054
(305) 685-5966

RCBS, Inc. (reloading tools)
See Blount, Inc.

Redding Reloading Equipment (reloading tools)
1089 Starr Road
Cortland, New York 13045
(607) 753-3331

Redfield (scopes)
5800 East Jewell Avenue
Denver, Colorado 80224
(303) 757-6411

Remington Arms Company, Inc. (handguns, rifles, shotguns, ammunition, primers)
1007 Market Street
Wilmington, Delaware 19898
(302) 773-5291

Rooster Laboratories
2833 15th Avenue S.
Minneapolis, Minnesota 55407
(612) 721-5157

Rossi (handguns, rifles, shotguns)
Available through Interarms

Rottweil (shotguns)
Available through Dynamit Nobel/RWS

Ruger (handguns, rifles, shotguns, black powder guns)
See Sturm, Ruger & Company, Inc.

Ruko Products, Inc. (rifles and shotguns)
P.O. Box 1181
Buffalo, New York 14240-1181
(416) 826-9192

RWS/Diana (rifles)
See Dynamit Nobel

Sako (rifles, actions, scope mounts)
Available through Stoeger Industries

J. P. Sauer & Sohn (rifles and shotguns)
P.O. Box 37669
Omaha, Nebraska 68137
(402) 339-3530

Savage Arms (rifles, shotguns)
Springdale Road
Westfield, Massachusetts 01085
(413) 568-7001

Schmidt and Bender (scopes)
Schmidt & Bender U.S.A.
P.O. Box 134
Meriden, New Hampshire 03770
800-468-3450

Shilo Rifle Mfg. Co., Inc. (Shiloh Sharps black powder rifles)
P.O. Box 279, Industrial Park
Big Timber, Montana 59011
(406) 932-4454

Shooting Systems Group, Inc. (gun holsters, cases)
1075 Headquarters Park
Fenton, Missouri 63026
(314) 343-3575

Sierra Bullets (bullets)
P.O. Box 818
1400 West Henry St.
Sedalia, Missouri 65301
(800) 223-8799

Sigarms Inc. (handguns)
Corporate Park
Exeter, New Hampshire 03833
(603) 772-2302

Simmons Outdoor Corp. (scopes)
14530 SW 119th Ave.
Miami, Florida 33186
(305) 252-0477

SKB Shotguns (shotguns, Nichols Scopes)
4325 South 120th Street
P.O. Box 37669
Omaha, Nebraska 68137
(402) 339-3530

Smith & Wesson (handguns)
2100 Roosevelt Avenue
Springfield, Massachusetts 01102-2208
(413) 781-8300

Speer (bullets)
See Blount, Inc.

Springfield Armory (handguns, rifles, scopes)
420 West Main Street
Geneseo, Illinois 61254
(309) 944-5631

Star (handguns)
Available through Interarms

Steyr-Mannlicher (rifles)
Available through Gun South Inc.

Stoeger Industries (Sako rifles, Llama handguns,
Stoeger shotguns, Tikka rifles, shotguns; InterAims
sights; mounts, actions)
55 Ruta Court
South Hackensack, New Jersey 07606
(201) 440-2700

Sturm, Ruger and Company, Inc. (Ruger handguns,
rifles, shotguns)
Lacey Place
Southport, Connecticut 06490
(203) 259-7843

Swarovski American (scopes)
2 Slater Road
Cranston, Rhode Island 02920
(401) 942-3380

Swift Instruments, Inc. (scopes and mounts)
952 Dorchester Avenue
Boston, Massachusetts 02125
(617) 436-2960

Tasco (scopes and mounts)
7600 N.W. 26th Street
Miami, Florida 33122
(305) 591-3670

Taurus International, Inc. (handguns)
16175 N.W. 49th Avenue
Miami, Florida 33014
(305) 624-1115

Thompson/Center Arms (handguns, rifles, black
powder guns, scopes)
Farmington Road, P.O. Box 5002
Rochester, New Hampshire 03867
(603) 332-2394

Tikka (rifles, shotguns)
Available through Stoeger Industries

Traditions, Inc. (black powder guns)
P.O. Box 235
Deep River, Connecticut 06417
(203) 526-9555

Trius Products, Inc. (traps, clay targets)
221 South Miami Avenue, P.O. Box 25
Cleves, Ohio 45002
(513) 941-5682

Uberti USA, Inc. (handguns, rifles, black powder
rifles and revolvers)
362 Limerock Rd., P.O. Box 469
Lakeville, Connecticut 06039
(203) 435-8068

Ultra Light Arms Company (rifles, black powder
rifles)
214 Price Street, P.O. Box 1270
Granville, West Virginia 26534
(304) 599-5687

U.S. Repeating Arms Co. (Winchester rifles,
shotguns)
275 Winchester Avenue
New Haven, Connecticut 06511
(203) 789-5000

Walther (handguns, rifles)
Available through Interarms

Weatherby, Inc. (rifles, shotguns, scopes,
ammunition)
2781 Firestone Boulevard
South Gate, California 90280
(213) 569-7186

Weaver (scopes, mount rings)
See Blount, Inc.

Wesson Firearms Co., Inc. (handguns)
Maple Tree Industrial Center, Route 20
Wilbraham Road
Palmer, Massachusetts 01069
(413) 267-4081

Whitworth (rifles)
Available through Interarms

Wideview Scope Mount Corp. (mounts, rings)
26110 Michigan Avenue
Inkster, Michigan 48141
(313) 274-1238

Wildey Inc. (handguns)
P.O. Box 475
Brookfield, Connecticut 06804
(203) 355-9000

Wilkinson Arms (handguns, rifles)
Route 2, Box 2166
Parma, Idaho 83660
(208) 722-6771-2

Williams Gun Sight Co. (sights, scopes, mounts)
7389 Lapeer Road, P.O. Box 329
Davison, Michigan 48423
(313) 653-2131

Winchester (ammunition, primers, cases)
See Olin/Winchester

Winchester (domestic rifles, shotguns)
See U.S. Repeating Arms Co.

Winslow Arms Co. (rifles)
P.O. Box 783
Camden, South Carolina 29020
(803) 432-2938

Zeiss Optical, Inc. (scopes)
1015 Commerce Street
Petersburg, Virginia 23803
(804) 861-0033

Antonio Zoli (shotguns)
Via Zanardelli 39
Gardone V.T. (BS)
Italy 25063

GUNFINDER

To help you find the model of your choice, the following list includes each gun found in the catalog section of SHOOTER'S BIBLE 1993. A supplemental listing of **Discontinued Models** and the **Caliberfinder** follow immediately after this section.

HANDGUNS

PISTOLS

American Arms
Models Sabre, P-98, PK-22 & CX-22 ... 98

American Derringer
Models 1, 3, 7, 10, 11, Lady Derringer,
 Double Action 38 Double Derringer ... 99
Model 4 ... 100
Model 6 ... 100
Semmerling LM-4, Alaskan Survival,
 Mini-Cop Derringer ... 100

AMT
Automag II ... 101
AMT 380 Backup ... 101
45 ACP Longslide ... 101
On Duty Double Action ... 101
Javelina ... 102
Automag III & IV ... 102

Anschutz
Exemplar ... 103
Exemplar XIV ... 103
Exemplar Hornet ... 103

Auto-Ordnance
Model 1911A-1 Thompson ... 104
Model 1927 A-5 ... 104
Model 1911 "The General" ... 104

Beeman
P-08 & MP-08 Semiauto ... 105
Unique 2000-U ... 105
Beeman/Korth Semiauto Pistol ... 105
Unique 69U Target ... 105
Hammerli Models 208 and 212 Target ... 106
Hammerli Model 232 Rapid Fire ... 106
Hammerli Model 150 Free Pistol ... 107
Hammerli Model 152 Electronic ... 107
Hammerli Model 280 Sport ... 107

Beretta
Model 21 ... 108
Model 950 BS ... 108
Model 84 ... 108
Model 85 ... 109
Model 86 ... 109
Model 87 ... 109
Model 89 Target ... 109
Model 92F & 92F-EL ... 110
Model 96 ... 110

Bersa
Model 23 DA ... 111
Model 83 DA ... 111
Models 85 & 86 ... 111

Browning
9mm Hi-Power ... 112
Model BDM 9mm ... 112
Buck Mark 22 Series ... 113
Model BDA-380 ... 113

Chinasports
Type 54-1 Tokarev ... 117
Type 59 Markarov ... 117
Norinco Type M1911 ... 117
Type 77B ... 117

Colt
Double Eagle ... 118
Combat Commander ... 118
Lightweight Commander ... 118
Gold Cup National Match ... 119
Government Model ... 119
Government Model 380 Auto/Pocketlite ... 119
Delta Elite & Delta Gold Cup ... 120
Mustang 380 ... 120
Officer's 45 ACP ... 120
Colt All American Model 2000 ... 121
Model M1991 A1 ... 122

Daewoo
Model DP51 9mm ... 124

Davis
Model D-22 Derringer ... 124
Model P-32 ... 124
Model P-380 ... 124

Erma
Model ESP 85 Sporting ... 127

Glock
Model 17 ... 129
Model 17L Competition ... 129
Model 19 Compact ... 129
Model 23 Compact ... 129
Model 20 ... 129

Grendel
Model P-12 ... 130
Models P-30, P-30M ... 130

Heckler & Koch
Model P7M8 & P7M10 Self-Loading ... 131
Model P7K3 ... 131
Model SP 89 ... 131

KBI
Model PSP-25 ... 132
Model 941 Jericho ... 132
FEG Models MBK-9HP & PMK 380 ... 132

L.A.R.
Mark I & Mark IV Grizzly ... 133
Grizzly Win. Mag. Model G ... 133

Llama
9mm Para Standard ... 136
Compact 45 ... 136
Small-Frame Auto ... 136–137
Large-Frame Auto ... 138
Model M-82 9mm ... 139
Model M-87 Comp ... 140
Duo-Tone Finish ... 141

Magnum Research
Desert Eagle Mark I ... 142
Desert Eagle Mark VII ... 142
SSP-91 Single Shot ... 143
Mountain Eagle & Baby Eagle ... 143

Mauser
Models 80-SA, 90-DA & 90-DAC ... 144

Mitchell Arms
Pistol Parabellum '08 Luger ... 145
Single Shot Sharpshooter ... 145

M.O.A.
Maximum ... 146

Navy Arms
TI-Olympia ... 146

QFI (Quality Firearms)
Model LA 380 ... 150
Model 722 TP Silhouette ... 150
Model SA25 ... 150
Victory MC5 ... 150

Remington
Model XP-100 Bolt Action Models ... 151
Model XP-100 Long-Range Custom ... 151
Model XP-100R KS Custom ... 151

Ruger
Model P-85 Mark II ... 157
Models P90 & P91 ... 157
Mark II Target ... 158
Mark II Standard ... 158
Mark II Bull Barrel ... 158

Sig Sauer
Model P220 "American" ... 159
Model P225 ... 159
Model P226 ... 159
Model P228 ... 160
Model P229 ... 160
Model 230 SL ... 160

Smith & Wesson
Model 422 ... 161
Model 41 ... 161
Model 52 ... 161
Model 1000 Series ... 162
Model 3900 Series ... 162
Model 4000 Series ... 163
Model 4500 Series ... 163
Model 5900 Series ... 164
Model 6900 Series ... 164

Springfield Armory
Model 1911-A1 ... 173
Model 1911-A2 ... 173
"R" Series ... 174–175
Model P9, P9C, P9 LSP ... 174

Star
Model 31M & 31 PK ... 176
Model M40 & M43 Firestar ... 176

Taurus
Model PT 22 ... 176
Model PT 92 & PT 92C ... 177
Model PT 58 ... 177
Model PT 99 ... 178
Models PT 100 & 101 ... 178

Thompson/Center
Contender Bull & Octagon Barrels ... 182
Contender "Super 14" & "Super 16" ... 182
Contender Hunter ... 182

A. Uberti
1871 Rolling Block Target ... 183

Walther
Model PPK & PPK/S ... 184
Model TPH Double Action Automatics ... 184
Model P-5 DA ... 185
Model P-88 DA ... 185
Model P-38 DA ... 185
GSP Match ... 186
OSP Match Rapid Fire ... 186
GSP Jr. ... 186

Wichita Arms
Silhouette ... 192
International ... 192

Wildey
Gas-operated Survival & Hunter Pistols ... 192

REVOLVERS

American Arms
Regulator SA ... 98

RIFLES

CENTERFIRE, AUTOLOADING & SLIDE ACTION

CENTERFIRE, BOLT ACTION

Pedersoli English Dueling/Mang Target	400
Pennsylvania	400

Gonic Arms

Model GA-90	410

Navy Arms

LePage Flintlock	417
LePage Percussion	417
LePage Double Cased Set	417
Kentucky Flint/Percussion	418
Harper's Ferry	418

Thompson/Center

Scout	432

Traditions

William Parker	432
Trapper	432
Pioneer	432

REVOLVERS

Armsport

Models 5145/5152/5153/5154	388
Models 5133/5136/5138/5120/5139/5140	389

CVA

1858 Remington Army Steel Frame	390
1858 Remington Target	390
Colt Walker	390
New Model Pocket Remington	390
1861 Navy Brass-Framed	391
1851 Navy Brass-Framed	391
Sheriff's Model	391
1860 Army	391

Wells Fargo Model	392
Remington Bison	392
Third Model Dragoon	392
Pocket Police	392

Dixie

Remington 44 Army	398
1860 Army	398
Navy Revolver	398
Spiller & Burr	398
"Wyatt Earp"	398
RHO200 Walker	399
RHO301 Third Model Dragoon	399

EMF

Sheriff's Model 1851	405
Model 1860 Army	405
Model 1862 Police	405
Second Model 44 Dragoon	405

Euroarms

Rogers & Spencer (Model 1005)	409
Rogers & Spencer Army (Model 1006)	409
Rogers & Spencer (Model 1007)	409
Remington 1858 New Model Army	409
1851 Navy Confederate	410

Mitchell Arms

1851 Colt Navy	412
Remington New Model Army	412
1860 Colt Army	412
Remington "Texas" Model	412

Navy Arms

1862 Police	414
Lemat (Army, Navy, Cavalry)	414

Colt Walker 1847	414
Rogers & Spencer	414
Reb Model 1860	415
Army 1860	415
1851 Navy "Yank"	415
Stainless Steel 1858 Remington	416
Target Model Remington	416
Deluxe 1858 Remington-Style	416
Remington New Model Army	416
Army 60 Sheriff's	416

A. Uberti

1st, 2nd & 3rd Model Dragoons	436
1861 Navy	436
Walker	436
1851 Navy	436
1860 Army	436
1858 Remington Army 44	437
Paterson	437

SHOTGUNS

Dixie

Double Barrel Magnum	401

Euroarms

Single-Barreled Magnum Cape	406

Navy Arms

Model T&T	424
Mortimer Flintlock	424
Fowler	424
Steel Shot Magnum	424

Thompson/Center

New Englander	429

DISCONTINUED MODELS

The following models, all of which appeared in the 1992 edition of SHOOTER'S BIBLE, have been discontinued by their manufacturers or are no longer imported by U.S. distributors.

HANDGUNS

ASTRA
Model A-100
Constable 380 ACP
BERETTA
Model 84
Model 86
Model 89 Target
BERNARDELLI Model P018
CHARTER ARMS
Police Bulldog (32 Mag.)
New Police Bulldog (44 Sp.)
Target Bulldog
COLT
Double Eagle (9mm & 38 Super)
Officer's ACP (40 S&W)
DETONICS
Ladies Escort 45 ACP
Servicemaster
Combatmaster
Compmaster
EMF/DAKOTA 1894 Bisley
FEDERAL ORDNANCE
Peters Stahl PSP-07 Combat Compensator
Ranger Alpha
Ranger Ambo
Ranger EXT
GRENDEL Model P-10
NAVY ARMS 1890 Single Action
QFI-QUALITY FIREARMS
Model S038 DA
Arminius DA
MAGNUM RESEARCH Desert Eagle Mark VII
REMINGTON Model XP-22LR Rimfire
RUGER
Redhawk KRH-41S, KRH-41, KRH-41R,
RH-41S, RH-41, RH-41R
SPRINGFIELD ARMORY
Omega Match
Model M6 Single Shot

STAR Model BKM & BM 9mm
Model PD (45 ACP)
VICTORY ARMS Model MC5
WALTHER Model FP (Free Pistol)
SMITH & WESSON
Model 31 & 34
Model 5943 SSV & 5944
Model 3914 LadySmith
ZASTAVA ARMS Model CZ99 & CZ40
Drulov 75 Target

RIFLES

ANSCHUTZ Model 1449
Biathlon Model 1427
BROWNING Model 53 (ltd. ed.) lever action
CHINASPORTS Model 64/70
COLT Sporter Conversion Kit
HEYM Model SR20 (Magnum & Standard)
HOWA Lightning Sporting Rifles
KIMBER
Model 89 Big Game
Model 89 African
Model 82 Rimfire Sporting
Model 82 Rimfire Gov't Target
Model 84 Mini-Mauser Centerfire Sporter
McMILLAN Standard Sporter
NASS (North Am. Shooting Systems)
Canadian Classic (now avail. as Custom
Hunter)
REMINGTON Model 581-S Sporstman
Model 700 AS
RWS/DIANA Match Rifle Model 820L & 820F
SAVAGE Model 110B
SPRINGFIELD ARMORY
Model SAR-4800 Sporter
Model SAR-8 Sporter
VARNER Favorite Hunter models
WALTHER Model GX-1
Model KK/MS Silhouette Target
WEATHERBY Mark V Euromark
ZASTAVA Model CZ99 Precision

SHOTGUNS

ARMSPORT Model 1127 Takedown Single Barrel
BENELLI Black Eagle Slug
BERETTA
Model 303 Slug
Waterfowl Turkey (now Model 390)
BERNARDELLI
S. Uberto 2E S/S
Model 192-MC over/under
Model 115 Skeet
BROWNING BPS Pump (Youth & Ladies)
CHURCHILL
Royal S/S & Windsor I S/S
Windsor III O/U & Regent V O/U
Competition model
KBI/KASSNAR Omega Deluxe O/U
LAURONA
Grand Trap Model GTO & GTU
Model 85 MS Special Sporting
MERKEL
Models 210, 210E, 211, 211E
Double Rifles S/S
Models 220, 221, 223 double rifles
Model 122E Boxlock
REMINGTON Parker AHE
WINCHESTER
Model 1300 Defender Combo, Custom &
Waterfowl

BLACK POWDER

CVA
Stalker Rifle (Premium Grade)
Ozark Mountain Rifle
O/U Carbine
Hawken Rifle (Premier Grade)
Blazer Rifle
MODERN MUZZLE LOADING
Backcountry Carbine
Model BK 89 Squirrel Rifle
PARKER-HALE Model 1200M Super Magnum

CALIBERFINDER

How to use this guide: To find a 22LR handgun, look under that heading in the **Handguns** section. You'll find several models of that description, including Beretta Model 21. Turn next to the **Gunfinder** section and locate the heading for **Beretta** (pistols, in this case). Beretta's **Model 21,** as indicated, appears on p. 108.

BLACK POWDER

HANDGUNS

30

Gonic Arms Model GA-90

31

CVA New Model Pocket Remington, Wells Fargo Model, Vest Pocket Derringer

36

Armsport Models 5136, 5154
CVA Models 1851 & 1861 Navy Brass-Framed Revolvers, Sheriff's Model, Pocket Police
Dixie Navy Revolver, Spiller & Burr Revolver
EMF 1851 Sheriff's Model, Model 1862 Police
Euroarms 1851 Navy & Navy Confederate Revolver
Mitchell Arms 1851 and 1861 Colt Navy, Remington "Texas" Model, Remington New Model Army
Navy Arms 1862 Police Revolver, Reb Model 1860, Army 1860 Sheriff's Model, 1851 Navy "Yank" Revolver
A. Uberti 1851 Navy, 1858 Navy, 1862 Pocket Navy, Paterson

38

Dixie Pedersoli Mang Target Pistol
Gonic Arms Model GA-90

41

Dixie Abilene & Lincoln Derringers

44

Armsport Models 5138, 5120, 5136, 5139, 5140, 5145, 5152, 5153
CVA 1861 Navy Brass-Framed, 1860 Army Revolvers, Walker, Third Model Dragoon, Remington Bison, 1858 Remington Target Model and Army Steel Frame Revolver (also Brass Frame)
Dixie Walker Revolver, Remington Army Revolver, Pennsylvania Pistol, Third Model Dragoon, Wyatt Earp Revolver
EMF Model 1860 Army, Second Model 44 Dragoon
Euroarms Rogers & Spencer Models 1005, 1006 & 1007 Remington 1858 New Model Army (and Target), 1851 Navy
Gonic Arms Model GA-90
Mitchell Arms 1851 and 1861 Colt Navy, 1860 Army Model, Remington "Texas" Model, Remington New Model Army
Navy Arms Colt Walker 1847, Reb Model 1860 Revolver, 1860 Army Revolver, Army 60 Sheriff's Model, Rogers & Spencer Revolver, Target Model Remington Revolver, Stainless Steel 1858 Remington, Remington New Model Army, LeMat Revolvers, 1851 Navy Yank Revolver, Deluxe 1858 Remington-Style Revolver, Le Page Flintlock/Percussion & Cased Sets
Uberti 1st, 2nd & 3rd Model Dragoon, Walker, 1858 Remington, 1860 Army

45

CVA Colonial, Philadelphia Derringer, Siber Target Pistol
Dixie Pedersoli English Dueling Pistol, LePage Dueling Pistol
Gonic Arms Model GA-90
Traditions Trapper Pistol, Pioneer Pistol, William Parker Pistol

50

CVA Kentucky Pistol, Hawken Pistol
Thompson/Center Scout Pistol
Traditions Trapper Pistol, William Parker Pistol

54

Thompson/Center Scout Pistol

58

Navy Arms Harper's Ferry Pistol

RIFLES & CARBINES

30

Gonic Arms Model GA-87 Rifle/Carbine

32

Dixie Tennessee Squirrel
Navy Arms Pennsylvania Long

36

CVA Squirrel
Traditions Frontier Scout

38 & 44

Gonic Arms Model GA-87 Rifle/Carbine

44-40

Dixie Winchester '73 Carbine

45

Dixie Kentuckian, Hawken, Pedersoli Waadtlander, Tryon Creedmoor, Pennsylvania
Gonic Arms Model GA-87 Rifle/Carbine
Navy Arms Pennsylvania Long
Thompson/Center Hawken, White Mountain Carbine
Traditions Frontier, Frontier Scout, Pennsylvania,
Ultra Light Arms Model 90

451

Navy Arms Rigby-Style Target Rifle, Tryon Creedmoor
Parker-Hale Whitworth Military Target & Sniper Rifles, Volunteer
White Model Super 91

45-70

Shiloh Sharps Model 1874 Sporting Rifle #1 & #3/Business/Military/"Civilian" Carbine

45-90

Shiloh Sharps Model 1874 Sporting #1 & #3; Model 1874 Business/"Civilian" Carbine

45-120

Shiloh Sharps Model 1874 Sporting #1 & #3, Business

50

American Arms Hawkeye
CVA Frontier, Kentucky, Stalker, Tracker Carbine, Pennsylvania Long Rifle, Bushwacker, St. Louis Hawken, Apollo 90, Apollo Sporter & Shadow, Hawken, Express Double Rifle & Carbine, Frontier Carbine, Plainsman, Hawken Deerslayer (rifle & carbine)
Dixie Hawken, Tennessee Mountain
Gonic Arms Model GA-87 Rifle/Carbine
Lyman Great Plains, Trade Rifle, Deerstalker Rifle and Carbine
Modern Muzzleloading Knight MK-85 Series, Model BK-92 Black Knight
Navy Arms Ithaca-Navy Hawken, Japanese Matchlock, Smith Carbine
Thompson/Center Renegade, Renegade Hunter, Scout Carbine, Hawken, New Englander, Pennsylvania Hunter, White Mountain Carbine
Traditions Frontier Scout, Hunter, Hawken, Frontier, Pennsylvania, Hawken Woodsman, Pioneer, Trophy, Buckskinner Carbine
Uberti Santa Fe Hawken
Ultra Light Arms Model 90

50-70

Shiloh Sharps Model 1874 Business, Sporting #1 & #3, Military

50-90

Shiloh Sharps Model 1874 Business, Sporting #1 & #3

50-140

Shiloh Sharps Model 1874 Business, Sporting #1 & #3

504

White Model Super 91

54

American Arms Hawkeye
CVA St. Louis Hawken, Apollo Shadow, Apollo 90, Express Double Barrel, Stalker (rifle & carbine)
Dixie Hawken
Euroarms 1803 Harper's Ferry
Gonic Arms Model GA-87 Rifle/Carbine
Lyman Great Plains, Trade Rifle, Deerstalker Rifle
Modern Muzzleloading Knight MK-85 Series, BK-92 Black Knight
Navy Arms Sharp's Cavalry Carbine, Mortimer Flintlock, 1841 Mississippi, 1803 Harpers Ferry
Shiloh Sharps Model 1863 Sporting
Thompson/Center Renegade, Renegade Hunter, Hawken, New Englander, Scout Carbine, White Mountain Carbine
Traditions Hunter, Hawken, Hawken Woodsman, Pioneer, Trophy
Uberti Sante Fe Hawken

Parker-Hale 1853 & 1858 Enfields, 1861 Enfield Musketoon

58

CVA St. Louis Hawken
Dixie U.S. Model 1861 Springfield, 1841 Mississippi, 1863 Springfield Civil War Musket, 1862 Three-Band Enfield Rifle Musket, 1858 Two-Band Enfield rifle
Euroarms Model 2260 London Armory Company Enfield 3-Band Rifle Musket, Models 2270 and 2280 London Armory Company Enfield Rifled Muskets, Model 2300 Cook & Brother Confederate Carbine, J. P. Murray Carbine, 1841 Mississippi, 1861 Springfield, 1863 Zouave
Navy Arms 1861 Enfield Musketoon, 1861 Springfield, 1862 C.S. Richmond, 1863 Springfield, Mississippi Model 1841, J.P. Murray Carbine, 1853 Enfield Rifle & Musket
Thompson/Center Big Boar Caplock

69

Dixie U.S. Model 1816 Flintlock Musket
Navy Arms 1816 M.T. Wickham Musket

75

Dixie Second Model Brown Bess Musket
Navy Arms Brown Bess Musket & Carbine

SHOTGUNS (Black Powder)

CVA Trapper (12 ga.)
Dixie Double Barrel Magnum (12 ga.)
Euroarms Model 2295 Magnum Cape (single barrel)
Navy Arms Model T&T, Fowler (12 ga.), Mortimer Flintlock 12 ga., Steel Shot Magnum 10 ga.
Thompson/Center New Englander

HANDGUNS

17 Rem

Thompson/Center Contender "Super 14"

22LR

American Arms Models CX, PK & PX, Model P-98
American Derringer Models 1 and 7
Anschutz Exemplar and Exemplar XIV
Beeman Model P-08, Unique 69U Target, Beeman/Hammerli Model 150 Free Pistol, Model 152 Electronic, Model 208 Target & Model 212 Target, Model 232 Rapid Fire, Model 280, Beeman/Korth
Beretta Model 21, Model 87, Model 89
Bersa Model 23
Browning Buck Mark 22 Series
Charter Arms Pathfinder, Off-Duty
Davis Model D-22
EMF/Dakota Model 1873, Dakota Target, Custom Engraved Single Action Revolver
Erma ESP 85A Sporting Pistol, Model 772 Match
Freedom Arms Model 252, Silhouette & Competition Models
Harrington & Richardson Sportsman 999
Heckler & Koch Model P7K3
Llama Automatic (Small Frame)
Magnum Research SSP-91 Pistol, Mountain Eagle
Mitchell Arms SA Sharpshooter
Navy Arms Model TT-Olympia
New England Firearms Standard Revolver, Ultra Revolver

North American Arms Mini-Revolvers and Mini-Master Series
QFI-Quality Firearms Western Ranger SA, Plains Rider, Model 722 TP Silhouette Pistol
Rossi Model 515
Ruger New Model Single-Six, Mark II Pistols, Model SP101 Revolver
Smith & Wesson Models 17, 34, 63, 41, 422, 2206, 2214 Rimfire "Sportsman"
Springfield Armory Model 1911-A2 SASS
Taurus Model 94, 96, PT 22
Thompson/Center Contender
A. Uberti 1871 Rolling Block Target Pistol
Walther Model TPH-DA, Model PP-DA, Models OSP & GSP, Models PPK & PPK/S
Wichita Arms International

22 Rimfire Magnum

American Derringer Model 1, Model 7 Mini-Cop DA Derringer
AMT 22 Automag II
Grendel Model P-30
Mitchell Arms Single Shot Sharpshooter
Taurus Model 941
Dan Wesson 22 Rimfire Magnum
Wichita Arms International

22 Short

Beeman Unique 2000-U, Beeman/Hammerli Model 232 Rapid Fire
Beretta Model 950 BS
Harrington & Richardson Sportsman 999
New England Firearms Standard
Walther OSP Match Rapid Fire

22 Hornet

Anschutz Exemplar Hornet
Magnum Research SSP-91 Pistol
MOA Maximum
Thompson/Center Contender
Uberti 1871 Rolling Block Target Pistol

22 Win. Mag.

Davis Model D-22
Magnum Research SSP-91 Pistol
New England Firearms Ultra Revolver
North American Mini-Revolvers and Mini-Master Series
QFI-Quality Firearms Plains Rider, Western Ranger SA
Rossi Model 515
Smith & Wesson Model 651
Thompson/Center Contender
Uberti 1871 Rolling Block Target Pistol, 1873 Cattleman Quick Draw
Dan Wesson 22 Win. Mag. Revolvers

22-250

Remington Model XP-100 LR and Custom Repeater

223 Remington

Magnum Research SSP-91 Pistol
Remington Model XP-100, XP-100R Long Range Custom Repeater and XP-100 Silhouette Target and "Varmint Special" Pistols
Springfield Armory Model 1911-A2 SASS
Thompson/Center Contender, Hunter
Uberti 1871 Rolling Block Target Pistol

223 Rem. Comm. Auto

American Derringer Model 1
Thompson/Center Contender, "Super 14"

6mm BR

Magnum Research Model SSP-91
Remington XP-100 Long-Range Custom

243

Springfield Armory Model 1911-A2 SASS

25 Auto

American Arms PX-25
Beretta Model 21, Model 950BS
Davis Model D-22 Derringer
KBI/Kassnar Model PSP-25
QFI-Quality Firearms Model SA25
Springfield Armory Lynx

270 Remington

Thompson/Center Contender

7mm BR

Magnum Research Model SSP-91
Remington Model XP-100 and XP-100 Silhouette Target and Varmint Special Pistols
Springfield Armory Model 1911-A2 SASS

7mm T.C.U.

Thompson/Center Contender, "Super 14"

7mm-08

Magnum Research Model SSP-91
Remington Model XP-100 Long-Range Custom and Custom Repeater
Springfield Armory Model 1911-A2 SASS

7-30 Water

Thompson/Center Contender, Hunter
Wichita Arms International

30 Luger

Beeman Korth Semiauto
Walther Model P-38

30 Carbine

AMT Automag III
American Derringer Model 1
EMF Dakota Model 1873
Ruger Model Blackhawk SA
Thompson/Center Contender

30-30 Win.

American Derringer Model 1
Magnum Research SSP-91 Pistol
Thompson/Center Contender, Hunter
Wichita Arms International

308 Win.

Remington XP-100 Long Range Custom and Custom Repeater
Springfield Armory Model 1911-A2 SASS
Wichita Arms Silhouette

32 Mag.

American Derringer Models 3 & 7, Lady Derringer
Charter Arms Bonnie & Clyde
Ruger Model SP101
Dan Wesson Six-Shot

32 Auto

Davis Models D-22 and P-32
Llama Auto (Small Frame)
Walther Model PP-DA

32 H&R

Charter Arms Police Undercover
New England Firearms Ultra Revolver
QFI-Quality Firearms "RP" Revolvers
Ruger New Model Single-Six SSM
Smith & Wesson Model 16
Taurus Model 73

32 S&W Long

American Derringer Model 7 and Lady Derringer
Beeman/Hammerli Model 280 Sport Pistol
Erma Model ESP 85 Sporting, Model 773 Match
QFI-Quality Firearms "RP" Revolvers, Arminius DA
Smith & Wesson Model 52

32 S&W Wadcutter

Erma ESP 85A Sporting Pistol
Walther Model GSP Match and OSP Pistols

32-20

American Derringer Model 1
EMF/Dakota Model 1873, Hartford Models
Magnum Research Model SSP-1
Thompson/Center Contender

35 Remington

Remington Model XP-100, XP-100R Long Range, Custom Repeater and XP-100 Silhouette Target and "Varmint Special" Pistols
Thompson/Center Hunter

357 Mag.

American Arms Regulator SA
American Derringer Models 1, 6, 38 DA and Mini-Cop Double Derringers
Beeman Korth
Charter Arms Bulldog Tracker, Pit Bull
Colt King Cobra, Python
EMF/Dakota Target, 1875 Outlaw, 1890 Remington Police, Model 1873, Model 1813 Premier SA, Custom Engraved SA
Erma Model 777 Sporting Revolver
Freedom Arms Model 353, Silhouette & Competition Models
L.A.R. Grizzly Mark I
Llama Comanche III
Magnum Research Desert Eagle, Model SSP-91
Mitchell Arms SA Army revolvers, 1875 and 1890 Remington Revolver, Sharpshooter
Rossi Model 971
Ruger Model GP-100, Model SP101, Blackhawk SA, Bisley
Smith & Wesson Models 13, 19, 27, 65, 66, 586
Springfield Armory Model 1911-A2 SASS
Taurus Models 65, 66, 669, 689
Thompson/Center Contender
Uberti 1875 Remington Army Outlaw, 1871 Rolling Block Target pistol, 1873 Cattleman Quick Draw, Buckhorn SA
Dan Wesson 357 Mag., 357 Super Mag., Action Cup/PPC
Wichita Arms International

357 Maximum

American Derringer Models 1 and 4
Thompson/Center Contender, Hunter
Dan Wesson 357 Super Max.

358 Winchester

Magnum Research Model SSP-91
MOA Maximum
Springfield Armory Model 1911-All SASS

38 Special

American Derringer 1, 3, 7, 11, Lady Derringer, DA 38 and Cop Double Derringers
Charter Arms Police Undercover, Off-Duty, Undercover 38 Special, Bonnie & Clyde, Pit Bull
Colt King Cobra DA, Python Premium DA
QFI-Quality Firearms Model RP Revolvers
Rossi Models 68, M88, 851
Ruger Model SP101
Smith & Wesson Models 649, LadySmith

Taurus
Taurus Models 66, 80, 82, 83, 85, 86
Dan Wesson 38 Special, Action Cup/PPC

380 Auto

American Derringer Models 1 and 7
AMT Model 380 Backup
Beeman Model MP-08
Beretta Model 85
Bersa Model 83 DA, Model 85
Browning Model BDA-380
Chinasports Type 59 Makarov
Colt Government Model, Mustang, Mustang Plus II, Mustang Pocket Lite 380
Davis P-380
Grendel Model P-12
Heckler & Koch Model P7K3
Llama Automatic (Small Frame), Duo-Tone
QFI-Quality Firearms Model LA 380
Sig Sauer Model 230 SL
Springfield Armory Bobcat
Taurus Model PT 58
Walther Model PPK & PPKS, Model PP-DA

38 Super

American Derringer Model 1
Auto-Ordnance Model 1911A-1 Thompson
Chinasports Type 54-1 Tokarev
Colt Combat Commander, Government Model, Double Eagle MK Series 90
Llama Compact
QFI-Quality Model Victory MC5
Sig Sauer Model 220 "American"
Springfield Armory Model 1911-A1 Standard

38 S&W

Smith & Wesson Models 10, 13, 14, 15, 36, 38, 49, 52, 60, 64, 65

38-40

EMF/Dakota Model 1873
Uberti 1873 Cattleman Quick Draw

9mm Federal

Charter Arms Target Bulldog

9mm Luger

American Derringer Model 1, Model DA 38 Double Derringer, Cop and Mini-Cop
AMT On Duty DA Pistol
Browning Model BDM DA
Wilkinson Arms Model "Linda" Pistol

9mm Win. Mag.

AMT Automag III

9mm Parabellum

American Derringer Semmerling LM-4
Auto Ordnance Model 1911A-1 Thompson
Beretta Model 92F and 96
Browning 9mm Hi-Power
Charter Arms Pit Bull
Colt All-American Model 2000
Daewoo Model DP51
Glock Models 17, 17L Competition, Model 19 Compact
Heckler & Koch Models P7M8 & P7M13, Model SP89
KBI/Kassnar Model 941 Jericho
Llama Automatics (Compact Frame), Model M-82, Duo-Tone, M-87 Comp
Magnum Research Baby Eagle
Mauser Models 80-SA and 90 DA
Mitchell Arms Pistol Parabellum '08
QFI-Quality Victory MC5
Ruger Model P-85, Model SP101
Sig Sauer Models 220, 225, 226, 228

Third Generation Pistols
Smith & Wesson Third Generation Pistols (Model 3900 Compact Series, 5900 and 6900 Compact Series); Model 642 Centennial Airweight, Model 940 Centennial
Springfield Armory Model 1911-A1 Standard, Model P9 DA
Star Models 31P, 31PK, M43 Firestar
Taurus Models PT92 & PT99
Walther Models P-38, P-88DA, P-5DA

10mm

American Derringer Model 1
AMT Javelina and Automag IV
Auto-Ordnance Model 1911-A1 Thompson
Colt Delta Elite, Delta Gold Cup, Double Eagle
Glock Model 20
L.A.R. Grizzley Mark I
QFI-Quality Firearms Victory MC5
Smith & Wesson Model 1000 Series

10mm Auto

Colt Double Eagle MK Series 90
Thompson/Center Contender

41 Action Express

Magnum Research Baby Eagle

40 S&W

American Arms Sabre Semiauto
American Derringer Model 1
AMT On Duty DA Pistol
Auto-Ordnance Model 1911A-1
Colt Double Eagle Officer's and Combat Commander, Government Model MK Series 90
Glock Model 23 Compact, Model 22
Heckler & Koch Model P7M10
KBI/Kassner Model 941 Jericho
Magnum Research Baby Eagle
QFI-Quality Model Victory MC5
Sig Sauer Model P229
Smith & Wesson Model 4000 Series
Springfield Armory 1911-A1 Standard, "R" Series, Model P9 DA
Star Models 31P & 31PK, M40 & M43 Firestar
Taurus Model 100/101

40 Auto

Ruger Model P91

41 Mag.

American Derringer Model 1
Magnum Research Desert Eagle
Ruger Model Bisley, Blackhawk SA
Smith & Wesson Models 57, 657
Dan Wesson 41 Mag Revolvers

.410

American Derringer Models 1, 4 and 6
Thompson/Center Contender Super "16"

44 Magnum

American Derringer Model 1
Colt Anaconda
Freedom Arms Premier & Field Grades, Silhouette and Competition Models
L.A.R. Grizzly Mark 4
Llama Super Comanche IV
Magnum Research Desert Eagle, Mark IV
Mitchell Arms SA Army Model Revolvers
Ruger Redhawk, Model Bisley, Super Blackhawk SA, Super Redhawk DA, Super Blackhawk Hunter
Smith & Wesson Model 29 and 629
Springfield Armory Model 1911-A2 SASS
Thompson/Center Contender, Hunter
Uberti Buckhorn SA
Dan Wesson 44 Mag. Revolvers

44 Special

American Derringer Models 1, 4 and 7
Charter Arms Bulldog Special
EMF/Dakota Hartford Models
Rossi Model 720
Smith & Wesson Model 629
Uberti 1873 Cattleman Quick Draw

44-40

American Arms Regulator SA
American Derringer Model 1
Colt Single Action Army
EMF/Dakota Models 1873, 1875 Outlaw, 1894 Bisley, Custom Engraved SA, Model 1890 Remington Police
Navy Arms 1873 SA
A. Uberti 1873 Cattleman Quick Draw, 1875 Remington Army Outlaw, Buckhorn SA

445 Supermag

Dan Wesson 445 Supermag

45 Auto

American Derringer Models 1, 4, 6, 10 Semmerling LM-4
AMT Longslide & Government Models
Auto-Ordnance Model 1911A-1 Thompson, Model 1911 "The General," Model 1927A-5
Chinasports Norinco Type M1911 Pistol
Colt Combat Commander, Lightweight Commander, Gold Cup National Match, Officer's ACP, Government Model, Double Eagle, Combat Elite MKIV Series 80
Glock Model 21
L.A.R. Grizzly Mark I
Llama Automatics (Large and Compact Frames), Duo-Tone
QFI-Quality Victory MC5
Ruger Model P90
Sig Sauer Model 220 "American"
Smith & Wesson Third Generation (Model 4500 Series), Model 625
Springfield Armory Model 1911-A1 Standard, "R" Series, Model P9 DA
Uberti 1873 Cattleman Quick Draw, 1875 Army SA Outlaw

45 Colt

American Arms Regulator SA
American Derringer Models 1, 4, 6, 10
Colt Model M1991 A1 Pistol, Single Action Army Revolver
EMF/Dakota Target, Models 1873, 1875, Hartford Models, "Outlaw", Model 1890 Remington Police, 1894 Bisley, 1873 Premier SA, Custom Engraved SA, Hartford Models
Freedom Arms Premier & Field Grades
Mitchell Arms SA Army Model Revolvers, 1875 and 1890 Remington Revolver, Sharpshooter
Navy Arms 1873 SA and 1895 Cavalry
Ruger Model Bisley, Blackhawk SA
Smith & Wesson Model 25
Thompson/Center Contender Super "16"
Uberti 1873 Cattleman Quick Draw, 1875 Remington Army Outlaw, 1871 Rolling Block Target pistol, Buckhorn SA

45 Win. Mag.

AMT Automag IV
American Derringer Model 1
L.A.R. Grizzly Mark I
Wildey Pistols

454 Casull

Freedom Arms Casull Premier & Field Grades, Silhouette and Competition Models

45-70 Government

American Derringer Model 1
Thompson/Center Hunter

475 Wildey Mag.

Wildey Pistols

50-70

American Derringer Model 4

50 Mag. AE

Magnum Research Desert Eagle Express

RIFLES

CENTERFIRE BOLT ACTION

Standard Calibers

17 Bee

Francotte Bolt Action

17 Rem.

Remington Model 700 BDL, ADL, Safari
Sako Hunter, Lightweight, Varmint, Deluxe
Ultra Light Model 20 Series
Winslow Varmint

22 Hornet

Browning A-Bolt Short Action
Ultra Light Model 20 Series

220 Swift

McMillan Varminter
Ruger Model M-77R, M-77V Varmint

22 PPC

Sako PPC Varmint/BR, Hunter, Deluxe

220 Swift

Remington Model 700 Classic

222 Rem.

Francotte Bolt Action
Heym Drilling Model 33, 37
Remington Model 700 BDL, ADL, Safari, Varmint Special
Sako Varmint, Hunter, Lightweight, Deluxe
Steyr-Mannlicher Model SL, Varmint
Ultra Light Model 20 Series
Winslow Varmint

223 Rem.

Browning A-Bolt Short Action
Howa Trophy Sporting, Varmint, Model 1500 Series
Jarrett Lightweight Varmint
Mark X Barreled Actions, Mini-Mark X
McMillan Varminter
Remington Model 700 BDL, ADL, Varmint Special, Model Seven
Ruger M-77 Mark II Varmint, All-Weather
Sako Hunter Lightweight, Varmint, Deluxe
Savage Model 110 Series, Model 112FV & 116FSS
Steyr-Mannlicher Model SL, Varmint
Tikka Continental, New Generation, Premium Grade
Ultra Light Model 20 Series
Weatherby Vanguard Classic I, Weatherguard
Winchester Models 70 Featherweight, Sporter, Lightweight, Varmint, Ranger
Winslow Varmint

22-250

Blaser Model R84
Browning Short Action A-Bolt
Heym SR20 Classic Sporter
Howa Trophy Sporting, Varmint, Model 1500 Series
KDF Model K15
Mark X Barreled Actions, Viscount Sporter, Whitworth
McMillan Varminter, Classic, and Stainless Sporters, Talon Sporter
Parker-Hale Models M81, 1200, 1100 LWT, 2100 Midland
Remington Model 700 ADL, CS, Model 700 BDL, Varmint Special
Ruger Models M-77V Varmint, Model 77R, M-77RL Ultra Light
Sako Deluxe, Varmint, Carbine, Hunter Lightweight, Fiberclass, LS, Whitetail/Battue
Savage Model 110 Series, Model 112FV
Steyr-Mannlicher Sporter Model L
Tikka Continental, New Generation, Premium Grade
Ultra Light Model 20 Series
Weatherby Mark V, VGX Deluxe, Vanguard Classic II
Winchester Model 70 Featherweight, Lightweight, Sporter, Varmint, Ranger
Winslow Basic

243 Win.

Blaser Model R84
Brno Model ZKK 601
Browning A-Bolt Short Action
Chinasports Model 64/70
Francotte Bolt Action
Heym Model SR20 Classic Sporter Series, SR20 Alpine Series Trophy Series, Drilling 33, 37
Howa Trophy Sporting, Model 1500 Series (barreled actions)
KDF Model K15
Mark X Barreled Actions, Viscount Sporter, Whitworth
Mauser Model 66 & 99 Standard
McMillan Varminter, Benchrest, Classic, Talon, Standard & Stainless Sporters
Parker-Hale Models M81, 1200, 1100 LWT, 2100 Midland, 1300C Scout
Remington Models 700 BDL, LS, 7400, 7600, 700 Mountain, Varmint Special 700 ADL Deluxe, Model Seven, 700 CS
Ruger Varmint, M-77 Mark II Varmint & All-Weather
Sako Varmint, Fiberclass, Hunter Lightweight, Deluxe, LS, Mannlicher-Style Carbine, Whitetail/ Battue
Savage Models 110 Series, Model 116FSS
Steyr-Mannlicher Models Luxus, SSG, Sporter L, Varmint
Tikka Continental, New Generation, Premium Grade
Ultra Light Model 20 Series
Weatherby Vanguard Classic I, Classic II, Weatherguard, VGX Deluxe
Winchester Models 70 Featherweight, Lightweight, Varmint, Sporter, Ranger and Ranger 70
Winslow Basic
A. Zoli Model AZ 1900C

244 Rem.

Winslow Basic

6mm BR

McMillan Benchrest Rifle, Talon & Classic Sporters

6mm Rem.

Blaser Model R84
KDF Model K15
McMillan Benchrest, Classic, Talon & Stainless Sporters, Varminter
Parker-Hale Models 81, 1100 LWT, 1200 Super, Model 2100 Midland
Remington Model Seven, Model 700 BDL, ADL, Varmint Special
Ruger Model M-77 Varmint, M-77 Mark II
Steyr-Mannlicher Sporter Model L
Ultra Light Model 20 Series

250-3000 Savage

Ruger Model M-77RSI International
Ultra Light Model 20 Series

6mm PPC

McMillan Benchrest
Sako PPC Varmint, BR/Varmint, Hunter, Deluxe

25-06

Blaser Model R84
Browning A-Bolt
K.D.F. Model K15
Mark X Barreled Actions, Viscount Sporter, Whitworth, Mauser System Actions
Mauser Model 99 Standard
McMillan Classic, Stainless Sporters, Talon Sporter & Safari, Varminter
Remington Model 700 Mountain, BDL, ADL, Safari
Ruger Models M-77V Varmint, 77RS, 77R
Sako Fiberclass, Hunter Lightweight, Carbine, Deluxe, LS, Whitetail/Battue, Left-Handed Models
Sauer Model 90
Steyr-Mannlicher Model Luxus M
Ultra Light Model 24 Series
Winchester Model 70 Sporter Walnut
Winslow Basic

257 Ackley

Ruger Model M-77RL Ultra Light
Ultra Light Model 20 Series

257 Roberts

Browning A-Bolt Short Action
Dakota Arms Model 76 Classic
Remington Model 700 Mountain
Ruger Model M-77R
Ultra Light Model 20 Series
Weatherby Mark V Fibermark, Euromark, Lazermark
Winslow Basic

270 Win.

Blaser Models R84
Brno Model ZKK 600
Browning A-Bolt
Chinasports Model 64/70
Churchill Highlander
Dakota Arms Model 76 Classic
Francotte Bolt Action
Heym Model SR20 Classic Sporter Series, SR20 Alpine Series, Trophy Series, Drilling 33, 37
Howa Trophy Sporting, Model 1500 Series (barreled action)
KDF Model K15
Mark X Viscount Sporter, Barreled Actions, Whitworth, Mauser System Actions
Mauser Model 66 & 99 Standard
McMillan Alaskan LA, Titanium Mountain, Classic & Stainless Sporters, Talon Sporter & Safari
Parker-Hale Models M81, 1100, 1200, 2100 Midland

Remington Models 700 LS, KS & CS, 7400,

Remington Models 700 LS, KS & CS, 7400, 7600, 700 ADL Deluxe & BDL, 700 Mountain
Ruger Model M77 RS, RLS Ultralight, 77RSI, International, 77R
Sako Deluxe, Fiberclass, Hunter Lightweight, LS, Fiberclass Carbine, Whitetail/Battue, Left-Handed Models
Sauer Model 90
Savage Model 110 Series, Model 114CU & 116FSS
Steyr-Mannlicher Luxus Model M (Sporter & Professional)
Tikka Whitetail/Battue, New Generation, Premium Grade
Ultra Light Model 24 Series
Weatherby Models Mark V Lazermark, Deluxe, Fibermark, Vanguard Classic I & II, VGX Deluxe, Classicmark, Weathermark, Alaskan, Weatherguard
Winchester Models 70 Lightweight, Featherweight, Ranger, Winlite, Sporter
Winslow Basic
A. Zoli Model AZ 1900 C

280 Rem.

Blaser Models R84
Browning A-Bolt
Dakota Arms Model 76 Classic
KDF Model K15
McMillan Titanium Mountain, Classic & Stainless Sporters, Alaskan LA, Talon Sporter & Safari
Remington Models 700, Mountain, KS, 7400, 7600, 700 BDL, ADL, CS
Ruger Model M-77R
Sako Fiberclass, Hunter, LS, Deluxe, Whitetail/Battue, Left-Handed Models
Winchester Models 70 Featherweight, Winlite, Super Grade, Lightweight
Winslow Basic

280 IMP

Jarrett Standard Hunting

284 Win.

McMillan Classic, Talon & Stainless Sporters
Ultra Light Model 20 Series
Winslow Basic

7mm Ackley

Ultra Light Model 24 Series

7mm BR

McMillan Talon Sporter, Classic & Stainless Sporters

7mm Mauser

Remington Model 700 Mountain
Ultra Light Model 20 Series
Weatherby Mark V Fibermark, Euromark, Lazermark
Winslow Basic

7mm STW

Jarrett Model 3

7mm-08

Browning A-Bolt Short Action
McMillan Varminter, Talon, Classic & Stainless Sporters, National Match
Remington Model Seven, Model 700 Mountain, Model 700 BDL, ADL, Varmint, CS
Sako Hunter Lightweight, Deluxe, LS, Varmint, Fiberclass, Whitetail/Battue
Ultra Light Model 20 Series
Weatherby Classic I, Weatherguard
Winchester Model 70 Featherweight

30-06

A-Square Caesar and Hannibal
Blaser Model R84
Brno Model ZKK 600
Browning A-Bolt
Chinasports Model 64/70
Dakota Arms Model 76 Classic
Francotte Bolt Action
Heym Model SR20 Classic Sporter Series, SR20 Alpine Series, Trophy Series, Drilling 33, 37
Howa Trophy Sporting, Model 1500 Series (barreled action)
K.D.F. Model K15
Mark X Viscount Sporter, Barreled Action, Whitworth, Mauser System Actions
Mauser Model 66 & 99 Standard
McMillan Classic & Stainless Sporters, Alaskan LA, Talon Sporter & Safari, Titanium Mountain
Parker-Hale Models M81 Classic, 1100 Lightweight, 1200 Super, 2100 Midland
Remington Models 700 LS, KS, BDL Deluxe, ADL, CS, 7400, 7600, Model 700 Mountain
Ruger Model M-77RS, 77RLS & 77RL Ultra Light, 77RSI International, 77R
Sako Carbine, Fiberclass, Hunter Lightweight, Deluxe, LS, Whitetail/Battue, Left-Handed Models
Sauer Model 90
Savage Model 110 Series, Model 114CU & 116FSS
Steyr-Mannlicher Models M (Sporter & Professional), S (Professional)
Tikka Whitetail/Battue, New Generation, Premium Grade
Ultra Light Model 24 Series
Weatherby Mark V Fibermark, Lazermark, Deluxe, Vanguard Classic I & II, Weatherguard, VGX Deluxe, Classicmark, Weathermark, Alaskan
Winchester Models 70 Featherweight, Winlite, Lightweight, Sporter, Super Grade, Ranger
Winslow Basic
A. Zoli Model AZ 1900 C

30-06 Carbine

Remington Model 7400, 7600 and Models 7400 Carbine and 7600 High Gloss Carbine

300 Phoenix

McMillan .300 Phoenix

300 Savage

Remington Model 700 ADL, BDL, Safari
Savage 110 Series
Ultra Light Model 20 Series

308 Win.

Brno Model ZKK-601
Browning A-Bolt Short Action
Chinasports Model 64/70
Heym Model SR20, Classic Sporter Series, SR20 Alpine Series, Trophy Series
Howa Trophy Sporting, Model 1500 Series (barreled action), Varmint
KDF Model K15
Mark X Mauser System Actions, Barreled Action, Viscount Sporter, Whitworth
Mauser Model 66 & 99 Standard
McMillan Varminter, Benchrest, National Match, Classic & Stainless Sporters, Talon Sporter
Parker-Hale Models M81, 1100, 1200, 2100 Midland, Model 1300C Scout, M-85 Sniper
Remington Models Seven, 700 Mountain, 7400, 7600, 700 ADL Deluxe & BDL, 700 CS, Varmint Special
Ruger Models 77RSI International, 77V Varmint, M-77 Mark II

Sako Carbine, Varmint, Fiberclass, Hunter Lightweight, LS, Whitetail/Battue, Deluxe
Savage Model 110 Series
Steyr-Mannlicher Sporter L, Models Luxus, SSG, Match UIT
Tikka Continental, Whitetail/Battue, New Generation, Premium Grade
Ultra Light Model 20 Series
Weatherby Vanguard Classic I, Weatherguard
Winchester Model 70 Lightweight Win-Tuff, Featherweight, Heavy Barrel Varmint, Ranger Youth
Winslow Basic
A. Zoli Model AZ 1900C

---
35 Whelen

Remington Models 700 ''KS'' Mountain, 7400, 7600

---
358 Win.

Ultra Light Model 20 Series
Winslow Basic

MAGNUM CALIBERS (RIFLE)

---
17 Mag.

Winslow Varmint

---
222 Rem. Mag.

Steyr-Mannlicher Model Sporters L
Ultra Light Model 20 Series

---
224 Weatherby Mag.

Weatherby Mark V Lazermark, Deluxe, Fibermark

---
240 Weatherby Mag.

Weatherby Mark V Classicmark, Weathermark, Alaskan

---
257 Weatherby

Blaser Model R84
Mauser Model 99
Weatherby Ultramark, Mark V Deluxe, Lazermark, Fibermark, Classicmark, Weathermark, Alaskan

---
264 Win. Mag.

Blaser Model R84
Ultra Light Model 26 Series
Winchester Model 70 Sporter
Winslow Basic

---
270 Weatherby Mag.

K.D.F. Model K15
Mauser Model 99
Weatherby Vanguard Classic II and VGX Deluxe, Classicmark, Weathermark, Alaskan
Winchester Model 70 Sporter
Winslow Basic

7mm Imp. Mag.

NASS Custom Hunter

7mm Rem./Wby. Mag.

A-Square Hannibal and Caesar
Blaser Model R84
Browning A-Bolt
Chinasports Model 64/70
Dakota Arms Model 76 Classic
Heym Model SR20 Classic Sporter Series, Trophy Series
Howa Trophy Sporting, Model 1500 Series (Barreled Actions)
K.D.F. Model K15
Mark X Viscount Sporter, Barreled Action, Mauser System Actions, Mark X, Whitworth
Mauser Model 66 & 99

McMillan Alaskan, Titanium Mountain, Classic & Stainless Sporters, Talon Sporter & Safari, Long Range
Navy Arms/Parker-Hale Model M81 Classic, Model 2100 Midland
Remington Models 700 LS & KS, 700 ADL, CS, Deluxe, AS, BDL, ''KS'' Mountain
Ruger Models M-77RS, 77R
Sako Fiberclass, Hunter Lightweight, Carbine, Deluxe, LS, Whitetail/Battue, Left-Handed Models
Sauer Model 90
Savage Model 110 Series, Model 116 FSS & 114 CU
Steyr-Mannlicher Sporter & Professional S Models
Tikka Whitetail/Battue, New Generation, Premium Grade
Ultra Light Model 26 Series
Weatherby Mark V Fibermark, Deluxe, Lazermark, Vanguard VGX, Classic I & II, Weatherguard, Classicmark, Weathermark, Alaskan
Winchester Model 70 Winlite, Sporter, Super Grade, Featherweight
Winslow Basic
A. Zoli Model 1900C

7mm Weatherby Mag.

Weatherby Classicmark, Weathermark, Alaskan
A. Zoli Model AZ 1900C

8mm Rem. Mag.

A-Square Hannibal and Caesar
Remington Model 700, ''KS'' Mountain, Safari Grade

---
300 Phoenix

McMillan Long Range, Safari

---
300 Weatherby Mag.

A-Square Hannibal and Caesar
Blaser Model R 84
KDF Model K15
Mauser Models 66 & 99
McMillan Alaskan MA, Classic & Stainless Sporters, Talon Sporter & Safari
Remington Model 700 CS, ''KS'' Mountain, ADL Deluxe
Sako Hunter Lightweight, Deluxe
Sauer Model 90
Weatherby Mark V Fibermark, Deluxe, Lazermark, Vanguard Classic II, VGX Deluxe, Classicmark, Weathermark, Alaskan
Winchester Model 70 Sporter
Winslow Basic

---
300 Win. Mag.

A-Square Caesar and Hannibal
Blaser Model R 84
Brno Model ZKK 602
Browning A-Bolt
Chinasports Model 64/70
Dakota Arms Model 76 Safari & Classic
Heym Model SR Classic Sporter Series, Trophy Series
Howa Trophy Sporting, Model 1500 Series
KDF Model K15
Mark X Mauser System Actions, Barreled Action, Viscount Sporter, Whitworth
Mauser Model 66, 99
McMillan Titanium Mountain, Safari, Classic & Stainless Sporters, Alaskan, Talon Sporter, Long Range
Remington Model 700 KS Mountain, BDL, ADL, Safari
Ruger M-77R, M-77RS

Sako Fiberclass, Hunter Lightweight, Carbine, LS, Deluxe, Whitetail/Battue
Sauer Model 90
Savage Model 116FSS & 114CU, Model 110 Series
Steyr-Mannlicher Varmint & Sporter S Models
Tikka Whitetail Battue, New Generation, Premium Grade
Ultra Light Model 26 Series
Weatherby Vanguard Classic II, VGX Deluxe
Winchester Model 70 Winlite, Super Grade, Sporter, Featherweight
Winslow Basic
A. Zoli Model AZ 1900C

---
300 H&H

A-Square Caesar and Hannibal
McMillan Alaskan MA, Safari, Talon Sporter, Classic & Stainless Sporters
Winchester Model 70 Sporter
Winslow Basic

---
300 & 311 Imp. Mag.

NASS Custom Hunter

---
308 Norma

Winslow Basic

---
338 Lapua

McMillan Long Range, Safari

---
338 Win. Mag.

Blaser Model R84
Browning A-Bolt
Dakota Arms Model 76 Safari
Heym SR20 Classic Sporter Series, Trophy Series
Howa Trophy Sporting, Model 1500 Series
KDF Model K15
Mauser Model 99
McMillan Classic & Stainless Sporters, Talon Sporter & Safari
Remington Model 700 ADL, Safari, BDL, ''KS'' Mountain
Ruger Model 77R, M-77RS
Sako Safari Grade, Hunter Lightweight, Carbine, Deluxe, LS, Fiberclass, Whitetail/Battue, Left-Handed Models
Sauer Model 90
Savage Model 116FSS
Tikka Whitetail/Battue, New Generation, Premium Grade
Weatherby Vanguard VGX Deluxe, Classic II
Winchester Model 70 Winlite, Sporter, Super Grade
Winslow Basic

---
340 Weatherby Mag.

A-Square Caesar and Hannibal
KDF Model K15
McMillan Alaskan MA, Classic & Stainless Sporters, Talon Sporter & Safari
Weatherby Mark V Fibermark, Deluxe, Lazermark, Classicmark, Weathermark, Alaskan

---
350 Rem. Mag.

McMillan Classic & Stainless Sporters, Varminter, Talon Sporter

---
35 Whelen

Remington Model 700 ADL, BDL, ''KS'' Mountain, Models 7400 & 7600
Ruger Model M-77RS

---
358 Win.

McMillan Alaskan MA
Winslow Basic

360 Imp. Mag.

NASS Custom Hunter

375 H&H

A-Square Caesar and Hannibal
Blaser Model R84
Brno Model ZKK 602
Browning A-Bolt
Dakota Arms Model 76 Safari, Classic
Francotte Bolt Action
Heym Model SR20 Classic Sporter Series, Trophy
  Series, Express, Classic Safari
KDF Model K15
Mark X Barreled Action
Mauser Model 66 Safari & 99
McMillan Safari, Alaskan MA, Classic & Stainless
  Sporters, Talon Sporter
Parker-Hale Model M81 African, 1100M African
Remington Model 700 Safari Grade, "KS"
  Mountain
Ruger Magnum
Sako Safari Grade, Carbine, Fiberclass, Hunter
  Lightweight, LS, Deluxe, Whitetail/Battue, Left-
  Handed Models
Sauer Model 90
Steyr-Mannlicher Models S & S/T
Weatherby Classicmark, Weathermark, Alaskan
Winchester Model 70 Super Express Walnut
  Magnum
Winslow Basic

375 Weatherby

A-Square Caesar and Hannibal

378 Win./Wby. Mag.

A-Square Caesar and Hannibal
Heym Express
McMillan Safari
Weatherby Mark V Lazermark, Deluxe,
  Fibermark, Classicmark, Weathermark, Alaskan

404 Jeffrey

A-Square Caesar and Hannibal
Heym Model SR 20 Classic Safari
McMillan Safari

411 KDF

KDF Model K15

416 Rem./Weatherby Mag.

A-Square Caesar and Hannibal
KDF Model K15
McMillan Alaskan MA, Safari, Classic & Stainless
  Sporters, Talon Sporter
Remington Model 700 Safari Grade
Sako Fiberclass, Deluxe, Hunter Lightweight,
  Laminated Stock Models
Weatherby Mark V Euromark, Deluxe, Lazermark,
  Classicmark, Weathermark, Alaskan

416 Rigby

A-Square Hannibal & Caesar
Francotte Bolt Action
Heym Express
McMillan Safari
Ruger Magnum

416 Taylor & Hoffman

A-Square Hannibal & Caesar

425 Express

A-Square Hannibal & Caesar
Heym Model SR20 Classic Safari Series

450 Ackley

A-Square Caesar and Hannibal
Heym Express

458 Win. Mag.

A-Square Hannibal & Caesar
Brno Model ZKK-602
Dakota Arms Model 76 Safari, Classic
Heym Model SR20 Classic Safari
KDF Model K15
Krieghoff Ulm & Teck
Mark X Barreled Action
Mauser Model 66 Safari
McMillan Safari
Parker-Hale Model 1100M African
Remington Model 700 Safari Grade
Ruger Magnum
Sauer Safari
Steyr-Mannlicher Model S-S/T
Winchester Model 70 Super Express Walnut
  Magnum
Winslow Basic

460 Win./Weatherby Mag.

A-Square Hannibal & Caesar
Francotte Bolt Action
Heym Express
McMillan Safari
Weatherby Mark V Lazermark, Euromark, Deluxe,
  Classicmark, Weathermark, Alaskan

500 N.E.

Heym Express

505 Gibbs

Francotte Bolt Action

600 N.E.

Heym Express

CENTERFIRE LEVER ACTION

218 Bee

Marlin Model 1894 Classic

22LR

A. Uberti Model 1866 Sporting, Model 1871
  Rolling Block Baby Carbine, Model 1866
  Yellowboy Carbine

22 Hornet

A. Uberti Model 1871 Rolling Block Baby Carbine

22 Magnum

A. Uberti Model 1866 Sporting & Yellowboy
  Carbine, Model 1871 Rolling Block Baby
  Carbine

222 Rem./223 Rem.

Browning Models 81 BLR

22-250

Browning Model 81 BLR

243 Win.

Browning Model 81 BLR
Savage Model 99C

25-20 Win.

Marlin Model 1894 Classic

257 Roberts

Browning Model 81 BLR

284 Win.

Browning Model 81 BLR

7mm-08

Browning Model 81 BLR

7-30 Waters

Winchester Model 94 Standard Walnut

307 Win.

Winchester Model 94 Big Bore Walnut

308 Win.

Browning Model 81 BLR
Savage Model 99C

30-30 Win.

Marlin Models 336CS, 30AS
Navy Arms Cowboys Companion
Winchester Models 94 Ranger, Win-Tuff,
  Standard, Trapper Carbine

30-06

Browning Model 1885 Single Shot, 53 Ltd. Ed.

32 Win.

Winchester Model 94 Standard Walnut

32-20 Win.

Marlin Model 1894 Classic

35 Rem.

Marlin Model 336CS

356 Win.

Winchester Model 94 Big Bore Walnut

357 Mag.

Marlin Model 1894CS
Mitchell Arms 1873 Winchester
Rossi Puma Models M92 SRS & SRC
Uberti Models 1871 Rolling Block Baby Carbine,
  Model 1873 Sporting & Carbine
Winchester Model 94 Trapper Carbine, Walnut

358 Win.

Browning Model 81BLR

38 Special

Marlin Model 1894CS
Mitchell Arms 1866 and 1873 Winchesters
Rossi Puma Models M92 SRS & M92 SRC
A. Uberti 1866 Sporting, Model 1873 Carbine and
  Sporting, Model 1866 Yellowboy Carbine &
  Sporting

44 Special

Marlin Model 1894S
Uberti Henry
Winchester Model 94 Trapper Carbine, Walnut,
  Wrangler

44 Rem. Mag.

Marlin Model 1894S
Rossi Puma Model M65 SRC
Winchester Model 94 Trapper Carbine, Walnut,
  Wrangler

444 Marlin

Marlin Model 444SS

44-40

Mitchell Arms 1858 Henry, 1866 and 1873
  Winchesters
Navy Arms 1873 Rifle, 1866 "Yellowboy" (rifle &
  carbine), Henry Military, Iron Frame & Trapper
  Models
Uberti Model 1866 Sporting, Yellowboy Carbine,
  Model 1873 Sporting & Carbine, Henry Rifle &
  Carbine

45 Colt

Marlin Model 1894S
Mitchell Arms 1873 Winchester
Navy Arms 1873 Rifle
Uberti Model 1873 Sporting & Carbine, Model 1866, Henry, Model 1866 Yellowboy Carbine & Sporting
Winchester Model 94 Trapper Carbine, Walnut

45-70 Government

Browning Model 1886 Carbine
Marlin Model 1895SS
Navy Arms Sharps Cavalry Carbine and Plains Rifle

CENTERFIRE PUMP

38 Special

Action Arms Timber Wolf

357 Magnum

Action Arms Timber Wolf

44 Magnum

Action Arms Timber Wolf

SINGLE SHOT

22S,L,LR

Dakota Arms Model 10
Walther Model GX-1, UIT Match, Model KK/MS Silhouette

22 BR Rem.

Remington Model 40-XBBR Bench Rest

22 Hornet

Thompson/Center Hunter

220 Swift

Ruger No. 1V Special Varminter, No. 1B Standard
Thompson/Center Hunter

222 Rem.

Remington Models 40-XB, Bench Rest
Thompson/Center Hunter

222 Rem. Mag.

Remington Model 40-XBBR

223

Browning Model 1885
Remington Model 40-XBBR Bench Rest
Ruger No. 1B Standard, No. IV Special Varminter
Thompson/Center Hunter

22-250 Rem.

Browning Model 1885
Remington Model 40-XB Rangemaster
Ruger No. 1B Standard, Special Varminter
Thompson/Center Hunter

243 Win.

Remington Model 40-XB Rangemaster
Ruger No. 1A Light Sporter, No. 1B, No. 1 RSI International Standard
Thompson/Center Hunter

25-06

Remington Model 40-XB Rangemaster
Ruger No. 1V Special Varminter, No. 1B Standard

6mm BR Rem.

Remington Model 40-XBBR Bench Rest

6mm Rem.

Remington Model 40-XB Rangemaster
Ruger No. 1B Standard, No. IV Special Varminter

257 Roberts

Ruger No. 1B Standard

270 Weatherby

Ruger No. 1B Standard

270 Win.

Browning Model 1885
Ruger No. 1A Light Sporter, No. 1B Standard, RSI International
Thompson/Center Hunter

280 Rem.

Ruger No. 1B Standard

7mm-08

Thompson/Center Hunter

30-06

Browning Model 1885
Remington Model 40XB Rangemaster
Ruger No. 1A Light Sporter, No. 1B Standard, RSI International
Thompson/Center Hunter

300 Weatherby Mag.

Ruger No. 1B Standard

300 Win. Mag.

Remington Model 40-XB Rangemaster
Ruger No. 1B Standard
Thompson/Center Hunter

308 Win.

Remington Model 40-XB and 40-XBBR
Thompson/Center Hunter

7mm Rem. Mag.

Browning Model 1885
Remington Model 40-XB Rangemaster
Ruger No. 1B Standard & 1S Medium Sporter
Thompson/Center Hunter

338 Win. Mag.

Ruger No. 1S Medium Sporter, No. 1B Standard
Thompson/Center Hunter

375 H&H

Ruger No. 1H Tropical
Thompson/Center Hunter

416 Rem.

Ruger No. 1H Tropical
Thompson/Center Hunter

458 Win. Mag.

Ruger No. 1H Tropical

45-70 Govt.

Browning Model 1885
Navy Arms No. 2 Creedmoor Target, Remington Style Rolling Block Buffalo
Ruger No. 1S Medium Sporter

50

Iver Johnson Long Range Model 5100A1

AUTOLOADING

22 LR

AMT Lightning and Small Game Hunting Rifle
Auto-Ordnance Thompson Deluxe Model 1927-A1
Mitchell Arms Models M-16A1 & CAR-15
Norinco Model 22D & Model JW-15
Ruger 10/22 Carbine, Sporter & Stainless Models

22 Hornet

Dakota Arms Sporter

223 Rem.

Colt Sporter Lightweight and Competition, Match H-Bar, Target Gov't Model
Eagle Arms Model EA-15
Ruger Mini-14, Mini-14 Ranch

243 Win.

Browning BAR Semiauto

270 Win.

Browning BAR Semiauto

280 Rem.

Browning BAR Semiauto

300 Win. Mag.

Browning BAR Semiauto

30-06

Browning BAR Semiauto

308 Win.

Browning BAR Semiauto
Heckler & Koch Models SR-9 and PSG-1 Marksman's
Mauser Model 86
Springfield Armory MIA Standard, Match; MIA-A1 Bush

338 Win. Mag.

Browning BAR Semiauto

45 Auto

Auto-Ordnance Thompson Models M1, 1927A1
Marlin Model 45

7mm Rem. Mag.

Browning BAR Semiauto

9mm

Colt Sporter Lightweight
Iver Johnson M-1 Carbine
Marlin Model 9 Camp

10mm

Auto-Ordnance Model 1927-A1

RIMFIRE BOLT ACTION

22S,L,LR

Anschutz Match 54 & Match 64 Sporters: Models 1403D, 1416D, 1418D, 1516D, 1518D, 54.18S, 54.18S-REP, 64MS, 1803D, 1903D, 1907, 1910, 1911, 1913, 1808, Model 1700, Achiever, Biathlon Models 1827 B/BT, 1403 B, Model 2013, Model 2007 ISU
Beeman/Weihrauch Models HW60 Smallbore, HW 60J-ST, HW660 Match
Beeman/FWB Model 2600
Browning Model A-Bolt 22, Model 52
Chinasports Norinco Type EM-332

Dakota Arms Sporter
Lakefield Sporting Models 91 & 91TR, Mark I,
Mark II, 90B & 92S
Marlin Models 15YN ''Little Buckaroo'', 880, 881,
25N, Model 2000 Target
Mauser Model 201, 107
Navy Arms Model TU-KKW
Remington Models 40-XR, 541-T
Ruger Model 77/22RS
Ruko Model M14P
RWS Diana Model 820L and 820F
Walther U.I.T. Match
Weatherby Accumark Classic 22

22 Hornet

Anschutz Model 1700D Custom, Classic, & 1700
Bavarian

22 Magnum

Anschutz Model 1700D Custom, 1700 Bavarian,
1700D Classic, Match 64 Sporters

22 WMR

Marlin Models 25MN, 882, 883
Mauser Model 201
Ruger Model 77/22 RS
Ruko Model M1500

222 Rem.

Anschutz Model 1700 Bavarian, Custom and
1700D Classic
Beeman/Weihrauch Model HW 60J-ST

7.62mm NATO

Remington Model 40-XC KS

RIMFIRE AUTOLOADING

22S,L,LR

Anschutz Model 525
Browning Model 22 (Grades I & VI)
Feather Model AT-22 & F2 AT-22
Marlin Models 70P, 70HC, 60, 995, 990L
Ruger Model 10/22
Ruko Model M20P

RIMFIRE LEVER ACTION

22S,L,LR

Browning Model BL-22 (Grades I & II)
Lakefield Model 64B
Marlin Models 39TD, Golden 39AS
Winchester Model 9422

22 WMR Mag.

Winchester Model 9422

9mm

Feather Model F9 AT-9

44

Navy Arms Henry Military and Iron Frame (rifles
and carbines)

RIMFIRE PUMP ACTION

22 S, L, LR

Chinasports Model EM-321
Remington Model 572 BDL Deluxe Fieldmaster
Rossi Models M62 SAC & SA

DOUBLE RIFLES

308

Krieghoff Models Ulm & Teck

30-06

Chapuis S/S Express
Heym Model 88B Safari
Krieghoff Models Ulm & Teck

300 Win. Mag.

Krieghoff Models Ulm & Teck

9.3 X 74R

Tikka Model 412S

375 H&H

Chapuis S/S Express
Heym Model 88B Safari
Krieghoff Model Ulm

458 Win.

Chapuis S/S Express
Heym Model 88B Safari
Kreighoff Models Ulm & Teck

470 N.E.

Heym Model 88B Safari
Chapuis S/S Express

500 N.E.

Heym Model 88B Safari

RIFLE/SHOTGUN COMBOS

22 Hornet/12 ga.

Heym Model 22S
Savage Model 24F (20 ga. also)

222 Rem./12 ga.

Heym Model 22S2

222 Rem. Mag./12 ga.

Heym Model 22S2

22-250

Heym Model 22S2

223 Rem./12 ga.

Heym Model 22S2
Savage Model 24-F (20 ga. also)

243 Win./12 ga.

Heym Model 22S2

30-06

Heym Model 22S2

308 Win./12 ga.

Heym Model 22S2

30-30/12 ga.

Savage Model 24F (20 ga. also)